A Companion to Shakespeare's Sonnets

Blackwell Companions to Literature and Culture

1. *A Companion to Romanticism*   Edited by Duncan Wu
2. *A Companion to Victorian Literature and Culture*   Edited by Herbert F. Tucker
3. *A Companion to Shakespeare*   Edited by David Scott Kastan
4. *A Companion to the Gothic*   Edited by David Punter
5. *A Feminist Companion to Shakespeare*   Edited by Dympna Callaghan
6. *A Companion to Chaucer*   Edited by Peter Brown
7. *A Companion to Literature from Milton to Blake*   Edited by David Womersley
8. *A Companion to English Renaissance Literature and Culture*   Edited by Michael Hattaway
9. *A Companion to Milton*   Edited by Thomas N. Corns
10. *A Companion to Twentieth-Century Poetry*   Edited by Neil Roberts
11. *A Companion to Anglo-Saxon Literature and Culture*   Edited by Phillip Pulsiano and Elaine Treharne
12. *A Companion to Restoration Drama*   Edited by Susan J. Owen
13. *A Companion to Early Modern Women's Writing*   Edited by Anita Pacheco
14. *A Companion to Renaissance Drama*   Edited by Arthur F. Kinney
15. *A Companion to Victorian Poetry*   Edited by Richard Cronin, Alison Chapman, and Antony H. Harrison
16. *A Companion to the Victorian Novel*   Edited by Patrick Brantlinger and William B. Thesing
17–20. *A Companion to Shakespeare's Works: Volumes I–IV*   Edited by Richard Dutton and Jean E. Howard
21. *A Companion to the Regional Literatures of America*   Edited by Charles L. Crow
22. *A Companion to Rhetoric and Rhetorical Criticism*   Edited by Walter Jost and Wendy Olmsted
23. *A Companion to the Literature and Culture of the American South*   Edited by Richard Gray and Owen Robinson
24. *A Companion to American Fiction 1780–1865*   Edited by Shirley Samuels
25. *A Companion to American Fiction 1865–1914*   Edited by Robert Paul Lamb and G. R. Thompson
26. *A Companion to Digital Humanities*   Edited by Susan Schreibman, Ray Siemens, and John Unsworth
27. *A Companion to Romance*   Edited by Corinne Saunders
28. *A Companion to the British and Irish Novel 1945–2000*   Edited by Brian W. Shaffer
29. *A Companion to Twentieth-Century American Drama*   Edited by David Krasner
30. *A Companion to the Eighteenth-Century English Novel and Culture*   Edited by Paula R. Backscheider and Catherine Ingrassia
31. *A Companion to Old Norse-Icelandic Literature and Culture*   Edited by Rory McTurk
32. *A Companion to Tragedy*   Edited by Rebecca Bushnell
33. *A Companion to Narrative Theory*   Edited by James Phelan and Peter J. Rabinowitz
34. *A Companion to Science Fiction*   Edited by David Seed
35. *A Companion to the Literatures of Colonial America*   Edited by Susan Castillo and Ivy Schweitzer
36. *A Companion to Shakespeare and Performance*   Edited by Barbara Hodgdon and W. B. Worthen
37. *A Companion to Mark Twain*   Edited by Peter Messent and Louis J. Budd
38. *A Companion to European Romanticism*   Edited by Michael K. Ferber
39. *A Companion to Modernist Literature and Culture*   Edited by David Bradshaw and Kevin J. H. Dettmar
40. *A Companion to Walt Whitman*   Edited by Donald D. Kummings
41. *A Companion to Herman Melville*   Edited by Wyn Kelley
42. *A Companion to Medieval English Literature and Culture c.1350–c.1500*   Edited by Peter Brown
43. *A Companion to Modern British and Irish Drama 1880–2005*   Edited by Mary Luckhurst
44. *A Companion to Eighteenth-Century Poetry*   Edited by Christine Gerrard
45. *A Companion to Shakespeare's Sonnets*   Edited by Michael Schoenfeldt

A COMPANION TO

SHAKESPEARE'S SONNETS

EDITED BY **MICHAEL SCHOENFELDT**

Blackwell
Publishing

BLACKWELL PUBLISHING
350 Main Street, Malden, MA 02148-5020, USA
9600 Garsington Road, Oxford OX4 2DQ, UK
550 Swanston Street, Carlton, Victoria 3053, Australia

First published 2007 by Blackwell Publishing Ltd

1   2007

Library of Congress Cataloging-in-Publication Data

A companion to Shakespeare's sonnets / edited by Michael Schoenfeldt.
p. cm.—(Blackwell companions to literature and culture ; 45)
Includes bibliographical references (p.) and index.
ISBN-13: 978-1-4051-2155-2 (acid-free paper)
ISBN-10: 1-4051-2155-6 (acid-free paper)
1. Shakespeare, William, 1564–1616. Sonnets.   2. Sonnets, English—History and
criticism.   I. Schoenfeldt, Michael Carl.   II. Series.

PR 2848.C66 2006
821'.3—dc22
2006012850

A catalogue record for this title is available from the British Library.

Set in 11/13 pt Garamond 3
by SNP Best-set Typesetter Ltd, Hong Kong
Printed and bound in Singapore
by Markono Print Media Pte Ltd

The publisher's policy is to use permanent paper from mills that operate a sustainable forestry policy,
and which has been manufactured from pulp processed using acid-free and elementary chlorine-free
practices. Furthermore, the publisher ensures that the text paper and cover board used have met
acceptable environmental accreditation standards.

For further information on
Blackwell Publishing, visit our website:
www.blackwellpublishing.com

Contents

Notes on Contributors   viii
Acknowledgments   xii

Introduction   1

PART I   *Sonnet Form and Sonnet Sequence*   13

1   The Value of the Sonnets   15
    Stephen Booth

2   Formal Pleasure in the Sonnets   27
    Helen Vendler

3   The Incomplete Narrative of Shakespeare's Sonnets   45
    James Schiffer

4   Revolution in *Shake-speares Sonnets*   57
    Margreta de Grazia

PART II   *Shakespeare and His Predecessors*   71

5   The Refusal to be Judged in Petrarch and Shakespeare   73
    Richard Strier

6   "Dressing old words new"? Re-evaluating the "Delian Structure"   90
    Heather Dubrow

7   Confounded by Winter: Speeding Time in Shakespeare's Sonnets   104
    Dympna Callaghan

PART III   *Editorial Theory and Biographical Inquiry:*
                 Editing the Sonnets   119

   8   *Shake-speares Sonnets*, Shakespeare's Sonnets, and Shakespearean
        Biography   121
        Richard Dutton

   9   Mr. Who He?   137
        Stephen Orgel

  10   Editing the Sonnets   145
        Colin Burrow

  11   William Empson and the Sonnets   163
        Lars Engle

PART IV   *The Sonnets in Manuscript and Print*   183

  12   Shakespeare's Sonnets and the Manuscript Circulation of Texts in Early
        Modern England   185
        Arthur F. Marotti

  13   The Sonnets and Book History   204
        Marcy L. North

PART V   *Models of Desire in the Sonnets*   223

  14   Shakespeare's Love Objects   225
        Douglas Trevor

  15   Tender Distance: Latinity and Desire in Shakespeare's Sonnets   242
        Bradin Cormack

  16   Fickle Glass   261
        Rayna Kalas

  17   "Th' expense of spirit in a waste of shame": Mapping the "Emotional
        Regime" of Shakespeare's Sonnets   277
        Jyotsna G. Singh

PART VI   *Ideas of Darkness in the Sonnets*   291

  18   Rethinking Shakespeare's Dark Lady   293
        Ilona Bell

  19   Flesh Colors and Shakespeare's Sonnets   314
        Elizabeth D. Harvey

PART VII *Memory and Repetition in the Sonnets* 329

20 Voicing the Young Man: Memory, Forgetting, and Subjectivity in the
Procreation Sonnets 331
Garrett A. Sullivan, Jr.

21 "Full character'd": Competing Forms of Memory in Shakespeare's
Sonnets 343
Amanda Watson

PART VIII *The Sonnets in/and the Plays* 361

22 Halting Sonnets: Poetry and Theater in *Much Ado About Nothing* 363
Patrick Cheney

23 Personal Identity and Vicarious Experience in Shakespeare's Sonnets 383
William Flesch

PART IX *The Sonnets and* A Lover's Complaint 403

24 "Making the quadrangle round": Alchemy's Protean Forms in
Shakespeare's sonnets and *A Lover's Complaint* 405
Margaret Healy

25 The Enigma of *A Lover's Complaint* 426
Catherine Bates

Appendix: The 1609 Text of Shakespeare's Sonnets and *A Lover's
Complaint* 441

Index 502

Notes on Contributors

Catherine Bates is Reader in Renaissance Literature at the University of Warwick. She is author of *The Rhetoric of Courtship in Elizabethan Language and Literature*, and *Play in a Godless World: The Theory and Practice of Play in Shakespeare, Nietzsche and Freud*, as well as numerous articles on Renaissance literature.

Ilona Bell, Professor of English at Williams College, is the author of *Elizabethan Women and the Poetry of Courtship* and the editor of the Penguin Classic *John Donne: Selected Poems*. She has written widely on Renaissance poetry, early modern women, and Elizabeth I. Her previous essays on Shakespeare's sonnets and *A Lover's Complaint* have appeared in *Shakespeare's Sonnets: Critical Essays* (ed. James Schiffer, 1999), *The Greenwood Companion to Shakespeare*, and *Critical Essays on Shakespeare's "A Lover's Complaint": Suffering Ecstasy*.

Stephen Booth, Professor of English at the University of California at Berkeley, is the author of *An Essay on Shakespeare's Sonnets* (1969), *Shakespeare's Sonnets, Edited with an Analytic Commentary* (1977), *King Lear, Macbeth, Indefinition, and Tragedy* (1983), and *Precious Nonsense: The Gettysburg Address, Ben Jonson's Epitaphs on His Children, and Twelfth Night* (1998).

Colin Burrow is Senior Research Fellow in English at All Souls College, Oxford. He edited *The Complete Sonnets and Poems* for The Oxford Shakespeare (2002), as well as the poems for the forthcoming *Cambridge Edition of the Works of Ben Jonson*. He is the author of *Epic Romance: Homer to Milton* (1993), as well as numerous articles on early modern literature.

Dympna Callaghan is Dean's Professor in the Humanities at Syracuse University. Her published work includes *The Impact of Feminism in English Renaissance Studies* (2006), *Romeo and Juliet: Texts and Contexts* (2003), *Shakespeare Without Women* (2000), *John Webster's* The Duchess of Malfi*: Contemporary Critical Essays* (2000), *Woman and Gender* *in Renaissance Tragedy: A Study of* Othello, King Lear, The Duchess of Malfi, *and* The White Devil (1989), *The Weyward Sisters: Shakespeare and Feminist Politics* (co-authored with Lorraine Helms and Jyostna Singh, 1994), *The Feminist Companion to Shakespeare* (2000), Winner of Choice Award for Outstanding Academic Title, and *Feminist Readings In Early Modern Culture: Emerging Subjects* (edited with Valerie Traub and Lindsay Kaplan, 1996). She is currently completing an anthology of Renaissance poetry for Oxford University Press.

Patrick Cheney, Professor of English and Comparative Literature at Penn State University, is the author of *Shakespeare, National Poet-Playwright* (2004) and *Shakespeare's Literary Authorship: Books, Poetry, and Theatre* (forthcoming 2007), as well as editor of *The Cambridge Companion to Shakespeare's Poetry* (2006).

Bradin Cormack is Assistant Professor of English at the University of Chicago. His book *A Power to Do Justice: Jurisdiction in English Literature, 1509–1625* is to be published by the University of Chicago Press. He has written articles on early modern law and literature, and is co-author, with Carla Mazzio, of *Book Use, Book Theory: 1500–1700* (2005). He is currently at work on a study of Shakespeare's sonnets.

Margreta de Grazia is the Joseph B. Glossberg Term Professor in the Humanities at the University of Pennsylvania. She is the author of *Shakespeare Verbatim* (1991) and *"Hamlet" Without Hamlet* (2006). She has also co-edited *Subject and Object in Renaissance Culture* (1996) with Maureen Quilligan and Peter Stallybrass, and the *Cambridge Companion to Shakespeare* (2001) with Stanley Wells.

Heather Dubrow, Tighe-Evans Professor and John Bascom Professor at the University of Wisconsin-Madison, is the author of five single-authored books, most recently *Shakespeare and Domestic Loss: Forms of Deprivation, Mourning, and Recuperation*. Her other publications include a recently completed book on lyric, numerous articles on teaching, and poetry appearing in two chapbooks and in journals.

Richard Dutton is Humanities Distinguished Professor of English at Ohio State University. He is author of *Mastering the Revels: The Regulation and Censorship of Renaissance Drama* (1991) and *Licensing, Censorship and Authorship in Early Modern England: Buggeswords* (2000) and co-editor with Jean Howard of the four-volume *A Companion to Shakespeare's Works* (2003 and 2006). He has edited Jonson's *Epicene* (2003) for the Revels Plays and is currently editing *Volpone* for the new Cambridge Ben Jonson.

Lars Engle is Associate Professor and Chair of the English Department at the University of Tulsa. He is the author of *Shakespearean Pragmatism* (1993) and an editor of *English Renaissance Drama: A Norton Anthology* (2002). Earlier essays on Shakespeare's sonnets have appeared in *PMLA* and in *Shakespeare's Sonnets: Critical Essays* (ed. James Schiffer, 1999).

William Flesch is Professor of English at Brandeis University. His books include *Generosity and the Limits of Authority: Shakespeare, Herbert, Milton*. His most recent book, on narrative and vicarious experience, will be published in 2007, and he is completing a study of literary quotation.

Elizabeth D. Harvey, Professor of English at the University of Toronto, is the author of *Ventriloquized Voices: Feminist Theory and Renaissance Texts* and, most recently, editor of *Sensible Flesh: On Touch in Early Modern Culture* and co-editor of *Luce Irigaray and Premodern Culture*.

Margaret Healy is a Senior Lecturer in English at the University of Sussex. She is the author of *Fictions of Disease in Early Modern England: Bodies, Plagues and Politics* and *Writers and Their Work:* Richard II, and has published extensively in the field of literature, medicine, and the body.

Rayna Kalas is Assistant Professor of English at Cornell University, where she teaches sixteenth- and seventeenth-century poetry and prose. She has published articles on the "framing" of language and on Renaissance mirrors. Her book *Frame, Glass, Verse: The Technology of Poetic Invention in the English Renaissance* is forthcoming from Cornell University Press.

Arthur F. Marotti, Professor of English at Wayne State University, is the author of *John Donne, Coterie Poet* (1986); *Manuscript, Print, and the English Renaissance Lyric* (1995); and *Religious Ideology and Cultural Fantasy: Catholic and Anti-Catholic Discourses in Early-Modern England* (2005). He has written extensively on early modern English literature and culture.

Marcy L. North is Associate Professor of English at Pennsylvania State University. She is the author of *The Anonymous Renaissance: Cultures of Discretion in Tudor–Stuart England* (2003), as well as articles and chapters on early modern anonymity, print culture, and manuscript culture.

Stephen Orgel is the Jackson Eli Reynolds Professor of Humanities at Stanford University. He is the author of *The Jonsonian Masque* (1965), *The Illusion of Power* (1975), *Impersonations: The Performance of Gender in Shakespeare's England* (1996), *The Authentic Shakespeare* (2002), and *Imagining Shakespeare* (2003).

James Schiffer is Professor and Head of the English Department at Northern Michigan University. He has published essays on the poems and plays, and is editor of the volume *Shakespeare's Sonnets: Critical Essays* (1999). At present he is editing the New Variorum edition of *Twelfth Night* as well as *Twelfth Night: New Critical Essays*.

Michael Schoenfeldt is Professor of English Literature and Associate Dean for the Humanities at the University of Michigan. He is the author of *Bodies and Selves in Early*

Modern England: Physiology and Inwardness in Spenser, Shakespeare, Herbert, and Milton (1999) and of *Prayer and Power: George Herbert and Renaissance Courtship* (1991), and co-editor of *Imagining Death in Spenser and Milton* (2003).

Jyotsna G. Singh, Professor of English at Michigan State University, is the author of *Colonial Narratives/Cultural Dialogues*, co-author of *The Weyward Sisters: Shakespeare and Feminist Politics*, and co-editor of *Travel Knowledge: European "Discoveries" in the Early Modern Period*. She has also published several essays and reviews.

Richard Strier, Frank L. Sulzberger Professor, University of Chicago, is the author of *Love Known: Theology and Experience in George Herbert's Poetry* and *Resistant Structures: Particularity, Radicalism, and Renaissance Texts*; he has co-edited a number of cross-disciplinary collections, and published essays on Shakespeare, Donne, and Milton, and on twentieth-century critical theory.

Garrett A. Sullivan, Jr., Professor of English at Pennsylvania State University, is author of *Memory and Forgetting in English Renaissance Drama: Shakespeare, Marlowe, Webster* and *The Drama of Landscape: Land, Property and Social Relations on the Early Modern Stage*. He is co-editor of *Early Modern English Drama: A Critical Companion*.

Douglas Trevor, Associate Professor of English at the University of Iowa, is the author of *The Poetics of Melancholy in Early Modern England*. He has also published numerous articles and a collection of short stories, *The Thin Tear in the Fabric of Space*.

Helen Vendler is the A. Kingsley Porter University Professor at Harvard University. She is the author of many books on lyric poetry, including *On Extended Wings: The Longer Poems of Wallace Stevens* (1969), *The Poetry of George Herbert* (1975), *The Odes of John Keats* (1983), *The Music of What Happens: Essays on Poetry and Criticism* (1988), *The Art of Shakespeare's Sonnets* (1997), *Coming of Age as a Poet: Milton, Keats, Eliot, Plath* (2003), and *Invisible Listeners: Lyric Intimacy in Herbert, Whitman, and Ashbery* (2005).

Amanda Watson, recently a Council on Library and Information Resources Post-doctoral Fellow at the University of Virginia Library, is now working on a degree in library and information science. A previous essay of hers appeared in *Forgetting in Early Modern English Literature and Culture: Lethe's Legacy*.

Acknowledgments

This collection has from its initial inception to its last punctuation check been a collaborative enterprise, and so has engendered myriad opportunities for the expression of gratitude. I want first to thank Andrew McNeillie, who conceived and commissioned the collection. Since then, everyone with whom I have worked at Blackwell has been a consummate professional as well as a delightful individual. I have never dealt with such a punctual and efficient lot; their graceful proficiency at once exposed my own ineptitude and helped me conceal it. I want in particular to thank Jennifer Hunt, Astrid Wind, Karen Wilson, Emma Bennett, and Rosemary Bird. Gillian Somerscales was an impeccable copy-editor, respecting the integrity of the various individual contributions while uniformly improving them.

I have been very lucky in the many exceptional students with whom I have worked at Michigan, two of whom, Marcy North and Amanda Watson, are represented in this collection. Students who have marred their summers in order to work on the collection include Aaron McCollough, Kentston Bauman, Jonathan Smith, and Rebecca Wiseman. I completed this collection during a term of administrative indenture, and owe a concomitant debt of gratitude to the extraordinarily accomplished and supportive staff of the LSA Dean's Office at the University of Michigan.

Finally, I am deeply grateful to the contributors for their rare combination of brilliance, patience, and perseverance. I learned an immense amount about the sonnets, and about contemporary criticism, in the process of editing the collection, and I hope that readers of all levels will have a similarly edifying experience. I am grateful for the opportunity to reprint previously published work by three influential and prominent critics – Stephen Booth, Helen Vendler, and Stephen Orgel – alongside the twenty-two essays composed specifically for this volume. I am particularly pleased to inaugurate the volume with an essay from Stephen Booth's wonderful first book on the sonnets. One of my teachers in graduate school, he taught us all how to read the sonnets anew.

Introduction

Michael Schoenfeldt

There has perhaps never been a better time, since their publication almost four hundred years ago, to read Shakespeare's sonnets. Subjects that were formerly the source of scandal – the articulation of a fervent same-sex love, for example, or the clinical exploration of the harmful effects of love, imagined as the ultimate sexually transmitted disease – are now sites of intense scholarly interest. Similarly, issues to which earlier readers and cultures were largely deaf – the implicit racism inherent in a hierarchy of light and dark, the myriad ways that social class can distort human interaction, and the subjugation of women in an economy of erotic energy – have been the subject of rigorous critical scrutiny for at least thirty years. With the privilege, and the inconvenience, of some historical distance, we are now better able to apprehend the hidden injuries and byzantine delicacies of the class structure in early modern England. The purpose of this collection is to exploit this opportunity; it intends to celebrate the achievement of the sonnets, to investigate what they have to say to us at this moment in our critical history, and to exemplify the remarkable range and intelligence of current engagements with the sonnets.

By including in this collection of essays the text of the 1609 quarto volume entitled *Shake-speares Sonnets. Never before Imprinted.*, I hope to make available to the contemporary reader a text that is at once of great historical interest and easily approachable by an intelligent reader. Indeed, I would argue that the 1609 quarto edition is the perfect venue for beginning readers of the poems; the occasional strangeness of early modern spelling and typography can actually help counteract the uncanny familiarity of certain Shakespearean utterances. Compared to those besetting most early modern poetry, moreover, the editorial problems of the sonnets are relatively minor. Indeed, there is only one serious and insoluble textual crux – sonnet 146, which repeats in its second line the last words of the first:

> Poore soule the center of my sinfull earth,
> My sinfull earth these rebell powers that thee array . . .

Among the more plausible suggestions as substitutes for the second "my sinfull earth" are "feeding," "fenced by," "foil'd by," and "pressed with." But the sonnets are generally free of the kinds of textual issues that challenge and baffle readers today. Although original spelling and punctuation can occasionally pose problems for the modern reader, they can also provide opportunities to explore that particularly Shakespearean mode of generating layers of significance via riddling inference and syntactic suspension – modes that modernized texts sometimes disguise.

The text of the 1609 poems, then, is in comparatively good shape; but the volume is cloaked with a kind of mystery that has served as an open invitation both to conspiracy theorists and to reasoned scholarly speculation. Indeed, if one set out intentionally to create a copy-text of tantalizing irresolution, it would be hard to achieve the level attained in this volume by the accidental contingencies of history and biography.

We do not know when Shakespeare wrote the sonnets – they might have been penned during a brief burst of productivity while the theaters were closed because of the plague, or worked on throughout his career. The poems were first published in Shakespeare's lifetime, possibly many years after their composition, and dedicated to a mysterious Mr. W.H. with an elusive utterance signed not by the poet but by the printer Thomas Thorpe. We do not know whether Shakespeare approved this publication or not; he certainly did not rush into print with his own authorized edition, as writers so frequently did on the heels of pirated publication of their works (Duncan-Jones 1997). But there survives no dedication from Shakespeare of the collection of sonnets to a particular patron, such as he gave to his two previous non-dramatic publications, the narrative poems *Venus and Adonis* and *The Rape of Lucrece*. Rather, many of the energies of dedicatory tropes of deference and submission seem to have been absorbed within the collection itself. In fact, sonnet 26, "Lord of my love," sounds so much like a dedicatory epistle that some critics, hungry for biographical clues to the identity of the addressee, have used resemblances between this poem and Shakespeare's dedication of *The Rape of Lucrece* to the Earl of Southampton to argue that the Earl must be the young man of the sonnets.

Perhaps this thick aura of mystery explains in part why the most significant and substantial scholarly engagements with the sonnets over the last several years have been editorial.[1] While the 1609 title-page attests to the established reputation and concomitant marketability of a new work by Shakespeare – *Shake-speares Sonnets. Never before Imprinted.* – the dedication by the printer Thomas Thorpe employs enigmatic initials and allusive language to imply a kind of côterie knowledge of the central players in the collection (knowledge to which we are not privy):

> *TO.THE.ONLIE.BEGETTER.OF.*
> *THESE.INSVING.SONNETS.*
> *M˚.W.H. ALL.HAPPINESSE.*
> *AND.THAT.ETERNITIE.*
> *PROMISED.*

BY.

OVR.EVER-LIVING.POET.

WISHETH.

THE.WELL-WISHING.

ADVENTVRER.IN.

SETTING.

FORTH.

T. T.

We do not know what "begetter" means here – does it refer to the patron of the poems, or to the inspirer of the poems, or to the person who helped Thorpe obtain a copy of the poems, or even to the poet himself? – nor do we know who Mr. W.H. is.[2] It is clear that Thorpe has read the poems closely, and is aware that one of their central tropes is the promise of eternal recognition (one of the ironies of literary history is that we are ignorant of the identity of the young man, and know a good amount about the poet). We do know that some of the poems circulated in manuscript before their publication – in 1598 (eleven years before the publication of *Shake-speares Sonnets*) Francis Meres refers in *Palladis Tamia* to "Mellifluous & hony-tongued Shakespeare, witness his . . . sugred Sonnets among his private friends" (Meres 1598). But we do not know which sonnets he refers to here. Despite the vendor's claims that the sonnets were "never before imprinted," sonnets 138 and 144 had been published in a variant form in a popular anthology, *The Passionate Pilgrim*, in 1599, ten years before *Shake-speares Sonnets* appeared.

There are other layers of uncertainty shrouding the collection. We are not certain whether these poems were intended to be read as a sequence, or whether they were written as individual verses and published by Thorpe as a sequence simply to suit the fashion of the time. Even if we assume that Shakespeare was writing a deliberate sequence, we cannot be certain that the 1609 text sets the poems in the precise order Shakespeare intended. But various themes and narrative strands do emerge over the course of the volume. The collection, first of all, is divided into two large sequences: sonnets 1–126, which are written to a beautiful young man, and sonnets 127–52, which are written to a "dark lady." In addition, there are many small thematic or narrative sequences: sonnets 1–17 urge the young man to reproduce, and also meditate on poetry as a mode of reproduction and immortality. Sonnets 91–6 suggest the poet and the young man quarrel and then reconcile, perhaps after some erotic betrayal. Sonnets 133–4 depict the dark lady's unfaithfulness with the young man, while sonnets 135, 136, and 143 develop puns on the poet's name, "Will," and his desire, or "will." Sonnets 153 and 154, the last sonnets in the collection, depict the whimsical yet all-conquering power of Cupid; they describe the futility of any human attempt to "cure" the disease of love. The 1609 sequence concludes with *A Lover's Complaint*, a 329-line narrative poem spoken by a jilted female desolated by erotic abandonment. Although many earlier critics doubted whether the poem was Shakespeare's, John Kerrigan and others have argued decisively for its thematic importance to the collection (Kerrigan in Shakespeare

1986; Burrow in Shakespeare 2002). Many Elizabethan poets had concluded their sonnet sequences with complaints – Samuel Daniel's *Delia* (1592) and Thomas Lodge's *Phillis* (1593) are two celebrated examples. The tone of despair in *A Lover's Complaint*, moreover, provides an apt conclusion to the frequently cynical collection of sonnets that precedes it. Just as the last sonnet suggests that the effort to contain love only gives it further fuel, ending with the line "Love's fire heats water, water cools not love," so the abandoned female in *A Lover's Complaint* admits in her final lines that she would do it all again.

Indeed, one of the most striking things about the sonnets is how utterly unsentimental and rigorously tough-minded their account of love and friendship is. Although they contain some of the most justly celebrated accounts of love and friendship in the English language – sonnet 18, "Shall I compare thee to a Summers day?" and sonnet 116, "Let me not to the marriage of true mindes / Admit impediments" are among the most famous descriptions of the tenderness and authenticity which love is capable of producing – the collection also contains two of the most haunting portraits of the mad compulsions and intemperate behaviors of love in the English language: sonnet 129, "Th'expence of Spirit in a waste of shame" and sonnet 147, "My love is as a feaver longing still." In these poems, love is inseparable from lust, and entails an invariably torturous experience; even its longed-for satisfactions, as 129 (one of the first poems in English to depict orgasm) makes clear, are ephemeral and unsatisfying. Like the miniature of the Young Man in Flames whose portrait graces the cover of this book, these poems depict love as a kind of auto-da-fe, searing all who experience its burning heat (Fumerton 1991). The last two sonnets (153 and 154) pay tribute to the contagious and intractable power of Cupid's "heart inflaming brand" (154. 2). The caloric economy of the sonnets includes the warming fires of passionate commitment and the corroding flames of venereal disease described in the bitter conclusion of sonnet 144.

Whether intended to be read as such or not, the collection as a whole provides a fascinating study of the various pathologies and occasional comforts of erotic desire. Unlike most early modern sonnet sequences, which tend to explore only a single relationship in fastidious (if not repetitive) detail, Shakespeare's sequence explores love in an impressively wide range of moods, situations, and expressions. It describes love between two men, as well as love between men and women. It depicts love between the old and the young. It portrays love traversing putative social and gender-based hierarchies in both directions. It characterizes love as a highly idealized emotion, and as a deeply degrading passion. With all their various love objects, the sonnets explore an enormous range of emotional temperatures, from cool deference to fevered passion.

The sequence as a whole is haunted by the related phenomena of death and change. The poems struggle to find a satisfying answer to the question of what might abide in a world whose only constant is change. Some of the answers that are offered provisionally include progeny (sonnets 1–14), poetry (sonnets 15–17, 54–5, 60), love (*passim*), memory (sonnets 1–18, 54, 64–5, 77, 107, 121–2), and beauty (sonnets 63–8). The poems wonder if anything, including the composition of poetry, can challenge the inherent transience of existence. As a result, the poems engage in the recursive and self-fulfilling claim that as long as they are being read, they prove that poetry can survive (see, for example, the conclusions of sonnets 18 and 55). The poems also wonder whether the ephemerality of an object itself enhances the value of and love for that object or diminishes them; as sonnet 73 concludes: "This thou percev'st, which makes thy love more strong, / To love that well, which thou must leave ere long." Haunted by the transience of love objects and the mobility of desire, the poems aspire to discover what might survive the ravages of time.

The sonnets analyze love in its most heterodox incarnations. The first group of seventeen sonnets, dedicated to the effort to persuade an aristocratic young man to preserve his beauty through procreation, signal that the poems inhabit territory very different from that of the conventional Elizabethan sonnet sequence, typically addressed to a distant mistress. Women are important in these poems primarily as sites of biological reproduction – "From fairest creatures we desire increase," remarks the first line of the first sonnet. Even the beauty of women – the source of so much poetic description in the period – is here merely an indicator of their potential as vehicles for reproducing the young man's beauty.

Shakespeare's sonnets, moreover, scrutinize both heterosexual and same-sex love with great conviction and insight. Only Richard Barnfield and Christopher Marlowe explore love between males with similar vigor (Pequigney 1985; Smith 1991; Hammond 1996). While many of the sonnets do not bear overt markers of the gender of the addressee, some deliberately flout the conventions of heterosexual courtship. Sonnet 20 in particular is addressed to the "Master Mistris" of "my passion," a beautiful young man who encapsulates all that is good in women and men. Nonchalant antifeminism here underwrites praise of the young man, who has "A womans gentle hart but not acquainted / With shifting change as is false womens fashion" (ll. 3–4). This fascinating fable about the complex origins of same-sex love cleverly employs in every line the final unaccented syllable that we still call "feminine rhyme." Bawdy puns on "quaint" (l. 3) and "prick" (l. 13) preclude the poem's resolution into the comfortable neoplatonism to which so many readers have tried to consign it.

Sonnet 144, "Two loves I have of comfort and despair," turns the tropes of traditional homophobia on their head. The speaker of this poem is divided between same-sex and heterosexual commitments. Strikingly, his "femall evill" is opposed to "my better angel." Heterosexuality here entails a world of evil and disease; it is same-sex love which is seraphic. The speaker, moreover, is deeply worried that his two lovers will betray him, and in the process his female evil will infect his better angel with the fiery corruptions of venereal disease. The female lover, furthermore, belies traditional definitions of beauty; while the young man is "right faire," the "worser spirit" is "a woman colloured ill" (ll. 3–4). Her darkness, which may only be an indication of hair or skin coloring, demonstrates how easily western culture has translated differences of color into hierarchies of morality (Hall 1995, 1998; Floyd-Wilson 2003; Iyengar 2005). This sonnet provides the nightmarish consummation of the various scenarios of erotic betrayal that suffuse the sonnets.

Shakespeare, then, discovers little comfort in the pursuit of erotic pleasure. Indeed, sex is troubling because its pleasures are so fleeting, and because it is inherently an act that entails the loss of control. Sexual intercourse is not, for the author of the sonnets, a consummation devoutly to be wished, but a nightmare from which one wishes to awake. The sonnets, though, make available to the reader other forms of comfort and pleasure. Of primary importance among these is the sensuous pleasure that emerges from reading words combined carefully into patterns of expectation and surprise. Allied with this pleasure is the profoundly comforting rhythm of the Shakespearean sonnet form – identifying a problem or situation in the first quatrain, discussing it in the two subsequent quatrains, and resolving, restating, or revealing an essential paradox in the couplet. As one reads through the sequence, one senses a developing aura of logical inevitability about the final couplet. Indeed, the kinds of control the poems discuss provide on the verbal and formal plane a central component of the pleasure they offer. When synchronized with the pendular erotics of iambic pentameter and blended with the visceral pleasure of finding rhythmical and tonal sounds to convey apt emotions, this emergent liturgy of desire produces a soothing inevitability in the concluding couplet. Indeed, one could argue that one of the central pleasures of the sonnets emerges from the tension between their syntactic smoothness and formal regularity and their radical and radically disordered content.

The capacity of these remarkable poems to embody complex emotional states in formally accomplished language remains a draw to readers almost four centuries after their composition. Repudiating traditional paradigms both of the sonnet and of romantic love, their taut formal structures and loose narrative configurations explore the ethical import of aesthetic and erotic effects. Indeed, Shakespeare's accomplished fluency of syntax sometimes causes us to miss the deep tensions and heightened drama contained in the sonnets. But Shakespeare the poet learned much from Shakespeare the dramatist, and vice versa. Shakespeare is not just writing sonnets with the left hand, as John Milton would say of his own composition of polemical prose. Indeed, when Shakespeare seeks in his plays to achieve a kind of heightened affect, it is the formal appurtenances of poetry – meter and rhyme – to which he turns (Cheney 2004). Yet Shakespeare's lyric poetry is not as overtly dramatic as that of his contemporary John Donne, whose poems aspire to the staccato immediacy of dramatic utterance. Shakespeare achieves in his sonnets a remarkable confluence of syntax and form that can sometimes seem to mute rather than amplify the drama implicit in the poetry. This surface smoothness – a valued effect in Shakespeare's day – should not lead us to underestimate the drama that seethes under the surface. Shakespeare's sonnets participate in various dramatic scenarios, both within individual poems and within clusters of various poems.

Compared to Shakespeare's plays, which were published in several unauthorized editions while he lived, and in an "authorized" edition, the First Folio, seven years after his death, the sonnets were published only once in Shakespeare's lifetime, in an edition that may or may not have been authorized. The volume seems not to have been a major hit; a second edition did not appear until 1640, and this was a highly revised and reordered production, John Benson's *Poems: Written by Wil. Shake-speare. Gent.*[3] It is telling that this second edition advertises Shakespeare's status as a gentleman (he had used his profits from the theater to buy the family a coat of arms). It is also telling that the sonnets were excluded from the First Folio of Shakespeare's plays, assembled in 1623. There were no reprintings of the sonnets between 1640 and 1709.

*

This collection of essays aspires to represent the myriad ways that are available today for appreciating the remarkable achievement of the sonnets. The chapters are informed by the latest theoretical, cultural, and archival work, but never forget the accomplishment of earlier generations of scholars and close readers. They are designed to be at the cutting edge of critical thinking about the sonnets, yet accessible to undergraduates and the informed general reader, for whom the sonnets have always held a great interest. Together, they offer a kind of tutorial in current critical engagement with the sonnets by some of the best minds working on Shakespeare and poetry today.

The collection deliberately mixes scholars with established reputations and those whose voices are just emerging. All of the contributors are attentive to the pleasures and rigors of close reading, a method pioneered and honed in the twentieth century for dealing particularly with lyric poetry. But they are also alert to the avenues opened by literary theory, as well as the most recent engagements of archival scholarship. By using these critical and scholarly tools, the essays together begin to delineate some of the aesthetic accomplishment of these fascinating and elusive lyrics.

The essays have been divided into nine parts addressing discrete but overlapping themes, a structure which overall constitutes a kind of deep but not exhaustive core sample of current thought about the sonnets. It is telling that the two largest sections are devoted to exploring, in turn, editorial theory and models of desire, since these have been such fruitful venues for writing on the sonnets.

Part I, "Sonnet Form and Sonnet Sequence," is focused on the two competing modes of significance and attention that all readers of the sonnets must confront: the aesthetic integrity of the highly wrought individual sonnet versus the inviting threads of theme, imagery, and narrative that connect individual poems. We begin where most significant work on the sonnets in the second half of the twentieth century commenced, with Stephen Booth's deeply intelligent account of the aesthetic value of their formal complexity. We then move to the work of one of the finest close readers working today, Helen Vendler, before proceeding to the larger questions of narrative and sequence in the work of James Schiffer, himself an editor of one of the signal collections of essays on the sonnets (Schiffer 1999). In the final essay in this section, Margreta de Grazia explores the ethics implied by the larger narrative patterns of the sonnets.

Part II, "Shakespeare and His Predecessors," is focused on Shakespeare's particular transmutation of the poetic forms he inherited. Richard Strier explores how Shakespeare aggressively remakes the rich materials of his Petrarchan literary inheritance, while Heather Dubrow shows Shakespeare dealing with the model provided by a

near-contemporary, Samuel Daniel. Dympna Callaghan shows Shakespeare working
through his predecessors as well as his contemporaries – primarily Spenser and
Sidney – in developing his particular ideas about time.

Part III, "Editorial Theory and Biographical Inquiry: Editing the Sonnets," looks at
two related areas in scholarship on the sonnets. Beginning with an essay by Richard
Dutton on the implicit if unstated relations between biography and editorial theory,
this part contains essays by Stephen Orgel and Colin Burrow – two major editors of
Shakespeare – discussing the complex, cumulative, and unending project of editing the
sonnets. It concludes with an essay by Lars Engle on the ways in which biography tacitly
informs the work of the highly influential twentieth-century critic William Empson,
one of the best close readers of the sonnets.

Part IV, "The Sonnets in Manuscript and Print," analyzes the scribal and print
cultures from which the sonnets emerged. While Arthur Marotti looks at the sonnets
as they circulated in various manuscripts in the period, Marcy North explores the published sonnets through the history of the publishing conventions of sonnet sequences.

Part V, entitled "Models of Desire in the Sonnets," explores the various patterns of
erotic utterance that emerge in the sonnets. The first essay, by Douglas Trevor, looks
at the distinctly nonplatonic nature of the objects for whom the various speakers express
affection. Bradin Cormack, by contrast, explores Shakespeare's Latinate linguistic
resources for articulating desire. Rayna Kalas uses a close reading of the pivotal sonnet
126 to explore the poetics of subjection and the trajectory of desire. Jyotsna Singh
concludes the section by considering Shakespeare's particular development of a resonant
vocabulary of emotional experience. Part VI, "Ideas of Darkness in the Sonnets,"
contains essays by Ilona Bell and Elizabeth Harvey that explore in very different ways
the discourses emerging around the issues of race, gender, complexion, and aesthetics
that suffuse the sonnets.

In Part VII, "Memory and Repetition in the Sonnets," Garrett Sullivan focuses on the
centrality of memory to notions of identity in the poems, while Amanda Watson looks
at the arts of memory, and how these models of memorialization are assimilated into
the sonnets' repeated efforts to commemorate the young man. Part VIII, "The Sonnets
in/and the Plays," is devoted to the symbiotic relationship between Shakespeare's
dramatic and lyric productions. Where Patrick Cheney looks at how Shakespeare uses
the sonnet form in the plays, William Flesch explores how the plays and the sonnets are
part of a continuous project of delineating personal identity.

The final Part IX, "The Sonnets and *A Lover's Complaint*," reconsiders the importance
of the poem with which the 1609 volume ended. Here Margaret Healy highlights the
alchemical imagery pervading the poem, and Catherine Bates analyzes the appropriateness of the posture of female abjection as a conclusion to the volume.

No party line was followed in the solicitation or composition of these essays; indeed,
I tried to encourage a wide range of critical commitments, and to foster some productive tensions among the various essays. If there was a tacitly governing paradigm at
work, it was simply an aspiration to emphasize the kinds of scholarly, critical, and
archival work that interrogate the theories that inform it; an aspiration rooted in

admiration for a variety of practitioners in whose work theories are subjected to texts and contexts just as rigorously as texts have been subjected to theories. The poems, of course, remain far richer and more interesting than anything we can say about them. We must never forget, moreover, that we read them in large part for the complex pleasures they give us.

In her introduction to *The Art of Shakespeare's Sonnets*, Helen Vendler, a vigorous and articulate advocate of the exquisite pleasures of poetry, asserts that political concerns and aesthetic interests are inevitably opposed, and further, that recent criticism has erred in its emphasis on the former at the expense of the latter:

> I . . . wish to defend the high value I put on them [the sonnets], since they are being written about these days with considerable jaundice. The spheres from which most of the current criticisms are generated are social and psychological ones. Contemporary emphasis on the participation of literature in a social matrix balks at acknowledging how lyric, though it may *refer to* the social, remains the genre that directs its *mimesis* toward the performance of the mind in *solitary* speech. (Vendler 1997: 1–2)

I would agree that the aesthetic has been ignored in recent criticism, to the detriment of our comprehension and appreciation of these remarkable poems. I would argue, though, that the political and the aesthetic are not necessarily opposed, and are in these poems absolutely inseparable. I would also argue that the following essays offer eloquent testimony to that effect. Our appreciation for the aesthetic accomplishment of the sonnets is enhanced by our attention to the poems' shrewd transmutation of social, historical, and psychological materials. I would assert, furthermore, that the sonnets' deliberate and obsessive participation in the partial fiction of deeply social speech constitutes a substantial portion of their aesthetic accomplishment. In their profound exploration of the psychological dimensions of such speech, and their provisional struggle to stave off in formally accomplished language the harrowing transience of existence, they still have much to say to us.

NOTES

1 Since Stephen Booth's marvelous and prize-winning edition of 1978, the sonnets have been edited by John Kerrigan (1986), G. B. Evans (1996), Katherine Duncan-Jones (1997), Helen Vendler (1997), and most recently, Colin Burrow (2002).

2 Viable candidates for the mysterious Mr. W.H. include Henry Wriothesley, the Earl of Southampton, whose initials may have been accidentally transposed by an otherwise careful printer, and William Herbert, the third Earl of Pembroke, co-dedicatee of the First Folio of Shakespeare's plays.

3 Benson claims, almost certainly disingenuously, that his edition, which frequently combines several sonnets into a single poem to which he devotes a thematic title, and which mingles those conglomerate poems with poems that are not by Shakespeare from an anthology entitled *The Passionate Pilgrim* (the expanded second edition of 1612), allows the poems finally to "appear of the same purity, the Author himselfe then living avouched" (Shakespeare 1640).

References and Further Reading

Barnfield, Richard (1990). *The Complete Poems*, ed. George Klawitter. Selinsgrove: Susquehanna University Press.

Bate, Jonathan (1997). *The Genius of Shakespeare*. London: Macmillan-Picador.

Booth, Stephen (1969). *An Essay on Shakespeare's Sonnets*. New Haven: Yale University Press.

Cheney, Patrick (2004). *Shakespeare, National Poet-Playwright*. Cambridge, UK: Cambridge University Press.

Cheney, Patrick, ed. (2007). *The Cambridge Companion to Shakespeare's Poetry*. Cambridge, UK: Cambridge University Press.

Crystal, David, and Crystal, Ben (2002). *Shakespeare's Words: A Glossary and Language Companion*. Harmondsworth: Penguin.

Dubrow, Heather (1997). *Captive Victors: Shakespeare's Narrative Poems and Sonnets*. Ithaca, NY: Cornell University Press.

Duncan-Jones, Katherine (2001). *Ungentle Shakespeare: Scenes from His Life*. London: Thomas Nelson. (The Arden Shakespeare.)

Empson, William (1930). *Seven Types of Ambiguity*. London: Chatto & Windus.

Edmondson, Paul, and Wells, Stanley (2004). *Shakespeare's Sonnets*. Oxford: Oxford University Press.

Fineman, Joel (1986). *Shakespeare's Perjured Eye: The Invention of Poetic Subjectivity in the Sonnets*. Berkeley: University of California Press.

Floyd-Wilson, Mary (2003). *English Ethnicity and Race in Early Modern Drama*. Cambridge, UK: Cambridge University Press.

Fumerton, Patricia (1991). *Cultural Aesthetics: Renaissance Literature and Practice of Social Ornament*. Chicago: University of Chicago Press.

Greenblatt, Stephen (2004). *Will in the World: How Shakespeare Became Shakespeare*. New York: Norton.

Hall, Kim F. (1995). *Things of Darkness: Economies of Race and Gender in Early Modern England*. Ithaca, NY: Cornell University Press.

Hall, Kim F. (1998). " 'These bastard signs of fair': Literary Whiteness in Shakespeare's Sonnets." In Ania Loomba and Martin Orkin (eds.), *Post-Colonial Shakespeares*, 64–83. London and New York: Routledge.

Hammond, Paul (1996). *Love between Men in English Literature*. Basingstoke: Macmillan.

Hyland, Peter (2003). *An Introduction to Shakespeare's Poems*. Basingstoke: Palgrave Macmillan.

Iyengar, Sujata (2005). *Shades of Difference: Mythologies of Skin Color in Early Modern England*. Philadelphia: University of Pennsylvania Press.

Kay, Dennis (1998). *William Shakespeare: Sonnets and Poems*. New York: Twayne.

Meres, Francis (1598). *Palladis Tamia, or Wit's Treasury*. London.

Pequigney, Joseph (1985). *Such Is My Love: A Study of Shakespeare's Sonnets*. Chicago: University of Chicago Press.

Roberts, Sasha (2003). *Reading Shakespeare's Poems in Early Modern England*. New York: Palgrave Macmillan.

Schalkwyk, David (2002). *Speech and Performance in Shakespeare's Sonnets and Plays*. Cambridge, UK: Cambridge University Press.

Schiffer, James, ed. (1999). *Shakespeare's Sonnets: Critical Essays*. New York: Garland.

Schoenfeldt, Michael (1999). *Bodies and Selves in Early Modern England: Physiology and Inwardness in Spenser, Shakespeare, Herbert, and Milton*. Cambridge, UK: Cambridge University Press.

Shakespeare, William (1640). *Poems: Written by Wil. Shake-speare. Gent.*, ed. John Benson. London.

Shakespeare, William (1977). *Shakespeare's Sonnets*, ed. Stephen Booth. New Haven: Yale University Press.

Shakespeare, William (1986). *The Sonnets and A Lover's Complaint*, ed. John Kerrigan. Harmondsworth: Penguin. (The New Penguin Shakespeare.)

Shakespeare, William (1996). *The New Cambridge Shakespeare: The Sonnets*, ed. G. B. Evans. Cambridge, UK: Cambridge University Press.

Shakespeare, William (1997). *Shakespeare's Sonnets*, ed. Katherine Duncan-Jones. London: Thomas Nelson. (The Arden Shakespeare.)

Shakespeare, William (2002). *The Complete Sonnets and Poems*, ed. Colin Burrow. Oxford: Oxford University Press. (Oxford World's Classics.)

Smith, Bruce (1991). *Homosexual Desire in Shakespeare's England: A Cultural Poetics.* Chicago: University of Chicago Press.

Spiller, Michael G. (1992). *The Development of the Sonnet.* London: Routledge.

Vendler, Helen (1997). *The Art of Shakespeare's Sonnets.* Cambridge, Mass.: Harvard University Press.

Wall, Wendy (1993). *The Imprint of Gender: Authorship and Publication in the English Renaissance.* Ithaca, NY: Cornell University Press.

Wells, Stanley (2004). *Looking for Sex in Shakespeare.* Cambridge, UK: Cambridge University Press.

PART I
Sonnet Form and
Sonnet Sequence

1

The Value of the Sonnets

Stephen Booth

Shakespeare and the Essence of Verse

An artist usually presents a given object or idea in one relationship to other objects and ideas; if he opens his reader's consciousness to more than one frame of reference, he focuses on the object in one of its relationships and subordinates all other relationships to it. The essential action of the artist in creating the experience of an audience is the one that in grammar is made by indicators of relationship like "although," "but," "after," "because," "however." In literature such indicators of relationship tell the reader that he is not in the borderless world outside art where he himself has always to work upon what he perceives, to arrange it around a focal point chosen and maintained by himself. Syntactic organization tells the reader that he is dealing with what we are likely to label "truth," experience sorted, classed, and rated, rather than with "what is true," the still to be sorted data of "real" experience.[1]

The great distinction between the experience of life and of art is that art, by fixing one or more sets of relationships, gives its audience an experience in which objects *are* as they must be to be thought about, in which the audience can see what I have called "truth" without having to hunt it out and pull it out, in which "what is true" and "truth" can be the same. Art presents the mind with an experience in which it is at home rather than one in which it must make itself at home by focusing, stressing, and subordinating. All works of literary art, from the simplest sentence of the simplest mind to *King Lear*, are alike in that they are fixed orderings that place their audiences in an experience ready fitted to the experiencer's manner and means of experiencing.

Such orderings incline to be self-defeating. What we ask of art is that it allow the mind to comprehend – know, grasp, embrace – more of experience than the mind can comprehend. In that case, art must fail because the impossibility of its task is one of

Excerpt from *An Essay on Shakespeare's Sonnets* by Stephen Booth, pp. 169–87. New Haven, CT: Yale University Press, 1969.

its defining factors. To state it simplemindedly, we demand that the impossible be done and still remain an impossibility. When an artist focuses his audience's mind and distorts what is true into a recognizable, graspable shape to fit that mind, he not only does what his audience asks but what cannot long satisfy audience or artist just because the desired distortion *is* a distortion. Art must distort; if it is to justify its existence, it must be other than the reality whose difficulty necessitates artistic mediation. It must seem as little a distortion as possible, because its audience wants comprehension of incomprehensible reality itself. We do not want so much to live in *a* world organized on human principles as to live in *the* world so organized. Art must seem to reveal a humanly ordered reality rather than replace a random one. Our traditional values in art exhibit its self-contradictory nature; all the following adjectives, for example, regularly say that the works of art to which they are applied are good: "unified," "sublime," "clear," "subtle," "coherent," "natural." In a style we are likely to value both simplicity and complexity; we ask that a character be both consistent and complex. Above all, what we want of art is the chance to believe that the orderliness of art is not artificial but of the essence of the substance described, that things are as they look when they have a circle around them. We don't want to feel that art is orderly. We want to feel that things are orderly. We want to feel that art does not make order but shows it.

There are as many ways of trying for the contradictory effects of art as there are artists. All of them aim at replacing the complexities of reality with controlled complexities that will make the experience of the orderly work of art sufficiently similar to the experience of random nature, so that the comfort of artistic coherence will not be immediately dismissed as irrelevant to the intellectual discomfort of the human condition. No work of art has ever been perfectly satisfactory. That is obvious. No work of art has ever satisfied the human need to hold human existence whole in the mind. If a work of art ever succeeded perfectly, it would presumably be the last of its kind; it would do what the artist as theologian describes as showing the face of God. All works have failed because the experience they are asked for and give is unlike nonartistic experience. Neither reality nor anything less than reality will satisfy the ambitions of the human mind.

Of all literary artists, Shakespeare has been most admired. The reason may be that he comes closest to success in giving us the sense both that we know what cannot be known and that what we know is the unknowable thing we want to know and not something else. I have tried to demonstrate that in the sonnets Shakespeare copes with the problem of the conflicting obligations of a work of art by multiplying the number of ordering principles, systems of organization, and frames of reference in the individual sonnets. I have argued that the result of that increase in artificiality is pleasing because the reader's sense of coherences rather than coherence gives him both the simple comfort of order and the comfort that results from the likeness of his ordered experience of the sonnet to the experience of disorderly natural phenomena. In nonartistic experience the mind is constantly shifting its frames of reference. In the experience of the sonnet it makes similar shifts, but from one to another of overlapping frames of reference that are firmly ordered and fixed. The kind and quantity of mental action necessary in nonartistic experience is demanded by the sonnet, but that approximation of real experience is made to occur within mind-formed limits of logic, or subject matter, or form, or sound.

Shakespeare's multiplication of ordering systems is typically Shakespearean in being unusual not in itself but in its degree. The principle of multiple orders is a defining principle of verse in general. Although "verse" and "prose" are not really precise terms, verse is ordinarily distinguishable from prose in that it presents its materials organized in at least two self-assertive systems at once: at least one of meaning and at least one of sound. Here, as an almost random example, are the first lines of Surrey's translation of the *Aeneid*, Book II:

> They whisted all, with fixed face attent,
> When prince Aeneas from the royal seat
> Thus gan to speak: "O Quene! it is thy will
> I should renew a woe cannot be told,
> How that the Grekes did spoile and ouerthrow
> The Phrygian wealth and wailful realm of Troy.[2]

As the principle of multiple ordering is common to poems at large, so its usual operation is different only in degree from its operation in a Shakespeare sonnet. Where one system tends to pull things together, another tends to separate. In the sample above, the syntax tends to unify and the form to divide. Similarly, in all literature any single system of organization is likely both to unify and to divide. Since not only verse but any literature, any sentence, is a putting together, the very nature of the undertaking evokes an awareness both of unity and of the division that necessitates the unifying. Thus, at the risk of belaboring the evident, the statement *They whisted all, with fixed face attent* is a clear unit of meaning made up of clearly articulated parts. The larger whole of the Surrey passage is similarly a unit made of distinct clauses and phrases. Formal organizations work the same way. The second line looks like the first and rhythmically is pointedly similar, but they are not identical either in appearance or sound. They look and sound as different from one another as they look and sound alike. Inside a line the same unifying and dividing exists. What is on one side of the pause, *They whisted all*, is roughly the same length as *with fixed face attent*, which balances it. Moreover, the fact that they make up a single line is just as active as the fact that they are divided by the pause.

The addition of rhyme to syntactic and metrical organization is the addition of one more independent system of organization. This is Dryden's version of the opening of the *Aeneid*, II:

> All were attentive to the godlike man,
> When from his lofty couch he thus began:
> "Great queen, what you command me to relate
> Renews the sad remembrance of our fate:
> An empire from its old foundations rent,
> And every woe the Trojans underwent[3]

Rhyme also adds another manifestation of the principle of unification and division. Aside from puns, rhyme presents the best possible epitome of the principle. Two rhyming words are pointedly like and unlike in sound, and they pull apart and together with equal force.

Any verse is capable of this kind of analysis. Since what it demonstrates is obvious, there is no need to prolong it. Still, if such analysis is unnecessary in most verse, what it reveals is nonetheless true: verse in general is multiply organized.

Shakespeare and the Sonnet Form – Sonnet 15

Although Wordsworth's "Scorn not the Sonnet" is not a good advertisement for the justice of its plea, the fact that Wordsworth himself wrote sonnets, that he wrote them when nobody else was writing sonnets, that Milton wrote them when almost nobody else was writing sonnets, and that Shakespeare wrote his well after the Elizabethan sonnet vogue had passed suggests that there may be something about the sonnet form that makes it not to be scorned. In an earlier chapter I said that the sonnet form in any of its varieties is simultaneously unifying and divisive. Those contradictory coactions result from its unusually high number of systems of organization. In the limited terms of my thesis that multiplicity of structures is an essence of verse, the sonnet is an especially poetic form. The first line of an English sonnet participates in a metrical pattern (fourteen iambic pentameter lines), a rhyme pattern (*abab*), a trio of quatrains (alike in being quatrains, different in using different rhymes), and an overall pattern contrasting two different kinds of rhyme scheme (three quatrains set against one couplet). I suggest that the concentration of different organizing systems active in the form before any particulars of substance or syntax are added is such as to attract the kind of mind that is particularly happy in the multiple organizations of verse: witness Shakespeare, Milton, and Wordsworth. The different patterns inside the sonnet form pull together and pull apart just as the different patterns do in verse forms less crowded with coherences. The sonnet does what all verse does; it just does more of it.

As the sonnet form extends the basic verse principle of multiple organization, so Shakespeare's sonnets reflect and magnify the tendencies of the form itself. In superimposing many more patterns upon the several organizations inherent in the form, Shakespeare marshals the sonnet the way that it was going. Having talked at length about the kind, quantity, and operation of the patterns in which Shakespeare organizes his sonnets, I propose to pull together what I have said and summarize it, but to do so in the abstract would not, I think, be meaningful. Instead, I will take one sonnet, number 15, and use it to make a summary demonstration of the kinds and interactions of patterns in Shakespeare's sonnets generally:

> When I consider everything that grows
> Holds in perfection but a little moment,
> That this huge stage presenteth nought but shows

Whereon the stars in secret influence comment;
When I perceive that men as plants increase,
Cheered and checked even by the selfsame sky,
Vaunt in their youthful sap, at height decrease,
And wear their brave state out of memory:
Then the conceit of this inconstant stay
Sets you most rich in youth before my sight,
Where wasteful Time debateth with Decay
To change your day of youth to sullied night;
    And, all in war with Time for love of you,
    As he takes from you, I ingraft you new.

On top of the formal pattern (4, 4, 4, 2) is a logical pattern (8, 6) established in the syntactical construction *when/then*. In the first eight lines, which are formally two quatrains and logically an octave, a 2, 2, 4 pattern arises from the three object clauses: [*that*] *everything* . . . (two lines), *that this huge stage* . . . (two lines), *that men as plants* . . . (four lines).

In addition to these three major structures and structuring principles, the nonformal phonetic patterns that operate in the poem are probably literally innumerable. They tend to interact with the other patterning systems in much the same way that the other systems interact with each other: an informal sound pattern will link elements that are divided, or divide elements that are linked, by the formal or logical or syntactical or rhythmic patterns.

Considering the great many words it takes to talk about sounds, it would not be profitable to talk about them here. [. . .] It should suffice here to say that informal sound patterns do what I have said the multiple patterns of the sonnets do generally. The mere fact of their presence adds to the reader's sense that he is engaged in an ordered, coherent, nonrandom, humanly geared experience. They help the poem give a sense of the intense and universal relevance of all things to all other things. The companion fact of their great number helps maintain in the reader an accompanying sense that, for all the artistic order of his reading experience, it is not a limited one. No one of the sound patterns dominates the others over the whole length of the poem; similarly, no one pattern of any kind dominates the whole poem. From moment to moment incidental sound patterns keep the reader aware of the orderliness, the rationality, of the experience, but the principal patterning factor does not stay the same from moment to moment. The multiplication of sound patterns, like the multiplication of structures generally, increases the reader's sense of order, while at the same time it diminishes the sense of limitation that a dominant pattern can add to the limitation inherent in the focusing of the reader's attention on particular subjects in particular relationships. In short, by fixing so many phonetic relationships and by putting a single word in so many of those relationships, Shakespeare overcomes the limitation that order entails. The reader is engaged in so many organizations that the experience of the poem is one both of comprehending (for which order, limit, pattern, and reason are necessary) and of having comprehended what remains incomprehensible because it does not seem to have been limited. Nothing in the poem strikes the reader as seen only "in terms of." Everything is presented in multiple terms — more as it is than as it is understood.

Shakespeare and the Sonnet Tradition – Sonnet 15

I have said that the peculiarly Shakespearean effect of these sonnets arises in part from a bold extension of a principle basic to verse generally and to the sonnet form particularly. The same can be said about an extension of the basic principle of courtly love in general and the sonnet convention in particular.

More than a writer in any other genre, a sonneteer depends for his effects on the conjunction or conflict of what he says with what the reader expects. Like the basic courtly love convention from which it grew, the sonnet convention is one of indecorum. Its essential device is the use of the vocabulary appropriate to one kind of experience to talk about another. The writer talked about his lady and his relation to her as if she were a feudal lord and he a vassal, or as if she were the Virgin Mary and he a supplicant to her. A witty emphasis on the paradoxically simultaneous pertinence and impertinence of the writer's language and stance to his subject matter is of the essence of the convention. The lady was not a deity or a baron, but she was virtuous, powerful, beautiful. In all stages of its development, the courtly love tradition relies upon a reader's sense of the frame of reference in which the writer operates and the writer's apparent deviation from that pattern in a rhetorical action that both fits and violates the expected pattern.

By the time the first Italian and French sonnets were written, the conventions of courtly love were traditional, and a decorum, albeit a decorum of indecorum, was firmly established for aristocratic secular love poetry. Followers of Petrarch wrote to be judged on their success in introducing variations within a narrow and prescribed space, using set vocabulary and subject matter. To be appreciated, the sonneteer presupposed an audience whose presuppositions he could rely on. An audience for a sonnet had to be able to recognize a new surprise in a convention of long established paradoxes.

Perhaps the poems most typical of all the rhetorical actions of courtly love writers are those which exploit the apparently inexhaustible surprise of returning the language of religion to religious subject matter inside the courtly love and sonnet conventions. Dante did it in the thirteenth century; Donne did it in the seventeenth. A good example is this sonnet which George Herbert sent home to his mother from Cambridge:

> My God, where is that ancient heat towards thee,
>   Wherewith whole showls of *Martyrs* once did burn,
>   Besides their other flames? Doth Poetry
> Wear *Venus* Livery? only serve her turn?
> Why are not *Sonnets* made of thee? and layes
>   Upon thine Altar burnt? Cannot thy love
>   Heighten a spirit to sound out thy praise
> As well as any she? Cannot thy *Dove*
> Out-strip their *Cupid* easily in flight?

> Or, since thy wayes are deep, and still the same,
>   Will not a verse run smooth that bears thy name?
> Why doth that fire, which by thy power and might
>   Each breast does feel, no braver fuel choose
>   Than that, which one day Worms may chance refuse?[4]

Exaggerated predictability and surprise, pertinence and impertinence, are in the nature of the convention; and all the devices I have talked about have a common denominator with the more grossly effective conjunction of frames of reference in the earliest courtly love poetry, in Donne's *Holy Sonnets*, and in such collisions of value systems as that between the last line of this Sidney sonnet and the rest of the poem:

> It is most true, that eyes are form'd to serve
> The inward light: and that the heavenly part
> Ought to be king, from whose rules who do swerve,
> Rebels to Nature, strive for their owne smart,
>   It is most true, what we call *Cupid's* dart,
> An image is, which for our selves we carve;
> And, fooles, adore in temple of our hart,
> Till that good God make Church and Churchman starve.
>   True, that true Beautie Vertue is indeed,
> Whereof this Beautie can be but a shade,
> Which elements with mortall mixture breed;
>   True, that true Beautie Vertue is indeed,
>   And should in soule up to our countrey move:
>   True, and yet true that I must *Stella* love.[5]

Sometimes, as in the following sonnet from *Arcadia*, the whole effect of a poem will depend upon a reader's familiarity with the genre being so great that for an instant he will hear only the poet's manner and not his matter:

> What length of verse can serve brave *Mopsa's* good to show,
> Whose vertues strange, and beuties such, as no man them may know?
> Thus shrewdly burdned then, how can my Muse escape?
> The gods must help, and pretious things must serve to shew her shape.
>   Like great god *Saturn* faire, and like faire *Venus* chaste:
> As smooth as *Pan*, as *Juno* milde, like goddesse *Isis* faste.
> With *Cupid* she fore-sees, and goes god *Vulcan's* pace:
> And for a tast of all these gifts, she borowes *Momus'* grace.
>   Her forhead jacinth like, her cheekes of opall hue,
> Her twinkling eies bedeckt with pearle, her lips of Saphir blew:
> Her haire pure Crapal-stone; her mouth O heavenly wyde;
> Her skin like burnisht gold, her hands like silver ure untryde.
>   As for those parts unknowne, which hidden sure are best:
>   Happie be they which well beleeve, and never seeke the rest.[6]

Like his predecessors, Shakespeare plays openly on his reader's expectations about
the sonnet convention in poems like sonnet 130 (*My mistress' eyes are nothing like the
sun*) and in the bawdy conclusions of sonnets 20, 144, and 151. Shakespeare's dark lady
is traditionally cited as contrary to the traditional beloved, but the very impropriety
of a technically unattractive and morally vicious beloved is a consistent enlargement
on the standard rhetorical principle of the convention; and, whatever other significance
there may be, certainly addressing love sonnets to a man is an all but predictable
extreme of courtly love technique. Shakespeare's surprises, like Dante's, Donne's,
and George Herbert's, come from going farther in the direction natural to the
convention.

Although Shakespeare exploits the reader's expectations in the largest elements of
the sonnets, similar smaller plays on the reader's expectations about syntax and idiom
are more numerous. Moreover, their effects are more typical of the general rhetoric of
the sonnets. Where both the traditional clashes of contexts in courtly love poetry, and
Sidney's sudden shifts in clearly distinguished systems of value call attention to themselves, the comparable actions in the syntactical fabric of sonnets like number 15 do
not fully impinge on the reader's consciousness, and so do not merely describe inconstancy but evoke a real sense of inconstancy from a real experience of it. In sonnet 15
the reader is presented with the subject, verb, and direct object of the potentially complete clause *When I consider everything that grows*. The next line continues the clause and
requires an easy but total reconstitution of the reader's conception of the kind of sentence
he is reading; he has to understand *When I consider [that] everything that grows / Holds in
perfection but a little moment*. The kind of demand on the reader made syntactically in
the first two lines is made in lines 11 and 12 by a nonidiomatic use of the common
construction "debate with":

> . . . wasteful Time debateth with Decay
> To change your day of youth to sullied night. . . .

Having newly learned to understand *with* as "in the company of," the reader is forced
by the couplet to readjust his understanding when essentially the same idiom appears
in a variation on its usual sense, "fight against":

> And, all in war with Time for love of you,
> As he takes from you, I ingraft you new.

Just as the reader's mind moves from one to another formal or logical or phonetic
structure, it also moves back and forth among metaphoric frames of reference. The
terms in which the speaker presents his meaning, the "things" of the poem, are from
a variety of ideological frames of reference, and the reader's mind is in constant motion
from one context to another. Like all the other stylistic qualities I have talked about,
the variation and quick change in the metaphoric focus of the sonnets presents in little
the basic quality of courtly love and sonnet convention.

The first active metaphor of the poem, *grows*, carries a vaguely botanical reference over into line 2, whose substance lends itself to overtones of traditional floral expressions of the *carpe diem* theme. The overtones would have been particularly strong for a reader accustomed to *perfection* in its common Renaissance meaning, "ripeness":

> When I consider everything that grows
> Holds in perfection but a little moment

Line 3 begins a new object clause, logically and syntactically parallel with the first. That parallelism helps the reader accept the new theatrical metaphor as an alternative means of simply restating the substance of the first clause. Moreover, the theatrical metaphor continues and reinforces the *watcher–watched* relationship established first in line 1 for the speaker and what he considers, and fully mirrored when line 4 introduces a new metaphor, the secretly influential stars, which are to the world-stage roughly as the powerless speaker was to the mortal world in line 1:

> That this huge stage presenteth nought but shows
> Whereon the stars in secret influence comment

The tone of the quatrain is matter-of-fact as befits a declaration so simple and so obviously justified that it is a subordinate prologue to the statement proper. That the matter-of-fact tone withstands coexistence with three distinct metaphors would be remarkable if each new metaphor were not introduced into the reader's mind as if it were already there.

Parallel syntax and parallel relationships suggest equation between the two object clauses – an equation which gives the reader a sense that what is both new and separate from the first two lines is at the same time neither new nor separate. In short, the physics of the quatrain's substance are the same as those of its rhyme scheme. The three metaphors pull both apart and together. The stars in line 4 are both new to the poem and have been in it covertly from the start. Probably only a mind as pun-ready as Shakespeare's own could hear the echo of Latin *sidus, sider-*, "star," in *consider*, but for any reader the act of imagining *this huge stage* presupposes the vantage point of the stars; the reader is thinking from the heavens, and, when the stars themselves are mentioned, their propriety is immediately further established because the stars comment, like critics at a play.[7]

Just as such an incidental sound pattern as *cheerèd and checked* emerges (from *perceive* and *increase*) into dominance and then submerges again (in *sky* and *decrease*) into the music of the whole, so the substance of the poem slips into and out of metaphoric frames of reference, always in a frame of reference some of whose parts pertain incidentally to one of the other metaphors from which and into which it moves.

> When I perceive that men as plants increase,
> Cheerèd and checked even by the selfsame sky,
> Vaunt in their youthful sap, at height decrease,
> And wear their brave state out of memory

At the beginning of quatrain 2, *plants increase* returns the botanical metaphor to clear prominence. The next line, *Cheerèd and checked even by the selfsame sky*, pertains very well to a growing plant (*Cheerèd* – smiled upon – *and checked* – restrained, held back, by the vagaries of the weather), but the primary syntactical object here is *men*, and *Cheerèd and checked* suggests the theatrical metaphor, particularly in the second half of the line, when the encouragement and rebuke turn out to be given *by the selfsame sky* that has earlier been audience to the shows on the huge stage.[8] In line 7, *Vaunt* confirms the metaphoric dominance of boastful, strutting actors, but in the phrase that follows, *youthful*, which pertains directly to men (actors), is coupled with *sap*, a word from the botanical frame of reference to which *youthful* applies only figuratively, and which itself is only metaphorically descriptive of the humors of men: *Vaunt in their youthful sap, at height decrease*. *At height* is metaphorically applicable to the careers of men and the performances of haughty actors, and it is literally descriptive of a plant at its full growth, but the context to which *height* more usually belongs is astronomy (its context in sonnet 116). The phrase *at height decrease* confirms an earlier suggestion of the sun's passage across the sky or of the waxing moon – a suggestion that does not conform logically to the other use of astronomical metaphor, but that does persist throughout the quatrain. At the end of line 5, *increase* pertained obviously to *plants*. Its noun-meaning "fruit of the harvest," appears prominently in sonnets 1 and 11 which precede this one in the 1609 sequence; here, however, astronomical senses of *increase* also pertain. The *OED* reports Renaissance uses of the noun form of *increase* to mean "the rising of the tide . . . the advance of daylight from sunrise to noon; the waxing of the moon," and cites Renaissance examples in which forms of *decrease* indicate the negative of all three astronomical senses of *increase*. In this context *at height decrease* suggests the waning of the moon (taking *at height* figuratively to mean "fullness"), the descent of the sun (taking *at height* literally, and *decrease* to mean the decline of daylight from noon to sunset), and a tidelike ebbing of once *youthful sap*.

The last line of the quatrain, *And wear their brave state out of memory*, brings back the actors strutting in their finery, but its juxtaposition with *at height decrease* and the vague, cosmic immensity of *out of memory* give the line a majestic fall more appropriate to the descent of the sun than the perseverance of a player king. The reader's experience of this line is a type of his experience of this sonnet and the sonnets in general. The line is easy to understand, but it would be hard to say just what it says or how it says it. *Wear* in combination with *their brave state* says something like "wear their fine clothes." Following on *at height decrease*, *and wear* has reference to movement in space (*OED*, s.v. *Wear*, v. 21), and so, still under the influence of *Vaunt*, the half line says: "continue to advance in their pomp and finery." Thus, when he comes upon *out of*, the reader is likely to take it spatially (as in "out of the country"). On the other hand, *out* is in the same line with *wear* and *brave state*, and so leads the reader's understanding into a context of wearing out clothes, a context that is an excellent metaphor for the larger idea of the decay in time of everything that grows. The syntax of the line presents *memory* as if it were a place, but its sense makes it capable of comprehension only in terms of time. In common idiom "out of memory" refers to the distant, unseen past; but in *wear their brave state out of memory* the reference must be to the unseeable future. The statement of the octave takes in everything that has grown, grows, or will grow, and the multiple reference made by the conflict between standard usage and the use of *out of memory* in this line allows the reader an approximation of actual comprehension of all time and space in one.

The last six lines of the sonnet are more abstract than the first eight, and the three metaphors become more separable from each other, from a new metaphor of warfare, and from the abstract statements that they figure forth. In line 10 the beloved is set before the speaker's sight in a refrain of the theatrical metaphor; in line 12 the astronomical metaphor appears overtly in a commonplace; in the last line *ingraft* brings the botanical metaphor into a final statement otherwise contained entirely in the metaphor of warfare:

> Then the conceit of this inconstant stay
> Sets you most rich in youth before my sight,
> Where wasteful Time debateth with Decay
> To change your day of youth to sullied night;
>   And, all in war with Time for love of you,
>   As he takes from you, I ingraft you new.

After the experience of the octave, the experience of the sestet is a clear awareness of the simplicity hidden in a great – a lifelike – complexity of relationships. The couplet describes a facile and fanciful triumph over time. The reader's experience of it, however, is the justified culmination of a small but real intellectual triumph over the limits of his own understanding.

The Value of the Sonnets

A formulated idea – written down, ordered, settled, its elements fixed in permanent relationship to one another as parts of a whole – accentuates its reader's incapacity to cope fully with what is outside the description. Like a fort, any statement presupposes, and so emphasizes, the frailty of the people it serves. Wordsworth made the point more cheerfully and in specific praise of the sonnet:

> Nuns fret not at their convent's narrow room;
> And hermits are contented with their cells;
> And students with their pensive citadels;
> Maids at the wheel, the weaver at his loom,
> Sit blithe and happy; bees that soar for bloom,
> High as the highest Peak of Furness-fells,
> Will murmur by the hour in foxglove bells:
> In truth the prison, unto which we doom
> Ourselves, no prison is: and hence for me,

> In sundry moods, 'twas pastime to be bound
> Within the Sonnet's scanty plot of ground;
> Pleased if some Souls (for such there needs must be)
> Who have felt the weight of too much liberty,
> Should find brief solace there, as I have found.⁹

The many different patterns that exist in any sonnet by virtue of its form make it seem crowded or, if that word has irremediably derisive connotations, full. Shakespeare's enlargement of the number and kinds of patterns makes his sonnets seem full to bursting not only with the quantity of different actions but with the energy generated from their conflict. The reader has constantly to cope with the multitudinous organizations of a Shakespeare sonnet; he is engaged and active. Nonetheless, the sonnets are above all else artificial, humanly ordered; the reader is always capable of coping. He always has the comfort and security of a frame of reference, but the frames of reference are not constant, and their number seems limitless.

The solace to be found in a Shakespeare sonnet is brief indeed, but it is as great a solace as literature can give – the feeling that the weight of liberty is not too much. That is a remarkable achievement for a reader and for the writer who gives it to him. I think it is that achievement which readers acknowledge when they praise Shakespeare's sonnets.

NOTES

1 It might be argued that, strictly speaking, no experience is completely unorganized, since, by definition, experience implies a perceiver who in various ways shapes the raw materials, whatever they are, which provide the ingredients of any perception. But even if, philosophically speaking, the disjunction between organized and unorganized experience is false, it nevertheless remains valid to speak of degrees of organization and to distinguish as sharply as I have done between the highly organized world of art and the comparatively shapeless world of everyday existence. Whether or not this difference is one of degree, it is so great as to warrant speaking of it for critical purposes as if it were a difference in kind.

2 *Poems of Henry Howard Earl of Surrey*, ed. F. M. Padelford (Seattle: University of Washington Press, 1920).

3 *The Poetical Works of John Dryden*, ed. George R. Noyes (New York: Macmillan, 1908), p. 536.

4 *The Works of George Herbert*, ed. F. E. Hutchinson (Oxford: Oxford University Press, 1941), p. 206.

5 *The Poems of Sir Philip Sidney*, ed. William A. Ringler, Jr. (Oxford: Clarendon Press, 1962), p. 157.

6 *Poems of Sir Philip Sidney*, p. 12.

7 Moreover, in the pattern in *s* and *t* that runs across both lines, *stars*, the fourth syllable of line 4, alliterates with *stage* in the same metrical position in line 3.

8 "Cheer" has a specifically theatrical meaning for a modern reader that it did not have for Shakespeare, but, even though it did not yet refer to shouts of applause, "cheer" did have the general meaning "encourage," from which the later meaning presumably developed.

9 *The Poetical Works of Wordsworth*, ed. Thomas Hutchinson, rev. Ernest de Selincourt (Oxford: Oxford University Press, 1950), p. 199.

2

Formal Pleasure in the Sonnets

Helen Vendler

The Art of the Sonnets, and the Speaker They Create

With respect to the *Sonnets* – a text now almost four hundred years old – what can a commentary offer that is new? It can, I think, approach the sonnets, as I have chosen to do, from the vantage point of the poet who wrote them, asking the questions that a poet would ask about any poem. What was the aesthetic challenge for Shakespeare in writing these poems, of confining himself (with a few exceptions) to a single architectural form? (I set aside, as not of essential importance, the money or privileges he may have earned from his writing.) A writer of Shakespeare's seriousness writes from internal necessity – to do the best he can under his commission (if he was commissioned) and to perfect his art. What is the inner agenda of the *Sonnets*? What are their compositional motivations? What does a writer gain from working, over and over, in one subgenre? My brief answer is that Shakespeare learned to find strategies to enact feeling in form, feelings in forms, multiplying both to a superlative degree through 154 poems. No poet has ever found more linguistic forms by which to replicate human responses than Shakespeare in the *Sonnets*.

Shakespeare comes late in the sonnet tradition, and he is challenged by that very fact to a display of virtuosity, since he is competing against great predecessors. His thematic originality in his *dramatis personae* makes the sequence new in Western lyric. Though the sharing of the speaker by the young man and the lady, and the sharing of the young man by the lady and the rival poet, could in other hands become the material of farce, the "plot" is treated by Shakespeare elegiacally, sardonically, ironically, and tragically, making the *Sonnets* a repository of relationships and moods wholly without peer in the sonnet tradition. However, thematic originality alone never yet made a memorable artwork. Nor did psychological depth – though that is at least a prerequisite for lyric profundity.

Excerpt from *The Art of Shakespeare's Sonnets* by Helen Vendler, pp. 17–37. Cambridge, Mass.: The Belknap Press of Harvard University Press, 1997.

No sufficient description exists in the critical literature of how Shakespeare makes his speaker "real." (The speaker is the only "person" interiorized in the *Sonnets*, though there are other *dramatis personae*.) The act of the lyric is to offer its reader a script to say. The words of a poem are not "overheard" (as in the formulations of J. S. Mill and T. S. Eliot); this would make the reader an eavesdropping voyeur of the writer's sensations. Nor is the poet "speaking to himself" without reference to a reader (if so, there would be no need to write the poem down, and all communicative action would be absent). While the social genres "build in" the reader either as listener (to a narrator of a novel) or as audience (to a play), the private literary genres – such as the Psalms, or prayers printed in prayer books, or secular lyrics – are scripted for repeated personal recitation. One is to utter them as one's own words, not as the words of another. Shakespeare's sonnets, with their unequaled idiomatic language-contours (written, after all, by a master in dramatic speech who shaped that speech into what C. S. Lewis called their lyric *cantabile*), are preeminently utterances for us to utter as ours. It is indispensable, then, if we are to be made to want to enter the lyric script, that the voice offered for our use be "believable" to us, resembling a "real voice" coming from a "real mind" like our own.

It is hard to achieve such "realness." Many lyrics are content with a very generalized and transient voice, one of no determinate length of life or depth of memory. In a drama, the passage of time and the interlocking of the web of events in which a character participates allow for a gradual deepening of the constructed personality of even minor characters. But Shakespeare must render his sonnet-speaker convincing in a mere fourteen lines. He is helped, to this end, by the fact that a "thick description" of his speaker accretes as the sequence progresses; but since few readers read the sequence straight through, the demand for evident "realness" in each poem, even were it to stand alone in an anthology, remains. The *Sonnets* cannot be "dramatic" in the ordinary sense because in them, as in every lyric of a normative sort, there is only one authorized voice. True drama requires at least two voices (so that even Beckett's monologues often include an offstage voice, or a tape of a voice, to fulfill this requirement). Some feminist critics, mistaking lyric for a social genre, have taken offense that the women who figure as *dramatis personae* within sonnet sequences are "silenced," meaning that they are not allowed to expostulate or reply. In that (mistaken) sense one would have to see *all* addressees in lyric as "silenced" (God by George Herbert, Robert Browning by E. B. Browning) since no addressee, in normative lyric, is given a counter and equal voice responding to that of the speaker.[1] Since the person uttering a lyric is always represented as alone with his thoughts, his imagined addressee can by definition never be present. The lyric (in contrast to the dramatic monologue, where there is always a listener present in the room), gives us the mind alone with itself. Lyric can present no "other" as alive and listening or responding in the same room as the solitary speaker. (One of Herbert's witty genre-inventions, depending on this very genre-constraint, was to assert that since God is everywhere, God could be present in the room even in the speaker's "solitariness" and could thus offer a reply, as God the Father does in "The Collar" and as Jesus does in "Dialogue.")

Shakespeare's speaker, alone with his thoughts, is the greatest achievement, imaginatively speaking, of the sequence. He is given "depth" of character in each individual sonnet by several compositional strategies on Shakespeare's part. These will be more fully described and demonstrated in the individual commentaries below, but in brief they are:

1. *Temporal.* The establishment of several retreating "panels" of time, representing episodes or epochs in the speaker's past, gives him a continuous, nontransient existence and a continuity of memory. (See, for example, sonnet 30, *When to the sessions of sweet silent thought.*)

2. *Emotional.* The reflection, within the same poem, of sharply conflicting moods with respect to the same topic (see, e.g., sonnet 148, *O me! what eyes hath love put in my head*). This can be abetted by contradictory or at least nonhomogeneous discourses rendering a topic complicated (see, e.g., sonnet 125, *Wer't aught to me I bore the canopy*). The volatility of moods in the speaker (symbolized by the famous *lark at break of day arising* of sonnet 29) suggests a flexibility – even an instability – of response verbally "guaranteeing" the presence of passion.

3. *Semantic.* The speaker's mind has a great number of compartments of discourse (theological, legal, alchemical, medicinal, political, aesthetic, etc.). These compartments are semipervious to each other, and the osmosis between them is directed by an invisible discourse-master, who stands for the intellectual imagination.

4. *Conceptual.* The speaker resorts to many incompatible models of existence (described in detail in the commentary) even within the same poem; for example, sonnet 60 first describes life as a homogeneous steady-state succession of identical waves/minutes (a stoic model); then as a sharply delineated rise-and-eclipse of a sun (a tragic model); and next as a series of incessant violent extinctions (a brutal model). These models, unreconciled, convey a disturbing cognitive dissonance, one which is, in a philosophical sense, intolerable. The alert and observant mind that constructs these models asserts the "truth" of each for a particular occasion or aspect of life, but finds no "supramodel" under which they can be intelligibly grouped, and by which they can be intelligibly contained. In this way, the mind of the speaker is represented as one in the grip of philosophical conflict.

5. *Philosophical.* The speaker is a rebel against received ideas. He is well aware of the received topoi of his culture, but he subjects them to interrogation, as he counters neoplatonic courtly love with Pauline marital love (116), or the Christian Trinity with the Platonic Triad (105), or analogizes sacred hermeneutics to literary tradition (106). No topics are more sharply scrutinized than those we now subsume under the phrase "gender relations": the speaker interrogates androgyny of appearance by evoking a comic myth of Nature's own dissatisfaction with her creation (20); he criticizes hyperbolic

praise of female beauty in 130; he condones adultery throughout the "will" sonnets and elsewhere (and sees adultery as less criminal than adulterated discourse, e.g., in 152). This is not even to mention the interrogations of "love" and "lust" in 116 and 129 (sonnets of which the moral substance has not been properly understood because they have not been described in formal terms). No received idea of sexuality goes uninvestigated; and the thoroughly unconventional sexual attachments represented in both parts of the sequence stand as profound (if sometimes unwilling) critiques of the ideals of heterosexual desire, chastity, continence, marital fidelity, and respect for the character of one's sexual partner. What "ought to be" in the way of gender relations (by Christian and civic standards) is represented as an ideal in the "marriage sonnets" with which the sequence opens, but never takes on existential or "realist" lived validation. Shakespeare's awareness of norms is as complete as his depiction, in his speaker, of experiential violation of those norms.

6. *Perceptual.* The speaker is also given depth by the things he notices, from damask roses to the odor of marjoram to a canopy of state. Though the sonnets are always openly drifting toward emblematic or allegorical language, they are plucked back (except in extreme cases like 66) into the perceptual, as their symbolic rose is distilled into "real" perfume (54) or as an emblematic April is *burned* by *hot* June (104). The speaker stands poised between a medieval emblematic tendency and a more modern empirical posture; within his moral and philosophical systems, he savors the tang of the "sensual feast."

7. *Dramatic.* The speaker indirectly quotes his antagonist. Though no one but the speaker "speaks" in a lyric, Shakespeare exploits the usefulness of having the speaker, in private, quote in indirect discourse something one or the other of the *dramatis personae* previously said. Many of the sonnets (e.g., 76 and 116) have been misunderstood because they have been thought to be free-standing statements on the speaker's part rather than replies to the antagonist's implicitly quoted words. Again, I support this statement below in detail; but one can see what a difference it makes to interpretation whether in sonnet 76 the poet-speaker means to criticize his own verse – "Why is my verse so barren of new pride?" – or whether he is repeating, by quoting, an anterior criticism by the young man: "Why [you ask] is my verse so [in your words] 'barren of new pride'?" In the (often bitter) give-and-take of prior-criticism-answered-by-the-speaker (in such rebuttal-sonnets as 105, 117, 151, and the previously mentioned 76 and 116), we come closest, in the sonnets, to Shakespeare the dramatist.

More could be said of the strategies that create a credible speaker with a complex and imaginative mind (a mind which we take on as our own when stepping into the voice); but I want to pass on to the greatest strength of the sonnets as "contraptions," their multiple armatures. Booth sees these "overlapping structures" as a principle of irresoluble indeterminacy; I, by contrast, see them as mutually reinforcing, and therefore as principles of authorial instruction.

Organizing Structures

When lyric poems are boring, it is frequently because they possess only one organizing structure, which reveals itself unchanged each time the poem is read. *If* the poet has decided to employ a single structure (in, say, a small two-part song such as "When daisies pied and violets blue"), then the poem needs some other principle of interest to sustain rereading (in that song, a copious set of aspects – vegetative, human, and avian – of the spring). Shakespeare abounds in such discourse-variety, and that in part sustains rereadings of the sonnets; but I have found that rereading is even better sustained by his wonderful fertility in structural complexity. The Shakespearean sonnet form, though not invented by Shakespeare, is manipulated by him in ways unknown to his predecessors. Because it has four parts – three isomorphic ones (the quatrains) and one anomalous one (the couplet), it is far more flexible than the two-part Italian sonnet. The four units of the Shakespearean sonnet can be set in any number of logical relations to one another:

successive and equal;
hierarchical;
contrastive;
analogous;
logically contradictory;
successively "louder" or "softer."

This list is merely suggestive, and by no means exhaustive. The four "pieces" of any given sonnet may also be distinguished from one another by changes of agency ("I do this; you do that"), of rhetorical address ("O Muse"; "O beloved"), of grammatical form (a set of nouns in one quatrain, a set of adjectives in another), or of discursive texture (as the descriptive changes to the philosophical), or of speech act (as denunciation changes to exhortation). Each of these has its own poetic import and effect. The four "pieces" of the sonnet may be distinguished, again, by different phonemic clusters or metrical effects. Booth rightly remarks on the presence of such patternings, but he refuses to establish hierarchy among them, or to subordinate minor ones to major ones, as I think one can often do.

I take it that a Shakespearean sonnet is fundamentally structured by an evolving inner emotional dynamic, as the fictive speaker is shown to "see more," "change his mind," "pass from description to analysis," "move from negative refutation to positive refutation," and so on. There can be a surprisingly large number of such "moves" in any one sonnet. The impression of an evolving dynamic within the speaker's mind and heart is of course created by a large "law of form" obeyed by the words in each sonnet. Other observable structural patterns play a subordinate role to this largest one. In its

Shakespearean incarnation, the sonnet is a system in motion, never immobile for long, and with several subsystems going their way within the whole.

The chief defect in critical readings of the *Sonnets* has been the critics' propensity to take the first line of a sonnet as a "topic sentence" which the rest of the poem merely illustrates and reiterates (a model visible in Berowne's sonnet quoted above). Only in the plays does Shakespeare write nondramatic sonnets in this expository mode. In his lyrics, he sees structure itself as motion, as a composer of music would imagine it. Once the dynamic curve of a given sonnet is perceived, the lesser structuring principles "fall into place" beneath it. See, e.g., my commentary on 129 for a textbook example of a trajectory of changing feelings in the speaker about a single topic (lust); it is the patterns and underpatterns of the sonnet that enable us to see the way those feelings change. If the feeling were unchanging, the patterns would also remain invariable. The crucial rule of thumb in understanding any lyric is that every significant change of linguistic pattern represents a motivated change in feeling in the speaker. Or, to put it differently, if we sense a change of feeling in the speaker, we must look to see whether, and how, it is stylistically "guaranteed." Unless it is deflected by some new intensity, the poem continues by inertia in its original groove.

I deliberately do not dwell in my Commentary on Shakespeare's imagery as such, since it is a topic on which good criticism has long existed. Although large allegorical images (*beauty's rose*) are relatively stable in the *Sonnets*, imagery is meaningful only in context; it cannot be assigned secure symbolic import except with respect to the poem in which it occurs. The point, e.g., of the fire in sonnet 73 (*That time of year*) is that it is a stratified image: the glowing of the fire *lies upon* the ashes of youth. The previous images in the sonnet have been linear ones (*time of year* and *twilight*) referring to an extension in time (a year, a day), rather than superposition in space. By itself, the image "fire" does not call up the notion of stratification, nor does it in the other sonnets in which it appears; but in this poem, because of the poet's desire for variance from a previously established linear structure, the fire is called upon to play this spatial role, by which youth appears as exhausted subpositioned ashes rather than as an idyllic era (*the sweet birds*; *sunset*) lost at an earlier point in a timeline. Previous thematic commentators have often missed such contextual determination of imagistic meaning.

In trying to see the chief aesthetic "game" being played in each sonnet, I depart from the isolated registering of figures – a paradox here, an antimetabole there – to which the practice of word-by-word or phrase-by-phrase commentary inevitably leads. I wish to point out instead the larger imaginative or structural patterns in which such rhetorical figures take on functional (by contrast to purely decorative) significance. I do not intend, by this procedure, to minimize the sonnets' ornamental "excess" (so reprehensible to Pound); no art is more pointedly ornamental (see Puttenham) than the Renaissance lyric. Yet Shakespeare is happiest when an ornamental flourish can be seen to have a necessary poetic function. His changes in discursive texture, and his frequent consciousness of etymological roots as he plays on Anglo-Saxon and Latin versions of the "same" meaning ("with my *extern* the *outward* honoring"), all become more striking when incorporated into a general and dynamic theory of the poem. (Rather than invoke the terms of Renaissance rhetoric, which do not convey much to the modern reader, I use ordinary language to describe Shakespeare's rhetorical figuration.)

To give an illustration: I myself find no real functional significance in Shakespeare's alliteration when the speaker says that in *the swart complexioned night, / When sparkling stars twire not, thou {the young man} gildst the even*. Such phonetic effects seem to have a purely decorative intent. But an alliterative "meaning-string" – such as sonnet 25's *favour, fortune, triumph, favourites, fair, frown, painful, famousèd, fight* (an emendation), *foiled*, and *forgot* – encapsulates the argument of the poem in little, and helps to create and sustain that argument as it unfolds. Grammar and syntax, too, can be functionally significant to argument; see, for instance, the way in which 66 uses phrases of agency, or the way in which 129 uses its many verbals. In his edition of the *Sonnets*, Booth leaves it up to the reader to construct the poem; I have hoped to help the reader actively to that construction by laying out evidence that no interpretation can afford to ignore. Any number of interpretations, guided by any number of interests, can be built on the same foundation of evidence; but an interpretation ignoring that evidence can never be a defensible one.

I believe that anyone seriously contemplating the interior structures and interrelations of these sonnets is bound to conclude that many were composed in the order in which they are arranged. However, given the poems' variation in aesthetic success, it seems probable that some sonnets – perhaps written in youth (as Andrew Gurr suggested of the tetrameter sonnet 145, with its pun on "Hathaway") or composed before the occurrence of the triangular plot – were inserted *ad libitum* for publication. (I am inclined to believe Katherine Duncan-Jones's argument that the *Sonnets* may have been an authorized printing.) The more trifling sonnets – those that place ornament above imaginative gesture, or fancifulness above depth (such as 4, 6, 7, 9, 145, 153, and 154) – do seem to be less experienced trial-pieces. The greater sonnets achieve an effortless combination of imaginative reach with high technical invention (18, 73, 124, 138), or a quintessence of grace (104, 106, 132), or a power of dramatic condensation (121, 147) that we have come to call "Shakespearean," even if, as Kent Hieatt has persuasively shown, they were composed in groups over time.

The speaker of Shakespeare's sonnets scorns the consolations of Christianity – an afterlife in heaven for himself, a Christian resurrection of his body after death – as fully as he refuses (except in a few sonnets) the learned adornment of classical references – a staple of the continental sonnet. The sonnets stand as the record of a mind working out positions without the help of any pantheon or any systematic doctrine. Shakespeare's speaker often considers, in rapid succession, any number of intellectual or ideological positions, but he does not move among them at random. To the contrary: in the first quatrain of any given sonnet he has a wide epistemological field in which to play, but in the second quatrain he generally queries or contradicts or subverts his first position (together with its discourse-field). By the third quatrain, he must (usually) advance to his subtlest or most comprehensive or most truthful position (Q_3 therefore taking on, in the Shakespearean sonnet, the role of the sestet in the Petrarchan sonnet). And the couplet – placed not as resolution (which is the function of Q_3) but as coda – can then stand in any number of relations (summarizing, ironic, expansive) to the preceding argument. The gradually straitened possibilities as the speaker advances in his considerations give the Shakespearean sonnet a funnel-shape, narrowing in Q_3 to a vortex of condensed perceptual and intellectual force, and either constricting or expanding that vortex via the couplet.

The Couplet

The Shakespearean couplet has often been a stumbling block to readers. Rosalie Colie's helpful distinction (in *Shakespeare's Living Art*) between the *mel* (honey) of love-poetry and the *sal* (salt) of epigram – a genre conventionally used for satiric purposes – represents a real insight into the mind of Shakespeare's speaker: the speaker is a person who wishes to analyze and summarize his experience as well as to describe and enact it. The distance from one's own experience necessitated by an analytic stance is symbolized most fully by the couplet, whereas the empathetic perception necessary to display one's state of mind is symbolized by the quatrains. In speaking about the relation of quatrain to couplet, one must distinguish the fictive speaker (even when he represents himself as a poet) from Shakespeare the author. The fictive speaker gradually becomes, over the course of the poem, more analytic about his situation (and therefore more distanced from his first self-pathos) until he finally reaches the couplet, in which he often expresses a self-ironizing turn:

> For thee watch I, whilst thou dost wake elsewhere,
> From me far off, with others all too near.
>
> (sonnet 61)

This we can genuinely call intrapsychic irony in the fictive speaker. But the author, who is arranging the whole poem, has from the moment of conception a relation of irony to his fictive persona. The persona lives in the "real time" of the poem, in which he feels, thinks, and changes his mind; the author has planned the whole evolution of the poem before writing the first line, and "knows" conceptually the gyrations which he plans to represent taking place over time in his fictive speaker. There is thus a perpetual ironizing of the living temporality of the speaker by the coordinating spatial overview of the author. Although the speaker seems "spontaneous" in his utterance, the cunning arrangements of the utterance belong primarily to Shakespeare (even if dramatically ascribed to the speaker). It is at the moment of the couplet that the view of the speaker and the view of the author come nearest to convergence.

One of Shakespeare's strategies for the couplet which has disappointed some readers is the turn of the speaker to the *consensus gentium*, either via a known proverb or via a discourse which resembles the characteristic idiom of proverb:

> For sweetest things turn sourest by their deeds;
> Lilies that fester smell far worse than weeds.
> (sonnet 94)

Such a turn toward the proverbial always represents the speaker's despair at solving by himself, in personally formulated language, the conundrum presented by the sonnet. "*I* don't know; what does the common wisdom say about this situation?" Unless one senses the reason for the speaker's turn to the proverbial, and of course "hears" the proverbial tone lurking "under" the "personal" language of the speaker, one is at a loss to know how to utter the couplet. It should be uttered with implied quotation marks around each of its proverbial sayings:

> For [as everyone says] "Sweetest things turn sourest by their deeds";
> [And it is also said] "Lilies that fester smell far worse than weeds."

The "meaning" carried by such a turn to the *consensus gentium* is that the speaker has run out, absolutely, of things to say from his own heart. He has to turn to old saws to console himself in his rejection, and to warn the young man that no good can come of his infidelities.

It might be thought that the couplet is the likeliest place for proverbial expression. Yet, knowing that the proverbial implies that the speaker "gives up" on the conundrum as insoluble, we are glad to see the displacement upward of proverbial closure into the body of the poem. I insert the mental quotation marks and emphasis implied by the following displaced-upward "closures":

> [Everyone knows that] "It is a greater grief
> To bear love's wrong than hate's known injury."
> (sonnet 40)
>
> No marvel then that *I* mistake *my* view,
> "The sun itself sees not till heaven clears."
> (sonnet 148)

When proverbial matter – implying a desire for unquestionable closure – is displaced upward into Q_3, it makes room for a new departure in the couplet, such as the fresh sensual address in sonnet 40 (*Lascivious grace*, etc.). Or, as in 148, the upward displacement of the proverbial idiom into lines 11–12 can enable a change of reference from third-person *love* (meaning successively "Cupid" or "the experience of love" or "emblematic Love") to a more mordantly "aware" second-person use of *love* in the couplet to mean the dark lady (a meaning certified by the obscenely punning adjective "cunning"):

> O me! what eyes hath *love* put in my head
> . . . . .
>   *love* doth well denote
> *Love's eye* is not so true as all men's: no,
> . . . . .
> No marvel then though I mistake my view;
> The sun itself sees not till heaven clears.
>   O *cunning love*, with tears thou keep'st me blind,
>   Lest eyes well seeing thy foul faults should find.

A reader alert to the way that boilerplate idiom, when it is found in the couplet (*as black as hell, as dark as night*, sonnet 147), carries the speaker's despair of a solution, and who sees how in other sonnets the speaker finds a "way out" by displacing despair from the couplet to a few lines above (thereby providing room in the couplet for a fresh view), will not find couplets of either sort uninteresting.

Readers intent only on the propositional statement made by the couplet have often found it redundant. When one looks at what a given couplet permits by way of functional agency, one sees more. A telling comment on the couplet was made by Jan Kott in his introduction to Jerzy Sito's edition of the *Sonnets*: "The closing couplet of each sonnet is addressed directly to the protagonist [by himself]. It is almost spoken. It is an actor's line." While this is not true of the couplets in all the sonnets, Kott's remark shows us a critic perceiving a crucial *tonal* difference between the body of the sonnet and the couplet, even if what they "say" is "the same." A theory of interpretation that is interested only in the paraphrasable "meaning" of a poem tends to find Shakespeare's couplets uninteresting; but such a theory merely betrays its own inadequacy. It is more productive to look for what Shakespeare might have had in mind to make his couplets "work" than to assume that, because they "restate" semantically the body of the sonnet, they are superfluous. Poetically speaking, Shakespeare was not given to idle superfluity. In my Commentary I have pointed out, for each sonnet, the significant words from the body of the poem that are repeated in the couplet, calling the aggregate of such words the Couplet Tie. These words are usually thematically central, and to see Shakespeare's careful reiteration of them is to be directed in one's interpretation by them. There are very few sonnets that do not exhibit such a Couplet Tie. Shakespeare clearly depended on this device not only to point up the thematic intensities of a sonnet, but also to show how the same words take on different emotional import as the poem progresses.

Reading the Sonnets

Shakespeare encourages alertness in his reader. Because he is especially occupied with literary consolidation (resuming the topics, the images, the consecrated adjectives, and the repertoire of tones of previous sonneteers), one can miss his subversive moves: the "shocking" elements of the sonnets in both subsequences; the parodies, by indirect quotation, of Petrarchan praise in sonnets 21 and 130 (though the latter has been sometimes read as denigration of the mistress, it is no such thing); the satire on learned language (78, 85); on sycophantic poets (79) and newfangled poets (76); the revisionism with respect to Christian views of lust (129) and continence (94) and with respect to Petrarchan views of love (116); the querying of eternizing boasts (122), of the Platonic conventions (95), of dramatic plot (144), of enumerative praise (84), of "idolatry" (105), of the Lord's Prayer (108) and of love-pursuit (143). That is, readers of the sonnets find themselves encountering – and voicing – both the most conventional images (*rose, time, fair, stars, love*) and the most unsettling statements. Many quatrains, taken singly, could well be called conventional, and paraphrases of them by critics make them sound stultifying. What is *not* conventional is the sonnet's (invisibly predicated) set of relations – of the quatrains to one another and to the couplet; of the words and images to one another; of the individual grammatical and syntactic units to one another. Even though the appearance of logic is often smoothly maintained by a string of logical connectives (*When . . . When . . . Then*), some disruptive or contradictory force will enter the poem to pull one quatrain in two directions at once – toward its antecedent quatrain by one set of words, toward its consequent by another; toward the couplet by its temporality; toward a preceding quatrain by its spatiality. Since quatrains often participate in several patterns simultaneously, their true "meaning" is chartable only by charting their pattern-sets.

Though antithesis is Shakespeare's major figure for constructing the world in the sonnets, it is safe to say that the ever antithetically minded Shakespeare permitted his antitheses to breed and bring to birth a third thing (see sonnet 66). His second preferred figure, chiasmus, contends in the sonnets against the "natural" formulation of a sentence (linear, temporal, ongoing). Chiasmus refuses to let a phrase or a sentence dilate "naturally": instead, it makes the syntax round on itself. Not "Least contented with what I most enjoy" (the linear or parallel formation), but rather *With what I most enjoy contented least* (the chiastic formulation). The chiastic formulation always implies an analytic moment in the speaker. "Spontaneous" moments say things "naturally"; but when the speaker has had time to think things out and judge them, he speaks chiastically. *Consumed with that which it was nourished by* – where *consumed* and *nourished* bracket *that* and *which* – is a formulation that simply could not occur in Q_1 or Q_2 of 73. The first two quatrains of that sonnet are the epitome of linearity, as phrase follows phrase in a "natural" imitation of life's gradual leakage:

> In me thou seest the twilight of such day
> As after sunset fadeth in the west,
> Which by and by black night doth take away,
> Death's second self that seals up all in rest.

On this narrative of pathos, there supervenes the superb analytic moment of Q₃: the stratified fire does not fade, it glows; and the analytic law of consumption and nourishment refuses a linear statement of itself: "As the fire was nourished by heat, so it is consumed by heat". Between the glowing fire and the physical law, however, there is one line of linear "leakage": *As the death-bed whereon it must expire.* If that were the last line of the poem, the speaker's stoic resolve could be said to have left him, and he would have submitted to a "natural" dying fall. But he pulls himself up from that moment of expiring linearity into his great chiastic law, that we die from the very same vital heat which has nourished us in life. It is (as this example shows) always worth noting whether a Shakespearean statement is being made "linearly," in a first-order experiential and "spontaneous" way, or whether it is being made chiastically, in a second-order analytic way. These represent very different stances within the speaker.

Strategies of Unfolding

One of the strategies making many sonnets odd is that the utterances of the speaker are being generated by invisible strings "behind" the poem – the concurrent deducible actions or remarks of an implied other. Such poems are like the rebuttal sonnets mentioned earlier, except that the invisible prompt is not an earlier speech-act by another but rather a series of actions or speech-acts which are, imaginatively speaking, *in process while* the sonnet is being uttered. (See my comments on 34, which explain why the changes of metaphor in the poem – storm, rain, slave, physic, cross, pearl, ransom – are not inexplicable or unintelligible.) And then there are the "shadow-poems" (as I think of them), where one can deduce, from the speaker's actual statements, what he would really like to say to the young man (in the case of the "slavery" sonnet, 57) or to the mistress (in, say, 138) if he could speak clearly.

Yet another recurrent strategy for Shakespeare is to "mix up" the order of narration so that it departs from the normal way in which such an event would be unfolded. It would be "normal" to say, "He abandoned me; and what did that feel like? It felt like seeing the sun go behind a cloud." In "normal" narration, the literal event is recounted first, and then a metaphor is sought to explain what the narrator felt like. But in sonnet 33 (*Full many a glorious morning have I seen*), the metaphor – not perceived as such because not introduced by "Just as" – precedes the literal event. After seeing the sunny landscape clouded, and thinking we have been admitted to the literal level of the poem, we hear *Even so my sun one early morn did shine.* In order to understand such a poem, we must ask why the poet has rearranged the normal order of narration. In 97, for example, it would be "normal" to state literal perception first, and let an emotional contradiction follow – to say, "It was summertime, *and yet* it seemed like winter to me with you away." Instead, the poet puts the speaker's emotional perception ahead of his sense-perception: "How like a winter hath my absence been / From thee . . . ! / *And yet* this time removed was summer's time." Similarly, the very peculiar order of narration in 62 (*Sin of self-love*) has to be both noticed and interpreted.

I want to say a word here about Shakespeare's fancifulness. It ought not surprise us that the author of *A Midsummer Night's Dream* might also be fanciful in his poems. Modern readers have shown little admiration for the sonnets that play with the convention of the contest between eye and heart (such as 46 or 47) or the sonnet about flowers stealing their odor and hue from the young man (99, *The forward violet*), or the sonnets of elaborate wordplay (43, *When most I wink*), or the more whimsical complimentary sonnets, such as 78 (*So oft have I invoked thee*). Such sonnets may be fanciful, but they are not frivolous, as I hope to have shown in the Commentary. Read from the right angle, so to speak, they can be very beautiful, or at least delightful; and in them, as elsewhere, Shakespeare is inventing some game or other and playing it out to its conclusion in deft and surprising ways.

Shakespeare the Writer

The purpose of my Commentary is to point out strategies of the sort I have been enumerating – strategies that make the speaker credible, that generate an evolutionary dynamic, that suggest interaction among the linguistic ingredients of the lines, that "use" the couplet, that beguile by fancifulness, and so on. There are hundreds of such strategies in the sonnets, since Shakespeare rarely amuses himself the same way twice. He is a poet acutely conscious of grammatical and syntactic possibility as one of the ingredients in "invention," and he routinely, but not idly, varies tense, mood, subject-position, and clause-patterns in order to make conceptual or rhetorical points. These *differentia* contribute to our sense that his mind was discriminating as well as copious. His inventories are sometimes exhaustive (as he reels off the forms of prognostication in sonnet 14, or the forms of social trespass by *lust till action* in 129) but at other times rigidly repetitive (as in the implication, by the almost invariant organization of 66, that the anatomy of evil is less complex than the world would like to believe). In any given case of enumeration in the *Sonnets*, an implicit table of organization is constructed, frequently through the "places" of logic ("who," "where," "when," "in what manner," "by what means," "with what aid," etc.). Items may then be further accumulated, contrasted, subtracted, and so forth, either from this table of organization or from another organizational grid superimposed on it as a corrective (as love and its obligations are superimposed on the masque of social evil in 66). A formidable intellectual command of phenomena (both physical and moral), of means (both human and cosmic), of categories (both quotidian and philosophical), and of discourses (both learned and popular) lies behind the *Sonnets* in the person of their invisible author. It is this intellectual command which accounts for the *Sonnets'* serene and unfaltering air of poetic resource, even (or perhaps especially) in the moments of the speaker's greatest psychological distraction. Though I cannot hope to have caught all of Shakespeare's strategies, or to have understood them all properly, or to have assigned them their proper weight with respect to one another, I do hope that I will have shown Shakespeare as a poet constantly inventing new permutations of internal form, designed to match what he was recording – the permutations of emotional response.

Sometimes I have not been sure of the "game" of a given sonnet, but I am happy to ask others to try their wits after me. There is always something cryptographic in Shakespeare's sonnet-surfaces – sometimes literally so, as in the anagrams of 7, or as in the play on *vile* and *evil* in 121, but more often merely an oddness that catches the eye and begs explanation. The obviousness of the *Sonnets'* "content" – love, jealousy, time's depredations – simply leaves readers obscurely conscious that their reactions to these poems exceed the rather commonplace matter they have understood. Poetry is not generally in the matter of its utterance philosophical; but it is philosophical insofar as its dynamic (when well constructed) represents in abstract or "geometric" form one or several of the infinite curves of human response. Shakespeare's *Sonnets* are philosophical insofar as they display interrelationships among their parts which, as they unfold, trace a conflict in human cognitive and affective motions. The surface of any poem is what John Ashbery calls its "visible core" ("Self-Portrait in a Convex Mirror"), and I have tried, by examining the surfaces of these poems as a writer would see and interpret them, to make the core visible. And though my main concern has been to show the unifying forces in each sonnet, the whole sequence displays, when taken as a single object, dispersive gaps and uncertainties between its individual units. It is on just such large uncertainties that the smaller certainties of single sonnets float and collide.

Shakespeare the Poet

What sort of poet is Shakespeare, as we meet him at work composing sonnets? The answer generated by each sonnet, or even by each part of a sonnet, is a particular one. Consider for a moment sonnet 54:

O how much more doth beauty beauteous seem
By that sweet ornament which truth doth give!
The rose looks fair, but fairer we it deem
For that sweet odour which doth in it live.
The canker blooms have full as deep a dye
As the perfumèd tincture of the roses,
Hang on such thorns, and play as wantonly,
When summer's breath their maskèd buds discloses;
But for their virtue only is their show,
They live unwooed, and unrespected fade,
Die to themselves. Sweet roses do not so,
Of their sweet deaths are sweetest odours made:
　　And so of you, beauteous and lovely youth,
　　When that shall vade, my verse distils your truth.

"What sort of poet?" "A poet of deep sensuous relish," one might say after reading the second quatrain of 54, with its play of deep-dyed maskèd rosebuds. Yet, reading the first two lines of the same sonnet, one might have said that the author was a metaphysical homilist, discoursing on truth and beauty. And, reading the couplet of the same poem (as generally emended), we might simply say: "This is a love-poet." Looking to the third quatrain, seeing the roses used as figures of human vice and virtue, we might see the author as a writer of ethical emblems, contrasting inner virtue to outward show. And yet each of these descriptions is inadequate. A poet of pure sensuous relish would not have needed to insert the moral pointer of *wanton play* into his descriptive attention to the roses. A metaphysical homilist would not have referred to truth as an *ornament* to beauty. A love-poet does not, unless he is also a poet of moral emphasis, give death-warnings to his beloved. An emblematic poet usually cancels from the interpretation of his emblem the lingering sensual overtones which Shakespeare retains in the word *unwooed* and the repetition *sweet . . . sweet . . . sweetest*. What is always unsettling in Shakespeare is the way that he places only a very permeable osmotic membrane between the compartments holding his separate languages – pictorial description, philosophical analysis, emblematic application, erotic pleading – and lets words "leak" from one compartment to the other in each direction. Rather than creating "full-fledged" metaphor, this practice creates a constant fluidity of reference, which produces not so much the standard disruptive effect of catachresis ("mixed metaphor") as an almost unnoticed rejuvenation of diction at each moment. The most famous example of this unexampled fluidity arrives in sonnet 60:

　　Nativity, once in the main of light,
　　Crawls to maturity, wherewith being crowned,
　　Crookèd eclipses 'gainst his glory fight.

This passage, in which Shakespeare allows free passage of language from compartment to compartment, behaves as though the discourses of astrology, seamanship, astronomy, child development, political theory, deformity, religion, and warfare were (or could be) one. Such freedom of lexical range suggests forcefully an *ur*-language (occurring in time after the Kristevan *chora* but before even the imaginary in the Lacanian order of things) in which these discourses *were* all one, before what Blake would call their fall into division. As Shakespeare performs their resurrection into unity, we recognize most fully that this heady mix of discourses *is* (as with the peculiar interfusion of spaniels and candy once noticed by Caroline Spurgeon) Shakespeare's "native language" when his powers of expression are most on their mettle.

And yet there is no "ambiguity" in this passage. A lesser poet would have clung to one or two chief discourses: "Man, once born onto the earth, crawls to maturity, but at that very moment falls, finding his strength failing him"; or "Our sun, once in its dawn of light, ascends to its zenith, whereupon crooked eclipses obscure it." The inertial tendency of language to remain within the discourse-category into which it has first launched itself seems grandly abrogated by Shakespeare. Yet we know he was aware of that inertial tendency because he exploited it magisterially; every time a discourse shifts, it is (he lets us know) because the mind has shifted its angle of vision. Unpacked, the three lines above from sonnet 60 show us that the speaker first thinks of a child's horoscope, cast at birth; then he thinks of dawn as an image for the beginning of human life, because the life-span seems but a day; then he reverts to the biological reality of the crawling infant; then he likens the human being to a king (a dauphin perhaps in adolescence, but crowned when he reaches maturity); then (knowing the necessity of human fate) he leaves the image of a king behind (since the uncrowning of a king is contingent – on, say, a revolution – but death is a necessary event) and returns to the natural world. We assume the speaker will predict, as his emblem of necessity (as he does in 73), the darkness of night overtaking the sun that rose at dawn; but instead, feeling the "wrongness" of death's striking down a human being just at maturity, the poet shows nature in its "wicked" guise, as the eclipse "wrongfully" obscuring the sun in the "glory" of his noon. Yet, remembering how death is not without struggle, the speaker shows the man being "fought against," not simply blotted out, by the dark. If we do not see each of these shifts in discourse as evidence of a change of mental direction by the speaker, and seek the motivation for each change of direction, we will not participate in the activity of the poem as its surface instructs us to do.

In conceptual matters, Shakespeare displays an exceptionally firm sense of categories (logical, philosophical, religious), together with a willingness to let them succeed each other in total aspectual contradiction. Within the process of invention itself, as I have said above, his mind operates always by antithesis. As soon as he thinks one thing, he thinks of something that is different from it (though perhaps assimilable to it under a larger rubric). If one believes, as I do, that in many of the sonnets successive quatrains "correct" each other, and that in the "philosophical" sonnets Q_3 generally offers an ampler, subtler, or truer view of the problem than those voiced in Q_1 or Q_2, then it is true to say that these aspectual contradictions – like those offered by 60 as it presents models of life that are successively stoic, tragic, and brutal – are ranked hierarchically and climactically with respect to their "truth-value." The stratified erotic fire in Q_3 of sonnet 73 (*That time of year*) is therefore a "truer" picture of human life (*Consumed with that which it was nourished by*) than the earlier "pathetic" autumnal tree or the subsequent "rest-awaiting" twilight. And yet Q_1 and Q_2 are not repudiated as *un*true: in 73, the whole question of how we picture our life has been thrice answered (once physically, once emblematically, and once philosophically). If the third formulation is better than the others, because intellectually more comprehensive (no villain robs us of life, we die of having lived, and our *calor vitae*, even in old age, makes us "glowing" rather than "ruined" or "fading"), it does not invalidate the psychological "truth" of the two earlier models. The proffering and hierarchizing of several conceptual models at once is, as I see it, Shakespeare's main intellectual and poetic achievement in the *Sonnets*.

Yet conceptual models, though necessary for the architectonics of poems, do not guarantee poetic interest. Although the conceptual models ("conceits") govern the working-out of compositional order, they do not repress other poetic energies, but rather act to stimulate them. As Keats put it (in a letter to J. H. Reynolds of November 22, 1817): "I neer found so many beauties in the sonnets – they seem to be full of fine things said unintentionally – in the intensity of working out conceits." The passage that drew this comment from Keats (Q_2 of sonnet 12) struck him so powerfully, we may suppose, because its theme – one that never failed to move him – was the consuming of beautiful and benevolent nature by death ("Is this to be borne?" Keats wrote in the margin; "Hark ye!"):

> When lofty trees I see barren of leaves,
> Which erst from heat did canopy the herd,
> And summer's green all girded up in sheaves
> Borne on the bier with white and bristly beard . . .

Even transfixed as he was by Shakespeare's theme of autumnal mortality, what Keats comments on is the "fine things" said (as if unintentionally) as the conception is worked out. Here, Shakespeare's metaphorical "leakages" occur in the words *barren, canopy, green, girded up, bier,* and *beard,* which "replace," with anthropomorphic emphasis, plausible words either more literal or more abstractly all-embracing, such as *shed, shade, corn, gathered into, wagon,* and *awn.* Here (with apologies) is a "literal" version of the quatrain:

> When lofty trees I see have shed the leaves
> Which erst from sultry heat did shade the fawn,
> And summer's corn all gathered into sheaves,
> Borne on the wain with white and bristly awn . . .

One can see the lessening of pathos in such a formulation.

But it was not merely the anthropomorphic reference in the metaphorical leakages that so affected Keats. I believe he was also moved by the apparently gratuitous insertion of *herd* (perhaps conceived "in the intensity of working out" the rhyme for *beard*, a word necessary to the bier-deathbed scene underlying the close of the quatrain). The trees at the opening of the quatrain are not only beautiful in their foliage, they are also virtuous (if unconsciously so) in the benefit they confer on the herd by their *canopy* (the Shakespeare Concordance shows that Shakespeare uses *herd* to mean *flock* rather than *shepherd*). That Shakespeare had the virtue as well as the beauty of the trees in mind is proved by the summary in line 11, "*sweets* and beauties do themselves forsake," in which the only conceptual antecedent in the sonnet for *sweets* is the charitable trees. In the sonnets, while *beauty* is used of appearance, *sweet* is used of substance and virtue. To Keats, the fact that Shakespeare wanted his trees kind as well as beautiful answered to his deepest wish that his "Presider" (as he called Shakespeare) be as exemplary in breadth of vision as in talent of execution.

NOTE

1   I do not include eclogues, debate-poems, etc. in the definition of normative single-speaker lyric. Such poems are constructed against the norm, and derive their originality from bringing into the public (dramatic) arena of shared speech thoughts that in normative lyric remain intrapsychic.

3

The Incomplete Narrative of Shakespeare's Sonnets

James Schiffer

> And more, much more than in my verse can sit,
> Your own glass shows you, when you look in it.
>
> (103: 13–14)[1]

There is much that we do not know with certainty, and probably will never know, about Shakespeare's sonnets. We do not know if Shakespeare authorized publication of the 1609 quarto; therefore, we do not know if the order of the 154 sonnets and the inclusion of *A Lover's Complaint* represent Shakespeare's arrangement, publisher Thomas Thorpe's, or someone else's. Most commentators acknowledge the presence of narrative elements in the sonnets, ranging from individual poems structured at least in part as narrative (for example, sonnets 99 or 143) to sonnets in which there is a rich interplay, as Heather Dubrow has written, of narrative, lyric, and dramatic modes (1999: 1) and to references in other sonnets to an imperfectly rendered story that may have relevance to all the sonnets – references, that is, to characters such as the poet speaker and the unnamed young friend, rival poet or poets, and dark lady, as well as references to specific actions and events, to the passage of time, to separations and reunions, to gifts and transgressions, to shifts in fortune, power, mood, and feeling. This imperfectly told overarching story will be the focus of this essay. Considerable disagreement exists among critics about many elements of the story, if any, that the sonnets tell, or about the relation, if any, of that story to Shakespeare's life. At most, the sonnets (or the sonnets and *A Lover's Complaint* combined) give hints of a narrative; but they do so sporadically (as in sonnets 40–2, 33–6, or 133, 134, and 144), at times obscurely, inconsistently (as when in sonnet 105 the poet calls the beloved "fair, kind, and true" long after having accused him of a "sensual fault" in sonnet 35), and in any case incompletely.

Lack of narrative clarity, coherence, and completion has been viewed by many scholars over the past two centuries as evidence that the order of the 1609 quarto cannot be trusted, that the publication may not have been authorized, and that the poems were perhaps never meant to be collected in a single cohesive volume, much less read as a narrative. Although her most recent work (Dubrow 1995, 1999) explores the presence of narrative elements in the sonnets, Heather Dubrow, for example, had earlier argued that the "sequence . . . eschews the narrative and dramatic modes more than most contemporaneous sequences do" (1996: 299; cf. Dubrow 1987, esp. 181–90). In addition, she has raised serious questions about the general critical acceptance of Edmond Malone's theoretical division of the sequence into two parts, the first 126 addressed to the young male friend, the last 28 to or about the dark lady (Dubrow 1996). Many have also concluded that the fragmentary narrative within the sonnets is a sign that these are poems written over time in response to real people and changing situations, and further, that the sonnets are autobiographical rather than fictive. A. C. Bradley speaks for a number of critics over the past two centuries when he writes:

> No capable poet, much less a Shakespeare, intending to produce a merely dramatic series of poems, would dream of inventing a story like that of the sonnets, or, even if he did, of treating it as they treat it. The story is very odd and unattractive. Such capacities as it has are but slightly developed. It is left obscure, and some of the poems are unintelligible to us because they contain allusions of which we can make nothing. Now all this is perfectly natural if the story is substantially a real story of Shakespeare himself and of certain other persons; if the sonnets were written from time to time as the relations of the persons changed, and sometimes in reference to particular incidents; and if they were written for one of these persons (far the greater for only one), and perhaps in a few cases for other friends – written, that is to say, for people who knew the details and incidents of which we are ignorant. But it is all unnatural, well-nigh incredibly unnatural, if, with the most skeptical critics, one regard the sonnets as a free product of imagination. (1909: 330–1)

There is much to ponder in Bradley's comments about the sonnets' anti-narrativity, and critics like Arthur Marotti, well versed in the literary practices of the age, would strongly agree with Bradley's inference of sporadical composition for a very limited audience, probably a single person in most instances, "who knew the details and incidents of which we are ignorant."[2] Perhaps Bradley had in mind sonnets like 120, which refers vaguely to specific, yet unnamed events:

> That you were once unkind befriends me now,
> And for that sorrow which I then did feel
> Needs must I under my transgression bow,
> Unless my nerves were brass or hammered steel.
> For if you were by my unkindness shaken,
> As I by yours, y' passed a hell of time,
> And I, a tyrant, have no leisure taken
> To weigh how once I suffered in your crime.
> O that our night of woe might have rememb'red

My deepest sense, how hard true sorrow hits,
And soon to you as you to me then tend'red
The humble salve which wounded bosoms fits!
  But that your trespass now becomes a fee;
  Mine ransoms yours, and yours must ransom me.

At least two separate offenses are referred to here: the poet's "transgression" in recent time, and the friend's apparent betrayal at an earlier time. Perhaps the allusion to the friend's earlier "unkind[ness]" concerns the "sensual fault" mentioned in sonnets 33–6. Yet making this connection does not provide any further information; we still do not know the details of either offense, with whom they were committed, or even if they ever occurred. While Bradley assumes the poem refers to real people and incidents, and asserts that only those with adequate information (which we do not have) can fully apprehend the poem's meaning and intended power, he would perhaps agree that the poem is still accessible, and even moving, to readers who know only that the poet asks forgiveness for "his sportive blood" (sonnet 121). That is, very few sonnets are so marred by obscurity as to be incomprehensible to later readers. Nevertheless, Bradley assumes the power and meaning of the poem for its original addressee cannot be recovered.

On the other side of this particular critical divide, that of authorization and audience, recent theories by Katherine Duncan-Jones, John Kerrigan, and others contend that Shakespeare probably did shape the sequence and perhaps even approved its publication. Duncan-Jones and Kerrigan would actually agree with Bradley that the poems reflect real relationships and were probably not originally intended to be part of a carefully designed collection. Duncan-Jones has gone so far as to weigh in with those who identify William Herbert, the Earl of Pembroke, as the young friend (1997: 57–64), while Kerrigan observes that there are so many points where "obscurity appears to stem not from failing verbal powers but from an unwillingness to grapple painful emotions into form. . . . It seems reasonable to infer a troubled author behind the poet 'I'" (1986: 11). Unlike Bradley, however, both Duncan-Jones and Kerrigan emphasize the resemblances between the 1609 quarto and collections published in the 1590s. They argue that Q would have looked familiar to contemporary readers, from the two anacreontic narrative poems that conclude the sequence to the female complaint that follows. Even the sonnets' incompletely told narrative would have seemed familiar. "There are probably no sonnet sequences of the period which do satisfy a modern reader's desire for continuity," writes Duncan-Jones. "The structural principles on which the Elizabethans built their sequences were only partly thematic or narrative. In profound ways, Shakespeare's sequence is very unlike all the others: but in such a superficial matter as ordering, I suggest, it would have been recognized by contemporaries as adequately answering expectations of continuity and coherence" (1983: 155). Later she adds: "To readers of Daniel's *Delia* and *Rosamond*, or of Lodge's *Phillis* and *Elstred* volume, the overall look of the 1609 *Sonnets* volume would have been by no means strange" (p. 170). Kerrigan also contends that the narrative looseness of Q would not have baffled its early readers. He finds "subtle modulation of material from poem to poem into the form of the whole which makes reading Shakespeare's sonnets such a concentrated yet essentially cumulative experience" (1986: 8). Recent computer-based, rare-word studies by A. Kent Hieatt, Charles W. Hieatt, and Anne Lake Prescott, as well as by Donald Foster, indirectly support Duncan-Jones's and Kerrigan's hypothesis about authorization in that they suggest Shakespeare was writing or revising at least some sonnets during the 1600s. This might well indicate a pattern of "fragmentary composition followed by careful selection and arrangement into a sequence" that, according to Carol Thomas Neely, is exactly the Italian model established by Dante and Petrarch (1978: 359).

I myself am agnostic about the issue of Q's authority, as I am about the issue of autobiography. Yet for the sake of critical speculation about form, and as a way of testing the authorization hypothesis of Duncan-Jones and Kerrigan, this essay will take as its imaginative starting point the idea that Shakespeare did shape the 1609 quarto into a collection. I will therefore hypothetically assume that the narrative elements have the form their author wanted. I will then ask: If Q does reflect his careful selection and arrangement of sonnets, perhaps after he wrote and revised them over a long period of time, why did Shakespeare present in the sonnets' "final form" the story of and behind these poems (real or fictive) in an "obscure," at times "unintelligible," inconsistent, incomplete, unsatisfying (at least, to readers who expect a story such as a novel might tell) way? Here are some thoughts about possible motives behind the sonnets' anti-narrativity.

Dramatic Effect

There is a prior question to the one about Shakespeare's incomplete rendering of narrative, which is why there are narrative elements at all in the sequence. If not the whole story, why any story at all? Here the motives of establishing a dramatic situation and enhancing lyric intensity become relevant, since so many of the sonnets are dramatic as well as lyric. This is true not just because so many are addressed to a specific person (the unnamed "you" or "thou"); it is also true because, as Barbara Hardy has written, "The time of each poem is a new present, renewed feeling" (1989: 94). "Like [Wallace] Stevens," she explains,

> [Shakespeare] is engrossed by the present, entranced by its immediacy, its experiences and images . . . He may have been a phenomenologist before his time. And his chosen genre of drama, in which all narratives must be rooted in the present tense of performance and audience, may have played its part, as cause or effect, in this absorption in the present. It was there in that breath-taking sense of the reader's breathing. (p. 100)

When we read the sonnets in sequence, this dramatic effect is heightened in many poems because of what we have learned about characters and the story, however incomplete, from previous poems. For example, our reading of sonnet 20 is influenced by what we have inferred from the procreation sonnets about the developing relationship between the poet speaker and the young friend (see Pequigney 1985; Crosman 1990; Bell 1999). Sonnet 20 seems like a development (however cryptic), seems to follow from the earlier poems and lead to later poems. (The creation narrative about Nature and the "master mistress," by the way, structures sonnet 20.) Similarly, I find it impossible to read sonnet 147 without taking into account the love triangle described in 144 and earlier dark lady poems (as well, perhaps, as in sonnets 40–2, which also describe a love triangle). Sonnets 147 and 144 are too closely related in thought, mood, imagery, and tone for the similarities to be accidental. The torment the speaker suffers in 147 seems to arise in part from the uncertainty of 144 –

> And, whether that my angel be turn'd fiend,
> Suspect I may, yet not directly tell,
> But being both from me both to each friend,
> I guess one angel in another's hell
>
> (9–12)

– which itself recalls the misogyny of 129. Perhaps the conclusion to 147 suggests that his earlier uncertainty is now resolved:

> For I have sworn thee fair, and thought thee bright,
> Who art as black as hell, as dark as night.
>
> (13–14)

To a certain limited degree, then, narrative can enhance the dramatic and lyric power of a poem or group of poems. The narrative provides a frame, a context in which dramatic and lyric situations can develop.

The relation between modes, however, always threatens to deteriorate into contestation. As Dubrow and others have shown, lyric has the potential to delay or disrupt narrative; but Dubrow also writes that "rather than impeding narrative, lyric and its separable but closely related cousin lyricism may be the end to which narrative tends, its final cause" (1999: 7). This description certainly seems to apply to *A Lover's Complaint*, which ends with the female complainant's aria – the narrator who begins the poem never returns to provide the closure complaint usually requires. However, if the narrative line in a sonnet sequence is too detailed and compelling, the lyric power of individual poems is weakened or even effaced. Thus, we might wish to regard narrative in the sonnets as a kind of Goldilocks's bed, neither too big nor too small, but just right: big enough to enable dramatic and lyric moments to develop, yet not so big as to disrupt or dilute lyric intensity. Both narrative and dramatic modes are subordinated, as they are in most Elizabethan sonnet sequences, to lyric. At the same time, the very dramatization of changing emotions over time that a sequence of lyrics like the sonnets provides creates the impression of narrative progression. That is, changes in emotion displayed in the sequence suggest changes in situation over time. Narrative is as much an effect as a cause of lyric modulation and contrast from sonnet to sonnet. Even if the order of the 1609 quarto were different, this effect of change over time, of narrative, would still be present.

Voyeuristic Pleasure

The obscurities about the story (for example, the fact that young friend, rival poet, and dark lady are unnamed) may well be evidence that the collection was addressed to a single person or small group of knowledgeable readers – as Bradley and others contend – but was never meant to be published for the general public. The motive for obscurity might then be to protect the identities of the real people the poems concern. Yet these same obscurities could also be part of a brilliant strategy to make the collection *seem* as if it originally had an exclusive primary audience. By referring elliptically to events known only to the speaker and the addressee, the poet affords the early modern general reader the voyeuristic privilege of overhearing one half of a private correspondence (perhaps with an aristocratic youth; perhaps regarding homoerotic, adulterous, and/or miscegenetic liaisons) at a time when literature was moving from a manuscript to a print culture. Our first reference to Shakespeare's sonnets from Meres – "his sugred sonnets among his private friends" – advertises this very quality. By affording what Barbara Hardy calls "access to privileged discourse" (1989: 96–7), the poems perhaps fed early modern curiosity about the lifestyles of the rich, powerful, and famous – as Shakespeare was by 1609. If there was a desire to arouse voyeuristic pleasure, the dedication to Mr. W.H. was perhaps a calculated element in this strategy, as Bruce Smith has suggested; Smith assumes that printer Thomas Thorpe is the shrewd author of the dedication (1991: 242). While there is little evidence that Shakespeare's dedication provoked much curiosity when it was first published, subsequent readers, especially since the birth of bardolatry in the late eighteenth century, have been eager to pry into Shakespeare's life. The same can be said for the identities of the unnamed characters in the sequence: there is no evidence of reader curiosity about them for almost two hundred years. Nonetheless, such evidence of voyeuristic curiosity about the sonnets during or in the decades right after Shakespeare's lifetime might once have existed, or might even still exist, waiting to be discovered.

Pleasures of Detection and Invention

A third possible motive, to stimulate the pleasures of detection and invention, follows clearly from the second, the stimulation of voyeuristic desire. It is a well-established effect of anti-narrativity to stimulate readers into creative speculation. According to Robert Scholes, "Our need for chronological and causal connection defines and limits all of us – helps to make us what we are" (1980: 211). When readers hear a story that is incomplete, one impulse is to fill in the gaps and forge their own narrative connections. I don't think this is just a modern phenomenon. Shakespeare delighted in such "misprisions." Think of the many characters in *Much Ado About Nothing* who form theories, usually mistaken, based on insufficient information, usually obtained by eavesdropping, by hearing just half a conversation. Inquiring minds want to know, and if the facts are lacking, they can be invented (as with J. F. Forbis's theory that the sonnets record Shakespeare's struggles with alcoholism, the dark lady standing for a wine bottle). If creative interpretation does not work, the sonnets can be reordered to suit the invented narrative. When there's a paucity of evidence and so much at stake with Shakespeare's biography on the line, detection easily turns into invention.

Would an early modern author, would Shakespeare, possibly have wanted to stimulate such curiosity, much of it about his life? To a limited degree, perhaps he did wish to tease the first readers of the 1609 quarto into limited speculation about the unnamed youth, rival poet, and dark lady; but he could not have dreamed of the kind of interest in his life that has led to so much obsessive speculation about story. Gary Taylor has noted that "as isolated individuals only a handful of the 154 [sonnets] have ever attracted or rewarded as much enthusiasm as the story told outside and between them" (1989: 158). Most of what has been written about the sonnets since the late eighteenth century has consisted of futile attempts to identify the young friend, the dark lady, and the rival poet or poets. The Southampton–Pembroke debate grossly outweighs in pages formalist readings like Helen Vendler's. Surely Shakespeare cannot have intended to generate this much detection. But we can imagine his wanting to stimulate sufficient interest in a story to keep readers turning the pages.

Replication

Yet another possible motive for keeping the time- and story-line impossible to unravel is a desire to replicate in the reader the speaker's experience of disorientation, confusion, and uncertainty, his "thoughts and . . . discourse as madmen's are / At random from the truth vainly expressed" (147. 11–12). This is a point suggested by Dubrow when she writes, in *Captive Victors*, "To read Shakespeare's sonnets is to become lost in the herte's forest and to realize that in many ways that heart is our own" (1987: 171). Later she adds, "For just as form mirrors content to an unusual degree in the sonnets, so the experiences of the reader mirror those of the speaker to an extent unusual in even the greatest art" (p. 257). John Kerrigan also speaks of Shakespeare's successful attempt "to disconcert the reader" (1986: 42), while Michael J. B. Allen writes of the dark lady sub-sequence: "we are compelled to switch moods, thoughts and evaluations in a vertiginous, continuously creative way; to make instantaneous adjustments that violate our needs for predictability, for causality, for various kinds of logic" (1978: 129). Colin Burrow makes a similar claim about the entire collection:

> The Sonnets are best viewed . . . as poems which develop the methods of the earlier narrative poems to their utmost point – a point at which one is not quite sure who is male and who is female, who is addressed or why, of what their respective social roles are. If

the Sonnets are viewed in this light, then the many empirical uncertainties as to when and to whom they were written seem less like damaging gaps in our knowledge, and more like an enabling condition of the delighted mystification which all readers of these poems have felt, and which they repeatedly invite. (2002: 91–2)

Here it may be worth noting Helen Vendler's comment that "Perhaps total immersion in the Sonnets – that is to say, in Shakespeare's mind – is a mildly deranging experience to anyone" (1997: 1). Elsewhere, too, she writes of her realization "with trepidation that the sonnets are a lightning rod for nuttiness" (1994: 24). Could much of that nuttiness be a response to the unsolved and unsolvable mysteries of these poems? Could Shakespeare have plotted his revenge against critics yet unborn?

Deflection

Robert Scholes has written that "the function of anti-narrative is to problematize the entire process of narration and interpretation for us" (1980: 211). With the fifth motive, deflection, we come full circle. By arousing and then frustrating the desire for story and narrative closure, the poet forces the reader (or at least some readers) into lyric attentiveness; here Helen Vendler, who eschews narrative in the sonnets almost entirely, comes to mind. Instead of plot, of linear progression, at least some readers come to appreciate patterns of subtle contrast and juxtaposition within and between individual sonnets. By frustrating our desire for story, Shakespeare teaches his readers – especially later readers – how to read in a new way. Again, Allen is helpful here: "By denying us the prop of narrative consistency, Shakespeare undermines our faith in time, conventionally conceived, and propels us towards non-chronological relationships, the relationships generated by what, from a chronological viewpoint, are arbitrary juxtapositions" (1978: 134).

As John Kerrigan states, one finds in the sonnets "subtle modulation of material," of mood and thought from poem to poem; the narrative elements offer just enough context and framework to enable contrasts, especially among those sonnets closely linked by theme, language, and imagery, as sonnets 33–6 or 71–4. These narrative elements fail to achieve resolution in the way a dramatic plot, tragic or comic, normally does (that is, with death or marriage). Instead we get sequential variation, variation that often involves significant incremental repetition, which nevertheless can often seem like narrative stasis. What seems to be most on display are shifting lyric moods over time, a principle of organization that links the sonnets to Sidney's *Astrophel and Stella* as well as to later collections like Donne's *Songs and Sonets*, where love poems radically different in tone bump against each other. Much of the pleasure in these collections lies in the reader perceiving and experiencing the contrasting moods and attitudes from poem to poem. Even the certainties of sonnet 116, so often recited and invoked at weddings to express the spirit of unchanging love, express just a moment's feeling of confidence against time and alteration. The poems surrounding sonnet 116 make clear that feelings of surety and permanence cannot be long sustained in an ever-changing relationship in a highly mutable world. (Sometimes, of course, we get the sense that the main problem in the sonnets is that the relationship between speaker and young friend, especially the young man's love, does not change, does not increase enough, over time.)

To say, as do Kerrigan and Duncan-Jones, that early modern readers would have found Q familiar does not really explain why the 1609 quarto or other collections published in the 1590s took the form they did, a form in some ways not unlike Dante's and Petrarch's. Perhaps it does suggest that early modern readers had aesthetic expectations about a collection of sonnets very different from ours. Perhaps the narrative of the sonnets is not developed more because it is far less important than other elements, above all lyric intensity, revelations of contrasting states of mind and feeling, and display of poetic virtuosity.

*

Examining the possible motives for the narrative in the sonnets, such as it is, does not prove that Shakespeare arranged or authorized the 1609 quarto. Neither does such an examination disprove authorization. Most of the possible motives I have outlined are actually drawn from reception history, from the various ways different readers have responded to the sonnets' anti-narrativity at different times over the past four hundred years. We have little direct evidence of how the sonnets were initially received. We do know that *Venus and Adonis* and *The Rape of Lucrece* went through many editions during and immediately after Shakespeare's lifetime, while the sonnets had only one, which suggests the sonnets were not nearly as popular or as profitable for booksellers as his first two lengthy narrative poems. Many scholars note that by 1609 the sonnet vogue of the previous decade had long passed.

In his introduction to his 1640 edition of the sonnets (*Poems: Written by Wil. Shakespeare. Gent.*), the first after 1609, John Benson claims the poems had never before been published, though clearly his copy text is the 1609 quarto and *The Passionate Pilgrim*. What little narrative clarity the sonnets had in Q Benson silently dismantles, eliminating some poems, changing the order of others, combining two or more sonnets to form longer single poems, providing titles to lyrics where none had existed before, and, most notoriously, changing pronouns so that at least some of the poems previously addressed to a male now addressed a female beloved. How do we read Benson's motives? Most commentators, including Hyder Rollins and Duncan-Jones, think he was simply disguising his piracy. Others, like Margreta de Grazia (1994) think Benson was trying to provide sense to a collection that to him lacked order and clarity. If it was the sonnets' lack of narrative cohesion and completion that led to the liberties Benson took, would Shakespeare have minded? Would he have been pleased? How would he have responded to Sasha Roberts's discovery that many seventeenth-century transcribers of the sonnets, like Benson, altered the pronouns in poems originally addressed to a male to denote a female beloved? These transcribers felt free to make other textual changes as well, and, again like Benson, they frequently provided titles for individual sonnets (Roberts 2003: 143–90). The practice of Benson and other early modern readers may well reflect a very different practice of reading, as well as very different notions of authorship and literary property from those we have today. Their actions may also, of course, suggest an aversion to love poems written by one man to another. On this question, and many others, we will no doubt continue to speculate.

What we can also do, however, is practice agnostic tolerance and healthy skepticism, while also eschewing dogmatism of any kind about the sonnets' story, by recognizing all that we do not know. Highly intelligent critics, using the skills of close reading and many other productive methodologies, continue to make substantial claims about the story implied by these poems and then to build elaborate interpretations based on these claims, which somehow slip from the status of possibility to that of fact. Such arguments often advance our understanding of the sonnets' possible meanings, yet they are unlikely to persuade those who disagree or to settle anything once and for all. An interesting example of such disagreement can be seen in the contrasting theories about the relationship between the poet and young friend in the work of Joseph Pequigney and David Schalkwyk. For Pequigney, whose larger purpose in *Such Is My Love* is to argue that the sonnets are "the grand masterpiece of homoerotic poetry" (1985: 1), the young friend is not an aristocrat. The references to patronage (sonnet 26) and servitude (sonnets 89 and 90) are for him metaphors for an imbalance of feeling between a sensitive older man and a less loving, beautiful younger man. In arguing that the friend is not an aristocrat, Pequigney fights a long tradition of interpretation. Most of his few predecessors in this line of argument, Oscar Wilde and Samuel Butler among them, also argued for an erotic relationship between Shakespeare and the friend, whom they both name Willie Hughes. Wilde propounded this notion of Willie Hughes as a boy actor in Shakespeare's company in a work of fiction, *The Portrait of W.H.*, while in *Shakespeare's Sonnets Reconsidered* Butler claims Willie Hughes was a sea cook with whom Shakespeare had a brief affair. The name Willie Hughes originated with Edmond Malone, who was one of the first to attempt to identify the "Mr. W.H." of Thorpe's dedication by pointing to a possible pun on "hues" in sonnet 20.

In *Speech and Performance in Shakespeare's Sonnets and Plays*, Schalkwyk reads the imagery and rhetoric of patronage and servitude as evidence that the young friend is indeed an aristocrat. He sidesteps almost entirely the possibility of a homosexual bond, seeing instead poems addressed to a social superior, a patron, from a poet ashamed of his profession as an actor and playwright. Both Pequigney and Schalkwyk see the sonnets as a coherent sequence; they accept Malone's important theory of a division between the first 126 poems and the last 28. Further, they also both argue that the sequence is autobiographical, though they use very different kinds of evidence to make their case.[3] For Schalkwyk, the anxieties and self-abasement expressed by the speaker are the result of a difference in class rather than of an imbalance of feeling. Perhaps these two readings could be reconciled: perhaps the young man was an aristocrat as well as the poet's often unkind lover. Or maybe not.

What the disagreement between Schalkwyk and Pequigney illustrates is the paucity of "hard evidence" about the overarching story the sonnets suggest. It also supports the truth that what is obvious to one serious critic is not to another. Each uses internal evidence to support his reading, and each is highly persuasive. All that is missing in their strong analyses is the admission that their theories are built on speculation rather than fact. All that is missing is greater acknowledgment of that which cannot be known with certainty.

NOTES

1 All quotations of the sonnets are from Booth's edition (Shakespeare 1977).
2 I doubt Marotti would find the story, such as it can be inferred, "very odd and unattractive." Is Bradley's reference to homoeroticism in the poems? Or to confessions of adultery?
3 In *Such Is My Love* Pequigney avoids making the claim that the sonnets are autobiographical, but in a later essay, "Sonnets 71–74: Texts and Contexts," he argues that they are.

REFERENCES

Allen, Michael J. B. (1978). "Shakespeare's Man Descending a Staircase: Sonnets 126–154." *Shakespeare Survey* 31, 127–38.

Bell, Ilona (1999). "'That which thou hast done': Shakespeare's Sonnets and *A Lover's Complaint*." In James Schiffer (ed.), *Shakespeare's Sonnets: Critical Essays*, 455–74. New York: Garland.

Benson, John (1640). *Poems: Written by Will. Shake-speare. Gent.* London.

Bradley, A. C. (1909). "Shakespeare the Man." In *Oxford Lectures on Poetry*, 311–57. London: Macmillan.

Burrow, Colin (2002). "Introduction." In William Shakespeare, *The Complete Sonnets and Poems*, ed. Colin Burrow. Oxford: Oxford University Press.

Crosman, Robert (1990). "Making Love out of Nothing at All: The Issue of Story in Shakespeare's Procreation Sonnets." *Shakespeare Quarterly* 41, 470–88.

de Grazia, Margreta (1994). "The Scandal of Shakespeare's Sonnets." *Shakespeare Survey* 46, 35–49.

Dubrow, Heather (1987). *Captive Victors: Shakespeare's Narrative Poems and Sonnets.* Ithaca, NY: Cornell University Press.

Dubrow, Heather (1995). *Echoes of Desire: English Petrarchanism and Its Counterdiscourses.* Ithaca, NY: Cornell University Press.

Dubrow, Heather (1996). "'Incertainties now crown themselves assur'd': The Politics of Plotting Shakespeare's Sonnets." *Shakespeare Quarterly* 47: 3, 291–305.

Dubrow, Heather (1999). "Have Lyre Will Travel: Lyric and Narrative in the Early Modern Sonnet Sequence." Paper presented to MLA, Chicago, 1999.

Duncan-Jones, Katherine (1983). "Was the 1609 *Shake-speares Sonnets* Really Unauthorized?" *Review of English Studies* n.s. 34, 151–71.

Duncan-Jones, Katherine (1997). "Introduction." In *Shakespeare's Sonnets*, ed. Katherine Duncan-Jones. Nashville: Nelson (The Arden Shakespeare).

Forbis, John F. (1924). *The Shakespearean Enigma and an Elizabethan Mania.* New York: American Service Library.

Foster, Donald (1991). "Reconstructing Shakespeare Part 2: The Sonnets." *The Shakespeare Newsletter*, Fall, 26–7.

Hardy, Barbara (1989). "Shakespeare's Narrative: Acts of Memory." *Essays in Criticism* 39, 93–115.

Hieatt, A. Kent; Hieatt, Charles W.; and Prescott, Anne Lake (1991). "When Did Shakespeare Write *Sonnets* 1609?" *Studies in Philology* 88, 69–109.

Kerrigan, John (1986). "Introduction." In William Shakespeare, *The Sonnet and A Lover's Complaint*, ed. John Kerrigan. Harmondsworth: Penguin.

Marotti, Arthur (1990). "Shakespeare's Sonnets as Literary Property." In Elizabeth D. Harvey and Katherine Eisaman Maus, eds., *Soliciting Interpretation: Literary Theory and Seventeenth-Century English Poetry*, 143–73. Chicago: University of Chicago Press.

Meres, Francis (1598). *Palladis Tamia*. London.

Neely, Carol Thomas (1978). "The Structure of English Renaissance Sonnet Sequences." *English Literary History* 45: 359–89.

Pequigney, Joseph (1985). *Such Is My Love: A Study of Shakespeare's Sonnets*. Chicago and London: University of Chicago Press.

Pequigney, Joseph (1999). "Sonnets 71–74: Texts and Contexts." In James Schiffer, ed., *Shakespeare's Sonnets: Critical Essays*, 285–304. New York: Garland.

Roberts, Sasha (2003). *Reading Shakespeare's Poems in Early Modern England*. Basingstoke: Palgrave Macmillan.

Schalkwyk, David (2002). *Speech and Performance in Shakespeare's Sonnets and Plays*. Cambridge, UK: Cambridge University Press.

Scholes, Robert (1980). "Language, Narrative, and Anti-Narrative." *Critical Inquiry* 7, 204–12.

Shakespeare, William (1977). *Shakespeare's Sonnets*, ed. Stephen Booth. New Haven: Yale University Press.

Smith, Bruce (1991). *Homosexual Desire in Shakespeare's England: A Cultural Poetics*. Chicago: University of Chicago Press.

Taylor, Gary (1989). *Reinventing Shakespeare: A Cultural History from the Restoration to the Present*. Oxford: Oxford University Press.

Vendler, Helen (1994). "Reading Stage by Stage: Shakespeare's Sonnets." In Russ McDonald, ed., *Shakespeare Reread: The Text in New Contexts*, 23–41. Ithaca, NY, and London: Cornell University Press.

Vendler, Helen (1997). *The Art of Shakespeare's Sonnets*. Cambridge, Mass.: Harvard University Press.

4

Revolution in *Shake-speares Sonnets*

Margreta de Grazia

Is there anie thing, whereof one may say,
Beholde this, it is newe?

(Eccl. 1: 10)

In 1986 John Kerrigan broke with editorial tradition by adding *A Lover's Complaint* to his edition of Shakespeare's sonnets. Like so many innovations, this one took the form of a restoration: when first published in 1609, *Shake-speares Sonnets* included 154 sonnets followed by a 329-line narrative poem. Editors have known this, of course, since at least the eighteenth century, when the 1609 quarto was for the first time edited. But in the subsequent editions of almost two centuries, *A Lover's Complaint* tended to be severed from the sonnets and either expelled from the canon or classified among Shakespeare's spurious works or his miscellaneous or narrative poems. That the 1609 *Sonnets* had included *A Lover's Complaint* was, editors assumed, a printing-house decision. For Kerrigan, however, it was Shakespeare who intended the combination. In keeping with a convention introduced in 1592 by Samuel Daniel's *Delia* and deployed by Thomas Lodge, Giles Fletcher, Richard Barnfield, Edmund Spenser, and others, Shakespeare concluded his series of sonnets with a complaint poem.[1] Subsequent editors have followed Kerrigan's precedent, so that the Arden editor can now proclaim, "[T]he Complaint has been confidently restored to its original position as an integral component of the sequence."[2] The Oxford editor concurs: "There is no doubt that *A Lover's Complaint* belongs where it is found in the Quarto, as a coda to the Sonnets."[3] The editor of Everyman's *Sonnets* also regards the complaint as integral, as does the editor of Norton's.[4]

The discovery of the convention has had the additional benefit of accounting for another anomaly in the 1609 quarto. The last two sonnets of the series, both originating in a fifth-century Greek epigram, hardly seem an appropriate conclusion to a series of intimate first-person lyrics.[5] Modern commentaries invariably set off the pair from the preceding 152 sonnets by identifying them as Cupid poems, little allegories, etiological myths, anacreontics (after the sixth-century BCE Greek poet Anacreon), or epigrams, as they will be called in this essay.[6] Indeed, had the two poems not been numbered 153 and 154 and had they not conformed to the fourteen-line standard, they might well have suffered the same checkered canonical career as *A Lover's Complaint*. Editors often feel the need to apologize for their presence, attributing it to the haphazard compiling practices of early modern printing houses; critics have tended to ignore them altogether. Kerrigan's discovery, however, justifies their presence too, for the conventional Delian structure was typically tripartite, with anacreontic verses interposed between sonnets and complaint: *Delia* consists of fifty sonnets, a short poem in anacreontic meter, and a complaint in rhyme royal. As Thomas Roche has pointed out, Lodge, Fletcher, and Barnfield also interpose cupidic poems between their sonnets and complaints.[7] Once *A Lover's Complaint* is fixed in final position, the Cupid poems can be seen to occupy an interludic or medial space. The effect of the new organization should not be underestimated. It has done nothing less than convert the 1609 *Shake-speares Sonnets* into a multi-generic work, consisting not of 154 uniform sonnets, but rather of 152 sonnets, two epigrams, and one complaint.[8]

It must be stressed, however, that the innovation is based on no new textual evidence. The 1609 quarto remains the sole authority for the sonnets, and its layout hardly articulates the conventional tripartite structure. On the contrary: the title-page names only *Shake-speares Sonnets*; the 154 sonnets conclude with a bold upper-case and full-stopped FINIS. *A Louers complaint* begins on a new page, with an independent attribution and a separate running title; in addition, the two cupidic epigrams are in no way divided from the preceding 152 sonnets. The warrant for the enlargement and restructuring is entirely extratextual, deriving from other collections where the formatting is typographically signaled. Early readers of the 1609 quarto, it is assumed, familiar with these other collections, would have automatically superimposed the schema onto their reading of the sonnets. The reattachment of *A Lover's Complaint* combined with the installation of the tripartite structure now makes it possible, according to Kerrigan, to read the sonnets as those first readers read them: as part of a larger whole, "They would have read the volume *as* a volume, and their sense of the parts would have been modified by the whole."[9]

Or, at least, that is *one* way in which they might have been read – if read in the 1609 quarto volume and by readers so well versed in sonnet collections that they had the tripartite layout in mind. We have more compelling material evidence, however, in both manuscript and print, that they were read in other contexts. As many as twenty-five manuscripts of the sonnets bear witness to their having circulated individually or in different groupings, in poetic miscellanies or anthologies, sometimes set to music.[10] And then there is John Benson's 1640 *Poems*, the only printed form in which they were published for some 150 years, which regrouped all but eight of the sonnets in combinations of up to five, assigned the groups generalizing rubrics, and interspersed them with other poems, by Shakespeare as well as other poets.[11] Thus the foregrounding of the tripartite structure gives us not the way the sonnets were first read but rather another way of reading them now: in relation to two epigrams and a complaint.

Taking advantage of this new opportunity, this essay begins with the simple observation that the three poetic units of the 1609 quarto are distinguished not only generically but also temporally. In contrast to the here-and-now of the sonnets, the anacreontics,
originating in a Greek epigram, revert back to antiquity, and *A Lover's Complaint*,
written in archaic vocabulary and diction, reaches back to old-fashioned medieval
ballads and complaints. The one antiquated and the other archaized, both tell very old
stories. The epigrams repeat, not once but twice, the little myth of the unquenchability
of desire. *A Lover's Complaint* rehearses "a plaintfull story" (l. 2) of seduction and abandonment as old as the hills in which it is heard to reverberate. Despite the prospect of
change held out by each poetic unit, in the form of first a therapeutic well and then a
clerical "Father" (l. 71), both the "ancient" epigrams and the "medieval" complaint
conclude with anticipations of more of the same.

*

In the two Cupid poems, Diana's maids plunge Cupid's torch in a cool fountain, but
the water, rather than extinguishing the torch, catches fire: desire overwhelms chastity
and recovers its "datelesse liuely heat still to indure" (153. 6).[12] A close analogue to
these poems has been found in an epigram by the fifth-century Byzantine poet, Marianus Scholasticus.[13] But as editors note, there are numerous other precedents, in Greek
and Latin as well as French and Italian. When Shakespeare penned sonnets 153 and
154, Kerrigan observes, "he was elaborating a conceit already at least a thousand years
old."[14] The poet rewrites what has been written many times before, in ancient and
modern tongues, to record what had been experienced before, time and again in legend
and history. Colin Burrow is certainly correct in seeing the cupidic pair as a demonstration of how "Shakespeare refashions or rerenders what has been written before";[15] the
two exercises in imitation each retell the primal myth of Cupid's irresistible passion.
In the very last line of the last sonnet, the poet offers up his own experience, his return
to the venereal hotspot, "my mistres eie" (153. 14) as proof of this myth's validity: "this
[the following proverb] by that [the preceding narration] I proue, / Loues fire heates
water, water cooles not loue" (154. 13–14). But the deictic "that" also references the
entire group of sonnets to the mistress; all of them bear witness – sometimes comically
and sometimes dead seriously – to the truth of desire's perennial inflammability.

A Lover's Complaint is also distanced from the contemporaneity of the sonnets. The
complaint genre reinvokes ancient England, as registered in what sonnet 106 terms "the
Chronicle of wasted time." Indeed its model, Daniel's *The Complaint of Rosamond*,
recounting the seduction of Rosamond by Henry II, draws its material from several
chroniclers; following suit, Thomas Lodge sets his *The Tragical Complaint of Estred* even
further back in time in narrating the woes of the cast-off mistress of the legendary
British king Locrine. The poem is written in seven-line iambic pentameter stanzas that
became known only in the nineteenth century as rhyme royal, in reference to its use
by the fifteenth-century King James I of Scotland in writing *The Kingis Quair*, a collection of poems in Middle Scots. Before James, however, the verse was associated not

with royalty but with the native English tradition of Chaucer, primarily, but also of
Gower and Lydgate. In his 1589 *Art of English Poesie*, Puttenham calls the verse "a staff
of seven or settaine" and associates with it with "our old Poets *Chaucer* and others in
their historicall reports and other ditties."[16] *A Lover's Complaint* also pretends to such
antiquity by its scant use of caesura; as Puttenham also relates, "our ancient rymers, as
Chaucer, Lydgate and others vsed these *Cesures* either very seldome, or not at all."[17] In
addition, as is always noted, the poem cultivates bygone times through techniques made
familiar by Spenser's use of what Samuel Johnson termed his "studied barbarity":[18] the
use of archaic vocabulary and arcane locutions which, here as in Spenser, pose a particular challenge to editors who would modernize a poem that the poet has taken pains to
archaize. Old words are resurrected ("feate," "teene," "maund," "browny"). New words
are coined to look old ("blusterer," "acture," "empleacht," "daft").[19] The rusticated landscape, the period-piece costume ("plattid hiue" for straw hat, "fillet" for ribbon, "greynd
bat" for staff); even the maiden's auditor, the "reuerend man" (l. 57) bearing promise
of "the charitie of age" (l. 70) might be a throwback to the olden days of the old faith.
The "plaintfull story" (l. 2) she tells is already an echo: she herself acknowledges the
many before her bewitched by the same lover, and he offers as ocular proof of his prior
multiple conquests ornamented locks of hair, "deepe brain'd sonnets" (l. 209) and gems.
Such betrayals are hardly news: they are the stuff not only of complaints, but of legends,
tales, ballads, and even casebook studies. They testify to the failure of admonitory
proverbs, as the maiden allows in admitting that when pressed by her lover, "what are
precepts worth / Of stale example?" "Aye me I fell," she confesses (ll. 267–8, 321), but
is content to fall again into what Colin Burrow terms "a cycle of seduction and
complaint."[20]

Both the epigrammatic pair and the complaint have long traditions of having been
sounded before. Bygone poetic forms and styles are simulated to tell the same old story
in antiquated and archaized forms, ancient and gothic. In both cases, the possibility for
change is held in view – of quenching the flame, of converting the fallen mistress. Yet
both end in relapse: the diseased lover returns to the wellspring of his desire, seeking
cure at the source of his infection; the fallen woman resigns herself to falling again for
her seducer. In the epigrams the lover, inflamed by Cupid's brand, seeks out "new fire"
(153. 14). In the complaint, the undone woman looks forward to being "new peruert[ed]"
(l. 329). At these end points, the "new" indicates no opening up of a future, but a return
to what was before. The "new fire" will be just like the old; the "new" perversion will
be just like the old. The two poetic codas to the sonnets, then, end in foreclosing the
possibility of change. Caught up in cycles of repetition, they shut out the possibility of
anything new. To quote the wise Solomon, credited with three thousand proverbs,[21] "Is
there anie thing, whereof one may say, Beholde this, it is newe?" (Eccl. 1: 10).[22] The
preacher has already answered his own question, for his time and all time. "As it hath
bene already in the olde time it was before us; there *is* no new thing under the sunne"
(Eccl. 1: 9).

*

Sonnet 59 begins by echoing this very proverb.

> If their bee nothing new, but that which is,
> Hath beene before, how are our braines beguild,
> Which laboring for inuention beare amisse
> The second burthen of a former child?

By echoing Ecclesiastes, the opening lines confirm the Ecclesiast's wisdom: what they say now has been said before, and so often as to be proverbial: "There is nothing new under the sun." There is no point in "laboring for inuention," for as Solomon has taught, "What remaineth unto man in all his travail . . . under the sunne?" (Eccl. 1: 3) The poetic struggle to bring something new into the world has been futile, like all efforts surveyed by the wise preacher: "I have considered all the workes that are done under the sunne, and behold as *is* vanities, and vexation of the spirit" (Eccl. 1: 14). Indeed a poem, often called a *vanity*, might be considered the "Vanitie of vanities" (Eccl. 1: 12), especially when presuming to create something new. The very metaphor the poet introduces to describe poetic brainwork might appear to bear out Solomon's axiom. To describe the futile labor of such an attempt, the poet lights on the most common topos for the poetic act: childbirth. A poem, like a child, is conceived and, after labor, delivered. In the first sonnet of the collection that precipitated the sonnet convention in England, for example, Sidney's Astrophil flails about laboring for this kind of invention, "Thus great with child to speake, and helplesse in my throwes";[23] similar references to poetic conception, gestation, delivery may be found in virtually every sonnet collection of the period. In Shakespeare's, the metaphor undergirds the opening sonnets to the friend in which the poet's petitions that he survive by begetting children are first supplemented and then superseded by his promises to keep him alive through poems.

And yet this "second burthen of a former child" is no ordinary baby. When was there ever such a thing? In straining for invention, the poet has forced out a new trope for poetic offspring, a far cry from the conventional metaphor, less a child than a freak of nature. For this newborn comes into the world with an unheard-of distinguishing feature: it has been born already. Not a twin, not an aborted foetus, not a false pregnancy, but a new kind of offspring: a *pre-nati* or déjà-né. Hence the post-partum stupefaction of the newly delivered cerebral parent: "how are our brains beguiled!"

The poet, as if in defiance of Solomon's wisdom, has dared to give birth to something new. And the attempt goes badly wrong. The upset is more serious than those caused by untimely familiar births: instead of coming too early or too late, this one comes after it has already come. No new-born, the child is an after-born. Like the monsters and prodigies featured in both early modern broadsheets and medical treatises, this one may signal a moral transgression of some kind.[24] An illicit thought might have generated the aberrant brainchild, just as in Book II of Milton's *Paradise Lost* Satan no sooner conceives of rebellion than he gives spontaneous birth to the portentous creature Sin. In this instance, the pressure to come up with something new appears to have produced an inconceivable conceit for poetic conception, or more accurately *mis*conception. If it were a mere untimely birth, it would qualify as a figure of speech, *hysteron proteron*, a setting before of that which should be behind, or vice versa. But parturition after delivery goes beyond temporal inversion by contorting the generational process beyond not only nature, but also beyond usage and even comprehension. Sixteenth-century rhetorics might have termed such a linguistic infraction *catachresis*, the result of straining too hard, of forcing resemblance beyond the bounds of intelligibility, and thereby causing metaphor – the figure of transport, the bearer or carrier of meaning (meta + phorein) – to "beare amisse" or miscarry. The most natural metaphor in the rhetorical laboratory is thus distorted into something Frankensteinian. The inflective rise indicated by the punctuation of both the quarto (a question mark) and modern editions (an exclamation point) registers understandable incredulity – *eureka!* – before the shock of the new.

The freakish metaphor notwithstanding, the poet seems convinced that what he has written has already been written before. If his poetry seems new, it is only because the poetic record does not extend far back enough to reveal its selfsame antecedent. In Francis Bacon's neat compression of Solomon's proverb, "all novelty is but oblivion" . . . or *ignorance*, he might have added.[25] The unknown no less than the unremembered appears unprecedented. The poet's sonnets are like the pyramids or obelisks erected in honor of James I's triumphal entry to London: they may have seemed novel when erected in 1604, as sonnet 123 observes, but they had been standing in Egypt for several millennia:[26]

> Thy pyramyds buylt vp with newer might
> To me are nothing nouell, nothing strange,
> They are but dressings of a former sight:

So, too, if the poet's verse seems new, it is only because literary history does not go back all the way to the time when writing was first invented (the days of Cadmus? of Thoth? of Adam?): "Since minde at first in carrecter was done" (59. 9), an elliptical and unidiomatic construction, with a touch of the "pseudo-primitive" as Stephen Booth suggests, mirroring less a writing in the earliest language (Phoenician? Egyptian? Hebrew?) than the clumsy earliest attempts at writing.[27] The poet yearns for long-distance hindsight or "a back-ward looke," an inversion of the prophetic foresight of the *vates*, an impossibly high-powered optics enabling him to discern images as far back as eons ago, or "fiue hundreth courses of the Sunne." With inverted visionary powers, he would spot in some dusty obsolete "antique book" (a tablet? a scroll? a codex?) the image he is convinced to have been long extant: the picture of the first "burden" or "former child" of which his own is the secondary epigone.

> Oh that record could with a back-ward looke,
> Euen of fiue hundreth courses of the Sunne,
> Show me your image in some antique booke,
> Since minde at first in carrecter was done.
> (59. 5–8)

This retrospective far-sightedness would enable him to see the two portraits as if side by side, the extinct poem of the "antique book" cheek by jowl with the modern rewrite of the 1609 quarto. So paired in his bifurcated vision, they could then be matched, his own "composed wonder" with the wondrous compositions of "wits of former daies." "[W]hat the old world could say" in praise of the friend could then be compared to what he himself is currently saying, including in sonnet 59. Solomon's wisdom would once again be confirmed: what is, hath been. The new is simply a rerun of the old, better or worse, perhaps, unless exactly the same:

> Whether we are mended, or where better they,
> Or whether reuolution be the same.

The poet's quandary over old and new recalls the debate recurring from the four-teenth through the seventeenth centuries over the relative value of the ancients and the moderns in both the arts and the sciences. In relation to the arts, that contest, as in sonnet 59, remains irresolvable – until toward the close of the seventeenth century, when the question is mooted by the realization scholars now use to mark the inception of modern historical consciousness.[28] Past and present are incomparable: the present is not a replay of the past but rather something altogether new and different, and to be measured, therefore, by a new set of literary standards. In his recent discussion of the emergence of modernity, Fredric Jameson gives a jaunty summary of the shift:

> the "quarrel" between ancients and moderns as it were unravels and undoes itself, and both sides unexpectedly come to the same conviction, namely that the terms in which the judg-ment is to be adjudicated – the superiority or not of antiquity, the inferiority or not of the present and of the modern times – are unsatisfactory. The conclusion on both sides is then that the past, and antiquity, is neither superior nor inferior, but simply different.[29]

But sonnet 59 allows for no such way out. The word that is positioned to introduce the possibility of radical difference in fact shuts it down. In the elliptical, "Or whether reuolution be the same" (l. 12), modern literary history is imagined to follow the same cycle followed by the ancient: it might, at the time of the writing, be higher or lower than the ancient, or at exactly at the same point. The word "reuolution" here has nothing of the explosive political charge it would carry in the next century; it refers to no dis-ruptive break with the past, but rather a cyclical return to it, like the imagined diurnal revolution of the Ptolemaic sun around the earth – because cyclical, literary history, both ancient and modern, is revolutionary. Thus the difference between the ancient and the modern is no greater than that between an old sun and a new, the latter a recur-rence of the former.

As we shall see, also following the rotational movement of literary history is the poet's own heliotropic poetics:

> For as the Sun is daily new and old,
> So is my loue still telling what is told,
> (76. 13–14)

Having racked his brains in the first quatrain and strained his eyes in the second and third, the poet relaxes into the comfort of a prosaic couplet:

> Oh sure I am the wits of former daies,
> To subiects worse haue giuen admiring praise.

After the risky speculation of "If their bee nothing new" and the extensive fantasy of "Oh that record could with a back-ward looke," the sonnet concludes in the unearned certainty of "Oh sure I am." The poet returns from his experimentation with ground-breaking novelty to the business of praise-per-usual, with the figure of *meiosis*, what Puttenham anglicizes as "the debaser," praising his friend as less bad than the "subiects worse" of "former daies."[30] But the unusual deployment of "the debaser" to praise a subject is not the couplet's only oddity. If the "antique book" contains an "image" of Mr. W.H., wouldn't the "subiect" of the image have to have been present to sit for the portrait? And by the principle of "reuolution be the same," wouldn't the modern Mr. W.H. be no better or worse than the ancient Mr. W.H.? Perhaps this bit of wit is intended as a modern challenge to the "wits of former daies," a submission, perhaps, to the ancient/modern poetry competition – though hardly likely to win any prizes.

*

The witty and flat coda, however, should not detract from the metaphysical daring of the body of the sonnet, with its miscarrying conception of "The second burthen of a former child" and its futuristic travel into the backward abyss of time. The conceits seem all the more audacious when measured against the only poetic standard the poet professes in the sonnets to the friend, the revolutionary poetics of the proverbial "There is nothing new under the sun." The poet commits himself repeatedly to the poetic routine of: "I must each day say ore the very same" (108. 6). With nothing new remaining to be said – "What's new to speake, what now to register . . . Nothing" (108. 3, 5) – the only option is repetition: "Spending againe what is already spent" (76. 12); "still telling what is told" (76. 14); "Counting no old thing old" (108. 7). Invariability – "so far from variation or quicke change" (76. 2) – becomes his poetic signature, the stylistic feature by which his verse can be identified as his: "euery word doth almost [t]el my name" (76. 7). His uniform "noted weed" distinguishes him from the new-fangled "quicke change" of his contemporaries (76. 6, 2). In addition to professing repetition, he practices it, most conspicuously in the thrice-repeated trinitarian litany of "Faire, kinde, and true" of sonnet 105. Like prayers divine, the poet's reiterations give voice to his unwavering devotion: "One thing expressing, leaues out difference" (105. 8). Of course, repetition is easier said than done, as Joel Fineman points out in commenting on that very line: " 'one thing expressing,' even as it is spoken, seems, to some extent, duplicitous, just as 'difference,' even left unspoken, does not seem entirely 'left out.' "[31]

Whatever the result in practice, the poet espouses no other poetic ideal. And it answers perfectly to the conservationist project announced by the collection's very first line:

> From fairest creatures we desire increase,
> That thereby beauties *Rose* might neuer die,
>
> (1. 1–2)

In order for "beauties *Rose*" to survive it must be reproduced as faithfully as possible: a mimesis closer to mechanical duplication than artful imitation, "Let him but coppy what in you is writ" (84. 9). The glamorizing cosmetics of rhetorical color are rejected as adulterate and therefore contaminating of his custodial mission of transmitting "What beauty was of yore" (68. 14) through the accurate replication of the "map of daies out-worne," and the untampered delivery of "what welth [Nature] had, / In daies long since, before these last so bad" (67. 13–14). Embellishment would introduce change, and change is precisely the force that must be withstood in order to keep "beauties *Rose*" freshly intact. Alteration is the sign of Time's ravaging passage, the result of its free-wheeling disfiguring scythe which the poet, "all in war with Time" (15. 13), challenges with his stilling stylus. The desire to preserve "beauties *Rose*" leads to what Richard Halpern has termed "a poetics of sublimation," the distillation of the essential friend in the antiseptic glass of verse (the *vers* of *vers*): "A liquid prisoner pent in walls of glasse" (5. 10); "by verse distils your truth" (54. 14).[32] In a number of sonnets, the sublimation is best achieved by verbatim repetition; the pure tautology of "you alone, are you" (84. 2) constitutes highest praise. The achievement is all the more arresting when the repetition is merely phonetic, as when a single sound unites two different signifiers as well as two different parts of speech, so that the friend's being conflates with the poet's verse: "thou art all my art" (78. 13). In an even flashier display of monotoning, three different signifieds are sunk into the same syllable, the object of sight (the friend's *eye*), the organ of sight (the poet's *eyeing*) and the beholding poet (his *I*): "when first your eye I eyde" (104. 2). Tautology is the best policy, too, when the poet repudiates change with the same formula by which the Godhead asserted selfsameness: "I am that I am" (121. 9). The poet's constancy guarantees the invariation of his praise: "O let me true in loue but truly write" (21. 9). And that invariation in turn wards off change in both the object ("My loue") as well as his love for that object ("My loue"): "My loue shall in my verse euer live young" (19. 14). In these sonnets, change is always for the worse, whether in the form of absence, betrayal, aging, or sickness. The poet generally reserves figurative language to describe less what he would preserve than the mutations that threaten to destroy it. The metaphorically rich sonnets, for example sonnet 18 ("Shall I compare thee to a Summers day?") or sonnet 73 ("That time of yeeare thou maist in me behold"), ponder or decry the transmogrifications of mortality, always in dread anticipation of what will eventually occur: "Time will come and take my loue away" (64).

The poet's repeated disavowal of change in favor of repetition is crucial to his poetic project of protecting "beauties *Rose*" from the ravages of Time. Monotony defends against mutability, "Yet doe thy worst ould Time dispight thy wrong, / My loue shall in my verse euer liue young" (19. 13–14); "No! Time, thou shalt not bost that I doe change" (123. 1); "Finding the first conceit of loue there bred / Where time and outward forme would shew it dead" (108. 13–14). The poet's poetics, as well as his subject and his love for his subject, will triumph over change by remaining selfsame. Immortality, whether for himself or for the friend, can be attained only through such poetic reiteration, the medium for transmitting "beauties patterne to succeding men" (19. 12). Indeed, the poems to the friend imagine a future awaiting its legacy through its numerous apostrophes to the "age to come" (17. 7), "times in hope" (60. 13), "ages yet to be" (101. 12). These unborn generations take the surreal synecdochic form of so many reading eyes ("eyes of all posterity" [55. 11], "eyes not yet created" [81. 10]), hearing ears ("heare this thou age vnbred" [104. 13]), and reciting mouths and tongues ("where breath most breaths, euen in the mouths of men [81. 14], "toungs to be, your beeing shall rehearse" [81. 11]). Readers-to-be – so many eyes, ears, mouths, and tongues – stand proleptically in wait for their poetically sealed legacy till the end of time, "til the iudgement that your selfe arise" (55. 13).

*

But the manifesto that is sonnet 127 changes everything: "In the ould age blacke was not counted faire." This sonnet leaves behind the "ould age" of the previous 126 sonnets, and rings in a new: "now is blacke beauties successiue heire." The succession is hardly lineal: fair cannot by any stretch beget black, at least not by due process. A rupture has occurred, one that approximates the modern sense of *revolution*, the kind Marx called for in 1851 that would tolerate no regress in its "forcible overthrow of all existing conditions," making "all turning back impossible."[33] Old values have been purged. "Sweet beauty," in the sonnet's allegoric bulletin, is stripped of her title ("hath no name") and of her sanctioned place ("no holy boure"), cast out into the contaminating open air ("prophan'd": *pro*, forth, + *fanum*, temple) and thereby exposed to abuse and violation ("in disgrace"). In the place of "beauties *Rose*" now rules Black. The proclamation is attended by an apology; the overthrow was necessitated by the pervasive simulations of sovereign Fair: "each hand hath put on Natures power." As a result, all distinction is lost: what is truly and naturally fair looks the same as what is seemingly and artificially fair.

At this transitional moment, the poet's loyalties seem divided. There is a touch of nostalgia in his report of "Sweet beauty['s]" demise. After all, he was just a sonnet or two ago a fervent believer in the "Faire, kinde, and true" of "beauties *Rose*." By the sestet, however, his allegiances are clear:

> Therefore my Mistersse eyes are Rauen blacke,
> Her eyes so suted, and they mourners seeme,
> At such who not borne faire no beauty lack,
> Slandring Creation with a false esteeme,

> Yet so they mourne becoming of their woe,
> That euery toung saies beauty should looke so.

The nostalgia for the old regime surfaces here as well, but this time projected onto his mistress with the improbable fantasy that her black eyes are in mourning for those made-up faces now suddenly fallen out of both fashion and favor: "such who not borne faire no beauty lack." As if to allay suspicion that her pity for the old guard might be mistaken for treason, he condemns those false pretenders for "Slandring Creation with a false esteeme." The charge of slander, however, seems less applicable to the glamorizing hands of the octave than to the lip-serving tongues of the couplet. The extreme crime of "Slandring Creation" better suits the poet's own disposition "[t]o swere against the truth" (152. 14). Taken seriously, swearing that "black is fairest" commits the linguistic crime of negating of the Vulgate's "*Fiat lux*" with a dictatorial "Let there be Dark."

Sonnets 127–52 play out, sometimes in jest and sometimes in earnest, the psychic consequences of the radical perjury committed when black hell and dark night are sworn to be fair (147. 13–14). The monotonous prayers to the friend's "Faire, kinde, and true" are replaced by relentless appeals to the mistress's "foul" (137. 12), "cruell" (149. 1), and "vniust" (138. 9), and they, too, are repetitive. The importuning desire of 135 and 136, for example, spins maniacally around homonyms and synonyms of the poet's first name; every word in sonnet 136 could be shown to signal its appetitive referent, its fourteen lines reducible to *Will wills will*, giving something like literal truth to the poet's earlier claim to distinction, "euery word doth almost [t]el my name" (76. 7).[34] But the frenzied repetition in the sonnets to Dark differs from the studied repetitions of those to Fair. In the second group, no future is designated. The testamentary project, implicit in the same name, is lost to the haywire temporality of "Had,hauing,and in quest, to haue extreame" (129. 10). It is only fitting, then, that sonnet 152, the last of the dark sonnets, should end in repetition that is compulsive rather than programmatic. As Helen Vendler precisely observes, "the speaker returns obsessively to the same words over and over," above all to the *I / eye* homophone, repeated eight times.[35] The 152 sonnets, like the cupidic epigrams and *A Lover's Complaint*, end with renewed recommitment to the same course of action, repeating a cycle of vows broken and mended: "new faith torne, / In vowing new hate after new loue bearing" (152. 3–4). The final sonnet locks itself in the past, no future in sight except as recapitulation: *da capo*.

Shakespeare uses the word "new" twice as many times in the sonnets as in any other work, but the word does not designate the "never before" of, say, the self-advertisement of the quarto's title-page: "Neuer before Imprinted." It denotes instead only a more recent version of what has already been. So, too, do the revolutionary poetics of *Shake-speares Sonnets*. When read as a tripartite work, each of its three units ends in chronic repetition: the 152 sonnets remain stuck in the cycle of hating-after-loving and loving-after-hating; the Greek epigrams in that of rekindling-after-quenching and quenching-after-rekindling, and the gothic complaint in that of perversion-after-reconciliation and reconciliation-after-perversion. On three temporal and generic registers, the recently re-authorized contents of the 1609 quarto rehearse programs of return, and with no end in sight other than the quarto's final typographic FINIS, terminating in a period, and re-terminating with an ornamental border.

FINIS.

NOTES

1 *The Sonnets and A Lover's Complaint*, ed. John Kerrigan (London and New York: Penguin, 1986), 13–14.

2 *Shakespeare's Sonnets*, ed. Katherine Duncan-Jones (London: Thomas Nelson, 1997; The Arden Shakespeare), 45.

3 *The Complete Sonnets and Poems*, ed. Colin Burrow (Oxford: Oxford University Press, 2002; Oxford World's Classics), 140.

4 *The Sonnets and A Lover's Complaint*, ed. Martin Dodsworth (Vermont: J. M. Dent; London: Charles E. Tuttle, 1995), xvii; The Sonnets and "A Lover's Complaint," ed. Walter Cohen, in *The Norton Shakespeare*, gen. ed. Stephen Greenblatt (New York and London: Norton, 1997), 1916.

5 Sonnets 153 and 154 have been traced back to a six-line epigram by the Byzantine poet Marianus Scholasticus published in the collection of 3,000 Greek poems known as the Greek Anthology. For the fifth-century epigram, the sixteenth-century editions of the collection in which it appeared, and its translations and parallels in Latin, French, Italian, and English, see James Hutton, "Analogues of Shakespeare's Sonnets 153–4: Contributions to the History of A Theme," *Modern Philology* 38 (May 1941), 385–403.

6 On the affinity between the sonnet and the epigram, see Rosalie Colie, *The Resources of Kind: Genre-Theory in the Renaissance* (Berkeley: University of California Press, 1973), 75.

7 Thomas P. Roche, Jr., *Petrarch and the English Sonnet Sequences* (New York: AMS Press, 1989), 436, 514, n. 68.

8 The fifteen-line sonnet 99 and the twelve-line sonnet 126 are the exceptions to the fourteen-line standard.

9 *Sonnets*, ed. Kerrigan, 14.

10 *Sonnets*, ed. Burrow, 106. See also Sasha Roberts, "Textual Transmission and the Transformation of Desire: The *Sonnets*, *A Lover's Complaint*, and *The Passionate Pilgrim*," in Sasha Roberts (ed.), *Rereading Shakespeare's Poems* (Basingstoke: Palgrave Macmillan, 2003), 143–90.

11 On the shift from John Benson's 1640 *Poems* to Edmond Malone's 1790 *Sonnets*, see Margreta de Grazia, *Shakespeare Verbatim: The Reproduction of Authenticity and the 1790 Apparatus* (Oxford: Clarendon, 1991), 152–76.

12 The sonnets and *A Lover's Complaint* are quoted throughout from the facsimile edition of the Bodleian Library *Shake-speares Sonnets* of 1609 (Menston, Yorks.: Scolar, 1970). Line numbers for *A Lover's Complaint* are given parenthetically, and are taken from Burrow's edition.

13 On this epigram, see *Sonnets*, ed. Duncan-Jones, headnote to 153–4, 422.

14 *Sonnets*, ed. Kerrigan, headnote to 153, 387.

15 *Sonnets*, ed. Burrow, 117.

16 George Puttenham, *The Art of English Poesie* (1589; facs. Menston: Scolar, 1968), 101.

17 Puttenham, *The Art of English Poesie*, 89. When the "ancient rymers" do use caesura, Puttenham continues, they do so "licentiously," so that their rhymes run unrestrained and "ryme dogrell" results.

18 *The Rambler*, ed. Walter Jackson Bate and Albrecht B. Strauss, in the Yale Edition of the *Works of Samuel Johnson* (New Haven: Yale University Press, 1969), vol. 3, 203.

19 On the category of "coined archaisms" or neologisms made to look obsolete, see *Sonnets*, ed. Kerrigan, 432–3. Burrow counts forty-nine neologisms: *Sonnets*, ed. Burrow, 139.

20 *Sonnets*, ed. Burrow, 146.

21 "And he spake three thousand proverbs" (1 Kings 4: 32).

22 All quotations from the Bible follow *The Geneva Bible* (1560 facs. rpt. Madison, Milwaukee, and London: University of Wisconsin Press, 1969).

23 *Astrophil and Stella* (1. 12), in *The Poems of Sir Philip Sidney*, ed. William A. Ringler, Jr. (Oxford: Clarendon Press, 1967), 165.

24 For the identification of early modern "monsters" with the issue of various kinds of illicit copulation, and the possibility that such issue might now be the source of "new social imaginings, new social actors, new ways of thinking," see Jonathan Goldberg's remarkable *Tempest in the Caribbean* (Minneapolis: University of Minnesota Press, 2004), 147 and esp. 41–9.

25 Sir Francis Bacon, "Of Vicissitude of Things," in *The Essays*, ed. John Pitcher (London and New York: Penguin, 1985), 228.

26 On the pyramids erected at the accession of King James, see *Sonnets*, ed. Burrow, 626 n. 2.

27 *Shakespeare's Sonnets*, ed. Stephen Booth (New Haven: Yale University Press, 1977), 237 n. 8.

28 On H. R. Jauss's thesis that the quarrel between the ancients and the moderns marks the start of a modern sense of history, see Paul de Man, *Blindness and Insight: Essays in the Rhetoric of Contemporary Criticism*, 2nd edn. (Minneapolis: University of Minnesota Press, 1983), 153.

29 Fredric Jameson, *A Singular Modernity: Essay on the Ontology of the Present* (London and New York: Verso, 2002), 22.

30 Puttenham, *The Art of English Poesie*, 195, 227–9.

31 Joel Fineman, *Shakespeare's Perjured Eye: The Invention of Poetic Subjectivity in the Sonnets* (Berkeley: University of California Press, 1986), 242.

32 Richard Halpern, *Shakespeare's Perfume: Sodomy and Sublimity in the Sonnets, Wilde, Freud and Lacan* (Philadelphia: University of Pennsylvania Press, 2002), 27.

33 *The Eighteenth Brumaire of Louis Bonaparte*, in *The Marx–Engels Reader*, ed. Robert C. Tucker (New York and London: Norton, 1978), 598.

34 See Margreta de Grazia, "The Scandal of Shakespeare's Sonnets," in James Schiffer (ed.), *Shakespeare's Sonnets: Critical Essays* (New York: Garland, 1999), 109.

35 Vendler continues the tally: "*swear* and its variants (*swore forsworn swearing*) alone occur seven times (1, 2, 2, 9, 12, 13, 14); *oaths* four times (5, 7, 9, 10); *vow(s)* (3, 4, 7), *love* (2, 4, 10) and *new* (3, 4, 4) thrice; and the punning *I'eye(s)* appears eight times. *Perjured* (6, 13), *truth* (10, 14), *faith* (3, 8), and *deep* (9, 9) are repeated once": Helen Vendler, *The Art of Shakespeare's Sonnets* (Cambridge, Mass., and London: Harvard University Press, 1997), 644.

PART II
Shakespeare and His Predecessors

5

The Refusal to be Judged in Petrarch and Shakespeare

Richard Strier

The funniest interchange in Petrarch's *Secretum* occurs at a very intense moment in the dialogue, a moment in which Franciscus and Augustinus are focusing on the stakes and value of Petrarch's love for Laura. Augustinus pulls out the big gun; Petrarch is guilty of idolatry: "She has distracted you from love of the Creator to love of one of the creatures."[1] Franciscus defends himself by asserting that "loving her has increased my love of God." Augustinus counters that loving God for having created Laura reverses "the right order of things" and places the physical over the spiritual. Franciscus insists that he has not "loved her body more than her soul"; his proof of this is that his feelings have not changed as Laura has grown older: "The bloom of her youth has faded with the passage of time, but the beauty of her mind – which made me love her in the first place and [made me] afterwards continue to love – has increased." Augustinus responds with the *coup de grâce*: "Are you serious? You mean that if that same mind had been in an ugly, gnarled body, you would have loved it just as much?" (p. 63). At this point, of course, Franciscus starts to backpedal.

My point in beginning with this passage is to suggest that "Augustinus" was right, and that Petrarch, and not only "Franciscus," knew this. But "Augustinus" was right from a descriptive point of view – not necessarily from a moral one. I want to argue, and attempt briefly to demonstrate, that in Petrarch's most important lyric poems, the "scattered rhymes" (*Rime sparse*) that he so carefully collected and arranged, there is a sustained insistence on the importance and value of the bodily and the mortal. I want to argue that Petrarch resists the Platonism – or the platonized Christianity – of which he is very intensely aware. He accepts the soul–body dualism of Platonism, but refuses to give the soul an absolute priority, and to dismiss and devalue the body. He refuses, in other words, to adopt a transcendental perspective – though, as we shall see (and as the *Secretum* aptly demonstrates), he was fully aware of such.[2] John Freccero has praised Donne's love poetry for its "rescuing" of human love from "angelic mysticism," for defending the distinctly human sphere of love from "the neo-Petrarchan and neoplatonic dehumanization of love."[3] I want to argue that, regardless of what "neo-Petrarchans" did, Petrarch does exactly what Freccero credits Donne with doing (Freccero does not address this issue in his direct treatment of Petrarch because he insists that Petrarch's lyrics do not actually have a subject matter).[4]

However, Augustinus' critique of Franciscus goes even deeper than the latter's attitude toward the body. After Augustinus has successfully critiqued Franciscus' erotic obsession, Franciscus says, "I am ashamed, I suffer for it, and I repent it; but I cannot get beyond it" ([p. 80]; "*Pudet, piget et penitet, sed ultra non valeo*").[5] This brings up the issue with which the *Secretum* both begins and ends: the matter of the will. At the beginning of the dialogue, Augustinus claims that Franciscus has willed his "unhappy state" (not yet specified). As a good Platonist in ethics as well as metaphysics, Augustinus holds that "anyone who has fully recognized his unhappiness wants to be happy; and anyone who wants this tries to achieve it" (6). He also holds the optimistic view, important for this kind of ethics, that "anyone who tries to achieve it [happiness] is able to achieve it." Franciscus has difficulty believing that the whole issue of happiness is a matter of knowledge and the will, but the problem that emerges is whether the movement from recognition (or "full" recognition) of the condition of being unhappy leads as directly as Augustinus asserts to the desire to be happy (this leaves aside the questions of whether the desire leads to action on its basis, and action to its success). Franciscus seems to grasp very clearly everything that Augustinus says, and yet, in their very last exchange, Franciscus says, "But I cannot restrain my desires" ("*Sed desiderium frenare non valeo*") and Augustinus rightly notes, "We are getting back to the old bone of contention. You are saying your will is impotent" ([93]; "*voluntatem impotentiam vocas*").[6] Petrarch shows in the dialogue the failure of Socratic ethics.[7] In the lyrics, Petrarch goes further and at times seem to accept the perversion of his will, his inability to desire what he knows to be the highest good. My largest point in this essay is that once we have seen Petrarch in this way, the deep continuity between Petrarch's sonnets and some of Shakespeare's will emerge — despite what seem to be significant differences.[8]

I

Anyone who thinks that Petrarch's sonnets are somehow simple and straightforward pieces should be disabused by opening the volume and reading the poem that he placed first (there is abundant evidence that Petrarch carefully arranged the order of the *Canzoniere*).[9] I can think of no other authorially arranged collection of lyrics – other perhaps than "The Church" section of George Herbert's *The Temple* – that begins with so complex a poem.[10] Moreover, I can think of no other collection of love lyrics that opens with what is essentially a palinode. Petrarch begins by addressing his readers – there is no pretense that these poems are not written to be widely read – and by doing so in an oddly intimate way, as if his readers were already familiar with the poems – "You who hear" ("*Voi ch' ascoltate*") rather than "You who will hear."[11] And the self that is writing to these readers (or hearers) has a complex relation to what the readers "hear."[12] They hear "those sighs with which I nourished my heart during my first youthful error" ("*quei sospiri ond' io nudriva 'l core / in sul mio primo giovenile errore*"). One would think that the speaker would distance himself from such "*errore*," but he states, with extraordinary care and precision, that he was then "in part another man from what I am now" ("*quand' era in parte altr' uom da quel ch' i' sono*"). The speaker is not wholly reformed; he is still "*in parte*" the person caught in the juvenile error. The reader is justifiably mystified. In what sense can one still participate in what one recognizes as a "juvenile error"? Augustine's (the real Augustine's) theory of imperfect conversion would seem to be at work here.[13]

Instead, however, of continuing to elaborate on the complexity of the relation between his past and present selves, the speaker of poem 1 returns to thinking about his readers. He hopes that they will be connoisseurs of poetry, appreciating the "varied style in which I weep" (l. 5). Most of all, he hopes that they will see and share the experience behind the style, and offer the poet not only moral but emotional understanding – "I hope to find pity, not only pardon" ("*spero trovar pietà, non che perdono*"). The sestet shifts to the way the speaker is in fact different from his past self. He is now afflicted with shame (or is it embarrassment? – "I was the talk of the town" ["*come al popol tutto / fabula fui*"]), and presents his "*vario stile*" as mere "raving" ("*mio vaneggiar*") that has produced in him not only the feelings that have already been named and enacted – shame and repentance – but a particular cognitive ability. He now has the ability to know something clearly, and what he has thus come to know constitutes the last line of the sonnet: "that whatever pleases in the world is a brief dream" ("*che quanto piace al mondo è breve sogno*"). The upshot of the whole process described and evoked in the poem is a grand metaphysical reflection, not an identifiably Christian moral. Obviously a "brief dream" is different from a solid and enduring reality, but it is also not necessarily something one would want to reject.

As we move through Petrarch's volume, the complexities of the opening sonnet develop. There continues to be a contrast between the speaker's present and his past, but this conflict persists in being different from the one we would expect. In the 55th poem (not a sonnet), the speaker recounts that in his "no longer fresh" age, he is still basically the same person that he was earlier, still burning with love. Instead of improving, he fears that "my second error will be the worse" (l. 6). Error, along with love and pain, seems to be a constant. Poem 59, "*Perché quel che mi trasse ad amar*," begins to raise the issue of the will. The speaker has to decide how to deal with the fact that he has apparently been barred from the sight of his beloved. This situation does not lead to any diminishment of the lover's passion, and this steadiness is seen not as a natural fact but as something like a decision or a commitment; the current deprivation "by no means dissuades me from my firm desire" (the willfulness is even stronger in the Italian, where the words for volition are more prominent: "*del mio firmo voler già non mi svoglia*"). The power of the bodily presence of the lady is evoked, but memory is seen as equally strong. The poet laments the loss of the "*dolce vista*" of the lady, but insists that his commitment to continuing his feelings, despite their cost to him, is a matter of honor ("*ben morendo onor s' acquista*"), and the poem ends with a clear assertion: "*non vo' che da tal nodo Amor mi scioglia*" ("I do not wish Love to loose me from such a knot").[14]

This *"nodo"* (and, as we shall see, others) recurs throughout the poetry. The poet's bondage is always seen as having, at least potentially, a relation to his will that is not simply negative. Poems 61 and 62, both sonnets, are an odd pair, but dramatize Petrarch's position. Each section of poem 61 begins with a formal blessing, some version of the opening *"Benedetto sia."* The poet accepts, sees as sacred, his entire situation – his pain, his poems, the fame they have garnered (ll. 12–13), and his bondage (her eyes have "bound" him [*"duo begli occhi che legato m' ànno"*]). In the following sonnet, the poet (let's call him "Petrarch") addresses the Christian God and asks to turn to another life (*"ad altra vita"*).[15] Petrarch notes that he has now been in bondage ("subject to a pitiless yoke") for eleven years, and asks that his "wandering thoughts" be led to "a better place." We learn what the better place is – Calvary – by learning that the day of the poem is Good Friday. The contrast with the asserted "blessedness" of the previous poem could not be sharper. Yet it is important to see that *"Padre del Ciel"* (poem 62) is entirely in the optative mode. There is no suggestion that the "turn" to a different life for which the speaker asks has actually occurred, or has even begun. His thoughts, in the present, still wander.

In poem 68, the "holy sight" of the city of Rome leads the poet to bewail his evil past, but – and Petrarch's poems are filled with significant adversatives – "with this thought another jousts" (*"Ma con questio pensier un altro giostra"*): namely, the thought that time is passing and the poet should "return to see our lady." The poem ends with the speaker in a state of puzzlement as to the outcome of this conflict within himself – *"Qual vincerà non so"* – and with the admission that this conflict is hardly new to him. The next poem, however, presents the poet as having experienced some sort of momentary and miraculous feeling (beyond what "natural counsel" can do) that allowed him freedom from "the hands" of Amor. In the final tercet, however, a counter-miracle, sponsored by Love, occurs – *"ecco i tuoi ministri"* – and the speaker realizes that it is bad to resist or hide from one's destiny (*"al suo destino / mal chi contrasta et mal chi si nasconde"*). "Destiny," a pagan concept, and one that does not allow for free will, shows (to return to the puzzlement of the previous sonnet) which side will win. The interesting question, however, is not whether heaven or destiny is the more important term for the speaker – though that is interesting – but how the speaker feels about this *"destino."* He seems, in this poem (69), rather calmly resigned to it. In the next poem, a canzone in which the speaker puts himself in the whole tradition of Provençal and *stilnovisti* love poetry,[16] Petrarch (who quotes himself in the poem) denies that his condition of erotic longing is externally caused: "who deceives me but myself . . . Nay, if I run through the sky from sphere to sphere, no planet condemns me to weeping" (ll. 31–4). The poem ends with the speaker contemplating his inability to appreciate the inner, moral structure of the creation,[17] and noting that if he ever returns to "the true splendor" (*"al vero splendor"*), his eye will not be able to stay still, it is so weakened by its own fault (*"l' occhio non po star fermo, / così l' à fatto infermo / pur la sua propria colpa"*),[18] for which even the transforming power of the lady's beauty cannot be blamed (the final line of poem 70 refers the reader back to the great metamorphosis canzone [poem 23]).

Again, this poem (70) seems very calm about its *"propria colpa."* In another (poem 99, a sonnet), Petrarch turns his inability to pursue the highest good (which he recommends to others) into comedy; an unnamed voice at the end rebukes him for his inability "now more than ever" to follow his own advice. The sonnet on the sixteenth year of Petrarch's devotion (poem 118), may seem more genuinely conflicted, but it too seems to present the will's puzzlement as a kind of comedy. The play with terms for will and capacity is too willful – *"vorrei piu volere, et più no voglio, / et per più non poter fo quant' io posso."*[19] The final line, again, seems more resigned and accepting than anguished – "nor for a thousand turnings about have I yet moved." The canzone *"Di pensier in pensier"* (poem 129) confronts the fact that Petrarch enjoys his life of sighs and tears – "I would hardly wish to change this bitter, sweet life of mine" (ll. 20–1) – and it celebrates, as Oscar Büdel argues, "the mode of conscious adoption of illusion."[20] The poet confesses that he finds his soul "satisfied with its own deception" (*"del suo proprio error l' alma s' appaga"* [l. 37]). The *"propria colpa"* (of poem 70) has turned into *"proprio error"* here. Self-reproach has disappeared, though analytical awareness has not. The poet knows that he is in "error," and consciously prefers "sweet deception" (*"dolce error"*) to the bleakness of *"il vero"* (ll. 49–52).

"Di pensier in pensier" is not Petrarch's final word on the matter, but it is a major statement. In the questioning sonnet *"S' amor non è"* (poem 132), Petrarch seems truly and deeply puzzled by his enjoyment of his sufferings, by the role of his will in his sufferings, and by the question of "consent" (*"s' io 'l consento, a gran torto mi doglio"* – "if I consent to [my suffering], it is very wrong of me to complain"). Yet in poem 141, a sonnet meditating on the self-destructive behavior of butterflies, the poet notes, quite calmly, that his soul "consents to its own death" (*"al suo morir l' alma consente"*). In another canzone, *"Ben mi credea passar mio tempo"* (poem 207), Petrarch returns to the position of *"Di pensier in pensier,"* though now in moral rather than in cognitive terms: *"dolce veneno"* replaces *"dolce error"* – "still I do not repent that my heart is overwhelmed with sweet poison" (ll. 83–4). He returns to the matter of honor (from poem 59) – "I shall stand firm on the field" (poem 207, ll. 92–3) – and *"Ben mi credea"* ends with Petrarch happily proclaiming that evil is his good: *"ben non à mondo che 'l mio mal pareggi."*[21] The monumental canzone (poem 264) that begins the second section of the *Rime* is another poem about "thoughts" – *"I' vo pensando."*[22] Here one voice (one thought), like Augustinus in the *Secretum*, insists on the freedom and potency of Petrarch's will – "as long as the body is alive, you have in your own keeping the rein of your thoughts" (*"Mentre che 'l corpo è vivo, / ài tu 'l freno in bailia de' penser tuoi"* [ll. 32–3]).[23] But the poem replaces a Platonic vision of the soul's (or intellect's) wings (ll. 6–8) with an Aristotelian insistence on habit (*"costume"* in l. 105, *"usanza"* in l. 125), and it ends, "I see the better, and I lay hold on the worse" (*"veggio 'l meglio et al peggior m' appiglio"*).[24] This line is translated from Ovid's *Medea*, but the context seems more resigned than tragic.[25] Pleasure remains "by habit" strong in Petrarch, even in the face of death (ll. 125–6).[26] In one of the last poems on the matter of choice (poem 296, a sonnet), Petrarch decides, first, not to accuse himself, as he has done in the past, but rather to excuse himself – or rather, to praise himself (*"I' mi soglio accusare, et or mi scuso, / anzi*

mi pregio") – for his erotic devotion. The sestet of the sonnet explains that any soul would change its natural mode ("*'l suo natural modo*") of loving (something like) life, liberty, and the pursuit of happiness ("*d'allegrezza . . . di libertà, di vita*") and choose, as the final line of the sonnet states, "to die content with such a wound, and to live in such a knot" ("*di tal piaga / morir contento, et vivere in tal nodo*").

The "knot," as we have seen, is Petrarch's recurrent image for the bondage of the will; it is also his image for what makes the human condition ontologically unique. In writing of "That subtle knot that makes us man," Donne is (whether consciously or not) echoing Petrarch.[27] In poem 214, a sestina, Petrarch states that he will not be cured from the "wound" he received on first seeing Laura until "my flesh shall be free / from that knot for which it is more prized" ("*la carne sciolta / fia di quel nodo ond' è 'l suo maggior preggio*"). Throughout the *Rime*, Petrarch remains committed to the special status of the "knot" that body and soul together form. He is constantly aware of Platonic dualism, and he constantly resists it.[28] Even in his most visionary moments, as in "*Erano i capei d' oro*" (poem 90), Petrarch is aware that even though Laura's walk seemed to him "not that of a mortal thing" ("*Non era l' andar suo cosa mortale*"), Laura is not, like Virgil's Venus (the model for the line), as Greene says, "a goddess who looks like a woman" but rather "a woman who looks like a goddess."[29] At the very end of the sonnet, Petrarch insists on this, asserting that if Laura "were not such now" ("*se non fosse or tale*"), it would not matter. She is not a goddess – whatever the impact of her appearance on the poet.

"*Erano i capei*" knows, then, that Laura is, in fact, "*cosa mortale.*" The phrase recurs in poem 248 ("*Chi vuol veder*"), a sonnet written, as David Kalstone puts it, in Petrarch's "majestic public manner."[30] Here Petrarch invites everyone interested in seeing the most sublime of sublunary sights – "all that Nature and Heaven can do among us" ("*tra noi*") – to gaze upon Laura, but the whole poem is a *carpe diem* addressed to such would-be admirers. It has the full classical sense of the vulnerability of the extraordinary – "*immodicis breves est aetas et rara senectus,*" says Martial.[31] Petrarch takes it as a fact that death "steals first the best," and he knows, in a full sense, that "this beautiful mortal thing passes, and does not endure" ("*cosa bella mortal passa et non dura*") – like a brief dream. Laura's mortality was built into the sequence from the beginning, and Petrarch's awareness of it is part of what makes him see her qualities as to be especially prized. Poem 311, the sonnet about the nightingale ("*Quel rosigniuol che sì soave piagne*"), comments directly on the fantasy that "*Erano i capei*" both voiced and subtly resisted. In "*Quel rosigniuol,*" written after Laura's death, Petrarch hears and appreciates the sweet mourning of the bird's song; it reminds him of his own hard lot ("*dura sorte*"), but he quickly takes personal responsibility for his grief, stating that "I have no one to complain of but myself, who did not believe that death reigns over goddesses" ("*'n dee non credev' io regnasse Morte*" [ll. 7–8]). As the repeated references to luck or destiny ("*sorte . . . ventura*") and the mention of "*dee*" suggest, the content here is, again, purely classical, so that the final recognition comes across as philosophical rather than Christian – "nothing down here both pleases and endures" (poem 311, l. 14).[32]

Yet, in the face of this, Petrarch does not flee to the transcendental. He sees Laura's death in Platonic terms, as untying the "knot" that links soul to body, but he almost never full-throatedly celebrates this untying, and he never denigrates the body. When, in the sonnet that begins *"O misera et orribil visione!"* (poem 251), Petrarch is trying, as in *"Chi vuol veder"* (poem 248), to prepare himself for Laura's death, he speaks of the possibility that she has exited from "her lovely inn" (*"uscita . . . del bell' albergo"*). Whenever he speaks of Laura's inanimate body, Petrarch always, as here, softens the Platonic ontology with a positive adjective. In poem 283, he describes Death as having loosed Laura's ardently virtuous soul from "the most charming and most beautiful knot" (l. 4).[33] In poem 300, he envies Heaven for having greedily (*"cupidamente"*) gathered to itself Laura's spirit "freed from her beautiful members" (*"de le belle membra sciolta"*). Even when Petrarch uses the body-as-prison metaphor for Laura's body, he speaks of *"la bella pregione . . . suo bel carcere terreno"* (poem 325, ll. 9, 101). For the most part, he does not present the "naked" soul as beautiful (poem 278, with its oddly erotic presentation of bodilessness, is an exception). Poem 301 builds on the appreciation of poem 300 for "the beautiful members" from which Laura's spirit has been freed (*"lo spirto da le belle membra sciolto"*). Petrarch returns to the place of Laura's death, "whence she went naked to Heaven" (poem 301, l. 13). But instead of celebrating and ending on this celestial nudity, the final line salutes what she left behind – "leaving on earth her beautiful vesture" (*"lasciando in terra la sua bella spoglia"* [l. 14]). In the canzone beginning *"Che debb' io far"* ("What shall I do?" [poem 268]), Laura's invisible form is in Paradise, set free not from a loathsome sink but, in a phrase that captures both physicality and temporality, "from the veil that here shadowed the flower of her years" (*"di quel velo / che qui fece ombra al fior degli anni suoi"*). Moreover, the truly consoling thought is the Pauline, anti-Platonic one that Laura "will be clothed with it [this veil, her body] another time" (*"per rivestersen poi / un' altra volta"*). In poem 302, a sonnet, Petrarch imagines Laura in heaven, where, although (she is presented as saying) she experiences a well-being that cannot be held by the human intellect (*Mio ben non cape in intelleto umano"*), she nonetheless is also imagined as waiting for two things: for Petrarch, "and for that which you loved so much, and which remained down there, my lovely veil" (*"quel che tanto amasti / et là giuso è rimaso, il mio bel velo"*), which she also misses.

Petrarch's task as a poet is to celebrate Laura's earthly existence – her walk, her voice, her face, even her clothing (poem 282). *"Che debb' io far"* (poem 268), in which we have already seen Petrarch's commitment to Laura's reincarnation, ends with the poet imagining Love telling him "not to extinguish" Laura's fame, "which sounds in many places still by your tongue." Unlike what Apollo tells the young Milton in "Lycidas," fame, for Petrarch, *is* an earthly matter (defended as such by Franciscus in in the *Secretum* [87] and presented similarly in *"I' vo pensando"* [poem 264; ll. 66–7]).[34] In poem 308, an autobiographical sonnet, Petrarch sees his poetic goal as a literally incarnational one – to attempt *"col mio stile il suo bel viso incarno"* (l. 8). The best he can do is to shadow forth (*"ombreggiare"*) some of Laura's earthly virtues. Her *"divina parte"* is entirely beyond him – "there fails my daring, my wit, and my art" (*"ivi manca l' ardir, l' ingegno, et l' arte"*). In the sonnet that is poem 345, Petrarch tries to take consolation in Laura's heavenly existence – "her being in Heaven ought to quiet my cruel state" – and he does so through imagining her "more beautiful than ever" there. But in poem 359, a visionary canzone where Petrarch imagines the beatified Laura sitting "on the left side of [his] bed," she rebukes him for his inability to celebrate her life in heaven ("Does it displease you so much that I have left this misery . . .?"). She urges him to use the wings of his soul and leave his poetry behind. But the poetry is here characterized in one of those oddly positive Platonic formulations – "these sweet deceptive chatterings of yours" ("*queste dolci tue fallaci ciance*").[35] In imagining this colloquy, Petrarch sees himself still admiring and bound by the "golden knot" of Laura's hair. She explains to him that she is a naked spirit ("*Spirito ignudo sono*"), and that what he admires has been dust for years, yet "to help you from your troubles, it is given to me to seem such" – that is, to appear to him in her bodily form (ll. 60–63a). Petrarch can be comforted only by a vision of Laura as clothed in her body – which, as "she" points out, she will be again (l. 63b). The final poem of the sequence (poem 366), is a prayer to the Virgin to free Petrarch from his devotion to "*mortal belezza*" (l. 85); yet in it he offers as his most promising feature his ability "to love with such a marvelous faith a bit of frail mortal earth" ("*poca mortal terra caduca / amar con si mirabile fede*" [ll. 121–2]).[36]

II

With this picture of Petrarch's *Rime* in mind, we can now approach Shakespeare's sonnets, and see the continuities, as well as the differences, between these poems and Petrarch's. At times, the continuities are obvious. The sonnet numbered 106 in the Shakespeare collection,[37] "When in the chronicle of wasted time," is unproblematically Petrarchan; it celebrates the beauty of the beloved as appropriate to the pens of the poets and prophets of the past, whose powers exceeded those of writers in the present (including the author) – though for Shakespeare the framework of the past writers is medieval rather than, in Petrarch's case, classical (see *Rime*, poem 186, in which Homer and Virgil would have praised Laura, and poem 187, in which they are needed to do so). Even the "blasphemy" that Helen Vendler attributes to Shakespeare's sonnet "in secularizing Messianic prophecy"[38] (ll. 9–11) is matched or perhaps exceeded by Petrarch, who, in poem 4 (a sonnet) sees a direct parallel between the circumstances of Christ's birth and those of Laura's ("He, when he was born, did not bestow himself on Rome . . . And now from a small village, He has given us a sun").

Heather Dubrow has shrewdly remarked that "anti-Petrarchism" is as difficult to define as "Petrarchism," and that the terms have a way of melding into each other.[39] Even some of the most obviously "anti-Petrarchan" poems in the volume of *Shake-speares Sonnets* turn out to be, in some ways, deeply Petrarchan. Sonnet 130, "My mistress' eyes are nothing like the sun," is a textbook case of "anti-Petrarchanism." It refuses to apply to the person of the woman in question any of the standard descriptive hyperboles. The speaker presents himself as a determined "realist" – he knows what is what ("If snow is white, why then her breasts are dun"). But there is more to the poem than this. If it were merely a "plain man" rejection of hyperbole, it would be nothing more than the "trifle" that Stephen Booth takes it to be.[40]

The sestet introduces a new element. After we are told that "in some perfumes there is more delight / Than in the breath that from my mistress reeks,"[41] we are somewhat surprised to hear this speaker straightforwardly expressing "delight" in his mistress – "I love to hear her speak" (l. 9). The final lines seem to answer *"Erano i capei"* directly. We recall "Her walk was not that of a mortal thing"; Shakespeare's speaker tells us that "I grant I never saw a goddess go; / My mistress when she walks treads on the ground" (ll. 11–12). But Shakespeare's speaker's point is not that his beloved is inferior; it is, rather, that she is in fact quite special. He uses a word that comes close to asserting absolute value. His mistress is "as *rare* / As any she belied with false compare."[42] This is a love poem, and even Booth has to concede that it is a "winsome" trifle. When we put it in the context of Petrarch's treatment of mortal things, and of his own "recantation" in *"Quel rosigniuol"* (poem 311) of "Her walk was not that of a mortal thing" – "I did not believe that Death reigns over goddesses" – we can see the poem as continuing Petrarch's stress on what it means for his beloved to be a "mortal thing."

The continuity is deeper in Shakespeare's sonnets 104 and 108. These pick up on the most extraordinary moment in *"Erano i capei,"* the ending in which Petrarch allows himself to have the thought that Laura may not be, in the present, as she was in the epiphanic moment evoked in the first twelve lines of the sonnet (*"et se non fosse or tale"*), and then dismisses this thought as irrelevant ("a wound is not healed by loosening of the bow"). Shakespeare fully develops the idea that his beloved is "a beautiful mortal thing" (see *"cosa bella mortal"* in *Rime*, poem 248). Shakespeare's sonnet beginning "To me, fair friend, you never can be old" (104) echoes Petrarch's habit of precisely recording the time that has elapsed between the beginning of the speaker's love for the beloved and the moment of the poem's composition: "Three winters cold . . . three beauteous springs."[43] But sonnet 104 is distinctively Shakespearean in its grand sense of natural development[44] – "process of the seasons" – and, in the sestet, in its evocation of the uncanny way that time seems both to move and to stand still: "Ah, yet doth beauty, like a dial hand, / Steal from his figure, and no pace perceived." The poem ends with a gesture rather like that on which Petrarch's poem 248 ends – addressing persons who may miss (in Petrarch) and who will miss (in Shakespeare) the beloved in full bloom. In "What's in the brain that ink may character" (108), Shakespeare's focus is not the poignancy of the beloved's beauty but the ability of love to keep "the first conceit of love" in place – that is, in mind, when, as Shakespeare wonderfully puts it, "time and outward form would show it dead" (ll. 13–14).[45] And "necessary wrinkles" (108. 11) is a phrase that combines realism with tenderness in a way related to but much deeper than the mode of sonnet 130.[46]

The assertion of the power of the lover's mind to contradict or contravene external reality is one of Petrarch's great themes (as in *"Di pensier in pensier"* [poem 129]), and it is developed by Shakespeare in ways that show both the continuities and the differences between the poets. "Since I left you, mine eye is in my mind" (sonnet 113) develops the Petrarchan motif directly – whatever external things the poet's eye takes in, he tells the beloved, the poet's mind "shapes them to your feature" (l. 12). As in Petrarch, Shakespeare's soul is here "satisfied with its own deception" (*"Di pensier in pensier,"* l. 37): "My most true mind thus maketh mine [eye] untrue."[47] The sonnet that follows continues – with some self-mockery ("my great mind most kingly drinks it up")

– this approving stance, echoing Petrarch's praise of "sweet poison." The approving
stance toward the power of the "true mind" over reality culminates in the famous sonnet
beginning "Let me not to the marriage of true minds / Admit impediments" (116).[48]
This expository sonnet (not a Petrarchan mode) has caused a great deal of critical confusion, since its opening praise of mutuality seems to be inconsistent with the rest of
its development, which praises autonomous and self-contained constancy in the face of
all possible sorts of change. This problem disappears, however, when one recognizes
that the poem is, throughout, a philosophical account of the nature of the "true mind"
in love. The plural of the opening line does not, as it turns out, refer to two persons
in a relationship but to how all persons of a certain sort ("true minds") conduct themselves. The poem is about how persons who are "true minds" love (that is, with constancy to their object, regardless of how the object behaves); it is not, despite how the
famous opening line and a half sounds, about how "true minds" love each other.[49]
Shakespeare seems to want to trick us into thinking that the poem is a simpler and
more easily adoptable statement than it in fact is (why Shakespeare wants to do this is
a deep and interesting question). On rereading, the poem should be seen as a grander,
more "credal" version of number 108 ("What's in the brain"). "Love's not Time's fool,"
regardless of what "time and outward form" show, or do.

The distinctive way that Shakespeare develops the "mind over matter" theme – the
basis for Joel Fineman's claim for Shakespeare's uniqueness – seems to emerge in sonnet
141, "In faith I do not love thee with mine eyes." This line could open a sonnet like
"What's in the brain" or "To me, fair friend" (104). But "In faith I do not love thee
with mine eyes" goes on to acknowledge not merely that the beloved is aging, but that
the beloved is flawed. The poet's eyes "in thee a thousand errors note." These "errors"
seem to be physical rather than moral. The poet loves what his eyes "despise" (l. 3),
and he insists, in the second quatrain of the octave, that none of his senses (systematically enumerated) are pleased by the beloved. In this sonnet, however, the inner item
that prevails over the senses is not the "mind" but the heart – "'tis my heart that loves
what they [mine eyes] despise." The sestet is entirely taken up with describing the
hopelessly enslaved condition of "one foolish heart" (l. 10). The hard question here is
the speaker's attitude toward the picture of the self that he is providing in the poem.
This sonnet is clearly not self-approving in the way that sonnets 113 and 116 are, but
is it unequivocally self-hating? If so, it does break with Petrarch, who, as we have seen,
always presents his self-condemnations ambivalently. His "*errore*" is always "*dolce*." The
couplet with which Shakespeare ends "In faith I do not love thee with mine eyes" may
attain something like this level of tonal and psychological complexity:

> Only my plague thus far I count my gain,
> When she that makes me sin awards me pain.

Obviously this is bitter, and plays off the appropriateness of "pain" to "sin," but does
the speaker accept his state? Petrarch presents himself, in the *Rime*, as having lived
most of his life in something like this condition. Petrarch would have added his

characteristic "*dolce*" to the mention of pain here – that is probably the most prevalent of all his oxymorons – and Shakespeare does not. Yet are we, in reading the couplet of Shakespeare's sonnet, to forget that his heart "is pleased to dote" in line 4 of the sonnet? And the tone of "one foolish heart" in line 10 is (at least) indulgent, if not approving; it is certainly not straightforwardly self-condemnatory.

In "O me! what eyes hath love put in my head" (sonnet 148), Shakespeare's speaker pretends to be puzzled by the problem of subjective erotic perception, but drops the issue for a mock-explanation in the sestet – tears distort "love's eye" – and ends the poem with a couplet that seems to be truly bitter, both self- and other-reproaching: "with tears thou keep'st me blind, / Lest eyes, well seeing, thy foul faults should find." A poem that almost immediately follows this one returns to the puzzled mode – "O from what pow'r hast thou his pow'rful might . . .?" (150). Here the speaker seems to accept as a fact that love has the power to overcome both sensory and moral perception, both to "give the lie to my true sight" (l. 3) and to present as "becoming . . . things ill" (l. 5).[50] After ten lines of questions – which start to become descriptive rather than interrogatory – the speaker seems to accept, although not happily, that he loves "what others do abhor" (l. 11). This acceptance – if that is what it is – connects to Petrarch's most scathing self-analysis (as in "*I' vo pensando*" [poem 264]), and produces some of the most distinctive moments in Shakespeare's sonnets. Again, the question is whether Shakespeare is able to transcend, or mitigate, or at least present some nuance or counter-current within self-loathing.

The great sonnet beginning "'Tis better to be vile than vile esteem'd" (121) is one in which Shakespeare refuses to be abhorred. In this poem, the lover, not the beloved, is the object of the world's negative judgment, and in this poem, Shakespeare (or his "speaker") is able, as Lars Engle well puts it, to clear an autonomous "evaluative space" for himself.[51] Petrarch had something of this autonomy – he flees the "Babylon" of the papal court (poem 114 *et alia*) – but he never approximates the boldness of "I am that I am," where Shakespeare seems to be asserting a self beyond ethics rather than merely an ethical self.[52] But could Shakespeare establish such a realm in relation to his own moral judgments on himself? The famous sonnet beginning "When my love swears that she is made of truth, / I do believe her" (138) seems to exist purely in the realm of moral and psychological self-loathing. But a closer reading reveals it to be more complex than that. The poem says, "I do believe her," not "I do pretend to believe her." What would it mean to take "I do believe her" seriously? There is a kind of grim utopianism here, one that emerges in the poem's insistence on intersubjectivity and (if there is a difference) either cooperation or collusion.[53] The final couplet continues both the bitterness and the subtle counter-movement to or within it:

> Therefore I lie with her, and she with me,
> And in our faults by lies we flattered be.

Christopher Ricks has called attention to the depth of the pun on "lie with" in the first line of the couplet here; he sees the pun as resisting (not reversing) complacent moral application.[54] The word to which I wish to call attention is the penultimate one. "Flattered" is something of a surprise here. We were surely expecting something harsher, something like "smothered" in the *Passionate Pilgrim* version ("Since that our faults in love thus smother'd be").[55] "Flattered," moreover, is not merely a softer and less violent word than "smothered"; flattery, in various nominal and verbal forms, is also something of a "complex word" in Shakespeare's sonnets.[56] The word is used in contexts of purely negative self-deception, as here and perhaps in sonnet 114, which speaks of "the monarch's plague, this flattery" (l. 2), and develops this conceit with non-humorous self-mockery in lines 9–10 ("'tis flattery in my seeing, / And my great mind most kingly drinks it up"). But the word is also used in the context of providing genuine beauty – "Full many a glorious morning have I seen / Flatter the mountain tops with sovereign eye" (sonnet 33). And, perhaps most hauntingly, the word is used in the evocation of a joy that is brief and delusive, but potent while it lasts:

> Thus have I had thee as a dream doth flatter,
> In sleep a king, but waking no such matter.
> (87. 13–14)

"As a dream doth flatter" – this resonates with Petrarch's sense that all earthly joy is like this: *"quanto piace al mondo è breve sogno"* (poem 1). So, to return to the final couplet of sonnet 138, these lines lines on "lying with" and being "flattered" may point to some genuine accommodation with the human condition.[57] We recall Büdel's claim that Petrarch's great contribution to the love tradition is "to acknowledge illusion and consciously live by it – even though he clearly perceives it as self-deception."[58] Shakespeare adds sex and company to Petrarch's solitary commitment to *"errore"* to produce a *folie à deux*.

Yet surely Shakespeare's sonnet on lust (129) is absolute in its loathing and self-condemnation? This is another poem that is easily classified as "anti-Petrarchan." Certainly Petrarch never wrote a sonnet about the horrors of compulsive copulation. But he did write a poem about self-destructive pleasure that has become deeply habitual, and about the impotence of knowledge in the face of such a condition (*"I' vo pensando"* [poem 264], ll. 125–36).[59] And Shakespeare's sonnet 129 is not a sober piece of self-examination. We must take "Past reason hated" as seriously as we take "Past reason hunted" (ll. 6–7). The poem is mad in presenting sexual activity only as self-destructive madness. After the repetition of "extreme" at the end of line 10 (the word already appeared in line 4), the poem comes, conceptually and rhetorically, to a full stop. Its whole movement changes at the beginning of line 11, "A bliss in proof." Suddenly there is a reason why this action is "hunted." "A very woe," which ends line 11, is much softer, conceptually as well as phonically, than "a swallowed bait"; and line 12, "Before, a joy proposed; behind, a dream," even leaves some pleasure in retrospection.[60] The couplet is extremely sober and somber, but does acknowledge that it is a heaven "that leads men to this hell." Something like a Petrarchan balance – "a pleasure so strong in me by habit that it seems to bargain with Death" (*"I' vo pensando,"* ll. 125–6) – is restored.[61]

For an utterly bleak picture, one must turn to "My love is as a fever" (sonnet 147). Here, pleasure is fully devalued and there is no autonomy or nobility in error. Yet the other poem of direct sexual self-disgust in the volume, "Love is too young to know what conscience is" (151), ends, for all its phallic comedy and self-disgust, on an oddly tender note – and this despite the continuation of the dirty joke: "No want of conscience hold it that I call / Her 'love,' for whose dear love I rise and fall." The poem might actually be hinting at an alternative notion of conscience. In general, we can say that some of Shakespeare's distinctive sonnets are most Petrarchan when they are most complex and modulated. The one religious poem in Shakespeare's strikingly secular volume, "Poor soul, the center of my sinful earth" (146), revels in the harsh dualism that Petrarch tried to soften. The poem attains a Petrarchan note when it sees the body not as dross or as food for worms, but as, in a phrase worthy of Petrarch, a "fading mansion."[62]

AUTHOR'S NOTE

For helpful comments on this essay, I am indebted to Paul Alpers, Gordon Braden, Bradin Cormack, Lars Engle, Ted Leinwand, David Quint, William Veeder, and Robert Von Hallberg.

NOTES

1 Francis Petrarch, *My Secret Book*, trans. J. G. Nichols (London: Hesperus, 2002), 63. Further page references to this translation are given in the text.

2 For neoplatonism in the *Secretum*, see *My Secret Book*, 23–4; for how directly the Platonism of "Augustinus" in the *Secretum* contradicts the position of the historical Augustine, and on the fact that Petrarch certainly knew this, see Carol Everhart Quillen, *Rereading the Renaissance: Petrarch, Augustine, and the Language of Humanism* (Ann Arbor: University of Michigan Press, 1998), ch. 5 (esp. 191–5).

3 John Freccero, "Donne's 'Valediction: Forbidding Mourning,'" *English Literary History (ELH)* 30 (1963), 335–76 at 336. I do not mean, hereby, to endorse this as a view of Donne's love poetry as a whole, though Freccero is convincing (if perhaps overly systematic and Dantescan) on the poem that he analyzes. Donne's attitude toward the body varies wildly within the "Songs and Sonets."

4 Oscar Büdel brilliantly contrasts Petrarch's poetry with the Platonism of the *stilnovisti* in

"Illusion Disabused: A Novel Mode in Petrarch's *Canzoniere*," in Aldo Scaglione (ed.), *Francis Petrarch, Six Centuries Later* (Chapel Hill: University of North Carolina Press, 1975), 128–51, esp. 129–30. See also J. W. Lever: "Laura was indeed the living manifestation of heavenly virtue; but she remained part of the natural world, not to be spirited away in concept and symbol" (*The Elizabethan Love Sonnet* [London, 1956], 3). For Freccero on Petrarch, see "The Fig-Tree and the Laurel: Petrarch's Poetics," in *Literary Theory / Renaissance Texts* (Baltimore: Johns Hopkins University Press, 1986), 20–32, esp. 21: Petrarch's is "a poetry whose real subject matter is its own act"; Freccero mocks those who think to find a representation of psychology (or anything else) in Petrarch's "autonomous universe of autoreflexive signs without reference to an anterior logos" (27).

5 Francesco Petrarca, *Prose*, ed. G. Martellotti et al. (Milan: Ricciardi, 1955), 184.

6 Gordon Braden argues that this is a slight mistranslation, and that the Latin (*Prose*, 214)

is even stronger here, and should be translated not as "you are saying your will is impotent," but as "what you are calling impotence is actually willfulness" (personal communication). This seems to me a useful, and clarifying, correction.

7   Needless to say, my reading of the *Secretum* differs from that of Thomas P. Roche, Jr., *Petrarch and the English Sonnet Sequences* (New York: AMS Press, 1989), p. 7, who says of the dialogue, "There can be no doubt who is right" (meaning "Augustinus"). My reading of the *Secretum* is in accord with that of Quillen (see note 2 above), and with Hans Baron, *Petrarch's* Secretum (Cambridge, Mass.: Harvard University Press, 1985), esp. 221–2. My readings of the *Canzoniere* and of Shakespeare's sonnets are equally opposed to those of Roche.

8   This thesis puts me in line with the perspective of Gordon Braden, "Shakespeare's Petrarchism," in James Schiffer (ed.), *Shakespeare's Sonnets: Critical Essays* (New York: Garland, 1999), 163–83, and against that of Joel Fineman, *Shakespeare's Perjured Eye: The Invention of Poetic Subjectivity in the Sonnets* (Berkeley: University of California Press, 1986).

9   On Petrarch's careful and continuous arranging of the order of the *Rime*, see Ernest Hatch Wilkins, *The Making of the "Canzoniere" and Other Petrarchan Studies* (Rome: Edizioni di storia e letteratura, 1951); for the composition, dating, and placement of *Rime* poem 1, see 151–2, 190–3. On the richness of the opening sonnet, in itself and in relation to the volume as a whole, see Bruce Merry, "*Il primo sonetto del Petrarca come modello di lettura*," *Paragone* 25 (1974), 73–9.

10   "The Church" section of *The Temple* begins with "The Altar," on the complexities of which see, most recently, Richard Strier, "George Herbert and Ironic Ekphrasis," in Shadi Bartsch and Jas' Elster (eds.), *Ekphrasis* (forthcoming as a special issue of *Classical Philology*, 101, Jan. 2007). For the care with which George Herbert arranged his lyrics, one has only to compare the earlier version of the volume (the "Williams manuscript" version) and the final version. There is a schematic version of this comparison in *The Works of*

George Herbert, ed. F. E. Hutchinson (Oxford: Clarendon, 1945), pp. liv–v.

11   Quotations from Petrarch's *Rime* are taken from *Petrarch's Lyric Poems: The* Rime Sparse *and Other Lyrics*, ed. and trans. Robert M. Durling (Cambridge, Mass.: Harvard University Press, 1976). Translations are Durling's unless otherwise noted. Wilkins, *Making*, 152, notes that "the writing of No. 1 proves that Petrarch now had in mind the idea of publication."

12   On the role of the reader in the *Canzoniere*, see William J. Kennedy, *Rhetorical Norms in Renaissance Literature* (New Haven: Yale University Press, 1978), 241.

13   For the differences between "Augustinus" in the *Secretum* and the historical Augustine, see note 2 above. For the historical Augustine's theory of incomplete conversion, and on how this differed from the prevailing way of conceiving of conversion in his time, see Peter Brown's discussion of Book X of *The Confessions* in *Augustine of Hippo: A Biography* (Berkeley: University of California Press, 1967), pp. 177–81.

14   Durling's translation of poem 59 weakens the force of this ending by reversing the penultimate and final lines.

15   Durling's translation is somewhat misleading here, since he translates "*ch' io torni*" as "that . . . I may return."

16   For excellent overviews of these traditions, see, *inter alia*, Maurice Valency, *In Praise of Love: An Introduction to the Love Poetry of the Renaissance* (New York: Macmillan, 1958), and Mariann Sanders Regan, *Love Words: The Self and the Text in Medieval and Renaissance Poetry* (Ithaca, NY: Cornell University Press, 1982).

17   These lines (70. 44–5) are quite difficult (conceptually, not linguistically); my paraphrase is an approximation of their meaning.

18   The tense structure of these lines, in which the future inability is expressed in the present tense ("*non po*") intensifies the assertion of inability.

19   "I wish I wished more, *and* I do not wish more, and by not being able to do more, I do as much as I can" (translation slightly altered from that of Durling, who, I think, improperly interrupts the series of "and"s by chang-

ing the italicized one to a "but"). Heather Dubrow quotes this sonnet and comments usefully on it in *Echoes of Desire: English Petrarchism and its Counterdiscourses* (Ithaca, NY, and London: Cornell University Press, 1995), pp. 18–19, but she does not, I believe, see any comedy or self-mockery in the poem.

20 Büdel, "Illusion Disabused," 139; see also Gordon Braden, *Petrarchan Love and the Continental Renaissance* (New Haven: Yale University Press, 1999), 18.

21 Durling's translation, "there is no good in the world that is equal to my ills," seems to me to soften the force and starkness of the line.

22 On the way the status of this canzone is marked in Petrarch's manuscript, see Wilkins, *Making*, 190–3.

23 On the closeness of *"I' vo pensando"* to the *Secretum*, see Baron, *Petrarch's* Secretum, 47–57. Baron argues, along with Wilkins, in *Making*, 153 (though not in later works), that the canzone and the original version of the *Secretum* were composed in the same year, namely 1347 (before Petrarch had heard of Laura's death, and in the same period in which he composed *De otio religiosum*). For Baron's dating of the composition of the *Secretum*, see 1–46. Wilkins, *Making*, 190–3, makes the intriguing suggestion that poems 1 and 264, the opening poems for each section of the *Rime*, were composed at about the same time.

24 Again, as in sonnet 118 (see note 19 above), Durling translates an *et* as "but."

25 For *"video meliora proboque, / deteriora sequor,"* see *Metamorphoses*, VII. 21–2: Ovid, *Metamorphoses*, 2 vols., trans. Frank Justus Miller, LCL (Cambridge, Mass.: Harvard University Press, 1977), vol. 1, 342.

26 As Wilkins, *Making*, p. 191, says, poem 264 is "not a poem or moral conversion – it is rather a poem of profound moral conflict."

27 "The Exstasie," l. 64. One would think from the title of Marianne Shapiro's *Dante and the Knot of Body and Soul* (New York: St. Martin's, 1998) that Dante uses the image in this way, but he, in fact, uses the image differently, as Shapiro's own analysis shows (15–16).

28 This assertion places me in opposition to Thomas M. Greene in *The Light in Troy: Imita-*tion *and Discovery in Renaissance Poetry* (New Haven: Yale University Press, 1982), where he seems to equate Christianity (rather than platonism) with body–soul dualism (125, 129), and to see in Petrarch the absence "of qualifications to pathos" (129). Greene is committed to a view of literary history that sees enacted in most Renaissance texts, and especially Petrarch's, "a disruption of classical equilibriums by a modern metaphysical fissure" (142). This view seems to me to darken Petrarch's poetry, and to understate the equilibrium that, as I will try to show, it often attains. At one point in his discussion (with regard to poem 188, *"Almo sol"*), Greene does suggest a less schematic view (140).

29 Greene, *The Light in Troy*, 112.

30 David Kalstone, *Sidney's Poetry: Contexts and Interpretations* (Cambridge, Mass.: Harvard University Press, 1965), 114.

31 *Epigrams* VI. 29, l. 8, translated (awkwardly) as "To unwonted worth comes life but short, and rarely old age" in Martial, *Epigrams*, 2 vols., trans. Walter C. A. Ker, LCL (Cambridge, Mass.: Harvard University Press, 1968), vol. 1, 374–5. I am not claiming that Petrarch knew this poem, but am using it, rather, as an illustration of a widespread classical topos. Petrarch certainly knew some of Martial's poetry, but how much is unclear. See Guido Martelotti, *"Petrarca e Marziale," Rivista de cultura classica e medioevale* 2 (1960), 388–93.

32 Greene's darkening of Petrarch's poetry (see note 28 above) is quite clear in his treatment of this final line of *"Quel rosigniuol."* Greeene says, "The closing line will deny that any earthly thing pleases" (123). But the line does not deny that. It denies that any earthly thing that pleases *also endures*. So committed is Greene to denying the presence of pleasure in the line that he later misquotes it by leaving the reference to pleasure out. *"Nulla qua giù dura,"* quotes Greene (125), rather than *"nulla qua giù diletta et dura."*

33 Durling's addition of "bodily" before "knot" here seems clarifying, but is actually misleading.

34 See Jacob Burckhardt, "The Modern Idea of Fame," in *The Civilization of the Renaissance in Italy*, intr. Benjamin Nelson and Charles

Trinkaus (New York: Harper & Row, 1958), vol. 1, 151–62, and the discussion in William Kerrigan and Gordon Braden, *The Idea of the Renaissance* (Baltimore: Johns Hopkins University Press, 1989), 19–34.

35 On the attitude toward poetry here, see Brenda Deen Schildgen, "Overcoming Augustinian Dichotomies in Defense of the Laurel in Canzoni 359 and 360 of the '*Rime Sparse*,'" *Modern Language Notes* 111 (1996), 149–63.

36 I have departed from Durling's translation ("a bit of deciduous mortal dust") here.

37 The role that Shakespeare played in the publication of the quarto volume, *Shake-speares Sonnets*, by Thomas Thorpe in 1609 is undetermined. The prevailing view has been that the sonnets were "pirated," but this has been challenged by Katherine Duncan-Jones in "Was the 1609 *Shake-speares Sonnets* Really Unauthorized?," *Review of English Studies* 34 (1983), 151–71, and in her Arden edition of the sonnets (London: Thomson Learning, 1997), 12–13, 31–41. Shakespeare's authorship of the sonnets that appear in the 1609 quarto is widely accepted, the only ones in dispute being the two sonnets that appear last in the volume. The order of the sonnets in the 1609 quarto may or may not be authorial, and so the arrangement of the volume has a very different status from that of Petrarch's volume. Unless otherwise noted, I have used, for my modernized text of the sonnets, the Duncan-Jones Arden edition (though I have at times Americanized spellings); for the quarto text, I have used the reproductions of the pages in *Shakespeare's Sonnets*, edited with analytic commentary by Stephen Booth (New Haven: Yale University Press, 1978), hereafter cited as Booth.

38 Helen Vendler, *The Art of Shakespeare's Sonnets* (Cambridge, Mass.: Harvard University Press, 1997), 451.

39 Dubrow, *Echoes of Desire*, 123–4.

40 Booth, 452.

41 On the trickiness of "reeks," see Booth, 454–5.

42 That "rare" is an extremely strong value term in Shakespeare is easily demonstrated. See e.g. *Pericles*, ed. Suzanne Gossett (London: Thomson Learning, 2004), III. iii. 103, 105; V. i. 152.

43 For poems of Petrarch's that do this, see *Rime* 30 (7 years), 62 (11 years), 79 (14 years), 118 (16 years), 122 (17 years), 212 and 221 (20 years), 364 (21 years up to her death; 10 years since).

44 On the way in which Shakespeare's sonnets open up grand cosmic vistas, see C. S. Lewis, *English Literature in the Sixteenth Century Excluding Drama* (Oxford: Clarendon, 1954): "In Shakespeare each experience of the lover becomes a window through which we look out on immense prospects" (549).

45 It is worth noting that my treatment here has simplified Shakespeare's couplet, since he emphasizes place as well as time: "*there* bred, / *Where* time . . ." "There" in line 13 refers both to the past beginning of the love, and, I think, to "conceit"; and line 14 continues this complex reference.

46 For the exact valence of "necessary" here – as neutral (or positive) rather than as negative – see "a harmless necessary cat" in *The Merchant of Venice*, ed. John Russell Brown (London: Methuen, 1959), IV. i. 55.

47 There is a textual crux here. In the 1609 quarto (Q), the final line of sonnet 113 reads, "My most true minde thus maketh mine untrue." Most editors have emended as in my text above, but Booth cleverly changes "mine" to "m'eyne," thus getting the effect of the emendation while keeping the sound of the line as it is in Q, while Duncan-Jones prints the line (in modern spelling) just as it appears in Q. I think the emendation is fully justified by the logic of the poem (contrasting eye and mind), and that Booth's suggestion is too clever by half.

48 As Booth explains (384), this sonnet appears between 115 and 117 in all the (thirteen) surviving copies of the 1609 quarto, but in twelve of these, it is misnumbered 119.

49 Braden is, I think, getting at this when he notes that "the true minds being celebrated are not necessarily marrying each other" ("Shakespeare's Petrarchism," 175).

50 On Shakespeare's development of the idea of "things ill" as "becoming," see the discussion in Strier, "Shakespeare against Morality," forthcoming in Marshall Grossman (ed.), *Reading Renaissance Ethics* (New York: Routledge, 2006).

51 Lars Engle, "'I am that I am': Shakespeare's Sonnets and the Economy of Shame," in James Schiffer (ed.), *Shakespeare's Sonnets: Critical Essays* (New York: Garland, 1999), 195; cf.

Vendler, *Art*, 515: "recognition of independent moral self-identity." Both contra Booth, 410.

52 See Strier, "Shakespeare against Morality," and G. Wilson Knight, *The Mutual Flame: On Shakespeare's Sonnets and "The Phoenix and the Turtle"* (London: Methuen, 1955), 49–52. Hilton Landry, in *Interpretations in Shakespeare's Sonnets* (Berkeley: University of California Press, 1967), 92–3, pointed out a striking parallel between Shakespeare's "I am that I am" and the refrain (and entire stance) of a poem by Wyatt (probably) to which Shakespeare may or may not have had access in manuscript. The poem in question begins, "I am as I am, and so will I be, / But how that I am none knoweth truly: / Be it evil, be it well, be I bond, be I free, / I am as I am, and so will I be" (see Sir Thomas Wyatt, *Collected Poems*, ed. Joost Daalder [London: Oxford University Press, 1975], 179).

53 On the way in which the pronouns in the poem work to diminish the independence and assert the mutuality of the lovers in this sonnet, see Booth, 481. For a truly "utopian" reading of the sonnet, see Edward Snow, "Loves of Comfort and Despair: A Reading of Shakespeare's Sonnet 138," *ELH* 47 (1980), 462–83. Although I think that Snow underestimates the negative, truly revolted dimension of the poem, I think that the direction in which he errs is an extremely productive and helpful one.

54 Christopher Ricks, "Lies," *Critical Inquiry* 2 (1975), 132.

55 "When my love swears that she is made of truth" is one of two sonnets in the 1609 volume that was published earlier, and in a different version. It appeared, together with a version of "Two loves I have, of comfort and despair" (number 144 in 1609) and two sonnets and a lyric from *Love's Labor's Lost* (and fifteen non-Shakespearean poems) in an octavo volume published in 1599 by William Jaggard entitled *The Passionate Pilgrim* and stated to be entirely

"By W. Shakespeare." For the 1599 versions of the two sonnets that appear in altered form in 1609, see Booth, 476–7 and 496. It should be noted that in the final line of the 1599 version, the aural pun on "mothered" might mitigate the harshness of this line, and be another Ricksian "deep" pun (see Janet Adelman, *Suffocating Mothers: Fantasies of Maternal Origin in Shakespeare's Plays*, Hamlet *to* The Tempest [New York: Routledge, 1992]). This element may remain in the 1609 version in the persistence of "our faults," where both lovers are feminized, since "fault" was a slang term for the female genitalia (compare Gloucester's "Do you smell a fault?"; see King Lear, *a Parallel Text Edition*, ed. René Weiss [London: Longman, 1993], I. i. 14–15 in both Q and F).

56 See William Empson, *The Structure of Complex Words* (London: Chatto & Windus, 1964).

57 Snow notes that "flattered" comes "as a final clinching grace," but does not offer much by way of analytical support for this intuition ("Loves of Comfort and Despair," 478).

58 Büdel, "Illusion Disabused," 129.

59 Compare Braden, "Shakespeare's Petrarchism," 178.

60 This is noted by Richard Levin, "Sonnet CXXIX as a 'Dramatic' Poem," *Shakespeare Quarterly* 16 (1975), 179. Giorgio Melchiori credits Levin with being the first to notice "the progressive toning down of the [negative] connotative features" of the poem's language (*Shakespeare's Dramatic Meditations: An Experiment in Criticism* [Oxford: Clarendon, 1976], 147).

61 Melchiori, in *Shakespeare's Dramatic Meditations*, 152–8, comes to a view somewhat close to this, but, like Snow on "When my love swears" (see note 53 above) seems to me to move away too far from the element of loathing. Again, however, if one has to err in a direction, this seems to me the better one.

62 Compare the "bell' albergo" of "O misera et orribil visione" (*Rime*, poem 251).

6

"Dressing old words new"? Re-evaluating the "Delian Structure"

Heather Dubrow

Tormented, uncertain, and volatile though the human relationships in Shakespeare's sonnets are, in the past two decades many critics have confidently posited far more stable literary relationships for these poems: published with *A Lover's Complaint*, they are seen as a typical, even prototypical, instance of an early modern predilection for bringing out volumes that link sonnet sequences to other texts, especially narratives. So well established was the tradition in question, John Kerrigan influentially asserts, that "When those first Jacobean readers opened Shakespeare's volume in 1609, they found something perfectly familiar."[1] In seconding his assumptions, critics have accepted and analyzed two interlocking sources for that familiarity: structural parallels in the organization of the texts within a given volume, and semantic connections in the ideas within and among those volumes, most notably a concern with the workings of desire and of its tricky servant rhetoric. But if we re-examine the books in question, we will come to discredit or at least substantially modify the first of those two tenets, the putatively recurrent structural repetitions, while tempering the second, the thematic parallels, to recognize issues more subtle and no less significant than desire.

Surrogacy in its many and divergent forms is central to both these challenges to the conventional wisdom. The structural relationships among texts in a given collection involve types of substitution and redefinition more varied and often more unstable than many readers have acknowledged – indeed, on occasion as indeterminate as the dark lady's behavior. In particular, often the concluding text is not conclusive: that is, it provides another perspective on rather than an answer to the problems in previous poems. And, not coincidentally, an exploration (and in some instances enactment) of several versions of surrogacy is among the most intriguing preoccupations of many of the texts in question. Recognizing this preoccupation, like questioning the putative structural connections critics have found in the texts where it appears, invites new approaches to Shakespeare's nondramatic poetry.

I

Editions meticulously prepared by Katherine Duncan-Jones and John Kerrigan, as well as Thomas P. Roche Jr.'s critical book *Petrarch and the English Sonnet Sequences*, are the primary if not the only begetters of the theory that Kerrigan and others call the "Delian tradition" because of its appearance in Daniel's *Delia*.[2] In this tradition, so the argument goes, a sonnet sequence is followed by other texts, generally including a narrative poem, that develop from different perspectives issues treated in the preceding fourteen-line poems. More specifically, celebrating *Delia* as a "decisive document" (p. 13) in the development of the tradition, Kerrigan suggests that its tripartite structure was closely imitated by other writers, hence establishing the pattern of a series of sonnets followed by a short poem, often though not invariably in tetrameters, such as the ode in Daniel's book or the anacreontics in Shakespeare's, and in turn followed by a complaint or other long poem. His emphasis on the normativity of this tripartite structure shapes many of his interpretations; for example, rather than reading Lynche's *Diella* as a dyad of sonnet and narrative, he maintains that one of its sonnets fills the role of the epigram or ode found in other collections. Among the principal reasons for juxtaposing these "mutually illuminating" (p. 14) texts, Kerrigan asserts, is achieving some form of closure, with the later poem typically resolving issues in the sonnets; thus he adduces as prototypical the relationship among the texts in Spenser's 1595 volume, echoing the widespread though not uncontroversial assumption that the "Epithalamion" substitutes its values for the more dubious ones of the Petrarchan tradition.

Kerrigan prints *A Lover's Complaint* together with the sonnets in his important and influential 1986 Penguin edition, thus instituting in practice the connections he posits in theory. Versions of this structure have also been identified by him and others in the work of Richard Barnfield, Alexander Craig, Giles Fletcher the Elder, Thomas Lodge, Richard Lynche, William Shakespeare, and Edmund Spenser; Roche tentatively suggests including Sir David Murray of Gorthy (p. 343). To this list we could add, an as yet unregistered instance, the succession of sonnets by a melancholic complaint in the work of the little-known early modern poet Robert Parry.[3]

Although the concept of the Delian tradition has met with widespread acceptance, its principal progenitors, Duncan-Jones, Kerrigan, and Roche, model it somewhat differently. For example, Duncan-Jones posits a two-part, not a three-part, form and genders the relationship between the two texts in question: "Some contrast and/or complementarity between a male-voiced sonnet sequence and an appended female-voiced 'complaint' was a normal feature of the two-part form" (p. 88). Seconding Kerrigan's contention that the final text engineers some sort of resolution, she locates that closural move in Shakespeare's collection in terms of "the sense of a sexual balance being redressed" (p. 88). Roche in turn analyzes the connections among poems within such volumes in terms of the putative numerological structures and the Christian preoccupations that he traces throughout *Petrarch and the English Sonnet Sequences*. A handful of other critics have questioned the very idea of the Delian tradition, though they have done so briefly, generally through passing observations in the course of another argument; for example, John Roe cautions us that the many different arrangements of sonnets and complaints make it dangerous to establish Daniel's as the normative pattern that shaped subsequent volumes.[4] Roger Kuin asserts that Shakespeare is less concerned to imitate Daniel's structure than to challenge Spenser's.[5]

Nonetheless, the ayes have it: the theory of the structural and thematic connections among texts in such volumes has met with widespread and generally uncritical acclaim from many otherwise divergent academics. Focusing on the issues of transmission and reception that have interested so many contemporary students of English literature, Sasha Roberts grounds her arguments in the assumption that the 1609 volume is a composite of closely connected texts; like Duncan-Jones, she is particularly interested in how the complaint challenges the misogyny of the sonnets that precede it.[6] And Ilona Bell's otherwise persuasive essay declares that "Thanks to Kerrigan's and Duncan-Jones's editions, it is now possible to read *A Lover's Complaint* without being put off by the genre or stymied by the literal meaning of the lines"; this article culminates in the assertion that "the pervasive and insistent links between the ways the young man beguiles the sonnet speaker and the ways the male lover beguiles the female complainant indicate that Shakespeare conceived *A Lover's Complaint* as the conclusion to and commentary upon Sonnets 1609."[7]

It is the theory in question that has beguiled many Shakespeareans, despite the demurrals of readers like Roe; a more detailed and systematic reconsideration of it is due, even overdue. First, neither the tripartite model nor its two-part alternative adequately responds to the varieties in these collections. In lieu of either of those structures, Richard Barnfield, for example, opens his volume with "Cynthia," a mythological poem that reshapes the story of the Olympian version of an Atlantic City beauty contest into a tribute to Elizabeth; he then moves to the sonnets, to an ode that refers specifically to the first poem, and finally to his narrative poem "Cassandra," which includes passages of complaint but cannot be confidently classified in that category. If Giles Fletcher the Elder includes in *Licia* a series of sonnets, a tetrameter ode, and a long narrative poem about and ostensibly by Richard III, he also places between the ode and that poem a pastoral dialogue from Lucian, three other love poems in sixains, and one in quatrains. Lodge's sonnets, like many other cycles, are interspersed with an elegy and two pastoral poems, whose presence anticipates and complicates their relationship to the poems that succeed them.

If the concept of an essentially stable and predictable Delian structure is compromised by the distinctive content of volumes too often grouped together in this regard, both verbal markers and printing conventions establish additional differences between the interrelationships of the texts within one volume and those in the next – in so doing demonstrating yet again the limits on and challenges to authorial agency in determining structure.[8] The wording on the title-page is likely to have been determined by the publisher, given that this sheet was a form of advertisement, and the presence or absence of a half-title (that is, a sheet bearing the title of the succeeding work and often some engraving as well) was probably decided by the publisher or printer. In deciding whether or not to use the term "finis" that printer might have been guided by its presence or absence in the manuscript – but he might also have inserted it to fill blank space. In short, many of the signals that can either emphasize or undermine the connections between texts in a putative Delian structure cannot be read as products of authorial intentions. Sometimes these markers give clear signals about the relationships among texts, flags consistent with the agency the author expresses in other ways. Elsewhere the signals are mixed or contradictory.

Also telling are the different conjunctions and participles title-pages use to describe the relationship of the shorter poems to the final one – "with" in the case of Daniel's 1592 edition, "annexed" in Lodge's *Phillis*, "adjoyned" in Lynche's *Diella*, and so on. This diction does not necessarily correspond to the reader's perceptions about how closely related the writings themselves are, perhaps because a printer was responsible for the wording; for example, although Lynche's "Dom Diego and Ginevra" is merely "adjoined" to the earlier poems, in fact it is, as we have already seen, thoroughly integrated. You can't judge a book by its title-page.

Salient distinctions separate not only different instances of the "Delian structure" but even versions of its paradigmatic originary moment in Daniel's own text: markers of the relationships among the texts, notably the use of "finis" and of half-titles, differ from edition to edition, including variants published in the same year.[9] In the first 1592 edition (STC 6243.2) "finis" appears between the sonnets and ode and between the ode and complaint; the latter is not, however, introduced with a half-title. In the same year, however, the same printer and publisher brought out a version (STC 6243.3) that corrects some errors within sonnets noted on a prefatory corrigenda sheet in the previous volume. More to my purposes, the relationship between the sonnets and "The Complaint of Rosamond" changes significantly: although the placement of "finis" remains the same, the two texts are distinguished by the use of the half-title; the complaint is further set off by the use of a large capital, lacking in the ode and the first sonnet. All these patterns are further complicated by the inclusion of *Cleopatra* in some later editions; for example, because it, unlike the complaint, acquires its own half-title in 1598, the connections among the lyric members of the volume are implicitly emphasized through the contrast. In short, although we cannot be certain how closely aligned Daniel considered the two texts in question, he must have been aware of the thematic and imagistic links between them, and by referring to Delia within the complaint he encourages the reader to note connections. Hence, rather than assuming that he requested changes in this revised version that would increase the separation between the texts, it is likely that the publisher added them, quite possibly hoping that the separate half-title would make readers think they were getting more for their money. In any event, these editions remind us that the semantic and the visual content of a book could give a reader mixed messages about how unified the volume is, encouraging her to debate that issue and uncover or suppress signs of unity or disunity. Thus author, printer, and reader all interact, not necessarily cooperatively, in determining structure.

In other words, in this as in the other volumes we have examined, not the least implication of the composite authorship stressed from so many different perspectives by critics today is that the architecture attributed to volumes like these was not likely to be controlled by the author: it could be built, or in significant ways dismantled, by printer and publisher. These complications invited the participation of the reader as well. For, rather than approaching such texts with straightforward expectations of a "Delian structure," the early modern reader received mixed signals about the interrelationship and integration of texts from reading other volumes of the type; in many instances the volume at hand did not definitively resolve those ambiguities, ensuring that its audience was invited, indeed challenged and impelled, to think through (in several senses of that preposition) a set of complex and sometimes opaque structural relationships.

More specifically, what do these conventions suggest about how readers negotiate the texts in the volumes in question? At one extreme of the spectrum, the poems in Lynche's *Diella* are so closely linked to the narrative poem that follows as to justify his description of the two as "intermingled" even though they follow each other sequentially:[10] the final sonnet advises the lady to read the ensuing story, which is a thinly disguised commentary on her own situation. The intimate connection between that lyric and the ensuing narrative is flagged by a catchword, "The," that in effect offers the reader precisely the same invitation that final sonnet extends to its diegetic reader, the disdainfully chaste Diella: "Harken awhile (Diella) to a storie . . . Reade all" (sonnet 38.1, 13). Yet in many other instances the links between texts are less firm, the signals of those links less clear, or both, challenging the reader to determine to what extent, in what ways, the poems are allied. Thus semantic and visual markers enjoy an uneasy coexistence; thus structure is again fluid in the sense of involving conflicting and indeterminate possibilities.

Spenser's 1595 volume offers a particularly intriguing challenge to the reader. Positing a template for Reformed and reformed love within this collection, many critics have interpreted its wedding poem as closely connected to the sonnets, functioning as rebuttal or culmination or both to their Petrarchism.[11] But Spenser's 1595 volume in fact gives mixed messages visually about such relationships. To be sure, the poems all obviously present different perspectives on love, with the epithalamium apparently more closely connected to the sonnets than either of them is to the anacreontics. Yet the sonnets are linked to the anacreontics with a catchword, and "finis" appears at the end of the anacreontics but not between them and the sonnets; the "Epithalamion," in contrast, is not linked to the anacreontics with a catchword; preceded by a half-title page, it too ends in "finis." Moreover, as I have demonstrated elsewhere, semantically the final poem is by no means clearly established as an ethical and generic solution to the problems of Petrarchism.[12] Thus the collection impels its readers to think about the relationship between Petrarchan and married love rather than insistently offering the second as answer and antidote to the first.

Another limitation in many analyses of the structural connections characteristic of this tradition anticipates the thematic parallels we will shortly re-examine. Exemplifying the attraction to teleology that informs so many literary paradigms (and finds its analog in the assumption, now discredited in many quarters, that in art history the imperfections of the early Renaissance culminate in the High Renaissance), many discussions of the texts in question, as we have seen, assume that the final poem in the collection decisively answers or rebuts earlier ones. The critical tendency to impose on collections of sonnets the type of linearity that encourages us to think in terms of "sonnet sequences" rather than "sonnet cycles," a predilection I have challenged elsewhere, not coincidentally mirrors the desire to read such collections of sonnets in terms of a linear relationship with the poem or poems that follow them.[13] Yet, as indicated above, even Spenser's 1595 volume, ostensibly the paradigmatic instance of this pattern, does not necessarily present its wedding poem as the solution to earlier problems. The final poem is often a surrogate not in the sense of a superior rendition that supersedes, but rather in that of an alternative that is compared to and contrasted with earlier visions, without a clear-cut victory. I will return to the thematic implications of these relationships and to their workings in Shakespeare later in this essay; and we might fruitfully debate in other venues why this type of teleological imperative survives even – or especially – in an academic climate that privileges poststructuralist paradigms.

In short, then, not only are the collections in question too inconsistent in their structures to posit either a two- or a three-part pattern as normative; differences between one author's text and another author's, from one variant of the same author's text to another variant, and even from one section of the same volume to another section within it are also created and emphasized by a range of paratextual materials and printing practices. This is not to deny the presence of some structural similarities, as we have seen. But the texts connected by those similarities are variable, volatile, experimental in their structures.

II

Desire and its interactions with rhetoric is clearly a problem that runs through many of these texts; but at the same time they are diverse in their preoccupations as well as in the architectural respects we have just traced. First of all, on the semantic level, as on the level of structure, the extent of the similarities among the collections differs considerably. Certain concerns, such as the emphasis on *carpe diem* that unites the principal poems in Daniel's volume, are specific to particular volumes, or emphasized considerably more in certain volumes than others, once again warning us against unqualified generalizations about these collections.[14] Similarly, the dangers of representation are among the most crucial questions in the volumes by Barnfield, Daniel, and Shakespeare, whereas Giles Fletcher the Elder's portrait of Richard III, surely an exemplum of misrepresentation if one ever existed, channels little energy into such concerns.

Moreover, the central issues in these volumes vary, and many though by no means all of them are united by a preoccupation more implicit and often more intriguing than the depredations of desire or the rapacity of rhetoric. Always based on a structure in which texts offer substitute visions and genres, often impelled by a latent agenda of replacing one emotion or interpretation with a more acceptable one, the books not only stage but also thematize many versions of surrogacy. These versions, like the collections in which they appear, are varied enough on first glance to complicate, if not call into question, an aggregation of them: they range from types of succession, whether by an heir in the most literal, familial sense or by a substitute storyteller, to types of representation, whether by an iconic ghost or shadow or by a mimetic text, to types of figuration, whether in a trope like metaphor or in its demonic parody catachresis. But this variety is less an impediment against than an impetus to studying these collections in terms of substitution: the interaction among the many forms that pattern may take are themselves intriguing. Moreover, these diverse forms of surrogacy are typically linked by certain characteristics in many of these texts; for example, they gesture toward the possibility of absence, of displacing, replacing, and changing places and hence genders, and of competition, all of which, as we will see, are central to such texts. And, more germane to my purposes here, it is through versions of substitution that these volumes variously allude to and attempt to conceal their own workings and agendas, not least the connections among their constituent parts.

To begin with, translation and imitation are figured in terms of surrogacy. Fletcher's collection focuses particularly on a type of proxy through his habit of starting a sonnet with a couple of lines translated from another writer, which he then deploys in his own way. Announced on the title-page ("to the imitation of the best Latin Poets"), this practice at once emphasizes the agency of the translator and draws attention to lyric as a form that can readily be appropriated by someone other than its original author, much as the seducer in Shakespeare's *Lover's Complaint* deploys both stories and their material analogs, love tokens.

As we have already seen, the relationships among texts within a given volume may fruitfully be mapped in terms of types of substitution, though often those connections are not teleological. At times a subsequent version offers a situation that, although not unproblematic in its own right, provides an alternative vision; in so doing, it may release some sort of blockage. In particular, when a tetrameter ode follows the sonnets, it often sets up a situation that, though like the one in the sonnets, differs in some salient way and frequently though not invariably creates a proxy or stand-in. In Barnfield's collection, the muse starts to faint at the end of the sonnet sequence; in the ensuing ode she is in a sense re-energized, arguably because the distancing involved in translating the first-person love of the sonnets to a third-person pastoral setting (a move anticipated within the fifteenth sonnet, a pastoral) allows the love that dare not speak its name to return to speaking. Fletcher's *Licia* turns from the frustrations of the sonnet sequence to an ode that substitutes another mistress, another meter, and another genre.

Substitution also occurs on the level of character and plot. Often these texts include both the narrative situation in which one story or storyteller or audience takes the place of another and the cognate judicial situation in which an erstwhile or would-be listener in effect becomes an attorney rehearsing a tale he or she has heard. As Katharine A. Craik penetratingly asks, "Is *A Lover's Complaint* 'told right', or is there a suggestion of narrative rivalry between the complainant's version of the story, the young man's report of the seduction, and the first auditor's record of it? In what ways is the reader, as third auditor, implicated in the narratological competition?"[15] A no less significant form of surrogacy is introduced by the deployment of ghosts, at once present and absent, who are so often the narrators in these complaints. Their ontological status as surrogates for a living person anticipates and models their agenda of demanding that someone will substitute for them by retelling the story they have just recounted; witness above all the ways Rosamond's ghost tries to impress the poet, thus linking together more than one sense of that verb. The discursive interaction among the texts in these volumes also contributes to substitutions on the level of character. For example, in the final sonnet of Lynche's *Diella*, the sonneteer enjoins his lady to read the ensuing tale, "The Love of Dom Diego and Ginevra," which tells of a woman who, having rejected her lover, eventually repents and marries him; in terms of suasive function, the narrative is substituted for the sonnets that have failed in its mission, and if it succeeds it will do so precisely because Diella will recognize Ginevra as a surrogate for herself. Thus the tale introduces the exemplarity whose successes and failures are charted through various forms of surrogacy in these volumes. Or, to put it another way, the final text in the volume offers not a resolution of the problems in the sonnet sequence but rather a demonstration of the problematic process of attempting to effect that resolution.

As the neurological mishap suffered by Barnfield's muse suggests, what often impels the substitution of one genre or character for another is a threat, and in many of the texts in question here it is a threat engendered by writing lyrics. Substitution allows the expression of an anger, especially misogynistic aggression, that was partly or entirely suppressed in the preceding sonnet sequence. Or, to put it another way, the gendered tensions involved in writing sonnets are variously and sometimes simultaneously disguised, defused, and declaimed through the complaints and other poems in these collections. In that process, on occasion one character, and on occasion one genre, stands in for another. In the volumes by Barnfield and Daniel, for example, the largely (though not entirely) laudatory portrayal of a beloved creates or suppresses antagonisms for which the complaint is a safety valve. From another perspective, however, to the extent that Barnfield's sonnets show a speaker wooing Ganymede, that speaker and the poet behind him are in the position of Apollo in the ensuing narrative; in presenting Apollo as Cassandra's victim – not to say Cassandra's mug – Barnfield is arguably expressing anxiety about his own role in the sonnets. And in blaming Cassandra he is in a sense blaming Ganymede for leading him on, deflecting the criticism by changing the gender of its recipient. Similarly suggestive (though similarly inconclusive) is the possibility that, having subordinated himself to his female patroness and to Licia in the earlier part of the sequence, Fletcher at once expresses and represses his own gendered antagonism in the complaint, when Richard in effect complains that three female figures have received more attention, more press coverage than he has. Richard's subsequent critique of the poets who praise women "Who are too light, for to be fortunes balles" (l. 36) may also deflect and gender Fletcher's guilt, expressed and countered in his prefatory matter and his first sonnet, about devoting time to the light pursuit of love poetry.[16] Wendy Wall develops cognate points when she argues that the complaint following Daniel's sonnets allows that poet to assume the moral high ground.[17] In other words, the poems following sonnet sequences generally do not offer the reader the clear-cut moral resolution many critics have found in them; but they may offer the writer a way of finessing moral dilemmas.

The most intriguing version of surrogacy in many of these collections is the voicing of someone else's story or song. That process is best illustrated by Daniel's *Complaint of Rosamond*, which deserves and repays close scrutiny for this and many other reasons, not least its unequivocal rebuttal of the widespread misapprehension that its author writes mere bagatelles.[18] Displacement and replacement occur on many levels in this text, demonstrating the potentially hazardous breadth of the overarching concept of surrogacy but also revealing the connections that may unite the many manifestations of that concept. Rosamond is, for example, tempted by a woman who is clearly a stand-in for the king, as well as resembling Rosamond herself in the ways the passage insistently announces:

> And safe mine honor stoode till that in truth,
> One of my Sexe, of place, and nature bad:
> Was set in ambush to intrap my youth,
> One in the habit of like frailtie clad,
> One who the liv'ry of like weakenes had.
>   A seeming Matrone, yet a sinfull monster,
>   As by her words the chaster sort may conster.
>   (ll. 211–17)[19]

Notice that the passive of "Was set in ambush" (213) serves the straightforward purpose of warning us that the woman was the king's stand-in – and arguably the less straightforward one of, however briefly, playing down her own agency and own guilt at the same time as they are emphasized earlier in the passage. Although the accusations directed toward her in the rest of the stanza more than counterbalance this passing hint that the controlling and conniving matron is herself controlled by a conniver, that momentary impression is worth noting; for Rosamond, as so many readers have observed, similarly swerves back and forth within the poem between acknowledging her own guilt and deflecting it onto other agents.

A singularly telling example of all these patterns, however, occurs earlier in the poem. Rosamond, we read,

> Comes to sollicit thee, since others faile,
> To take this taske, and in thy wofull Song
> To forme my case, and register my wrong.
>   (ll. 33–5)

Notice her segue from invitation and solicitation to cooption only a few lines later: "*Delia* may happe to deygne to read our story" (l. 43).[20] The shift from the trochaic opening foot to the string of monosyllabic iambs slows down the line, thus creating an impression of calm deliberation that clashes with how insistently the pronoun "our" forges an alliance.[21] In this version of surrogacy invitation has become interpellation.

On another level, however, a very different form of substitution, similar to the one we have encountered in other collections, is involved: a male writer is deflecting onto Rosamond and thus regendering his own guilt for recounting her story, much as she deflected her guilt onto the matron, whose responsibility, as we have just seen, is itself briefly displaced. Whatever other parallels connect this poem and the sonnets that come before it, might not their author be reacting misogynistically against the worshipful stance encouraged by his prior engagement with Petrarchism?

III

If, then, the collections sometimes amalgamated as a Delian tradition are in fact far more amorphous in their structure than that term suggests – and yet linked by a number of thematic preoccupations – what are the consequences for Shakespeare's 1609 volume and for its critics? Although a comprehensive answer to that question would require a separate essay, one can at least gesture toward some directions for future inquiries. First, my arguments have implications for how the sonnets were written and, perhaps more to the point, read. *Pace* Kerrigan's assertion, cited above, that, "When those first Jacobean readers opened Shakespeare's volume in 1609, they found something perfectly familiar" (p. 14), what they would have found, and would have been aware of finding, was yet another instance of an amorphous and varying predilection for publishing sonnets together with other poems. They would have asked to what extent and in what ways the texts within the collection were connected, knowing that its author's predecessors had offered a wide range of models on those issues. And Shakespeare himself confronted not a clearly established pattern but rather a range of ways of conceiving his sonnets to other texts – including thinking of them primarily in relation to the plays, as John Roe suggests is in fact the case.[22] The existence of so many possibilities renders the choices he did make especially telling.

From those options and invitations he chose revealing structural patterns. His collection resembles others in that, again *pace* Kerrigan, its final poem does not resolve what has come before. The ending of *A Lover's Complaint*, as abrupt and indeterminate as the conclusion of a New Wave film, synecdochally mimes the refusal of the whole volume to offer closural pronouncements.[23] At the same time the 1609 collection differs from some of its counterparts in one related respect: whereas those collections generally do not deploy their final poem to establish closure thematically or ethically, they do use it to close off, close out, and close down the poet's guilt. *A Lover's Complaint*, in contrast, intensifies the guilt driving the sonnets, even focusing attention on some of its sources. Thus the "fickle maid" (l. 5), though more sinned against than sinning, resembles the speaker in the sonnets in exemplifying the perils of using excuses to justify oneself; her seducer resembles him in exemplifying the dangers of using rhetoric to satisfy one's own desires. *A Lover's Complaint* is cast in the 1609 volume not as an all-forgiving duke but rather as a Malvolio or a Jaques, refusing to let the poet off the hook as those characters refuse to forgive those who trespass against them.

In addition, confronted with the range of thematic preoccupations in other collections, Shakespeare emphasizes substitution, another issue central to his own interests. To be sure, the texts in that 1609 volume are linked as well by many of the other concerns we find in cognate volumes, not least by the preoccupation with desire, rhetoric, and their interaction traced perceptively by many readers. The connections between the young man of the sonnets and the seducer of the complaint are apparent; John Kerrigan has posited and Ilona Bell has re-examined possible parallels between the dark lady and the seduced woman in *A Lover's Complaint*.[24] Colin Burrow, the most acute student of connections among Shakespeare's nondramatic poems, enumerates among the many parallels in this instance a preoccupation with eavesdropping. But surrogacy is, I suggest, one of the most intriguing connections between Shakespeare's sonnets and his complaint – and one of the most important links between his collection and the cognate volumes.

A Lover's Complaint, as I have demonstrated at length elsewhere, keeps substituting one narrator for another, with the lack of quotation marks in early modern texts both contributing to and figuring the blurring of attribution and consequent blurring of subjectivities.[25] Most notably, the seduced woman speaks the words she says her seducer has spoken to her, some of which are observations he attributes to other women; thus, discursively as on so many other levels, she assumes the role of the earlier victims with whom the young man is ostensibly contrasting her. The sonnets also record many diverse forms of substitution. Some are beneficent or apparently so: an heir can take the place of an aging father: "This were to be new made when thou art old" (2.13);[26] a dear friend can take the place of other losses: "Thy bosom is endeared with all hearts / Which I by lacking have supposed dead" (31. 1–2). The celebration of the immortalizing potentiality of poesy is rooted in its role as substitution for a living presence, reminding us of the new historicist play on re-presentation. And arguably the couplet of a sonnet is itself not only a culmination but also a substitution, proffering its epigrammatic certainties in lieu of prior meditations. But, as the simulacrum that is poetry reminds us, and as the many couplets in Shakespeare's collection that reverse or confuse rather than resolving demonstrate, surrogacy can also be associated with deceit and dissolution. In Shakespeare's collection, these darker versions contrast ironically with the beneficent replacement of an aged parent with an heir, one of many instances in which the range of forms surrogacy can assume becomes part of the meaning of the text. Thus jealousy and betrayal are repeatedly evoked in terms of substituting one lover for another. And sonnet 35 indelibly connects the substitution of one role and one player for another with an erosion of subjectivity: "Thy adverse party is thy advocate— / And 'gainst myself a lawful plea commence" (ll. 10–11).

I do not, of course, mean to suggest that the volumes explored in this essay are Shakespeare's only impetus for focusing on substitution in the ways he does: that preoccupation is as multi-determined as it is multi-faceted, as even the briefest survey of other texts in the canon demonstrates. Familial relations, literal and otherwise, are often cast in terms of substitution, in part because Shakespearean families are so often defined in terms of loss and absence: Falstaff becomes a father to Hal, Duke Senior a father to

Orlando, and that master of demonic parodies Claudius attempts to do the same to the nephew who is too much in the son. *Measure for Measure*, as critics have often observed, pivots on forms of substitution. The dialogue of genres in Shakespeare's canon also involves versions of the process in question, with the romances, for example, not erasing but attempting to offer alternatives, substitutions for characteristics of both comedy and tragedy.

Even when we acknowledge the pervasiveness of these issues elsewhere in the canon, however, their presence in the 1609 volume is especially insistent, and arguably one reason is its author's memories of and engagement with cognate volumes; the influence of Daniel's collection on Shakespeare's is especially marked in other ways, as many critics have observed, and its impact is no less apparent in the arena of substitutions of various sorts.[27] And reading the sonnets crystallizes two additional reasons why he is attracted to this constellation of ideas, two additional and interwoven reasons why he imitates this characteristic of volumes like Daniel's. Throughout these fourteen-line tomes, substitutions on the characterological level stage those enacted by figurative language, to whose dangers and delights the sonnets repeatedly recur (returning to sonnet 35, witness, for example, the line, "Authorizing thy trespass with compare" [6]). And arguably figurative language, that Mobius strip of equivalence and difference, itself deflects the central undertow of substitution in this sequence: the possibility that same-sex love may substitute for the love that speaks its name confidently if not without occasional challenge, in the conclusions of its author's comedies.

Author's Note

I am grateful to Kimberly Huth for valuable assistance with this essay.

Notes

1   John Kerrigan, "Introduction," in William Shakespeare, *The Sonnets and A Lover's Complaint*, ed. John Kerrigan (Harmondsworth: Penguin, 1986), 14. Future citations from this volume appear in parentheses within my text.

2   On the theory, see Kerrigan, "Introduction," esp. 13–15; William Shakespeare, *Shakespeare's Sonnets*, ed. Katherine Duncan-Jones (London: Thomas Nelson, 1997; The Arden Shakespeare), 88–95; Thomas P. Roche, Jr., *Petrarch and the English Sonnet Sequences* (New York: AMS Press, 1989), 343–4, 440–61. Subsequent citations from Duncan-Jones and Roche are included within my text in parentheses. Although Kerrigan's work appeared earlier, he credits Duncan-Jones with recognizing the structure in question earlier (p. 13); Roche explains in a note that his version of this theory was largely developed independently of those critics (p. 514 n. 72).

3   I am indebted to the late Gwynne Blakemore Evans for this and many other insights about Parry.

4   William Shakespeare, *The Complete Sonnets and Poems*, ed. Colin Burrow (Oxford: Oxford University Press, 2002; Oxford World's Classics), esp. 140; William Shakespeare, *The Poems: Venus and Adonis, The Rape of Lucrece, The Phoenix and the Turtle, The Passionate Pilgrim,*

A Lover's Complaint, ed. John Roe (Cambridge, UK: Cambridge University Press, 1992; The New Cambridge Shakespeare), 62–4.

5   Roger Kuin, *Chamber Music: Elizabethan Sonnet-Sequences and the Pleasure of Criticism* (Toronto: University of Toronto Press, 1998), 86–100.

6   Sasha Roberts, *Reading Shakespeare's Poems in Early Modern England* (Basingstoke: Palgrave Macmillan, 2003), esp. 146–53.

7   Ilona Bell, "'That which thou hast done': Shakespeare's Sonnets and *A Lover's Complaint*," in James Schiffer (ed.), *Shakespeare's Sonnets: Critical Essays* (New York: Garland, 1999), 455, 471. For another instance of the acceptance and application of this theory, see Catherine Bates, *The Rhetoric of Courtship in Elizabethan Language and Literature* (Cambridge, UK: Cambridge University Press, 1992), esp. 139.

8   I am indebted to Harold Love for valuable help with this section of the essay.

9   Also see the expanded discussion of this issue about Daniel in my essay "'Lending soft audience to my sweet design': Shifting Roles and Shifting Readings of Shakespeare's 'A Lover's Complaint,'" *Shakespeare Survey* 58 (2005), 26. John Roe also draws attention to Daniel's title-page, but rather than comparing different versions of it, he focuses on the contrast between the 1592 title-page and its counterpart in Thorpe's edition of Shakespeare, arguing that Daniel's paratextual material offers an encouragement to connect the ensuing texts that is absent in the Shakespearean edition (*The Poems*, 63).

10 R[obert] L[ynche], *Diella, Certaine Sonnets* (London, 1596), A3–A3ᵛ. All subsequent citations are to this edition.

11 See e.g. Lisa M. Klein, "'Let us love, dear love, lyke as we ought': Protestant Marriage and the Revision of Petrarchan Loving in Spenser's *Amoretti*," *Spenser Studies* 10 (1992), 109–37.

12 See my book *Echoes of Desire: English Petrarchism and Its Counterdiscourses* (Ithaca, NY: Cornell University Press, 1995), 76–81.

13 Cf. my essay "'Incertainties now crown themselves assured': The Politics of Plotting Shakespeare's Sonnets," *Shakespeare Quarterly* 47 (1996), 299.

14 On this and other thematic connections between the poems, see Zara Bruzzi, "'I find

myself unparadis'd': The Integrity of Daniel's *Delia*," *Cahiers Élisabéthains* 48 (1995), 1–15; Elizabeth Harris Sagaser, "Sporting the While: Carpe Diem and the Cruel Fair in Samuel Daniel's Delia and The Complaint of Rosamond," *Exemplaria* 10 (1998), 145–70.

15 Katharine A. Craik, "Shakespeare's *A Lover's Complaint* and Early Modern Criminal Confession," *Shakespeare Quarterly* 53 (2002), 443. I am indebted to the author for sharing an earlier version of this essay with me prior to publication.

16 I cite Giles Fletcher, the Elder, *The English Works of Giles Fletcher, the Elder,* ed. Lloyd E. Berry (Madison: University of Wisconsin Press, 1964).

17 Wendy Wall, *The Imprint of Gender: Authorship and Publication in the English Renaissance* (Ithaca, NY: Cornell University Press, 1993), 256–8.

18 For an expanded discussion of these issues, on which this section of the article at hand is closely based, see my essay "'Lending soft audience,'" 24–6.

19 I cite Samuel Daniel, *"Poems" and "A Defence of Ryme,"* ed. Arthur Colby Sprague (Chicago: University of Chicago Press, 1930). Here and elsewhere in this essay, the usage of u/v and i/j has been regularized.

20 Cf. Elizabeth Harris Sagaser's points about how *Delia* conflates the woman's beauty and the poet's song ("Sporting the While," 156–7). Sagaser's acute observation that the poem is "about being seen and being read" (p. 161) is also germane to my argument.

21 Wall also analyzes this pronoun, but from a perspective very different from mine, arguing that the identification it creates stems from the fact that both Rosamond and Daniel seek Delia's sympathy and that Rosamond's problems deflect Daniel's (*The Imprint of Gender*, 255–6).

22 Roe, ed., *The Poems*, 62–4.

23 For an alternative explanation of the ending, see Ilona Bell, "Shakespeare's Exculpatory Complaint," in Shirley Sharon-Zisser (ed.), *Critical Essays on Shakespeare's "A Lover's Complaint": Suffering Ecstasy* (Aldershot: Ashgate, 2006).

24 *The Sonnets and A Lover's Complaint,* ed. Kerrigan, 396; Ilona Bell, "That which thou hast done," esp. 464, 468.

25 Dubrow, "'Lending soft audience.'"

26 I cite throughout William Shakespeare, *The Riverside Shakespeare*, 2nd edn., ed. G. Blakemore Evans et al. (Boston: Houghton Mifflin, 1997).

27 On the influence of Daniel on Shakespeare, see e.g. Burrow, "Introduction," in Shakespeare, *The Complete Sonnets and Poems*, esp. 111–12; Mark Rasmussen, "Petrarchan Narrative in *A Lover's Complaint*," paper delivered at conference on "Shakespeare's Narrative Poems," University of London, July 2000. I thank the latter author for sharing his work prior to publication.

7

Confounded by Winter: Speeding Time in Shakespeare's Sonnets

Dympna Callaghan

The rapid tempo of life and love since Petrarch's death in 1374 has probably offered few opportunities for intense introspection to rival those that motivated the most famous vernacular sonnet sequence of the Italian Renaissance.[1] I will begin this essay with Petrarch because I believe that the juxtaposition of Shakespeare with his most illustrious predecessor in the genre discloses the sheer *speed*, the agitated urgency, which I take to be the hallmark of Shakespeare's sonnets. While Petrarch spends a lifetime of excruciating introspection on the *Canzoniere*, it is precisely *time* that the poet in the sonnets, hustling for patronage in the burgeoning metropolis, simply does not possess. As Shakespeare puts it at the end of the young man poems, in sonnet 126 – a twelve-line poem that itself runs out before its fourteen lines are up – Time's bill must be paid: the "*Audite* (though delayd) answer'd must be." Even the pervasive imagery of debts, leases, and loans becomes a way of figuring the persistence of life in relation to an inevitable mortality, while the beauty of the heedless youth only anticipates his inevitable decay. What is at stake in the sonnets, then, is not merely a change in the metaphor and language of love, but the transformation of the pace and therefore of the nature of desire itself – and in the temporal and lyrical framework in which it can unfold.

The poet, so pressed for time, money, and love, is right to worry: by the time of the sonnets' publication in the commercial bustle of London's urban metropolis in 1609, with the sonnet vogue over for a decade, these lyrics constitute the self-consciously belated articulation of the genre, far removed from the early Renaissance world in which the *Canzoniere* was written.

Starting with Petrarch's sonnet time, in what follows I will explore various lyrical and conceptual facets of Shakespeare's accelerated sonnet temporality, as he speeds up the natural rhythms of lifetimes and seasons. The effect produced by this new relation to time is that remarkably contemporary business (debt, dearth, and distillation, among other elements) imposes itself on the ostensible timelessness that is the leisurely inactivity of lyric.

Petrarchan Time

On a fateful day in 1327, there occurred one of the most truly momentous encounters in the annals of world literature.[2] On April 6, Petrarch first saw Laura:

> Mille trecento ventosette, a punto
> Su l'ora prima, il dì sesto d'aprile,
> Nel laberinto intrai, né veggio ond' esca.
> *In thirteen twenty-seven, and precisely*
> *At the first hour of the sixth of April*
> *I entered the labyrinth, and I see no way out.*
> (Canzone 211)

This moment of the poet's erotic epiphany is in fact "the subject of the entire *Canzoniere*."[3] In canzone 3 Petrarch tells us: "Era il giorno ch'al sol si scoloraro / per la pietà del suo factore i rai" ("It was the day the sun's ray had turned pale / with pity for the suffering of his Maker"). In his copy of Virgil, Petrarch is also specific about the location of the encounter, the Church of St. Clare in Avignon. This spring meeting was marked by the date of "commune dolor," universal woe: the anniversary of the crucifixion of Jesus. This was, in fact, a Monday (not Good Friday, the annual commemoration of the Passion) because it is the *feria sexta aprilis*, the date of Christ's death fixed in absolute time.[4] *Tempo* (time) is the first word of the second quatrain, and is made all the more emphatic by the space that precedes it: "Tempo non mi parea da far riparo / contra colpi d'Amor" ("It seemed not time to be on guard against / Love's blows"). The calendar is the portal through which Petrarch enters the labyrinth where Cupid, who does not observe the protocols of liturgical time, inflicts on him the wound that will forever fracture his identity. Although it should not be confused with biographical facticity, the date of the disintegration of Petrarch's emotional world is surprisingly precise.

Petrarch's sense of time, though it belongs to the order of temporal progression registered by books of hours, those popular devotional manuals dedicated to guiding the reader in prayer and meditation appropriate to the hours of the day and the seasons of the church year, does not so much secularize liturgical temporality as become its erotic counterpart. The atemporal dimensions of the labyrinth are those of eternity and infinity. The *Canzoniere* is shaped *not* by the urgency of desire, described in canzone 6 as a "slow run"/ "lento corer," or by the haste toward consummation (which, in the Petrarchan scheme of things, never arrives), but by *waiting*.[5] In the *Canzoniere* focused, expectant waiting is connected both to submission and to suffering (the poet's despair), as indeed it is in Christian theology,[6] while the relationship of the lover to the beloved is based on the paradigm of feudal service (attendance upon a social superior) and its related dynamics of distance and even antagonism.

Bemoaning the coldness and chastity of his beloved, and the hopelessness of his suit, the poet turns, with almost monastic meditative discipline, to the innermost recesses of his own psychological landscape. It is the extent to which Petrarch delves into the depths of the interiority of the suffering lover, and crucially, the *time* he takes to do this, that are simultaneously the hallmark and the achievement of the *Canzoniere*. That the sequence persists even thirty years after the death of his beloved Laura bespeaks a concern with the protracted nature of the poet's obsession rather than with any thought of a narrative resolution to the relationship. The emphasis is not on resolution but on continuity, and even the prospects of the poet's own demise provoke an arguably conventional renunciation of worldly love for the heavenly mistress, the Blessed Virgin, in the realms beyond time and space. Far from signaling the end of his passion, then, Laura's death from plague in 1348 prompts Petrarch to plunge even more deeply into self-reflection, his thoughts "evidently less focused on entering a life of philosophy than on finding a philosophically satisfactory manner of leaving this life. At the same time, he adapts the view of life as a preparation for death to his worldly concerns."[7] Petrarchan temporality, even when most precisely dated, is protracted, and its rhythm is that of the eternal cycle.

Time and Transformation

Perhaps predictably, while the form of Shakespeare's sonnets is invariably indebted to Petrarch, their pace, one of "continual haste" (123. 12), owes more to his favorite poet, Ovid. The brisk Latin hexameters of the *Metamorphoses*, which lend the poem its "irresistible readability," take the reader through the course of human history from "Chaos to Cleopatra,"[8] that is, from creation to the moment Ovid finishes his poem, so that time is telescoped, and human beings, overpowered by divine forces, suffer a rapid diminution of their human identity.[9]

Although the poet in the sonnets concentrates on transformations wrought by Time *within* the *vitae summa brevis*, the brief span of life, as Horace called it[10] (rather than, as in Ovid, *from* human life to that of a plant or an animal), he often traverses the changes from youth to the grave and back again in the space of a mere fourteen lines. There is a sense in which the flight from Time in the sonnets intensifies the young man's beauty. Like Daphne's flight from Jove in the *Metamorphoses*, under the pressure of acceleration, "his literally fleeting loveliness is '*auctaque forma fuga est,*' augmented by flight."[11] In a key lyric from this point of view, sonnet 5 (a poem I will return to a number of times in the course of this analysis), Time is both the instigator and the instrument of metamorphosis.

> Those howers that with gentle worke did frame
> The lovely gaze where every eye doth dwell
> Will play the tirants to the very same,
> And that unfair which fairely doth excell:
> For never resting time leads Summer on
> To hidious winter and confounds him there,

> Sap checkt with frost and lusty leav's quite gon.
> Beauty ore-snow'd and barenes every where,
> Then were not summers distillation left
> A liquid prisoner pent in walls of glasse,
> Beauties effect with beauty were bereft,
> Nor it nor noe remembrance what it was.
>> But flowers distil'd though they with winter meet,
>> Leese but their show, their substance still lives sweet.

Here, as in all the sonnets, time's accelerated progress ultimately distorts beauty in the course of the lifespan into such grotesque forms that the young man and the poet are confronted with the abrupt and horrifying – the confounding – transformation from youth to decay: "For never resting time leads Summer on, / To hidious winter and confounds him there" (5. 5–6). "Led on" to his destruction – the reader following across the now perilous precipice that is the enjambment of lines five and six – the young man is literally misled, but also enticed and seduced, by Summer, only to be confounded by Winter, who again in sonnet 6 is set to desecrate the young man's beauty: "Then let not winter's wragged hand deface / In thee thy summer" (ll. 1–2). The *threat* of winter carries strong connotations of sexual threat, and the young man's "confounding" bears a resemblance to Ovidian sexual violation. Summer personified, the young man is "led on," that is, he makes an initial misjudgment at the critical moment that offered his only opportunity for resistance. Ovidian rape not infrequently involves Jove chasing down his prey, but there are also instances of the now obsolete notion of "rape" as abduction, that is, the sense of being swept away. Thus, for example, in the rape of Europa, Jove, harmless-looking in taurine form, succeeds in luring his hapless victim into the ocean. Naïve Europa, "nerawhit appalde" (II. 1086), is led on, as Golding's translation puts it, "Amid the deepe where was no meanes to scape with life away" and is carried off to Crete. "[N]o meanes to scape" intimates an explicitly sexual danger that is, furthermore, precisely congruent with the way Shakespeare's young man is imperiled by Time. The ravages of time, too, constitute a species of rape, carrying off and overpowering both the beauty and the will of its victim.

The first poems in the 1609 edition of the sonnets also carry the force of a sexual threat, albeit an unusual one since the poet demands that the young man engage in reproductive sex: "thou . . . diest, unlesse thou get a sonne" (7: 13–14). Here, it is the poet himself, rather than a personification of Time, who brandishes time's scythe over the head of the young man and issues his threats about the necessity of reproduction. Harping relentlessly on the ticking time-bomb that is the young man's biological clock, the poet of the sonnets resorts to a curious combination of both *carpe diem*[12] and *memento mori* decrees, even though traditionally these reminders of death sought to shape behavior in opposite directions (the former tended to encourage sensual indulgence while the latter cautioned it was better to refrain).

The time pressure on human reproduction is insistent: "Thou by thy dial's shady stealth mayst know / Time's thievish progress to eternity" (77. 7–8). Time is "thievish" not because it is slow, but because its progress is clandestine and its movements imperceptible even when looking at the clock face, or at one's own: "Thy dial how thy precious minutes waste" (77. 2).

The beloved's annihilation proceeds at a frenetic pace: by line 8 of sonnet 5, the shadow of the Petrarchan "turn," the young man is done for. Although the passage of time is both inevitable and rapid, the poet makes no argument for surrendering to temporal inevitability, or gracefully accepting the progress of growth and the change of seasons. The progress of time is not stately and orderly as in classical and medieval models of time, but careening, so that youth and beauty come crashing into oblivion. This is because the changes brought by nature and time resemble the sudden and start-ling transformations of Ovidian metamorphoses, when from one minute to the next perfectly attractive young people are reduced to animal life, or less. Alternatively (and indeed, often simultaneously), young lovelies of both sexes have their beauty captured in some emblematic way that is analogous to the process of distillation the poet envis-ages for the young man. Notably, in the case of Daphne, her transformation is preceded by an invocation to the gods ("help your daughter here"), that is, by an assertion of her will which counters the force of the rapacious Jove who pursues her: ". . . and thus of that she earst had benne, / Remayned nothing in the worlde, but beautie fresh and greene" (I. 675–6). John Kerrigan has suggested that this aspect of the sonnets is in part the result of the advent of unnatural, mechanical time: "The invention and dis-semination of mechanical time in the renaissance brought about a complete reordering of sensibility . . . Those who explain the Elizabethan obsession with Time by invoking the iconography of Saturn and Chronos (the god of Chronology) confuse symptoms with cause."[13] Crucially, *time* – not just the means by which it is measured – also undergoes transformation. Thus the Nature that unfolds this accelerated temporality, while not mechanical as such, is not quite natural either. No sooner is the young man out of the womb, Time's crucible at the beginning of sonnet 5, than he is enjoined to fend off approaching winter. If one can be forgiven the anachronism, as the young man grows old, his "substance" is to be preserved like a semen sample in a laboratory, and within the logic of the poem, the cycle of procreation is curiously (albeit temporarily) suspended.

Time Distilled and Mechanized

The instigator of seasonal change hurrying the young man on toward winter and death in sonnet 5, "never-resting time" (l. 5) offers a sharp contrast with the unmotivated cyclical progression of the natural order, as presented for example in the Garden of Adonis in Spenser's *Faerie Queene*, Book III:

> Ne needs there Gardiner to set, or sow,
> To plant or prune: for of their owne accord
> All things, as they created were, doe grow,
> And yet remember well the mightie word,

Which first was spoken by th'Almightie lord,
That bad them to increase and multiply.[14]

The stately pace of Spenser's verse here conveys the measured pace of growth and reproduction, and the rhyme of "sow" and "grow" works to lengthen the sound of these lines, in a way that offers a stark contrast with the compression of ideas and images in the sonnets. Crucially in Spenser, "the Almightie" has set the processes of reproduction on automatic. Order is established here without human agency, so there is no need for the poet, or even a gardener, to intrude on this divinely ordained scheme of things in order to urge the garden to get a move on and reproduce.

Notably, two of the poems most keenly concerned with time in Shakespeare's sequence are given symbolically significant numbers: Sonnet 12 is about the twelve hours on the clock face, while sonnet 60 reflects "our minutes":

When I do count the clock that tells the time,
And see the brave day sunk in hideous night;
When I behold the violet past prime,
And sable curls, all silvered o'er with white;
When lofty trees I see barren of leaves,
Which erst from heat did canopy the herd,
And summer's green all girded up in sheaves,
Borne on the bier with white and bristly beard,
Then of thy beauty do I question make,
That thou among the wastes of time must go,
Since sweets and beauties do themselves forsake
And die as fast as they see others grow;
   And nothing 'gainst Time's scythe can make defence
   Save breed to brave him when he takes thee hence.
(12. 1–14)

While the strokes of the scythe refer to an ancient image of death derived from the manual labor of the harvest time, the clock bespeaks mechanical time, and the alliterative monosyllables of the first line count out the seconds of a ticking clock. Counting by the clock is simultaneously the precise record of time and its complete abstraction, while the organic register of temporality is akin to the medieval rhythm of abundance and scarcity, of time on a human scale and the dignified ritual of death. The last, heavily alliterative line of the octave,[15] which John Keats regarded as an aesthetic lapse, forges in fact a deliberate metrical connection between the kind of archaic, mnemonic verse of a world dominated by agricultural labor, the remnant of the language and lyricism of medieval, and even Anglo-Saxon, temporality. This archaic view of time survived in popular images of both the Seven Ages of Man and the seasons, whose remnants are found in alliterative and even visually alliterative moments of lyric like "winter's wragged hand" in sonnet 6. Most practically and instrumentally, however, this well-nigh obsolete temporality survived in Shakespeare's England in the legal fictions wrought in an effort to secure land tenure in perpetuity. For example, in April 1564, the month of Shakespeare's birth, Solomon Saunders sold a lease for 2,995 years; Thomas Sharpham purchased a lease in Devon until AD 3607; and John Hodge's family bought property on a lease that ran out in AD 4609.[16] Such contracts are of the order of the "dateless bargain to engrossing death" made by the lovers in *Romeo and Juliet*. Yet they bespeak a temporality that is no longer the reality of Shakespeare's England, where "reckoning time" (115. 5) asserts its demands even on the most privileged members such as Shakespeare's young man: "O thou, my lovely boy, who in thy power / Dost hold Time's fickle glass, his sickle, hour" (126: 1–2).

   Although they are obsessed with time, aging, and encroaching death, Shakespeare's sonnets do not index time's passing with any reference to the specifically numerical arrangement of the calendar. Such is Shakespeare's singular treatment of time in the annals of the sonnet tradition, that even those poems that register longing in response to the lovely boy's absence fail to reflect the conventional impatience of courtship, the idea that "Time goes on crutches till love have all his rites" (*Much Ado About Nothing*, II. i. 357–8). We learn in sonnet 104 (a poem that races through the seasons) that "Three Winters colde" have passed since the poet first met the young man, but the exact moment and circumstances of their meeting we are never told, and the poet alludes only to the abstract idea of "date": "beauty's doom and date" (14. 14) "too short a date" (18. 4); "So long as youth and thou are of one date" (22. 2); "death's dateless night" (30. 6); and, finally, the "dateless lively heat" of the hell-fire that is venereal disease (153. 6). The poet emphasizes not the dates but the *duration* or *tide*, not in our modern sense of the rising or falling of the sea, but in a sense which is both proverbial (the sense of time and tide, that is, of a season of time) and contractual: "bonds do tie me day by day (117. 4) "summer's lease," "brief minute," and so on.

Time and Husbandry

In this un-Spenserian view of time and the cycles of life, sonnet 5, urging the young man to "distill" his substance, has arguably much in common with one rather less illustrious contemporary poem, the concluding "*sonet*, or brief rehersall of the properties of the twelue monethes afore rehersed" from Thomas Tusser's *A Hundred Points of Good Husbandry*. The function of this poem is the archaic one of mnemonic practicality: it details the more mundane ways in which human labor seeks to harmonize itself with the passing seasons. The pace of the poem is anything but frenetic, of course, and the seasons pass by with comforting regularity.

> As Ianeuer fryse pot, broth corne kepe hym lowe:
> And feuerell fill dyke, doth good with his snowe:
> A bushel of Marche dust, worth raunsomes of gold:
> And Aprill his stormes, be to good to be tolde:
> As May with his flowers, geue ladies their lust:

And Iune after blooming, set carnels so iust:
As Iuly bid all thing, in order to ripe:
And August bid reapers, to take full their gripe.
September his fruit, biddeth gather as fast:
October bid hogges: to come eat vp his mast:
As dirtie Nouember, bid thresh at thine ease:
December bid Christmas to spende what he please:
So wisdom bid kepe, and prouide while we may:
For age crepeth on as the time passeth away.

In this fallen condition, quite unlike Spenser's self-generating bounty, Tusser's human agents do not observe the Spenserian pattern and "yet remember well the mightie word." Tusser's audience needs verse as a mnemonic reminder of the activities appropriate to each season. As Tusser puts it, "Thinges thriftie . . . teacheth the thriuing to thriue"; in other words, the "sonet" urges the expenditure of energy in the present for future use – and that is precisely the subject of Shakespeare's early sonnets, which also castigate the youth for his "unthrifty lovelinesse" (4. 1). In contrast to the Spenserian "God bade," which needs no further iteration, Tusser's repetition of "bid" as a metrical filler in this poem, nonetheless bespeaks the human will that urges on the progress through the calendar even though that progress is something over which human beings have no control.

Both sonnets 5 and 6 and Tusser's "sonnet" are essentially concerned with how to survive winter by means of advance preparation, so that in the latter, by August, we move from a description of seasonal change and weather patterns to the necessity of human industry. Such comparison discloses the potentially elaborate alchemical image of Shakespeare's "distillation" as instead a curiously domestic strain of metaphor concerning the culinary task of preserving liquids. Like Tusser's long poem, too, this one has a pithy mnemonic conclusion that serves as a reminder to the young man: "But flowers distil'd though they with winter meet, / Leese but their show, their substance still lives sweet." John Partridge, in *The Treasurie of Hidden Secrets*, confirms: "{D}istill *your water in a Stillitorie*," and describes the process for making rose-water (used as a cooking ingredient as well as a fragrance) as follows: "[T]hen put it in a faire glasse, and take the budes of Roses . . . and put the leaves into the stilled water."[17] The poet displays an almost housewifely thrift in his impatience to have the young man bottled,[18] "a liquid prisoner pent in walls of glass" (5. 9). Further, these domestic concerns about preservation over time (or, perhaps, more adversarially, *against* time) as the chief mechanism of a kind of thriving husbandry ("husbandry," 3. 6, 13. 10; "husband nature's ritches from expence," 94. 6; "pittiful thrivors," 125. 8) connect the poem not so much with the exalted tradition of the continental sonnet as with the commonplaces of popular and indigenous poetry, such as the lovely medieval lyric "Spring it is acummin in," which registers with a joyful anticipation about the passage of the seasons that is quite antithetical to the sonnets, or the sententious couplet John Taylor records finding on the walls of the Star Inn in Rye: "No flower so fresh, but frost it may deface."[19]

The inevitable effects of time – decay and death – require, then, not passive acceptance on the part of the young man, in Shakespeare's sonnets, but active intervention via the repeated image of distillation. The specific distillation here, an image borrowed from Sidney's *Arcadia* (1590), refers to the preservation of sonnet 1's "beauty's rose," as "pure rosewater kept in a crystal glass":[20] "Make sweet some vial; treasure thou some place, / With beauty's treasure ere it be selfe-kil'd" (6. 3–4). The process (distillation), the thrifty activity required of the young man by the poet, is that he inseminate ("make sweet") a woman, the unspecified container ("some vial," "some place") of his perfume/semen. Pent-up and imprisoned, that is, corked in a bottle ("a liquid prisoner pent in walls of glass" or, as *Merry Wives* has it, "stopped in like a strong distillation," III. v. 112–13), his is not an ideal situation, but it is the youth's best and last resort in the face of the ravages of time. His beauty's substance will be detained, yet preserved, by a vessel whose transparency, at least, will not obscure or impair its integrity.

The disturbing association of unused or unsaved semen with suicide, the "selfe-kil'd" is reminiscent of the connection between sex and death explored in the tragedies. Negligent husbandry is linked in the sonnets quite specifically to negligent husbands: "For where is she so faire whose un-eared wombe / Distdaines the tillage of thy husbandry?" (3. 5–6). Although it is a qualitatively different substance from the "leprous distill-ment" with which Claudius, an evil husband, murders his brother, a potentially negligent one, in *Hamlet* (I. v. 64), both the perfume and the poison are insistently seminal images. Significantly, too, the poet urges precisely the kind of control over domestic expenditure that Hamlet disparagingly ascribes to his mother's union with Claudius: "Thrift, thrift, Horatio. The funeral baked meats did coldly furnish forth the marriage table" (*Hamlet* I. ii. 180–1).[21] The content of the vial, the "substance" (5. 14), that is, the object of preservation, prefigures the poet's famous question in sonnet 53: "What is your substance, whereof are you made?" In Shakespeare's sonnets, this enigmatic "essence" of the young man's beauty and identity is to be understood primarily (albeit counter-intuitively for 21st-century readers) to the theological and Platonic sense of the word, to the nonmaterial, to that which transcends matter. Far from indicating the kernel of the young man's identity – that is, a denser, more concentrated form of matter – the "substance" in fact refers to the young man's liquid assets: both to seminal fluid and to the fluidity of money. In this sense, far from being of a totally different order from biological "substance" (seminal "stuff," "self-substantial fuel" [1. 6]) the pervasive financial language of the sonnets in fact shares the vital propensity for duplication and increase, the enactment of the biblical injunction to "increase and multiply."

Financial Time

In the sonnets, as in banking and husbandry, time the destroyer is paradoxically the medium of "number," that is, of accumulation, propagation, and increase. The contents of sonnet 5's vial in sonnet 6 ("Then let not winters wragged hand deface, / In thee thy summer ere thou be distil'd" [ll. 1–2]) assume the less archaic connotations of storage as a hedge against dearth by the second quatrain, and take on a more familiar financial figuration:

> That's for thy self to breed another thee,
> Or ten times happier be it ten for one,
> Ten times thy self were happier than thou art,
> If ten of thine ten times refigured thee
> (ll. 7–10)

Sonnet 6 is careful not to urge violation of the Christian prohibition on usury: "That use is not forbidden usury, / Which happies those that pay the willing loan" (ll. 5–6). Rather, the poet argues that this form of self-preservation is not ethically opprobrious hoarding but morally commendable thrift. The young man is urged not so much to enjoy his own blossoming, or to seize the day (*carpe diem*), as to have himself put into storage and preserved immediately for use at the onset of winter.

With Shakespeare, we move from the Petrarchan formula of love, interminable desire, dissatisfaction, and deferral to the experience of love as a more specifically material form of deprivation, as dearth, "making a famine where abundance lies" (1. 7). A rash of bad harvests in the 1590s made famine more than a poetic metaphor. The threat of starvation was in fact very real, especially when hoarders forced up the price of grain. Faced with such parlous conditions, the Queen's Council cracked down on hoarding and grain speculation in Stratford in 1598, when Shakespeare himself was found to have the rather copious supply of eighty bushels. Indeed, the prospect of popular insurrection in the face of such manufactured dearth seems to have made Shakespeare change his investment strategies in his home town.[22]

Throughout the sonnets, the poet is keen both to elucidate the differences between hoarding (self-preservation that disregards the needs of others) and thrift (the practical measures that permit survival in seasons of dearth) and to condemn idle profligacy, "wast" or "ruining" (125. 4). Crucially, however, what is being saved and squandered here is not food or money but life itself, which is diminished, atrophied, and depleted by the wastrel, Time: "the chronicle of wasted time" (106. 1); "wasteful time" (15. 11); "among the wastes of time" (12. 10).

Saving Time

In the sonnets, the young man's attempts to preserve the integrity of the self, just like those of Shakespeare's Adonis in *Venus and Adonis*, do not reckon on impending mortality and constitute a form of miserliness. (If there were time to grow into ripeness, Adonis's arguments against sexual congress with Venus might make more sense; but of course, Adonis will be dead even before the morning hunt is over.) There is a further word which Shakespeare and Sidney (from whom, as we have seen, Shakespeare borrowed his image of distillation), have in common: "niggard" ("niggard truth," 72. 8; "beauteous niggard," 4. 5), or in Shakespeare's first sonnet "niggarding" (hoarding):

> And, tender churl, mak'st waste in niggarding:
> Pity the world, or else this glutton be,
> To eat the world's due, by the grave and thee.
> (1. 12–14)

Like the "hungry ocean" of sonnet 64 (l. 5), the gluttonous young man is linked to the notion of devouring time, Ovid's *tempus edax rerum*.[23] "Niggarding" (or the adjectival form "niggardly") suggests hoarding or parsimony. As Stephen Booth points out, because "churl" was used as a synonym for miser, the "tender churl" of line 12 "embodies suggestion of another oxymoron: generous miser."[24] In Sidney, the word comes up in the "Second Song" of *Astrophel and Stella* in a similarly oxymoronic sense: "Giving frankly niggard No," in other words very freely giving rejection, and thus not giving at all. This is certainly the sense – an indictment of greed – that "churl" has in *Romeo and Juliet*, when Juliet sees the poison drunk by Romeo: "O churl! – drunk all, and left no friendly drop / To help me after? (V. iii. 163–4).[25] In *As You Like It*, the word comes up when a note of the harsh economic realities of life intrudes hard upon the heels of the pastoral dialogue between Corin and Silvius, the shepherds who represent respectively youth and age. Corin tells the disguised Rosalind that he cannot assist the travel-weary Celia: "My master is of churlish disposition, / And little recks to find the way to heaven / By doing deeds of hospitality" (II. iv. 80–2). In other words, Corin's master has not made the requisite investment in the future that was characteristic of medieval Catholicism. Celia immediately revives at the prospect of such a charming rural retreat and uses language that echoes something of the tenor of the sonnets when she tells the homely shepherd: "we will mend thy wages. I like this place, / And willingly could *waste* my time in it" (II. iv. 94–5, emphasis added).

"Waste" here connotes "spend" rather than "squander," but it suggests again an aristocratic leisure that the moral voice of the sonnets unquestionably despises, and it resonates also with the paranomasic sense of "waste" invoked in relation to the dark mistress, the notorious "waste" in the first line of sonnet 129: "Th'expense of spirit in a waste of shame." The connection here is not primarily a pun on "waist," on female anatomy, as several critics have suggested, but with profligacy, with the misspending of emotional and seminal (potentially reproductive) energy.[26]

In Sidney's "Fourth Song," while everyone else is in bed, including Stella's mother who thinks she is up writing letters, Astrophel tries to seduce Stella, but, as usual, to no avail, despite the Sidneian iteration of the *carpe diem* theme:

> That you heard was but a mouse;
> Dumb sleep holdeth all the house;
> Yet, asleep, methinks they say,
> Young folks, take time while you may:
> Take me to thee, and thee to me.
> "No, no, no, no, my dear, let be."
> *Niggard Time* threats, if we miss
> This large offere of our bliss,
> Long stay ere he grant the same.[27]

It is not so much time itself as opportunity and occasion to consummate desire that is scarce here, and the scarcity is generated principally by Stella in the role of the Petrarchan lady.

Readers have long recognized that time is the key theme of the sonnets, but for all that it has been addressed more as an abstract category rather than as an integral part of the fabric through which these poems were composed. Time hacks away with a demented speed and fury that registers the shaping pressures of the conditions in which Shakespeare's poems were composed. This goes against of some of our most deeply held ideas about the act of lyrical composition. We "mystify" such a process, perhaps, in an attempt to account for the aesthetic mysteries that are the sonnets themselves. Be that as it may, as Jonathan Bate points out, "Shakespeare was not a Romantic poet who just sat down and wrote a sonnet when he felt one coming on"[28] – which is not to say that the reverse is true and that Shakespeare cranked out poems to order. Rather, Shakespeare always wrote for an audience – in the most literal sense when he wrote for the theater and his company's aristocratic patrons, and for patronage in the narrower sense when he wrote *Lucrece* and *Venus and Adonis* for Henry Wriothesley, third Earl of Southampton. We have no evidence whatsoever that Shakespeare ever "just wrote," that is to say that he ever wrote outside the financial and cultural context of clientage.[29] Cryptic though the dedication of the sonnets may be, "the onlie begetter of these insuing sonnets" bespeaks composition as much as publication (and, since the poem is begotten of the patron, metaphoric paternity) within the system of patronage, even if the specific networks of connections and relationships that apply in this particular instance have now become obscure to us. Crucially, writing for patronage meant that there were constraints and pressures, specifically those of time and occasion, surrounding Shakespeare's poetic production. It is certainly the case that his sonnets are irredeemably shaped by the context of a very different world from that of his courtly predecessors, namely the pressured world of urban life, a world where love often has a cash equivalent, and where *tempus fugit*, but not as it did in classical and medieval precedent, as a reminder of the ephemerality of human life, but with a pace that overwhelms the natural temporal rhythms of human reproduction to require a mechanical one: "Thou shouldst print more, not let that coppy die" (11. 14).

The contouring pressures of patronage are everywhere in the sonnets' rendition of temporality. The organizing principle of the 1609 quarto is far from arbitrary, and while it is arguable whether the arrangement of the volume constitutes a narrative, it is beyond doubt that there is a coherent pattern of tone, pace, and tempo. While the sonnets may or may not describe relationships synonymous with those in Shakespeare's own life, it is certainly the case that the first 126 poems addressed to the young man resonate with the life of an author who struggled to get even a coat of arms and was ridiculed for it when he did (Ben Jonson famously rendered *non sans droit* as "not without mustard"), and who entered the sonnet tradition, then, from a very different vantage point from that of his aristocratic predecessors. That is, the powerful demands upon the poet's labor, his attention, his energy, and – crucially – *his time* exerted by patronage are to be found in the aggressive impatience, intensity, and concentration that so often characterize Shakespeare's sonnets: determined, energetic exercises in assuming personal initiative in relation to their addressee, nowhere more evidently than in the poet's badgering the young man to reproduce in the opening poems.

> Being your slave what should I do but tend
> Upon the hours, and times of your desire?
> I have no precious time at all to spend;
> Nor services to do, till you require.
> Nor dare I chide the world without end hour,
> Whilst I, my sovereign, watch the clock for you.
>
> (57. 1–6)

The life of "service" is precisely that of attentive waiting (albeit resentfully) on the will and pleasure of a social superior. Jonathan Bate points out: "The sonnets could accordingly be read as a plea to the fair youth to share his bounty in material ways, not least by reciprocally 'inriching' the industrious sonneteer who is celebrating the adornments."[30]

Winter

Shakespeare, writing a decade later than Sidney and working over his verse at the beginning of the seventeenth century, represents a marvelously unapologetic deviation from aristocratic Petrarchanism. Peter Herman has for this reason aptly described these poems as the "embourgeoisement" of the sonnet form,[31] although for him sonnets necessarily "exemplify the reduction of human subjects to the status of things" that occurs when the marketplace governs human relationships.[32] In the sonnets' stress on the way time diminishes or ruins beauty and finally extinguishes existence altogether, however, they also demonstrate Ovidian transformation, which, as we have seen, involves the attrition or instantaneous reduction of human life to an inert or gravely diminished form of existence.

> Then ugly winter last
> Like age steales on with trembling steppes, all bald, or overcast
> With shirle thinne heare as whyght as snowe. Our bodies also ay
> Doo alter still from tyme to tyme, and never stand at stay.
> We shall not be the same wee were today or yisterday.
>
> (*Metamorphoses*, trans. Golding, XV. 228–38)

Shakespeare is Golding's Ovid at speed. In Shakespeare's sonnets, there is no sweet season that can evade the confrontation with winter; and we are a world away from Petrarch, whose encounter with Laura and Cupid metamorphoses him into the evergreen laurel, which, as he reminds us in canzone 23, "foglia non perde," does not lose its leaves in winter.

AUTHOR'S NOTE

I am indebted to Heather James for her intellectual generosity and helpful suggestions on my argument.

NOTES

1   For Petrarch and the early humanists, solitude – albeit solitude witnessed by an audience – was a precondition of self-understanding. As Brian Stock observes, this involved a shift "from the town to the countryside, from the business of life to inward and calm reflectiveness." Petrarch is "not a hermit: he admits a companion or two, provided that he can retreat into a private meditative realm alone in order to write": Brian Stock, *After Augustine: The Meditative Reader and the Text* (Philadelphia: University of Pennsylvania Press, 2001), 80.

2   See e.g. William J. Kennedy, *Authorizing Petrarch* (Ithaca, NY: Cornell University Press, 1994), 228.

3   Francis Petrarch, *The Canzoniere or Rerum Vulgarium Fragmenta*, trans. with notes and commentary by Mark Musa (Bloomington: Indiana University Press, 1996), 532.

4   Musa cites this as "a matter of general agreement": Petrarch, *The Canzoniere*, 522.

5   In canzone 6, the urgency of desire, likened to a galloping horse, is attached to Ovidian allusions about flight and pursuit.

6   Christ, the Messiah whose coming was so long awaited by the Jews of the Old Testament, must endure suffering and death in order to secure humanity's salvation, and his disciples must wait for the second coming.

7   Stock, *After Augustine*, 75.

8   Ovid, *Metamorphoses*, trans. Charles Martin (New York: Norton, 2005), xxiv.

9   Ovid, *Metamorphoses: The Arthur Golding Translation of 1567*, ed. John Frederick Nims (Philadelphia, Pa.: Paul Dry Books, 2000; first publ. 1969), xviii.

10   Horace, *Odes*, I. 4.

11   See Lynne Enterline, *The Rhetoric of the Body from Ovid to Shakespeare* (Cambridge, UK: Cambridge University Press, 2000), 32.

12   J. B. Leishman has argued that there are no *carpe diem* pleas in Shakespeare's sonnets; but, on the contrary, the poet is incessantly enjoining the young man to "seize the day." See J. B. Leishman, *Themes and Variations in Shakespeare's Sonnets* (New York: Harper & Row, 1963; first publ. 1961), 99.

13   William Shakespeare, *The Sonnets and A Lover's Complaint*, ed. John Kerrigan (Harmondsworth: Penguin, 1995; first publ. 1986), 34.

14   David Norbrook and H. R. Woudhuysen, eds., *Penguin Book of Renaissance Verse* (Harmondsworth: Penguin, 1992), 221.

15   Stephen Booth, *An Essay on Shakespeare's Sonnets* (New Haven: Yale University Press, 1971; first publ. 1969), 75.

16   Park Honan, *Shakespeare: A Life* (Oxford: Oxford University Press, 1998), 172.

17   Quoted in Wendy Wall, *Staging Domesticity: Household Work and English Identity in Early Modern Drama* (Cambridge, UK: Cambridge University Press, 2002), 119; Peggy Muñoz Simonds, "Sex in a Bottle: The Alchemical Distillation of Shakespeare's Hermaphrodite in Sonnet 20," *Renaissance Papers* 1999, 97–105.

18   Other critics have seen the poet as more the alchemist than the housewife and have pursued the idea that the glass container is analogous to the sonnet itself. See e.g. Richard Halpern, *Shakespeare's Perfume: Sodomy and Sublimity in the Sonnets, Wilde, Freud, and Lacan* (Philadelphia: University of Pennsylvannia Press, 2002), 14; Helen Vendler, *The Art of Shakespeare's Sonnets* (Cambridge, Mass.: Harvard University Press, 1997), 67.

19   Malcolm Jones, "'Such pretty things would soon be gone': The Neglected Genres of Popular Verse, 1480–1650," in Michael Hattaway (ed.), *A Companion to English Renaissance Literature and Culture* (Oxford:

Blackwell, 2002), 442–63; Thomas M. Greene, *The Vulnerable Text: Essays on Renaissance Literature* (New York: Columbia University Press, 1986), 176.

20 Sir Philip Sidney's *New Arcadia* (1590), quoted in *Sonnets*, ed. Kerrigan, 178.

21 Thomas M. Greene notes that "a terrible fear of cosmic destitution overshadows the husbandry of the procreation sonnets": *The Vulnerable Text*, 178.

22 Honan, *Shakespeare*, 240.

23 Leishman, *Themes and Variations*, 95.

24 *Shakespeare's Sonnets*, ed. Stephen Booth (New Haven: Yale University Press, 1977), 136.

25 Miles Coverdale's translation of Isaiah also conjoins the words "niggard" and "churl": "Then shall the niggard be no more called gentle, nor the churl liberal" (32: 5). See William Shakespeare, *The Complete Sonnets and Poems*, ed. Colin Burrow (Oxford: Oxford University Press, 2002; Oxford World's Classics), 382.

26 Similarly, in *Julius Caesar*: "The deep of night is crept upon our talk, / And nature must obey necessity, / Which we will niggard with a little rest" (IV. iii. 226–8). The sense here is that of stinting one's rest, a grudging minimum.

27 Emphasis added.

28 Jonathan Bate, *The Genius of Shakespeare* (New York: Oxford University Press, 1998), 38.

29 For a brilliant extrapolation of this fact see Lukas Erne, *Shakespeare as Literary Dramatist* (Cambridge, UK: Cambridge University Press, 2003).

30 Jonathan Bate, *Shakespeare and Ovid* (Oxford: Clarendon, 1993), 98.

31 Peter Herman, "What's the Use? Or, the Problematic of Economy in Shakespeare's Procreation Sonnets," in James Schiffer (ed.), *Shakespeare's Sonnets: Critical Essays* (New York: Garland, 1999), 264.

32 Ibid.

PART III
Editorial Theory and Biographical Inquiry: Editing the Sonnets

8

Shake-speares Sonnets, Shakespeare's Sonnets, and Shakespearean Biography

Richard Dutton

> When the legend becomes fact, print the legend.
> *The Man Who Shot Liberty Valence* (1962)

John Ford's infamous dictum about the American West aptly characterizes the way many biographers have approached Shakespeare's sonnets, about which there have always been far more myths than facts.[1] My subject here is how recent biographers have repeatedly printed the legend (or rather, variations on several myths) in their attempts to read the sonnets into the poet's life, or the life into his sonnets. "Myth" here is meant to be a neutral term, denoting a narrative for which we have no empirical evidence: it is for you, gentle reader, to decide what myths are more plausible than others. I have rarely attempted to identify where particular myths originated, a topic that would take up at least an essay of its own: my focus has been on how they have been deployed, revised, discarded or resurrected.

The new *Oxford Dictionary of National Biography* points up differences between biographical treatment of the sonnets a century ago and today. Sir Sidney Lee in the 1897 *DNB* was discretion itself: "While Shakespeare's poems bear traces of personal emotion and are coloured by personal experience, they seem to have been to a large extent undertaken as a literary exercise" (p. 1301). He concedes that in the dark lady sonnets "a more personal note is struck" (p. 1302), but is unwilling to inquire about the biographical urge behind it. The Earl of Southampton is nominated as the likeliest "fair youth," since he is known in other contexts to have been Shakespeare's patron – a role identified in the sonnets; but there speculation ends. Lee was, of course, treading on hot coals. Oscar Wilde's risqué *Portrait of Mr W.H.* (1889) had identified the dedicatee of the poems, and the "fair youth," with one Willie Hughes, an androgynously attractive boy actor; when Wilde himself was convicted of homosexuality the book became positively scandalous. That was Lee's Scylla; his Charybdis was the unavoidable fact that, if any dark lady existed at all, she was certainly not the national poet's wife. The sonnets as a "literary exercise" is a masterly stroke for averting prurient minds.[2]

In our own time Peter Holland has no qualms about calling a spade a spade. He acknowledges that the sonnets may be purely works of fiction: "Shakespeare, the consummate dramatist, may of course be constructing a drama set out in sonnets without any real figures behind it, but if the poems do tell of events in Shakespeare's life the identities of the participants come to matter greatly."[3] While arguing that all attempts to identify the "rival poet" and dark lady have been unconvincing, he offers a clear and considered preference for William Herbert, third Earl of Pembroke, as the W.H. of the dedication and the "fair youth." (As I suggest later, this reflects a recent alteration to a consensus which had all but settled on Southampton.) And he is much more forthcoming about the personal feelings betrayed by the sonnets, whomever they addressed: "Their explicit homoeroticism suggests that Shakespeare's sexuality was consciously bisexual in its desires, though the modern concept of bisexuality and one appropriate to Shakespeare's lifetime may be significantly different." He also suggests that they "make plain that fidelity to Anne [Hathaway] was not something Shakespeare was much concerned about, though adulterous sex with the 'dark lady' induced deep shame." Note that, by this point, the hypothetical "consummate dramatist" has been subsumed by a flesh-and-blood confessional poet, who had bisexual desires and adulterous sex – a rhetorical elision that goes with the territory of Shakespeare's biography.

Both Lee and Holland were finely attuned to debates about the sonnets current in their day, and what they might (or might not) be said to tell us about the man who wrote them. I shall not trace the whole evolution of thought between them, but pick up the story at a critically illuminating moment: the early 1970s. Even then I cannot pretend to be comprehensive. The impossibility of writing Shakespeare's biography has not prevented a great many people (including yours truly) from trying. It would not be feasible to do justice to them all or even to draw meaningful circles around what constitutes biography. My yardstick for inclusion here, a feebly subjective one, is the illuminating intervention – those formulations that allow us, for good or ill, to see life–text relations between Shakespeare and the sonnets in a newly productive light. (If a few examples fall short of that standard, they may help to keep the others in perspective.)

The 1970s

Little escaped the political and sexual revolutions of the 1960s unscathed, and Shakespeare was no exception – though in his case it took time for the political to catch up with the sexual. Written shortly after the obscenity trial of *Lady Chatterley's Lover*, Anthony Burgess's novel *Nothing Like the Sun* (1964) pointed the way forward, typically mingling bawdry with Freud and philosophy. As the *New York Times* reviewer put it, his implicit thesis was that "Shakespeare's talent had its origins in his sexual drives . . . his topless towers of words were founded on his immense desire and will."[4] When Burgess then wrote a popular biography, he kept his imagination in check, but similar emphases emerged. He writes with a breezy iconoclasm, sweeping aside any

Lee-style fig-leaf that the sonnets are merely patronage-work: "There is a measure of convention in the Sonnets . . . but the characters are real people and the emotions unfeigned . . . Will would not be shocked by evidence of homosexuality: he may have been inclined to it himself: he was, after all, a member of the theatrical profession" (Burgess 1970: 127–8). But heterosexual passion, as in the novel, looms much larger: "It was about this time [1594/5] that he was heavily in love. Anne in Stratford was forgotten or, if remembered, remembered guiltily; his affections were centered on a lady cultivated enough to play the virginals . . ." (p. 145). He inventively speculates about whether the "darkness" of the lady relates only to hair and eyes or whether she was actually black. This is clearly of more interest to him than who she might have been: "There have been many candidates or, to be pedantic, nigrates" (p. 146). But, in the end, the creative artist in him prefers not to know: "It is best to keep the Dark Lady anonymous, even composite . . . Shakespeare was no John Keats mooning over Fanny Brawne, but a realist aware of self-division, the tugging of the black and the white spirits, and the irresistible lure of the primal darkness that resides in all women, whether white or black" (p. 148).

In 1967 the law in Britain decriminalized homosexual acts between consenting males over twenty-one. The following year the historian G. P. V. Akrigg published the first extended study of Shakespeare's only known literary patron, the Earl of Southampton, who he had no doubt was the "fair youth" of the sonnets. The law in Britain was one thing (Akrigg was Canadian), but he did not see this as a relationship that Shakespeare could have been comfortable with, however deep the passion:

> Let Southampton be identified as the sonnet Friend, and a flood of light is cast upon the basic relationship between poet and patron. To most contemporaries who were aware of the connection, it probably seemed a squalid association between a libertine young aristocrat and a player with a homosexual bias. Shakespeare himself was aware of how sordid the whole affair must appear . . . One is forced to suspect that some element of homosexuality lay at the root of the trouble . . . The love which he felt for Southampton may well have been the most intense emotion of his life. (Akrigg 1968: 236–7)

Unlike Burgess, Akrigg clearly did not glory in the dark waters of Shakespeare's sexuality: "It is difficult to conceive of some of these sonnets being handed to the Earl of Southampton as it is to imagine some of the Dark Lady sonnets being given to that lady . . . Probably Shakespeare put many of his sonnets in some private drawer" (p. 239).

Despite these reticences, Akrigg's book contributed to a decisive shift that established Southampton as virtually the default candidate for the "fair youth" for almost thirty years and his patronage as critical to their understanding. A very different contributor to this shift was another historian, A. L. Rowse. Rowse, a tireless and tiresome blower of his own trumpet, wrote *William Shakespeare: A Biography* in 1963. In this he ridiculed the undisciplined speculation of literary scholars: "All kinds of wild-cat notions have been proposed as to the identity of the Dark Lady. In fact we do not know, and are never likely to know, who she was" (1963: 197). Within a year, however, he began a one-man industry in Shakespeare's sonnets (see References and Further Reading below), based on his utter conviction that he had identified the unidentifiable in Emilia Lanier (or Aemilia Lanyer), *née* Bassano, born of a notable musical family, one-time mistress of Lord Hunsdon (Lord Chamberlain and patron of the first actors with whom we can associate Shakespeare) and one of the earliest women to publish poetry in England.

This conviction was integrated into a biography in *Shakespeare the Man* (1973). Rowse starts modestly enough:

> With a full knowledge of the age and the conditions in which Shakespeare lived and wrote, I have been able to reduce the unnecessary confusion to order and make sense of both life and work, with unanswerable certainty. As an Elizabethan historian I have been able to settle once and for all the dating of the sonnets . . . In short, we now have the definitive biography of the greatest writer, all confusions cleared up and problems settled. (Rowse 1973: x)

Among these "confusions," Rowse also saw patronage as critical, and Southampton as the patron: "It is pitiable that people should not have perceived that the sonnets are sonnets of duty from the poet to his patron, from beginning to end, obvious throughout and evident in many of the sonnets individually . . . one sees that the poet–patron relationship is fundamental, the basis of the whole thing" (pp. 56–7). He differs profoundly from Akrigg, however, in his sense of the nature of that relationship: "The high flown language was in keeping, the terms of endearment not going beyond the bounds of affection and decorum. For, make no mistake about this, Shakespeare's interest in the youth is not at all sexual – as Marlowe's or Bacon's might have been: that was clean contrary to Shakespeare's highly heterosexual nature" (p. 58). Rowse's conviction on this point remained unshaken to his death, which is odd, not least because he himself was widely understood to be homosexual and wrote openly about writers like Marlowe and Wilde. But Shakespeare for him was always unimpeachably heterosexual.

On the other hand, heterosexuality does not emerge here as an unmixed blessing: "The poet, with his sensitive nature, his extreme susceptibility to women, was abnormally vulnerable" (Rowse 1973: 72) – unlike, apparently, Southampton. "Towards the end of 1592 a serious complication had entered the relationship to endanger it. The snake had already entered Paradise, and destroyed its pristine innocence, with a woman" (p. 74). Hardly an auspicious entrance for Lanier. Rowse had encountered her in the records of the astrologer and quack physician Simon Forman, to whom Lanier confided some of her history. But Forman never actually mentions either Shakespeare or Southampton, despite Rowse's blustering that "[w]hat he tells us completely corroborates what Shakespeare tells us in the Sonnets . . . dates and respective ages fill out and confirm the story" (p. 95). This includes the fact that Hunsdon gave her up when she became pregnant in 1592, marrying her off to Alfonso Lanier, with whom she may not therefore have been close. She certainly came from a musical family – her husband was also a court musician; and the Italian Jewish descent made dark features likely enough.

Many have found Emilia Lanier a plausible candidate for the dark lady, but hardly the *necessary* one Rowse insists upon. The fact that her book of verse, *Salve Deus Rex Judaeorum*, with a preface trenchantly defending the virtue of women, appeared in the same year as the *Sonnets*, is an intriguing additional angle. Rowse in fact lessens his own case by insisting on a very precise and narrow dating of the sonnets to 1591–4. This largely concurs with one of the great myths: that Shakespeare wrote the sonnets, along with *Venus and Adonis* and *Lucrece*, when he was prevented from working in the theater by the prolonged plague of 1592–3. (In some versions, Southampton's patronage is construed as very much second best to writing for the stage, to which he returned with alacrity when the plague relented.)

Rowse is less interested in Shakespeare's theatrical leanings than in his own prowess as a historian: "We are still in the year 1592, for Sonnet 25 has a transparent reference to the fall of Sir Walter Ralegh from the Queen's favour . . ." (1973: 62). (That courtier after courtier made the same fall, for the same reasons, does not trouble his convictions.) Most critically, Rowse insists that "The mortal moon hath her eclipse endured" (107. 5), refers to Elizabeth I's deliverance from the Lopez plot of 1594. Akrigg followed earlier speculation that this relates to Elizabeth's *death* in 1603, while "this most balmy time" refers to James I's peaceful succession and Southampton's release from the Tower, where he had been since the 1601 Essex rebellion. This of course suggests that Shakespeare's relations with Southampton extended long after *Lucrece*, and with them the writing of the sonnets, which Rowse will not credit. Others, yet again, make "mortal moon" refer to Elizabeth's "climacteric" or sixty-third year, 1596 (see Burgess 1970: 128), where it conveniently serve the causes of either Southampton or Pembroke. Nothing better demonstrates how little we know for certain about the sonnets, and how inventive biographers are in either ignoring or disguising the fact.

No one recognized this better than Samuel Schoenbaum, whose wry, even-handed skepticism in *William Shakespeare: A Documentary Life* (1975; better known and quoted here in its 1977 *Compact* version) made it the most reliable Shakespeare biography of its era. His introduction sets the tone: "The *Sonnets* especially have invited biographical license. These are often entertaining, and sometimes instructive, but to my mind they enhance the place for a convenient narrative bringing together in up-to-date fashion all that we really know about Shakespeare, as revealed by the records," throwing in that "I have no new Dark Lady to offer a transiently curious world" (Schoenbaum 1977: viii). In that spirit he scrupulously records plausible candidates for the various *personae*, and has fun with the puzzles posed by Thomas Thorpe's dedication on the title-page of the 1609 quarto. He even resists plumbing individual sonnets for dating purposes, noting that "the ambiguous language of poetry resists the fragile certitude of interpreters" (p. 180).

He does not, however, carry even-handedness to the point of utter impartiality:

Southampton now [after *Lucrece*] departs from the biographical record. He does not, however, drop out of speculation. Many commentators, perhaps a majority, believe that the Earl is the Fair Youth urged to marry and propagate in the *Sonnets*, and there immortalized by the poet who addresses him in the extravagant terms of Renaissance male friendship. The object of his devotion, the Master-Mistress of the sonneteer's passion, has "a woman's face" but (worse luck for his heterosexual celebrant) a man's phallus [alluding to sonnet 20]. (p. 179)

So he does not endorse the Southampton case outright, but (oddly, because his personal instincts favored Pembroke) comes as close to it as makes little difference; and he deftly saves Shakespeare for the heterosexual camp. (Burgess aside, most people in the 1970s seemed to think of sexuality in either/or terms.) Even so, he is sufficiently disturbed by the content of the poems to suggest that "All the signs point to unauthorized publication" (Schoenbaum 1977: 268), a long-established proposition – Rowse concurs: "published by Thorp in 1609 (never by Shakespeare)" (1973: 98) – that was not to be challenged for another decade. It would be churlish to deny Schoenbaum the pat on the back he offers himself: "All the riddles of the *Sonnets* – date, dedication, sequence, identity of the *dramatis personae* – elude solution, while at the same time teasing speculation. This writer takes satisfaction on having no theories of his own to offer" (1977: 271). But it is not strictly true. Even he implicitly endorses some of the myths. What he actually offers is not absolute objectivity but something as close as we are ever likely to see to a consensual reading, determined by the prevailing scholarly wisdom of his era.

Lastly in the 1970s, a straw in a different wind was M. C. Bradbrook's *Shakespeare: The Poet in His World*. Throughout the twentieth century Shakespeare was acknowledged as a poet of the theater. But many of his admirers found the actualities of professional theater (ancient and modern) rather distasteful, and shaded him from it as much as possible. For some, that changed decisively in the last quarter of the century, when the idea of Shakespeare as a *professional* – a man with marketable skills, who worked for money – became widely acceptable, not least to those who wanted to rescue him from an elitist mystique, perhaps even reclaim him as a man of the people. This was also consonant with the editorial revolution (epitomized by the Wells–Taylor *Oxford Shakespeare* of 1986) which gave greater priority to the theatrical provenance of play texts than ever before.

Dame Muriel Bradbrook was hardly a populist, but her lack of interest in the non-dramatic poetry is almost palpable. Her view of the sonnets mythology is flagged in the preface to her *Shakespeare*, where she facetiously proposes Richard Burbage's wife, Winifred, as the dark lady: this "has the double advantage of novelty and plausibility. The lady was dark, musical and married – this is the sum of our direct information. Mrs Burbage's Christian name is Welsh; the Welsh are almost invariably dark and musical and not infrequently married" (p. ix). This snubs traditional biographers, who felt duty-bound to nominate a dark lady (preferably a fresh one), and in particular Rowse. It also betrays a deeper lack of interest in this side of Shakespeare's career. Bradbrook dutifully traces the sonnets in the tradition of courtly patronage verse; but it is all rather half-hearted, because she felt Shakespeare's own heart was not in it: "Yet the stage, evidently, was what Shakespeare chose, before anything else, before the beauty of his beloved youth or the beauty of the countryside" (p. 110). When she comes to the publication of the sonnets – "apparently without the consent of Shakespeare and his patron" – its interest lies in a possible connection to his writing of the death of Cleopatra: "The appearance of the *Sonnets*, unexpected, unwelcome, must have touched off memories" (pp. 214, 215). The poet was distinctly giving way to the playwright.

The 1980s

Shakespearean biography in the 1980s did not add much to what had gone before.[5] Russell Fraser in *Young Shakespeare* assigns the sonnets to his youth and early career, echoing Bradbrook's conviction that they represent a side-tracking from his true calling as a dramatist. He does believe that they reveal something of Shakespeare's inner being (for example, he's a pessimist: Fraser 1988: 189), and waxes ecstatic at what he perceives as bisexuality: "An androgynous personality, he combined in himself both halves of Plato's sorb apple. Back in the beginning a jealous God cleft the apple. Wanting to diminish us, He reserved a plenary form for Himself. But Shakespeare gets around Him, and his sonnets, notably inclusive, throb with erotic longing, devoted impartially to a woman or a man" (p. 186). But the sonnets' significance, he suggests, was transient to Shakespeare and perhaps should be for us too: "With his world-famous book, Shakespeare most likely had nothing to do. Misprints disfigure it, much chaff in the wheat. One sonnet is too short, another too long, and the same couplet turns up twice. Deploring publication, Shakespeare otherwise ignored it. Perhaps he had forgotten all about his youthful effusions" (p. 187).

Conversely, Peter Levi in *The Life and Times of William Shakespeare* evinces little interest in Shakespeare the man-of-the-theater. A poet himself, he has an Arnoldian notion of poetry, feeling greatness infallibly on his own highly refined pulse. His reaction to the theory (first floated by Andrew Gurr and now widely accepted) that sonnet 145 puns on Anne Hathaway's name and so relates to her wooing, is typical:

> I would be pleased to disregard the pun, but the Sonnets do seem to contain other naming puns, all jejune to my mind. It was a game the Elizabethans liked to play. The unusual and light metre of this sonnet, combined with its trivial theme, might sway a reasonable critic to believe that the poem is early and the pun intended . . . I find it almost too tasteless to credit, but not quite. (Levi 1988: 40)

He applies the same Brahmin instincts to other myths. The sonnets "are the most thrilling and intimately deep poems in our language" (p. 93), and yet they must all have been written, and probably organized, by the year Shakespeare dedicated *Lucrece* (1594). He takes it as read that most of them were written to Southampton: "If they are not about Southampton they are about someone of the same nature and circumstances, but no one like that exists" (p. 111). (Pembroke?)

Confronted with a body of opinion that the sonnets discuss events as late as 1603, he confutes it thus: "Wise men agree that sonnet 107 must be about the death of the Queen ('The mortal Moon hath her eclipse endured'), the arrival of James I ('this most balmy time') and Southampton's emergence from prison, but I do not agree with them" (Levi 1988: 98). Why not? It would conflict with his settled conviction that "the Sonnets were written almost at the beginning of his life's work, probably before he was thirty. He was in love with Southampton, in love with love, in love with poetry and in love with life" (p. 100). Levi is thrilled by the sonnets, but assumes that Shakespeare abandoned them early in life, to pursue (he implies) a lesser career on the stage.

Moreover, he finds it difficult to put into words quite what he means by "love" in this context: "Shakespeare and Southampton were not complete lovers, and the Sonnets are not about buggery" (Levi 1988: 100). He endeavors to identify Shakespeare's heterosexual credentials, mainly in *Venus and Adonis* and "A Lover's Complaint," whose "girls" he describes as "a tribute to his wife, who taught him some degree of humorous tenderness towards women which one would not learn from Ovid" (p. 53). The Sonnets themselves are tainted with adultery, which he also finds uncomfortable and blames on the dark lady, whom he would prefer to think of as entirely fictitious; failing that he will settle for Emilia Lanier, who can be blamed for being "no better than she should be" (p. xix). But all in all, the Sonnets are beside the point in respect of Shakespeare's deepest feelings: "And love? I think he loved his wife and children" (p. 101). He also clings to the myth that the 1609 edition was pirated: "the text it prints was certainly not supervised nor, I believe, authorised by Shakespeare" (p. 94). What Levi leaves out is any real reason why this family-loving Shakespeare, whose "fair youth" sonnets do not betoken buggery and whose dark lady ones may well be fictional, should be embarrassed by the publication. All in all, Levi is one of those whose enthusiasm for Shakespeare outstrips their qualifications to write coherently about his life.

The 1990s and 2000s

If the 1980s were a disappointment, the 1990s and early 2000s have been a Golden Age in Shakespearean biography, to which I shall hardly do justice.[6] Peter Thomson carried the trend we have seen in Bradbrook and Fraser to a logical conclusion. *Shakespeare's Professional Career* devotes just nineteen lines to the sonnets, concluding: "If they tell a story at all, it is an old story. Shakespeare may have approved their publication in 1609, confident that the past was another country and the wenching dead, or he may have known nothing about it. The dominant view is that Thorpe went ahead without authorization" (Thomson 1992: 185–6). Thomson, a theater historian, assumes that the nondramatic verse has little or no role in Shakespeare's *professional career*, which has become by definition the career in the theater. Even the patronage relations which fostered that verse, construed by some as early modern professionalism in another mode (making money by your skill with a pen), barely warrant attention. Publication of the *Sonnets* is a career event (he leans to the myth of piracy, as if to suggest that Shakespeare's own priorities match his own), but the rest is unexplored silence.

Jonathan Bate's *The Genius of Shakespeare* is biography only within severe limits of its own devising. "Genius" here is the unique power of art rather than a mysterious force within its author; that of the sonnets is treated in relation to the origins of that power, and is associated with Shakespeare's patronage relations with Southampton. While not ruling out the possibility that Shakespeare later adapted the sonnets for Pembroke, Bate develops the most clinical argument yet that Southampton was the original recipient of at least the earliest ones, applying Occam's razor:

> Occam's estimable principle was that for purposes of explanation things not known to exist should not, unless absolutely necessary, be postulated as existing. *All candidatures for the fair youth with the exception of Southampton's depend on things not known to exist; it is not necessary to postulate any of these things as existing, since the origin of the sonnets can be explained with things we do know exist.* (Bate 1998: 47; emphasis in original)

He thus pursues known facts about Southampton, including reluctance to marry: "Once all these facts are collected, the case for Southampton as the original patron/youth looks irrefutable" (p. 49). Facts may be facts, but, as we repeatedly see with the sonnets, interpretation is sacred. Bate partly dates them in the years associated with Southampton's patronage by reading the sequence 110–12 (where Shakespeare hints "at the social stigma attached to the trade of acting": p. 19) as a riposte to Robert Greene's notorious attack on the "upstart crow" in *A Groatsworth of Wit* (fall 1592). This is plausible but still a myth. Ingeniously, he does not think – as most do – that the first seventeen poems urge Southampton to marry: that would be contrary to his patron's known wishes. They are, rather, a parody of other attempts to argue that case. From that base, and playing on the conventional mixed language of patronage and love (which flows so much easier to a "mistress" than to a "master"), Shakespeare is supposed to think himself more deeply into the suitor/master situation: "The sonnets are best thought of as *imaginings of potential situations which might have grown* from the initial Southampton situation" (p. 53, emphasis in original).

So even as Bate seems concerned to establish "facts," he is really more interested in the imaginative context from which the "genius" of the sonnets might derive. In that spirit he ventures into the muddy waters of the dark lady's identity. "I would like to propose that our understanding of the [dark lady] sonnets will be assisted if we suppose – not confidently assert – that they are tied to some rather sordid intrigue in the South-ampton household around 1593–4" (1998: 54). He never asserts that this "sordid intrigue" actually happened, only that our "understanding" will be assisted if we suppose it so. Playing on (unproven) speculation that John Florio, Southampton's lan-guage tutor, was Burghley's known spy in the household, Bate announces: "My dark lady, then, is John Florio's wife, who happens to have been the sister of Samuel Daniel, the sonneteer" (p. 56).

The intrigue thus becomes a revenge of sorts on Florio as spy and on Daniel as a rival poetic suitor (not that there is any evidence that Daniel sought service with South-ampton). It is imaginatively apt rather than biographically true, evoking from Bate this "confession": "I began work on the sonnets with a determination to adhere to an agnostic position on the question of their autobiographical elements. But . . . I have been unable to hold fast to my unbelief. The sonnets have wrought their magic upon me . . . Their genius is still at work" (Bate 1998: 58). In which spirit he offers a coda on Thorpe's "Mr W.H.," celebrating the imaginative appropriateness of its mystery, but finally – with a nod to both poststructuralist indeterminacy and the material history of the book – ascribing it to a printer's oversight: "Of all the candidates for the identity of Master W. H., the misprint [i.e. for W. S. or W. SH.] seems to me the strongest" (p. 63).

Park Honan's *Shakespeare: A Life* is a more sober biography, perhaps the most thorough – and would-be objective – since Schoenbaum's. He too is firmly in the Southampton camp: "Pembroke, of course, may have influenced the sonneteer at some point . . . But there is no sign that Shakespeare met the future earl in the 1590s" (Honan 1998: 181). He finds in the sonnets possible narrower contexts – he sees in 56, with its description of a distinctive estuary like that of the River Ribble, possible support for the Lancashire theory (revived by Ernst Honigmann) of Shakespeare's "lost years" as a "schoolmaster in the country"; he too looks at 110–12 in relation to Greene's attack on Shakespeare; he assumes 107 refers to Elizabeth's death and James's succession, but does not link it to Southampton's release (pp. 161–2; 69; 297). But the lowly poet/actor's experience of Southampton's aristocratic lifestyle is for Honan the core of the sonnets: "Imaginatively, it was as a leisurely sonnet-writer that Stratford's poet most nearly entered his patron's privileged, less mercenary world" (p. 180).

This has become very much a modern theme, sometimes associated with feelings of envy or inadequacy on Shakespeare's part. Garry O'Connor puts it bluntly: "Shakespeare was exploring seriously the idea of becoming more closely identified with a great nobleman's entourage and way of life – as opposed to being a playwright dependent on market forces – he was enumerating in the Sonnets, with great care, the self-hugging, or hoarding, qualities that such a path entailed" (2000: 111). James C. Humes, a former presidential speech-writer, who sees Shakespeare as "self-made" and a "businessman," helpfully translates this into US terms: "Today a young man coming to Washington might seek the help of his senator, or a senator his family knows. In Shakespeare's day the "Senate" was the House of Lords, and Shakespeare chose the young Southampton as the most likely candidate for his friend in Court . . . So Shakespeare sought to gain the attention of Southampton" (2003: 58). Stephen Greenblatt, too, who is only incidentally interested in the biographical actuality behind the sonnets, settles readily for Southampton as the "fair youth" but is really focused on the social tension explored in the poems: "The sonnets represent the poet and the young man as excited by the immense class and status difference between them. Even while slyly criticizing his beloved – or perhaps because he is slyly criticizing him – Shakespeare plays at utter subservience" (2004: 250).

And what of sexuality within Southampton's world? Greenblatt is relaxed about the biographical actualities; he assumes that *something* went on – "whether they only stared longingly at one another or embraced, kissed passionately, went to bed together" (2004: 253) – but remains focused on the "staged" account of things in the poems. Honan explores in detail Southampton's possible bisexual or homosexual inclinations. On

Shakespeare's own appetites, however, he remains coy: "The Sonnets show Shakespeare's understanding of homoerotic feeling" (1998: 177). He is equally uninterested in the "Dark Woman," calling her a "composite portrait" (p. 189), offering no suggestions as to her identity, if indeed she existed. What matters about the sonnets lies in another sphere: "Certainly these poems take us inside Shakespeare's mind, and the real importance of the Sonnets in his life is that they become a means of developing his artistic sensibility," thus contributing to "his stunning progress as a dramatist in the 1590s" (p. 185). So Honan tiptoes around whatever might be biographically risqué. Nevertheless, he assumes that the intimacy and bawdiness of their subject matter was sufficient to make Shakespeare reticent about sharing them, indeed that he "wrote sonnets over the years for private perusal" (p. 180). But if he shuns biographical speculation about the poems themselves, he indulges it in respect of the person he supposes Shakespeare least wanted to see them: "Shakespeare had kept his Sonnets out of print while [Mary Arden, his mother] lived. Eight months after she died they were registered for publication . . . The most tangled and contradictory of his relationships, one suspects, was always with his mother. His troubled attitudes to women are too deep to be of anything but early origin" (p. 358).

Alongside this mother-myth, Honan also unostentatiously develops one of the author ("a leisurely sonnet-writer") working on these poems for fifteen years or more, and so reinforcing his artistic development. He shows no interest in whether the attachment to Southampton might have lasted that long, but seems confident that Shakespeare himself was involved with the final publication: "Months of plague [in 1607–8] would have given him ample time to order his sonnets in small groups with two main sections, followed by an interlude in Sonnets 153 and 154, and *A Lover's Complaint*" (1998: 360). He is the first biographer of substance to buy into Katherine Duncan-Jones's 1983 argument, denying the myth that the *Sonnets* were unauthorized or suppressed: "There is no sign that *Shake-speares Sonnets* was later withdrawn from publication or that it appeared in irregular circumstances" (1998: 360). Indeed, on the contrary, he suggests that "there was a tactical advantage, for Shakespeare's actors, in having these elegant lyrics in print in London at a crucial time in 1609 [as they were trying to move into the Blackfriars theater, against the protests of local residents] . . . It would have helped to have *Shake-speares Sonnets* in print to testify to their poet's courtly refinement" (pp. 362–3). So the sonnets, oddly, were not fit for his mother's eyes, yet a testament to the elevated circles Shakespeare moved in.

Katherine Duncan-Jones's *Ungentle Shakespeare* and her 1997 Arden edition of the sonnets together constitute the most radical rethinking of the biographical context of the sonnets in many years, resurrecting – with a vengeance – the case for William Herbert (Pembroke) as both W.H. and the primary "fair youth." With Honan, she sees the poems as written over many years, and does not rule out Southampton as the first recipient of some. But she associates the bulk of them, and the quasi-biographical narrative of their 1609 arrangement, with Pembroke. Her arguments include: that the 1623 Folio was dedicated to Pembroke and his brother, though Southampton was still alive; that the Dark Lady–fair youth relationship fits what is known of Pembroke's sexual habits – promiscuous with women, though averse to marriage; that, as the son of Mary Sidney, Pembroke grew up in a rich tradition of literary patronage, and wealthy enough to patronize more writers than anyone else of his generation; that the most obvious connotation of "onlie begetter" (in Thorpe's dedication) is "inspirer"; that the address to "Master" W.H. is intelligible if it carries over from before he inherited the title (January 1601); that one of Pembroke's own poems seems to echo one of the sonnets. The list is impressive, but lacks a smoking gun such as the dedications of *Venus* and *Lucrece* to Southampton.

But it is the location of the Pembroke connection within Shakespeare's career that is most impressive in *Ungentle Shakespeare*, a work bent on removing the romantic gloss still attaching to The Bard. Duncan-Jones suggests "that Shakespeare was strongly interested in sexual relationships with well-born young men, while his sexual relations with women, conversely, may have been more functional than sentimental" (2001: xi), noting for example "the maleness of all Shakespeare's major patrons" (p. 130) in an era when many rivals courted female patrons like the Countesses of Pembroke and Bedford. And she rounds on perversely romantic misreadings of the sonnets:

> The *Sonnets* were the only texts that could conceivably be wrenched to provide some testimony to Shakespeare, grotesquely inappropriate though this was, as an adoring, and heterosexual, lover and love poet. The dedication to Mr W. H. had to be sidelined as entirely the quirk of Thomas Thorpe; the great majority of the sonnets themselves had to be ignored or re-assigned; and the closing sonnets had to be read as if they were sonnets of romantic love, not anatomies of sexual obsession and disgust. (p. 130)

Recounting sexual tittle-tattle from John Manningham's *Diary*, she suggests:

> Though eagerly promiscuous women . . . might be a regular sexual convenience for him, they did not provoke any deep emotions beyond feelings of resentment and dislike. "Will" passionately resents the power that the woman has to draw him into the morally polluting "hell" of lust (129. 14), and of her possibly infected body. Even more intensely he resents her capacity to foul up his relationship with a male friend, for it is in upwardly mobile male friendship that his deepest emotions are invested. (2001: 133)

The sonnets, then, reveal an ambitious, status-conscious man, deeply committed to a homosocial world of patronage which catered to his most private needs. He wrote no memorial for Elizabeth I, perhaps mourning neither her passing nor the courtly love poetry to which her reign gave rise:

> Shakespeare's evolving *Sonnets*, composed of a sophisticated male-on-male sequence and a misogynistic coda in which the speaker explicitly mocks all those courtly love poets who have belied their ugly mistress "with false compare", would be well-tuned to the coming times. In the famous 107, "Not mine owne fears", his speaker looks forward to an "endless age" of male friendship presided over by a king." (Duncan-Jones 2001: 160)

The whole scenario is quite different from that associated with the Southampton myth, where Shakespeare is usually characterized as young and at the beginning of his career. This moves him decisively to mid-life, an older man whose son, Hamnet, has recently died. Duncan-Jones sees the sonnets "evolving" well into the seventeenth century: 123 ("pyramids built up") and 125 ("I bore the canopy") perhaps discuss the Magnificent Entertainment which greeted James I on his plague-delayed entry into London in 1604 and offer "the clearest statement Shakespeare ever made of his political and religious position" (Duncan-Jones 2001: 216). The sonnets were also published with Shakespeare's blessing and dedication. The rival poet – commonly for Southamptonites a choice between Chapman and Marlowe – might be any of those who sought Herbert patronage, including Daniel, Chapman, and Jonson. The dark lady fades into unremarkable anonymity, "a woman too stupid to realize that she is being set up as the butt of [Shakespeare's] wit," as she is characterized in the edition (Duncan-Jones 1997: 48).

Recent though this assessment is, it has already been enthusiastically endorsed. Ernst Honigmann (2000) has written of Pembroke as the "first reader" of the sonnets, much as Bate envisages Southampton. He disagrees on details: he does not think the woman in the poems is "stupid," nor is he convinced that Shakespeare authorized the publication; and he makes his own case for Jonson as the rival poet. But in general he reinforces the case for Pembroke. So too does the most impressive of recent popular biographers, Michael Wood. His four-part documentary on Shakespeare, first aired on the BBC in Britain in 2003, was accompanied by a book of the same title, *In Search of Shakespeare*. Material about the sonnets in the films was perhaps lost on the cutting-house floor: they are only mentioned in a truncated sequence in Episode 3.

> [*Shot*] the Stratford burial register recording Hamnet's death; [*cut to*] the glories of the Herbert estate. [*Wood's voice-over*]: "The next spring Shakespeare got a commission from one of the great literary patrons, Lady Mary Herbert of Wilton. He was to write sonnets for the seventeenth birthday of one of her children . . .

. . . and with elegiac tones he reads the sonnets in the sunshine of Wilton's grounds – but never discusses what Pembroke's patronage might have meant (indeed, Pembroke is never personally identified) or even the dedication of the First Folio.

The book, however, is much fuller.[7] Wood claims sonnet 145 as Shakespeare's "first poem," and is more charitable to Anne Hathaway than many: "He was vulnerable. Anne was twenty-six and knew the world. Reading between the lines, she would be the rock on which he relied through his life, supporting his career in London" (Wood 1978: 87). Southampton is characterized as "literary, beautiful, bisexual, and from a Catholic dynasty," but this is not related to the sonnets (p. 147). Shakespeare's supposed Catholicism is an important part of Wood's thesis; but again it is not associated with the sonnets (the Herberts were Protestant), the psychological roots of which Wood locates in the death of Hamnet:

There is . . . compelling evidence to suggest his response to the death of his son in poems
he wrote soon afterwards. These poems describe the love for a beautiful boy, and
his passionate sexual affair with a married woman, both of which might be seen in
some sense as response to personal tragedy, especially perhaps in a middle-aged man.
(p. 166)

So Wood largely sidesteps the homoeroticism of the sonnets, changing Duncan-
Jones's emphasis by dwelling on father–son relationships, a paid job of work turning
into something altogether more personal: "there are strong reasons to think that Shakespeare used his poems as ways of getting things off his chest . . . if they are not autobiographical, it is hard to imagine what is" (p. 177). He acknowledges that after the
"first seventeen, the poems swiftly take on a passionate tone, as if to a lover," but always
qualifies the implication: "his love is absolute, intense, overwhelming, in the way a
father feels for a child" and so reads sonnet 33 ("Full many a glorious morning")
as "very adaptive, a kind of transference. It was a way of coping with crushing grief"
(pp. 182, 184, 185). Pembroke is consistently sidelined as a means to Shakespeare's very
private end.

Wood is, I think, the first to nominate Emilia Lanier as dark lady to Pembroke's
"fair youth." What recommends her to him is her own poetic achievement, about which
Rowse was at best equivocal; she is now "accepted in her own right; her poetry is taught
on university courses, published in modern editions" (p. 200). He sees her unconventional accomplishment as befitting Shakespeare's attention, and argues that her Jewish
ancestry might have influenced *The Merchant of Venice c.*1597.[8] He also hints at a
meaningful connection between the publication of her poems and that of the *Sonnets*:
"within a year, strangely enough, Emilia Lanier registered her own religious poems,
which would be prefaced with a cry from the heart about men's abuse of women"
(p. 306). On Shakespeare's own volume, he follows Duncan-Jones: "Despite many later
critics' prudish hopes that the sonnets were pirated, the current consensus is that they
were taken from Shakespeare's own manuscript and were published with his authorisa-
tion" (p. 305). "Current consensus" is an exaggeration, but the tide is certainly flowing
that way.

I conclude with an item from a different but overlapping tide, Patrick Cheney's
Shakespeare, National Poet-Playwright (2004). This is not properly biography, but a
rethinking of the nature and shape of Shakespeare's career, within which Cheney
asserts a biographical pattern of sorts, where the *Sonnets* have a key place. He argues
that the poet-playwright was a distinctive mode of sixteenth-century authorship, of
which the clearest classical antecedent was Ovid (author of the lost play *Medea*), and
with which Shakespeare's career conforms. His book "discusses all of the poems as a
corpus in its own right, and does so by not severing the poems from the plays, but
precisely by embedding them within Shakespeare's career as a playwright, actor, and
shareholder in a theatre company . . . Such a view does not reduce Shakespeare's production of poetry to an 'interlude' in the theatrical career" (Cheney 2004: 3–4). He is
particularly scathing about "one of the most stubborn yet unexamined staples of

Shakespearean biography, endlessly repeated yet rarely pursued: Shakespeare wrote *Venus, Lucrece,* and a draft of the Sonnets because the theaters closed due to plague in 1592–93" (p. 23; see also 63–4). He cites Colin Burrow on the likelihood of the sonnets having occupied Shakespeare throughout his career: " 'Several of the Sonnets are very likely to have been composed at the start of Shakespeare's career, and the whole sequence should be thought of as approaching Shakespeare's life's work' " (p. 21).[9] So he speculates freely about the period "between 1600 and 1609, when he composes many of his sonnets and *A Lover's Complaint* and witnesses their publication (with or without his consent)" (p. 21). But the biographical specifics are secondary to the construction of the author: "not simply the writer of plays who assiduously avoids print and bookish immortality, but rather the author of both plays and poems whose works as a whole show a fascination with – sometimes also a fear and distrust of – print publication" (p. 209). As written by such an author, "[t]he Sonnets are poems not merely *by* a practicing man of the theatre but also *about* a theatrical man who tries to write them" (p. 238). It is an outright repudiation of the myth of Shakespeare as *definingly* a man of the theater. There are conscious parallels with Lukas Erne's *Shakespeare as Literary Artist* (2003), which is about the writing of the plays as works to be read. But both books, in radically reimagining Shakespeare as an author, inevitably also reimagine his life. It can only be a matter of time until this is printed as another legend by the biographers.

NOTES

1   See the bibliography for full details of all works cited within the text. I use sonnets (roman) to denote the body of poems, and *Sonnets* in italics to refer to the 1609 quarto; in quotations, however, I reproduce the authors' usages.

2   Lee's *DNB* piece was not simplistically consensual, representing an accepted view. In fact he himself changed his mind radically over the 1890s – an earlier draft committed him to Pembroke as "Mr. W.H." and the fair youth, with his mistress, Mary Fitton, as the dark lady. He became more disturbed by the possible biographical implications of the sonnets as time went on, and his *A Life of William Shakespeare* (1898) pushes the "literary exercise" line even more earnestly. See Bate (1998: 40–2).

3   http://www.oxforddnb.com.proxy.lib.ohio-state.edu/view/article/25200, accessed April 26, 2005. I only have access to the new DNB online, which does not offer pagination.

4   As cited on the cover of the current (1996) Norton paperback edition.

5   E. A. J. Honigmann's *Shakespeare: The "Lost Years"* (1985) is an honorable exception. Sadly, because of its focus, it had little to say about the sonnets.

6   I particularly regret not having space to work the biographies by Dennis Kay and Anthony Holden into my narrative: see Further Reading.

7   See my " 'If I'm right': Michael Wood's *In Search of Shakespeare*," forthcoming in Mark Burnett and Ramona Wray (eds.), *Shakespeare on Film in the Twenty-First Century* (Edinburgh: Edinburgh University Press).

8   Wood overstates the case in claiming her as "the first woman in England to publish a volume of poetry" (p. 201); Isabella Whitney published volumes in 1567 and 1573.

9   The quotation is from Burrow 1998: 17.

References and Further Reading

Akrigg, G. P. V. (1968). *Shakespeare and the Earl of Southampton.* London: Hamish Hamilton.

Bate, Jonathan (1998). *The Genius of Shakespeare.* New York: Oxford University Press.

Bradbrook, Muriel C. (1978) *Shakespeare: The Poet in His World.* London: Weidenfeld & Nicolson.

Burgess, Anthony (1970). *Shakespeare.* London: Jonathan Cape.

Burrow, Colin (1998). "Life and Work in Shakespeare's Poems." The Chatterton Lecture on Poetry. *Proceedings of the British Academy* 97, 15–50.

Cheney, Patrick (2004). *Shakespeare, National Poet-Playwright.* Cambridge, UK: Cambridge University Press.

Duncan-Jones, Katherine (1983). "Was the 1609 *Shake-speare's Sonnets* Really Unauthorized?" *Review of English Studies* n.s. 34 (1983), 151–71.

Duncan-Jones, Katherine (2001). *Ungentle Shakespeare: Scenes from His Life.* London: Thomson Learning. (The Arden Shakespeare.)

Erne, Lukas (2003). *Shakespeare as Literary Dramatist.* Cambridge, UK: Cambridge University Press.

Fraser, Russell (1988). *Young Shakespeare.* New York: Columbia University Press.

Greenblatt, Stephen (2004). *Will in the World: How Shakespeare Became Shakespeare.* New York: Norton.

Holden, Anthony (1999). *William Shakespeare: His Life and Work.* London: Little, Brown.

Honan, Park (1998). *Shakespeare: A Life.* Oxford: Oxford University Press.

Honigmann, E. A. J. (1985). *Shakespeare: The "Lost Years."* Manchester: Manchester University Press.

Honigmann, E. A. J. (2000). "The First Performances of Shakespeare's Sonnets." In Grace Ioppolo, ed., *Shakespeare Performed: Essays in Honor of R. A. Foakes,* 131–48. Newark: University of Delaware Press.

Humes, James, C. (2003). *Citizen Shakespeare: A Social and Political Portrait.* New York: University Press of America.

Kay, Dennis (1992). *Shakespeare.* New York: William Morrow.

Levi, Peter (1988). *The Life and Times of William Shakespeare.* London: Macmillan.

O'Connor, Garry (2000). *Shakespeare: A Popular Life.* New York: Applause.

Rowse, A. L. (1963). *William Shakespeare, a Biography.* London: Macmillan.

Rowse, A. L. (1973). *Shakespeare the Man.* London: Macmillan.

Rowse, A. L. (1985). *Shakespeare's Self-Portrait.* London: Macmillan.

Schoenbaum, S. (1977). *William Shakespeare: A Compact Documentary Life.* Oxford: Oxford University Press.

Shakespeare, William (1964). *Shakespeare's Sonnets,* ed. A. L. Rowse. London: Macmillan.

Shakespeare, William (1997). *Shakespeare's Sonnets,* ed. Katherine Duncan-Jones. London: Thomas Nelson. (The Arden Shakespeare.)

Shakespeare, William (2002). *The Complete Sonnets and Poems,* ed. Colin Burrow. Oxford: Oxford University Press. (Oxford World's Classics.)

Thomson, Peter (1992). *Shakespeare's Professional Career.* Cambridge, UK: Cambridge University Press.

Wood, Michael (1978). *In Search of Shakespeare.* London: BBC Books.

9
Mr. Who He?

Stephen Orgel

In his own time, Shakespeare was much better known to the reading public as a poet than as a playwright. *Venus and Adonis* went through ten editions before his death in 1616, and another six before 1640. His other long narrative poem, *The Rape of Lucrece*, was less popular, but it, too, circulated far more widely than any of the plays, appearing in six editions during his life, and in two more by 1640. The most popular of the plays were *Richard III* and *Richard II*, each of which went through five editions before 1616. *Romeo and Juliet* went through four; *Hamlet* appeared in three.

For readers since the 18th century, the narrative poems have been at best marginal to the Shakespeare canon. The sonnets, on the other hand, which were the least known of his non-dramatic poems until the end of the 18th century, had by the 20th century become essential to the construction of the canonical Shakespeare. This transformation, to be sure, involved a good deal of revision, emendation, and especially elucidation, for which the 18th-century editor Edmond Malone, who did more to define what we mean by "Shakespeare" than anyone since the editors of the First Folio, is chiefly responsible. Malone's versions of the most problematic of these poems vary significantly from the original texts, but they have essentially replaced them.

Since the publication of the First Folio in 1623, the canonical Shakespeare has been Shakespeare the playwright; which makes one wonder how Shakespeare would appear to us had his poems been included in the Folio – had the Folio been a volume of Complete Works, rather than Complete Plays. We are always told that the model for the First Folio was the first folio of Ben Jonson's *Works*, published in 1616. But this is, in a crucial way, incorrect: Jonson's folio comprised not only plays but poems, masques, entertainments and a good deal of prose commentary. Indeed, it was his epigrams that Jonson designated "the ripest of my studies", and he endured a certain amount of scorn for presuming to include the plays at all, for claiming the status of Works for scripts from the popular theatre. The Shakespeare Folio is evidence enough that by 1623 Jonson

"Mr Who He?" by Stephen Orgel, *London Review of Books*, 8 August 2002.

had made his point, and in that sense Jonson's *Works* were indeed an enabling precedent. Still, Jonson is for literary history as much a poet as a playwright, and his involvement in the world of aristocratic patronage and connoisseurship, amply revealed in his poems and masques, is an essential element in our sense of his career. Had Shakespeare's poems been, from the outset, part of the canon, we might at the very least take seriously his involvement in that same social world of patronage, erudite readers and aristocratic admirers. The dedications to his two long narrative poems, and the care with which they were prepared for and seen through the press, make clear that his ambitions extended beyond the stage.

Why weren't they included in the First Folio? Probably for practical reasons. The volume was put together by the King's Men, the acting company of which Shakespeare had been a principal shareholder, playwright and performer, as a memorial to their most admired colleague. What they owned the rights to – and what chiefly concerned them – was the plays. Since the narrative poems were still selling well in 1623, to have acquired the rights to reprint them would have been difficult, if not impossible. As for the sonnets, who knows? The quarto volume published in 1609 was the only edition in Shakespeare's lifetime, and it seems to have generated little interest: so little that a second edition, published in 1640, was able to imply that the poems had never been printed before. Perhaps the sonnets were simply not considered worth including.

The editorial history of Shakespeare's poems is an index to how complex and con-flicted our sense of Shakespeare the poet has been. The first quartos of *Venus and Adonis* (1593) and *The Rape of Lucrece* (1594) were well printed, elegant little books. They addressed an audience of readers who knew the classics, both Latin and English; they recalled, in both their physical presentation and versification, recent editions of Ovid, Spenser and Sidney. Both poems include fulsome dedications to the Earl of South-ampton, a glamorous young aristocrat (he was 19 when *Venus and Adonis* appeared) who was also the ward of William Cecil, Lord Burghley. This is the way ambitious Elizabethan poets got on in the world: they found a generous aristocratic patron, whose taste, praised in a lavish dedication, in turn constituted a marketable endorsement. That this worked for Shakespeare, at least initially, is indicated by the fact that the *Lucrece* dedication is significantly warmer than the dedication for *Venus and Adonis*; conversely, the fact that there are no further dedications to Southampton implies that it ultimately failed to pay off. Southampton was liberally endowed with taste and charm, but when at the age of 21 he came into his inheritance, it turned out to consist of debts: artistic patronage does not live by taste alone.

Venus and Adonis was witty, inventive and stylish; it was also daring, erotically explicit, even amoral. Though it seems to us sexually more comic than pornographic, its immense popularity was cited frequently in Shakespeare's own time as an index of the decline of morals among the young, or the literate classes, or – extraordinarily – the Roman Catholic Church. Thomas Robinson, a lapsed friar, in a pamphlet published in 1622 called *The Anatomy of the English Nunnery* at Lisbon, described the comfortable life of a father confessor to the nuns there: "Then after supper it is usual for him to read a little of *Venus and Adonis*, the jests of George Peele, or some such scurrilous book: for there are few idle pamphlets printed in England which he hath not in the house." *The Rape of Lucrece* is less obviously licentious – and certainly much less fun – but for all its moralising, there is a good deal here to feed the Renaissance erotic, and sadistic, imagination. Moreover, the elements that we find tiresome in the two poems – their formality, dilation, extensive description and digression; in short, the sheer undramatic quality of these narratives by our greatest dramatist – would have been a good part of what contemporary readers admired: these were the things that put Shakespeare, as a poet, in the league of Spenser and Marlowe. At the same time, their focus on the political implications of rape, on the one hand, and the sexual power of women, on the other, have a striking relevance to our own social and political history. Jonathan Crewe, in the recent, excellent Pelican Shakespeare *Narrative Poems* (1999), is particularly good on the sexual politics of these works, and the new and complex critical life they have taken on.

The sonnets are, editorially and bibliographically, another matter entirely. They were, to begin with, not a book. At least some of them circulated initially in manuscript – the miscellaneous writer Francis Meres in 1598 praises Shakespeare's "sugared sonnets among his private friends", and while it is difficult to imagine "sugared" applying to such poems as "They that have power to hurt and will do none" or "Th'expense of spirit in a waste of shame", the adjective certainly describes many of the sonnets written to the beloved young man. There was nothing secretive about this mode of publication; manuscript circulation was a normal form of transmission for much lyric poetry in the period. Even Sidney's *Astrophil and Stella*, Marlowe's *Hero and Leander* and Donne's *Songs and Sonnets*, all of them monuments of Elizabethan verse, were initially conceived as coterie literature: the poet was writing for an audience he knew. Donne refused to allow his lyric poetry to be published in his lifetime because he would then have no control over who read it. The Shakespeare who wrote the "sugared sonnets" is the Shakespeare of the social world implied by the dedications to *Venus and Adonis* and *Lucrece*. As for those tougher nuts, the obscure courtly allegory *The Phoenix and the Turtle* and the Spenserian lament *A Lover's Complaint*, they have seemed bafflingly unlike the Shakespeare of the plays, and it is only in the past few decades that *A Lover's Complaint* has been accepted as Shakespeare's at all; but if we look at them in the context of Shakespeare's other poetry, we will see that they are entirely consistent with its literary ideals and intellectual milieu.

How the sonnets got into print is unclear, but there is no reason to believe that there was anything surreptitious about the 1609 quarto. Thomas Thorpe, the publisher, had printed play quartos, including Jonson's *Volpone* and *Sejanus*, and Shakespeare might well have given him a manuscript of sonnets to publish. The manuscript was not, however, prepared with the care evident in the texts of *Venus and Adonis* and *The Rape of Lucrece*, and it seems more likely that Thorpe had some source other than the author for his copy, which would not necessarily even have been in Shakespeare's hand. Whether Shakespeare approved of the publication or not is unknowable, but the issue would not have been a significant one: intellectual property is largely a modern concept, and the rights to the poems would have belonged to whoever owned the manuscript.

Though there are occasional muddles in the book, Thorpe's copy must have been clear enough, because the text is on the whole satisfactory. Its editorial problems are undeniable, but they are not, for the most part, the fault of the printer.

Why, given the continuing success of *Venus and Adonis* and *Lucrece*, the sonnets were not popular in 1609 is difficult to say, but it should make us take with a grain of salt the claim that Shakespeare's name on a title page was enough to guarantee a publisher's profit. The tantalising evidence of emotional turmoil and non-vanilla sex that makes them irresistible to us apparently was not a big selling point for Shakespeare's contemporaries: it was in Sidney's sonnets (which strike us as relentlessly literary) that early readers found the satisfactions of autobiography and erotic revelation. The usual explanation for the neglect of Shakespeare's sonnets is that the vogue for sonnets was past; but in 1609 the vogue for Shakespeare certainly wasn't. Those sonnets that were in print remained coterie literature, experimental and daring both linguistically and erotically, and seriously playful. It is clear from the number of these sonnets that reappear in commonplace books of the period that their attractiveness to that coterie audience did continue: even after publication, people continued to copy the ones they liked, circulate them, make them their own. But there was no second edition until 1640, 24 years after Shakespeare's death.

That edition, however, involved wholesale revision. John Benson, the publisher, capitalising on the undiminished sales of *Venus and Adonis*, produced a volume of what looked to be not old-fashioned sonnets but new Shakespeare love poems. The transformation involved both format and erotics: many of the sonnets are run together, making them 28-line poems, and all are given titles, such as "True Admiration", "Self-Flattery of Her Beauty", "An Entreaty for Her Acceptance" – as the latter two indicate, most of the love poems addressed to the young man are now addressed to a woman. To effect this, it was necessary only to change three masculine pronouns in the poems to feminine ones and supply a few gendered titles, but since the sonnets to the young man form a fairly consistent narrative, that was sufficient to change the story. The motive for this was probably not any nervousness about Shakespeare's sexuality; Benson simply wanted to bring the poems up to date, and in so doing transformed the book from an Elizabethan sonnet sequence to a volume of Cavalier love lyrics.

Even this edition was not a great success, and there wasn't another until 1710, when a supplementary volume to Nicholas Rowe's edition of Shakespeare's plays reprinted Benson's text. Benson's revision remained the standard text until late in the 18th century; and indeed, these versions of the poems were still being reprinted in the 19th century. The return to the 1609 quarto was the work of Edmond Malone, who in 1780 produced an edition that finally brought the editing of the poems into line with the editing of the plays by taking the original texts into account. It rationalised Thorpe's text, certainly, but its clarifications have on the whole stood the test of time. In a few critical instances, however, Malone undertook wholesale rewriting to produce the kind of sense the 18th-century Shakespeare seemed to demand. The most famous of these involves a crux in Sonnet 129, "Th'expense of spirit in a waste of shame". Here "lust in action" is described, in the 1609 quarto, as "A blisse in proofe and proud and very wo". The line continued to read this way, with minor adjustments to modernise spelling and punctuation, throughout the next century – through John Benson's 1640 edition, Nicholas Rowe's in 1710, and the numerous popular editions of the 18th century – until Malone's edition, in which the line became "A bliss in proof, and prov'd, a very woe". Thereafter, with very few demurrals, this became the line: Malone was acknowledged to have restored Shakespeare's original.

Orthographically, the quarto's "proud" could in 1609 be read as either "proud" or "provd" – though for the latter, considering the compositor's practice in the rest of the volume, "prou'd" would have been the expected form – but, as with *travaill* meaning both "travail" and "travel" in Shakespeare's English, the reader of 1609 who saw "proved" in the word would not have seen only that, and would have read it as both: "provd" retained the sense of "proud". It is a sense that we should certainly not edit out of the poem: "pride", the Bible says, is what "goeth before . . . a fall" (Proverbs 16.18) – before the sonnet's "very woe", before "this hell" in which the poem ends. *Proud* also means "erect", or "tumescent" (as in Sonnet 151, line ten), a usage still current in the medical term "proud flesh". Therefore, whatever Shakespeare intended, the most we may reasonably argue is that both readings are possible; or to put it more strongly, that the two readings are not separable. It should be emphasised, however, that there is no evidence that anyone before 1780 ever read the word as anything but "proud". Simply to eliminate one of the word's senses, as Malone's emendation does, is both to falsify the text and abolish its history.

But the transformation of "proud" to "proved" required Malone to make another revision in the line, less noticeable, though arguably even more radical: the change of the second "and" to "a", so that the clause reads not "and proud and very wo" but "and prov'd, a very woe". This emendation transforms the view of sex from a tripartite act – a bliss both during action and when completed, and also true woe – to a simple before and after contrast: bliss in action, woe afterwards. There is no room for "proud" in this neatly balanced pair. If the 1609 quarto (or, for that matter, Benson's 1640 volume) was the form in which Donne, Jonson, Herbert, Milton, Marvell, Dryden read Shakespeare's *Sonnets*, Malone's poem is not the poem they read. But of course Malone's poem has its history, too. It is now not only our poem, but the poem of Keats, Wordsworth, Browning, Yeats, Eliot, Auden. Only Robert Graves and Laura Riding saw through it; but to return with them to the Shakespeare of Donne and Marvell is to abolish the Shakespeare of Keats and Yeats.

Malone's edition, of course, had a more problematic consequence for Shakespeare: it had him pining once more, in the first 126 of the poems, not for a woman but for a man; and when in 1793 the editor George Steevens explained his refusal to include the poems in his Shakespeare edition by asserting that "the strongest act of Parliament that could be framed, would fail to compel readers into their service," it is unlikely that metaphoric complexity or rhyme schemes were what bothered him. Everyone remembers that Wordsworth said of the sonnets that "with this key/Shakespeare unlocked his heart", but he also declared them "abominably harsh, obscure, and worthless". For the 19th and a good part of the 20th century it was customary to deal with what looks, from the perspective of the past thirty years, like an overtly homoerotic sequence by arguing, when this fact was acknowledged at all, that the homoeroticism was purely conventional, or that the sonnets were not autobiographical – the lovestruck poet was a persona, and the sonnets to the young man no more implied that Shakespeare was gay than *Macbeth* implied that he was a murderer. Of course, in an age in which it is being argued that Internet pornography featuring virtual sex with computer-generated minors should be a prosecutable offence, claiming that Shakespeare was a pederast only in his imagination doesn't help much. But in fact, recent editors have accepted the sonnets' gayness without worrying much about Shakespeare's, and contemporary commentary on these poems is sexually much more open than in comparable editions of the plays.

For Shakespeareans of my generation, the great edition was that of W.G. Ingram and Theodore Redpath, first published in 1964, which intelligently rethought the texts and offered a detailed, thoughtful and untendentious commentary – it is an admirable edition, which may still be consulted with profit. The sex is acknowledged, though in a fashion that today seems absurdly gingerly, with terms like *"membrum pudendum"* and "carnal innuendo"; of the frankly obscene Sonnet 151 ("Love is too young to know what conscience is") Ingram and Redpath merely observe that "the numerous double meanings . . . are too obvious to need an explanation." (Reason not the need: Helen Vendler, in *The Art of Shakespeare's Sonnets*, glosses "conscience" as "knowledge of cunt".) Ingram and Redpath approach the young man in an especially gingerly fashion, suggesting that "the relationship was one of profound and at times agitated friendship, which involved a certain physical and quasi-sexual fascination emanating from the young Friend and enveloping the older poet, but did not necessarily include pederasty in any lurid sense." The discomfort expressed here seems positively quaint (rescuing the author of *Titus Andronicus* from the imputation of luridness is especially nice), but the notion that the way to deal with sex in Shakespeare is to assume that he wouldn't have done anything we wouldn't do cuts both ways, and as our society grows more sexually open, so inevitably does Shakespeare.

What might be considered the enabling document for contemporary editorial practice was Stephen Booth's remarkable *Essay on Shakespeare's Sonnets*, published in 1969. This articulated, brilliantly, a poetics of indeterminacy as a way of reading the sonnets, arguing that the poems are essentially open, and that their interpretation is a function of the process of reading, a process that will, inevitably, vary from reader to reader and age to age. Booth's commentary, it follows, is a world of alternatives and possibilities, and the essay, when it appeared, was genuinely exciting. Indeterminacy stopped, however, at the texts: no questions were asked of Malone's modernisations. Eight years later Booth paid his debt to bibliography with a monumental edition, including facsimiles of the 1609 texts, new modernisations *en face* and an exhaustive commentary. I confess to finding the commentary exhausting as well as exhaustive: Booth worries every possible ambiguity at great length; but in the end, the book is curiously conservative – it almost invariably decides that the standard reading is after all the right one, and Malone's texts are the ones we should stick with.

Two more recent editions seem to me especially notable. Helen Vendler's *The Art of Shakespeare's Sonnets* (1997) offers long, energetic readings, poem by poem. Vendler is one of the great readers of poetry writing today; her essays on contemporary verse are critical classics – she has a genius for selection, and writes about the most complex and arcane poets with clarity and without condescension. She clearly loves the sonnets, and treats them as contemporary poems. Though her interests are not historical, she does prefix to her commentary a facsimile of each poem with a modernisation that is for the most part Malone's. Nevertheless, she occasionally acknowledges that the facsimile and the modernisation are different works, observing of her reading of Sonnet 144, for example, that "the following remarks are equally true if one uses the quarto spelling." I find her readings far more coherent than Booth's, though there is a sense of the poems being kept under control, almost disciplined: they are supplied with key words (sometimes *defective* key words) and "couplet ties", and there are occasional terrifying diagrams. Vendler is not the most comfortable guide to the sonnets, but she is an intense, exciting and observant one.

John Kerrigan's *Sonnets and "A Lover's Complaint"* (1986) is very much concerned with history. His readings are learned, his glosses wide-ranging and exceptionally informative, and his sense of the poems often genuinely unsetting. He argues that we cannot properly appreciate the sequence unless we see *A Lover's Complaint* as part of it, and understand the sonnets' relation to earlier poetry by Daniel, Marlowe, Spenser and the overtly homoerotic Richard Barnfield. The critical tone is tough and often confrontational. Of "Let me not to the marriage of true minds/Admit impediments" he writes: "this sonnet has been misread so often and so mawkishly that it is necessary to say at once, if brutally, that Shakespeare is writing about what cannot be obtained." His introduction is a model of intelligent contextualisation, and includes the best treatment I know of both homosexuality and autobiography in the sequence.

Colin Burrow, editor of the Oxford *Complete Sonnets and Poems*, is in Kerrigan's league as a scholar and an editor: both are erudite, critically and philosophically sophisticated, and treat textual issues with the seriousness they require. But Burrow works on a larger canvas: it was a brilliant idea to produce the narrative poems and sonnets as a single edition, and the result is that he has been able to offer, in his book-length introduction, the best study there is of Shakespeare as a poet. Burrow writes wonderfully about the interplay between the various poems and genres, and is especially good on the implications of the sonnets' original mode of circulation, in manuscript among Shakespeare's "private friends", where both the mystification and the playfulness that have so frustrated later readers were entirely appropriate. He briskly and amusingly disposes of Mr W.H., observing that all the proposed candidates are nonsensical, and offers instead "Who He?" This seems to me probably correct: the great bibliographer Arthur Freeman has suggested to me that the initials stand for "Whoever He (may be)", and has found a parallel in a contemporary pamphlet. A major theme throughout the edition is what the original readers of these volumes would have expected of them and assumed about them, and therefore a number of poems ascribed to Shakespeare in his lifetime are included, as an indication of the kind of poet his contemporaries considered him. (Like Crewe in the New Pelican, Burrow does not include the notorious "Funeral Elegy for William Peter", now ignominiously demoted to a poem by John Ford: Burrow never believed in it, nor did I.) As for the sonnets' place in Shakespeare's poetic career, Burrow writes that they are "best viewed not as Shakespeare's final triumphant assertion of poetic mastery, but as poems which develop the methods of the earlier narrative poems to their utmost point – a point at which one is not quite sure who is male and who is female, who is addressed and why, or what their respective social roles are". I would not want to be without Crewe, Booth, Vendler or Kerrigan, but if the bookshelf had room for only one edition of Shakespeare's poems, Burrow's would be the one.

10
Editing the Sonnets

Colin Burrow

Most readers don't think twice about editors or the editions they create. In the case of Shakespeare's sonnets this is more than usually unwise. Every known text of the poems, from the first quarto of 1609 (Q) up to popular modern paperback editions, has been worked upon by agents other than Shakespeare. Although Q is entitled *Shake-speares Sonnets*, it is partly Compositor A's sonnets and partly Compositor B's sonnets and partly perhaps the publisher Thomas Thorpe's sonnets. In modern editions the text becomes also partly John Kerrigan's or Helen Vendler's or Colin Burrow's or Katherine Duncan-Jones's sonnets. Although this chapter will eventually argue for a constructive alliance between readers of the sonnets and their editors, I would like to start with a provocative claim which is designed to encourage readers of this volume to take a critical attitude to the texts they read. Editors do dreadful things to texts. That is their job. We now expect them to do their dreadful things consistently and accurately and on the basis of principles rather than of instinct or whim or tradition, and to tell us what they have done. The sonnets invite close inward attention. Their language seems to slip in sense from line to line and from phrase to phrase: probably if you do not find at least four different currents of meaning in each clause you have missed something, and even if you find more than four you probably still have missed something. As a result these poems pose particular problems for editors, who, as a breed, tend to want to be certain about what texts are and about what they mean. They also pose problems for readers of edited texts, who might want more fluidity from the poems than most editors want to allow.

The Problems

There are probably only two or three facts about the sonnets with which no one could argue. A volume called *Shake-speares Sonnets* appeared in 1609. It was published by Thomas Thorpe and printed in the workshop of George Eld. After that the arguments

begin. Thorpe has been presented as an unscrupulous pirate, who obtained a manuscript
of the sonnets from an unknown source, without Shakespeare's consent, and who made
a bad job of printing it (see e.g. Lee 1904: 93–9). Thorpe has also been seen as a reliable publisher with excellent connections to theatrical circles, who oversaw the careful
printing of a manuscript which he obtained at least with Shakespeare's consent and
possibly from Shakespeare himself (Duncan-Jones 1983). The truth is we do not know
how he obtained the manuscript of the sonnets or how close the manuscript from which
he worked was or was not to Shakespeare's drafts. Thorpe was no saint: he sometimes
sailed close to the wind by printing works which were the property of other printers,
as he did with Marlowe's translation of Lucan in 1600 (Greg 1943) and with Thomas
Coryate's *Odcombian Banquet* in 1611. But he also published Ben Jonson's *Sejanus* and
Volpone in editions which clearly had Jonson's blessing. Q may have been "authorized"
by Shakespeare, or it may be that Thorpe obtained a manuscript of the sonnets by illicit
means and appended *A Lover's Complaint* to the volume (Vickers 2003). We do not
know. Most editors will have a favored hypothesis about the origins of Q, and that will
influence in a hundred tiny ways what they do to the text of the sonnets.

Despite the many uncertainties which surround the 1609 volume, there are many
respects in which Shakespeare's sonnets ought to be very easy texts to edit. All printed
editions derive from the quarto of 1609. As a result, editors of the sonnets do not face
the irresolvable problems which beset editors of, say, *Troilus and Cressida*, who are confronted with a quarto and a folio text of apparently roughly equal authority with about
five thousand variations between them. It is likely, however, that at least some of the
sonnets existed in earlier versions. Two sonnets from the 1609 volume had appeared in
print before 1609. Sonnets 138 and 144 were given pride of place in William Jaggard's
pirated volume called *The Passionate Pilgrim*, which appeared in 1598–9 (the exact date
is not known, since the title-page of the first edition does not survive). *The Passionate
Pilgrim* version of 138 deals in relatively simple antitheses between youth and age, truth
and untruth:

> I smiling, credite her false speaking toung,
> Outfacing faults in Loue, with loues ill rest.
> But wherefore sayes my Loue that she is young?
> And wherefore say not I, that I am old?
> O, Loues best habite is a soothing toung,
> And Age (in Loue) loues not to haue yeares told.
> Therfore Ile lye with Loue, and Loue with me,
> Since that our faults in Loue thus smother'd be.
>   (ll. 7–14)

The 1609 version of the same poem offers a much more complex mixture of deception
and self-deception:

> Simply I credit her false speaking tongue,
> On both sides thus is simple truth supprest:

> But wherefore sayes she not she is vniust?
> And wherefore say not I that I am old?
> O loues best habit is in seeming trust,
> And age in loue, loues not t'haue yeares told.
> > Therefore I lye with her, and she with me,
> > And in our faults by lyes we flattered be.

Did Jaggard "edit" the text he received? Did he obtain a text which was simplified by scribal or memorial transmission (as Roe argues in Shakespeare 1992, ad loc.)? Did Shakespeare "edit" or revise the text? How should editors present these two versions? There are no certain answers to any of these questions. The rhymes "young" and "tongue" in *The Passionate Pilgrim* become "vniust" and "trust" in 1609, and these are perhaps the most significant differences between the two versions: they turn a poem on lying about your age into an edgy work on mutually knowing deception. But even here the arguments could run either way. Rhymes are more likely than other features of a text to be preserved in memorial transmission; but in this case the "young"/"tongue" rhyme of *The Passionate Pilgrim* version repeats the rhyme of the second quatrain. This repetition could indicate that Shakespeare was stumped for a fresh rhyme in the earlier version, or it could result from an imperfect attempt to remember the text on the part of a copyist.

Other evidence of authorial revision is similarly double-edged. Versions of sonnets 2 and 106 that differ significantly from those in Q are found in a number of poetical miscellanies from the early seventeenth century (see Taylor 1985; full list in Beal et al. 1980: 452–55, and chapter 5 above). Here again it is almost impossible to distinguish with certainty between scribal and authorial variants. The first four lines of sonnet 2 in Rosenbach MS 1083/17 (where it is named "The Benefitt of Mariage") look like this:

> When forty yeares shall beseige thy browe
> and drench deep furrowes in yt louely field
> Thy youths fairer field so accounted now
> Shall be like rotten weeds of noe worth held

Q reads as follows:

> When fortie Winters shall beseige thy brow,
> And digge deep trenches in thy beauties field,
> Thy youthes proud liuery so gaz'd on now,
> Wil be a totter'd weed of smal worth held:

The Rosenbach manuscript is late, and it displays many signs of a text that derives from a game of scribal Chinese whispers: it is alone among manuscript versions in reading "yeares" (others have "winters"), "drench" (others have "trench"), and "fairer" (others have "fair" or "proud"). These are typical of the kinds of errors that arise from repeated transcription. But some of its features are harder to explain away. The manuscript versions do not exploit the heraldic sense of "field" ("the surface of a shield"), which is expanded in Q's "liuery." Nor do they register a pun on "weeds" meaning "clothing" (hence "totter'd" or "tattered"). Read one way, these features could be taken as indicators that the manuscript versions are the result of a deadening mistransmission, a view supported by the relatively inert repetition of "field" in the Rosenbach text (see Duncan-Jones 1997: 453–66). Read another way, however, these variants could suggest that lexical play dawned on Shakespeare in the process of composition or revision: revise the second "field" to "liuery" and suddenly organic growth, clothing, and heraldry all come into play.

Editors can be helped a little in deciding between these two options by detailed arguments about the provenance and character of particular manuscripts and scribes; but beliefs about the status of the manuscript versions of the sonnets tend finally to depend on the kind of self-supporting evidential loop that is all too common in arguments about texts from this period. Someone who believes that Shakespeare's language is characterized by immediate and unsettling confluences of multiple senses, and who believes that these confluences occurred as he wrote, will probably maintain that the manuscript versions have been massacred by copyists. Someone, on the other hand, who thinks that Shakespeare may have added layers of imagery to his writing after its first composition will find confirmation of that belief in the manuscript versions. It is no accident that Gary Taylor was one of the first scholars to take the manuscript versions seriously. He, as one of the editors of the Oxford Shakespeare, was committed to the thesis that Shakespeare revised his plays. It may seem reasonable to suppose that Shakespeare also revised his poems; but if the manuscript versions and *The Passionate Pilgrim* versions do show how Shakespeare revised the sonnets by enriching their language, then they bear witness to a rather different kind of revision from the theatrically motivated excisions and revisions that scholars have found in the different versions of the plays. The manuscript and early printed versions may testify to the ways in which Shakespeare revised his poems, but they also, and perhaps only, bear witness to other kinds of alteration that texts can undergo in the process of copying and recopying.

Life after Q: The 1640 Edition

Whether or not Shakespeare revised the poems, editors certainly revised them for him after his death. In 1640 the second "edition" of the sonnets appeared. And here we should perhaps pause over the different things that the word "edition" can mean. John Benson's octavo volume of *Poems: Written by Wil. Shake-speare. Gent.* was not quite a second edition in the sense that we would use the word today of a new or expanded version of a work; nor was it exactly a reprint of Q; nor was it an "edition" in the sense of a text which had been critically examined by an editor with a view to eliminating errors of earlier editions. Benson worked from a copy of Q (Alden 1916). He made about seventy verbal changes to the text, some of which introduced new errors, and others of which may have been emendations. He also reordered the sonnets, and in several cases combined up to five together to form single poems, to which he gave headings such as "Familiaritie breeds contempt" (52), "Vpon the receit of a Table Booke from his Mistris" (122), and the consciously Donnean "A Valediction" (71). Benson also included the poems from the 1612 edition of *The Passionate Pilgrim*, a collection that had been augmented by the addition of a number of poems by Thomas Heywood.

Benson's edition used to be regarded as an act of piracy and textual vandalism performed by an unscrupulous printer (Rollins 1944: vol. 2, 18–28; cf. Bennett 1968). It may have had the more innocent purpose of adapting Shakespeare's sonnets for an audience attuned to Cavalier lyrics about time and love. Whatever the motives behind the 1640 text, though, it was extremely influential. Its order, titles, and (with a few emendations, modernizations, and the occasional misprint) texts were followed in the majority of editions through the eighteenth century. For Charles Gildon in 1709 (in a volume designed to pass itself off as the seventh volume of Rowe's collected edition of the plays), for George Sewell in 1725 (who presented his edition of the poems as a supplementary volume to Alexander Pope's edition of Shakespeare's works), and so for most readers of the sonnets in the eighteenth century, Shakespeare wrote poems of twenty-eight, forty-two, or fifty-six lines with epigrammatic titles, as well as several poems by Heywood. He owes that much to his editors.

It used to be said that Benson censored the homoerotic elements of Shakespeare's sequence (Rollins 1944: vol. 2, 20; cf. de Grazia 1994). He does on three occasions change male pronouns to female, but it is extremely unlikely that he systematically sought to eradicate traces of a male addressee. He began his collection, after all, with very masculine addresses: a version of sonnets 67 ("Ah wherefore with infection should he live"), 68 ("Thus is his cheeke the map of daies out-worne"), and 69 ("Those parts of thee that the worlds eye doth view") is printed first under the catch-all title "The glory of beautie" as the first poem in the volume. The originator of this particular criticism of Benson was Hyder E. Rollins, the author of the magisterial variorum edition of 1944. Rollins regarded substantive emendations of the text of Q as the ultimate means by which the interpretation of the sonnets could be changed: he therefore attached great weight to Benson's degendering of sonnet 108's "boy" to "love." What Rollins did not fully acknowledge was the extent to which not just the wording of the text but the "paratexts" of an edition – its notes, even its title-page and preface – could shape readers' responses as much as and sometimes more radically than emendations of the text. If these aspects of an edition are taken into account, then the process of transforming the addressee of the sonnets began a little later than Benson, and in a very surprising place. In July 1711 the printer Bernard Lintott published effectively the first facsimile edition of Q. This included even the mysterious dedication to Mr. W.H., and printed the poems in the order in which they appear in Q, in a text very close to that of 1609. Modern scholars have praised this edition for avoiding the corruptions and un-Shakespearean contaminations of Benson (Rollins 1944: vol. 2, 37), but it shows that editions can change how poems are read without even altering a single word. It was called *A Collection of Poems, in Two Volumes; Being all the Miscellanies of Mr William*

Shakespeare, which were Publish'd by himself in the Year 1609. and now correctly Printed from those Editions. The Second Volume, which contains I. One Hundred and Fifty Four Sonnets, all of them in Praise of his Mistress. II A Lover's Complaint of his Angry Mistress. It is worth imagining how sonnet 1 would sound to a person who believed that he or she had bought 154 sonnets "all of them in Praise of his Mistress":

> From fairest creatures we desire increase,
> That thereby beauties *Rose* might never die,
> But as the riper should by time decease,
> His tender heire might beare his memory:

Apart from following eighteenth-century usage for u and v, this makes no changes to the text of Q, and even retains the italic form of "*Rose.*" And yet the effect of reading the poem as a panegyric to a mistress is radically transformative. Is a reader to imagine this was written to a girl called Rose? Are the masculine pronouns in line 4 implicitly identified with the poet, who wants his own blood-line to be continued by his coy mistress? Lintott's title-page probably has at least as great an effect on how the sonnets are read as Benson's modifications of three pronouns, and it suggests that editors can do dreadful things to a text without changing a single word.

Malone: The Birth of Modern Editing

The example of Lintott indicates that the word "innocent" probably does not belong in the same sentence as the word "edition." The modern academic editor is no innocent, though he is a relatively recent phenomenon. He (Shakespeare's sonnets were not edited by a woman until the last years of the twentieth century) began life in the late eighteenth century. In 1780 Edmond Malone presented a regularized and, by the standards of its day, modernized text of Q, setting out the poems in the order in which they had first appeared. It was printed along with the narrative poems as a supplement to the edition of Shakespeare presided over by George Steevens, and in 1790 was revised and extended to become the final volume of Malone's edition of the plays.

Malone is sometimes presented as a heroic lone scholar who brought the rationality of the Enlightenment to the process of editing Shakespeare. Rollins risks a rare panegyric flight on the subject: "Truly, one knows not whether to marvel more that he in that misty time could see so clearly, or that we in the supposedly clear age walk so stumblingly after him" (1944: vol. 2, 39). More recently Malone has been presented as having brought the characteristic blindness of post-Enlightenment individualism to the text of Shakespeare (de Grazia 1991). His edition is a stranger thing than either of these descriptions would allow. It was a hybrid and collaborative enterprise. In his textual decisions Malone may have had access to a number of emendations made by Edward Capell in a copy of Lintott's reprint of the quarto (now in the library of Trinity College, Cambridge). In his annotations, too, Malone is seldom alone: he frequently argues with other scholars – notably with George Steevens, who thought that the sonnets were an abomination. The dialogues between these two scholars, which grow in the notes to the 1790 edition in parallel with the increasing animosity between them, are a vital part of the reception history of the poems, and are extremely revealing about changing attitudes to editing the sonnets in the later eighteenth century.

The third quatrain of sonnet 25 of Q reads:

> The painefull warrier famosed for worth,
> After a thousand victories once foild,
> Is from the booke of honour rased quite,
> And all the rest forgot for which he toild:

Malone painstakingly argues that the aberrant rhyme on "worth" and "quite" indicates textual corruption, and emends "worth" to "fight." Steevens tartly retorts: "This stanza is not worth the labour that has been bestowed on it," but then goes on to propose the hopelessly unmetrical transposition "for worth famousèd" and "quite rasèd." Malone comes back querulously: "Why it should not be worth while to correct this as well as any other manifest corruption in our author's works, I confess, I do not comprehend. Neither much labour, nor many words, have been employed upon it" (Malone 1790: 213).

These arguments between the two scholars are more than displays of spleen and rivalry (though they certainly are that): they signal to the readers of the 1790 text that informed authorities can disagree over the text and over interpretation of the poems, and they give exemplary instances of how to conduct arguments about textual corruption. The editorial apparatus of the 1790 edition does not simply fix or rationalize the text of the sonnets: it presents that text as a suitable subject for argument between competent authorities, and encourages its readers to participate in those arguments.

One of those arguments is about sexuality – or rather, about style and sexuality. George Steevens disliked the sonnets partly because he was suspicious of their sexuality and partly because he thought they were painfully obscure. Malone's commentary is formed partly in response to Steevens's attitudes. Malone's most-quoted note is on "thy deceased lover" in sonnet 32:

> The numerous expressions of this kind in these Sonnets, as well as the general tenour of the greater part of them, cannot but appear strange to a modern reader. In justice therefore to our author it is proper to observe, that such addresses to men were common in Shakespeare's time, and were not thought indecorous. That age seems to have been very indelicate and gross in many other particulars beside this, but they certainly did not think themselves so.

Malone goes on to cite parallel uses of the word "lover" by men to men from Jonson and Drayton. This note conflates stylistic and sexual indecorum and allows the former to mask the latter. Shakespeare's age was gross in conversation in Malone's eyes not because it fostered homoerotic desire, but because it allowed men to *call* each other "lover." But he does not leave the matter there, with sexuality swept under the carpet of stylistic indecorum: he goes on to record that the literary historian Thomas Wharton had shown that "whole sets of Sonnets were written with this sort of attachment." Malone does not say what sort of thing "this sort of attachment" was, but that phrase – combined with the fulminations that pepper the notes from Steevens about the stylistic and moral ugliness of the poems – does leave it open to the polite readership of the 1790 edition to suppose that the relationship between Shakespeare and his addressee was homoerotic.

And that supposition becomes the central repressed truth about the sonnets in Malone's edition. He is often said to have been the first editor to make explicit connections between the sonnets and Shakespeare's life, and to invite his readers to believe that the first 126 sonnets were addressed to a single man. Malone's role in this development is indisputable, but was more tentative and dialectical than is sometimes suggested. His note on the dedication to Mr. W.H. records Farmer's opinion that "many of these Sonnets are addressed to our author's nephew Mr. William Hart"; this W.H., Malone argues, must have been too young. He goes on: "Mr. Tyrwhitt has pointed out to me a line in the twentieth Sonnet, which inclines me to think that the initials W.H. stand for W. Hughes . . . To this person, whoever he was, one hundred and twenty six of the following poems are addressed; the remaining twenty-eight are addressed to a lady." Malone's conjectures sit alongside and emerge from the work of other scholars, and they insist on their own uncertainty ("whoever he was"). They emerge not as a proud discovery of the biographical foundations of the sonnets, nor as part of Malone's "driving project of identifying the experience of the Sonnets with Shakespeare's own" (de Grazia 1994: 37); they constitute an implicit correction of the work of others. They are perhaps primarily directed at the claim on the title-page of Lintott's edition that all of the poems were addressed to a mistress. Later editors were of course far more dogmatic: by 1898 George Wyndham could say in his headnote to 127, "This Sonnet opens the Second series, where the poet addresses his mistress, or comments on the wrong she has done him," and by the same date scholars were deedily searching for new W.H.s on the basis of Malone's division of the sequence (see chapters 8 and 14 in this volume). But Malone does not present the sonnets as desexed biographical records: his dialogues with Steevens and other scholars frequently enact the contingency of judgment, and encourage their readers to debate the text and its biographical significance; they also temptingly construct a homoerotic reading of the sonnets by repeatedly withdrawing from such a reading.

Malone's often silent impositions of textual regularity on the quarto text had as profound an influence on the editorial tradition as his notes. He was presenting Shakespeare's sonnets to an audience that expected regularity in orthography and punctuation, and for whom the dominant model of a literary edition was that of a classical text. Malone wished to present the "original" and the "authentic" Shakespeare to that audience. As a result his attitude to Q was distinctly double: when he suspects its readings he generally calls it the "old copy," as though its antiquity makes it suspect; when, however, he trusts it more than a later edition he terms it "the original copy." The editor's job, Malone and his readers would have both felt, was to seek to emend texts that had been corrupted by copyists or printers, or, in the case of the plays, by "the players" who produced the texts. The most dangerous aspect of that process is the way in which conscious, argued decisions to emend are often accompanied by multiple unargued transformations of the text. Sonnet 129 shows this danger most clearly – and this particular sonnet was taken by Laura Riding and Robert Graves in 1969 as proof that modernizing editors edit out sense.

Lust in 1609 is

> Made In pursut and in possession so,
> Had, hauing, and in quest, to haue extreame,
> A blisse in proofe and proud and very wo,
> Before a ioy proposd behind a dreame,
> > All this the world well knowes yet none knowes well,
> > To shun the heauen that leads men to this hell.

In 1790 it is rather different:

> Mad in pursuit, and in possession so;
> Had, having, and in quest to have, extreme;
> A bliss in proof, —and prov'd, a very woe;
> Before, a joy propos'd; behind, a dream:
> > All this the world well knows; yet none knows well
> > To shun the heaven that leads men to this hell.

The Q text is a splurge of energy. The absence of punctuation in "Before a ioy proposd behind a dreame" may evoke a single temporal state ("in anticipation lust is a joy that is put to us in the appearance of a delicious dream"), in which the temporal sense of "behind" is secondary or marginal. "A blisse in proofe and proud and very wo" excitedly piles up indistinguishable attributes of sexual passion, and allows a pun on "proud" (which can mean "erect") to stand right by the woe that follows it, with no *cordon sanitaire* of a comma or a dash between the two.

Malone is not just removing textual corruption here. He duly records that "the old copy corruptly reads – *Made* in pursuit." He also notes his emendation of "and very wo" to "a very woe"; but as he does so he either misrecords or misreads or edits out what may be an obscene pun in Q: his note is a dry "The quarto is here evidently corrupt – It reads:—and prov'd *and* very woe." Q of course reads "proud" rather than "prov'd." Malone's invisible unsignaled modernization to "prov'd" – a perfectly possible way of modernizing "proud," but only one of several – is as significant perhaps as the "substantive" emendation of Q's reading. His emendation of "and proud and very wo" to "and prov'd, a very woe" may not be "stupid" (McLeod 1991: 250); but it does silence several undercurrents of sense which are fighting to be heard in Q.

A Very Woe: Editing the Sonnets Today

The present state of thinking about editing the sonnets is a minor case of cultural schizophrenia. Theorists of editing – notably Margreta de Grazia and Randall McLeod – have argued against the tendency of editors to perpetuate Malone's Enlightenment attitudes to the text, and have emphasized the unruliness and irregularity of early modern printing practices. They have argued, effectively, for "un-editing" the sonnets (see Marcus 1996), and have insisted that readers should attend to the ways in which changing practices in and attitudes toward printing materially influence the texts produced in the seventeenth century. None of these scholars – perhaps unsurprisingly, given how critical they are of the implied attitudes of editors – has ever edited a text, and no editor of the sonnets has yet attempted to put their ideas into practice, though some (including this one) have been shaken into thinking (sometimes editors can do this) as a result of their arguments. Meanwhile there has been a stream of excellent editions of the sonnets, with exceptionally good introductions, perceptive notes, and all the annotations and paraphernalia designed to help most modern readers to make sense of Shakespeare. Most of these editions recommend that their readers also consult a facsimile of the quarto (and those who wish to follow this excellent advice could do well to consult the excellent digital facsimile available from Octavo.com). Some reproduce both a modernized text and a facsimile version (notably Booth and Vendler). But all of these editions also do all the things that are anathema to the un-editors: they regularize spelling and punctuation, and they emend the texts in dozens of places, often in ways that are influenced by the tradition that goes back to Malone and Capell.

This self-contradictory state of affairs is one consequence of the cultural position of Shakespeare today. On the one hand the sonnets are prime material for a graduate seminar, in which students would be encouraged to appreciate the multiplicity of senses of the words in the quarto text, and to examine the ways in which modernizing spelling and punctuation limits that multiplicity, and perhaps also marks quietly performed acts of cultural erasure or sexual formation on the text of the poems. Shakespeare for the educational elite is increasingly a Shakespeare of blots and typographical irregularities (see e.g. de Grazia and Stallybrass 1993). On the other hand, there is mass demand for the sonnets from readers who want to be guided through the texts in a form that does not continually unsettle their expectations about how sentences are shaped or words are spelled, or who want to think about what the sonnets say about time without worrying too much about the finer points of punctuation. This market appeals to publishers, for whom editions which look accessible spell sales in the tens of thousands rather than in the hundreds.

The scholarly editor of a modernized edition sits uncomfortably in between these different forces. Neither audience can be pleased fully all the time, and neither audience can be expected to realize that probably each semi-colon in each edition has been thought and rethought and removed and then replaced by the editor several times over. It would be theoretically possible to produce an XML tagged variorum text of the sonnets online, where a click could enable a reader to alternate between Q's, Malone's, Benson's, and Wyndham's texts, but even this technological wizardry would not replicate the full horror of what an editor sees in his or her dreams (or are they night-mares?) – a version of the sonnets in which every possible way of handling the text is *simultaneously* present to the mind. Until this digital nirvana or Neverneverland or hell arrives, probably all the editor can do is annotate liberally in both senses of the word: both copiously, and in a manner that reminds readers of the edition that these words could work rather differently if a comma were removed, or if they were emended in another way.

The "un-editors" have made principled attacks on two distinct cultural movements. The first is, broadly speaking, an Enlightenment attempt to impose regularity on texts deriving from a culture that held very different attitudes to printing, to the concept of regularity, and to variations in spelling and grammar. Early modern texts often accom-modate unruliness, and authors and printers from this period did not seek, let alone achieve, perfect regularity in their ways of presenting texts. The un-editors often also, and rightly, remark that editors perpetuate each others' errors – or that, as McLeod (writing as Random Cloud) has colorfully put it, "Editing in our tradition is largely hear-say" (McLeod 1994: 148). The second strand in the arguments for un-editing is an attack on the editorial principles that underlie much of the editorial theory and practice of the "new bibliography" of R. B. McKerrow and W. W. Greg, as refined by Fredson Bowers and Thomas Tanselle. According to the later adherents of this group of bibliographers (which is by no means either as simple or as unified as this cursory summary implies), the leading criterion for selecting one particular reading over another would be a search for "the nearest approximation in every respect of the author's final intentions" (Bowers, quoted with approval in Tanselle 1990: 28). The un-editors would argue against this position: they would claim that books are material rather than nou-menal things, and result from material processes rather than from mental acts. They would also note that authors do not necessarily leave one "authorized" version (and the biblical flavor of that phrase suggests how those who use the word "authorized" are often smuggling in a quasi-religious dimension to their claims about texts). An author is not a sole agent of creation, they would say, and texts emerge from irregular and collaborative processes (see e.g. McGann 1983, 1991; McKenzie 1999). The material objects that result – early modern books – are therefore, in all their sublime irregular-ity, the sole proper objects of our attention.

In the course of this argument, however, the un-editors run the risk of making a fetish, not of the idea of authorial intention, but of the materiality of the book and of the outcomes of the processes of book production. Where texts exist in multiple versions the un-editors can quite rightly insist that readers and editors should not attempt to delimit textual flux by conflating those various versions into a single text; but in the case of the sonnets their emphasis on the materiality of print can lead them to make a fetish of Q. Randall McCleod (writing this time as Random Clod), for example, has written acutely on the crux in sonnet 106, which says of future poets "They had not still enough your worth to sing." Most editors follow Malone (who follows Tyrwhitt), and emend "still" to "skill." Clod, who is a self-proclaimed gadfly to editors, argues that "skill" is an unnecessary and improbable emendation for "still" because "st" is presented in a text as a ligature, achieved by a single piece of type (McLeod 1991: 253–61). The compositor therefore could not have picked up a "t" by mistake from the section of his box of type which was supposed to contain "k"s, since ligatures were positioned far away from either of these two letters in his "case" of type. This is a strangely over-material argument, since it ignores the obvious possibility that the compositor simply misread his copy as "still" and so reached (incorrectly) for an "st" ligature. The error is easily made when reading Elizabethan handwriting, and as it happens "skill," the emended reading of Malone, is also found in seventeenth-century manuscript sources of which Malone was unaware, and which may represent a separate line of textual descent from that of the 1609 quarto.

Printing is a complex process, which like any other human activity involves material objects – boxes of type, wads of ink, marks on paper – as well as mental processes – recognizing letters in a manuscript, construing sense. In printing, as in life, percept and concept are not distinct: a belief can change what you see. Printing can go wrong in a number of ways at a number of stages: type can be in the wrong box, a compositor can take a scrawl on a page as corresponding to one figure rather than another, and so on. The material form of the printed book has a manifest worth, but it should be interpreted as the outcome of a set of processes which we only partially but do at least partially understand, and we should not shrink from recognizing that those processes can go wrong.

"Wrong" is a heavy word to use, and is one which anxious postmoderns like to put in scare quotes; but it is clear that early modern printers did have the concept of error. Lists of corrigenda at the start or end of a volume, and press variants within it (that is, occasions on which printers would stop the presses and reset words or occasionally whole lines or pages of type if they spotted something which looked wrong) are clear evidence that printers operated with a concept of error, even if that concept of error was different from that of a modern printer, for whom any departure at all from his copy constitutes error. (The most perfect illustration of this modern conception of error is the erratum slip inserted into volume two of the Oxford Byron, which reports that "The following examples of Byron's faulty Greek transcription were inadvertently corrected by the printer": Byron 1980). Early modern printers did not print exactly what was before them. Authors would expect to have spelling and punctuation modified in the process of transition from manuscript to print: when Riding and Graves claim of the text of sonnet 129 in Q that "Shakespeare's punctuation allows the variety of meanings he intends" (Riding and Graves 1969: 74) they are being extremely naïve. The punctuation of Q is very unlikely consistently to reflect anything that issued from Shakespeare's hand. Early modern texts were not closed books that embodied the authority of the author. Printers changed what they read, and assumed that readers read texts with a pen in hand, ready to change, correct, and annotate the text before them (Kerrigan 1996). So when the text of sonnet 73 in Q reads "Bare rn'wed quires" it is likely that most early modern readers, and most printers too, would have thought something was wrong with the text that they were reading. When a modern editor emends Q's phrasing, following one of Benson's relatively few emendations, to "bare ruined [or "ruin'd"] choirs," that editor is not necessarily imposing anachronistic conceptions of accuracy on the volatile early modern text: he or she is making inferences about the ways in which the process of setting a manuscript might have gone wrong, even according to the standards of the early seventeenth century. In this case the assumption is that the minims in "ruin'd" were misread by Compositor B as "rn'wed."

This argument is vulnerable to at least two objections, which are answerable only by a kind of pragmatism that will not seem reasonable to everyone. At the theoretical level any argument about error rests on judgments about probability, about early modern grammar, about Shakespearean usage, and perhaps about methods in early modern print-shops. It therefore implies that some measure of system can be reconstructed in order to postulate error. Most editors would agree that on fourteen occasions Q prints "their" where Shakespeare probably wrote "thy," and this is usually ascribed to some relatively consistent peculiarity in the manuscript from which Q was set. At 26. 12, for example, Q reads "To show me worthy of their sweet respect." The "their" in that line does not conform to what we think we know about expectations of consistent address in early modern English, since the addressee of the poem is referred to as "thou" earlier in the poem. Almost all editors emend it. When they do so they are assuming a system of two kinds: first, a system of grammatical expectations, and second, a more or less systematic or recurrent idiosyncrasy of the manuscript. In this respect any emended text is implicitly founded on a paradox: for it is founded on an inference of system derived from moments which depart from that system. In this respect too any emended text could be seen as participating in "Enlightenment" ideology, and be the little brother to Alexander Pope's infamously "systematized" and "reformed" edition of Shakespeare of 1725, both being founded on the assumption that irregularity is to be eradicated.

However, even this kind of system is subject to forms of decorum that are not simply textual. So, in the last line of sonnet 20, the poem to the "Master Mistris," there are two occurrences of "thy" and one of "their": "Mine be thy loue and thy loue's vse their treasure." No editor has ever suggested emending "their" to "thy" here, for obvious reasons: doing so would turn the addressee into a masturbator ("use of your love would be your own treasure"), and so would change what we take to be the point of the poem, which is generally taken as a complex piece of advocacy for breeding. Readers of any kind of emended text of the sonnets are in the hands of – sometimes perhaps they are even the victims of – their editors, who are constantly seeking methods of regularizing what could be entirely random processes of error, or phenomena that might not be error at all, and who repeatedly subject those regularizations to limits imposed by taste, judgment, and their sense of sexual decorum.

There is no way out of this problem except to be aware of it. The relation between reader and editor is one of trust, and like all relations of trust it is wise for the trusted person to show why he or she warrants trust and for the person trusting to question the grounds of that trust, since "well-placed trust grows out of active inquiry rather than blind acceptance" (O'Neill 2002: 79). A good editor is not a nerd who has worked out a perfect system for eradicating error; a good editor makes decisions about the needs of readers and about the probable actions of scribes, compositors, and authors, and is aware that he or she is presenting in a form which could encourage readers to believe it is certain a text that is founded on thousands of contingencies. Much of the recent resistance to editing has been a result of the rhetoric of certainty that many editors adopt. For them, as for Malone at his most dogmatic moments, "certainly" is good, while "probably" is bad, and "possibly" is worst of all. If everyone accepted that most of what they do is grounded on a measure of probability about which rational agents could reasonably disagree, many arguments in editing (and in the world) would end. Editing a text is part of a conversation about that text, and it is an act of accommodating a text to a particular audience. When modern editors undertake that task, which is by its nature impossible to get right, they should perhaps seek to emulate the dialogic aspect of Malone's edition rather than its rhetoric of certainty.

There is a second unanswerable problem with the argument from error. Although it is often possible to make inferences about occasions on which the process of printing a text has gone wrong, it is not always possible to know how the printed symbols before us would have looked had that process not gone wrong. Only an editor of very strong constitution would not whimper when presented with this at the start of sonnet 146 in Q:

> Poore soule the center of my sinfull earth,
> My sinfull earth these rebbell powers that thee array

Most editors would share Malone's unease, if not his confidence in uncertainty: "It is manifest that the compositor inadvertently repeated the last three words of the first verse in the beginning of the second, omitting two syllables, which are sufficient to complete the meter. What the omitted word or words were, it is impossible now to determine" (1790: 312). Conceivably the second line paraphrases the "sinfull earth" of the end of the first line; but if so it is odd to use the plural "these" of a singular antecedent, and the line contains two more syllables than the norm. Faced with this, editors often again resort to the closest thing to system that is open to them: they often try to use what they know about Shakespeare's usages elsewhere to try to patch in a phrase with which to begin the Sonnet. Editors have tried "Fool'd by those" (Malone), "Gull'd by these" (Seymour-Smith), "Feeding these" (Vendler). "Spoild by these" is suggested by Stanley Wells on the grounds that this is analogous to *Lucrece* 1172 (Wells 1985), a passage about an attack on the mansion of the body. I adopted this reading in my edition, not without an uneasy recognition that the principal reason for favoring it could also be a good reason for rejecting it: the use of a phrase closely analogous to another passage of Shakespeare violates perhaps the first law of reading Shakespeare, which is to expect the unexpected. We do not know that Shakespeare did not, on a wet Wednesday, while struggling with a sonnet on a theme that may have been uncongenial, leave a gap to which he never returned. The only solution to this problem of the unreconstructable is again pragmatic and interpersonal rather than theoretical. Editors can do no more than explain what they're doing, set out alternatives, and acknowledge that the process that is Shakespeare's sonnets does not stop with printers or editors: it finally involves readers and their decisions and responses, and these decisions and responses editors should try to inform and facilitate rather than direct. Explaining to readers what the text could have been in your judgment, had not something gone wrong somewhere along the line of producing a printed sonnet, here entails trusting readers as much as oneself to think about alternative ways in which the text could be (and no beating about the bush; this is not an emendation) rewritten.

This argument that the production of the Sonnets was not a single act by Shakespeare but a process that involves many agents and many uncertainties could be extended in directions that make it even more tendentious and vulnerable than even this extremely tricky (or should it be "spoiling" or "rebellious"?) example would indicate. Surely modernization goes well beyond the bounds of the early modern printing process? This is perhaps less obviously true than it appears to be. When Sir John Harington passed over the manuscript copy of his translation of *Orlando Furioso* to his printer Richard Field (the same careful workman who was to print Shakespeare's *Venus and Adonis* and *Lucrece*) he gave the printer instructions about the typeface in which the book should be set, and was probably as closely involved in the production of the book as any author from his period would have been (Greg 1923). But he showed no signs of objecting when Field's compositors often changed his rather old-fashioned spelling or his very relaxed punctuation. When writers from this period handed their copy to a printer (and of course we do not even know that Shakespeare did this with the sonnets) they *expected* the printed version to differ from what they wrote in spelling and punctuation. In that sense every printed text from the early modern period might be said to come to us already modernized: some of the spelling and punctuation might correspond in some texts to authorial fair copies, but in no cases (not even in the 1616 *Workes* of the notoriously careful Ben Jonson) would it *all* do so. Presenting a text to a public is a necessarily an act of mediation, and it was part of the early modern conception of authorship to accept that putting out a text (and that's all that the word "to edit" means; it derives from the Latin *edo*, which means to give out) involved subjecting it to a collaborative process. Therefore there is nothing wicked in presenting a text which is mediated by modernizing spelling and punctuation to a 21st-century reader, for the process of dissemination is a process of adapting texts to audiences. Shakespeare would not be spinning in his grave.

This argument is neither quite as good or as quite as bad as it might sound. Modernization is the most practiced but most under-theorized activity among editors: only Stanley Wells (Wells and Taylor 1979) has seriously attempted to justify and explicate the practice, and there is no firm agreement about how it should be done. Some modernized editions – such as the Riverside Shakespeare – retain a number of archaic forms; others – such as the Longman editions of Milton's and Marvell's poems – retain the punctuation of the first printed texts. Every editor who has produce a modernized text of the sonnets not only feels but knows that a thousand uncertainties, which might be vital to the flavor of the text, have been occluded by standardizing spelling and punctuation.

So how far does the poet soar in sonnet 29? Q brackets him firmly within the stratosphere:

> Haplye I thinke on thee, and then my state,
> (Like to the Larke at breake of daye arising)
> From sullen earth sings himns at Heauens gate,

Most modern editors, following Malone, turn the poet into a heavenly astronaut:

> Haply I think on thee,—and then my state
> (Like to the lark at break of day arising
> From sullen earth) sings hymns at heaven's gate:

I am in a small minority of editors who follow Q's placing of the brackets here, and because I did so a well-read medical colleague accused me of ruining his favorite poem, which he had read in a text that followed Malone. The arguments about changing a piece of punctuation that might be termed one of the "accidentals" of Q are here of exactly the same sort as arguments about "substantive" emendations. Q offers a paradox of a "state" stuck on "sullen earth" nonetheless singing hymns "at" heaven's gate. The argument for that reading is that it makes sense, although it has the poet paradoxically still excluded from joy when he is singing hymns at heaven's gate ("at" has in Q an almost aggressive force, as though the hymns are artillery). Malone's reading (which he does not note, since he does not regard it as an emendation) has the locational coherence that meant a lot to his period, and those who are skeptical about it would argue that it suits an age of Shakespeare-worshippers suspiciously well to have the poet soar aloft to heaven. It also daringly enjambs a line after a participle, as though lifting off, but in a way that does not comfortably fit my sense of the norms of Shakespearean usage (though norms are only norms, of course). The decision is not just about a bracket, and cannot be resolved simply by principle ("brackets in Q are authorial"): it is, like the decision about the status of manuscript versions of the poems, partly about what kind of Shakespeare an editor wants to believe in.

If "modernized" punctuation can restrict the height to which a soul soars, modern spelling can also damp down some of the faint reverberation of words within words in the text of Q which for many readers give it its life. Katherine Duncan-Jones has noted that Q favors the spelling "mynuits" or "minuites" for "minutes," and has suggested that these forms mark a buried pun on "midnight" via the French *minuit* (Duncan-Jones 1995). Since she believes that Q was authorized, and set from a manuscript close to Shakespeare or even in Shakespeare's hand, she is particularly conscious that modernizing loses a sinister overtone which is present in the text of Q here. Examples could be multiplied endlessly of cases where a reading in Q permits ambiguity as a modernized text does not. There is again simply no solution to this problem except for editors regularly to alert their readers to the quiet violence they may be performing by modernizing the text. To put it more strongly, modernizing editors, even more than non-modernizing editors, urgently need to be two-faced. Their job is to make the sonnets seem welcoming and approachable while at the same time reminding their readers that these poems are anything but either of those things.

In my edition of the sonnets I tried to be as two-faced as I could manage to be: for me it was axiomatic that the artifact called Q "was" the sonnets, and that this physical thing, rather than any abstract conception of Shakespeare's intentions, or any hypothetical authorial manuscript, was what it was my job to present to readers. I did not get it all right, and early impressions of my text contained errors, which several readers pointed out (a full list, for those curious about the dreadful things which even a reasonably diligent editor can do to a text, is in Rasmussen 2003). It was also axiomatic that Q was the outcome of processes which I only partially understood, and that at various points I could uncertainly infer that things had probably gone wrong in that process. I wanted my text to face its readers and their expectations, while as far as possible also facing the text of the quarto. I retained some of the more prominent aspects of Q's punctuation (brackets in particular) since I felt that these were less likely to be compositorial than the colons and stops which quite routinely fall at the end of quatrains, and which may reflect mechanical compositorial expectations about the shape of the Shakespearean sonnet.

Producing texts and understanding texts is a collaborative process. It does not stop with the author, and it is not finalized by an editor. Editors can be dangerous beasts if they think they are right; if they are prepared to regard themselves as part of a conversation about a text that will continue after they are dead, then they may be able to help readers think.

REFERENCES

Editions

S. Booth, ed. (1977). *Shakespeare's Sonnets*. New Haven: Yale University Press.

C. Burrow, ed. (2002). *The Complete Poems and Sonnets*. Oxford: Oxford University Press.

K. Duncan-Jones, ed. (1997). *Shakespeare's Sonnets*. London: Thomas Nelson. (The Arden Shakespeare.)

J. Kerrigan, ed. (1986).*The Sonnets and A Lover's Complaint*. Harmondsworth: Penguin.

E. Malone, ed. (1780). *Supplement to the Edition of Shakspeare's Plays published in 1778 by Samuel Johnson and George Steevens*. London: printed for C. Bathurst, W. Strahan, J. F. and C. Rivington, J. Hinton, L. Davis.

E. Malone, ed. (1790). *The Plays and Poems of William Shakspeare, in ten Volumes*. London: printed by H. Baldwin for J. Rivington and Sons, L. Davis, B. White and Son, T. Longman, B. Law.

H. E. Rollins, ed. (1944). *The Sonnets*, 2 vols. Philadelphia: Lippincott.

M. Seymour-Smith, ed. (1963). *Shakespeare's Sonnets*. London: Heinemann.

G. Wyndham, ed. (1898). *The Poems of William Shakespeare*. London: Methuen.

Secondary Works

Alden, R. M. (1916). "The 1640 Text of *Shakespeare's Sonnets*." *Modern Philology* 14, 17–30.

Beal, Peter, Croft, P. J., et al. (1980). *Index of English Literary Manuscripts*. London and New York: Mansell/Bowker.

Bennett, Josephine W. (1968). "Benson's Alleged Piracy of *Shake-speares Sonnets* and of some of Jonson's Works." *Studies in Bibliography* 21, 235–248.

Byron, George Gordon, Lord (1980). *The Complete Poetical Works*, ed. J. J. McGann, vol. 2. Oxford: Clarendon.

de Grazia, Margreta (1991). *Shakespeare Verbatim: The Reproduction of Authenticity and the 1790 Apparatus*. Oxford: Clarendon.

de Grazia, Margreta (1994). "The Scandal of Shakespeare's Sonnets." *Shakespeare Survey* 46, 35–49.

de Grazia, Margreta, and Stallybrass, Peter (1993). "The Materiality of the Shakespearean Text." *Shakespeare Quarterly* 44, 255–83.

Duncan-Jones, Katherine (1983). "Was the 1609 *Shake-speares Sonnets* Really Unauthorized?" *Review of English Studies* n.s. 34, 151–71.

Duncan-Jones, Katherine (1995). "Filling the Unforgiving Minute: Modernizing *Shake-Speares Sonnets* (1609)." *Essays in Criticism* 45, 199–207.

Greg, W. W. (1923). "An Elizabethan Printer and his Copy." [Richard Field and a MS of Harington's translation of "Orlando Furioso."] *The Library* 4, 102–18.

Greg, W. W. (1943). "The Copyright of Hero and Leander." *The Library* 24, 165–74.

Kerrigan, John (1996). "The Editor as Reader: Constructing Renaissance Texts." In J. Raven, H. Small, and N. Tadmor (eds.), *The Practice and Representation of Reading in England*, 102–24. Cambridge, UK: Cambridge University Press.

Lee, Sidney (1904). *A Life of William Shakespeare*. London: Smith, Elder.

Marcus, Leah S. (1996). *Unediting the Renaissance: Shakespeare, Marlowe, Milton*. London: Routledge.

McGann, Jerome J. (1983). *A Critique of Modern Textual Criticism*. Chicago and London: University of Chicago Press.

McGann, Jerome J. (1991). *The Textual Condition*. Princeton: Princeton University Press.

McKenzie, D. F. (1999). *Bibliography and the Sociology of Texts*. Cambridge, UK: Cambridge University Press.

McLeod, Randall (1991). "Information on Information." *Text: Transactions of the Society for Textual Scholarship* 5, 241–81.

McLeod, Randall, ed. (1994). *Crisis in Editing: Texts of the English Renaissance*. New York: AMS.

O'Neill, Onora (2002). *A Question of Trust*. Cambridge, UK: Cambridge University Press.

Rasmussen, Eric (2003). "Editions and Textual Studies." *Shakespeare Survey* 56, 349–56.

Riding, Laura, and Graves, Robert (1969). *A Survey of Modernist Poetry*. New York: Haskell House.

Shakespeare, William (1992). *The Poems*, ed. J. Roe. Cambridge: Cambridge University Press.

Tanselle, G. Thomas (1990). *Textual Criticism and Scholarly Editing*. Charlottesville, Va.: Bibliographical Society of the University of Virginia.

Taylor, Gary (1985). "Some Manuscripts of Shakespeare's Sonnets." *Bulletin of the John Rylands Library* 68, 210–46.

Vendler, H. (1997). *The Art of Shakespeare's Sonnets*. Cambridge, Mass.: Harvard University Press.

Vickers, Brian (2003). "'A Rum 'Do': The Likely Authorship of *A Lover's Complaint*." *Times Literary Supplement*, 5 Dec., 13–15.

Wells, Stanley (1985). "New Readings in Shakespeare's Sonnets." In J. P. V. Motten, ed., *Elizabethan and Modern Studies Presented to Professor Willem Schrickx on the Occasion of His Retirement*, 319–20. Gent: Seminarie voor Engelse en Amerikaanse Literatuur.

Wells, Stanley W., and Taylor, Gary (1979). *Modernizing Shakespeare's Spelling*. Oxford: Clarendon.

11

William Empson and the Sonnets

Lars Engle

This chapter offers a schematic account of William Empson's approach to literary reading, noting that Empson's first major interpretative project, the Cambridge long essay that became *Seven Types of Ambiguity*, was conceived after Empson read Laura Riding's and Robert Graves's analysis of the quarto version of Shakespeare's sonnet 129. The chapter then treats two post-Empson readings of sonnet 35, a poem never discussed in detail by Empson, focusing both on the reading possibilities Empson opens up and on the ways two strong readers of the sonnets, Stephen Booth and Helen Vendler, have responded to the sonnets and to Empson's example as a reader of them. The chapter closes with reflections on the relation between lyric and speculative biography.

Standing on the shoulders of theoretically inclined recent commentators on Empson like Christopher Norris and Paul Fry (Norris 1978; Fry 1991; Norris and Mapp 1993: 1–120), and profiting by the recent account of the first half of Empson's life in John Haffenden's new biography (Haffenden 2005: 2–5), it is possible to see William Empson's career as following up the consequences of two broad claims about reading literature:

(a) complex and multiple meanings can be reasonably read out of particular textual moments by close attention to their details;

(b) these meanings must ultimately take shape in the reader's mind as part of an author's struggle to live well, often a struggle to understand, embrace, combat, or reconcile himself or herself to particular opportunities and cruelties of the social, moral, or natural order.

I'll refer back to these as (a) and (b) below.

Before turning to the role of Shakespeare's sonnets in the formation and elaboration of these claims or themes in Empson's work, it may be helpful to reflect on what they demand in a reader who aspires to be Empsonian. To elaborate on claim (b): reading involves the reader in an effort to understand an author's life, but the struggle to live well must take place on the reader's side as well for process (b) to be complete, in part because no one who is not attempting to sort out the opportunities and cruelties of his or her own culture can sympathize effectively and imaginatively with such struggles on an author's part. As Empson remarked, "you can only understand people by having such a life in yourself to be their mirror" (Bevis 2004). Process (a) calls on the reader to develop an elastic, often playful, willingness to juggle options and enjoy the complexity of understandable expression, but also to exercise a rigorist belief that reading involves making sense of things as exactly as possible. Put more concisely, to do (a) the reader must combine exquisite sensitivity with belligerent rationality. Thus the fully equipped reader ("geared up," as Empson would say, to do both (a) and (b) at once) needs good cheer, moral sympathy, and an interest in resistance, as well as a highly developed faculty for logical and unsentimental exegesis.

It is evident that (a) and (b) pull in somewhat different directions, but it would be a mistake (though not an uncommon one) to imagine that Empson's career moves alphabetically from (a) to (b). I shall be demonstrating below that both strands are evident and well developed in *Seven Types of Ambiguity*, Empson's first book, published in 1930. It makes some sense to suggest that after *The Structure of Complex Words* (1967; first published in 1951) Empson largely sets aside (a), which he regarded as having been in many ways misappropriated by the New Critics, for (b). More (b) and less (a) allows the later Empson to polemicize vigorously, on the one hand against mere academic explication that ignores the possibility of genuinely meaningful authorial intention, and on the other against historicist orthodoxies that rule out the possibility of genuinely surprising meaning; the latter polemic has been emphasized recently by Richard Strier (1995: 7–26). Nonetheless it remains true that all of Empson's later work from *Milton's God* through *Using Biography* involves passages of remarkably tight analysis, however far the general arguments are from theorizing local meaning.

The way (a) and (b) intertwine at the beginning of Empson's career can be seen, more or less symbolically, in a famous passage from the opening chapter of *Seven Types of Ambiguity*, perhaps the first passage in which new readers of that book became certain that they were dealing with a writer of genius. I quote at length:

> Not unlike the use of a comparison which does not say in virtue of what the two things are to be compared is the use of a comparative adjective which does not say what its noun is to be compared with . . . I shall give an example from one of Mr. Waley's Chinese translations, to insist upon the profundity of feeling which such a device may enshrine.

> > Swiftly the years, beyond recall.
> > Solemn the stillness of this spring morning.

> The human mind has two main scales on which to measure time. The large one takes the length of a human life as its unit, so that there is nothing to be done about life, it is of an animal dignity and simplicity, and must be regarded from a peaceable and fatalistic point of view. The small one takes as its unit the conscious moment, and it is from this that you consider the neighbouring space, an activity of the will, delicacies of social

tone, and your personality. The scales are so far apart as almost to give the effect of defining two dimensions; they do not come into contact because what is too large to be conceived by the one is still too small to be conceived by the other. Thus, taking the units as a century and the quarter of a second, their ratio is ten to the tenth and their mean is the standard working day; or taking the smaller one as five minutes, their mean is the whole of summer. The repose and self-command given by the use of the first are contrasted with the speed at which it shows the years to be passing from you, and therefore with the fear of death; the fever and multiplicity of life, as known by the use of the second, are contrasted with the calm of the external space of which it gives consciousness, with the absolute or extra-temporal value attached to the brief moments of self-knowledge with which it is concerned, and with a sense of security in that it makes death so far off.

Both these time-scales and their contrasts are included by these two lines in a single act of apprehension, because of the words *swift* and *still*. Being contradictory as they stand, they demand to be conceived in different ways; we are enabled, therefore, to meet the open skies with answering stability of self-knowledge; to meet the brevity of human life with an ironical sense that it is morning and springtime, that there is a whole summer before winter, a whole day before night.

I call *swift* and *still* here ambiguous, though each is meant to be referred to one particular time-scale, because between them they put two time-scales into the reader's mind in a single act of apprehension. But these scales, being both present, are in some degree used for each adjective, so that the words are ambiguous in a more direct sense; the *years* of a man's life seem *swift* even on the small scale, like the mist from the mountains which "gathers a moment, then scatters"; the *morning* seems *still* even on the large scale, so that this moment is apocalyptic and a type of heaven. (Empson 1947: 23–4)

These two scales parallel, though they are not identical to, the intensity of the textual moment and the understanding of the text as part of a whole life, itself in relation to yet larger structures of belief and custom, that I have identified above as (a) and (b). Moreover, we can see both (a) and (b) in this passage, though they are clearer in the full text. There is no invocation of authorial biography in Empson's treatment of a translation of a Chinese text that is not credited with either an author or a date. Nonetheless, something like an authorial intention is created by treating the poem as contemplating, and enabling its readers to contemplate, with the goal of making experience more bearable, a general or even universal biological contrast between a moment of perception and the whole lifetime of a human being. Moreover, the passage contrasts short and long time – treating us to some dazzling if obscure calculations in the process – while ignoring the intermediate time structures that, for people like Empson and us, stand between the conscious moment and the lifetime, whether we are looking back in memory or forward in anticipation. I have in mind such structures as projects, career phases, epochs of relationship, periods of institutional affiliation, etc. In ignoring such intermediate structures, Empson parallels in a rather uncanny way his general lack of interest in the larger formal and generic traditions – the inherited structures within which artists work – that might be seen as intermediate between particular passages and grand struggles in the life of the author: Empson pays relatively little attention to most things that lie between (a) and (b) in the ways most literary critics approach literary texts.

Empson does comment wonderfully on form, but it tends to be local form, as can be seen in his discussion early in *Seven Types* of the predominant absence of ambiguity in *The Faerie Queene*. Meditating on "the dreamy repetition of the great stanza perpetually pausing at its close," Empson comments wakefully that "stanzas may . . . be classified by the grammatical connections of the crucial fifth line, which must give a soft bump to the dying fall of the first quatrain, keep it in the air, and prevent it from falling apart from the rest of the stanza" (Empson 1947: 33). He goes on to perform such a classification in a meaty paragraph that anatomizes a number of the kinds of voice and pace to be found in Spenser's epic, and then adds the following observation:

> The size, the possible variety, and the fixity of this unit give something of the blankness that comes from fixing your eyes on a bright spot; you have to yield to it very completely to take in the variety of its movement, and, at the same time, there is no need to concentrate the elements of the situation into a judgment as if for action. As a result of this, when there are ambiguities of idea, it is whole civilisations rather than details of the moment which are their elements; he can pour into the even dreamwork of his fairyland Christian, classical, and chivalrous materials with an air, not of ignoring their differences, but of holding all their systems of values floating as if at a distance, so as not to interfere with one another, in the prolonged and diffused energies of his mind. (Empson 1947: 34)

Here one can see Empson moving from (a) to (b) by way of trying to imagine the creative process of a great poet whose mind would be so untroubled as not to produce local ambiguities of diction. Empson returns to the matter in 1952 in a radio talk entitled "Edmund Spenser: Is He the 'Poet's Poet'?"; after again discussing Spenser's capacity to extend himself (often by placid self-contradiction) rather than concentrating his differences with himself in local complexity or ambiguity, he ends that talk by repeating, with evident admiration for his own youthful productions, this paragraph (Empson 1987: 247–9).

Empson's (a) and (b) premises, seen as a way to map lyric, may seem old-fashioned – though they seem less old-fashioned than they would have fifteen or twenty years ago, before books like Stephen Greenblatt's *Will in the World* or Katharine Duncan-Jones's *Ungentle Shakespeare* reminded us all of the possibilities of speculatively reading authorial biography out of a mixture of facts and fictions. Nonetheless, it is premise (b) that may seem controversial; premise (a), as a habit of reading or thought, is not overtly ideological. But premise (b), with its interest in the author as an imagined self, located in both an individual and a collective history, clearly is an ideological commitment, though a flexible one. On its basis Empson in his own time polemicized against formalist anti-intentionalism, and Empson now seems to weigh in from the grave on how we should go about imagining the subject's position in discourse. Given this, we might expect both poststructuralist readers and new historicist readers, or people who used to identify themselves by those terms and have not yet shed the commitments the terms signal, to be uncomfortable with premise (b), specifically with its reliance on an idea of the author as a historically located individual whose intentions can be inferred.

Deconstructive readers of lyric often use (a) against (b) — that is, they mobilize very detailed descriptions of textual events to demonstrate the implausibility of stabilizing structures like the author's selfhood. That said, it should be noted that some foundational instances of deconstructive reading, for instance Paul de Man's "The Rhetoric of Temporality," offer readings that fit very tidily into an Empsonian pattern. De Man's description of Wordsworth's "A Slumber Did My Spirit Seal," after describing the shock of the death in the white space between the poem's two stanzas, states that "there is no real disjunction of the subject; the poem is written from the point of view of a unified self that fully recognizes a past condition as one of error and stands in a present that, however painful, sees things as they actually are . . . Wordsworth is one of the few poets who can . . . speak, as it were, from beyond their own graves" (de Man 1983: 224–5). Nonetheless, a great deal of poststructuralist writing depends precisely on the notion that one should not expect one's (a)-type analyses to lead to a (b)-type understanding of another person's relation to his or her world. Michel Foucault offers this as a kind of axiom of his moment in the history of writing toward the beginning of "What Is an Author?":

> Writing unfolds like a game that inevitably moves beyond its own rules and finally leaves them behind. Thus the essential basis of this writing is not the exalted emotions related to the act of composition or the insertion of a subject into language. Rather, it is primarily concerned with creating an opening where the writing subject endlessly disappears. (Adams and Searle 1986: 139)

Materialist readers of lyric, while stressing against deconstructors that it is important to come to grips with the cruelty of history rather than to philosophize about the nature of language, tend to avoid Empson's robust intentionalism in a variety of ways. One is to stress the social significance of genres. Thus there are helpful treatments of English Renaissance lyrics as exchange items within côteries and as gifts (e.g. Marotti 1986; Fumerton 1991). Another is to stress the ways lyrics are shaped by some particular early modern discourse (e.g. Schoenfeldt 1999 on the sonnets and physiology). The historicizing projects are often linked to a more general Foucauldian or Althusserian stress on the idea that the subject is enmeshed in constitutive discourses that change over time, and that the real social power lies in the discourses rather than the subjects. In treating lyric, materialist readers subsume (a) within a version of (b) that stresses the social embeddedness of the versifying subject, his or her responsiveness to interpellation, etc. Again, this need not lie outside the parameters of Empson's very flexible account of (b); nor is an Empsonian critical path, alternating between meditation on the local logic of lyrics and very wide-ranging accounts of them as manifestations of the author's struggles, one that materialist critics avoid, though they tend to spend a good deal of time discussing the sets of constraints with which the author struggles as general historical phenomena, and to manifest skepticism about anyone who tries to move directly from (a) to (b) simply on the basis of shared experience. To cite (as I have with de Man and Foucault) a central figure in the evolution of contemporary historicist literary criticism, consider the version of (b) in Stephen Greenblatt's summing-up of his chapter on Sir Thomas Wyatt in *Renaissance Self-Fashioning*, which follows on a fine local account of Wyatt's "They flee from me that sometime did me seek" that in itself moves fluently between (a) and (b) (Greenblatt 1980: 150–4):

> We are now prepared to grasp how the gap between discourse and intention opens up in Wyatt and hence how it is possible for his greatest poems to engage in complex reflections upon the system of values that has generated them. The skillful merger of manliness, realism, individuality, and inwardness succeeds in making Wyatt's poetry, at its best, distinctly more convincing, more deeply moving, than any written not only in his generation but in the preceding century. But his achievement is dialectical: if, through the logic of its development, courtly self-fashioning seizes upon inwardness to heighten its histrionic power, inwardness turns upon self-fashioning and exposes its underlying motives, its origins in aggression, bad faith, self-interest, and frustrated longing. . . . The result is the complex response evoked by a poem like "They Flee from Me": on the one hand, acceptance of the speaker's claim to injured merit, admiration for his mastery of experience, complicity in his "manly" contempt for women's bestial faithlessness; on the other hand, recognition of the speaker's implication in his own betrayal, acknowledgement of the link between the other's imputed bad faith and his own, perception of an interior distance in the ideology so passionately espoused. (Greenblatt 1980: 156)

Certainly Greenblatt sees Wyatt's lyric as part of an author's struggle to live well – a struggle in which the author is, at least in part, failing because he has been fashioned by a courtly system that programs him for failure, but one in which he is also partly succeeding by including intense awareness of this fact in his lyric. Examples from Empson's sonnet criticism will show the frequency with which his own moves to imputed biography end in the imputation of a dialectical or ambivalent selfhood to his author.

I now turn to Shakespeare's sonnets. As is well known, the sonnets bear a privileged historical role in Empson's formation as a literary critic. He got the idea for what became *Seven Types of Ambiguity* from a 1928 essay by Laura Riding and Robert Graves that explored the punctuation, syntax, and meaning of sonnet 129 by reading an unedited version of that poem (Wellek 1986: 275; for the full, rather complicated story see Haffenden 2005: 216–26).

The first part of Empson's book to appear in print was an essay on sonnet 16 that pursued their method. A number of the analyses in *Seven Types* focus on sonnets, though commentators note that the book's treatment of the sonnets is fairly weak by comparison with its handling of other lyrics or of passages from Shakespeare's plays (Sale 1973: 126; Fry 1991: 89). Empson's central treatment of the sonnets comes in the chapter on sonnet 94, "They that have power to hurt," in *Some Versions of Pastoral*, and there are recurrent references to the sonnets in Empson's discussion of the plays and narrative poems ever after, notably in the chapter on "sense" in *Measure for Measure* in *Complex Words* and in the essay introducing the Signet edition of the narrative poems, now reprinted in *Essays on Shakespeare*.

I want to suggest, however, that Empson may have been drawn to the sonnets not merely because they are luminous beacons for any interpreter drawn to complex utterance. For it is in relation to the sonnets that Empson could be said to discover how to join (a) with (b), extremely close textual analysis with speculative authorial biography. And the reason for this is fairly obvious, so that it must long since have been clear where I am headed. After all, the sonnets are to a pre-eminent degree both locally complex and biographically suggestive. More crucially, without large-scale biographical inferences local ingenuity has a great deal of difficulty making sense of them (witness the debate over whether Stephen Booth's attempts to have a lot of (a) without much (b) produce satisfaction [see e.g. Vendler 1997: 2–4]). For Empson, at any rate, it is evidently both impossible and undesirable to do much type-(a) analysis of the sonnets without involving himself in a good deal of type-(b) hypothesizing about the life of the author. Empson moves from one to the other in the first two pages of *Seven Types*, citing line 4 of sonnet 73.

> To take a famous example, there is no pun, double syntax, or dubiety of feeling in,
>
> > Bare ruined choirs, where late the sweet birds sang,
>
> but the comparison holds for many reasons; because ruined monastery choirs are places in which to sing, because they involve sitting in a row, because they are made of wood, are carved into knots, and so forth, because they used to be surrounded by a sheltering building crystallised out of the likeness of a forest, and coloured with stained glass and painting like flowers and leaves, because they are now abandoned by all but the grey walls coloured like the skies of winter, because the cold and Narcissistic charm suggested by choir-boys suits well with Shakespeare's feeling for the object of the Sonnets, and for various sociological and historical reasons (the protestant destruction of monasteries; fear of puritanism), which it would be hard now to trace out in their proportions; these reasons, and many more relating the simile to its place in the Sonnet, must all combine to give the line its beauty, and there is a sort of ambiguity in not knowing which of them to hold most clearly in mind. Clearly this is involved in all such richness and heightening of effect, and the machinations of ambiguity are among the very roots of poetry. (Empson 1947: 2–3)

(The final sentence in the passage shows that Empson feels that his (b)-drenched exploration of (a) gets at something central about the nature of lyric.)

This is a baroque passage, richer and more startling than most of the later treatments of whole sonnets in *Seven Types*, and it encapsulates an Empsonian movement from specific words through the mind of the author (Shakespeare's feeling for the young man) to various aspects of the author's culture that may have pressed on the author's consciousness. These include Shakespearean ambivalence about the destruction of English

Catholicism, possibly an historically prescient awareness that religious intolerance in England is always part of a struggle for power and property between one group and another, and a "fear of puritanism" that seems to involve both a professional wariness of the consequences of Puritan anti-theatricalism and a more personal fear that puritanical resistance to the pursuit of bodily pleasure will not only oppress him but also possibly infect him, as it seems to be doing in some of the dark lady sonnets (cf. Empson 1967: 272).

Such speculative unpacking of Empson's own formulations is, surely, encouraged by Empson's general way of going about things. Moreover, Empson's biography supports the speculation. When he published *Seven Types* Empson himself was, we now know, a recent victim of what he clearly regarded as hypocritical puritanism. After his outstanding undergraduate results at Cambridge, Empson was, unsurprisingly, elected to a research fellowship at Magdalene and seemed headed for a career in the Cambridge English school. But servants found condoms in his luggage when helping him move into college rooms to take up his fellowship, and his testimony at an inquiry by the College Governing Board made it clear that he had, indeed, used them (see Haffenden in Empson 1986b: 11; see also Empson's poem "Warning to Undergraduates" in Empson 1986b: 115–17 and, for the full story, Haffenden 2005: 230–59). As a result of this shocking discovery, Magdelene College withdrew Empson's research fellowship and expelled him, and the university made it clear that he was not welcome in Cambridge. Thus Empson's biographical projection of a Shakespeare haunted by Puritanism and the casting-off of bad influences on the young – a projection that informs his close readings of the *Henriad* and *Measure for Measure* – seems linked to Empson's own biography from the start.

Empson's extended discussion of sonnet 83 in *Seven Types* furthers such reflections. The discussion comes at the beginning of his chapter on ambiguities of the fourth type: "when two or more meanings of a statement do not agree among themselves, but combine to make clear a more complicated state of mind in the author" (Empson 1947: 133). Thus Empson abstractly states one of the major relations between (a) and (b) in his criticism: a problem encountered in type-(a) local exegesis leads to, and is then retroactively fixed or transcended by, an advance in type-(b) imputed biography. The full sonnet, with punctuation and capitalization (though not spelling) according to the 1609 quarto, as quoted by Empson, is as follows:

> I never saw that you did painting need,
> And therefore to your fair no painting set,
> I found (or thought I found) you did exceed,
> The barren tender of a Poet's debt:
> And therefore have I slept in your report,
> That you yourself being extant well might show,
> How far a modern quill doth come too short,
> Speaking of worth, what worth in you doth grow,
> This silence for my sin you did impute,
> Which shall be most my glory being dumb,

> For I impair not beauty being mute,
> When others would give life, and bring a tomb.
> There lives more life in one of your fair eyes,
> Than both your Poets can in praise devise.
>   (Empson 1947: 133)

Empson comments of the whole:

> One must pause before shadowing with irony this noble compound of eulogy and apology.
> But one may notice its position in the sequence (Shakespeare seems to have been taunted
> for his inferiority, and is being abandoned for the rival poet); the mixture of extraordinary
> claims and bitter humility with which it is surrounded; and that the two adjacent Sonnets
> say: "Thou truly fair wert truly sympathised In true plain words by thy truth-telling
> friend," and "You to your beauteous blessings add a curse, Being fond on praise, which
> makes your praises worse." It is not true that the feeling must be simple because it is
> deep; irony is similar to this kind of lyrical self-abandonment, or they relieve similar
> situations; by the energy with which such an adoration springs forward one can measure
> the objections which it is overriding, by the sharpness of what is treated as an ecstasy
> one may guess that it would otherwise have been pain. (Empson 1947: 134)

Here Empson moves to a direct declaration, "it is not true that the feeling must be
simple because it is deep," that seems, in its generality, to be grounded in Empson's
own mind mirroring the imputed experience of Shakespeare as well as in his reading
of this particular sonnet. The claim makes Shakespearean ambiguity (at least as manifested in this sonnet) into the expression of Shakespeare's (and, perhaps, everyone's)
ambivalence, an ambivalence that can find "relief" in either lyric idealization or irony
or an ambiguous combination of the two. The particular biographical construction
Empson has in mind becomes clearer in his discussion of the final quatrain.

It too involves the characteristic movement from (a) to (b). Unlike modern editors,
who almost without exception insert a comma after "beauty" in line 11, thus making
it seem almost necessary to read line 12 as meaning "When the other poets who are
now writing about you intend to give you life but in fact give you a tomb," Empson,
reading the quarto punctuation, considers at length the possibility that lines 11 and
12 should rather be paraphrased together to allow the possibility that it is Shakespeare
who "bring[s] a tomb":

> It would be possible to regard line 12, which clinches the third quatrain, as an antithesis:
> "when others would bring life, I in fact bring a tomb." This might be Shakespeare's *tomb*;
> "I do not flatter you but I bring you the devotion of a lifetime." More probably it is
> W. H.'s; "I do not attempt to flatter you at the moment; I bring you the sad and reserved
> gift of an eternal praise." We may extract from this some such meaning as: "I do not
> describe your beauty or your faithlessness, but my love for you." However, there are two
> other ways of taking the syntax which destroy this antithesis: "When others would bring
> life, I, if I wrote about you, would bring a tomb," and "When others would try to write
> about you, would try to give you life, and thereby bring you a tomb"; for both of these

the *tomb* must imply some action which would *impair beauty*. The normal meaning is
given by Sonnet xvii:

> Who will beleeve my verse in time to come
> If it were fild with your most high deserts?
> Though yet Heaven knowes it is but as a tombe
> Which hides your life, and shows not halfe your parts.

This first use of the word has no doubt that it is eulogy; the Sonnet is glowing and
dancing with his certitude. But when the metaphor is repeated, this time without being
explained, it has grown dark with an incipient double meaning; "I should fail you, now
that you have behaved so badly to me, if I tried to express you in poetry; I should give
you myself, and draw from my readers, a cold and limited judgment, praise you without
sincerity, or blame you without thinking of the living man." (Empson 1947: 137–8)

This is something new. What is Empson doing when he, as Shakespeare, says to
"W.H." "now that you have behaved so badly to me, if I tried to express you in poetry . . . I should . . . blame you without thinking of the living man"? Surely we must
call this a kind of *performance* of the sonnet (this is well within our ideas of what one
does with lyric); but it is also a kind of *impersonation* of the poet (and this stretches
our normal thinking). Having followed premise (a) and explored the varieties of possible meaning in the quatrain, Empson takes premise (b) so far that he in effect
becomes the speaker/poet who voices the complex of feelings within it. Like a Stan-
islavskian actor, Empson constructs both a biography for the lyric speaker (mostly out
of the adjacent sonnets in the sequence and his general sense of it), and what he voices
is a kind of through line for the sonnet – a set of declarations in his own distinctive
prose. His tendentious paraphrase picks up the aspect of Shakespeare's relation to the
young man that most interests Empson by giving what most readers find the least
probable construction of lines 11–12. This "incipient double meaning" lets Empson,
having temporarily become Shakespeare, return and tell us what Shakespeare feels as
he writes, quoting Parolles's most famous line from *All's Well that Ends Well* in the
process:

> "I should . . . blame you without thinking of the living man." ("Simply the thing I am
> Shall make me live"; Shakespeare continually draws on a generosity of this kind. It is
> not "tout comprendre," in his view, it is merely to feel how a man comes to be a working
> system, which necessarily excites a degree of sympathy.) (Empson 1947: 138)

The idea that one of the goals of lyric is to anatomize the excitation of sympathy by
showing Shakespeare "feel[ing] how a man comes to be a working system" is quite
close, it seems to me, to the way that Greenblatt suggests that our response to Wyatt
involves both sympathetic admiration for Wyatt's expression of loss and awareness that
in his lyric Wyatt is worked by the system that he is working. And all this plausible
and powerful Empsonian generalization about Shakespeare emerges from a type (a)
problem in reading that most modern editions, by repunctuating, render invisible.

Let me close this part of the essay by briefly discussing the chapter on sonnet 94 in *Some Versions of Pastoral*, which offers a kind of exercise in moving through (a) to (b) and fully displays Empson's technique of Shakespeare impersonation. Following Graves and Riding, Empson quotes the Q version:

> They that haue powre to hurt,and will doe none,
> That doe not do the thing,they most do showe,
> Who mouing others,are themselues as stone,
> Vnmooued,could,and to temptation slow:
> They rightly do inherrit heauens graces,
> And husband natures ritches from expence,
> They are the Lords and owners of their faces,
> Others,but stewards of their excellence:
> The sommers flowre is to the sommer sweet,
> Though to itselfe, it onely liue and die,
> But if that flowre with base infection meete,
> The basest weed out-braues his dignity:
>   For sweetest things turne sowrest by their deedes,
>   Lillies that fester, smell far worse then weeds.
>   (Empson 1974: 88)

Empson begins by setting up the basic problem of interpretation posed by the unspecified terms that need to be placed in comparison with one another in the sonnet: "you can work through all the notes in the Variorum without finding out whether flower, lily, 'owner,' and person addressed are alike or opposed . . . the simplest view (that any two may be alike in some one property) . . . yields 4096 possible movements of thought." He concludes that "the niggler is routed here; one has honestly to consider what seems important" (Empson 1974: 89). There is no "person addressed" in 94 proper (just as line 4 of 73 is not a "simile"), but Empson will not be inhibited from biography by such minor matters of form, and, as he points out later, the idea of address is carried over from 93 and continues through 95, both sonnets on related themes. Empson's calculation of the number of possible movements of thought is famously wrong, incidentally.

Empson's treatment of the sonnet includes many of the kinds of meditation joining (a) and (b) I have talked about above. One occurs as Empson reflects on what kind of mental tool sonnet 94 turns out to be. It is both a map on which one can trace many routes, and an instrument on which the reader and the author are both imagined as performers. The mind of the reader and the mind of the author meet here in much the way they met in Empson's discussion of the Spenserian stanza in *Seven Types*:

The vague and generalised language of the descriptions [in sonnet 94], which might be talking about so many sorts of people as well as feeling so many things about them, somehow makes a unity like a crossroads, which analysis does not deal with by exploring down the roads; makes a solid flute on which you can play a multitude of tunes, whose solidity no list of all possible tunes would go far to explain. The balance of feeling is both very complex and very fertile; experiences are recorded, and metaphors invented, in the Sonnets, which he went on "applying" as a dramatist, taking particular cases of them as if they were wide generalisations, for the rest of his life. (Empson 1974: 90).

After an illuminating discussion of the passage (and as part of a generous and helpful discussion of Empson's brilliant contribution to studies of pastoral), Paul Alpers comments oddly in *What Is Pastoral?* that "the unity of a crossroads (such as it is) is a fact of social existence, with no grounding in nature or analogy to the human individual; the solid flute suggests the limits of the minds that write and interpret, for of course no tune can be played on it" (Alpers 1996: 37–8). But surely Empson means that the sonnet is fluid in that many various meanings can pass through it, yet solid in that it remains the singular and unchanging instrument on which such meanings are "played" by the author or by readers? I do not think, *pace* Alpers, that Empson intends the idea of a flute that has no hollow passage through which to blow air.

At any rate, this idea of the lyric as crossroads or instrument serves as Empson's segue to a wide-ranging account of links among this sonnet, all the sonnets, and a number of the plays. As he notes, "it is hard not to go off down one of the roads at the crossing, and get one plain meaning for the poem from that, because Shakespeare himself did that so very effectively afterwards; a part of the situation of the Sonnets, the actual phrases designed for it, are given to Prince Henry, to Angelo, to Troilus, to the Greek army; getting further from the original as time went on" (Empson 1974: 102). After exploring these, Empson concludes with a tendentious paraphrase that is both his own final attempt to read sonnet 94 and Shakespeare's final attempt to sum up his relation to the young man:

> It is not surprising that this sentiment [Bassanio's awareness that he is loved for his own success and superficial qualities] should make Shakespeare's mind hark back to the Sonnets, because it was there so essential; these poems of idealisation of a patron and careerist depend upon it for their strength and dignity. "Man is so placed that the sort of thing you do is in degree all that any one can do; success does not come from mere virtue, and without some external success a virtue is not real even to itself. One must not look elsewhere; success of the same nature as yours is all that the dignity, whether of life or poetry, can be based upon." This queer sort of realism, indeed, is one of the main things he had to say.
>
> The feeling that life is essentially inadequate to the human spirit, and yet that a good life must avoid saying so, is naturally at home with most versions of pastoral . . . (Empson 1974: 114–15)

Thus in his type (b) criticism of Shakespeare, Empson is preoccupied with, and vocalizes from the inside, a quasi-biographical question about Shakespeare that was probably at times an autobiographical question for Empson as well: how could someone so unimaginably successful in literary creation be so unhappy – or, to put it another way, how could someone with such extraordinary analytical gifts make such self-destructive object choices? Empson's answer comes here, in the idea that literary creation can come out of the acceptance that "life is essentially inadequate to the human spirit, and yet that a good life must avoid saying so." This intellectually enabling though not personally reassuring attitude, a kind of negative humanism, informs much of Empson's Shakespeare criticism.

Empson's example has had a considerable effect on later critics of the sonnets, most explicitly in their embrace of the (a) position outlined above. As Empson says in defense of his (a) premise at the end of *Seven Types of Ambiguity*,

> an advance in the machinery of description makes a reader feel stronger about his appreciations, more reliably able to distinguish the private or accidental from the critically important or repeatable, more confident of the reality (that is, the transferability) of his experiences; adds, in short, in the mind of the reader to the things there to be described, whether or not it makes those particular things more describable. (Empson 1947: 254)

Both Stephen Booth and Helen Vendler, in their sonnet-by-sonnet commentaries, seek to "advance the machinery of description" through precise elucidation of local semantic and aesthetic effects.

In the preface to his edition of the sonnets, Stephen Booth takes Empson's pioneering discussion of sonnet 16 – the first piece of criticism Empson published, subsequently included in *Seven Types* – as an example of how to admit and celebrate the extraordinary wealth of overlapping meanings in Shakespearean language (Empson 1947: 54–7; Shakespeare 1977: xiii–xvi). He also devotes a substantial segment of his 1969 *An Essay on Shakespeare's Sonnets* to a detailed demonstration (with much citation of other critics responding to Empson) that in his treatment of sonnet 94 in *Some Versions of Pastoral* Empson has sacrificed (a) to (b) by subordinating much of the play of signification in the poem to his beliefs about what the speaker means to say to the (non-)addressee – that is, the young man whom Empson sees as the target as well as the topic of the poem (Booth 1969: 152–68; for a recent critique that partly takes issue with Booth see Schoenfeldt 1999: 83–95). Like Empson, Booth is concerned to argue that extremely precise type (a) description – which brings out areas of puzzlement – need not and should not detract from the appreciation of beauty:

> My notes are as much occupied with investigating the sources of the greatness, the beauty, and, often, the obvious substantive meaning of Shakespeare's sentences as with reviving and revealing that meaning; the notes analyze the processes by which the relevant meanings of Shakespeare's words and phrases and the contexts they bring with them combine, intertwine, fuse, and conflict in the potentially dizzying complexity from which a reader's sense of straightforward simplicity emerges. It is the complexity, I think, that gives the sonnets what critics of eras less ambitious than this one for the clinical precision of natural science called the magic of the sonnets, the sense they give of effortless control of the uncontrollable. The notes to this edition investigate the particulars of the complexity. Any reader superstitiously fearful that the magic of a poem will vanish with knowledge

of its sources need not worry any more than a student of zoology need worry that gazelles will slow down if he investigates the reasons why they can run so fast. (Shakespeare 1977: xii–xiii)

As we have seen, then, Booth takes Empson as something of a model for the kind of registration of line-by-line complexity undertaken in his own commentary. But if he follows the (a) premise I've attributed to Empson, Booth is an overt foe of what he calls "inferential biography" and thus would seem to be at least wary of the (b) premise discussed throughout this chapter (see Shakespeare 1977: 543). His hostility to biographical imputation is suggested by a well-known comment in his Appendix 1: "HOMOSEXUALITY: Shakespeare was almost certainly homosexual, bisexual, or heterosexual. The sonnets provide no evidence on the matter" (Shakespeare 1977: 548). Although Booth might phrase the comment differently now, in light of arguments that the terms "homosexual" and "heterosexual" are anachronistic descriptors for early modern subjects, I doubt that the scholarship on the sonnets since 1977 would change his mind about the central claim that on this topic as others the sonnets are not biographically informative.

Helen Vendler sees Booth, almost alone among the critics she takes seriously, as offering (a) with too little (b), while other critics err by having far too much (b) with very little (a): that is, she credits Booth with appropriately stressing the variety and complexity of what goes on inside a lyric, but believes that he gives up too easily on the task of describing its fundamental or unifying shape (she avoids the idea that it is "meaning" one should be after). "Booth's critical stance – that the critic, helpless before the plurisignification of language and overlapping of multiple structures visible in a Shakespearean sonnet, must be satisfied with irresolution with respect to its fundamental gestalt – seems to me too ready a surrender to hermeneutic suspicion" (Vendler 1997: 13). She sees Empson as a pioneer of type (a) criticism, citing "brilliant beginnings" in the description of "what ideational and structural and linguistic acts by a poet result in a successful poem . . . by William Empson (on individual words and images)" (pp. 12–13). Empson does not seem to count for Vendler as a constructor of explanatory biographical imputations. Her own critical practice is declaredly anti-thematic, but she does put emphasis on the way lyrics invite personalization when she writes that "the poet's duty is to create aesthetically convincing representations of feelings felt and thoughts thought" (p. 16), and she herself engages in something like speculative biography in such comments as "the infatuation of the speaker with the young man is so entirely an infatuation of the eye – which makes a fetish of the beloved's countenance rather than of his entire body – that gazing is this infatuation's chief (and perhaps best and only) form of intercourse" (p. 15). The difference from Empson here is that Vendler draws a sharp and consistent distinction between the speaker and the author, evidently seeing it as appropriate that we admire the author's amazing mastery even as we experience and reproduce the speaker's occasional abjection: "a formidable intellectual command . . . in the person of their invisible author . . . accounts for the *Sonnets'* serene and unfaltering air of poetic resource, even (or perhaps especially) in the moments of the speaker's greatest psychological distraction" (p. 32). Empson fervently embraces the "intentional fallacy," a phrase for which he never forgave William Wimsatt (see e.g. Empson 1986a: 158); Vendler avoids it, at least with respect to this set of lyrics. Vendler also, unlike Empson, rarely seems to be puzzling her way through a poem; rather she presents herself as utterly sure she has the tone and stance of every line just right. In this, she avoids the kind of interpretative autobiographical provisionality that is such a feature of Empson's criticism (Strier 2006).

Despite this, she can, like Empson, sometimes seem intimately aware of the creative process of her author. As Empson does in his description of the Spenserian stanza, Vendler discusses the form of a Shakespearean sonnet as it might be experienced in the process of repetitive composition:

> The sonnets stand as the record of a mind working out positions without the help of any pantheon or systematic doctrine. Shakespeare's speaker often considers, in rapid succession, any number of intellectual or ideological positions, but he does not move among them at random. To the contrary: in the first quatrain of any given sonnet he has a wide epistemological field in which to play, but in the second quatrain he generally queries or contradicts or subverts his first position (together with its discourse-field). By the third quatrain he must (usually) advance to his subtlest or most comprehensive or most truthful position (Q_3 therefore taking on, in the Shakespearean sonnet, the role of the sestet in the Petrarchan sonnet). And the couplet – placed not as resolution (which is the function of Q_3) but as coda – can then stand in any number of relations (summarizing, ironic, expansive) to the preceding argument. The gradually straitened possibilities as the speaker advances in his considerations give the Shakespearean sonnet a funnel-shape, narrowing in Q_3 to a vortex of condensed perceptual and intellectual force, and either constricting or expanding that vortex via the couplet. (Vendler 1997: 25)

Vendler ties her commitment to the endeavor of describing the mechanisms of the sonnet to a comment by W. H. Auden that neatly summarizes (and is, I think, at least somewhat indebted to) Empson's commitments to (a) and (b) in his earlier criticism:

> The questions which interest me most when reading a poem are two. The first is technical: "Here is a verbal contraption. How does it work?" The second is, in the broadest sense, moral: "What kind of guy inhabits this poem? What is his notion of the good life or the good place? His notion of the Evil One? What does he conceal from the reader? What does he conceal even from himself?" (Vendler 1997: 10–11, citing Auden 1968: 55)

Vendler links her own descriptions of the sonnets, which she represents as dealing with technical poetic issues that are thereby prior to thematic interpretation, specifically to the discourse of mechanism in Auden: "[b]ecause many essays on the sonnets attempt moral and ethical discussion without any close understanding of how the poems are put together, I have emphasized in this Commentary the total 'contraptionness' as the first necessary level of understanding" (1997: 11). And she clearly believes that Auden's interest in imputed biography, the Empsonian premise (b) interest in "What kind of guy inhabits this poem," must properly go on inseparably from, and as a consequence of close attention to, the technical, premise (a) activity of noticing and describing how the poem's elements work together. (While the question of Empson's influence on Auden as critic is beyond the scope of this essay, it is perhaps worth noting that they were friends – Auden loaned Empson money after a robbery so that Empson could get back to England in 1939 – and that Auden quotes *Some Versions of Pastoral* in the Shakespeare lectures he gave in New York in 1940–1, when he was formulating ideas that he published in *The Dyer's Hand* [Bevis 2004; Carpenter 1981: 279; Auden 2000: 138, 143].)

In describing above why Shakespeare's sonnets were so formative in Empson's emergence as a literary critic, I implicitly suggested that for readers of the sonnets, whether disposed in their other work toward attentive exegesis or toward biographical inference or toward neither of these things, type (a) explication and type (b) imputation tend to follow from the nature of Shakespeare's lyric sequence. Given this claim, I want to look briefly at the ways Booth and Vendler treat sonnet 35, a sonnet that Empson never deals with in any detail, though there is a short discussion of its use of the word "sense" in *Complex Words* (Empson 1967: 272–3).

I quote from Booth's edition (Vendler, who emends line 8 differently, thus discusses a slightly different poem):

> No more be grieved at that which thou hast done:
> Roses have thorns, and silver fountains mud,
> Clouds and eclipses stain both moon and sun,
> And loathsome canker lives in sweetest bud.
> All men make faults, and even I in this,
> Authorizing thy trespass with compare,
> Myself corrupting salving thy amiss,
> Excusing thy sins more than thy sins are;
> For to thy sensual fault I bring in sense—
> Thy adverse party is thy advocate—
> And 'gainst myself a lawful plea commence.
> Such civil war is in my love and hate,
>   That I an áccessary needs must be
>   To that sweet thief which sourly robs from me.
>   (Shakespeare 1977: 32)

Booth begins his commentary with line-by-line glosses – including some of the registration of semantic static for which his edition is famous: "*make faults* Shakespeare's contemporaries may have heard a pun here on 'make farts' (a pun that would have given cogency to a complementary pun on *in sense* in line nine)" (Shakespeare 1977: 190). But he ends (as he often does in glossing sonnets he thinks particularly exemplary or important) with a summary note on the sonnet as a whole. It begins "This sonnet is a variation of Shakespeare's habits of damning with fulsome praise (as in 87. 1) and of making flattering accusations (as in 33)" (Shakespeare 1977: 191). Booth then characterizes the first quatrain: apparently "a loving effort to relieve the beloved's sense of guilt," it is undermined by "the easiness of its not-quite-appropriate platitudes" so that it "advertises the speaker's earnest benevolence rather than the justice of the defense he offers" (p. 191). The next quatrain "develops a competition in guilt between the speaker and the beloved," which Booth details with short tendentious paraphrases of an Empsonian kind: " 'you are no more guilty than other mortals'; . . . 'I am guilty too; I am in the act of sinning now,' . . . 'I am more guilty than you' . . . 'I have become so for your sake' " (p. 191). A glance back at the second quatrain will show that these imputed statements, though highly suggestive, and nicely capturing the accelerating rhythm of accusation and self-accusation, are paraphrases only in a very extended (and, again, very Empsonian) sense of the word "paraphrase." The speaker in 35 never says, for instance, that he is "more guilty" than the addressee (or at any rate I would not so construe "more than thy sins are" in quite this way, despite the proverb "a fault once excused is twice committed" that Booth aptly cites in his line-by-line commentary: p. 190). Like Empson, Booth here revels creatively in the experience of being Shakespeare. Having established the rhythm with these short quotations, Booth's description picks up further speed: "From there the speaker goes on to belittle the beloved (ll. 8 and 9), to call attention to his own superiority as both sinner and sacrificer (ll. 9–11), and to reassert the beloved's wrongdoing" (p. 191). It is clear by this time that the close attention to the multiplicity and undecidability of sonnet meaning for which Booth is well known has given way to an excited and attractive conviction that he knows just what is going on and can rival the vigor of its presentation:

> The poem leaves the beloved diminished and under a new guilt – the guilt of being beneficiary of the speaker's ostentatious sacrifice. All in all, the manner of this poem is that of a long-suffering and relentlessly selfless wife. The facts the poem reports should make the speaker seem admirable in a reader's eyes; the speaker's manner, however, gives conviction to the idea that he is worthy of the contempt he says he deserves. Everything about the poem – its substance, its structure, its syntax, its effect – suggests *civil war* (courteous, legalistic, *and* intestine). (Shakespeare 1997: 191–2)

We see Booth driven by the power of the sonnet (to some extent against his own declared resistance to single story-lines) into a strongly Empsonian reading that moves from premise (a), registration of verbal complexity, to premise (b), speculative recreation of a recognizable human situation fraught with pain and ambivalence.

Helen Vendler's handling of sonnet 35 is more elaborate: among other things, it persuasively bears out her description of the general funnel-shaped logical pattern in the sequence. A key paragraph lays out the relations between the first two quatrains, seen in the light of the superior analytic clarity achieved in the third:

> The *dédoublement* by which the speaker now bitterly scrutinizes his past exculpatory commonplaces (roses with thorns, fountains with mud, suns with eclipses, cankers in buds) is visible chiefly in the violent departure from those Q₁ commonplaces in the knotted language of Q₂. The "same person" cannot speak both the first quatrain and the second: the speaker of the first was misguided, and even corrupt, according to the speaker of the

second. Therefore, the speaker resorts to the subsequent analytic metaphor of civil war: the first quatrain was spoken (according to subsequent analysis) by *love* (not besottedness or moral fatuity) and the second by *hate* (a far cry from clear moral logic). But although the closing judgment will name Q$_1$ *love* and Q$_2$ *hate*, as we actually encounter the poem we hear the sentences of Q$_1$ *as quoted* by the present speaker of Q$_2$; the sentences are therefore given in a foolish, flat, and debased form, which would not convince a flea, and which in fact amount (so cunningly is *hate* arranging them) to a progressive indictment of the friend ("You are a rose with thorns, you are a fountain with mud, you are a stained sun, you have a loathsome worm living in you"). One imagines that when these excuses were made in the true voice of love (rather than the voice of love summarized by hate), they sounded passionate and convinced. (Vendler 1997: 186)

Unlike Booth, Vendler does not believe that the sonnet's ending presents a speaker "worthy of the contempt he says he deserves" (Shakespeare 1977: 192). Though she employs tendentious declarative paraphrase in moving from logical detail to human situation in an Empsonian way, she does not follow Booth in continuing to paraphrase the poem according to the human situation of the speaker excusing, berating, and guilt-tripping the beloved. Instead, she works with the opposed voices of love and hate she has identified as formally present in quatrains one and two:

"I have corrupted myself" is a statement that presupposes a *true* "higher" self which has, by a "lower" self, been corrupted, and which should once again take control. Even the metaphor of lawsuits implies that one side, in each suit, is "lawful" and should win. In the close, *love* and *hate* have equal civil voices, and the robbed plaintiff (feeling *hate*) is at the same time the willing criminal accessory (feeling *love*). Though this expressed dualism cannot be called self-integration, it is an epistemological advance over the attempt by the voice of *hate* to suppress, in lines 1–8, the voice of *love* (which, so long as it speaks from a feeling that still exists, cannot in poetry be suppressed without formal crime). (Vendler 1997: 189)

Vendler's commitment to the idea that the sonnets are the work of an artist who stands well above the emotional turbulence of his speaker doubtless contributes to the sort of balance her description of the action of the poem achieves. Booth, though in general less prone than Empson to throwing himself into the speaker's situation and imagining it as the author's, offers a reading of sonnet 35 that dramatizes the poem as a gesture in an ongoing human struggle rather than seeing it, as Vendler does, as a progressive meditation on such gestures. But Vendler ends her comment on this sonnet with a quite Empsonian glance at the sequence as a whole, seen as an ongoing human crisis in which, at the end, fulfillment is rather magnificently forgone in favor of art:

The difficulty of maintaining love for an unpredictably unfaithful beloved will henceforth preoccupy the sonnets to the friend. The speaker's final solution will be, in 124, to separate completely the act of love from its object, and to make it absolute in its own grandeur, without respect to the worth of the beloved. It is a drastic but sublime (and also tragic) solution. (Vendler 1997: 189)

At this point, though she sticks to the term "speaker," Vendler is talking about the architecture and curve of feeling of the sequence as a whole – something we would normally attribute to the poet rather than the speaker: she here comes as close as she ever does to an Empsonian biographical imputation.

I have chosen Stephen Booth and Helen Vendler for detailed comparison with Empson because I regard them highly, not because I regard them as uniquely Empsonian in their ways of moving between precise formal analysis and resonant generalization. Indeed, my point is that the sonnets impose this Empsonian oscillation on many readers, including these two very strong and theoretically self-aware ones, neither of whom would accept Empson's premise (b) in the form stated at the opening of this chapter. I do not claim to have caught Booth or Vendler channeling Empson and losing their resistance to intentional criticism. But I have shown how each of them, at the end of a wonderfully revealing close analysis of a great sonnet, moves along paths Empson has marked: ventriloquizing the variety of different lines of lyric thought as tendentious addressed statement, and then moving yet further (as Vendler does) to general description of the preoccupations and strategies of a larger poetic project that involves drastic, sublime, and tragic personal relations.

If my description of Empson is persuasive – both as an account of Empson and as an approach to the sonnets – it may contribute to readings of the sonnets by linking them to a general account of the power of lyric that is, as we have seen, partly derived from reading the sonnets. Precisely because the (a) and (b) premises I have attributed to Empson seem so obvious and (though disputable) innocuous, they may sort uneasily with the professional critic's imperative to say something new. But the examples I have explored, both in Empson's own work and in that of Booth and Vendler, show how nigglingly precise exegesis (involving logical mastery and apparent detachment) and openness to the performance of lyric intentionality (involving emotional vulnerability and evident attachment) combine in some exemplary sonnet readers.

Author's Note

My thanks to David Goldstein, Holly Laird, and Richard Strier for commentary. An earlier version of the essay was composed for an MLA session at the invitation of David Mikics and Jenn Lewin and expanded for an SAA seminar led by Paul Edmondson and Stanley Wells.

References

Adams, Hazard, and Searle, Leroy, eds. (1986). *Critical Theory since 1965*. Tallahassee and Gainesville: University Presses of Florida.

Alpers, Paul (1996). *What is Pastoral?* Chicago: University of Chicago Press.

Auden, W. H. (1968). *"The Dyer's Hand" and Other Essays*. New York: Viking.

Auden, W. H. (2000). *Lectures on Shakespeare*, ed. Arthur Kirsch. Princeton: Princeton University Press.

Bevis, Matthew (2004). "William Empson." *The Literary Encyclopedia*. www.LitEncyc.com.

Booth, Stephen (1969). *An Essay on Shakespeare's Sonnets*. New Haven and London: Yale University Press.

Carpenter, Humphrey (1981). *W. H. Auden: A Biography*. London: Allen & Unwin.

de Man, Paul (1983). *Blindness and Insight*, 2nd rev. edn. Vol. 7 of *Theory and History of Literature*. Minneapolis: University of Minnesota Press.

Duncan-Jones, Katherine (2001). *Ungentle Shakespeare: Scenes from His Life*. London: Thomson Learning. (The Arden Shakespeare.)

Empson, William (1947). *Seven Types of Ambiguity*, rev. edn. New York: New Directions. (First publ. 1930.)

Empson, William (1965). *Milton's God*, rev. edn. London: Chatto & Windus. (First publ. 1961.)

Empson, William (1967). *The Structure of Complex Words*, rev. edn. Ann Arbor: University of Michigan Press. (First publ. 1951.)

Empson, William (1974). *Some Versions of Pastoral*, corr. edn. New York: New Directions. (First publ. 1935.)

Empson, William (1984). *Using Biography*. Cambridge, Mass.: Harvard University Press.

Empson, William (1986a). *Essays on Shakespeare*, ed. David Pirie. Cambridge, UK: Cambridge University Press.

Empson, William (1986b). *The Royal Beasts and Other Works*, ed. John Haffenden. London: Chatto & Windus.

Empson, William (1987). *Argufying: Essays on Literature and Culture*, ed. John Haffenden. Iowa City: University of Iowa Press.

Foucault, Michel (1986). "What Is an Author?" In Hazard Adams and Leroy Searle, eds., *Critical Theory since 1965*. Tallahassee and Gainesville: University Presses of Florida.

Fry, Paul (1991). *William Empson: Prophet Against Sacrifice*. London: Routledge.

Fumerton, Patricia (1991). *Cultural Aesthetics: Renaissance Literature and the Practice of Social Ornament*. Chicago: University of Chicago Press.

Greenblatt, Stephen (1980). *Renaissance Self-Fashioning from More to Shakespeare*. Chicago: University of Chicago Press.

Greenblatt, Stephen (2004). *Will in the World: How Shakespeare Became Shakespeare*. New York: Norton.

Haffenden, John (2005). *William Empson*, vol. 1: *Among the Mandarins*. Oxford: Oxford University Press.

Marotti, Arthur (1986). *John Donne: Coterie Poet*. Madison: University of Wisconsin Press.

Norris, Christopher (1978). *William Empson and the Philosophy of Literary Criticism*. London: Athlone.

Norris, Christopher (1993). "Introduction: Empson as literary theorist, from Ambiguity to Complex Words and beyond." In Christopher Norris and Nigel Mapp, eds., *William Empson: The Critical Achievement*, 1–120. Cambridge: Cambridge University Press.

Norris, Christopher, and Mapp, Nigel, eds. (1993). *William Empson: The Critical Achievement*. Cambridge: Cambridge University Press.

Sale, Roger (1973). *Modern Heroism: Essays on D. H. Lawrence, Willilam Empson, and J. R. R. Tolkien*. Berkeley: University of California Press.

Schoenfeldt, Michael (1999). *Bodies and Selves in Early Modern England: Physiology and Inwardness in Spenser, Shakespeare, Herbert, and Milton*. Cambridge, UK: Cambridge University Press.

Shakespeare, William (1977). *Shakespeare's Sonnets*, ed. Stephen Booth. New Haven: Yale University Press.

Strier, Richard (1995). *Resistant Structures: Particularity, Radicalism, and Renaissance Texts*. Berkeley: University of California Press.

Strier, Richard (2006). Personal communication.

Vendler, Helen (1997). *The Art of Shakespeare's Sonnets*. Cambridge, Mass.: Harvard University Press.

Wellek, Rene (1986). *A History of Modern Criticism*, vol. 5: *English Criticism, 1900–1950*. New Haven: Yale University Press.

PART IV
The Sonnets in Manuscript and Print

12

Shakespeare's Sonnets and the Manuscript Circulation of Texts in Early Modern England

Arthur F. Marotti

Despite the growing importance of print in sixteenth- and seventeenth-century England and the gradual incorporation of lyrics in print culture, the manuscript system of literary transmission remained a vital one for poetry. There survive from the period hundreds of manuscripts that were either collections of verse or documents that included verse in their contents, testifying both to the social character of lyric poetry and to the participation of a wide range of individuals in the circulation and use of poetic texts. When their poems were released into or captured for manuscript circulation, authors lost control of their texts and others felt free to transcribe, alter, and arrange them as they saw fit. Compilers also sometimes wrote answer poetry in response to the verse they received, or included in their personal anthologies other pieces they themselves wrote. In such a context the lines between literary producer and consumer were blurred. Some poets of the time, such as Sir Walter Ralegh and John Donne, wrote for manuscript circulation and, for the most part, avoided print publication; others, such as Samuel Daniel, Edmund Spenser, and Michael Drayton, preferred print as a medium; and still others, such as Ben Jonson and Robert Herrick, deliberately worked within both systems of literary transmission (Marotti 1995).

We know that at least some of the poems that were published by Thomas Thorpe in 1609 as *Shake-speares Sonnets* were circulated in manuscript before that edition was printed. The reference in Francis Meres's 1598 book, *Palladis Tamia*, to Shakespeare's "sugred Sonnets among his private friends"[1] has been cited repeatedly as external evidence of this phenomenon. To produce his (falsely advertised) volume, *The Passionate Pilgrim by William Shakespeare* (1599 and 1612), William Jaggard appropriated circulating manuscript copies of sonnets 138 and 144, three songs from *Love's Labor's Lost*, and three "Venus and Adonis" sonnets that might also have been written by Shakespeare (Hobday 1973). The statement on the title-page of Thorpe's 1609 quarto, "Never before Imprinted," indicates that the poems in the volume were presented to a general readership by a publisher who took them from a restricted sphere of manuscript circulation and made them available for purchase – the same situation advertised by Richard Tottel sixty-two years earlier for his landmark *Miscellany*, which offered for the "profit and pleasure" of readers some socially restricted texts "which the ungentle horders up of such treasures have heretofore envied thee" (Rollins 1965: vol. 1, 2). Despite the evidence of the early manuscript transmission of the sonnets, these poems were not transcribed in very many collections in the half-century following their publication in the quarto. Scholars who have examined hundreds of surviving manuscript collections of verse from the sixteenth and seventeenth centuries have discovered only eleven whole sonnets in twenty different manuscripts: a surprisingly small number if we consider how many copies of poems by such writers as Sir Walter Ralegh, John Donne, Ben Jonson, and Thomas Carew appear in these collections. Donne's verse, for example, shows up in some 250 manuscripts and Carew's in fifty-nine.

It is hard to not to draw two conclusions about the relative paucity of manuscript copies of Shakespeare's sonnets: the first is that Thorpe's quarto had a remarkably weak impact on the literary scene; the second is that the manuscript transmission of the sonnets was so restricted or the poems that circulated were so few that this body of poetry did not really enter a wider sphere of manuscript copying the way the work of many other poets did. The near-disappearance of the verse from circulation may be due to the fact that sonnets, at least those of the traditional Petrarchan amorous kind, ceased being fashionable in Jacobean and Caroline England. The sonnet craze of the 1590s had passed and, although some sequences, such as Drayton's, continued to be reissued in new editions, Shakespeare's 1609 volume had a quality of belatedness, coming after the Renaissance tradition of amorous sonneteering had effectively run its course. In the first two-thirds of the seventeenth century, Donne's and Jonson's lyric poetry captured the attention of new generations of readers and collectors, especially in the period from 1620 to 1650 when so many of the surviving manuscript anthologies of poetry were compiled. Still, given the numerous examples we have of individuals transcribing poems for their collections from printed, as well as manuscript, sources – for example, British Library MS Harley 6910 – one would expect Thomas Thorpe's 1609 quarto of *Shake-speares Sonnets* and John Benson's 1640 *Poems: Written by Wil. Shakespeare. Gent.* to have stimulated more manuscript transcription than they did.

With regard to the manuscript transmission of the poems, one can surmise that at least those sonnets Shakespeare wrote to the young man (sonnets 1–126) were held to very restricted circulation. There are references to poems' being sent to an addressee singly and in groups, an act that was connected to their functions within the context of a relationship of patronage and clientage. It is no accident, I believe, that the poems that found their way into *The Passionate Pilgrim* are from the "dark lady," or more miscellaneous, section of the collection (127–52),[2] rather than from the other, larger body of poems. The young-man poems have an aura of privacy and exclusiveness to them. They are portrayed as gifts of the poet to his patron: sonnet 83 is characterized as "The barren tender of a poet's debt" (l. 4); in this poem and in sonnets 100, 101, 102, and 103, the poet apologizes for his slacking off in sending new poems of praise, assuming that offering his patron sonnets on a regular basis was expected of him as a client. Some poems have a clearly indicated "for your eyes only" message: sonnet 26, for example, is an epistolary poem serving as a "written ambassage" (l. 3) sent out of "Duty" (l. 4) to his benefactor; in it the poet states that it is the "good conceit" (l. 7) of the patron, as a receptive reader, that makes this poem, and the others he sends, complete. In fact, the value of such sonnets partly lies in their being given to a single recipient, not to a larger circle of friends and acquaintances.

Either with or without Shakespeare's cooperation (and I side with those who think the Thorpe quarto was unauthorized), the sonnets were published in 1609 and then again, but with aggressive editorial intervention, in 1640. Largely because of the existence of these printed copies of the poems and of the publication of sonnets 138 and 144 in *The Passionate Pilgrim*, the poems were available for transcription in personal manuscript collections of verse, including the following:

Bodleian Library, Oxford, MS Rawlinson Poetical 152: sonnet 128 on fol. 34^r
British Library, MS Additional 10309: sonnet 2 on fol. 143^r
British Library, MS Additional 15226: sonnet 8 on fol. 4^v
British Library, MS Additional 21433: sonnet 2 on fol. 114^v
British Library, MS Additional 25303: sonnet 2 on fol. 119^v
British Library, MS Additional 30982: sonnet 2 on fol. 18^r
British Library, MS Sloane 1792: sonnet 2 on fol. 45^r
Folger Shakespeare Library, MS V.a.162: sonnet 71 on fol. 12^v and sonnet 32 on fol. 26^r
Folger Shakespeare Library, MS V.a.170: sonnet 2 on pp. 163–4
Folger Shakespeare Library, MS V.a.339: sonnet 138 on fol. 197^v
Folger Shakespeare Library, MS V.a.345: sonnet 2 on p. 145
New York Public Library Music Division, MS Drexel 4257, no. 33: sonnet 116
University of Nottingham, Portland, MS Pw V 37: sonnet 2 on p. 69
Pierpont Morgan Library, MS MA 1057: sonnet 106 on p. 96
Rosenbach Library, MS 1083/16: sonnet 106 on pp. 256–7
Rosenbach Library, MS 1083/17: sonnet 2 on fols. 132^v–33^r
St. John's College, Cambridge, MS S.23: sonnet 2 on fol. 38^{r-v}
Westminster Abbey, MS 41: sonnet 2 on fol. 49^r
Beinecke Library, Yale, Osborn Collection, MS b 205: sonnet 2 on fol. 54^v

(Beal et al. 1980: vol. 1, pt. 2, 452–5)

These nineteen manuscripts have copies of eight of the 154 sonnets, sonnet 2 being the one most reproduced (in twelve manuscripts). Another manuscript, Folger Shakespeare Library, MS V.a.148, includes whole versions of sonnets 33, 68, and 107, bringing the total number of complete sonnets found in manuscript collections to eleven.

This last manuscript is a special case.[3] It is a small notebook that seems to have been used, probably by a student, to record material from sermons and scripture, some of it in shorthand; notes on Hebrew grammar; astronomical calculations; many epigrams, including a group by Thomas Fuller (fols. 24^v–25^r); and other poems by such major and minor Caroline authors as Ben Jonson, Henry King, Richard Crashaw, William Strode, Thomas Carew, J. Ravenshaw, and J. Gibbon. Peter Beal claims that

all the poems are taken from printed sources (Taylor 1985: 215). The collector transcribed fifty-one poems and excerpts of poems from Benson's edition, but only thirty-
one from sonnets clearly by Shakespeare (fols. 22ʳ–24ʳ), for Benson not only reordered,
conflated, and supplied titles to Shakespearean sonnets, but also included in his edition
falsely attributed poems from Jaggard's *The Passionate Pilgrim* as well as a short anthology of lyrics by other, mostly Caroline, authors. What the scribe-collector of Folger
MS V.a.148 obviously did was to go through Benson's volume and, more or less following the order of the pieces found there, either copy whole poems or excerpt particular passages, often modifying them to create independent clauses or memorable phrases.[4]
While he copied only three whole Shakespearean sonnets, he took passages from
twenty-eight others.[5]

The excerpts in this manuscript vary in size from one phrase to two quatrains and
a couplet. The shortest one is the expression "Summers front" (fol. 23ʳ) from line 7 of
sonnet 102. The scribe selected some lines for their gnomic value: "The Canker bloomes
have full as deepe a dy / As the Perfumed tincture of the roses" (54. 5–6) (fol. 22ʳ);
"Love alters not with his briefe hours & weeks / But bears It out even to the Edge of
Doome" (116. 11–12) (fol. 23ʳ); "Love suffers not in smiling Pomp nor falls / Under the
blow of thrilling discontent / Nor fears It Heretick Policy" (124. 6–8) (fol. 23ʳ). He
obviously found some expressions and metaphors attractive and memorable: "The
stormy gusts of winters day / And Barren rage of deaths eternall cold" (13. 11–12) (fol.
22ᵛ); "The Heavenly Rhetorick of thy ey / Gainst which the world cannot Hold Argument" (*PP* 3. 1–2) (fol. 22ᵛ); "Gilding the object whereupon It gazeth" (20. 6) (fol. 22ᵛ);
"Celestial as thou art" (*PP* 5. 13) (fol. 22ᵛ); "Beaten & Chopt with Tan'd Antiquity"
(62. 10) (fol. 23ʳ); and

> Not the Morning sun of heaven
> Better becomes the grey cheeks of the East
> As those two morning ys become thy face
> (132. 5–6, 9) (fol. 23ʳ)

Sometimes the scribe not only excerpted, but also modified and rewrote passages.
For example, he took lines 9–12 of sonnet 28,

> I tell the Day to please him thou art bright,
> And do'st him grace when clouds doe blot the heaven:
> So flatter I the swart-complexiond night,
> When sparking stars twire, not thou guil'st th'even[6]
> (Benson, sig. B4ᵛ)

and reduced them to the following: "Clouds blot the heaven & make me flatter / The
swart Complectiond night when sparkling stars twire" (fol. 23ʳ). He took lines 10–12
of sonnet 29,

> Haply I thinke on thee, and then my state,
> (Like to the Larke at breake of day arising)
> From sullen earth sings hymns at Heavens gate,
>   (Benson, sig. B5ʳ)

and reduced them to "To sing from sullen earth hymnes at heavens gate" (fol. 23ʳ). He expanded the phrase from the second line of sonnet 97, "the pleasure of the fleeting yeare," to "Thou art the Pleasure of the fleeting yeare" (fol. 23ʳ). He converted lines 5–7 of sonnet 142,

> Or if it doe, not from those lips of thine,
> That have prophan'd their scarlet ornaments,
> And seal'd false bonds of love as oft as mine,
>   (Benson, sig. F3ʳ)

into a two-line unit: "Thy lips Profane their scarlet ornaments / And seald fals bonds of love" (fol. 23ᵛ).

This manuscript may not have any particular value for textual scholars, since it does not connect to any possible alternative Shakespearean versions of individual sonnets and since, in copying Benson, who used not only the quarto but also the 1612 edition of *The Passionate Pilgrim* as his copy texts, the scribe was corrupting further already textually corrupted texts. But what he was doing points to a growing practice in the seventeenth century of appropriating texts to put them either in a commonplace book that served as a repository of valued quotations and useful information or in a personal anthology of poetry. In such a context, Shakespearean sonnets and passages from sonnets could be valued as memorable poetic gems or felicitous expressions, associated with verse from the compiler's own time and made part of a personal development of linguistic skills and intellectual sophistication. Such a collector made decisions about what to select, what to excerpt, what to modify. Although Shakespeare had a high cultural visibility and prestige, certainly after the First (1623) and Second (1632) Folios of his plays were published, this environment of collecting was not particularly author-centered, since many poems, including the sonnets, were transcribed without authorial ascription; and even where authorship was highlighted, this did not lessen the personal use-centered purpose of the activity.

In other manuscripts in which we find Shakespearean sonnets transcribed, the same process was at work. Most scholars have examined these documents primarily to determine whether the Shakespearean poems they contain have any textual interest, treating the pieces in isolation from the other poems surrounding them, but some, such as Marcy North (2003), Katherine Duncan-Jones (intr. to Shakespeare 1997), and Sasha Roberts (2003), have been more interested in other issues. North concentrates on the functions of anonymity in the presentation of the poems in manuscript, while Duncan-Jones and Roberts both emphasize the socioliterary contexts of particular manuscripts and the cultural transformation of the Shakespearean texts in a new era. Attending to the way in which the system of manuscript transmission operated and the effects of recontextualizing poetic texts, I would like to consider some of the manuscripts that record sonnet 2 and then examine other manuscripts that reproduce other Shakespeare sonnets.

In six of the twelve manuscripts that contain sonnet 2, there are titles that change the addressee from male to female: "to one that would dye a Mayd" (BL MSS Add. 30982 and Sloane 1792, Folger MS V.a.170, Westminster Abbey MS 41, Yale Osborn Collection MS b 205) and "A Lover to his Mistres" (University of Nottingham, Portland MS Pw V 37). The other titles used, "Spes Altera" (BL MSS Add. 10309, 21433, and 25303), "Spes Altera A song" (Folger MS V.a.345) and "The Benefitt of Mariage" (Rosenbach MS 1083/17) do not specify the gender of the addressee, but, in the context of a mass of poetry about heterosexual love, the implication is that the poem, which concentrates on the perpetuation of "beauty" (l. 5), is written to a woman. Isolated from the sequence in which it is embedded, particularly the initial procreation sonnets, the piece seems to be an eloquent restatement of conventional wisdom.

In the George Morley manuscript (Westminster Abbey MS 41)[7] we find a copy of sonnet 2, but, as Katherine Duncan-Jones (Shakespeare 1997: 454) observes, it apparently was added later in a hand differing from that of the poems preceding and following it to fill available space at the bottom of one page (fol. 49[r]), a common practice. This one Shakespeare sonnet is immersed in what is a model anthology of Christ Church, Oxford verse: it contains many of the poems of those other Christ Church poets, Richard Corbett and William Strode, and, given Morley's role in tutoring undergraduates throughout the period, his collection was probably lent to students who, in turn, compiled their own poetical collections (Hobbs 1992: 116–29). Including pieces transcribed from the early 1620s through to the late 1640s, this late Jacobean and Caroline anthology provides an environment for sonnet 2 very different from that of its original circulation and publication.[8]

In Yale Osborn MS b 205, a collection in which two main hands dominate, Hand A records sonnet 2 in a part of the manuscript (fols. 52[r]–72[r]) transcribed in a darker ink than that usually used by this scribe, and the poem is placed in the midst of a large number of poems by Christ Church poets.[9] This section begins with George Morley's "on the Nightingale" (fol. 52[r]), William Strode's popular poem "On the death of Mistris Mary Prideaux" ("Weepe not because thie child hath died so yong" [fol. 52[v]]), another (anonymous) popular elegy about a deceased child, "De Infante immatura morte perempta" ("As carefull mothers to their beds do lay" [fol. 52[v]]), and three more poems by William Strode: "To Sir John Ferrers" ("Gold is restorative how can I then" [fol. 53[r–v]]), "To the same" ("It greives me that due thankes I thus retan" [*sic*] [fols. 53[v]–54[r]]), and "To Sir Edmund Linge" ("Sir I had writ in Latine but I feare" [fol. 54[r]]). Shakespeare's sonnet follows, with the title "To one that would die a maide" (54[v]), succeeded immediately (on the same page) by Richard Corbett's poem about religious iconoclasm, "On Faireford windowes" ("Tell me you Antisaintes why glasse" [fols. 54[v]–55[r]]) and a run of twenty-one poems by Strode,[10] punctuated by two anonymous pieces that may or may not be by him: "To your memories recorder" ("keepe my charge in watchfull order" [fol. 55ʳ]) and "An Epitaph" ("Behind this brazen plate those ashes lie" [fol. 59ᵛ]) – neither of which appears in Margaret Crum's (1969) first-line index. Again, the Shakespeare sonnet is immersed in a group of Christ Church poems. The "W S" whose work was of great interest in this environment was William Strode, not William Shakespeare.

Folger MS V.a.170, which bears a copy of sonnet 2, is another typical Christ Church anthology.[11] In the sector of the manuscript in which we find Shakespeare's poem, we have also poems by Richard Corbett and William Strode – for example, Corbett's "On Fayrford windows" and the Strode poem on the same subject (pp. 153–7), pieces antago-nistic to radical Protestant iconoclasm. There is a poem on the bell of Christ Church (pp. 157–8) and an elegy for King Charles's dead child ("Tis vayne to weepe; or in a riming spite") (pp. 158–9) ascribed to "W:C:" (probably William Cartwright), followed by the two lyrics by Ben Jonson about Venetia Digby that most frequently appear in seventeenth-century manuscript anthologies, "The Body" and "The Minde" (pp. 159–63). Shakespeare's sonnet 2 immediately follows, with the title "To one that would dye a Mayd." Given the two preceding poems and the title under which it appears, address-ing it to a woman, this sonnet here becomes yet another Caroline poem concerned with female sexuality.

What follows it is another much-transcribed poem, "Mr [Robert] Herricks Welcome to Sacke" (pp. 164–7), a classic Cavalier lyric that in its celebration of drinking came to characterize Royalist alienation in the Civil War era (Potter 1989). This is followed by two Latin poems addressed to John King, Bishop of London (p. 168), the father of the Christ Church poet, Henry King; a poem entitled "I.D. to his Paper" ("Flye Paper: kisse those hands") (pp. 168–70), probably to ascribe it (wrongly) to John Donne;[12] and two poems ascribed to "W:S:" – initials that, in the Christ Church context, would be used to identify William Strode, not William Shakespeare: "A parallel between Bowling and Preferment" ("Preferment like a Game at bowles" [pp. 170–1]) and "The Capps" ("The Witt hath long beholden bin" [pp. 171–4]). Within such a local as well as general context in this manuscript, the anonymous Shakespearean sonnet appears as just one of many manifestations of Caroline wit and political conservatism.

British Library MS Sloane 1792, compiled by one "I.A." of Christ Church (Beal et al. 1980: vol. 1, pt. 2, p. 43; Hobbs 1992: 118), also contains sonnet 2, but recorded sloppily so as to introduce variants not found in the other examples of the alternate manuscript version (printed in Shakespeare 2002: 691) of the piece. It has "youth" for "youths" in line three; "like like" for "like" in line 4; the non-rhyming word "pleasure" for "praise" in line 8; and, violating the rhythm, "How better" in place of "O how much better" in line 9 of the alternate version of the poem. The sonnet is preceded by poems "On the death of Kinge James" ("All that have eyes now waile and weepe" [fol. 44ʳ⁻ᵛ]) and "an Epitaph on Mr Hen: Boling" ("If gentleness could tame the fates, or witt" [fol. 44ᵛ]), and followed by a poem also found in close proximity to the sonnet in Folger MS V.a.170, "I.D. to his paper" ("Flie paper kisse those hands" [fol. 45ʳ⁻ᵛ]). The rest of the collection resembles the contents of most other Christ Church anthologies – except that one finds here an unusual, and rearranged, version of a poem that is possibly an early piece by Shakespeare, appearing in *The Passionate Pilgrim* and, in whole form, in three other manuscripts: "When that thine eye hath chose the dame."[13] Here the scribe, or someone else whose work he might have copied, seems to have excerpted eighteen lines of this 54-line poem, rearranged them,[14] and supplied a unique title, "Upon one that went a wooing" (fol. 11ʳ). This, in effect, is a case of textual "sampling."

Another Christ Church collection, BL MS Add. 30982, associated with Daniel Leare and William Strode[15] – a small notebook such as a student might use – has a copy of Shakespeare's sonnet 2 in the original compilation found on fols. 1–89.[16] This Caroline collection contains quite a few pieces by Strode and by other Christ Church poets, many of which refer to persons and topics of interest to the Christ Church community. It inserts the Shakespearean sonnet into a run of poems that generalize the moral meaning of experience and present love and courtship through both an academic and a Cavalier sensibility. Immediately before the Shakespeare poem we find two poems by Thomas Carew, "On his mistris sickness" ("Must shee then languish and wee sorrow then") and "on lipps and eyes" ("In Celias face a question did arise") (fols. 14ᵛ–15ᵛ), and two poems by William Strode, "On a good foot and a bad leg" ("Yf Hercules tall stature might be gest") and "An answere made to Maudlins Rimes" ("If Ch[rist] Ch[urch] lads were sad they spent their breath") (fols 15ʳ–17ʳ). These are followed by a piece of prose bawdry, "A Law Cause":

A gentellman & a gentlewoman heald plea for entailed land, he shewed her in the common pleas on a former downe, the land in variance was called tough-grove plashy meadd & bushy close situate in the parish of Buttockeberry in the county of Harreford, the matter was to be tried in Hillary tearme, the gentelman tooke with him 3 of his men (waiting continually on him) naked, because it should not be counted a riot In the pasture before said betwixt 2 haunches is a Clife, he himselfe in proper person without any forcible entraunce drave a stake <did> downe in the middest, where by long tarriance he chanced to take & burne his evidence now the question is how he shall recover his evidence being the first suer. (fol. 17ʳ)[17]

This item is followed by a section of a poem by Benjamin Stone about Samburne, Sheriff of Oxford ("The sherriffe of oxford late is growne so wise") (fol. 17ʳ) (Crum 1969: vol. 2, 696; vol. 1, 237); an anonymous poem, "To his sister" ("Loving sister every line" [fol. 17ᵛ]);[18] and another Strode poem, to which his initials are attached, a complimentary piece "To Sr Edmond Ling" ("Sir I had writt in lattin but I heare" [fol. 17ᵛ]).

Sonnet 2, with the same title as in Folger MS V.a.170, follows these items, succeeded immediately by an anonymous poem on "Jealousy" ("There is a thing that nothing is") (fol. 18ʳ); another Strode poem, "On Westwell Downes" ("When westwell Downes I gan to treade" [fol. 18ʳ⁻ᵛ]); a poem from Sidney's *Arcadia* identified as "3 song Sr P: Sydney" ("What ever in Philoclea the faire" [fol. 18ᵛ]); a much-transcribed witty university poem "On Eggerlies wife the carrier" ("Nine days are past & yet the wonders new" [fol. 19ʳ⁻ᵛ]); and a rare anonymous poem "On a made not marriagable" (fol. 19ᵛ):

Would you have me leade the blind
Because thy Lydia proves unkind
Shees yet to young to know delight
And is not plumpe for Cupids flight
She cannot yet heigh [*sic*] of pleasure
Pay her love with equall measure
But like a rose new blowne doth feed
The eye alone but yeelds no seed
Autumn will come & shortly greet her
make her tast colour sweeter
Then hir ripeness will be such
That shee will fall over with a touch.

(fol. 19ᵛ)

We are back in the world of adolescent university wit and of the recreational poetry that found its way into such midcentury Royalist anthologies as *Wits Recreations* (1640), *The Academy of Complements* (1640), *The Harmony of the Muses* (1654), and *Parnassus Biceps* (1656), publications that picked up many of the ephemeral poems circulating in the universities and in fashionable circles before, during, and after the English Civil Wars. The Sidney poem is identified by its author, the Christ Church poets' pieces are often ascribed by using initials that would be understood by members of that community, but the Shakespeare sonnet is anonymous.[19]

Sonnet 2 appears in three numbered quatrains and a fourth numbered section comprising the couplet as "Spes Altera A song"[20] in Folger MS V.a.345, a huge collection of over five hundred poems, many of them with Christ Church origins and associations.[21] It is preceded by Bacon's "The worlds a buble and the life of man" (pp. 143–4), "A Charme Fran[cis]: Beaumont" ("Sleep old man let silence charme thee" [p. 144]), an anonymous and rare poem in three numbered stanzas with the simple title "A Sonnet" ("my mistres frownes when I am gon" [pp. 144–5]), and William Strode's much-transcribed poem, "On Dr Hut: daughter" ("I saw faire Cloris walk alone" [p. 145]), which in some versions has a musical setting and in others is presented as written about Richard Corbett's wife.[22] It is followed by a short epigram "On Sir William Sands" ("Unto our names, we must not trust / For I was Sands, but now am dust" [p. 145]) and two unascribed Donne poems, "Loves Diety" and "Loves Dyet" (pp. 146–7), the first with four, the second with five numbered stanzas.

The Shakespeare sonnet is associated with musical verse, one of the important contexts for the manuscript versions of the sonnets in seventeenth-century collections (Hobbs 1979; Shakespeare 2002: 106). In BL MS Add. 15226, sonnet 8, with the title "In laudem Musice et opprobrium Contemptorii [*sic*] eiusdem" ("In praise of music and in reproach of the despiser of the same"), is broken into three stanzas, perhaps for musical performance. Duncan-Jones suggests that this title "gives the sonnet the air of belonging to an academic debate" (Shakespeare 1997: 457). Henry Lawes's modified and expanded version of sonnet 116, which appears in NYPL MS Drexel 4257, is arranged in three six-line stanzas and set to music. Many seventeenth-century collections of verse include many songs and, in addition, numerous musical manuscripts survive from the period (Hobbs 1992: 93–6, 105–15).

Two of the manuscripts that include Shakespeare's sonnet 2 are associated with the social environment of the Inns of Court: BL MSS Add. 25303 and 21433, the second of which reproduces most of the contents of the first – though it does lift out funeral and elegiac poetry into a separate section instead of strictly adhering to the order of the poems of the first manuscript.[23] Both are large collections of verse probably compiled in the 1630s and 1640s. In BL MS Add. 25303, Shakespeare's poem follows pieces by or attributed to Strode ("Bee silent yow still musick of the spheares" [fol. 117ᵛ]), Ralegh ("Passions are likened beste to flouds & streames" [fol. 118ᵛ] and "What is our life? the play of passion" [fol. 118ᵛ]), Carew ("Thinke not cause men flattering say" [fol. 119ʳ]), and Benjamin Stone of Christ Church, Oxford ("Why death so sone did honest Owen catch" [fol. 119ᵛ]). It is followed by poems on "Sr Antony Benn recorder of London" ("In hell of late did growe some great disorder" [fol. 120ʳ]) and "On Mr Beaumonts death" ("Hee that hath such acuteness & such witt" [fol. 120ʳ]), Carew's "Kisse lovely Caelia and bee kinde" (fols. 120ᵛ–1ʳ), Henry Wotton's popular piece, "How happy is he borne and tought" (fol. 121ʳ), "An epitaphe on Berkely" ("He that's impryson'd in this narrow rome" [fol. 121ʳ]), and the comic poem on "The Lovinge Welshman" ("A modest shentell when hir see" [fols. 122ʳ⁻ᵛ]). In this collection of miscellaneous Caroline (and earlier) verse, the Shakespeare poem neither has special status nor thematic reinforcement. The same is true in BL MS Add. 21433, which has most of the poems in the same order.[24]

A professionally transcribed poetical collection associated with Margaret Bellasis, BL MS Add. 10309,[25] also reproduces sonnet 2, but locates it in a radically heterogeneous assemblage of verse, a diversity especially marked among the poems in close proximity to it. On the two folios preceding the one on which we find Shakespeare's poem, we find Ralegh's popular "Even such is Time, which takes on trust" (fol. 141ʳ), Donne's "The Indifferent" (fols. 141ᵛ–2ʳ), an anti-Puritan piece ("Puritie, if't should come to passe"), a rare piece about a religious dispute over whether Christ's soul descended into hell ("Our English church of late doth question make" [fol. 142ʳ]), a politically satiric piece on the Earl of Essex's 1601 failed coup ("Essex prayes, Southampton playes" [fol. 142ᵛ]),[26] one of John Harington's epigrams ("A Cobler & a Curate once disputed" [fol. 142ʳ]), and a poem and answer poem playing with the name of Lady Benbow ("There is a bow wherein to shoote I sue" and "You bended have the bow wherin to shoot you sue" [fol. 142ᵛ]).[27] Immediately following is a bawdy poem about Lord Lampus, who died in sexual intercourse ("Here sixe foote deepe, in his last sleepe" [fol. 143ʳ]), then a rare twenty-line poem addressed to a friend, with a thirty-line response ("Tell me (deere friende) what course is't we shall take" and "You ask'd your friend what courses we should take" [fols. 143ᵛ–4ʳ]), the first a pessimistic inventory of all the things that prevent happiness, the second a conventional list of the characteristics of a good and happy life. The variety of topics, of attitudes, of styles and of poetic forms is remarkable in this section of the manuscript and in the collection as a whole.

Among the seventeenth-century manuscripts that contain other Shakespeare sonnets, Folger MS V.a.162, which was apparently written in several different hands,[28] contains copies of sonnet 71 and sonnet 32. Probably using the quarto or a manuscript based on it as its copy text, it introduced four textual variants, all of which seem to be the products of scribal error: in sonnet 71, "me" for "you" in line 8 and "moone" for "moan" in line 13; in sonnet 32, "high" for "hight" in line 8 and "love" for "birth" in line 11, though the last of these might be a deliberate change on the scribe's part. The poems preceding and following each of the Shakespeare sonnets provide a context that not only reveals the collector's or collectors' interests, but also the new cultural circumstances in which transcription took place.

In the textual vicinity of sonnet 71, from the start of the manuscript, we encounter a run of rare or unique poems[29] interspersed with a few pieces found in other similar manuscripts: a poem on Sir Francis Bacon's fall ("When you awake dull Brittaines" [fols. 2^{r-v}]), a popular piece attributed to Bacon himself ("The world's a bubble" [fols. 5^{r-v}]), the first stanza of John Donne's "The Indifferent" (fol. 11^v), and George Herbert's "The Altar" (fol. 12^v) and "Redemption" (fol. 15^v). The unusual pieces, which, like the familiar ones, are all anonymous, deal with love, sex, marriage, friendship, socially prominent figures, and the meaning of life. There are witty poems: "Upon a chambermaid" (fol. 1^v), "On a curst wife" (fol. 4^v), on "Naked Love" (fol. 8^v), "on a loose bodied mistress" (fol. 10^r), "of a Wedding Ring" (fol. 10^r); poems about amorous experience, such as "A Passion" (fol. 13^v) and "On Jealousie" (fol. 14^r); poems on marriage, such as "On the choyce of a wife" (fols. 14^v–15^v) and "A Dialogue betwixt Anna and Mary" ("Into the bride yoake wilt thou madly fly" [fol. 16^r]); sexually cynical pieces such as "Like Mistres like Maide" (fol. 10^v), "Of Whores and their Maisters" (fol. 10^v), and "A Song" ("Maides in the chamber, or of the kitchen" [fol. 11^r]); and others such as an epitaph on "G.A. gent." (fol. 8^v), a piece "On Sir Thomas Overbury" (fol. 14^r),[30] an epistolary poem "To his deere frend Mr Stephen Jackson" (fol. 12^r), and an "Epigram of Cardinall Pooles Picture" (fol. 11^v), the last a strange item to appear in a document from the mid-seventeenth century, unless the collector were a Catholic or at least had a particular admiration for a long-deceased Catholic cardinal.

Shakespeare's Sonnet 71 is flanked in this manuscript by two religious poems, Herbert's "The Altar" and the anonymous "Of Man" (fol. 13^{r-v}). In this context, the young-man sonnet that is originally framed by the ongoing relationship of the poet and his patron–lover looks more like an exemplary set of reflections on personal mortality (Roberts 2003: 174) rather than an elegantly passive-aggressive attempt to stimulate reciprocity in love. The sentiments in the piece are departicularized and valued for their general religious and moral applicability.

Sonnet 32 is found in a section of the collection that begins with a transcription of a poem of disputed authorship printed in the 1633 edition of John Donne's poetry, "An Expostulation" (fols. 20^v–21^v), an acrostic poem for Sir Paul Pinder (fol. 21^r), a ring posy (fol. 21^r), and another poem addressed to Stephen Jackson (fol. 21^v). Many of the poems leading up to sonnet 32 are witty pieces, including a version of the much-transcribed epitaph on the deceased member of Christ Church, Oxford, "a Scholler . . . whose Name was Pricke" (fol. 21^v), an epigram from Henry Parrot's 1608 collection ("A scoffing mate; passing along Cheapeside" [fol. 21^v]), an epitaph "Upon a Love sicke youth" (fol. 23^r), and "A Canniball" (fol. 24^r). The scribe copied a piece from William Habington's

Castara, "On Joseph's Cloake" (fol. 23ʳ), and recorded both Sir John Suckling's verse ("I am confirm'd a woman can" [fol. 23ᵛ]) and an answer poem to it ("His witts ill forme'd that thinkes wee can" [fols. 23ᵛ–24ʳ]) – a rare case in this manuscript of an author's name being mentioned. This is followed by "A Passinate Sonnet" ("Speake, gentle heart, where is thy dwelling place" [fol. 25ʳ]), a piece found also in British Library MS Harley 3277 (fol. 4ʳ), and, without authorial ascription, Donne's song "Goe and catch a falling starre" (fol. 25ᵛ). Immediately preceding the Shakespeare sonnet is a rare religious poem, "Gods love":

> Noe mortall hath seen god, few heard him speake
> (hence is theire love so cold, theire faith so weake)
> yet all his goodness taste, which (like the shower
> on Gideons fleece) he on all flesh doth power.
>
> (fol. 25ᵛ)[31]

Shakespeare's sonnet 32, then, in its speculation about what might follow the death of the poet, not only resembles sonnet 71 in its subject matter, but here specifically maintains the focus on mortality of this short piece. The next poem, however, entitled "Idea" ("Nothing but NO and I, and I and NO" [fol. 26ʳ]), changes the subject. It is a rare item that portrays a frustrating game played by a lover and his mistress.[32] Most compilers of manuscript collections of verse did not arrange pieces thematically and, thus, in the course of serial transcription, miscellaneity emerged as a hallmark of such documents.

Folger MS V.a.339, a Caroline manuscript later owned by one Joseph Hall (not the famous satirist and bishop),[33] contains the version of sonnet 138 that appeared as the first poem in *The Passionate Pilgrim*. It is transcribed into this manuscript following four other poems from that volume – "Scarce had the sunne dride up the dewie morne," "Sweete Cytherea sittinge by a brooke," "Venus & Adonis sitting by her," and "Faire is my love, but not so faire as fickle" (poems 6, 4, 11, and 7) – and is itself followed by a poem that fuses two sonnets in the Shakespearean form into one poem:

> Befor that antient time that man & wife
> Joynd in atracted union & devotion
> betweene them was a stout & doubtfull strife
> which of the twaine should make the first loves motion
> yet for the world should not be desolate
> & of their strife to make an end intyre
> the Gods them selves theire cause to arbitrate
> gave women beauty & to man desire,
> so that although (in modesty of thought)
> women should not be made the first demaunders
> yet from theire beauties might such meanes be wrought
> that men might be induced to be no straungers
> and thus we men first undertake to woe

so that the cause is still deriv'd from you. /
'Tis questionlesse (mine honour'd Mistris)
beauties not given to you, desire to us
we to abuse your beauties happinesse
or you to frustrat our desires thus
If we should hould your beauties in disdayne
or you reward our loves with distent
then our desire was given us in vaine
and you unworthy beauties ornament
for beauty is made to teach, desire to move
if such an object then be set to view
as is your selfe the efficient cause of love
let me be blamelesse then in lovinge you
for since your beauty first doth dare the fielde
nedes must desire then strike to make you yeeld.

(fol. 198ʳ)

The tone and attitudes that characterize Shakespeare's sonnet 138 are consistent with those of this double sonnet. The manner of such pieces well suits the context of the other Caroline poetry found in this collection, which contains verse by Thomas Carew, George Morley, and Richard Corbett as well as older pieces by Nicholas Breton, Samuel Daniel, Henry Cuffe, Joshua Sylvester, John Dowland, Ben Jonson, and Sir Philip Sidney. In this environment the Shakespearean sonnet is part of a larger analytic, anti-romantic treatment of love and of the relationship of the sexes.

Sonnet 106 appears in Rosenbach Library MS 1083/16 in an interesting form – combined with a non-Shakespearean poem associated with someone who has been identified as a possible addressee of the young-man section of the sonnet collection, William Herbert, Earl of Pembroke.[34] The resulting conflated poem is entitled "On his Mistress Beauty":

When in the Annales of all-wasting time
I see descriptions of the fayrest wights
And beauty making beautiful old rime
In praise of Ladies dead and lovely knights,
Then in the Blazon of sweet beauties best
Of face, of hand, of lipps, or eye or brow
I see their antique pen would have exprest
Even such a beauty as you master now;
Soe all their praises were but prophecies
Of these our dayes all you pre figuring
And for they say but with deceving eyes
They had not skill enough thy worth to sing,
For me which now behold these pleasant dayes
Have eyes to wonder but noe tongue to praise,
When mine eies first admiring of your beauty

Secretly stole the picture of your face
They fearing they might ere, with humble duty
Through vnknowne pathese convayd it to that place
Where reason & true judgment hand in hand
Sate, and each workmanship of sences scand:
Reason could find noe reason but to love it
Soe rich of beauty was it, full of grace
True judgment scand each part and did approve it
To be the modell of some heavenly face
And both agreed to place it in my hart
Where they decreed it never should depart,
Then since I was not borne to be soe blest
Your reall selfe faire mistris to obtaine
Yet must your image dwell within my brest
And in that secrett closett still remaine,
Where all alone retyred, Ile sit and view
Your picture Mistris, since I may not you.

(p. 256)[35]

The text of sonnet 106 in this version differs in some significant ways from that of the quarto. In the first line, "Annales" replaces "Chronicle"[36] and "all-wasting" "wasted." The sixth line, "Of face, of hand, of lipps, or eye or brow" replaces "Of hand, of foote, of lip, of eye, of brow." In line 10, "Of these our dayes" replaces "Of this our time," and in line 11, "And for they say but with deceving eyes" replaces "And for they look'd but with devining eyes." In line 12, "skill" actually corrects what looks like a compositor error in the quarto, "still"; but the substitution of "me" for "we" in line 13 makes no sense. In line 14 "noe tongue" replaces "lack toungs," a change that might have, like most of the others, resulted from normal errors associated with memorial transcription.[37]

Although the part of this poem that is found in the Pembroke and Rudyerd edition is not identified in that volume as Pembroke's with the "P." usually used (not always accurately) for this purpose, most of the pieces in the anthology by these two figures alternate between the two authors, and this poem is flanked by two poems ascribed to Rudyerd. Fused into one poem, sonnet 106 and "When mine eies first admiring of your beauty" becomes an extended treatment of the perception of and love of beauty, addressed to the female beloved to whom the title and the language of the second part refer. Whether this handling of the Shakespeare poem was the result of scribal inventiveness or of the association of Shakespeare's "papers" (sonnet 17. 9) with Pembroke's, the resulting poem, like the many conflated sonnets of John Benson's 1640 edition of Shakespeare's verses, testifies to the freedom scribes and collectors had to manipulate the texts they received. I don't think we need conclude from the evidence that there was in circulation an alternative *authorial* version of sonnet 106. Given the malleability of texts in the system of manuscript transmission, it is more likely that the textual variants were the result of deliberate or accidental scribal changes.

Most of the compilers of manuscript collections of verse who transcribed particular sonnets by Shakespeare did so from printed editions rather than from manuscript sources. Although Gary Taylor argues that, of the Shakespeare sonnets found in the manuscripts, four (sonnets 2, 8, 106, and 128) are from manuscript sources with texts whose differences from those of the quarto suggest they may be earlier or alternative authorial versions of those poems (Taylor 1985: 225),[38] Katherine Duncan-Jones (Shakespeare 1997: 453–6) believes such textual variants are normal changes produced by the conditions of manuscript reproduction and that the source of the manuscript copies was the printed quarto. Although Duncan-Jones has good reasons for distrusting Taylor's main argument, if we look at some of the textual variants in the copy of sonnet 128 found in Bodleian MS Rawlinson Poetical 152,[39] we have reason to believe that this text was copied from a handwritten exemplar, not a printed one. For example, in line 2 this text has "mocions" rather than "motion" (Q) and in line 14 "youre fingers" for "their fingers" (Q). The first basic change comes from, I believe, a misperception of a secretary "t" for a "c," a mistake much easier to make when reading a handwritten text than a printed one. So too, the second example seems to show a reading of a handwritten and abbreviated "y^{r}" ("their") as "youre." The text in a handwritten source of this manuscript, of course, might itself have been copied from the quarto, instead of from another manuscript in a line descending from an alternative authorial version of the poem.

Duncan-Jones may be right in her basic argument that we should look to the transformations of texts that normally take place in the course of manuscript transmission rather than positing alternative authorial variants for the manuscript poems that differ textually from the ones in the quarto. If we look at the texts of sonnets 138 and 144 found in Jaggard's *The Passionate Pilgrim*, for example, in relation to the quarto versions, we can see, as I have argued elsewhere, that the variants look more like the result of corruption resulting from memorial transcription – a process in which, through faulty memory and/or unconscious revision, convoluted syntactical structures are simplified, more familiar words are substituted for unusual ones, and meter is regularized (Marotti 1990: 151–2). The manuscript texts Jaggard appropriated were probably the result of the kinds of changes characteristic of the system of manuscript transmission, where both deliberate and accidental alterations took place at the hands of the scribes who recorded poems.

Seventeenth-century collectors who included particular Shakespeare sonnets or excerpts of sonnets in their verse compilations valued the poetry as artful language, conventional wisdom, witty performances, social commentary, models of personal expression, or song. Roberts (2003: 189) says that, in such a context, Shakespeare sonnets "functioned . . . as typical love lyrics for their readers, compilers and editors; representative poems that met the taste for Caroline amatory verse. . . . their generic appeal – their familiar treatment of well-known subjects – . . . marked their inclusion in readers' miscellanies." The larger structures and contexts in which the poems are found in the 1609 quarto were of no interest to these later scribes. Like any other writing circulating in print or manuscript, the sonnets were open to appropriation and personal use, for the most part (unlike Shakespeare's plays) dissociated from originary authorship.

NOTES

1   In citing early modern texts I expand abbreviations and modernize u/v and i/j (except, in the case of initials, where an "I" might be either "I" or "J."

2   I view the anacreontic lyrics that conclude the collection as outside both previous sections, a feature used at the end of some other sonnet sequences, such as Spenser's *Amoretti*.

3   I discuss Folger MS V.a.148 in my essay, "Shakespeare's Sonnets as Literary Property" (1990: 163–5).

4   The poems and excerpts of Shakespeare's sonnets that appear in this manuscript are as follows (including the two sonnets from *The Passionate Pilgrim* [noted as *PP*]), cited by sonnet numbers and line numbers for the excerpts, with the signatures in Benson in parentheses): 60. 5–12 (A3^r), 65. 5–8 (A3^v), 107 (F6^{r-v}), 1. 5–14 (A5^v), 2. 1–4 (A5^v), 54. 5–6 (A4^v), 68 (A2^v), 13. 11–12 (A6^r), 15. 5–8 (A6^v), 5. 5–14 (A7^r), 8. 5–10 (A8^v), *PP* 3. 1–2, 13–14 (B2^{r-v}), *PP* 5. 11–12 (B4^r), 20. 6 (B4^r), *PP* 5. 13 (B4^r), 28. 10–11 (B4^v), 29. 12 (B3^r), 30. 1–2 (B6^r), 33 (C2^{r-v}), 62. 10 (D1^r), 116. 11–12 (D4^r), 82. 9–10 (D4^r), 83. 13 (D4^v), 95. 1–3 (D8^r), 97. 2 (D8^v), 107. 2 (E2^v), 112. 1–4 (E3^v), 115. 5–8 (E4^r), 121. 5–6 (E6^r), 124. 6–8 (E7^r), 132. 5–6, 9 (E8^v), 142. 5–6 (F3^r). The excerpts from Benson continue with non-Shakespearean items until fol. 24^r of the manuscript.

5   These include the following sonnets (in the order in which their excerpts appear): 60, 65, 1, 2, 54, 13, 15, 5, 8, *Passionate Pilgrim* 3 (sonnet 138), *Passionate Pilgrim* 5 (sonnet 144), 20, 28, 29, 30, 62, 116, 82, 83, 95, 97, 102, 112, 115, 121, 124, 132, 142.

6   The Quarto text reads "guil'st th'eauen." This is usually emended to "gild'st the even."

7   See the discussion of this manuscript in Hobbs 1992: 116–20.

8   This manuscript also contains William Basse's much-transcribed epitaph on Shakespeare ("Renowned Spencer lye a thought more nigh" [fol. 27^v]).

9   This manuscript is a small notebook of some eleven gatherings in a modern (re)binding, the first two of which of which are largely blank. At the start of the third gathering, among the scribblings on the first folio (where the modern penciled numbering starts), are found the name "Mathew" and the expression "Most deere Calisthea." There are many hands in this manuscript, as well as some pieces recorded in reverse transcription from the other end. Many of the poems recorded in Hand B are not found in Margaret Crum's (1969) first-line index and are possibly by the scribe, who subscribes three of them "MP" (fols. 3^r and 10^{r-v}). The section transcribed by Hand A, which also appears early in the manuscript and which copies the Shakespeare sonnet, runs from fol. 40^v through fol. 91^v.

10   "A Register for a Bible" ("I am that faithfull deputy" [fol. 55^r]), "A purse string" ("We hug, imprison, hang, and save" [fol. 55^v]), "A watch string" ("Times picture here invites your eyes" [fol. 55^v]), "A girdle" ("When ere the wast makes to much hast" [fol. 55^v]), "posies for bracelets" ("This keeps my hand" [fol. 55^v]), "Another" ("When you put on this little band" [fol. 56^r]), "Idem" ("Silke though thou be" [fol. 56^r]), "on a Dissembler" ("Could any show us here [where] plinies people dwell" [fols. 56^v–57^r]), "on Dr Corbets marrige day" ("Come all you muses and rejoyce" [fols. 56^v–58^r]), "Commendation of grey eyes" ("Looke how the russet morne exceeds the night" [fols. 58^v–59^r]), "on a watch made by a blacksmith" ("A Vulcan & a Venus seldome part" [fol. 59^r]), "The divines comendation of a good voice" ("O let me learne to be a Saint on earth" [fol. 59^v]), "A replie to a friend" ("have I a corner in your memory" [fol. 60^r]), "An Epitaph on Mistris Eliz: Neckham" ("As sin

makes gros the soule, & thickens it" [fol. 60^r]), "An Epitaph" ("Man newly borne is at full age to die" [fol. 60^v]), "On a blistered lip" ("Chide not thy sprouting lip, nor kill" [fols. 60^v–61^r]), "On the bible" ("Behold this little volume here inrold" [fol. 61$^{r–v}$]), "on one that died of an impostume in the head" ("Is Death so cunning now that all her blow" [fols. 61^v–62^v]), "on the death of a twinne" ("Where are you now astrologers, that looke" [fol. 62^v]), "on the death of the lady Caesar" ("Though death to good men be the greatest boone" [fol. 63$^{r–v}$]), and "on the death of Sir Tho: Leigh" ("You that affright with lamentable notes" [fols. 63^v–64^v]).

11 Its first twelve pages are missing and pages 13–244 are transcribed in a single italic hand. Other hands take the collection through page 333, after which pp. 334–400 are blank, more material is inserted on pp. 401–9, and pp. 410–540 are blank before the remains of ripped-out pages at the end.

12 This piece also appears in Bod. MS Ashmole 47, fol. 47^v; Bod. MS Douce f.5, fol 20^r; BL MS Add. 30782, fol. 13^v; and Folger MS V. a.345, p. 131.

13 See Marotti 2002: 74–9.

14 The order he creates is lines 43–8, 31–6, and 25–30. The two significant textual changes from the copytext are "Good sooth" for "In faith" (l. 36) and "cloudie lookes" for "frowning browes" (l. 25), both unique readings.

15 On fol. 1^v we find "Daniell leare his Book. Witness / William Strode."

16 Later additions follow, but also Leare's handwriting appears in reverse transcription on fols. 163^v–117^r, followed also by later additions.

17 This piece also appears in Yale Osborn MS b 62, p. 16.

18 This is a fairly rare item, appearing in no Bodleian manuscript and only one British Library manuscript (BL MS Sloane 1792, fol. 94^r, "A Gentleman to his sister").

19 Roberts (2003: 176) notes that of all the manuscripts that reproduce sonnet 2 only St John's College Cambridge MS S.23 attributes the poem to Shakespeare.

20 Taylor (1985: 223–4) notes that Hobbs and Beal believe the popularity of sonnet 2 in the

manuscript collections might be due to its having been set to music.

21 I briefly discuss this manuscript in my 2001 essay, "Folger MSS V.a.89 and V.a.345: Reading Lyric Poetry in Manuscript."

22 Crum (1969: vol. 1, 405) notes that it was printed in Walter Porter's *Madrigales and Ayres* (1632), *Wits Recreations* (1640), *Parnassus Biceps* (1656), and, with music, in *The Musical Companion* (1673) and Purcell's *The Theatre of Music* (1686), as well as in many manuscripts.

23 See BL MS Additional 21433, fols. 167^r–86^v.

24 It lacks "Uppon Owen Butler of Christ church" and moves the poem "One Mr Beaumonts death" to a later section of the manuscript (fol. 177^v) to place it in a group of epitaphs and elegies.

25 This manuscript is discussed both by Roberts (2003: 179–83) and Moulton (2000: 57–64).

26 This also appears in Bod. MS Rawlinson Poetical 26, fol. 2^r. See Bellany and McRae 2004: 99–100.

27 See Crum (1969: vol. 2, 902).

28 The first two seem to be variations of one person's writing, the second of which is more heavily italic in form, the former preserving more secretary forms. There are poems (for example, "Sonnett" [fol. 9$^{r–v}$] and "On the Choyce of a Wife" [fols. 14^v–15^v]) where the two hands alternate in the transcription. Many poems have the title in Hand B and the body of the text in Hand A (e.g. "Of Whores and theire Maisters" [fol. 10^v], "faith and love" [fol. 11^r], and "on Jealousie" [fol. 14^r]). The fourth or fifth hand begins on fol. 27 and continues to the last couple of folios of the manuscript, where the first hand returns. Although the whole collection was not produced by a single compiler, all of the scribes record poems with Oxford associations and the first two hands are found in the section in which the two Shakespeare sonnets are found.

29 None of these appear, for example, in Margaret Crum's (1969) first-line index of poetry in Bodleian Library manuscripts.

30 This poem appears in the 1616 edition of Overbury's *The Wife*.

31 This piece appears in none of the manuscripts found in the two largest repositories of

manuscript poetry from the period, the British Library and the Bodleian Library, Oxford.

32 This poem is found in no British Library or Bodleian Library manuscript.

33 Into this document John Payne Collier inserted eighty-three forged ballads (Dawson 1971).

34 The last eighteen lines are a poem found in *Poems Written by the Right Honourable William Earl of Pembroke . . . Many of which are answered by way of Repartee, by Sr Benjamin Ruddier* (1660), pp. 54–5. Robert Krueger (ed.), "The Poems of William Herbert, Third Earl of Pembroke" (B. Litt. Thesis, Oxford University, 1961), ascribes this poem to Pembroke.

35 I cite the text from the transcription in Redding (1960: 670–1). This poem also appears in the Holgate MS (Pierpont Morgan Library MS MA 1057, p. 140), which also has Sonnet 106 (on p. 96).

36 Burrow (Shakespeare 2002: 107) suggests that the change may be the scribe's "updating" of the older term, "chronicles," which was common in the 1590s, to the newer term, "annals," which, because of the publication of Tacitus' *Annals,* was the trendier word in the seventeenth century.

37 For a discussion of the practice of memorial transcription, see Leishman (1945).

38 John Kerrigan (Shakespeare 1986: 428) is also inclined to believe in the existence of alternative authorial versions of some of the sonnets.

39 This manuscript is a composite one made up of single sheets and booklets, written in several hands over an extended period of time. It is not, like some of the other manuscripts in which Shakespearean sonnets are found, a substantial compilation by a single individual.

References and Further Reading

Beal, Peter, Croft, P. J., et al. (1980). *Index of English Literary Manuscripts*, vol. 1, pt. 2. London: Mansell.

Bellany, Alastair, and McRae, Alastair, eds. (n.d.). *Early Stuart Libels: An Edition of Poetry from Manuscript Sources. Early Modern Literary Studies, Text Series I,* http://www.earlymodernweb.org.uk/emn/index.php/archives/2005/07/early-stuart-libels/.

Crum, Margaret (1969). *First-Line Index of English Poetry 1500–1800 in Manuscripts of The Bodleian Library, Oxford.* New York: Modern Language Association; Oxford: Clarendon.

Dawson, Giles (1971). "John Payne Collier's Great Forgery." *Studies in Bibliography* 24, 1–27.

Duncan-Jones, Katherine (2001). *Ungentle Shakespeare: Scenes from His Life.* London: Thomson Learning. (The Arden Shakespeare.)

Hobday, C. H. (1973). Shakespeare's Venus and Adonis Sonnets. *Shakespeare Survey* 26, 103–9.

Hobbs, Mary (1979). "Shakespeare's Sonnet II: A 'sugred sonnet'?" *Notes and Queries* 224, 112–13.

Hobbs, Mary (1992). *Early Seventeenth-Century Verse Miscellany Manuscripts.* Aldershot: Scolar.

Leishman, J. B. (1945). " 'You meaner beauties of the night': A Study in Transmission and Transmogrification." *The Library,* 4th ser., 26, 99–121.

Marotti, Arthur F. (1990). "Shakespeare's Sonnets as Literary Property." In Elizabeth D. Harvey and Katharine Eisaman Maus, eds., *Soliciting Interpretation: Literary Theory and Seventeenth-Century English Poetry,* 143–73. Chicago and London: University of Chicago Press.

Marotti, Arthur F. (1995). *Manuscript, Print, and the English Renaissance Lyric.* Ithaca, NY: Cornell University Press.

Marotti, Arthur F. (2001). "Folger MSS V.a.89 and V.a.345: Reading Lyric Poetry in Manuscript." In Sabrina Alcorn Baron, ed., *The Reader Revealed,* 45–57. Washington DC, Seattle, and London: Folger Shakespeare Library/University of Washington Press.

Marotti, Arthur F. (2002). "The Cultural and Textual Importance of Folger MS V.a.89." *English Manuscript Studies 1100–1700* 11, 70–92.

Moulton, Ian (2000). *Before Pornography: Erotic Writing in Early Modern England.* New York and Oxford: Oxford University Press.

North, Marcy (2003). "Rehearsing the Absent Name: Reading Shakespeare's Sonnets through Anonymity." In Robert J. Griffin, ed., *The Faces of Anonymity: Anonymous and Pseudonymous Publication from the Sixteenth to the Twentieth Century*, 19–38. New York and Basingstoke: Palgrave Macmillan.

Potter, Lois (1989). *Secret Rites and Secret Writing: Royalist Literature, 1641–1660*. Cambridge, UK: Cambridge University Press.

Redding, David Coleman, ed. (1960). "Robert Bishop's Commonplace Book: An Edition of a Seventeenth-Century Miscellany." Ph.D. diss., University of Pennsylvania.

Roberts, Sasha (2003). *Reading Shakespeare's Poems in Early Modern England*. Basingstoke: Palgrave Macmillan.

Rollins, Hyder, ed. (1965). *Tottel's Miscellany (1557–1587)*, 2 vols. Cambridge, Mass.: Harvard University Press.

Shakespeare, William (1986). *The Sonnets and A Lover's Complaint*, ed. John Kerrigan. New York: Viking Penguin. (The New Penguin Shakespeare.)

Shakespeare, William (1997). *Shakespeare's Sonnets*, ed. Katherine Duncan-Jones. London: Thomson Learning. (The Arden Shakespeare.)

Shakespeare, William (2002). *The Complete Sonnets and Poems*, ed. Colin Burrow. Oxford: Oxford University Press. (Oxford World's Classics.)

Taylor, Gary (1985). "Some Manuscripts of Shakespeare's Sonnets." *Bulletin of the John Rylands Library* 68, 210–46.

13

The Sonnets and Book History

Marcy L. North

Thomas Thorpe's edition of *Shake-speares Sonnets* made its appearance in 1609, a good ten years after the sonnet heyday of the 1590s. As critics have observed, its intense focus on time and mortality, frequent invocation of a male beloved, and misogynous depiction of a dark mistress also set it apart from most Elizabethan sequences. The late date and unique thematic perspectives are not the *Sonnets'* only anomalies, however. The volume also deviates in meaningful ways from the material standards that defined the 1590s vogue. Its organization and physical appearance – the patched-together arrangement, lack of an author's epistle, and even the asymmetrical page layout – are noticeably unconventional. This essay argues that the Thorpe edition's material anomalies are a key to understanding Shakespeare's sequence as a cultural and generic product, especially if they are analyzed through the frame of book history. More so than other approaches, book history shows us a sonnet vogue driven by print industry standards, some of which outlasted the 1590s to influence Thomas Thorpe. It thereby draws the distinctions between the typical Elizabethan sequence and Shakespeare's in much subtler terms. At the same time, however, book history also provides evidence that Shakespeare's sequence followed an unconventional path to publication and that Thorpe saw the *Sonnets* as generically divergent from the Elizabethan first-edition sequences.

Between 1591 and 1599, well over a dozen different Petrarchan sonnet sequences reached print as principal texts in quarto or octavo first editions. If one includes devotional sequences such as Barnabe Barnes's *Divine Centurie* (1595), translations such as the du Bellay sonnets in Spenser's *Complaints* (1591), and sequences couched within larger publications such as Richard Barnfield's sonnets to Ganymede (in *Cynthia*, 1595), one finds nearly two dozen first-edition sequences and a half-dozen second editions published in the nine years when sonneteering was most fashionable.[1] The sonnet craze is usually characterized as an Elizabethan phenomenon that ran out of steam before the turn of the century. The odd appearance of *Shake-speares Sonnets* a decade later has therefore generated numerous theories about Shakespeare's financial straits during plague years and Thomas Thorpe's piratical tendencies. It has sparked arguments about when and how the sonnets were composed, revised, and gathered for publication, and why the sonnets enjoyed only one edition before 1640, when John Benson published *Poems: Written by Wil. Shake-speare. Gent.* The late publication has both teased and defeated scholars trying to trace the influence of the 1590s fashions on Shakespeare and Thorpe, for no one early sequence stands out as a model.

Not surprisingly, "book history" has been employed enthusiastically in these debates. Book history traditionally chronicles the emergence and production methods of the print industry, but in the last several decades it has, together with bibliography and textual studies, developed into a more culturally based discipline, serving as a sociological and theoretical lens through which to examine the rich body of material evidence in early print and manuscript cultures (McKenzie 1986; Chartier 1987). Foundational to this new brand of book history, as David Scott Kastan phrases it, is the idea that "the specific forms and contexts in which we encounter literature, its modes and mechanisms of transmission, are intrinsic aspects of what it is, not considerations wholly external to it; and, no less than its semantic and syntactic organization, these exert influence over our judgments and interpretations" (Kastan 2001: 3). In Shakespeare scholarship generally, book history has long been employed in studies of the quartos and folios, and its newer theories have inspired much excellent criticism, particularly in editorial history and reception studies (Stallybrass 1993; de Grazia 1991; Marcus 1996). Book-historical approaches have also been foundational to sonnet scholarship, and they continue to be applied today, especially in the arguments about Shakespeare's role in the 1609 publication. Editors Colin Burrow and Katherine Duncan-Jones, for instance, both employ print-industry evidence to measure Shakespeare's approval of the Thorpe edition. Although their conclusions differ – with Duncan-Jones arguing that Shakespeare was closely involved in the *Sonnets'* publication and Burrow finding Shakespeare's hand in its organization but not necessarily in its printing – they share the belief that the Thorpe quarto's physical properties are inseparable from its poetry (Duncan-Jones 1997; Burrow in Shakespeare 2002). As Burrow observes, the puzzles surrounding the quarto have become "an enabling condition of the delighted mystification which all readers of these poems have felt, and which they repeatedly invite" (Shakespeare 2002: 91–2).

For these editors and for most sonnet scholars, the Thorpe edition is the starting point for any book-historical approach to the sonnets. For many, it is also the end point. Other than this quarto, there is little explicitly related to Shakespeare on which to build a convincing argument about his career as a sonneteer. A brief mention of Shakespeare's "sugred sonnets among his private friends" by Francis Meres in 1598 (*Palladis Tamia*, fols. 281ᵛ–2), the publication of a few Shakespeare sonnets and poems in *The Passionate Pilgrim* (1599, 1612), and the circulation of a few select sonnets in manuscript after Shakespeare's death (Taylor 1986; North 2003) offer only a few clues about the generation and development of the larger sequence. The 1640 Benson edition of Shakespeare's *Poems* proves valuable for the study of Shakespeare reception in the decades after the author's death, but the Thorpe quarto still stands as the most substantial material record of Shakespeare's interest in the sustained Petrarchan sequence.

The quarto, then, has become a kind of material icon – an elusive but essential key to understanding the genesis and development of the best-known sonnet sequence in English. Its status, however, is not without critics. Sasha Roberts and Patrick Cheney question the attention afforded to the quarto, arguing that the full significance of *The Passionate Pilgrim*, the Benson edition, and manuscript evidence has been overlooked (Roberts 2003: 143–97; Cheney 2004). The authority granted to the quarto has also, ironically, discouraged scholars from exploring a broader range of book-historical evidence that could illuminate Shakespeare's sonneteering and even the quarto itself.

Too few studies follow the lead of Wendy Wall (1993), Burrow (Shakespeare 2002), and Arthur Marotti (1990) to analyze the quarto in terms of the print-industry standards for compiling, framing, laying out, and introducing sonnet sequences. More attention could also be paid to minor sequences, which come closer to typifying industry practices than major sequences do. Similarly, Shakespeare scholars tend to date and define the sonnet craze using the better-known Elizabethan sequences even though several influential later editions and minor seventeenth-century sequences might have inspired Thorpe or Shakespeare to bring the sonnets out (Duncan-Jones 1997: 29–31). Scholars have also not fully foregrounded the extent to which the sonnet *sequence* – despite the côterie ethos and manuscript imagery within the sonnets themselves – was a print genre. In fact, recent book historians seeking to broaden the context for the sonnet craze have moved in the other direction to align sonneteering with the practices of manuscript culture. This is an understandable trend, given the general neglect of manuscript evidence in traditional Shakespearean scholarship. But in emphasizing the sonnet's côterie connections, scholars have not addressed the fact that there is no manuscript evidence for the majority of extant sequences, and what is available for the rest is slim compared to the manuscript evidence for other côterie genres.

My point in calling attention to these neglected areas of scholarship is to show that the selective application of book history to the study of Shakespeare's sonnets can prove more misleading than illuminating. Such an application has, I believe, further polarized the arguments about the quarto's authorization, reception, and uniqueness. Book history could be used more productively to situate the quarto in a broad material history of English sonneteering, a history that gives attention to less canonical sequences, to subsequent editions of more famous sequences, and to the two-way relationship between material and literary traditions. This broader perspective would bring to the fore the subtle choices that Thorpe (and perhaps Shakespeare) made in publishing the relatively anomalous *Sonnets* in 1609. In the following discussions I outline the possibilities in this approach. I pull together the scattered material evidence of sonnet sequence publication between 1590 and 1619 to argue that the sonnet sequence was a highly standardized print genre familiar to both Elizabethan and Jacobean readers. I set the Thorpe quarto in this context, looking at the page layout, material details, and particular sonnets to illuminate the quarto's generic affiliations with print and manuscript cultures. Studies that compare the *Sonnets* only to the better-known sequences are bound to miss some of the subtle characteristics that make the Thorpe edition unusual. Although the often-studied sequences of Sidney, Daniel, Constable, Drayton, and

Spenser are more conventional than the quarto, they each deviate from the norm in some way, either defying the odds to circulate in manuscript or reaching second editions. Sidney's unauthorized sequence, in particular, stands apart from the others. It is precisely because *Shake-speares Sonnets* is also an exception to the standards for sequence publication (in ways that may even invoke Sidney) that we need to pay more attention to the broader publishing norms for English sonnet sequences.

The Material Conventions of the Sonnet Craze

The fashionable sonnet sequences of the 1590s had a distinct appearance. They were typically printed in quarto, and the sonnets were arranged one per page, sometimes two, with a good deal of space in the margins and even between the lines. The poems were carefully numbered, but other headings were rare (Burrow in Shakespeare 2002: 97). Printers inserted decorative borders below and sometimes above the sonnets, framing them like portraits or jewels. The symmetry and simplicity of the open quarto page dictated a reader's first impression. The borders and mirrored layout discouraged a strictly narrative reading, for the poems were presented as individually whole and discrete.[2] Although many sequences were intentionally arranged, and several contained small groupings of sonnets linked rhetorically, their leaves *looked* as if they could be reordered or read out of sequence without any loss of text or sense (Fumerton 1991: 114–16). This layout suited nicely the dramatic pattern created by the genre's variety of tropes, the emotional vacillations of the lover, the recurring tests of his devotion, and the sporadic hints at progress or retreat as he sought his mistress's favor. The conventionally less narrative page arrangement also allowed authors to play fancifully with the ordering of sonnets as they revised and expanded, as both Samuel Daniel and Michael Drayton did. Although the symmetrical page set-up became fashionable and influential in print, it may have been inspired initially by early manuscripts of Sidney's sequence; of the three important manuscripts extant today, all were copied symmetrically and two were copied one poem per page (Ringler 1962: 538–42; Beal et al. 1980).[3]

The length of the first-edition sequences varied considerably, from twenty to well over one hundred sonnets, and many included other lyric genres, either interspersed or clustered at the end. Despite this variety, the prefatory materials attached to the sequences remained surprisingly consistent. The title-pages conventionally sported the pseudonym of the Petrarchan mistress who had inspired the sonnet writing, a figure who was both the nominal subject of the poems and a symbol for the book itself (Wall 1993: 61–71). She gave some unity to the variety of tropes and emotions conveyed by the individual sonnets. The sequences were also introduced to readers through authors' epistles, envoys, and commendatory verses – all but two 1590s first editions employ one of these authorizing conventions. Frequently, the first or first few sonnets of the sequence proper also served an introductory role. Paradoxically, they often described the author's infatuation prospectively and retrospectively, looking forward to the experiences recorded in the sequence and backward on the outcome of the affair (Neely 1978: 363). Authorial introductions are often cited as evidence that authors were involved in preparing their sequences for print (Duncan-Jones 1983: 165), but the introductory numbered sonnets suggest that authors also had print in mind during the composition of at least some of their sonnets proper.

All of these material conventions came to define the 1590s printed sonnet sequence very precisely, with most publishers adopting the majority of the industry standards. Daniel's *Delia* (1592) and Thomas Lodge's *Phillis* (1593) are typical examples, and a dozen other sequences fit the publication format almost exactly. Even sequences that lack traditional Petrarchan mistresses still demonstrate their publishers' familiarity with the genre's print conventions. Barnes's spiritual sequence, *A Divine Centurie* (1595), and Barnfield's sonnets to the young boy share the symmetry, borders, and reluctance to divide sonnets between pages that characterize Petrarchan first editions, and Barnfield's sequence appears in a publication conventionally titled *Cynthia* (1595). The exceptional standardization of the sonnet vogue argues that, after the first few exemplary sequences were published in the early 1590s, authors composed sonnet sequences to conform to print standards.

Shake-speares Sonnets shares some of the characteristics of the highly standardized 1590s sequences, such as quarto formatting, simple numbering of sonnets, and a fore-grounding of the sonnets within a multi-genre publication. In its scope and focus, too, it is aligned with the sonnet sequence tradition. The quarto nevertheless lacks other material attributes that commonly define the printed genre. Its title has no pastoral pseudonym, and its pages are not set up symmetrically or framed with decorative borders. It offers no authorial introduction to the sequence as a complete project. Even the connections and breaks between poems in the quarto do not follow the pattern of most printed sequences; many 1590s sonneteers employed formal rhetorical links to join poems, and several made an effort to space out poems that used similar tropes. Shakespeare's sequence, in contrast, tends to cluster related poems and to link them less formally through shared themes and verbal echoes. Whether the quarto was autho-rized or not, neither Shakespeare nor Thorpe molded the *Sonnets* into what print readers might have expected from a typical sonnet sequence.

For readers familiar with the 1590s traditions, the quarto's material anomalies would have been pronounced and significant. Since its compositor made no effort to keep poems to a single page, awkwardly isolated leading and trailing lines force the reader to flip pages back and forth to get the full sense of some sonnets. Most of sonnet 2, for instance, appears at the bottom of sig. B2^r, but the couplet, "This were to be new made when thou art ould, / And see thy blood warme when thou feel'st it could," sits at the top of the verso. Sonnet 137's first line, "Thou blinde foole love, what doost thou to mine eyes," sits alone at the bottom of sig. I1^r. Turning pages sequentially is a necessity for quarto readers. After the first nine sonnets, they must complete five pages or twelve poems in order to reach a page that ends with a couplet. This pattern is consistent throughout the edition, creating a kind of forward rhythm that cuts across the thematic divisions and connections in the sequence.

Is the quarto's page layout indicative of changing Jacobean expectations? Standards for sonnet layout became a bit more flexible in the Jacobean period in both stray first editions and reprints of 1590s sequences. Yet this flexibility may have been motivated by conservation of space rather than a major shift in the perception of the printed sonnet sequence. Paper accounted for well over half of a book's production cost in this period, and the 1590s layout had not been particularly economical. Most of the seventeenth-century first editions are still quartos, but they are typically organized with two sonnets per page. This is the case for sequences in William Drummond's *Poems* (1604), John Davies of Hereford's *Wittes Pilgrimage* (1605), and Sir David Murray's *Caelia* (1611). They maintain the symmetry of the 1590s but sacrifice the decorative borders. Of the eight sequences initially published in the first decade of James's reign, only William Alexander's *Aurora* (1604) and *Shake-speares Sonnets* have asymmetrical facing pages.

Seventeenth-century second editions of Elizabethan sequences also tended to be laid out symmetrically. It is worth noting that very few Elizabethan sequences ever reached second editions; thirteen of the 1590s sequences were never reprinted. In this light, the single edition of Shakespeare's sequence before 1640 was hardly unusual. Of the sequences that did reach a second edition, only the unauthorized *Astrophel and Stella* was reissued in a subsequent year in quarto.[4] Most second editions appeared instead as addenda to other texts. Beginning with Sidney's 1598 *Countess of Pembroke's Arcadia*, which contained the first authorized *Astrophel and Stella*, printers added sonnet sequences to the back of folio and octavo collected works, placing them after the epics, romances, histories, and even laments. Drayton's *Idea* was reprinted in half a dozen editions of his *Poems*, appearing after the *Heroical Epistles*. In the case of Daniel, the *Complaint of Rosamund*, which followed *Delia* initially, came to precede *Delia* in the 1601 *Works* and in subsequent Daniel collections. When adding sequences to collected editions, printers typically placed two to four sonnets on a page and avoided splitting sonnets across pages. In Sidney's 1598 and 1605 *Arcadia*s, the sonnets are arranged three per page until the interspersed songs throw off the line count. The 1599 *Arcadia* printed in Scotland, however, contains an asymmetrical *Astrophel and Stella*.

Altogether, over thirty editions of sonnet sequences were reissued or published between 1603 and 1612, and there is no reason to suspect that these editions went unnoticed. If Thomas Thorpe looked to the later editions as his publication models, he might have found a precedent in the 1599 Sidney or in Alexander's *Aurora*. The shorter sequences in Francis Davison's *Poetical Rhapsody* were symmetrical in the initial 1602 edition, but Thorpe might also have seen the asymmetrical second edition of 1608. More generally, he could have been influenced by the more economical use of paper and perhaps by the way that collected editions advertised the author's name rather than the volume's contents on the title-page. The title-pages and preliminaries to many collected editions do not even register the inclusion of the sonnet sequence. Coincidentally, just a couple years after *Shake-speares Sonnets* appeared, sequences by Spenser (*Colin Clouts*, 1611), Daniel (*Certain Small Works*, 1611), and John Davies of Hereford (*Muses Sacrifice*, 1612) were printed asymmetrically at the back of longer works. Asymmetrical layout was also typical for Thorpe generally, although he printed no other sonnet sequences

(Duncan-Jones 1983: 161–2). One wonders, then, if the quarto marks the beginning of a shift away from symmetrical layout and if Thorpe was at all influential in establishing this trend.

Some scholars have proposed that Thorpe's publication model comes not from the highly standardized editions of the 1590s or from the Jacobean sequences, but from the unauthorized Sidney sequence of 1591, which William Ringler deemed a pirated edition (1962: 542–3). *Astrophel and Stella* is credited with inspiring the Elizabethan sonnet craze, but the unauthorized edition was clearly not the model for the material conventions that came to define the sequence genre. In the 1591 and 1597 editions of *Astrophel and Stella* (STC 22536–8), the poems are set up continuously rather than symmetrically. They are unnumbered, and, with only a narrow space between them, they resemble stanzas in a narrative poem rather than individual sonnets. The songs are placed last, and sonnets by Daniel and a few poems by others are appended. The sequence contains no prefatory material by Sidney himself, and a letter from Thomas Nashe in STC 22536 was removed from the subsequent printings and may have been suppressed. For Burrow and Marotti, the similarities between the Shakespeare and Sidney editions are evidence that the quarto was not entirely authorized. Marotti observes that the Thorpe quarto lacks the unity typical of published sonnet sequences (1990: 154–8). Like the 1591 *Astrophel and Stella*, it bears the marks of a text pulled prematurely out of manuscript into print. Observing the similar layout of the two first editions, Burrow proposes a more explicit but also less decipherable connection:

> The resemblances to the pirated *Astrophil and Stella* can be interpreted in two quite contradictory ways: they could tell readers that this was another publisher's coup, in which a work by a notable author was smuggled into print by an unscrupulous printer; or they could support the view that Shakespeare's sequence consummates the Sidneian tradition by recognizing its great predecessor in its physical form. (Shakespeare 2002: 98)

Burrow's speculations lead one to ask if Thorpe was familiar enough with the unauthorized Sidney to imitate its page layout and presentation. Admittedly, no later *Astrophel and Stella* ever appeared in quarto with the sonnets as the principal text. Nevertheless, the authorized *Arcadia*s from 1598, 1599, and 1605 with the sonnets included would have been in circulation in the early seventeenth century, and Sidney's iconic status was much more visible in these folios than it had been in the unauthorized editions. Manuscripts of *Astrophel and Stella*, perhaps similar to the symmetrically copied manuscripts extant today, might also have been in circulation in the early seventeenth century. If Thorpe did model his quarto on the unauthorized Sidney and not on another source, it seems likely that he chose this prototype because it was the first edition, not because it was the only Sidney to which he had access. He may even have chosen it because it was pirated, perhaps hoping to market Shakespeare's sonnets as a text the author had wanted to keep private.

There is a Sidney connection that Burrow does not explore and that warrants more attention. In two of the folio *Arcadia*s that contain both Sidney's *Certain Sonnets* and

Astrophel and Stella (1598, 1605), the *Certain Sonnets* are not held to the same standards of layout and symmetry as the more organized Petrarchan sequence. With thirty-two sonnets and poems, Sidney's miscellaneous sequence is as substantial as some of the 1590s published sonnet sequences, yet it seems to be defined as a different sort of genre by the *Arcadia* printers. Little effort is made to keep sonnets on one page, and none of the facing pages are symmetrical. *Certain Sonnets* and *Astrophel and Stella* also have different manuscript transmission histories. Individual sonnets and small clusters from *Certain Sonnets* traveled more extensively in manuscript than material from *Astrophel and Stella* did. Perhaps Thorpe saw Shakespeare's sonnets as a more miscellaneous collection, along the lines of *Certain Sonnets*, rather than a sequence organized by the author, as *Astrophel and Stella* was. The generic title that the Thorpe edition and *Certain Sonnets* share could have been intended to distinguish these groups of sonnets from the sonnet sequence tradition.

There is some evidence that sonnet sequences printed from more miscellaneous manuscript copies were treated differently by printers. Barnes had not prepared *Parthenophil and Parthenophe* for publication when it reached a printer in 1593 – if one believes the printer's letter and author's reluctant envoy. Although there is internal evidence that Barnes intended to print the work, *Parthenophil and Parthenophe* is framed as a stolen manuscript, and its asymmetrical layout contributes to this generic identification. Marotti observes that Fulke Greville's *Caelica*, which was also set up with continuous, asymmetrical text, remained in manuscript many years before it was published with Greville's other works in 1633. The disjointed quality of the Greville sonnets, Marotti argues, is a consequence of their long gestation in manuscript. The Thorpe quarto's fragmentation, he posits, may be evidence of a similar transmission history (Marotti 1990: 155). More important than the symmetry alone, however, is the fact that a particular kind of page layout could come to define a particular genre. The symmetrical layout standards may have begun in manuscript, but they flourish and exercise their influence in print. That Thorpe did not adhere to this relatively simple though perhaps more expensive standard for sonnet sequence publication may indicate that he saw Sidney's first edition as a model. It is more likely, however, that he did not see Shakespeare's sonnets as belonging to quite the same genre as the sequences that the sonnet craze produced and reprinted. Rather than a sequence composed and organized for print, Thorpe acquired a partially organized collection of small côterie sequences and individual sonnets.

Framing a Print Genre

The material resemblance of the Thorpe edition to the unauthorized Sidney is also evident in the lack of authorial paratexts, framing devices whose functionality is detailed in Gerard Genette's *Paratexts* (1997). Sidney's death in 1586 goes a long way toward explaining the absence of an author's letter in 1591 and 1597, but not the whole way. Later editions of the *Arcadia* are tellingly prefaced by Sidney's letter to his sister, the Countess of Pembroke, as if even posthumous publications required an authorial frame. The absence of an author's introduction in *Shake-speares Sonnets* is more puzzling. There is no clear proof that the quarto was pirated, but the mysterious dedication from Thomas Thorpe to Mr. W.H. is unconventional for Shakespeare the author and for sonneteers generally. In publishing *Venus and Adonis* and *The Rape of Lucrece*, Shakespeare had taken pains to include letters to his patron, and most published sequences bore a similar record of the sonneteer's participation in preparing the work for publication.

Most sequences also had at least one numbered sonnet that served as a framing device, and although some scholars have read into Shakespeare's first sonnet an introductory tone, "From fairest creatures we desire increase" does not emphasize the transmission or function of the finished product in the way that the other initial sonnets do. The introductory sonnet has roots in Petrarch and the continental sonneteering tradition (Warkentin 1975: 18–20), but in the English fashion, these first poems are notable for framing the sonnets as a unified set, often by acknowledging the scope and labor of the project, its publication, or its affinity with the sonnet sequence genre. Like the title-page, they make a whole out of seemingly discrete pieces. "Mystrisse behold in this true-speaking Glasse," begins Barnabe Barnes in sonnet 1 of *Parthenophil and Parthenophe* (1593), describing the sequence as a mirror that holds "each Love ditty" (p. 1, ll. 1, 8). William Smith asks his mistress to "waigh the taske I undertake," a task clearly bigger than the composition of this one sonnet (*Chloris* 1596: sig. A3, l. 13). In sonnet 1 of *Coelia* (1594), William Percy promises to make public the sentence of misery passed against him, "that ev'rie sillie eye may view [it] most plaine" (sig. A3, l. 3). It seems unlikely that Shakespeare or Thorpe would neglect paratextual conventions as common as author's letters and introductory sonnets in order to *honor* Sidney. The absence of an authorial frame more likely marks a breach of communication between author and printer rather than a positioning of the author as a second Sidney. At the least, Thorpe and Shakespeare are flouting tradition rather than celebrating it, choosing not to identify Shakespeare's sequence with the highly conventional products of the broader sonnet craze.

Authors' preliminaries, of course, do much more than assure readers that works are not pirated. Much of the identification of the 1590s sonnet sequence as a print genre begins in the front matter, which justifies the author's decision to publish or acknowledges the world as the audience. In his first sonnet's couplet, Lodge promises to "show to the world tho poore and scant my skill is, / How sweet thoughts bee, that are but thought on *Phillis*" (1593: sig. B2ʳ). Prefatory materials, however, can always be added to a work after its composition, as was the Induction which precedes Lodge's sonnet. They can usher into print a text previously circulated in manuscript, and they do not necessarily offer evidence that authors originally composed their sequences for print (Wall 1993: 188–202). In fact, the preliminaries to sonnet sequences are just as likely to describe a sequence as a personal transmission of manuscript poetry, as in the case of Spenser's first sonnet, where the final couplet reads "leaves, lines, and rymes, seeke her to please alone, / whom if ye please, I care for other none" (*Amoretti* 1595: sig. A2ʳ). In this sonnet, only a subtle depiction of the sequence as a finished product belies the fiction of the intimate côterie exchange. What a careful reader finds in the front matter to many sequences therefore is a dual gesture as an author presents the sequence to the world as an ambitious, generically specific product and simultaneously tries to recast it as a loose collection of occasional rhymes (Wall 1993: 58–9). One of William Smith's dedicatory sonnets to Spenser concludes

> Therefore good Collin, graciously accept
> A few sad sonnets, which my muse hath framed
> Though they but newly from the shell are crept,
> Suffer them not by envie to be blamed.
>   (*Chloris*, 1596: sig. A2)

The image of a "few sad sonnets" hardly warrants the envy the author fears, and a reader is wise to observe this disparity. The material object at hand is an extended sequence in print, despite the humble designation of the sequence as a small number of côterie poems.

In preliminaries that mingle images of manuscript and print, there is no reason to assume that the manuscript images are originary and that the print images have been inserted just prior to publication. Côterie images could also be added before publication, as subsequent editions of Daniel's *Delia* illustrate. The envoy to the twenty-eight Daniel sonnets included in the 1591 *Astrophel and Stella* not only acknowledges publication, it uses it to threaten a cruel mistress. "Go wayling verse," Daniel writes, and be a "monument that whosoever reedes / May justly praise and blame my loveless *Faire*" (ll. 7–8). He concludes by asking his verse to "Knock at her hard hart: say, I perish for her, / And feare this deed wil make the world abhor her" (Sidney 1591: sig. I3ᵛ, ll. 13–14). When Daniel revised his sonnets for the first authorized edition, he moved this envoy to position number two, muted the allusion to publishing and enhanced the image of côterie exchange so that the couplet reads, "Knock at her hard hart, beg till you have moov'd her / And tell th'unkind, how deerely I have lov'd her" (Daniel 1592: sig. B1ᵛ). Instead of "Go wailing verse," another poem introduces the 1592 sequence, one that addresses the mistress more intimately and directly, but which in its image of the poet "unclasp[ing] the booke of my charg'd soule" still hints that the sequence was already a substantial achievement at the time this sonnet was composed (Daniel 1592: sig. B1).

In her astute analysis of the sonnet sequence as a genre at the intersection of manuscript and print cultures, Wendy Wall is careful to acknowledge the affectation in many côterie images, but she is also reluctant to see them as entirely fictional:

> It may well be that writers in an age of print construct an eroticized authorial and readerly presence within these poems precisely in order to combat the distance publication seemingly conferred on writing. But such inscriptions could as easily contradict the idea that writers felt this distance at all, suggesting instead that these erotic exchanges mimetically reproduce the losses and gains incurred by the actual exchange of manuscript texts. (Wall 1993: 49–50)

Daniel's revisions argue that the first of Wall's hypotheses deserves more attention, and that the côterie ethos in many sonnet sequences is a frame constructed for their publication rather than a vestige of an actual mode of exchange. Certainly the côterie images may invoke an existing côterie culture with which the author was familiar, but most published sonnet sequences did not participate in that culture. This is not to say that sequences had no life in *manuscript*. Even sequences composed specifically for print were at one point manuscripts, and some of their images are likely vestiges of a composition process involving quills, ink, and paper. The interest sonneteers took in thematizing the manual task of writing can make sequences seem more grounded in côterie culture than they probably were.

Although many 1590s sonneteers claim to have composed their poems over an extended period of time corresponding to their infatuation with the beloved, the actual process of composition was probably much more focused and directed. There is really no other way to explain the compactness of the 1590s sonnet craze, which was too short to allow authors the leisure to circulate poems extensively before publication. In the dedicatory epistle that prefaces *A Divine Centurie*, Barnes describes devoting his sonnet writing to God "daily to his honour and service by prescribed taske" (1595: sig. A2^{r-v}) Although not without inspiration, the task is disciplined and focused, not occasional or casual. In another example, the author of *Emaricdulfe* picked up his half-written sequence and completed it during a short illness. "By reason of an ague," E.C. writes, "I was inforced to keepe my chamber, and to abandon idlenes, I tooke in hande my pen to finish an idle worke I had begun, at the command and service of a faire Dame" (1595: sig. A3). The sequence may have originated as a type of côterie challenge, but it was set aside only to be finished in one concentrated effort. Many of the 1590s sequences may have been composed along these lines, with the authors adding côterie frames late in the game to give immediacy or credibility to the described love affair.

The available manuscript evidence for sonnet sequences is in line with this interpretation. Long sequences rarely traveled far beyond their authors' desks. Compared to other verse genres, they were kept surprisingly close. Of the dozen sonneteers listed in Peter Beal's *Index of English Literary Manuscripts* (1980), Barnfield, Lodge, Spenser, Drayton, and Shakespeare have left us no manuscript sequences. For some of these authors, including Shakespeare, one can find individual sonnets in manuscript, but no long clusters or complete sequences exist. The early sequences of Sidney and Constable circulated in manuscript, but not to the extent of these authors' other works. Only one seventeenth-century manuscript of Daniel's sequence is extant. William Drummond and Fulke Greville, who wrote their sonnets long before they published them, also did not circulate their sequences extensively. Sir John Davies sent a copy of his satirical "Gulling Sonnets" to Sir Anthony Cooke, but since the sequence runs to only ten sonnets, it is surprising that we have no more than this one extant copy. Donne's short "Corona" also did not travel as broadly as his other poems. From the perspective of Beal's index, sonnet sequences did not have a great deal of currency in manuscript.

Looking at the sonneteers not included by Beal, the manuscript evidence is also scarce. Cambridge Library MS Hh 3.8 contains a short sonnet sequence crowded onto fol. 145ᵛ (Coatalen 2003). There is one personal copy of Robert Sidney's sonnet sequence and an autograph copy of Mary Wroth's *Pamphilia to Amphilanthus*. Wroth may have circulated her sonnets, but her father, Robert Sidney, probably did not (Croft 1984: 1–2). Margaret Crum's first-line index of poetry in Bodleian manuscripts (1969) turns up no additional substantial sequences, and neither do the finding aids from the Folger Shakespeare Library, Cambridge Library, and British Library. Although a comprehensive search of seventeenth-century manuscripts is not yet possible, we appear to have no manuscript sequences for Barnes, Fletcher, Lok, Percy, Chapman, Linche, Smith, Rogers, Perry, or the authors of *Tears of Fancy*, *Zepheria*, and *Emaricdulfe*. There is a nineteenth-century manuscript of Griffin's *Licia* at the British Library.

What can we conclude from this evidence? Sonnet sequences, especially those longer than twenty sonnets, did not circulate broadly in manuscript. When it came to the longer sequences of the 1590s, most sonneteers probably composed the majority of the sonnets after having decided to print them and with print as their model. Those with no intention to print their sonnets tended to keep them close. If sonneteers had circulated their sonnets in whole or in substantial parts, and if the long sonnet sequence had been considered a manuscript genre, we might have patterns more like the ones we have for the other kinds of poetic sequences: for example, the Sidney *Psalms*, with seventeen extant manuscripts, or various combinations of poems from Spenser's *Complaints*, which appear in a half dozen manuscripts (Beal et al. 1980). Several groups of satirical poems by Sir John Davies circulated in manuscript much more extensively than his "Gulling Sonnets" (Beal et al. 1980). Certainly, many sonnet sequences probably began with a few poems shared among friends; but at the point when authors decided to compose a sequence, it is likely that many sat down to write the greater part of the sequence in a relatively prescribed amount of time, essentially preparing the manuscript for print as they wrote.

This pattern of relatively quick composition and preparation for print, however, was probably not the one Shakespeare followed. Most scholars believe Shakespeare composed sections of his sequence at different times and tinkered with the sequence over time (Schiffer 1999: 7–8). The quarto likely contains at least three sequences – the procreation sonnets, the middle section, and the sonnets to the female addressee (Duncan-Jones 1983: 165–6) – though some sonnets could fit into more than one group (Dubrow 1996). The procreation sonnets seem likely to have served a patronage function in manuscript long before 1609, though the sonnets to the mistress may be the earliest group (Burrow, in Shakespeare 2002: 105). Multi-sequence publications are not necessarily rare, but both John Davies of Hereford (*Wittes Pilgrimage*, 1605) and Richard Nugent (*Cynthia*, 1604) drew distinctions between the sequences that they published together. The Thorpe edition is unusual because the sub-sequences are placed together without new titles, new numbering, or other material divisions. If Thorpe worked from the author's miscellaneous manuscript of short sequences and clusters, he may have seen in the number of sonnets an ambitious sequence in the making and tried to position it as a coherent whole, or he may simply have printed faithfully the copy he had.

The revisions undertaken by Michael Drayton in subsequent editions of *Idea* and Samuel Daniel in editions of *Delia* are sometimes used as evidence that sonnet sequences have an openness characteristic of manuscript culture, but I would argue that both Drayton and Daniel took advantage of print's malleability, not manuscript's openness, in revising their sequences. Many of their revisions were made with print in mind and can be read as clues to the composition practices that enabled minor sonneteers to produce long sequences quickly. Unlike those of Daniel and Drayton, Shakespeare's sequence really does resemble a loose manuscript collection that he composed, gathered, and revised piecemeal. He may have begun to prepare some sections for print or circulation, but the collection was never molded into a conventional sonnet sequence. My final discussion considers some of the practices used by 1590s sonneteers to build, organize, and finish their sequences for print. Looking this time at internal evidence, I ask where and to what extent Shakespeare employed these techniques and imagined his sonnets as an ambitious sequence destined for print.

Sonnet Labors

It was no easy task to write over a hundred sonnets, even if one borrowed heavily from other sonneteers, as most poets did. This is another good reason to examine skeptically the notion that sonnet sequences were inspired by amorous occasions, written at leisure, and circulated among friends and patrons before reaching print. John Davies of Hereford confesses in sonnet 100 of *Wittes Pilgrimage* (1605) that fame rather than love motivates his sonneteering. "Why sing I then in this too loving Straine" he asks, when he generally feels "adverse to light Loves amity"? He concludes,

> Some cal it Fame, that nought but Aire respects,
> And, sooth to say, for It I sing of Love:
> And though they write best, that write what they feel
> Yet, edgd by Fame, I fetch Fire out of Steele.

How does one fetch fire out of steel to finish a long sequence? In sonnet 101, he explains:

> Thus far may Speculation help a Wit
> Unapt for love, to write of Loves estate
> Thus far can Art extend hir Benefit
> Past Natures Bounds, in shew of Love, or Hate.
> (sig. H3)

In the course of their sonnet labors, almost all poets confront the artificiality of composing a very large group of seemingly private côterie love expressions. Davies does so explicitly, turning the problem into a trope. Shakespeare is slightly more discreet in

Sonnet 76, claiming that any redundancy in his sonnets is evidence of his constant devotion. He admits, nevertheless, that the task of sonneteering is basically "dressing old words new, / Spending againe what is already spent" (1609: sig. E4ᵛ, ll. 11–2). Sonnet 18 of Barnes's *Parthenophil and Parthenophe* (1593) begins with a desperate invocation that depicts both the lover's and writer's doggedness: "Write write, helpe helpe, sweet muse and never cease / In endlesse labours pennes and papers tyer / Untill I purchase my long-wish't desier" (p. 12). These sonnets about the labor of writing a long sequence, even when dressed in the language of devotion, remind us that the production of a long sequence could be purposeful and focused.

The artifice poets needed to produce sonnet after sonnet often took a rhetorical form. Several sonneteers employed formal links between poems to aid continuous composition or to fill out a collection. One of the more popular linking devices was the use of the last line of one sonnet to begin the next. Daniel added several linked pairs of sonnets to *Delia* when he brought out the authorized edition in 1592. Interestingly, although some of Daniel's revisions invoke manuscript culture, these additions allude instead to the sequence's printing. Sonnet 6 ends by noting that if the mistress had offered some pity, "then who had heard the plaints I utter now. / O had shee not beene fayre, and thus unkind, / My Muse had slept, & none had knowne my minde" (fol. 6, ll. 13–14). Sonnet 7 extends this trope, repeating exactly the previous sonnet's line 13:

> O Had shee not beene faire and thus unkind,
> Then had no finger pointed at my lightnes:
> The world had never knowne what I doe finde,
> And clowdes obscure had shaded stil her brightnes.
> Then had no Censors eye these lynes survaide,
> Nor graver browes have judg'd my Muse so vaine.
> (fol. 7, ll. 1–6)

These images have been absorbed into the fiction of the love affair, as if printing the sequence was inevitable, at least as long as the mistress's refusals kept Daniel writing.

Daniel's addition of several linked poems in 1592 is not unusual. Most of the rhetorically linked poems in Constable's 1595 expanded edition of *Diana* were added after his first edition. Several one-edition sonneteers, Barnes and Smith, for example, make extensive use of these kinds of link, too, which suggests that the publication pressures driving Daniel and Constable were similar to the ones faced by the sonneteers who followed their lead. Coincidentally, there are very few formally linked sonnets in Sidney.[5] Though verbal echoes and thematic clusters dominate the sequence progression in *Shake-speares Sonnets*, like Sidney's sequence it has surprisingly few formally linked sonnets, especially for such a long sequence. One could argue that Sidney and Shakespeare did not require the artificial aids that lesser sonneteers employed, but a more likely explanation is that neither Shakespeare nor Sidney rushed to finish a sequence for print.

Although Shakespeare's sequence does not have the hallmarks of a quick revision, his thematic clusters indicate some initial expansion in anticipation of print. Almost all sonneteers recycle conceits and metaphors and develop them into new sonnets. Some poets separated these related poems to avoid redundancy. Others formalized their clusters with rhetorical connections. The odd informal pairing of so many poems in Shakespeare's sequence has led Heather Dubrow to suggest that certain pairs may be versions of the same poem that Shakespeare probably intended to trim or separate. For some reason he left the revision unfinished (Dubrow 1996: 298–9). On the other hand, Shakespeare would be in step with other sonneteers if he strove to retain as many sonnet attempts as possible. We know that Daniel, rather than editing out his introductory sonnets from the 1591 selection, moved them further into the sequence in 1592. Drayton also moved introductory sonnets around (Neely 1978: 362).[6] Several one-edition sequences also have internal sonnets that might have functioned as initial sonnets at one point during the composition of the sequence. Sonnet 4 of *Emaricdulfe* is decidedly introductory: "Mine artles pen that never yet was dipt / In sacred nectar of sweet Castalie . . . Shall now learne skill my Ladies fame to raise" (1595: sig. A2^v, ll. 5–6, 9). These false starts often bring into the center of a sequence an awareness of the sequence genre as a whole, so that in the midst of the côterie exchange between lovers, a reader is suddenly reminded of the author's finished product and publication plans. These sequence-aware sonnets also suggest that poets had the final printed product in mind early enough in the composition and revision process to test various introductions and arrangements. One could speculate, judging by the length of the shorter printed sequences and the few unpublished manuscript sequences, that as few as ten to twenty sonnets might point an author toward the press.

Although *Shake-speares Sonnets* lacks the conventional preliminaries and the introductory numbered sonnet, it does share some of the sequence-awareness that one finds reshuffled into the middle of published sequences, though the examples are not as frequent or as clear-cut as in other sequences. Sonnets 32 and 38 demonstrate the poet's awareness of the sequence by imagining "verse" as something greater than an individual poem. The invocation of the lover in 38 "bring[s] forth / Eternal numbers to out-live long date" (1609: sig. C4^v–D1, ll. 11–12). Before it was knit into a thematic cluster, Sonnet 55, "Not marble, nor the guilded monument," could have been an introductory sonnet promising to preserve the lover's memory in "these contents" (sig. D4, l. 3) Sonnet 26's lines, "To thee I send this written ambassage / To witnesse duty, not to shew my wit" (sig. C2, ll. 3–4), read very much like an introductory dedication. Sonnets 100 and 101, which scold Shakespeare's "truant muse" for a dry spell, are clearly invocations, perhaps intended to introduce a sub-sequence. Like the paired poems, these sonnets argue that Shakespeare, at some point during the composition of his sonnets, imagined that all or part of them would eventually reach print. It is interesting that the poems with introductory or sequence-aware gestures tend to be clustered together. None of them appear in the first seventeen poems or after sonnet 126. There are several examples between sonnets 26 and 55, around 77, and between 100 and 117. These clusters bear witness to Shakespeare's tinkering with potential beginnings and frames, either for the sequence as a whole or for sections of it. The fact that Shakespeare does not make use of the beginning and end of his sequence to frame the sonneteering project and that he does not employ the conventional rhetorical tricks for expanding or extending a sequence suggests that he did not complete the final revisions before print. Even though Shakespeare probably considered print at some point, there is no evidence that he proceeded apace with the preparation of the sequence. Indeed, he may have lived the côterie ideal described in many sequences, composing or revising poems a few at a time as occasion inspired him and keeping his sequences in manuscript for many years.

For most sequences, then, the image of a leisurely exchange of manuscript verse between the poet and his readers is a fiction or exaggeration, though not a meaningless one. It allows the lover's devotion and pain to seem longer-lasting, and it gives credibility and immediacy to the poetry. It was relatively easy to imitate this particular ethos in what was predominantly a print genre. But in many sequences one also finds competing evidence that authors had print in mind at a relatively early point in the composition process. There is both paratextual and internal evidence that they were framing their sonnets for print. The Thorpe edition goes only part of the way toward identifying itself with the 1590s standards. The quarto's "unfinished" state does not preclude Shakespeare's authorization, but neither does it suggest his full participation in making the sonnets into a *sequence*. Thomas Thorpe seems to have recognized that Shakespeare's sonnets did not adhere to the Elizabethan sequence standards and to have responded by creating a kind of hybrid publication. He framed *Shake-speares Sonnets* partly as an organized sequence and partly as a miscellaneous gathering of small sequences and pairings. His model for this type of hybrid was likely to have been a work like Sidney's *Certain Sonnets* that had been pulled from manuscript unrevised. His model might even have been the larger collected work in which *Certain Sonnets* and *Astrophel and Stella* appeared, which pieced together disparate titles under an author's name and made both Sidney sequences seem more miscellaneous than they would have seemed in quarto. These collected editions, after all, brought the sonnet craze into Thorpe's decade.

The anomalous quality of the 1609 Thorpe edition of *Shake-speares Sonnets* is material as well as aesthetic, and both material and aesthetic simultaneously. But the anomalies are vulnerable to misunderstanding when the Thorpe edition is compared only to the better-known first editions of Elizabethan sequences and when sonneteering is imagined to begin as a côterie activity. To understand the subtle ways that Shakespeare's sequence differs from those of his predecessors, *Shake-speares Sonnets* needs to be set within the fullest material context that book history can provide, a context in which the sonnet sequence is primarily a print genre. Against this backdrop, the vestiges of a manuscript origin found in the quarto are indeed unique.

NOTES

1   First editions published between 1591 and 1599 include P. Sidney, *Astrophel and Stella*, 1591; J. du Bellay, "Ruins of Rome" and "Visions of Bellay," trans. E. Spenser, *Complaints*, 1591; S. Daniel, *Delia*, 1592; H. Constable, *Diana*, 1592; B. Barnes, *Parthenophil and*

Parthenophe, 1593; T. Lodge, *Phillis*, 1593; G. Fletcher, *Licia*, 1593; T.W., *Tears of Fancie*, 1593; H. Lok, *Sundry Christian Passions*, 1593; M. Drayton, *Ideas Mirrour*, 1594; W. Percy, *Coelia*, 1594; anonymous, *Zepheria*, 1594; B. Barnes, *A Divine Centurie* 1595; E.C., *Emaricdulfe*, 1595; G. Chapman, "A Coronet for his Mistresse Philosophie," in *Ovids Banquet of Sence*, 1595; E. Spenser, *Amoretti and Epithalamion*, 1595; R. Barnfield, sonnets to Ganymede in *Cynthia*, 1595; B. Griffin, *Fidessa*, 1596; R. L[inche], *Diella*, 1596; W. Smith, *Chloris*, 1596; H. Lok, "Sundrie Sonnets" and "Affectionate Sonets," in *Ecclesiastes*, 1597; R. Perry, *Sinetes*, 1597; T. Rogers, *Celestial Elegies*, 1598; P. Sidney, *Certain Sonnets* and *Astrophel and Stella* in *The Countess of Pembroke's Arcadia*, 1598 (first authorized edition).

Elizabethan second editions include Daniel, *Delia*, 1594, 1595, 1598, 1599; Constable, *Diana*, 1594, 1595; Sidney, *Astrophel and Stella*, 1597, 1598; Drayton, *Idea*, 1599.

2 On this point, I disagree with Wall (1993: 70), who sees the single, numbered sonnets as having a forward progression.

3 British Library MS Additional 15232; University of Edinburgh MS De. 5. 96; manuscript in the possession of Arthur A. Houghton, Jr. as of 1980. Constable's sequence in the Arundel Harington Manuscript is also copied symmetrically.

4 Daniel's *Delia*, however, did appear at the back of STC 22536 in 1591 and was issued twice in 1592 in quarto. Barnfield's *Cynthia* was also issued twice in 1595.

5 Some shorter manuscript sonnet sequences, such as Robert Sidney's, Mary Wroth's, and Donne's, took the form of a corona, a set of poems linked in a ring by their first and last lines. This form was more difficult to handle than shorter linked sequences, and it was probably not used for expansion.

6 Daniel and Drayton also removed some early sonnets from later editions.

REFERENCES AND FURTHER READING

Beal, Peter, Croft, P. J., et al. (1980). *Index of English Literary Manuscripts*. London: Mansell.

Chartier, Roger (1987). *The Cultural Uses of Print in Early Modern France*, trans. L. Cochrane. Princeton: Princeton University Press.

Cheney, Patrick (2004). *Shakespeare, National Poet-Playwright*. Cambridge, UK: Cambridge University Press.

Coatalen, Guillaume (2003). "Unpublished Elizabethan Sonnets in a Legal Manuscript from Cambridge University." *Review of English Studies* 54, 553–65.

Croft, P. J., ed. (1984). *The Poems of Robert Sidney*. Oxford: Clarendon.

Crum, Margaret (1969). *First-line Index of English Poetry 1500–1800 in Manuscripts of the Bodleian Library, Oxford*. New York: Modern Language Association; Oxford: Clarendon.

de Grazia, Margreta (1991). *Shakespeare Verbatim: The Reproduction of Authenticity and the 1790 Apparatus*. Oxford: Clarendon.

Dubrow, Heather (1996). "'Incertainties now crown themselves assur'd': The Politics of Plotting Shakespeare's Sonnets." *Shakespeare Quarterly* 47: 3, 291–305.

Duncan-Jones, Katherine (1983). "Was the 1609 *Shake-Speares Sonnets* Really Unauthorized?" *Review of English Studies* n.s. 34, 151–71.

Duncan-Jones, Katherine (1997). "Introduction." In *Shakespeare's Sonnets*, ed. Katherine Duncan-Jones. London: Thomas Nelson. (The Arden Shakespeare.)

Fumerton, Patricia (1991). *Cultural Aesthetics: Renaissance Literature and the Practice of Social Ornament*. Chicago: University of Chicago Press.

Genette, Gerard (1997). *Paratexts: Thresholds of Interpretation*. Cambridge, UK: Cambridge University Press. (First publ. in French as *Seuils*, Editions du Seuil, 1987.)

Kastan, David Scott (2001). *Shakespeare and the Book*. Cambridge, UK: Cambridge University Press.

McKenzie, D. F. (1986). *Bibliography and the Sociology of Texts: The Panizzi Lectures 1985*. London: British Library.

Marcus, Leah S. (1996). *Unediting the Renaissance: Shakespeare, Marlowe, Milton*. London: Routledge.

Marotti, Arthur (1982). "'Love is not love': Elizabethan Sonnet Sequences and the Social Order." *English Literary History* 49: 396–428.

Marotti, Arthur (1990). "Shakespeare's Sonnets as Literary Property." In Elizabeth D. Harvey and Katherine Eisaman Maus, eds., *Soliciting Interpretation: Literary Theory and Seventeenth-Century English Poetry*, 143–73. Chicago: University of Chicago Press.

Neely, Carol (1978). "The Structure of English Renaissance Sonnet Sequences." *English Literary History* 45: 359–89.

North, Marcy (2003). "Reading Shakespeare's Sonnets Anonymously." In R. Griffin, ed., *Faces of Anonymity*, 19–38. Basingstoke: Palgrave.

Ringler, William A., Jr., ed. (1962). *The Poems of Sir Philip Sidney*. Oxford: Clarendon.

Roberts, Sasha (2003). *Reading Shakespeare's Poems in Early Modern England*. Basingstoke: Palgrave Macmillan.

Schiffer, James (1999). "Reading New Life into Shakespeare's Sonnets: A Survey of Criticism." Introduction to J. Schiffer, ed., *Shakespeare's Sonnets: Critical Essays*, 3–74. New York and London: Garland.

Shakespeare, William (1944). *A New Variorum Edition of Shakespeare: The Sonnets*, ed. H. E. Rollins. 2 vols. Philadelphia: Lippincott.

Shakespeare, William (2002). *The Complete Sonnets and Poems*, ed. Colin Burrow. Oxford: Oxford University Press. (Oxford World's Classics.)

Stallybrass, Peter (1993). "Editing as Cultural Formation: The Sexing of Shakespeare's Sonnets." *Modern Language Quarterly* 54, 91–103.

Taylor, Gary (1986). "Some Manuscripts of Shakespeare's Sonnets." *Bulletin of the John Rylands University Library* 68, 210–46.

Wall, Wendy (1993). *The Imprint of Gender: Authorship and Publication in the English Renaissance*. Ithaca, NY: Cornell University Press.

Warkentin, Germaine (1975). "'Love's sweetest part, variety': Petrarch and the Curious Frame of the Renaissance Sonnet Sequence." *Renaissance and Reformation* 11: 14–23.

PART V
Models of Desire in the Sonnets

14

Shakespeare's Love Objects

Douglas Trevor

> Let not my love be called idolatry,
> Nor my belovèd as an idol show,
> Since all alike my songs and praises be
> To one, of one, still such, and ever so.
>
> (105. 1–4)

Ever since they began to receive sustained critical attention, following Edmond Malone's edition in 1780, William Shakespeare's sonnets have occasioned an enormous degree of speculation regarding the objects of scorn and praise around which they circle. Scholars have puzzled over the identity of the speaker's male friend, debating whether or not he is one man or a composite, rooted in real life or a purely literary conjuring. They have scrutinized the initials "W.H." that ambiguously designate the dedicatee of the 1609 edition, in some cases questioning his proximity to Shakespeare, since the dedication is itself signed by "T.T.," presumably the edition's printer, Thomas Thorpe, while in other cases — most notably that of Oscar Wilde — an entire reading of the poems has been based upon speculating who in fact W.H. really was (Wilde 1994: 302–50).[1] And of course there is the dark lady, identified alternately as a nameless aristocrat, a commoner, Queen Elizabeth, her maid of honor Mary Fitton, the London prostitute Lucy Negro, the poet Aemilia Lanyer, and so on.

One need not read very extensively in secondary materials to find entire constellations of love objects connected to, and derivative of, the historical figures and literary personages mentioned above. The pursuit of biographical readings of the sonnets has waned in the past three decades, with previous attempts to introduce real-life characters into the poems now regarded by most scholars with disdain (see Duncan-Jones 1998: 50–2). Nonetheless, while critics have been less interested in establishing, for example, whether or not William Herbert is a more likely candidate for the role of the speaker's male friend than Henry Wriothesley, they have been more impassioned than in the past in arguing that the erotic sentiments expressed by Shakespeare were themselves truly felt, and that the sonnets are evidence of their authenticity. Thus does Joseph Pequigney set out to "prove" in his 1985 reading of the sequence "that the poet carnally enjoys him [the male friend] as well as her [the dark lady]," the reality of the poet's purported bisexual identity now figuring more prominently than any speculation about real figures with whom Shakespeare might have actually been involved, amorously or otherwise (Pequigney 1985: 4).

Indeed, tremendous critical intelligence and perceptivity have been brought to bear on Shakespeare's sonnets over the past several decades in order to read them as representing either an important shift in the history of gender relations or as a barometer for assuaging the sociocultural dimensions of male and female subjectivities in the period. As a result the sexual appeal, and abjection, of the love objects mentioned in the poems have been emphasized. Thus for Joel Fineman, in the sonnets Shakespeare "invents the poetics of heterosexuality" (Fineman 1988: 18), while – by contrast – for Pequigney, Shakespeare disparages love only "where it is lustful and heterosexual," not where it emerges out of male–male friendship and is homoerotic (Pequigney 1985: 100). Valerie Traub observes that "[w]hereas a formal goal of many Shakespearean comedies is to explore homoerotic desires within the safety of an overall heterosexual (en)closure, the Sonnets represent heteroerotic desires within a normative homoerotic economy" (Traub 1999: 439), a reading that builds on Eve Kosofsky Sedgwick's shrewd observation that "[t]he Sonnets present a male–male love that, like the love of the Greeks, is set firmly within a structure of institutionalized social relations that are carried out via women" (Sedgwick 1985: 35).

Critics made uncomfortable by the resonant homoeroticism of the sequence have historically resorted to neoplatonism as a way of anaesthetizing intimations of same-sex sexual desire by arguing that what sounds like erotic love is meant to sound like friendship (see Bush 1974: 13). "Neoplatonism," as I am using the word, would substantiate in philosophical terms the following beliefs: the soul is purer than and substantively different from the body and will eventually return to its creator, who is likewise immaterial; the soul lives for ever, while the body – in its earthly form at least – does not; *love* names the coupling of souls, not the pairing of bodies; in that love therefore is about spiritual and intellectual congress rather than physical, men might love men, and women might love women, without such love being besmirched by a lower, sexual appeal. With such tenets in mind, Rafael Koskimies asserts the following:

Since Shakespeare's Sonnets in no way imply homosexuality – apart from the occasional turn of phrase – and since on the other hand they have posed impossible problems to scholars striving to identify the noble youth in the background, no other conclusion is obviously possible except the following: The poet already knew enough of the general abstract ideas and imagery of Platonism, thanks to the contemporary literary mode and fashion, to adapt them to suit his sonnets with which he was deliberately competing with his contemporaries. (Koskimies 1970: 267–8)

The telling weaknesses of this approach, coupled with its evident homophobia, have been underscored in recent years, particularly in light of the poet's fondness for puns and wordplay that sexualize the relationship between the speaker and young friend. Dismissing such turns of phrase as only incidental to the thematics of the sequence means ignoring, for example, that in sonnet 135, *will* designates not only the poet's first name and possibly that of the male friend, but also both male *and* female sexual organs. Wordplay, otherwise put, does not merely embellish the literary conceit of the poem but *is* its conceit, with the resulting images hardly conforming to what Koskimies labels as "the general abstract ideas and imagery of Platonism" (1970: 268).

Scholars such as John Roe and Stephen Medcalf have uncovered traces of neoplatonic influence in Shakespeare, and have examined a multitude of texts in which it is likely a literate person of his generation might have encountered them.[2] Nonetheless, Roe and Medcalf also emphasize the degree to which Shakespeare's neoplatonic turns are "never quite circumscribed by the kind of seriousness which we associate with Bembo's speech [at the end of Book 4] in *The Courtier*" (Roe 1996: 108), and more pronounced in works such as *The Phoenix and the Turtle* and *Troilus and Cressida* than in the Sonnets (Medcalf 1996: 122). Indeed, even when Shakespeare appears on the surface to be reciting Platonic dictums, as for example when he confesses to his addressee in sonnet 36, that "we two must be twain, / Although our undivided loves are one" (ll. 1–2), or when he insists, in sonnet 53, that the addressee's "substance" is reflected by his or her "external grace" (ll. 1, 13), these moments of presumed immaterial yearning are quite quickly contained by metapoetic references that bring the reader back to the poems themselves. Thus in sonnet 36 it is the speaker's "good report," his poetry, that substantiates his love (l. 14), while in sonnet 53 Stephen Booth notices – rightly, I think – that the final words of the poem, "constant heart" (l. 14), are hard to distinguish phonetically from "constant art" (Shakespeare 1977: 226).

Shakespeare's sonnets, I will maintain in this essay, are defiantly anti-Platonic in their outlook and are innovative, within the tradition of sonnet writing, largely because they are so anti-Platonic. As evidenced by these poems, Shakespeare did not appear to privilege, or even consistently separate, the soul from the body. He did not demean earthly love – the love of objects – as deficient in comparison to a higher, spiritual love. In fact, he did not seem to believe in the vertical register of neoplatonism itself. Nonetheless, it is not necessarily true – as many critics have assumed – that because Shakespeare is so willing to oppose the kind of immaterial soul-coupling at times described in the works of Marsilio Ficino, Giovanni Pico della Mirandola, and other neoplatonists, the sonnets are principally about erotic attachment between a man and another man and woman (See Ficino 1999: 54–78, 72–80; Pico 1914: 33–4). It is not true, in other words, that with his rejection of Platonic binaries, Shakespeare opts wholly for Ovidian erotic abandon. Shakespeare's speaker, unlike his neoplatonic or Ovidian equivalents, derives neither satisfaction nor strength from the condensation of such desires; rather he bursts again and again with unrequited longing, doubts, and anxieties. In that the speaker's capacity either to contend with such heartbreak or transcend the effects of his disillusionment is so powerfully questioned by the poet, who leaves his narrator at the end of the sequence in a bubbling bath – one of the more popular means in the period of treating syphilitic lesions – having discovered that "Love's fire heats water, water cools not love" (154. 14), we as readers are left in contemplation of a resolutely unresolved situation: a situation in which the speaker cannot even take "joy" in his "woes," as Sidney permits his speaker at the end of *Astrophel and Stella* (Sidney 1983: 240).

Within the elastic but nonetheless identifiable generic boundaries in which Shakespeare chooses to write his sonnets, there is always something more in play than the speaker's speaking "I" – something that instantiates this voice while at the same time creating the sense of being greater, that is more expansive, than the voice itself. This something is the love-sonnet genre itself, which – I wish to argue – Shakespeare aims to reimagine in his sonnets, not merely to authenticate a new sexual self-identification, although that might seem like its principal aim from our vantage point, but rather in the hopes of reconceiving the kind of amorous attachment that could be authenticated by, and written into being through, sonneteering. Such an aim might strike us as decidedly less exciting than the creation of a new sexual order; but within the sonnet tradition in which Shakespeare worked, this reconceptualization is arguably more shocking than is its connected, but thematically subsidiary, evocation of an erotics of ceaseless expansiveness and endless deferral (deferred not because the speaker can never obtain his love objects, as is the conventional case in the Petrarchan tradition, but because the objects give themselves up and then just as easily slip away).

My characterization of the sonnets here follows most closely the work of Heather Dubrow, who has pointed out the striking degree to which Shakespeare's sequence is made up of monologues, avoids references to specific times and dates, refrains from describing either the young man or the dark lady in any physical terms other than vague ones, resists presenting actual scenes of confrontation, and emphasizes the psychological tumult experienced by the speaker (Dubrow 1981: 58, 60, 62). I do not go so far as to deny, as does Dubrow, that Shakespeare intended any order for his poems whatsoever; nor do I see the speaker as hopelessly "trapped in brooding," as the sonnets themselves permit a measure of solace and an arena – I maintain – within which love may still be idealized (pp. 60 n. 15, 67). Still, like Dubrow, Booth, John Hollander, and others, I am inclined to view attempts to establish corollaries between literary characters and potentially real-life sources with skepticism (Shakespeare 1977: 549; Hollander 2001: xxix–xxx); neither do I accept Fineman's desire to read the sequence itself in "novelistic" terms, whereby a discernible, characterological plot in the sonnets is uncovered, or agree with the kind of unequivocal statements that emerge out of an otherwise fine piece by Judith Kegan Gardiner, where she asserts, for example, that "the poet clearly loves the friend far more than the mistress" and "the friend's betrayal . . . moves the poet far more than the dark lady's adultery" (Fineman 1988: 84; Gardiner 1985: 336, 347). In reference to specific moments in the sequence such contentions are certainly true; but they are by no means always true. On the contrary, the sonnets appear constructed so as to work against perspectival fixity on the part of either the reader or the writer, except in their increasingly – as they proceed – high regard for, and even faith in, writing itself.

Shakespeare's reconceptualization of the sonnet tradition he inherits is more shocking than the erotic triangle his poems map because his sonnets intend to reconceive more than the bipartite, Petrarchan notion of the lover and the beloved – a conception whereby the (typically) male sonneteer pursues a (typically) female, unattainable love object. This arrangement is refashioned in, broadly speaking, the first section of the sequence, sonnets 1–126, where we see a male lover write in praise, and frustration, about a male love object (although he designates this object, as we shall see, often in ambiguous ways). Even more striking than this reconceptualization, and more at odds with the sonnet tradition he inherits, Shakespeare recalibrates the tripartite, Petrarchan and – eventually – neoplatonic conception of the lover, beloved, and God: a recalibration that occurs, for the most part, in the last section of the sequence, sonnets 127–54. The sonnets thus first introduce a new kind of character into the sonnet tradition, the figure of the sexually appealing, if ultimately disappointing, male friend; but the presence of this friend, eventually coupled with the dark lady, is less scandalous, I would argue, than what their presence – and the speaker's relation to loving and coveting physical objects – directly implies. No room is made, in this rearticulated love economy, for the ultimate love object of Petrarchan poetry, the Almighty, Christian Godhead; and with his exclusion, any stable, hierarchical progression that would order love objects, and pacify the speaker's longing, and sick, heart, is similarly renounced. Remarkably, even as the speaker recognizes the unsettling consequences of his restless love he finds himself powerless – and, more intriguingly, disinclined – to correct it.

Earthly love is, from the point of view of both early modern medicine and the general dictates of the sonnet-writing tradition, a fluctuating and potentially ruinous state in which to find oneself. As explained by the French physician Jacques Ferrand, "erotic passion is a form of dotage, proceeding from an inordinate desire to enjoy the beloved object, accompanied by fear and sorrow" (Ferrand 1990: 238). Love, quite literally, makes one sick, creating a melancholic humor that "being cold, chills down not only the brain but also the heart" (p. 240). The loss of self-control, ceded to another being who might or might not reciprocate one's affections, places the lover in a terribly dangerous predicament: one in which he (the sufferer is typically identified as male in this tradition) fails to marshal the defenses necessary to protect his body from the dangerous outside world. Paraphrasing the ancient poet Musaeus, Ferrand explains that a lady "of incontestably perfect beauty . . . wounds the heart through the eye more quickly than the feathered arrow, and from the eye love darts and glides into the vital organs where it generates malign ulcer and venomous bile" (p. 233).

Looks, in such a quasi-medical account, can in fact kill, and Shakespeare's speaker is similarly sickened by the sight of both the male friend and the dark lady. Indeed, the pathologies associated with these gendered objects of regard should call into question the degree to which love for either one or both of these figures is to be positively viewed by the reader. Love, we discover as we read well into the sonnets, disrupts the speaker's capacity to *see*: that is, both to understand the world around him and to view it accurately and in a healthy manner. "Most true it is, that I have looked on truth / Askance and strangely," the speaker admits in sonnet 110 (ll. 5–6), and then – in sonnet 113 – he explains in part how this process of self-corruption has occurred:

> Since I left you, mine eye is in my mind,
> And that which governs me to go about
> Doth part his function, and is partly blind,
> Seems seeing, but effectually is out.
>
> (ll. 1–4)

As the section of poems typically grouped as concerned with the male friend crest – in sonnets 110–26 – we find them fixated on the topic of corrupted vision: in sonnet 114, the speaker debates with himself whether he can trust what he thinks he sees, while in sonnet 119 he bemoans that his eyes have "out of their spheres been fitted / In the distraction of this madding fever!" (ll. 7–8). If the speaker does indeed turn away from the male friend at this juncture, he does so with a bitter taste in his mouth, convinced that "All men are bad and in their badness reign" (121. 14). Furthermore, degradation of the speaker's vision is powerful attestation to just how removed his experienced passion is from that approved by neoplatonists such as Ficino, for whom the sense of sight is the most trusted, and esteemed, means by which to enjoy the beloved (see Ficino 1999: 52–8).

The speaker's turn against the dark lady has been more commented upon in readings of the sonnets than has the speaker's disgust with the male friend, but I would suggest that both revulsions rehearse the same set of symptoms: that, in fact, the gender of these objects matters less than does the way both of them make the speaker renounce as dangerous any emotional attachment to other human beings. When the speaker rails against the dark lady, blaming himself for not trusting his own eyes and putting "fair truth upon so foul a face" (137. 12), it is the woman's deceitfulness he underscores, and yet the male friend has been no more trustworthy himself; he too has demonstrated an "inconstant mind" (92. 9). Thus, while these sonnets are deeply celebratory of love – as countless readers have noted – what we find when we look past the friend and lady is that the most appealing love object forwarded in the sequence is the sequence itself.

Indeed, it is the act of writing alone that can cure the speaker's malignant vision by recording its limitations and then – by virtue of this "good report" (36. 14; 96. 14) – reclaiming temporal failure as transcendent, artistic triumph. This process of reclamation through aesthetic refiguration is of course not a wholly unanticipated discovery for Shakespeare – as a sonneteer – to make. What is, perhaps, far more remarkable is that Shakespeare never bothers, in his sonnets, to qualify as morally questionable the project of sonnet-writing itself. He never bothers, as does Petrarch's speaker, to consider whether his investments in writing might be spiritually corroding or demeaning. Rather, he doubts only – as in sonnet 16 – his capacity as a poet to render what he loves in written form.

Sonnet 105, the opening of which serves as my epigraph, illustrates two of the central concerns toward which I have been working thus far, each of which demonstrates the poet's remarkably agile preoccupation with reconfiguring the dimensions of amorous attachment so that his sequence both draws from and changes the sonnet tradition. The first concern addressed in this sonnet has been taken as the poem's conceit: the speaker's desire to equate his love with the kind of love practiced by Christians who claim to love *a* God that is really three Gods in one. What strikes us immediately in this formulation is precisely what we might expect to confront at this juncture in the sequence but do not: the speaker's defense of the same-sex nature of his love for the male friend. That no such defense is forthcoming perhaps supports Stephen Orgel's observation that "English Renaissance culture does not appear to have had a morbid fear of male homoerotic behavior" (Orgel 1997: 58). Rather, what is defended is the idolatrous attitude toward beauty itself, which the speaker denies by turning to poetry.

> Let not my love be called idolatry,
> Nor my belovèd as an idol show,
> Since all alike my songs and praises be
> To one, of one, still such, and ever so.
> (ll. 1–4)

Shakespeare's evocation of the Athanasian Creed has perhaps made critics feel required to treat sonnet 105 as a mock-religious poem – which it is, but not in the way that it has generally been understood. Booth, for example, chides the poem for its "playful experiment in perversity [that] derives from the false logic resulting from the speaker's studiously inadequate understanding of idolatry" (Shakespeare 1977: 336). But Booth reads Shakespeare as if he were trying to turn a doctrinal understanding of idolatry back on itself and failing. What is lost in this reading is the *kind* of ambition that this poem reveals: not an ambition to poke fun at religious dogma, but rather to replace spiritual consolation with poetic.

As Fineman notes, "the young man is an ideal idol *because* the poetry of praise . . . displays him in its 'wondrous scope' [l. 12]" (Fineman 1988: 141). The key homonym, however, overlooked by Booth and Fineman, is *idol/idle*. Shakespeare's speaker defends his love because it is not a passive kind of love, but rather one written into being in the sequence itself. The potential problem is not that the male friend has been carnally enjoyed; that is rather, a consummation devoutly to be wished. The problem is that the male friend is so coveted, and coveted not for religious reasons but rather literary ones. Thus can the speaker maintain that this "one" love will live for "ever" (l. 4), because written words – in the poet's universe – exist until the end of time. Shakespeare is certainly not saying that the male friend will live for ever; indeed the progress of the "procreation" sonnets (1–17) witnesses the poet's gradual acceptance first that the reduplication of the young friend through sexual reproduction will result in only a "copy" (ll. 14), and ultimately that poetry alone will preserve the male friend for posterity

("So long lives this [i.e. eternal verse], and this gives life to thee": 18. 14). Instead, the speaker here argues that his love is made active, and worthy of eternal preservation, because it is written in verse and, by virtue of being written, made into a religious kind of love: one that grants its writer eternal presence through the expression of his affections.

The first concern that the poem addresses, then, is the speaker's insistence that his love of beauty can be made to last for ever by recording and substantiating this love through poetry. The speaker is not concerned, strikingly, with defending this love as spiritually robust. In fact, the spiritual quality of love that lords over Petrarch's *Rime sparse* has no purchase whatsoever in Shakespeare's sonnets. There is no retreat from the sequence's first stated desire – to preserve "beauty's rose" so that it "might never die" (1. 2) – only a re-evaluation of what strategy might best accomplish this task.

The second concern established in sonnet 105, already glimpsed in the opening quatrain and in what I have said, is that the "love" described by the speaker is a love put into being by poetry itself (l. 1). This is an enormously important point, without which the end of the poem makes little sense, and yet – excepting Fineman – critics have persistently missed it (Fineman 1988: 141). This point has been missed routinely because, even if Shakespeare studies have by and large disavowed biographical readings of the young friend and dark lady, the status of these figures as real objects in the purview of the speaker has ensconced itself in most critical appraisals of the sonnets. I have already suggested that many readers engaged with questions of erotics and the sex/gender system of early modern England have a particular investment in thinking about the friend and lady as real objects of desire, but even formalist critics have been seduced by this kind of approach.

The lines that bear our attention now are those that make up the second quatrain of sonnet 105:

> Kind is my love today, tomorrow kind,
> Still constant in a wondrous excellence;
> Therefore my verse to constancy confined,
> One thing expressing, leaves out difference.
>
> (ll. 5–8)

Is the "love" described here an animate object or a possessed affection? Does it name the feeling of love and the vehicle, the "One thing" that expresses it, or does it refer back *only* to the person or persons who generate it? Editors have, to my knowledge, unanimously read this *love* as a reference *only* to the male friend, but this interpretation – I would suggest – is not supported by the poem itself (see Shakespeare 1986: 309–11; 1996: 213–215; 2002: 590). Rather, it is indicative of the degree to which the critical preoccupation with mooring the speaker's love to human objects has caused readers to overlook how the sonnets so frequently function as the principal object of the poet's affections – the only means by which the speaker can subdue and reclaim the figures who, irrespective of gender, break his heart.

Helen Vendler's headlong rush into offering a declarative description of the speaker's "love" indicates the weakness of the kind of reading I am trying to refute. "First of all," she writes, "by identifying his beloved's qualities (*fair, kind, and true*) as those of the Platonic Triad (the Beautiful, the Good, the True), the poet opposes to his accuser's Christian Trinity an equally powerful, but classical, cultural totem as an emblem of the divine" (Vendler 1998: 445). The problem with this interpretation is that, by this point in the sequence, there is nothing unproblematically kind or true about the friend at all. In sonnet 95, for example, we learn that his "sins" are firmly lodged within him (l. 4), while in sonnet 96 it is "errors" that the speaker locates in him, errors rectified only by the speaker's "good report" (ll. 7, 14).[3] In sonnet 89, the friend offers no explanation for why he has forsaken the speaker, and indeed no clear explanation is ever given. In her reading, Sedgwick argues that all the "dissonance, doubleness, and self-division" associated with the fair youth is "described as located outside the youth himself" (1985: 41), but this reading is simply not sustainable once we have worked our way well into the sonnets. Rather, the young friend's many failings are rectified by the poetry offered by the speaker, the sonnets thus redeeming these failures by memorializing the friend as seen by the speaker, placing him in a "monument, / When tyrants' crests and tombs of brass are spent" (107. 13–14).

It is not, then, the beloved exactly that the speaker describes in these later sonnets, and in sonnet 105 specifically, but his own *love*: that is, the speaker's possession of amorous affection; and it is the vehicle by which this affection is authenticated – the verses that make up the sonnets – that persistently replaces objects such as the friend and/or dark lady with itself. Shakespeare typically concretizes the material features of the sonnets, for example turning them into a "monument" in sonnet 107 (l. 13), so that they seem almost as tactile to the reader who confronts them as they are to the writer who produces them. In sonnet 105 this is no different. The operative pun here, also curiously overlooked by critics, is the word "leaves" (l. 8). The speaker's verse, we are told, is confined to constancy not because any of his beloveds are ever constant (and with *any* we should bear in mind Dubrow's skepticism regarding the degree to which we may trust that the sonnets neatly divide their attention between the male friend in the first 126 and the dark lady in the last 28 [Dubrow 2000: 120]). Rather, only the speaker's verse itself bears out the overall constancy of his loving nature by permitting him to "leaf" out, from page to page, the various emotions that – otherwise untreated – would cause his love finally to become something else, something less noteworthy as an artistic artifact, indeed perhaps not an artistic artifact at all.

The third quatrain of sonnet 105 strengthens the poem's attention to its own composition:

> Fair, kind, and true is all my argument,
> Fair, kind, and true, varying to other words;
> And in this change is my invention spent—
> Three themes in one, which wondrous scope affords.
>
> (ll. 9–12)

With fairness, kindness, and truth the subject, or "argument," of his verse, the speaker now explains how he can write of such qualities only because they are contained by the "wondrous" or *one*-drousness of the sonnets themselves (ll. 9, 12).[4] It is his "scope," his range as a writer, that is here praised; not the beloveds who intermittently pass through his view. The poem's final claim of originality is precisely this ability on its author's part, not on the part of his love objects, to speak of the properties of his love in such a manner that proves both his originality and his satisfaction with poetry writing as a kind of religious practice: "Fair, kind, and true, have often lived alone, / Which three, till now, never kept seat in one" (ll. 13–14).

The progression we witness in sonnet 105 is, I am arguing, the general progression of many of the sonnets and of the sequence as a whole: a beloved is first gestured toward, then replaced by the feeling of love this object generates through poetic mediation, which then ushers in the object of poetry itself, an object – unlike either the male friend or the dark lady – that corrects human failing through aestheticization and thus merits the greatest of love, a love best – almost inevitably – described in religious terms. We see the same transference occur, for example, in sonnet 108, where the "ink" of the speaker's brain expresses the same "love" I described in my reading of sonnet 105, although here it is generated less ambiguously by the "sweet boy" himself, who is then promptly replaced by "prayers divine": poems in my reading that alone can etch the figure's "name" for posterity, such that this name can be termed "fair" precisely because it has been purified by the verse itself (ll. 1, 4, 5, 8).

I am arguing not that the most routinely mentioned love objects in the sonnets, the youth and the dark lady, are unimportant, but that they are loved in expressly literary terms – as literary creations, not real people – and that this kind of love is intended to direct both the writer and reader back to the verse itself, over and over again. There is, then, an overarching narrative in the sequence, but it is not a novelistic one; instead, though it twists around the speaker's tempestuous emotional travails, it does so without providing the kind of story-line we might expect from our 21st-century perspective. In place of plot, the sonnets expend incrementally more and more energy attempting first to recreate the initial fairness of the first love object – the male friend – as it is compromised through his inconstant, unbecoming behavior, and then, much more quickly, redressing the duplicity of the dark lady, fixing her infidelity within the poem's constant art.

The more closely we look at the high valuation of love objects in the sonnets, the more clearly we see that these high valuations refer more to poetry and less to seemingly real characters who are themselves rather creations of this poetry. As a result, it becomes more difficult to maintain, as does for example Pequigney, that any given poem, for example 116, is "undoubtedly intended for the eyes of the friend" (Pequigney 1985: 183). Instead, when we remind ourselves that everything we learn in the course of Shakespeare's sonnet sequence is either offered to us or shaped by the speaker, we recognize that the plot or facticity of the sequence is itself a projection: a dream – fantasy and nightmare alike – of the speaker's hopes, desires, and frustrations. But these emotive states are themselves only created for us; we have no proof of their status in the real world, no journal left by the Venetian Ambassador attesting to their performance, no rough draft of one of the lyrics in Shakespeare's hand, identifying real-life corollaries to the figures conjured on the page. Except for their artful, highly literary, laboriously structured manifestations, there is no way of knowing what, if anything, happened to spawn the creation of these poems, except that they pronounce themselves as literary traces of a certain type that then reconfigure this type, not so much as to no longer remain recognizable as love poetry, but not so little as to appear as poems that are only versions of kinds of poems that have already been written.

Any number of the sonnets could be turned to at this juncture to emphasize how skillfully the poems create a sense of something more real than the poems themselves, and thus can be taken to be about desires we intuit as real when – as I am arguing – they function more directly as symptoms of metapoetic concerns; but perhaps none of the lyrics thematizes this dynamic more strikingly than sonnet 40. The poem opens with the speaker presumably forsaking any claim on love whatsoever:

> Take all my loves, my love, yea, take them all:
> What hast thou then more than thou hadst before?
> No love, my love, that thou mayst true love call;
> All mine was thine, before thou hadst this more.
>
> (ll. 1–4)

The imperative demand to be stripped bare of his "loves" enables the speaker to trip up the addressee, who might erroneously assume that more loves have been gained when in fact "All" the speaker's loves were his – perhaps hers, the sonnet does not specify gender – from the beginning (ll. 1, 4). Katherine Duncan-Jones assumes, as do most other commentators, that the addressee "has betrayed his friend by taking one of the poet's *loves*, i.e. love-objects" (1998: 190), although – with sonnet 105 still in mind – I read "loves" (l. 1) as now naming the various, and unsettling, permutations of amorous affection that are splintering within the subject. Critics content to put off the dark lady's appearance in the sequence until much later, at least when imagining that ambiguous references to a love object must name the male friend, usually switch tactics at this confusing juncture in the sequence. As John Kerrigan explains, "the treachery described here and in the next two poems resembles so closely the poet's betrayal by the dark lady and his youthful friend – discussed in several sonnets between 133 and 152 – that it is usually assumed that the two situations are one" (Shakespeare 1986: 223–4). While introducing the dark lady here appears to solve a missing element of the sequence's plot, it does so very imperfectly. After all, the dark lady – never designated a lady by the poet – cannot grammatically satisfy the plural demands of "loves" (40. 1). Furthermore, if the speaker's mistress abruptly figures in this poem, why, we might ask, can she not serve as the addressee? The addressee's description as a "gentle thief" (l. 9) is the best indication provided by the poem that the addressee is of a higher class than the mistress, but of course "gentle" has tactile associations in the sequence as well, evoked for example with the "tender inward" of the dark lady's "hand" (128. 6).

I am suggesting here that readings that aim to distinguish one human love object from another in certain sonnets are in fact shakier readings than we might otherwise assume, and in fact that such analyses rest on assumptions that – in the sequence as a whole – are ever-receding. To give another example from sonnet 40, we might consider the poem's second quatrain, particularly its last line:

> Then if for my love thou my love receivest,
> I cannot blame thee for my love thou usest;
> But yet be blamed, if thou thyself deceivest
> By wilful taste of what thyself refusest.
>
> (ll. 5–8)

If "wilful taste of what thyself refusest" refers back to the friend's "capriciously engaging in sexual activity that, in the context of marriage, he refuses," as Duncan-Jones argues (1998: 190), then we are likewise assuming that evidence from earlier in the sequence is both relevant to this addressee's present situation and, in and of itself, clearly evincing an earlier tension in the poem between sexual activity and marriage bonds – a tension, we must recall, that the speaker himself projects onto the male friend. That is, we know only from what the speaker has told us that his friend has refused marriage, so to use this information as a lens by which to examine the friend in fact provides us only with information on the speaker's perspective, not anything having to do incontrovertibly with the friend himself.

Most of sonnet 40's thematic content is made up of a series of projections, foisted onto the addressee in an increasingly frenetic manner. An attempt to sustain the external (to the speaker), objectal reading of the "loves" from line 1 that I have summarized above would probably teeter most at line 10, when the speaker announces that the addressee, in taking his "loves" (l. 1), has managed only to rob him of what he paradoxically already lacks:

> I do forgive thy robb'ry, gentle thief,
> Although thou steal thee all my poverty;
>
> (ll. 9–10)

"[P]overty" could be read as a jab at the love objects taken by the addressee as themselves bereft of valuable qualities, in which case we must ask why *they* are *loves* in the first place; but the stronger reading is to locate the impoverishment of the word in the speaker himself, whose loves are worthless because they remain unreciprocated, but who would be immediately enriched if only someone, anyone, would play along. The speaker's manipulativeness is unrelenting throughout the poem, nowhere more so than in the concluding couplet, where he demands that the addressee "Kill me with spites" (l. 14). This final imperative, like the first, is just another attempt at provoking a response from a love object that appears to be maddeningly unmoved by the speaker's pleas. In fact, the gender of the object itself does not matter at all in the poem, only the speaker's perception of this object as cruel and therefore deserving of anger that can nonetheless, at this juncture, not be summoned.

Sonnet 40 performs in miniature what the entire sequence rehearses as a whole: the ceaseless creation of a fictive reality that, if it could be realized, would mitigate the speaker's sufferings, and yet, since it cannot, results only in dissimulation and wordplay. That is, the linguistic playfulness of Shakespeare's sonnets, like that of so many love sonnets that precede it in the western tradition, is playful in part because the speaker can successfully manipulate only words: the affections of the love objects that pass through the poems are emotionally unapproachable to the speaker, even when he appears to enjoy them carnally, as in sonnet 152. Indeed, when Shakespeare opts to introduce sexual congress in the sequence, his motivation – in my reading – is principally to see if this, the most presumably anti-Petrarchan move imaginable, can nonetheless be contained by the Petrarchan fixation on the unhappiness engendered by failed earthly love but assuaged by poetic success. What Shakespeare finds toward the end of the sequence, and so clearly delights in, is the realization that there is no greater performance of Petrarchan abjection than in acquiring the love object after all, for at such a moment one finds the object still unattainable, still cruelly indifferent, and still capable of provoking wrenching despair that then prompts only more fodder for the sequence itself.

As my interpretations of sonnets 40 and 105 suggest, I view the current fixation on gender issues in the sonnets as somewhat misguided if these objects are taken as important in and of themselves, rather than viewed relationally in terms of both the speaker's "I," itself a fabric of the poems in which its subjectivity, its very "I"-ness, is created, and the love-sonnet genre itself, in which one impetus for formal and thematic innovation is precisely to see how best to create an artistic engine for sonnet production that will run most effectively. It would be remiss to make such a case without considering the sonnet most acclaimed for its description – albeit allusive and elusive – of true love, sonnet 116. It is here, I want to argue, that Shakespeare's acceptance of unalterable love as achievable only in an artistic domain becomes clearest.

The sonnet begins by describing this highest form of love as itself unchanging and uninterested in affecting change on its object or objects of affection:

> Let me not to the marriage of true minds
> Admit impediments. Love is not love
> Which alters when it alteration finds,
> Or bends with the remover to remove.
>
> (ll. 1–4)

The imagined "marriage" here would pair "true" or faithful minds (l. 1); or, at least hypothetically, if such a union were to occur, the speaker would not intervene to disrupt it ("*Let me not* to the marriage of true minds / *Admit impediments*": my italics). Does such a formulation of true love necessarily place the speaker in the role of its proponent? Arguing against this traditional interpretation, Vendler insists that it does not, but that

rather sonnet 116 is a "dramatic refutation or rebuttal" of the claim which she paraphrases in the following manner: "You would like the marriage of minds to have the
same permanence as the sacramental marriage of bodies. But this is unreasonable –
there are impediments to such constancy" (Vendler 1998: 488). Indeed, the speaker
casts himself not within such a love economy, as he might have easily by inserting a
possessive pronoun (Let me not to the marriage of *our* true minds . . .), but slightly
outside it, watching, as it were, to see if the possible pairing occurs.

I agree with Vendler that in fact this pairing does not occur, or at least not as we
have been conditioned to consider it. In other words, if anything has characterized the
speaker's relations with human loves, it is alteration and removal (Vendler 1998: 493).
Unlike Vendler, however, I see the poem organized not from the top down but rather
the bottom up. The couplet's metapoetic emphasis on composition strikes me as incontrovertible, and in fact makes the reader realize that what is being described in the first
twelve lines of sonnet 116 is love as emblematized and created through poetry itself.
To begin, here is the couplet:

> If this be error and upon me proved,
> I never writ, nor no man ever loved.
> (ll. 13–14)

What would be required to invalidate what precedes the couplet would be, it turns
out, the poet's effacement as a poet ("I never writ"), linked with the seemingly larger
effacement of any experience of love at all ("nor no man ever loved"). I say *seemingly*
because the last line in fact structures the erasure of the poet's writing life as preceding,
and in effect conditioning, the erasure of love itself. Within the logic constructed by
the sonnets, if the poet never writes, no man ever loves.

Reading the sonnet now with this emphasis on writing in mind, we realize that the
poem's description of love is actually a description of the sequence as an aesthetic object:
one comprising units that record change and fluctuation but that nonetheless cohere
and amalgamate into a body of work. While the speaker attempts, especially in the
"procreation" sonnets, to change the friend's attitude toward sexual reproduction, and
while the friend's treatment of the speaker changes him, as he admits over and over
again, the sonnets alone can absorb such fluctuations without being compromised or
degraded by change. This bracketing of tumult and fluctuation within a larger economy
of constancy is evidence of Shakespeare's single – albeit enormous – debt to neoplatonism, perhaps gleaned from Nature's response to Mutabilitie in Edmund Spenser's
Two Cantos of Mutabilitie, first published in the 1609 folio edition of *The Faerie Queene*:

> I well consider all that ye haue sayd,
> And find that all things stedfastnes doe hate
> And changed be: yet being rightly wayd
> They are not changed from their first estate;
> But by their change their being doe dilate:

And turning to themselues at length againe,
Doe worke their owne perfection so by fate:
Then ouer them Change doth not rule and raigne;
But they raigne ouer change, and doe their states maintaine.

(Spenser 1977: 734)

Nature's rebuttal to Mutabilitie, which qualifies temporal alteration by situating it within a Platonic trajectory that returns everything to its original, perfect state, functions for Shakespeare only within the domain of art; writing alone can turn the male friend and dark lady "to themselues at length againe." In the natural world sketched in the sonnets, all houses "fall to decay" (13. 9), while "everything that grows / Holds in perfection but a little moment" (15. 1–2). The constancy of love in sonnet 116, the "it" of line five of the poem, is also – for the poet – the poetry, *the* object of love, *it*self:

O no, it is an ever-fixèd mark
That looks on tempests and is never shaken;
It is the star to every wand'ring bark,
Whose worth's unknown, although his height be taken.
Love's not time's fool, though rosy lips and cheeks
Within his bending sickle's compass come.
Love alters not with his brief hours and weeks,
But bears it out ev'n to the edge of doom.

(ll. 5–12)

Poetry will last longer than the male friend, longer than the dark lady, longer even then the speaker himself. This is no longer, as Fineman describes the sonnets, epideictic poetry, except insofar as its principal object of praise is its own emanation. Writing is, it turns out, the best thing the speaker has, even if it is not perhaps the best thing he might imagine having. Often read as if it has been "drained of particular personality," sonnet 116 in fact reveals a poet interested less in creating a persona than in fashioning an immutable, poetic *consolatio* in the face of rejection and scorn (Neely 1977: 88).

Among Shakespeare's most notable discoveries in his sonnets is the realization that by multiplying the scornful love objects in the poem and excising any appeal either to a higher being or to a potential on the poet's part for losing heart in writing itself – indeed, the poet's greatest doubts about his writing project appear early in the sequence rather than late – he can create a series of poems that, logically speaking, can be written for as long "as men can breathe or eyes can see" (18. 13). As well as creating a love triangle, or triangles, Shakespeare much more subtly, and no less importantly, replaces a single love object – the Laura or Stella figure of the Petrarchan sonnet tradition – with a literary object, the poems themselves, that contain "Two loves . . . of comfort and despair" (144. 1).[5] And rather than renounce this love as unsatisfying or merely idolatrous, Shakespeare instead leaves the sequence, the first perpetual-motion machine in English literature, more open-ended than any that preceded it: constantly capable of regenerating itself by ceaselessly absorbing the world's alterations so that it alone will remain unchanged, since it alone will comprise all of love's diverse effects.

The early annotator who wrote in his or her copy of the 1609 quarto "What a heap of wretched Infidel Stuff" has given us a useful hint as to what might have unsettled the sonnets' first readers: the poems' full absorption in the process of their composition, without mediation or qualification of any Christian kind (Shakespeare 1944: vol. 2, 348). Writing more than forty years ago, J. B. Leishman remarked that "Shakespeare's sonnets, like Petrarch's, are unworldly, but not, like Petrarch's, other-worldly" (Leishman 1963: 52). Indeed, they prefer to handle love, as in sonnet 130, by figuring it as treading "on the ground," rejecting a nod up to "heav'n" as a gesture of "false compare," not because heaven is demeaned by such a comparison, but rather because its comforts are too deferred, too immaterial, and too inconsequential when compared to more earthly, scribbled strivings (ll. 12, 13, 14).

NOTES

1 Wilde's conjectures, it is often overlooked, are made in the context of a fictional story.

2 Roe emphasizes the impact on Elizabethan erotic poetry of Thomas Hoby's 1561 translation of Baldassare Castiglione's *Il Cortegiano* (Roe 1996: 100). Medcalf hypothesizes that Ben Jonson might have introduced Shakespeare to Plato via Marsilio Ficino's Latin translation (Medcalf 1996: 118).

3 Compare the already mentioned sonnet 36, where the final line – "As thou being mine, mine is thy good report" – first claims the loved object and then immediately translates the figure into the possessed aesthetic representation of the sequence.

4 As Vendler remarks, this is the only sonnet Shakespeare writes in which the key word, *one*, "appears graphically or phonetically *twice* in each member" (Vendler 1998: 446).

5 Even the presumed male/female binary in sonnet 144, initially suggesting that the former is linked with purity and the latter with the "devil," collapses when both are revealed as relationally equidistant to the speaker: "both to each friend" (ll. 7, 11). The speaker can desire that the one angel "fire my good one out" (l. 14) only because he knows that such a firing will not occur, since they are part and parcel of the same vacillating dynamic that makes the poetry possible in the first place.

REFERENCES

Bush, Douglas (1974). "Introduction." In William Shakespeare, *The Sonnets*, ed. Douglas Bush and Alfred Harbage, 7–16. Baltimore: Penguin. (First publ. 1961.)

Dubrow, Heather (1981). "Shakespeare's Undramatic Monologues: Toward a Reading of the *Sonnets*." *Shakespeare Quarterly* 32: 1, 55–68.

Dubrow, Heather (2000). "'Incertainties now crown themselves assur'd': The Politics of Plotting Shakespeare's Sonnets" (first publ. 1996). In

James Schiffer (ed.), *Shakespeare's Sonnets: Critical Essays*, 113–33. New York and London: Garland (first publ. 1998).

Duncan-Jones, Katherine (1998). "Introduction." In *Shakespeare's Sonnets*, ed. Katherine Duncan-Jones, 1–105. London: Thomas Nelson. (The Arden Shakespeare.) (First publ. 1997.)

Ferrand, Jacques (1990). *A Treatise on Lovesickness*, ed. Donald A. Beecher and Massimo Ciavolella. Syracuse: Syracuse University Press. (First publ. 1610.)

Ficino, Marsilio (1999). *Commentary on Plato's Symposium on Love (De Amore)*, trans. Sears Jayne. Woodstock, Conn.: Spring.

Fineman, Joel (1988). *Shakespeare's Perjured Eye: The Invention of Poetic Subjectivity in the Sonnets*. Berkeley: University of California Press. (First publ. 1986.)

Fowler, Alastair (1973). "Emanations of Glory: Neoplatonic Order in Spenser's *Faerie Queene*." In Judith M. Kenney and James A. Reither (eds.), *A Theatre for Spenserians*, 53–82. Toronto: University of Toronto Press.

Gardiner, Judith Kegan (1985). "The Marriage of Male Minds in Shakespeare's Sonnets." *Journal of English and Germanic Philology* 84: 3, 328–47.

Hollander, John (2001). "Introduction." In William Shakespeare, *The Sonnets*, ed. Stephen Orgel, xxiii–xlii. New York: Penguin.

Koskimies, Rafael (1970). "The Question of Platonism in Shakespeare's Sonnets." *Neuphilologische Mitteilungen* 71: 2, 260–70.

Leishman, J. B (1963). *Themes and Variations in Shakespeare's Sonnets*. New York: Harper & Row. (First publ. 1961.)

Medcalf, Stephen (1996). "Shakespeare on Beauty, Truth, and Transcendence." In Anna Baldwin and Sarah Hutton (eds.), *Platonism and the English Imagination*, 117–25. (First publ. 1994.)

Neely, Carol Thomas (1977). "Detachment and Engagement in Shakespeare's Sonnets: 94, 116, and 129." *PMLA* 92: 1, 83–95.

Orgel, Stephen (1997). *Impersonations: The Performance of Gender in Shakespeare's England*. Cambridge, UK: Cambridge University Press. (First publ. 1996.)

Pequigney, Joseph (1985). *Such Is My Love: A Study of Shakespeare's Sonnets*. Chicago and London: University of Chicago Press.

Pico della Mirandola, Giovanni (1914). *A Platonick Discourse Upon Love*, trans. Thomas Stanley, ed. Edmund G. Gardner. Boston: Merrymount. (This trans. first publ. 1651.)

Roe, John (1996). "Italian Neoplatonism and the Poetry of Sidney, Shakespeare, Chapman, and Donne." In Anna Baldwin and Sarah Hutton (eds.), *Platonism and the English Imagination*, 100–16. Cambridge, UK: Cambridge University Press. (First publ. 1994.)

Sedgwick, Eve Kosofsky (1985). *Between Men: English Literature and Male Homosocial Desire*. New York: Columbia University Press.

Shakespeare, William (1944). *A New Variorum Edition of Shakespeare: The Sonnets*, ed. Hyder Edward Rollins. 2 vols. Philadelphia and London: Lippincott.

Shakespeare, William (1977). *Shakespeare's Sonnets*, ed. Stephen Booth. New Haven and London: Yale University Press. All quotations of the Sonnets are from this edition.

Shakespeare, William (1986). *The Sonnets and A Lover's Complaint*, ed. John Kerrigan. New York: Viking Penguin. (The New Penguin Shakespeare.)

Shakespeare, William (1996). *The Sonnets*, ed. G. Blakemore Evans. Cambridge, UK: Cambridge University Press.

Shakespeare, William (2002). *The Complete Sonnets and Poems*, ed. Colin Burrow. Oxford: Oxford University Press. (Oxford World's Classics.)

Sidney, Philip (1983). *Astrophel and Stella*, in *Sir Philip Sidney: Selected Prose and Poetry*, ed. Robert Kimbrough. Madison: University of Wisconsin Press. (This edn. first publ. 1969.)

Spenser, Edmund (1977). *The Faerie Queene*, ed. A. C. Hamilton. London and New York: Longman.

Steadman, John M. (1959). " 'Like two spirits': Shakespeare and Ficino." *Shakespeare Quarterly* 10: 2, 244–6.

Traub, Valerie (1999). "Sex Without Issue: Sodomy, Reproduction, and Signification in Shakespeare's Sonnets." In James Schiffer (ed.), *Shakespeare's Sonnets: Critical Essays*, 431–52. New York: Garland.

Vendler, Helen (1998). *The Art of Shakespeare's Sonnets*. Cambridge, Mass.: Harvard University Press. (First publ. 1997.)

Wilde, Oscar (1994). "The Portrait of Mr. W. H." In *Complete Works of Oscar Wilde*, ed. Merlin Holland, 302–50. Glasgow: HarperCollins. (First publ. 1889.)

15

Tender Distance: Latinity and Desire in Shakespeare's Sonnets

Bradin Cormack

The maze of repetitions, puns, and cross-references in Shakespeare's sonnets constitutes one of their principal seductions, a powerful version of the erotic pull whose structure they unfold in their analysis of friendship, love, desire, jealousy, hope, frustration, and self-deception.[1] In the close readings that make up this essay, I focus on a kind of pun through which Shakespeare exploits the fact that English vocabulary draws so heavily on Latin.[2] By attending to the effects of this peculiar allusiveness, my essay contributes to the large body of scholarly work on the relationship between Shakespeare's writings and the classical past as transmitted in the Tudor grammar-school curriculum, in humanist texts more generally, and in the various literary and philosophical texts that Shakespeare seems to have read and used.[3] As distinct from much work on Shakespeare's Latinity, however, I am not interested here in identifying classical sources or allusions. Instead, I model a way of reading the sonnets in which Shakespeare's training in Latin emerges as part of the poems' basic texture, as their way of hearing words and of approaching meaning through that hearing. Whereas identifying the intertextual support of the sonnets can help readers foreground the conventions within which the poems operate and on which they build,[4] I focus on the intratextual dynamics, sometimes within even a single word, that give an acoustic dimension to Shakespeare's analysis of form. Among several achievements, I argue, this intratextuality restages lyric's traditional concern with the distance separating lover and beloved as a linguistic concern: one mediated at the microtextual level by language's relation to its own history and crystallized in the semantic work of tenderness, a term that for Shakespeare defines the simultaneously psychological and material form of eros as a longing to be elsewhere, beyond one's own body.

My critical take on the Latinate vocabulary in Shakespeare's sonnets broadly resembles Colin Burrow's recent account of allusion in the plays. In an article on the creative possibilities that Shakespeare found in both the successes and the shortcomings of humanist reading method (including, for example, the practices of memorizing, double translation, and commonplacing), Burrow writes that *how* Shakespeare read the classics is fully as important as "*what* Shakespeare read." The "how" is reflected, Burrow argues, in the priority Shakespeare gave to the dramatic use of his allusions, according to the diverse needs of his characters, such that a classical reference can be understood not only in terms of its local textual particularity, but also as an instance of Shakespeare's "mobilizing a language of humanism, in which classical allusions can become part of the texture of conversation."[5] Like Burrow, I am pursuing a flexible sense of what Shakespeare's classicism entailed, one capable of accounting for the fact that in their diction the sonnets are suffused with a Latinity far in excess of the poems' relatively restrained references to classical texts.[6] I suggest that the critical interest in listening to Shakespeare listening to the layers of his language is philosophical rather than narrowly stylistic: Shakespearean etymology is a philology in the sense of being a love of the word, a trust not only in the signifying function of words but more essentially in their productive capacity for constituting form.[7]

Let me begin with two brief examples of the kind of linguistic effect I have in mind. When Shakespeare tells the beloved young man that "thou art all my art, and doost aduance / As high as learning, my rude ignorance" (78. 13–14), "thou art" wittily doubles "my art." The first "art" is native in origin,[8] the second Roman (Lat. *ars*, "art" or "skill"); juxtaposed, they bring together being and poetry, in order to reinforce the poem's argument that the beloved gives Shakespeare's verse its entire substance and being, rather than its mere "stile" (78. 12).[9] Typical here is how Shakespeare activates the pun through the line's internal symmetries, so that the two "arts," one the poet's and the other the beloved's, pivot around "all" and thus, in that balancing, absorb a little of one another's meaning. Technically, the pun involves the figure of antanaclasis, "which in repeating a word shifts from one of its meanings to another."[10] What I would emphasize is that Shakespeare's forms often work, as here, to apply pressure to particular elements in a line, thereby making connections suddenly present to the reader's ear or eye.

A second and more complex example, also wittily metaphysical in orientation, is found in sonnet 1, and involves a special instance of syllepsis, "the use of a word having . . . different meanings, although it is not repeated."[11] Comparing the young man's single-minded refusal to have a child to a rose's turning in on itself, the poet chastises his friend for refusing to spend the seed inside him by saying that "thou" "Within thine owne bud buriest thy content" (1. 11). The line is a visual and aural chiasmus, and to pause over it is to find oneself moving outwards from the line's center in the fifth and sixth syllables, backwards and forwards across the two pairs *bud/bur* and *thine/thy* to reveal a hidden third pair, *within/content*, in which the English "with" is directly answered by the Latin prefix *con-* (meaning "with" or "together"). And this is the point of the line's formal games: "content" holds a "with" in it. The "content" the young man buries in the bud that will never bloom is, of course, both his happiness (his contentment) and what he contains (his seed, his "sweet selfe" [1. 8], his substance). But heard against "within," "content" also captures the lesson of the whole poem, epitomizing it by announcing that what the friend contains is not even his, but something, rather, that has already put him in a relation "with." As the poem formally unfolds it, that is, content is a category pertaining to ethics in the sense of constituting a structure for the relation between persons. For its part, the "within" that opens the line aptly mirrors "content," by offering in English form the with-interior that the line discovers content (as that which is in the young man but does not belong only to him) to be: with-in. The auxiliary meanings that emerge through etymological hearing are produced by the poem rather than being prior to it: Shakespeare's line, that is, exerts a pressure on both words in order to make each one's etymological structure audible as philosophical.

These two lines from sonnets 1 and 78 show a poet deploying traditional and stylistic figures for untraditional and cognitive ends. As suggested by these examples, verbal wit in the sonnets is a serious game, because Shakespeare makes philology a way of thinking and of loving. In arguing that Shakespeare uses the linguistic connections between English and Latin to probe questions of ethical relation raised in the sonnets, I am opposing two views of how words do their work in the poems. John Hollander has recently warned against attributing to Shakespeare a historical interest in words, arguing that in the sonnets Shakespeare's "concern is not ordinarily to make the reader conscious of etymology – as if he cared himself, which he seems not to do most of the time. The history of words is not present for him, but the way they behave when thrust onstage with each other is central."[12] This argument relies on a picture of Shakespeare as untutored genius, a writer radically unlike "classicizing" authors such as Jonson or Milton. But Hollander's view is too extreme: although no Elizabethan possessed technical lexicographical skills, there was, as Sylvia Adamson has argued, "a general awareness of the etymological origins of words and an appreciation that the Saxon and Latinate elements in the word-stock had different and complementary expressive properties."[13] In relation to Shakespeare specifically, Hollander's implicit separation of the scholar (as historian of the word) from the dramatist is anachronistic; certainly, it is false to the poems, which if anything seem unusually alive to the Latin roots and prefixes that inhabit English. That said, I find Hollander's formulation suggestive as a corrective to his own point, since Shakespeare's etymological wordplay so often works exactly by thrusting two words onstage *within* a single word, exploiting Latin to mobilize a semantic range alternative or supplementary to the primary English one.

A second view about the language of the sonnets that I want to contest is exemplified by Stephen Booth's extraordinary analytical commentary on the sequence (or, more accurately, by how readers of the poems have reasonably enough used that commentary). This is the view that the poems' diction becomes complex through accretion, and is most easily approachable in terms of ambiguity. Booth is brilliant at cataloguing the semantic range of Shakespeare's vocabulary and at unfolding alternative readings to a passage as a line feeds off this or that meaning of a given word. But the commentary can have the effect, oddly, of deadening the experience of the poems as form: not because Booth's analytic copiousness weighs down the poems, but because the interpretative method tends to transform the poems' semantic play into a set of alternative but nonetheless fixed meanings. Booth, that is, tends to substitute for what I would call Shakespeare's experimental philology a more conventional philology of specifying historical meanings. This substitute complexity renders static the poems' exploration of their own language and terms, their restless testing of words to discover in them what arguments are available to be made. To put this in traditional terms, philology in the sonnets can most properly be thought of as a form of *invention*, that part of classical rhetoric dedicated to discovering what arguments are available to be made in the particular case.[14] More simply, we might say, in Stephen Greenblatt's formulation, that Shakespeare "heard things in the sounds of words that others did not hear" and "made connections that others did not make."[15]

As I read the sonnets, a central expression of Shakespeare's way of hearing is his treatment of words as acoustic matter, his mobilization of words as units of sound and significance not necessarily comprehended by the meaning they help constitute as the semantic "whole." For readers who attend to how Shakespeare brings his language under pressure, the experience of the poems is often the pleasure of experiencing that gap. The gap specifically between English and Latin had unusual importance in the 1590s, because of the place of Latin poetry in the grammar-school curriculum;[16] because of the place of Ovid in the poetic culture centered on the Inns of Court;[17] and because English literary nationalism, like its Italian and French counterparts, was imagined always as a conversation between the vernacular and learned languages.[18] In the connections between English and Latin, Shakespeare could test his own poetry in relation to the classical poetic canon, and his account of desire in relation to the canons of desire inherited from the Roman poets, pre-eminently from Ovid.[19]

Sonnet 38 explicitly takes up the relation of Shakespeare's English poetry to the poetry and language of the classical past, by transforming the young man into a tenth muse to supplement the Greek nine, and by audibly pitching English and Latin against one another:

> Be thou the tenth Muse, ten times more in worth
> Then those old nine which rimers inuocate,
> And he that calls on thee, let him bring forth
> Eternal numbers to out-liue long date.
>
> (ll. 9–12)

Scrupulously mirroring the mere rhymers' invocation (Lat. *in-* + *vocare*, "to call") of their muses, the poet instead "calls on" his new and English muse. Similarly, deriving from the Latin *aeternus*, the "eternal" numbers of immortal poetry receive a vernacular equivalent in "out-liue long date," a modest and even creaky formulation that nonetheless precisely captures the distinction, alive in Latin, between a perpetual endurance in time and an eternal elevation above time.

In a poem about what it takes to write poetry, it is especially telling that the opening lines juxtapose four sources for poetry or four ways of naming its cause, two in their Latinate form and two in easily heard English translation: rhetorical invention and argument, divine inspiration and infusion:

> How can my Muse want subiect to inuent
> While thou dost breath that poor'st into my verse,
> Thine owne sweet argument, to excellent,
> For euery vulgar paper to rehearse . . .
>
> (38. 1–4)

The friend's breath, of course, literalizes poetic inspiration. His pouring himself "into my verse" involves the same kind of semantic play but in reverse order, since this is to say that he infuses himself (Lat. *fundere*, "to pour") into the verse.[20] That he pours himself in as his "owne sweet argument" wittily explains, moreover, how in line 8 he can be said to be so effective for the speaker's poetry as to "giue inuention light," since the root of "argument" is *arguere*, "to make clear or bright." Here, as elsewhere, Shakespearean philology seems especially attracted to discovering a kind of tautological assertion – your brightness adds brightness to invention – in order to test its non-tautological implications. Governing all these categories is the excellence (Lat. *excellere*, "to raise high") of the young man's argument and self, as against the "vulgar paper" that would praise it, where "vulgar" takes from *vulgus*, Latin for "populace," the implication specifically of a vulgar tongue, a vernacular language unsuited to learned excellence. In this context, it is especially notable how, after the knotted assonance of the polysyllabic Latinate compounds in line 3, line 4 seems to relax, as though itself turning away from Latin, into the more vernacular language of "paper" and "rehearse": "Thine owne sweet argument, to excellent, / For euery vulgar paper to rehearse."[21] The point of the poem's playful responsiveness to linguistic difference is to figure the friend (who is his own "argument") as standing in the same relation to the poetry written in his praise as does Latin to vernacular English: he is the classic toward which Shakespeare's English reaches.[22] In order to make this argument, sonnet 38 is unusually explicit in seeking out Latin and English equivalents and thereby advertising its etymological concerns. By doing so, however, the poem identifies its work in terms not of a "pure" Englishness against Latin, but rather of a philology at the boundary between a Latin humanist culture and an English vernacular one, at the threshold where language works simultaneously to announce and then overcome historical distance.

Shakespeare's concern to figure poetry as the fitting of vulgar to learned, vernacular to classical, may seem to sit uneasily with the sonnet's effect as love poetry. But if it is a linguist's question to ask what it might take, in language, to repair the damage of time and allow England to reach back to Rome and Rome forward to England, that question is also broadly erotic, since the temporal gap that philology bridges is simultaneously an ethical (and, in one reading of humanism, ultimately tragic) gap between those persons who speak by means of the texts they share as author and reader.[23] The temporal distance between ancient and modern, that is, analogizes the gap that separates persons, in that reading already makes the temporal gap interpersonal. In the remaining pages of this essay, I will be concerned with how Shakespeare uses the shape of English words to imagine a poetic means for overcoming that distance, in both the erotic sense of reaching the beloved friend and the poetic sense of making him into a literary classic. There are, of course, multiple ways to explore the representation of distance in a sequence as concerned as this one with absence, trust, and betrayal. By approaching the theme of distance through the sonnets' Latinity, however, I mean to ask how it matters for that theme that it should be treated specifically in poetic language, in language subjected to a more than ordinary formal pressure.

I turn here to two poems among those in the sequence that take absence as their theme. Sonnets 44 and 45 are companion poems, which, as Michael Schoenfeldt has noted in an essay on the sequence's treatment of the Galenic humoral self, deploy "the conventional linkage between the four elements (earth, air, fire, and water) and the four humors (blood, phlegm, choler, and melancholy) to confront rather playfully an issue that haunts and blesses the Sonnets: the status of desire when distance separates one from the object of desire."[24] Using the elements both to figure the distance between lover and beloved and to analogize the material limitations of flesh (in 44) as against the efficacy of thought and desire across distance (in 45), the two poems, I argue, meditate on the material and immaterial dimensions of desire and poetry, probing the structure of distance itself (and its etymology) for the principle that will subvert it.

Sonnet 44 opens by turning the distance between the poet and the young man into injury:

> If the dull substance of my flesh were thought,
> Iniurious distance should not stop my way,
> For then dispight of space I would be brought,
> From limits farre remote, where thou doost stay,
> No matter then although my foote did stand
> Vpon the farthest earth remoou'd from thee,
> For nimble thought can iumpe both sea and land,
> As soone as thinke the place where he would be.
> But ah, thought kills me that I am not thought
> To leape large lengths of miles when thou art gone,
> But that so much of earth and water wrought,
> I must attend, times leasure with my mone.
>> Receiuing naughts by elements so sloe,
>> But heauie teares, badges of eithers woe.

The argument of the poem unfolds in a series of feints around the corporeal and incorporeal, spirit and matter. Because flesh is substance (that is, matter) and not thought, distance opposes itself to eros, exactly by becoming like matter, that is, an obstacle to "stop" the poet's "way." This is, curiously, to say that distance materially blocks, not just the poet's access to the beloved, but also the intervening distance (or "way") between them.[25] Immaterial and material, distance does injury by working against itself even as it works against the poet/lover.

Shakespeare locates something of this paradox in the word itself: distance, rooted in the Latin *dis-* and *stare* ("to stand" or "to stay"), is specifically a standing or a staying *apart*. The poem registers that parting in lines 4–6 in the difference between the foot's standing and the friend's staying; accordingly, the erotically charged distance between poet and friend is figured as a standing apart from a standing. Extending the pun deeper into the poem's syntax, Shakespeare makes distance the state of difference, also, between two moods of the same verb: in "did stand" (l. 5), the foot's removal from the beloved is marked as a di[d]stance and as a distance from "doost stay" (l. 4).

The poem is about overcoming these real and textual distances, about the desire, in despite of distance, to reach the beloved. The poem's linguistic playfulness contributes to this program, because the turning of and returning to the word's origins effectively unmakes the word; by so doing, Shakespeare reimagines the structure of distance itself, in order then to identify a way around it. As part of the analysis, the poem pitches "distance" against "dispight": "For then dispight of space I would be brought" (l. 3). The punning juxtaposition of the words makes distance's spite audible. But the proximity of the words is resonant also in a more important way, since "spight" has been identified in sonnet 36 as the very principle that separates the lovers from one another:

> In our two loues there is but one respect,
> Though in our liues a seperable spight,
> Which though it alter not loues sole effect,
> Yet doth it steale sweet houres from loues delight . . .
>   (36. 5–8)

The "seperable spight" here is some force, probably social, capable of separating the poet and beloved or keeping them at a distance from one another.[26] In sonnet 44, where the poet longs to be immaterial in order that "then dispight of space I would be brought, / From limits farre remote, where thou doost stay," part of the force of the formulation is that, in analogy with "di-stance" as a standing apart, "di-spight" momentarily splits the separating "spight" from itself. "Dispight," that is, gently reverses the work of "distance" by making the distance that spitefully separates loving poet and beloved friend stand apart from itself, exactly as a "dispight of space." The adverbial phrase thus provides, as a kind of pulse inside the syntactic meaning, a curiously apposite definition of "distance." Distance itself is a "dispight of space," a contempt for space in the sense of being the agent, as it were, of moving across itself by already including the space it semantically refers to. Just as the poem has materialized distance against itself (as its own material obstacle), so too, through the play of "distance" and "dispight," it finds in distance the dematerialization of space as the word's instantaneous absorption of the space it designates. This is, in language, already the equivalent of the poet's wish to collapse distance by thinking his flesh across space as "thought" (44. 1).

The poem's verbal materialization and dematerialization of distance grounds its argument about the nature of the erotic body, and it does so through a second and coordinated set of puns about standing. The play of material and immaterial through which Shakespeare understands "distance" is replicated in his treatment of "substance," a concept introduced in the first line: "If the dull substance of my flesh were thought"

(44. 1). Distance, the poem says, would be "no matter" (l. 5) if flesh were thought, that is, if flesh were precisely no *matter*. If flesh is a "substance" (l. 1), the foot that stands on "earth" in lines 5–6 reminds the reader that that substance is, etymologically, a standing under (Lat. *sub-* "under" + *stare*, "to stand"). The root meaning is supported and complicated in the third quatrain by the poet's lament that "so much of earth and water wrought, / I must attend, times leasure with my mone" (ll. 11–12). As the earth that stands under his own foot, the poet is materially the dull substance he desires not to be. His foot stands on earth, and is earth, and earth is that which stands under: the poet's flesh and substance.

That said, the curious circling back of standing and matter enabled by the play of Latin and English necessarily suggests another possibility: if earth is that which stands under the foot (as, therefore, its "substance"), flesh would seem not itself to be substance, but rather that under which substance stands. The suggestion is already present in line 1, in fact, in the two available ways of reading the genitive phrase "of my flesh": on the one hand, flesh is, as matter, simply the equivalent of "dull substance"; on the other, flesh is exactly that possessed *of* substance, substance being that which "stands under" flesh as a sustaining principle that is not (as the poet laments) thought. Just as with the poem's materialization of immaterial "distance," substance points equally toward the corporeal and beyond it. For all its despair about heavy fleshliness, the poem implies two ways of reading substance, posing a problem and in identical terms suggesting its solution. Just when flesh is defined as a dully material substance incapable of making its way past an equally material distance, the poem begins to look for a (non-dull) substantial principle that might be similarly commensurate with a dematerialized distance. The philosophical playfulness here is closely related to what Kenneth Burke identifies as the "paradox of substance" when he writes that "though used to designate something *within* the thing, *intrinsic* to it, the word etymologically refers to something *outside* the thing, *extrinsic* to it . . . since that which supports or underlies a thing would be a part of the thing's context."[27] What is notable about Shakespeare's version of the paradox, however, is that it does not depend upon the opposition between what is intrinsic and extrinsic to the corporeal, but rather upon alternative *aspects* of the corporeal, the constructions according to which the corporeal is understood and through which, in Schoenfeldt's formulation, a "purportedly immaterial subject is constituted as a profoundly material substance."[28]

Joel Fineman argues that sonnet 44 figures the poet as "conflicted, because weighed down and uplifted by the thoughts he thinks," locating him, through the internal difference "between an oxymoronic physicality and an ambiguous metaphysicality," at once "above his sodden flesh and below his high ideal."[29] The wordplay I am describing helps both to produce those oppositions and to undercut them, since through it the poem discovers how the claims of flesh on love might not necessarily be identical to those of substance, and that love's or poetry's answer to "iniurious distance" may depend on the difference between the two. Sonnet 45 extends the argument about the relation between body and substance by analyzing the different relation between body and thought. The poem looks past the elements of earth and water that keep the poet fixed in place to the elements of air and fire, which make him partly mobile. As against the slow and dull and heavy, this poem is about speed, swiftness, quickness. Here are the opening two quatrains:

> The other two, slight ayre, and purging fire,
> Are both with thee, where euer I abide,
> The first my thought, the other my desire,
> These present absent with swift motion slide.
> For when these quicker Elements are gone
> In tender Embassie of loue to thee,
> My life being made of foure, with two alone,
> Sinkes downe to death, opprest with melancholie.
>
> (45. 1–8)

The conceit of the poem is that, in the friend's absence, the poet's thought and desire are nonetheless present to the friend, because the poet is thinking of and longing for him. In their embassy, thought and desire are the poet's political and ethical agents, whose representations of love substitute for an embodied engagement. This mode of overcoming distance is, however, insufficient, since the body has its own continuous claims. In the friend's continuing absence, the splitting of the body from its own longing is a form of decomposition that can only ever be temporarily repaired, since the poet's desire must ultimately be wherever the beloved young man is.

The poet's melancholy, a function of the imbalance among the four elements that make up his life,[30] produces the poem's most striking metrical effect, since Shakespeare places the rhyme for "thee" onto the partially feminine ending of "melancholie," as though, like that word, the state of mind resulting from the beloved's absence were beyond the rational "measure" that is the pentameter line. In the poem's final six lines, that disruptive melancholy looks for the friend's reciprocal embassy, through which alone the healthful composition of the four elements can be restored:

> Vntill liues composition be recured,
> By those swift messengers return'd from thee,
> Who euen but now come back againe assured,
> Of their faire health, recounting it to me.
> This told, I ioy, but then no longer glad,
> I send them back againe and straight grow sad.
>
> (45. 9–14)

Reciprocity here is at heart a matter of the Latin prefix *re-*, which corresponds to the meanings "back" (as in "return" or "renege") and "again" (as in "renew" or "remake"). Fineman points out that, as against "remote" and "remoou'd" in the previous poem, sonnet 45 imagines the poet "literally 're-paired'" by and with the beloved, by means of a composition "recured," a messenger "return'd," a story in the "recounting."[31] As if to highlight the point, the phrase "back againe," which the poem repeats, offers the two alternative English translations for the prefix. Shakespeare's testing of the Latin syllable as a way to define reciprocity is made all the more poignant by the fact that the structure it helps delineate, in spite of the insistence of the semantic argument, seems curiously one-sided, since it is the poet's own messengers, not the beloved's, who "come back againe" to assure him of "their faire health," presumably a consequence of the beloved's own health, on which the lover's health must depend.[32]

In unfolding the claims of thought and desire on the erotic, the poem deploys an even more suggestive pun about distance, one that helps us think further about the nature of substance, as the earlier poem has begun to lay it out. In sonnet 44, the body (as earth and water) was fated to "attend, times leasure" (l. 12) as a servant might a master. Thought and desire, in contrast, are able (as air and fire) to go in "tender" embassy to the beloved. The Latin root of "attend" is *tendere*, "to stretch": the English word that most audibly preserves the root meaning is, of course, "extend," and it is a kind of extension across distance that the poet has longed for before lamenting that his body is destined instead to "attend." In sonnet 45, the "tender Embassie" of thought and desire thus adjusts the attending that in the previous poem has only weakly substituted for real extension. (It is relevant here that the connection between "tender" and "attend" works as a Latinate pun in English without working in Latin at all: "tender" comes from the adjective *tener*, "delicate," and not the homonymic *tendere*. Shakespeare's philological thinking, in other words, is etymological when it serves him, but it also looks to whatever acoustic forms are at hand.)

Read against sonnet 44's "attend," "tender" becomes both a conceptual and a material structure for love. The "Embassie of loue" is said to be "tender" not just because it is an embassy of *love*, but also, more simply, because it is an embassy, a representation of the self sent out by the lover and stretched across the distance separating him from the beloved. In this, the poet's embassy recalls the structure of erotic intention from an earlier poem grounded in the conceit that at night the poet's love for the absent friend keeps him awake: "For then my thoughts (from far where I abide) / Intend a zelous pilgrimage to thee" (27. 5–6). The difficulty for the weary poet here is that intending (Lat. *in-* + *tendere*) the pilgrimage is, as a stretching toward something, already to go on the journey. Like this intending toward the object of contemplation or desire, sonnet 45's tenderness constitutes a connection, answering the peculiarly materialized distance of sonnet 44 by itself materializing the relation that is to overcome such distance.

But if thought and desire are tender, and attending flesh correspondingly dull, Shakespeare's treatment of substance will not allow that opposition between material and immaterial to remain absolute. Indeed, the sequence as a whole has opened with an image of a material tenderness whose purpose is to extend beauty across time:

> From fairest creatures we desire increase,
> That thereby beauties *Rose* might neuer die,
> But as the riper should by time decease,
> His tender heire might beare his memory . . .
>
> (1. 1–4)

Against the hope of a tender heir, the poem pertinently opposes a second logic by which, unhappily, the young man finds himself "contracted to thine owne bright eyes" (1. 5), which is to say betrothed to them and shrunken into them.[33] From the Latin *con-* + *trahere* ("draw together"), "contracted" precisely undoes the elastic materiality of tenderness: whereas the heir promises to extend the young man's beauty into the future, his unhappy self-marriage only draws him inward to an isolated present.[34]

Tenderness works in the poems as materialization: if tender thought is like matter, tenderness is also the form that matter takes when it becomes capable of stretching beyond itself. As such, in opposition to dullness and bluntness, it is the defining attribute for a substance that can both be flesh and be under flesh as its subtending principle. The great sonnet 53 links substance and tending, but in doing so gives priority not (as in 44) to thought, but rather to the body, whose materiality the poem destabilizes so as to remobilize it as substance:

> What is your substance, whereof are you made,
> That millions of strange shaddowes on you tend?
>
> (ll. 1–2)

Just as the body tends on time's leisure (and in sonnet 57 the poet tends on the "times of your desire"), the shadows here tend because they wait on the young man as a servant might. They tend also because that is what shadows do: stretch out from the substantial matter that produces them. But this is a stretching, the poem announces, that unsettles what we know about matter. The shadows that attend the friend are strange (or alien) because they do not belong to him; the mystery of his substance is that it casts all shadows, as though it were all substances:

> Since euery one, hath euery one, one shade,
> And you but one, can euery shaddow lend . . .
>
> (53. 3–4)

The multiplicity of tending shadows is evidence of a body whose substance makes it miraculously polyvalent.

The opposition here between substance and shadow (as opposed to the Latin root of the first, the second word is audibly native and nonclassical[35]) is important for making sense of the paradox. As is well known, this opposition speaks to Plato's account of the forms, as well as to the idealizing neoplatonic account of love as transmitted to England during the sixteenth century, most famously in Thomas Hoby's translation of Castiglione's *Courtier*. But when the poems appeal to the idealist opposition between a real world of nonmaterial forms and a material world that consists merely of shadows of the real, they do so in order to test the reality so posited, to probe the idealist account of the real in order to determine its usefulness in the domain of experience. If as readers, then, we use Platonic or neoplatonic idealism as a way simply to name and so dispose of the poet's hyperbolic praise of the young man's beauty, we miss the point that the sonnets use that vocabulary, rather, to analyze what it might mean to say that form is real. The poems in this sense are experiments rather than doctrine.

In the sequence "shadow" can nearly always be glossed as mere "image," standing in implicit contrast with the real, as when sonnet 67 denigrates the "false painting" both of cosmetics and of visual representation by contrasting "Roses of shaddow" with "his Rose [which] is true" (l. 8); or when, in sonnet 61, the poet reports that, in the friend's absence, dream images or "shadowes like to thee" (l. 4) keep him awake. So, in sonnet 53, substance is the real against which the shadow is defined. Saying this, however, avoids the content of the question toward which the poems I am considering seem driven, and which sonnet 53 makes fully explicit: *What* is your substance? Which is to say, what is the nature of that real which is your real?

The relationship between shadows and substance in sonnet 53 is complex because while shadows imply substance, they do not indicate its nature. On the one hand, substance must be the friend's real (but absent) body, a counter to shadows as to the dream images of sonnet 61. But Shakespeare's sequence suggests a more complex relationship of shadow to body, since at times shadows behave strangely like substance, as in sonnet 27, when the friend's "shaddoe," the false image of him presented by the imagination to the poet's "sightles view," partly undoes the contrast by being as luminous as the real, making "blacke night beautious, and her old face new" (ll. 10, 12). Even more pointedly, sonnet 37 spectacularly reverses the usual relationship of shadow and substance, since there it is the young man's shadow, his mere social image or reputation, that gives substance to himself and thereby to the poet: "Whilst that this shadow doth such substance giue / That I in thy abundance am suffic'd" (ll. 10–11). And, most importantly, sonnet 43 playfully contrasts shadow not to body but to form, wittily inquiring after the power of the young man's "forme," in light of the extraordinary effect that his mere shadow or dream image has in making the speaker's dream world bright:

> Then thou whose shaddow shaddowes doth make bright,
> How would thy shadowes forme, forme happy show . . .
>
> (ll. 5–6)

In his edition of the poems, Colin Burrow helpfully notes that "thy shadowes forme" is "the substance which gives rise to the imaginary resemblance."[36] So it is; but Shakespeare's lines are stranger than the gloss allows, since by identifying form rather than the body with the substance responsible for shadows, the poem brings the real and the shadowed into very close proximity. This is an effect in part of the syntax of line 6, where it is difficult to say whether the verb is the "forme" that precedes "happy" or the "showe" following it. Is the line saying that the young man's real and substantial self would form a happy show or show a happy form? Read this way, the line works by yoking together the illusoriness of show and the reality of form, so as fully to disrupt the distinction between how a form answers an image and how a body does. The friend's absent body is substantial as a body and also as a form, and as form it is simultaneously like the mere shadow against which body and form are measured.

Returning to sonnet 53, it is as form, then, that the friend's body can be a substance capable of subtending the millions of shadows tending on it: "What is your substance, whereof are you made / That millions of strange shaddowes on you tend?" The curious feature of the poem's major opposition between substance and shadow is not only that it unravels in the saying, but also that it seems to do so in both directions at once. First, a substance construed as form becomes less like the body it seems to be and more like the shadow that attends it. For their part, shadows have come by this point in the sequence to seem rather like the body they attend, insofar as they are substantial – an equation that is nominally less puzzling in light of the fact that substance is form. The mystery, then, that the poem registers about the young man's nature is less the relation between a material body and its immaterial effect than a relation among dominant and attendant forms. Shakespeare's microformal analysis is the commensurate response to a world of forms emerging into and out of relation.

Tenderness as I have discussed it is pre-eminently erotic, the connection that desire effects between loving bodies. But it is also textual. After the first quatrain, in fact, Sonnet 53 turns to text, making a poem that has started as metaphysical speculation into a poem about the literary past. The distance between past and present is structured like that between lover and beloved, since as form the young friend's body lends shadows that stretch out, not only across space, but also across time. For the main examples of those whose shadows the friend appropriates are the classical exemplars of human beauty:

> Describe *Adonis* and the counterfet,
> Is poorely immitated after you,
> On *Hellens* cheeke all art of beautie set,
> And you in *Grecian* tires are painted new . . .
>   (ll. 5–8)

The mystery of the androgynous friend's body is not just that it surpasses the most beautiful male and female bodies from the classical world and classical literature, but that it is uncannily prior to those bodies, in the sense that any textual description of those bodies will turn out to be an imitation not of those bodies but of the friend's body. In a manner suggested also by sonnets 44 and 45, sonnet 53 thus commits itself to an account of the body as substantial matter and substantial form. The young man's body can be the substance on which all shadows tend, because the substance the poem asks after in line 1 is already in relation to itself: a substance that is the material body, but which also relates to the material body in a manner not unlike the shadow, as an immaterial substance standing under the corporeal substance evidenced by the shadow stretched out from it. A body crosses time or distance as substance. And it is as substance that the friend's body claims all shadows and thereby appropriates the bodies they imply.

Like the philological method of exploiting the distant Latin roots of English words, tenderness materially evokes distance: the distance between loving poet and beloved friend, between a literary past and literary present, between the exemplary Latin and Greek world and Shakespeare's English praise. If the friend's beauty overpowers the past, this argues too that the poetry in his praise has for that reason become classic. This is what Shakespeare imagines in a poem about the future reception of his own verse:

> Who will beleeue my verse in time to come
> If it were fild with your most high deserts?
> Though yet heauen knowes it is but as a tombe
> Which hides your life, and shewes not halfe your parts:
> If I could write the beauty of your eyes,
> And in fresh numbers number all your graces,
> The age to come would say this Poet lies,
> Such heauenly touches nere toucht earthly faces.
> So should my papers (yellowed with their age)
> Be scorn d, like old men of lesse truth then tongue,
> And your true rights be termd a Poets rage,
> And stretched miter of an Antique song.
>> But were some childe of yours aliue that time,
>> You should liue twise in it, and in my rime.
>
> (17. 1–14)

The poem seems doubly self-deprecating: first, it insists that the poet is unable to "write the beauty of your eyes" (l. 5) and instead "hides your life" (l. 4); second, even if the poetry were able sufficiently to praise, it would not do justice to the young man's beauty because it would not be believed. In this double self-criticism, however, Shakespeare paradoxically imagines his poetry exactly as a classic, being read in the future as his present now reads its "Antique" songs, such that the imagined reader and critic of the sonnets analogizes the classical philologist who glosses and emends the poetry of Rome and Greece. The sonnets, Shakespeare announces, will be subject to the critical work appropriate for a classic. Although the poem's principal argument in favor of the young man's having a son is that even a poetry "fild with your most high deserts" would not be believed, the poet simultaneously imagines poetry as a medium able powerfully to join present, past, and future. Read through the materiality of tenderness that we have been tracing, furthermore, the "stretched" meter of the "Antique song" that is Shakespeare's poem as imagined from the future captures this doubled account of poetic efficacy. Even if the meter is "stretched" in the negative sense of "exaggerated" – this is how editors usually gloss the word – it will be stretched, in respect of time, in a positive sense, too. Meter is that which measures the line in time. The line extends as far as the meter allows, and meter determines, too, the extension of individual words in time: here, notably, "stretched" is itself stretched into "stretchèd" to keep the pentameter line from being hypometrical. Most important, the song that is Shakespeare's poem is stretched exactly because it is "Antique," stretching forward across historical time to be read in another time as a classic. Poetic meter, a form like other forms, stretches between past and present, making the song, like the lover's embassy, a tender connection.

The poetry of tenderness involves the poet in a series of philological metamorphoses useful for overcoming distance, be it the spatial distance separating the lover from the absent beloved, the temporal distance separating the classical world from the Elizabethan literary present, or the ethical distance between persons. Distance is transformed into matter, matter into substance, and substance into form. The crucial transformation, of course, is that of the young man himself, whom the poems promise to make immortal by changing him into a tender version of himself, which is to say not only a self capable of persisting in time but a self, too, capable of reaching back to the lover who is reaching toward him. So it is notable that sonnet 53, having begun by asking after substance and having proceeded through the distance separating the classical world from the English, ends with a third kind of standing, this one about fidelity:

> In all externall grace you haue some part,
> But you like none, none you for constant heart.
> (ll. 13–14)

Helen Vendler acutely notes in her commentary the turn from substance to constancy and the implication therein that what may be at stake in the poems is ethics rather than metaphysics.[37] This ethics of con-stancy (and of "con-tent") finds its mechanics, I have argued, in tenderness. For if the young man is a "tender chorle" (1. 12) and the poet his slave, whose only role is to "tend, / Vpon the houres, and times of your desire" (57. 1–2), the shared sound (tender/tend), even as it differentiates between erotic roles, also promises a kind of reciprocity, the tenderness of the intending lover answered by the tenderness of the beloved: a "mutuall render onely me for thee" (125. 12).

Indeed, the sonnets propose a word for this reciprocal structure in a poem about the work of time:

> Like as the waues make towards the pibled shore,
> So do our minuites hasten to their end,
> Each changing place with that with goes before,
> In sequent toile all forwards do contend.
> (60. 1–4)

Read according to its modular parts as well as its more easily heard English meaning, "con-tend" expresses the stretching of the waves towards the shore in terms of a shared purpose, an intending together to the shore. On its own, this is, of course, too optimistic a reading of the word, since "contend" bespeaks principally a rivalry, the waves struggling against one another to reach their goal. The tension between the two ways of hearing "contend" thus indexes how unequal throughout the sonnets the structure put in place by tenderness is. The tenderness of the sonnets, like that of the young man, is never quite equal to the philological erotics it seems to offer the poet.

This failure of reciprocity that the sonnets document is analogized in one poem as the failed economy between the poet and the object of his praise, and, most pertinently for the present argument, as a radical undoing of tenderness:

> I Neuer saw that you did painting need,
> And therefore to your faire no painting set,
> I found (or thought I found) you did exceed,
> The barren tender of a Poets debt . . .
>
> (83. 1–4)

According to the economic metaphor, the "tender" or offer to repay the debt is necessarily "barren" because the poet's rhetorical currency will be unequal to the young man's excellence, which is itself the source of the debt incurred. Although the poem is outwardly concerned with the barrenness of what the poet offers, the parenthesized concession in line 3 brilliantly suggests, too, the barrenness of what the young man offers. Once heard, indeed, the phrase "barren tender" infects the whole logic of tenderness as it has emerged through the sonnets' philological experiments, punningly substituting an economy premised on the fixed distance between contracting parties for the other metaphysics by which a being (poet, lover, beloved, poem) becomes capable ethically of reaching backwards or outwards toward another.

Returning to Vendler's response to the tension in sonnet 53 between "distance" and "constancy," I find, then, that the familiar distinction between the ethics of relation and the metaphysics of being rings false for the sonnets. For the poems explored in this essay work by prying apart the categories that make for difference (the distance between times or persons; the content that makes one oneself; the material substance that is a principle of individuation); and they discover in those categories the mechanics of a being understood as grounded instead in a lack of absolute difference: this is what makes overcoming the distance between beings a possibility. If tenderness in the sonnets ends up seeming inefficacious, with the poems occupying their highly erotic philosophical territory almost exclusively in hope, as loss, or as absence, that fact should not make us think that the poems find their fullest meaning in a static opposition between the ideal and worldly. Indeed, the productive capacity of Shakespeare's puns, as I have attempted to describe it here, suggests that we misread the poems if we take words like shadow and substance to be directing us to a world of philosophical absolutes, as opposed to a world in which forms are real because they *become* real, over and over again. Far from reaching vertically toward prior forms in such a way as to make the play of substance legible as the play of worldly matter and divine idea, the sonnets are orientated horizontally toward the provisional forms that are the forms we have, those that language and relation produce as the posterior effects of their work in the social world.

AUTHOR'S NOTE

For their generous comments and suggestions, I thank Lauren Berlant, Bill Brown, Sean Keilen, Carla Mazzio, Michael Murrin, Stephen Orgel, Joshua Phillips, Michael Schoenfeldt, Joshua Scodel, Goran Stanivukovic, Richard Strier, Robert von Hallberg, and Candace Vogler.

NOTES

1   The *locus classicus* for the analysis of love and rhetorical language as mutually illuminating structures is Plato's *Phaedrus*. In Elizabethan England, Ovid's *Metamorphoses*, a text central to the grammar-school curriculum, provided in different terms the most important entry into that erotic argument.

2   On puns generally in the sonnets, see M. M. Mahood, *Shakespeare's Wordplay* (London: Methuen, 1957), esp. ch. 4 on the sonnets. For a deconstructive approach to Shakespeare's puns, see Patricia Parker, *Shakespeare from the Margins: Language, Culture, Context* (Chicago: University of Chicago Press, 1996); Geoffrey Hartman, "Shakespeare's Poetical Character in *Twelfth Night*," in Patricia Parker and Geoffrey Hartman (eds.), *Shakespeare and the Question of Theory* (London: Routledge, 1990 [first publ. 1985]), 37–5.

3   For Shakespeare's relation to the classical world, see e.g. the essays recently collected in Charles Martindale and A. B. Taylor, eds., *Shakespeare and the Classics* (Cambridge: Cambridge University Press, 2004). On Shakespeare as reader, see Robert Miola, *Shakespeare's Reading* (Oxford: Oxford University Press, 2000), esp. ch. 2 on the poems.

4   A valuable guide to the intertextuality of the sonnets is J. B. Leishman, *Themes and Variations in Shakespeare's Sonnets* (London: Hutchinson, 1961).

5   Colin Burrow, "Shakespeare and Humanistic Culture," in Martindale and Taylor (eds.), *Shakespeare and the Classics*, 21, 24. For the cultural significance of *how* classical languages and literature were taught, see also Leonard Barkan, "What Shakespeare Read," in Margreta de Grazia and Stanley Wells (eds.), *The Cambridge Companion to Shakespeare* (Cambridge, UK: Cambridge University Press, 2001), 31–47.

6   Rather little criticism on the sonnets, as opposed to the plays, has focused on the relation to the classical past. Raymond Waddington's fine account of the impact of the Prudence tradition on the shape and meaning of sonnet 15 is an exception. See his "Shakespeare's Sonnet 15 and the Art of Memory," in Thomas Sloan and Raymond Waddington (eds.), *The Rhetoric of Renaissance Poetry from Wyatt to Milton* (Berkeley: University of California Press, 1974), 96–122. More recently, A. D. Cousins has usefully placed the poems in the context of Ovid and especially the story of Narcissus. See his *Shakespeare's Sonnets and Narrative Poems* (Harlow: Longman, 2000).

7   For two recent approaches to the dense layers of Shakespeare's language, see Simon Palfrey, *Doing Shakespeare* (London: Thomson Learning, 2004; The Arden Shakespeare); Margreta de Grazia, "Shakespeare and the Craft of Language," in de Grazia and Wells (eds.), *Cambridge Companion to Shakespeare*, 49–64.

8   The relevant root is *art* or *eart*, from OE *am*, "to be."

9   All citations of the sonnets (by poem number and line) are to the 1609 quarto edition, as given in facsimile in *Shakespeare's Sonnets*, ed. Stephen Booth, rev. edn. (New Haven: Yale University Press, 1978 [first publ. 1977]). Booth's analytic commentary on individual poems (135–538) is cited as Booth, *Sonnets*.

10 Miriam Joseph, *Shakespeare's Use of the Arts of Language* (New York: Columbia University Press, 1947), 165. Joseph's indispensable study catalogues a wide range of figures of speech as they are found in the plays and (to a lesser extent) the poems. Another useful account of classical rhetoric and figures is Richard A. Lanham, *A Handlist of Rhetorical Terms*, 2nd edn. (Berkeley: University of California Press, 1992).

11 Joseph, *Shakespeare's Use of the Arts of Language*, 166.

12 John Hollander, "Introduction," in William Shakespeare, *The Sonnets*, ed. Stephen Orgel (New York: Penguin, 2001), xxxix.

13 Sylvia Adamson, "Literary Language," in Roger Lass (ed.), *The Cambridge History of the English Language*, vol. 3: *1476–1776* (Cambridge, UK: Cambridge University Press, 1999), 573. The place of Latin in the pedagogical culture seems of the essence for the shape of early etymological inquiry. Since

almost no one in the period knew Old English, for example, the same writers who were highly sensitized to Latin roots probably heard words with Old English roots as generically native, nonclassical or "English," rather than as having a "history" in the sense in which a Latinate word was audible as having one.

14 To take one formulation from the classical tradition, in a treatise widely read in the sixteenth century, Cicero defines *inventio* as "the discovery [*excogitatio*] of valid or seemingly valid arguments to render one's cause [*causam*] plausible [*probabilem*]." See his *De inventione*, trans. H. M. Hubbell, Loeb Classical Library (Cambridge: Harvard University Press, 1949), 19 (I. vii. 9).

15 Stephen Greenblatt, *Will in the World: How Shakespeare Became Shakespeare* (New York: Norton, 2004), 23. Shakespeare's language was, of course, a response to a highly fluid and rapidly changing linguistic context, On the social and cultural significance of linguistic variation in English prior to standardization, see Paula Blank, *Broken English: Dialects and the Politics of Language in Renaissance Writings* (London: Routledge, 1996).

16 On humanism and the grammar-school curriculum, see T. W. Baldwin, *William Shakespere's Small Latine and Lesse Greeke*, 2 vols. (Urbana: University of Illinois Press, 1944); Anthony Grafton and Lisa Jardine, *From Humanism to the Humanities* (Cambridge, Mass.: Harvard University Press, 1986).

17 On the importance of Ovid in the 1590s and for Shakespeare, see Jonathan Bate, *Shakespeare and Ovid* (Oxford: Clarendon, 1993). See also the essays collected in A. B. Taylor (ed.), *Shakespeare's Ovid: The Metamorphoses in the Plays and Poems* (Cambridge: Cambridge University Press, 2000); and the essays collected in Goran Stanivukovic (ed.), *Ovid and the Renaissance Body* (Toronto: University of Toronto Press, 2001).

18 See Richard Helgerson, "Two Versions of Gothic," ch. 1 in *Forms of Nationhood: The Elizabethan Writing of England* (Chicago: University of Chicago Press, 1992). For an account of literary eloquence and literary self-consciousness as they were defined through the meeting of the English vernacular with

classical myth, see Sean Keilen, *Vulgar Eloquence: On the Renaissance Invention of English Literature* (New Haven: Yale University Press, 2006).

19 For the importance of Petrarch and Petrarchanism for the Renaissance transmission of Ovid, see Lynn Enterline, *The Rhetoric of the Body from Ovid to Shakespeare* (Cambridge, UK: Cambridge University Press, 2000). On Shakespeare's Petrarchanism more generally, see Gorden Braden, "Shakespeare's Petrarchism," in James Schiffer (ed.), *Shakespeare's Sonnets: Critical Essays* (New York: Garland, 1999), 163–84.

20 A punning that, as in this poem, exploits a doubled movement between Latin and English, English and Latin, can probably be connected to the grammar-school practice of double translation, through which schoolboys were taught to translate from Latin into English and then from their English back into a Latin version of the original Latin.

21 "Paper" has its proximate and audible root in French (*papier*) and a more distant, almost certainly inaudible root in Latin (*papyrus*, "papyrus reed"). "Rehearse" has an old French origin (*rehercer*) and a distant Latin one (*re-* + *hirpex*, "harrow"). To be clear, my point here is simply that as against the audible Latin of the preceding lines, these words would have been heard as vernacular.

22 For a looser version of the comparison between lover and beloved as between low and high, see the final couplet of sonnet 78, as quoted above: "But thou art all my art, and dost aduance / As high as learning, my rude ignorance."

23 The classic account of the humanist discovery of historical distance as tragic is Thomas M. Greene, *The Light in Troy: Imitation and Discovery in Renaissance Poetry* (New Haven: Yale University Press, 1982).

24 Michael Schoenfeldt, "The Matter of Inwardness: Shakespeare's Sonnets," in Schiffer (ed.), *Shakespeare's Sonnets*, 305–24 at 307.

25 Booth notes the "quiet play on *way* meaning 'distance' – as in *Othello* III. iv. 200: ' 'Tis but a little way that I can bring you' " (*Sonnets*, 205).

26 Booth valuably accounts for the odd phrase in terms of Shakespeare's reversal of adjective and noun (*Sonnets*, 194).

27 Kenneth Burke, *A Grammar of Motives* (New York: Prentice-Hall, 1945), 23.

28 Schoenfeldt, "The Matter of Inwardness," 306.

29 Joel Fineman, *Shakespeare's Perjured Eye: The Invention of Poetic Subjectivity in the Sonnets* (Berkeley: University of California Press, 1986), 226. In an extended discussion of sonnets 44 and 45 (220–34), Fineman accounts for the failure of thought in the poems in terms of an irreconcilable split within the speaker between subject and object.

30 Following Booth, *Sonnets*, p. 207, Schoenfeldt points out that the poem's physiological "explanation for the sadness that afflicts one when separated from the object of desire" is inaccurate, "since earth and water would produce not melancholy but the far less appropriate phlegm" ("The Matter of Inwardness," 307).

31 Fineman, *Shakespeare's Perjured Eye*, 229.

32 Editors traditionally emend "their" in line 12's "Of their faire health" to "thy." The quarto reading seems, however, to register in a further sense the poem's representation of health as being fully dependent on an ideal reciprocity that remains only ever elusive.

33 As several critics have noted, the phrase "tender heire" depends on a bilingual etymological pun linking *mulier*, "woman," to *mollis aer*, "tender/soft air." See Booth, *Sonnets*, 579, citing Mahood, *Shakespeare's Wordplay*, 92, and, chiefly, W. L. Godshalk, "Puns in Shakespeare's Sonnet 1, Line 4," *English Language Notes* 16 (1979), 200–2.

34 Relevantly for the sonnets' larger argument, the "heir" can be said to be tender, in fact, because at law the heir is neither quite natural person nor material body, but rather a formal category that as form is useful for the transfer of substance across time.

35 The root of "shadow" is the Old English *sceadu*.

36 William Shakespeare, *The Complete Sonnets and Poems*, ed. Colin Burrow (Oxford: Oxford University Press, 2002; Oxford World's Classics), 466.

37 Helen Vendler, *The Art of Shakespeare's Sonnets* (Cambridge, Mass.: Harvard University Press, 1997), 258–9.

16

Fickle Glass

Rayna Kalas

This essay takes its point of departure – and its title phrase – from Shakespeare's sonnet 126. The poem is something of an oddity among the sonnets. Containing just twelve lines of verse, sonnet 126 is one of only three poems in the collection that deviates from the standard of fourteen lines in iambic pentameter: sonnet 99 is fifteen lines, and sonnet 145 is in iambic tetrameter (Ramsey 1979: 125). Sonnet 126 is composed entirely of rhyming couplets, and yet it lacks a couplet in the one place customarily reserved for them: lines 13 and 14, the last two lines of a sonnet. The absence of a closing couplet is graphically marked in the 1609 quarto edition by two sets of curved brackets designating the space where a reader would ordinarily find the final two lines of verse.

126

O Thou my louely Boy who in thy power,
　Doeſt hould times fickle glaſſe.his fickle,hower:
Who haſt by wayning growne,and therein ſhou'ſt,
Thy louers withering,as thy ſweet ſelfe grow'ſt.
If Nature(ſoueraine miſteres ouer wrack)
As thou goeſt onwards ſtill will plucke thee backe,
She keepes thee to this purpoſe,that her skill.
May time diſgrace,and wretched mynuit kill.
Yet feare her O thou minnion of her pleaſure,
She may detaine,but not ſtill keepe her treſure!
Her *Audite*(though delayd)anſwer'd muſt be,
And her *Quietus* is to render thee.
(　　　　　　　　　　　)
(　　　　　　　　　　　)

Noted more for its eccentricity than its exemplarity among the other sonnets, the poem is nevertheless pivotal to the sequence as a whole, when it is reckoned as the last of the sonnets addressed to the young man. A reductive paraphrase reveals that the poem's theme of fleeting youth is of a piece with those that precede it: "My lovely Boy, you hold time's glass in your power and you yourself will advance even as love dies.

But since Nature is sovereign over you, fear her. She may prolong your youth, if only to punish time, but ultimately your reckoning will come and she will give you up to death." As the last lines in the last poem to the young man, the curved brackets do not simply round out a poem, they complete a thought. And yet, the blank space held open by that pair of empty parentheses seems almost to mock the sense-making capacity of language and lines of verse.[1]

For many years, modern editors dropped the curved brackets from the text on the grounds that the poem is sufficient in its twelve lines of verse. Two accompanying claims went alongside this argument: the first is that any short lyric would have qualified as a "sonnet" in the sixteenth century; the second is that the curved brackets are most likely to have been added by a compositor who mistakenly thought the poem was incomplete.[2] More recently, editors and critics have observed that the blank parentheses seem to echo the language of the poem. The empty space at the end of the poem makes palpable the *"Quietus"* referred to in line 12 (Lennard 1991: 43). The individual curved brackets – which Erasmus termed "lunulae," or "little moons," as John Lennard notes – reinforce the image of the moon intimated by the shape of the "sickle" in line 2 and the mention of "wayning" in line 3 (Shakespeare 1977: 431). Taken together, the four brackets suggest the shape of an hourglass, which, along with the sickle and the mirror, is one of Time's attributes (Graves 1996: 205). And Katherine Duncan-Jones, the first modern editor to include the curved brackets in the printed text of the poem, points out that they may also answer to the *"Audite"* mentioned in line 11, since account books used similar notation to demarcate a final sum or reckoning (Shakespeare 1997: 366). Even if curved brackets are not authorial, that does not mean that they can be dismissed as mere accidentals (Lennard 1991: 43). In a scholarly milieu less orientated toward a single, transcendent meaning or authorial intention and more attuned to the history of the material text, the empty double parentheses at the end of sonnet 126 have come to seem more substantive and significant.

The curved brackets make a display out of the discrepancy between sonnet 126 and the others. They boost the number of lines in the poem to fourteen, rendering the poem comparable to the formal pattern of the other sonnets, even as they reveal the poem's deviation from that pattern. The left-hand brackets, indented like the last lines of every other sonnet in the collection, are typeset to reveal that what is missing is indeed the final couplet. The curved brackets also expose, albeit indirectly, the discrepant rhyme scheme of this sonnet. For the absence of the final couplet is further offset by the superabundance of couplets in the preceding twelve lines. The paired brackets follow upon six rhymed couplets – in a sonnet sequence in which every other poem contains quatrains of alternating rhyme.[3]

The curved brackets or lunulae at the end of sonnet 126 grant this poem integrity as a sonnet, and yet they also call attention to the very things that set this poem apart. They announce the poem's relation to the rest of the sequence, but in a manner that is double-edged. The lunulae bring the poem into conformity with the others around it, allowing it to signify as a complete poem, even as they expose as artifice the formal structure and sense-making function of the sonnet as an autonomous unit. Thus far critics have looked to the poem to make sense of those curved brackets. But a look toward the sequence as a whole is also warranted, especially in light of the fact that the one other distinguishing feature traditionally attributed to sonnet 126 (apart from its empty parentheses) is its place in the sonnet sequence.

Since Edmund Malone, in his 1790 edition of the sonnets, first split the sonnets into two groups – the first 126 poems addressed to the "fair youth" and the remaining poems addressed to the "dark lady" – sonnet 126 has been recognized as the last of the poems addressed to the young man. In John Dover Wilson's often-repeated phrasing, sonnet 126 is "an Envoy intended as [a] conclusion" to the first section of sonnets addressed to the "Friend" (Wilson 1964: 18). Though Malone's division has seemed to many readers an artificial one, it has also been a persistent one. Most critics at least tacitly observe the categorization of young man and dark lady sonnets; and for critics interested in sexuality, subjectivity, and narrative, that division has arguably been the defining feature of the sonnets in the past two hundred years of criticism. Under the circumstances, it is surprising that sonnet 126 has not figured more centrally in sonnet criticism. The poem holds a place in the criticism only to the extent that it can be recognized as an "envoy" or conclusion. As a poem of parting, sonnet 126 finalizes the young man poems and allows the two parts of the sequence to be construed as a narrative.

Yet sonnet 126 also expressly denies closure, and not only because it comes up one couplet shy of a sonnet. The poem speaks of accounts and quittances that have yet to be satisfied – such as Nature's *"Audite"* which "(though delayd) answer'd must be." In place of a summary couplet, the last lines are left blank, evoking the finality of death, but also suggesting that the poem is unfinished. That lacuna gives license for the reader to interject and perhaps even to inscribe the poem. It gives way to an imagined disclosure: the official written discharge of a *Quietus est* or the epitaph that might reveal the identity of the addressee (Shakespeare 1996: 95). It even withdraws the prospect that the poem itself will reveal the true reflection of the "lovely boy," leaving it to Nature to "render" the young man, as if only the *"Quietus"* of death – only the translation of living flesh into eternal spirit – could effect a truly ideal imitation of the boy's beauty. For Kerrigan, this sonnet conveys a sense of "poetic shortfall" (Shakespeare 1986: 351). The curved brackets reiterate the language of absence and death in the poem, but they also imprint a graphic echo of ending and silence. They are null and void, but they also convey incompleteness and expectation; they leave open for speculation that unmarked portion of the page bound by parentheses.

The poem offers no final image – neither physical description nor ideal reflection – of the "lovely Boy" whose beauty appears finally to have stopped time and left him holding, "in [his] power," "times fickle glasse, his sickle, hower." Though the young man of the sonnets repeatedly consults a looking glass, the poems say nothing of his physical appearance. Sonnet 126 is no exception. The poem gestures toward an image that would end all, but the mirror or "glasse" – the very device that most promises the imitation or reflection of such a timeless beauty – proves "fickle." The mirror proves, that is, to be another kind of "glasse," an hourglass. Never explicitly figured in the poem, the hourglass is evoked only by the proximity of "glasse" and "hower" and by the commonplace depiction elsewhere of Father Time holding the attribute of an hourglass (Panofsky 1962: 82–3). It is precisely the withholding of the image in the glass that allows the alternate figure of the hourglass to come through. Instead of presenting an eternal image of beauty, the poem describes what it means to be subjected to time; subjected, that is, to the threatened hour of one's death (the lovely boy's "sickle hower") but also to the relentless reminders of mortality that inhere even in the routine passage of time (Time's "sickle, [which is nothing other than] hower"). Where the reader expects to find an idealizing image – an image that might sublimate the beloved object into an absolute subject – the poem also presents the beloved as time's object, as one subjected to temporality and mutability.[4] This is not only to say that the poem contemplates the mortality of the beloved, though it certainly does do that. It is also to say that, in the mirror that is an hourglass, the poem discloses a mode of temporality that obtains in the very status of the object. The object has a temporality of its own that interrupts and inverts the narrative that would otherwise correspond with the progress of the subject (the lovely boy in relation to his mirror, but also the poem as a speaking voice) towards some promised end. Sonnet 126 indicates that the two parts of the sonnets might be read not only in sequence as a narrative, but also in dialogue, as reflections and inversions of one another.

An hourglass marks time through the reversion of stuff, sand, to its original repository. In the halting phrases, "times fickle glasse, his sickle, hower," and in the veiled disclosure of the mirror as an hourglass, the poem inverts both the linear progress of time and the subject–object relation. The "lovely Boy," the subject who holds time's mirror at the opening of the poem, is rather quickly made the object of time's sickle. The appositive regress from "*times* fickle glass" to "*his* sickle, hower" further complicates the syntactical orientation of these phrases. It almost seems that the implied figure of the hourglass in line 2 begins to take shape in the remaining lines of verse, finally acquiring form in the two sets of curved brackets that graphically render the approximate shape of an hourglass. The language of the poem reiterates the movement of sand in a hourglass with descriptions of simultaneous loss and gain: the lovely boy "who hast by wayning growne" and who shows "[his] louers withering, as [his] sweet selfe grow'st," or Nature personified, with her capacity to "plucke thee backe" as "thou goest onwards." Sonnet 126 makes reference to withering love and to death, but its figural underpinning is an hourglass. And in this way, the sonnet is not simply an ending, but a pivot on which the sequence can turn (and be turned, like hourglass, back on itself again). This poem suggests that the structure of the sonnet "sequence" may be dialectical as much as it is narrative, leading back onto itself as much as it leads to an end.

As a narrative, the sonnets will seem preoccupied with identity – the identity of the word with its concept, the identity of beauty with truth, the identity of the heir with its begetters, not to mention the identities of the personae in these poems. As a narrative, the sonnets are keyed to the progressive temporality of the subject. But as a dialectical work in the humanist tradition – one might think here of Thomas More's *Utopia*, which looks both backward to classicism and forward to the new world through a dialectical engagement of origins and ends, realities and imaginaries – the sonnets will seems equally concerned with the temporality of the nonidentical, the occasional, and the material, in short the temporality of the object. Sonnet 126 has not always made sense, or at least has not always been compelling, because it does not square with the emphasis readers have placed on poetic subjectivity. Readers have made sense of the poem by granting it a positional function within a narrative of poetic and subjective identity. But sonnet 126 also turns that narrative on its head. By inverting the orientation of the subject toward its object and its end, this poem allows for a way of reading backward through time. In so doing, it suggests how poetry, as dialectic, is uniquely able to disclose to the subject's apprehension an understanding of the object from the position of the object.

I

Those who have endeavored to analyze sonnet 126 – and Joseph Pequigney's reading in *Such Is My Love* is one of the more substantial efforts – have done so by considering the poem as one that completes the young man sonnets and separates them from the dark lady sonnets. Noting that the poem has often struck readers as substandard, awkward, and hastily composed, Pequigney argues instead that the poem does give the "impression of painstaking design," but only if it is read as the final acknowledgment of a great love that, having waned, is now finally "terminal and empty" (Pequigney 1985: 204, 206).[5] The authority of the 1609 quarto, the sequence of the poems, and the division of the sonnets into component sub-sequences to the young man and to the dark lady are essential to Pequigney's argument. Pequigney wants to demonstrate that "Shakespeare produced not only extraordinary amatory verse, but also the grand masterpiece of homoerotic poetry" (p. 1). One can see in Pequigney's language – poised as it is to anticipate its detractors – why his pioneering argument would have needed to make the poems to the young man a discrete and monumental sub-sequence. The aim is to show that Shakespeare's poems to the young man are not simply ancillary and titillating verses, but a substantive work of amatory verse addressed to an erotic love object of the same sex.

Though Pequigney's argument was radical in its insistence that the sonnets are a monument of homoerotic verse, it maintains a fairly traditional view of their place within the genre of love poetry. In Pequigney's reading, the speaker preserves the convention of "the single voice" (Pequigney 1985: 224); and the essential relation of subject to object has stayed the same. It is the identity of the love object that has changed. It may be that, to an audience at the time Pequigney was writing, the same-sex eroticism of the sonnets could only have been made visible as a question of identity. As Peter Stallybrass has pointed out, "sexual identity" is one effect of a culture that demands "unity of character" (Stallybrass 1999: 86). But "sexual identity" as such may not have been the primary rubric through which the late sixteenth- and early seventeenth-century audience of the sonnets would have understood the same-sex eroticism in the poems. Pequigney's argument, because it attaches homoeroticism to the traditional

Petrarchan subject, cannot go so far as to explain how homoeroticism might have been instrumental in rewriting the very relation of subject and object in the sonnet tradition.

For Pequigney, the sonnets present "a bisexual self who is the subject of these and other emotional responses and mental states" (Pequigney 1985: 224). But, as Bruce Smith has observed, the homoeroticism of the sonnets unsettles the very stability of the subject: for the love object is also a subject in his own right. "The problem with the male object of desire in Shakespeare's Sonnets is that 'he' is *not* the usual male object of desire in poems ranging from late antiquity all the way down to *Venus and Adonis*: to wit, a beardless boy with a lovely white neck and a ripe ass. Instead, he is an active subject in his own right, someone who can have sex with the mistress as readily as the speaker can" (Smith 1999: 421). The object of desire is also an agent – and anyway there are two objects of desire, the young man and the dark lady. The object of desire in this sequence is plural, and active.

Shakespeare's sonnets are unusual in specifying more than one beloved object. Maintaining a strict division between sonnets 126 and 127 – and between the sonnets to the young man and those to the dark lady – makes it possible to resolve the plurality of the love objects by placing them in sequence, thereby maintaining the appearance that, at least at a given moment in time, there is one primary love object. The insistence on that division thus preserves the expectation that love poetry concerns the relation of the lover to the beloved, the subject to the object. According to this logic, there may even be triangulations – as in sonnets 41 and 42, or again at 133 and 134 – so long as the lover remains primarily directed toward one beloved object.

The gendered division of the sonnets is not, in fact, as pat as it has been made to appear, as Margreta de Grazia has pointed out; and yet it is also the case that "Some kind of binary division appears to be at work" (de Grazia 1999: 98). Stanley Wells reckons that only thirteen poems are addressed to a woman and thirty to a man, but also observes that all of the explicitly gendered pronouns adhere to the division of the young man from the dark lady poems (Wells 2004: 53). The sonnets do suggest two distinct loves (one fair, one black; one male, one female; one young, one old; one of essence, one of appearance) and sonnet 126 does signal a shift in the lover's attention from one to the other of these substantively different objects: from a "compound sweet" that is "not mixt with seconds, knows no art" (sonnet 125) to its "successive heir" that has "prophan'd" "sweet beauty" with "Arts faulse borrow'd face" (sonnet 127).

But sonnet 126 does not simply mark a barrier between those two love objects; it also marks their intersection, suggesting that they are at least mutually informing, if not interarticulated. It is noteworthy that sonnet 126 recirculates some of the same language that appears in sonnet 20, the poem that, addressed to the "Master Mistris of my passion," clearly does not observe a stark distinction between the fair master and the dark mistress. In sonnet 20, the speaker addresses a womanish "man in hew [hue]" (not so fair after all?) who has "all *Hews* in his controwling." Sonnet 20 speaks of "nature" having interrupted the speaker's "purpose" and made of the young man a "treasure" for "womens pleasure," "since she prickt thee out." In sonnet 126, the speaker tells the "louely Boy" that Nature "will plucke thee backe," keeping the boy alive as "her tresure" but only as long as it is "her pleasure." For though the boy of sonnet 126 has "in [his] power" time's "sickle" (which "Hews" or cuts down everything), Nature observes her own "purpose." The distinction between the young man and the dark lady, though a real one, is not quite so tidy; and sonnet 126 offers clues that such distinctions are in place precisely to be queried.

Sonnet 126 refers not only to "my louely Boy," but also to a "soueraine misteres" whose "Audite" is yet to be "answer'd." And while the "soueraine misteres" clearly refers in sonnet 126 to the figure of Nature personified, the language that describes Nature echoes throughout the dark lady sonnets. The dark lady assumes Nature's place, albeit as a usurper. Sonnet 127 introduces the "Mistersse" with eyes of "Raven blacke" as one who by her "hand hath put on Natures power, / Fairing the foule with Arts faulse borrow'd face." And the dark lady is also figured, like Nature, as a holder of debts. The "louely Boy" of sonnet 126 is warned that he is Nature's "minnion": however he may be "detaine[d]" or "tresure[d]" by her, he will ultimately have to pay the debt of her "Audite" with his life. But in sonnet 133, it is presumably the dark lady to whom the speaker and his "sweet'st friend" are enslaved. And it is she, rather than Nature, who in sonnet 134 holds under bond both the speaker, who is "morgag'd" to her "will" and "a friend, came debter for my sake": "thou hast both him and me." Turning back upon sonnet 126 from the vantage of the subsequent poems in the fashion of the hourglass, one can read the dark lady into that earlier personification of Nature by virtue of their shared attributes. Sonnet 126 has even primed the reader to see how the attributes of a personified concept can be literally taken in hand by the personae of the poem. The "louely Boy" of the first line of sonnet 126 has "in [his] power," by the end of the second line, the attributes of Father Time: he "doest hould" "times fickle glass, his sickle, hower." The dark lady has a presence in sonnet 126 — that so-called "envoy" to the fair youth — if only by virtue of her proxy, Nature.

II

If the sub-sequencing of the sonnets reveals an investment in identity as a category of scholarly thought, the rendering of the sonnets as a narrative reveals an investment in subjectivity as a category of scholarly thought. In *Shakespeare's Perjured Eye*, Joel Fineman adheres to the order of sonnets in the 1609 quarto and to the division of the sonnets into young man and dark lady sub-sequences. For Fineman, these two groups of sonnets are interarticulated, but also sequential.

> The dark lady sonnets share many of the features of the young man sonnets – they employ, for example, similar cross-coupling conceits and similarly stress chiasmatic diction – but, in addition, the dark lady sonnets put directly into words a set of suspicions that are only suggested by the tonal reservations of the young man sonnets. (Fineman 1986: 243)

Cross-coupling and chiasmus characterize individual poems and, in the interaction of the two parts, the sequence as a whole. Fineman's argument is that "The sonnets show what happens to poetic subjectivity when a language of visionary presence is replaced and displaced by a language of verbal representation" (p. 1). As the visual ideality of the young man sonnets gives way to the verbal duplicity of the dark lady sonnets, the poems invent a novel form, indeed the modern form, of poetic subjectivity. Fineman's sensitivity to the dialectical character of the sonnets is not limited to the distinction between the young man and the dark lady, or to the distinction between verbal and the visual. He also notes, for instance, that "there is a specific materiality that complements the way the young man sonnets break with the poetics of ideal complementarity" (p. 250). The subtlety of these interarticulations, however, ultimately resolves into a more unequivocal, indeed a more univocal, argument. "The large claim that all of these subordinate claims lead to is that this produces an unusual, but, in the literature successive to Shakespeare's sonnets, a subsequently governing, poetic first person" (p. 250).

Lisa Freinkel has pointed out that Fineman's reliance on the trope of chiasmus allows him to "track the play of difference within the sonnets while still maintaining that unifying narrative that quilts together the sequence as a whole" (Freinkel 2002: 216). For Freinkel, chiasmus is a trope that construes linear syntax out of recursive movement: "its repetitions enforce rereadings – we double back and thus move forward" (p. 217). But the "universe of Shakespeare's sonnets," Freinkel contends, "is a world *in decline*" (p. 221). "In Shakespeare's post-Reformation world, time's wastes can only recount the continually renewed decline of flesh from spirit" (p. 208). The only consolation for the "continual erosion of time" (p. 233) and the "collapse of narrative fulfillment" (p. 232) is "beauty's in-creasing catachresis" (p. 236): not proper succession, but its polysemous name, "*Will*." "What is immortal, in the end, is not beauty, nor the figure of beauty, but the abuse of beauty's figure" (p. 236).

Freinkel's account also tells a narrative, albeit a narrative of decline, and that narrative is, in essence, the flip-side of Fineman's. The story of the sonnets, for Fineman, is ultimately the history of the modern poetic subject. Freinkel wants to resist this modernizing and secularizing tendency in sonnet criticism, and so she tells instead of the "decline of flesh from spirit." Freinkel's protagonist is not the modern poetic subject, but the theological author; the problem of authorial intention is not psychosexual, but theological; the speaker's challenge is to represent not homoerotic desire, but the Protestant understanding of the will; the agon opposes not identity and difference, but spirit and flesh; and the platform is not persona, but figura. Freinkel tells a story, not of the ascendancy of consciousness, but of the waning of ideality.

For Fineman, the waning of ideality is one part of the narrative of the modern subject: the sonnets invent modern subjectivity through the creation of a verbally duplicitous subject, but that subject is also occasioned by the waning of ideality. One the one hand, the sonnets evince the progressive teleology of the modern poetic subject; on the other, they demonstrate a falling away from the ideal complementarity of the traditional poetry of praise. These two trajectories, one ascending and one descending, comprise the chiastic narrative structure of Fineman's overall vision of the sonnets. Freinkel acknowledges that both of those narratives belong to the discourse of the modern subject, but cautions that the sonnets may not. Although, in her view, the sonnets imagine a world in decline, Freinkel is wary of hypostatizing the imagined universe of the poems. Historical narratives are imagined by the poems, but Freinkel resists ordering or sequencing the sonnets in any way that would suggest that historical narratives are inherent in the sequence itself. Catachresis is a figure, *the* figure, within the sonnets, but not a figure for the sonnets in history.

Freinkel's study has the effect of exposing some of the implicit narratives that undergird Fineman's argument. Though he claims to have discovered the origins of modern subjectivity in the sonnets, Fineman has in fact recast the historical figure of Shakespeare as the modern poetic subject *par excellence*. Despite his almost unfathomable attention to details in the sonnets – their attention to materiality, their odd contingencies, their inconsistent temporality – Fineman orchestrates "these subordinate claims" into one "large claim." He ends up with a thesis – that the sonnets innovate "a subsequently governing poetic first person" – that is, paradoxically, rather traditional. De Grazia has suggested that Fineman's study, precisely because it "overstresses the gender division at sonnet 126 . . . might be seen as the culmination of the Malonean tradition" (1999: 101). As de Grazia explains in *Shakespeare Verbatim*, Malone's edition left a powerful legacy for reading the sonnets in conjunction with biographical details. Insisting that the sonnets were poems of "experience" rather than "mere observation," and therefore correspondent with Shakespeare's interiority, Malone sought to calibrate the poems with the narrative of the poet's life (de Grazia 1991: 159). Malone inaugurated a way of reading the Sonnets whereby "true identity – feelings, thoughts, and meanings – remained deeply embedded in the verse" (p. 160). Though the Enlightenment construct of Shakespeare's interiority in Malone's reading has been replaced in Fineman's reading by the modern construct of the discursive subject, both read the sonnets as a narrative that discloses the true identity of the poetic first person.

What has perhaps made this approach so hard to get around is in part the generic form of the sonnets themselves. In his essay on the pronouns of the sonnets, Bruce Smith notes that "By Giorgio Melchiori's calculations, the proportion of pronouns to other words is higher in Shakespeare's sonnets than in the sonnets of Sidney, Daniel, Drayton, and Spenser: 14.7 percent. The most frequent of these pronouns, among the sonnet-writers, is the first person singular. To read Shakespeare's sonnets is, therefore, to acquire a certain identity as 'I'" (Smith 1999: 414). But, as Smith demonstrates, the "I" is always conditioned by language and culture, by other pronouns and the social relations that those pronouns codify. Those "contingencies should warn us against identifying with the speaking 'I'" (p. 427), even though the poems seem to present us with a universal speaking "I."

Freinkel has reminded us that the poems also present a "Will." This "Will" is a catachresis not only of beauty's proper succession, but also of the poetic first person; a catachresis not only of the subject of praise, but also of the speaking subject. In its second address to a second person, the poetic first person becomes a third person: the "I" becomes a "Will." Fineman claims that the Renaissance sonnet, by its very generic conventions, is concerned with the poetic self and that we have underestimated the extent to which the epideictic purpose of the poetry of praise is developed as the "the-matic motive of poetic first person" (Fineman 1986:1). Fineman may be right to shift our attention from the recipient of praise to the praising poet, but epideixis, by *its* very generic conventions, always reveals the dependency of the speaking subject upon the subject of its praise. Fineman finds in the sonnets an inaugural and triumphant poetic subject. But earlier twentieth-century commentators were at pains to explain why the sonnets were so filled with paroxysms of abjection. John Dover Wilson's reply was that, as a poet, "Shakespeare has no identity," and that as an author he was always subject to the terms of patronage (Wilson 1964: 2–6). It might also be said that in the sonnets, not only is the beloved objectified by praise, but the speaking subject is objectified by the poetic second person.

In their deictic purpose, the sonnets also explore not only "thou" as an object, but the very status of the object: the very condition of being subordinate, even to the point of nonbeing. Sonnet 126 is a prime example. Drawing the reader's attention to the space where there is no language, only blank page, the sonnet represents nonsentience: both death and thingness. Over the course of the poem, sonnet 126 describes what it means to be subject to both time and Nature. Through personification, the poem renders concepts as identities, and at the same time razes persons to mere mortal bodies. In sonnet 126, the opening apostrophe of praise – "O thou my lovely Boy" – is later echoed as an imperative addressed to an inferior: "Yet feare her O thou minnion." The poem's confused syntax confounds the grammatical order of subjects and objects; and its strange diction and orthography confound the relation of the word and the reality it presumably represents. Taking sonnet 126 as an example, it might be said that the sonnets explore not only the subject and its object, but also the subject as an object. They also seem to make a subject of the object. To Smith's list of pronouns, we might wish to add "it."

Thus what distorts Fineman's argument is perhaps not so much that he emphasizes the poetic subject, but that he de-emphasizes the poetic object, and subordinates it to the narrative of the poetic subject, to a consciousness that transcends the intractable particularity of the figures within the poems. Fineman explains the cross-couplings, prefigurations, and forswearings that trouble any semblance of a linearity in these poems as " revisionary recapitulations . . . of an idealizing poetics [that] are directly related by the poet to literary history, to the poet's sense that he now writes sonnets in the after-math of praise" (Fineman 1986: 244). The poems are perforce narrative because they are embedded in an external narrative of literary and intellectual history. The sonnets express from the outset an awareness of their place in time, their "literary belatedness, poetic secondariness, literary repetition." This is crucial to Fineman's argument, for he must explain how it could be that – despite the narrative claim that a poetics of visual ideality gives way to one of verbal duplicity – the very first poem already expresses a sense of "difference within the idea of the ideal." Fineman states concern for "the place of this difference *within* the commonplace reflexive reflection" (p. 248) and then suggests that the identity between persons in the young man sonnets trumps the experience of difference (materiality) that intrudes into the poet's idea of the ideal.

[I]t is this same "within" that the poet sees *in* the young man when he looks at "the lovely gaze where every eye doth dwell." The poet identifies himself, spatially, temporally, but also as will be seen, sexually, with the material feel of this divided "withinness," with "a liquid prisoner pent in walls of glass." This is what the poet now sees when he looks into "Idea's Mirrour": a dissolved liquidity within a brittle hardness, this hourglass being, again, the very image of the passing of an ideal time. (p. 249)

The "poet" who identifies himself with the material feel of what he sees in the young man and in the objects of his observation is the first-person speaker of the poems. But the "the poet [who] now sees" is Shakespeare the author, reader of Drayton's *Idea's Mirrour*, and poetic innovator. In Fineman's account, the speaker's observations of temporality and materiality are subordinated to the poet's idea. Fineman appears to have explained something of the narrative of the poems, the kind of movement that takes place *within* them, but in fact he has only imported a sense of literary history into the poems. Through the identification of the young man, the speaker, and the poet, we get "the very image of the passing of an ideal time" but not the actual passing of time, an "hourglass being" but not an hourglass. What Fineman has described is the temporality of the thinking subject, in which narrative is tied to the idea of identity; it is an idealist view of time as "'the moving image of eternity' as Plato describes it in the *Timaeus*" (Fineman 1986: 251).

Fineman acknowledges that there is a temporality of the object in the poems, but relegates the observation to a footnote, thereby actualizing his own logical and rhetorical subordination of the poetic object to the narrative of the poetic subject. In the text of a footnote whose reference appears at the end of the passage cited above, Fineman writes, "This material association – a formless, dissolved liquidity that is joined together with an overformed brittle hardness – is, in effect, a phenomenological description of a mirror. Throughout the young man sub-sequence, this materiality is used to figure the experience of temporal mutation and change, and it is also applied to the poet's verse." In order to put forward a thesis about the narrative of the poetic subject, Fineman must subordinate the temporality of the objects themselves. What happens, though, if we are to read these poems, not for the relation they establish between "idea's mirror" and its "hourglass being," but rather for the relation they establish between the mirror and the hourglass as poetic figures that are also objects?

III

The figure of the looking glass is regularly used in the sonnets as a didactic exemplum and as an image of time. The mirror is both a reflective surface and a *memento mori*. In sonnet 126, the poetic image that most promises an enduring imitation or reflection in language is in fact exposed not just as an image of time, but as a temporal instrument: the "fickle glasse," or looking glass, proves to be an hourglass. Whereas the figure of a looking glass is often an emblem of time's truth in many of the earlier sonnets, in 126 it seems to promise the true image of the young man. Sonnet 3 admonishes, "Looke in thy glasse and tell the face thou vewest, / Now is the time that face should forme an other." And sonnet 77 instructs, "Thy glasse will shew thee how thy beauties were." But sonnet 126 seems finally to have ceded power to the young man who holds the "glasse" that "therein shou'st" his own true image. In the end the poem offers neither a physical description nor an ideal imitation of the boy's true beauty. The poem does not reflect (upon) a true vision of the "lovely Boy," so much as it discloses the mutability and temporality in the very status of the object.

Sonnet 126 is set up as a meditation on the I–thou relation that is commonplace within the sonnet tradition. The poem, which begins "O Thou my lovely Boy who in thy power, / Doest hould times fickle glasse, his sickle, hower:" foregrounds the poet's apostrophe to his "lovely Boy"; and the "thou," "my," and "thy" of the first line establish the familiar subject–object relation of Petrarchan address. But the poem very quickly confounds this relation through its use of Time's attributes. Those things that typically reveal the identity of the personified figure of Time are here held by the lovely boy. And whereas Time's glass, as a *memento mori*, should function as the object that reveals to the observer his fleshly mortality, the poem seems to promise a view of the timeless essence of the boy's youthful beauty. The boy in his loveliness appears to have stopped time, appears to hold time in his power.

Time's "glasse" turns out, with the very next turn of phrase, to be Time's "sickle" and Time's "hower" or perhaps his "sickle hower." These objects, which are the attributes of Time and thus in some sense belong to Time, are nonetheless held by the boy in his power. But there is at least some suggestion that "his" might refer not to Time, but to the lovely boy: the boy holds Time's glass, which reveals his own "sickle hower," or hour of death. The ambiguity of "his" in the line suggests that the objects held by the subject also have a hold on the subject. By the end of the line, the confusing punctuation and diction confirm that the subject is no longer in command of these grammatical objects. Something needs to be cut out – the comma, for instance – or perhaps something already has been cut out, like the article that we would expect to precede "hower" if the appositive(s) to "times glasse" are to make sense. As an appositive to "times glasse," the "sickle" that represents not the image of a mortal, but the violence of mortality, has the effect of rather rapidly shifting the agency from the lovely boy to Time. The appositive (or appositives if one counts "sickle" and "hower" separately) to "times glasse" thus places the reader in time, or at least brings time abruptly into the practice of reading. The phrasing displaces the reader's illusion of being the subject of a promised view or reflection, and subjects the reader instead to rapid change. This apposition also makes the reader attentive to sequence and ordering in this line of verse. The "sickle, hower" asks the reader to think about what has happened or what needs to happen to make sense of the line: to what has been cut or what needs to be cut by the appositive addition of "sickle, hower." The "sickle," coming as it does between "times glass" and "hower," seems to reduce Time personified to the blunt expression of time as "hower." But if that "fickle glasse" has revealed the truth of time, it has not yet revealed the actuality of the youth's mortality. That revelation, in this poem, is left to Nature – left, that is, to a personification that is nonidentical to Time, but whose effects are the same (both will ultimately lead to the boy's demise).

If at the first mention of the "fickle glasse" the reader imagines a looking glass, fickle because it shows youthful beauty while also betokening its loss, by the end of that line ("Doest hould times fickle glasse, his sickle, hower") it is no longer clear that the glass is only a looking glass and not also an hourglass, fickle because turned over when it runs out. But "hower" is rarely used as shorthand for hourglass. And though the hourglass is one of Time's attributes, so too is the mirror. Unless the reader has assumed from the first that "glasse" means hourglass rather than mirror, it is only by literally reading backward that one gets an "howerglasse" in this poem. And there is ample reason to stop and read backward since the very confusing presence of a comma between "sickle" and "hower" makes it difficult to know whether "sickle" should be considered an adjective modifying "hower" (meaning the hour that life is cut off) or whether "hower" is simply lacking an article and should be read as yet another appositive, another attribute of Time, albeit an incongruous and strangely literal one in this context. The reader is prompted, that is, to read backward from the grammatical object to the grammatical subject. There is an uncanny logic in reading backward here, since to read backward is to mirror in reverse a passage that describes a boy holding a mirror. Indeed, the visual similarities in the "fi" and "si" ligatures make fickle and sickle appear to be mirror images of one another.

Reading backward, however, does not work like the "glasse" originally evoked. Reading backward does not yield the image of the young man that the passage, in its original forward-moving syntax, has conditioned us to expect. Reading backward works like the hourglass that the "glasse" has become with the addition of "hower." Reading backward requires the recognition of an hourglass that is never directly named, that has no "identity" as such, but that has a kind of real presence in the poem by virtue of the fact that its features and characteristics are repeated in the graphic representation at the end of the poem and in such phrases as "by wayning growne." Instead of a looking glass that demonstrates, to use Fineman's formulation, a poetics of ideal complementarity between the lovely boy and the poet, the glass as hourglass seems to get in the way of the I–thou relation and even the most basic grammatical and semiotic identities.

Reading backward from the object subverts the logic of succession, and the logic of figure, with a logic of material resemblance. Certainly the proximity of "hower" to the aforementioned "glasse" suggests this doubled meaning of the "glasse" as a mirror and an hourglass. But the possibility of this doubled meaning depends not only on the fact that the word "glasse" names both things; it also depends on the fact that glass, as a material substance, is constitutive of both objects. It is not only because "glasse" names, but also because glass *is*, both a mirror and an hourglass that the full sense of this line comes through. In order for "glasse" to cut both ways – in order for it to mean both mirror and hourglass – the reader must relinquish the singular identity of the word (as mirror) and imagine a material resemblance that links the mirror with the (implied) hourglass. And though the imagination plays its part here, this is not the "hourglass being" of "idea's mirror," not an hourglass in name or figure, but an hourglass indeed: not the image of eternity, but the matter of time itself.

In sonnet 3, the mirror serves as the exemplum to the young man to procreate ("Looke in thy glasse and tell the face thou vewest, / Now is the time that face should forme an other"). The identity of the youth with his heir is an entirely abstract one, an identity of succession. But the young man is also told that he is his "mothers glasse and she in thee / Calls backe the louely Aprill of her prime" (3. 9–10), an image that, with others in the poem, has prompted Booth to suggest that there is an hourglass evoked if not directly named in that poem (Shakespeare 1977: 138). The "mothers glasse" that is also an hourglass seems, by virtue of the shared material substance of glass, to link the original "glasse" or mirror of the poem with the "windows" mentioned in the final lines of sonnet 3, and thus to suggest an alternative poetic legacy to the legal system of inheritance whose ideology these poems must serve to reflect. The hourglass, and the temporality that it represents, may also assist in ensuring that, as Murray Kreiger has explained, these poems are both a formally self-reflexive mirror and a window onto historical reality (Kreiger 1964: 3–4). Mirrors are often conjoined to time, as in sonnet 77, where the mirror is likened to a dial. But this conjunction of the mirror with the hourglass seems specifically to connote the backward movement of time. Even Nature, the vaunted "soueraine misteres ouer wrack" in sonnet 126, cannot make time run backward. She can "plucke thee backe," she can disgrace time and "wretched mynuit kill," but only a poetry that attends to the temporality of the object can make time run backward, thereby interrupting and upsetting the narrative logic of proprietary identity, to expose the syntactical and semantic logic on which those identities are built.

What might it mean that this sonnet, this sonnet that is effectively an hourglass, lies at the pivotal moment where the young man sonnets end and the dark lady sonnets begin? It may mean, for one thing, that the promise of narrative progress is as fickle as the promise of an enduring ideality in these poems: that poetic time, because it is beholden to the temporality of the object (the temporality of the things of Nature), will always pluck back what appears to go onward. It may also suggest a way of reading the two sub-sequences of sonnets as hourglass inversions of one another: a way of reading that acknowledges chance resemblance, adjacency, and above all, movement, without attributing a teleology (be it mutability or progress) to such motion and flux. As a sequence that is also an hourglass, the sonnets appear to engage in a dialectic of subject and object that does not necessarily resolve itself in the absolute identity of the subject. The empty brackets at the end of the poem echo the hourglass as a figure of reading in that they encourage a kind of reversion in the ordinary patterns of poetic image and poetic signification, and in the expected narrative of literary and social heritage. Unlike, say, the use of capitals and italics in the printing of the word "Will," which Lisa Freinkel has discussed with subtlety and precision, the curved brackets and the space they contain are nonlinguistic (Freinkel 2002: 219–36). They draw attention to form and rhyme, but also to paper and ink, and to the fact that the poem consists in marks made on a page at a precise moment in time. This nonreferential bit of typography and material page is not without its set of resonances with the poetic language that precedes it. But it is also counterpoint to it. The empty space at the end of the poem stands in opposition to the personification and allegoresis that characterize so much of the poem. Rather than establishing an identity between the idea and the persona, the curved brackets offer a series of physical properties, italicized lunulae, empty bits of page, that belong to no one (not even to sonnet 126, as some early editors would have it). And because the attributes of this unusual but pivotal poem are also nonproprietary, they suggest something of the backward poetics of the object and its subject of subjection.

NOTES

1   All citations from the sonnets follow the facsimile of the quarto reprinted in Stephen Booth's 1977 edition (Shakespeare 1977). This essay is indebted to Tyler Smith's work on empty parentheses as "suppedital" places, textual lacunae that betoken meddling with signification (Smith: 2004), and from conversations with him about empty lunulae.

2   Omitted from John Benson's 1640 edition, the poem was included in Malone's 1790 *Works*, but without the parentheses (Shakespeare 1996: 95). Ingram and Redpath attribute the curved brackets to the printer, stating that the sonnet is complete as a twelve-line poem (1964: 288). John Kerrigan omits the brackets, but "not without regret": for Kerrigan, the poem falls short of being a sonnet (Shakespeare 1986: 350–1). On the sixteenth-century use of the word "sonnet," see Shakespeare (1977: 430).

3   The one poem in which the alternating rhymes are so close that they seem almost indistinct is also the one sonnet in iambic tetrameter, sonnet 145. The first quatrain reads: "Those lips that Loues owne hand did make / Breath'd forth the sound that said I hate, / To me that languisht for her sake, / But when she saw my wofull state . . ."

4   In amatory verse, the love object also becomes the subject of another object, his or her objectified reflection in verse. This dialectic is resolved in the absolute identity of the authorial voice: in the identity of the true idea of the beloved and the consciousness of the speaker (which likewise implies the absolute identity of speaker and beloved *as subjects*). For this dialectic to be resolved – for the speaking subject to be a universal subject – the poem cannot appear to be a mere thing. Only as ideal content can the words of the poem achieve identity with the authorial speaking subject. The materiality of the letter, which points up the poem as object, unsettles the absolute identity of the authorial poetic subject. Thus the physicality of the lovely boy, the materiality of the page, and the poetic disclosure of the looking glass as an hourglass (the revelation that the ideal image is in fact temporal) are all ways in which the poem exposes the status of the object.

5   Pequigney is in fact referring to the parentheses when he uses the phrase "terminal and empty." For Pequigney, the parentheses accentuate his sense that sonnet 126 finalizes Part 1 of the sequence. Pequigney speculates that the parentheses may be authorial, and are thus part of the poem's "painstaking design."

REFERENCES

de Grazia, Margreta (1991). *Shakespeare Verbatim: The Reproduction of Authenticity and the 1790s Apparatus.* Oxford: Clarendon.

de Grazia, Margreta (1999). "The Scandal of Shakespeare's Sonnets." In James Schiffer (ed.), *Shakespeare's Sonnets: Critical Essays*, 89–112. New York: Garland. (First publ. in *Shakespeare Survey* 46, 1993, 35–49.)

Fineman, Joel (1986). *Shakespeare's Perjured Eye: The Invention of Poetic Subjectivity in the Sonnets.* Berkeley: University of California Press.

Freinkel, Lisa (2002). *Reading Shakespeare's Will: The Theology of Figure from Augustine to the Sonnets.* New York: Columbia University Press.

Graves, Roy Neil (1996). "Shakespeare's Sonnet 126." *Explicator* 54: 4, 203–7.

Ingram, W. G., and Redpath, Theodore (1964). *Shakespeare's Sonnets*. London: University of London Press.

Kreiger, Murray (1964). *A Window to Criticism: Shakespeare's Sonnets and Modern Poetics*. Princeton: Princeton University Press.

Lennard, John (1991). *But I Digress: The Exploitation of Parentheses in English Printed Verse*. Oxford: Oxford University Press.

Panofsky, Erwin (1962). *Studies in Iconology: Humanistic Themes in the Art of the Reniassnace*. New York: Harper & Row.

Pequigney, Joseph (1985). *Such Is My Love: A Study of Shakespeare's Sonnets*. Chicago: University of Chicago Press.

Ramsey, Paul (1979). *The Fickle Glass*. New York: AMS Press.

Shakespeare, William (1977). *Shakespeare's Sonnets*, ed. Stephen Booth. New Haven: Yale University Press.

Shakespeare, William (1986). *The Sonnets and A Lover's Complaint*, ed. John Kerrigan. New York: Viking Penguin. (The New Penguin Shakespeare.)

Shakespeare, William (1996). *The Sonnets*, ed. G. Blakemore Evans, intr. Anthony Hecht. Cambridge, UK: Cambridge University Press. (The New Cambridge Edition.)

Shakespeare, William (1997). *Shakespeare's Sonnets*, ed. Katherine Duncan-Jones. Nashville, Tenn.: Thomas Nelson. (The Arden Shakespeare.)

Smith, Bruce (1999). "I, You, He, She, and We: On the Sexual Politics of Shakespeare's Sonnets." In James Schiffer (ed.), *Shakespeare's Sonnets: Critical Essays*, 411–29. New York: Garland.

Smith, Tyler (2004). "A Poetics of Indenture: Cases 'Peculiar' in English Renaissance Literature." Unpublished dissertation, University of Pennsylvania.

Stallybrass, Peter (1999). "Editing as Cultural Formation: The Sexing of the Sonnets." In James Schiffer (ed.), *Shakespeare's Sonnets: Critical Essays*, 75–88. New York: Garland. (First publ. in *Modern Language Quarterly* 54, 1993, 91–103.)

Wells, Stanley (2004). *Looking for Sex in Shakespeare*. Oxford: Oxford University Press.

Wilson, John Dover (1964). *An Introduction to the Sonnets of Shakespeare for the Use of Historians and Others*. Cambridge: Cambridge University Press.

17

"Th' expense of spirit in a waste of shame": Mapping the "Emotional Regime" of Shakespeare's Sonnets

Jyotsna G. Singh

He that should see Hercules raging, Orestes trembling, Cain ranging, Amnon pining, Dido consuming, Archimedes running naked would little doubt that Passions mightily change and alter the quiet temper and disposition of the Mind . . . Inordinate affections (as experience teacheth) many ways disquiet the Mind and trouble the peacable state of this petty commonweal of our soul . . .

Thomas Wright, *The Passions of the Mind in General* (1601), II. 141

I

Reading Shakespeare's sonnets, we enter a sharply delineated, yet highly changeable, emotional universe. Love, desire, fear, anger, obsession, pleasure, self-hate, and despair all jostle with one another as the speaker articulates his feelings, typically, toward the young man or the "dark lady"; but more broadly, he reveals his experience of the exigencies of human passions, especially of suffering in its varied manifestations. In sonnet 129, for instance, the speaker charts the unstable and disorienting dynamic of "lust in action," which he represents with a "perverse and self-defeating energy," evident in the two opening quatrains of the sonnet (Shakespeare 1977: 443).

> Th' expense of spirit in a waste of shame
> Is lust in action, and till action lust
> Is perjured, murd'rous, bloody, full of blame,
> Savage, extreme, rude, cruel, not to trust,
> Enjoyed no sooner but despisèd straight,
> Past reason hunted, and no sooner had,
> Past reason hated as a swallowed bait,
> On purpose laid to make the taker mad;
>
> (ll. 1–8)[1]

These lines signal both a self-address and a personification of "lust," referring "both to its qualities as well as to those of any person who is under the influence of lust, who is 'lust personified'"(Shakespeare 1977: 444). This poem does not refer to a specific addressee – the young man or the "dark lady" of so many other sonnets; rather, it evokes a generalized, though fraught, experience of consummation. In the opening lines (1–4), "lust" is negatively marked – "the expense of spirit" implies to expend oneself sexually and emotionally in a "waste of shame." Here the sonnet represents the passion of "lust in action" in terms of its destructive attributes: it is "murd'rous," "bloody," "Savage," "rude," "cruel," and "not to trust."

This emotional volatility in the exercise of lust continues past line 5, where the lust "Enjoyed" is also "despised," "hunted," and "hated." To "enjoy" itself evokes sexual possession and being "hunted" is later echoed in line 9: "Mad in pursuit, and in possession so." The psychic journey of the sonnet does not arrive at any feeling of fulfillment, as the concluding sestet articulates a continuing emotional struggle:

> Mad in pursuit, and in possession so,
> Had, having, and in quest to have, extreme,
> A bliss in proof, and proved, a very woe,
> Before, a joy proposed, behind, a dream.
>   All this the world well knows, yet none knows well
>   To shun the heav'n that leads men to this hell.
>
> (ll. 9–14)

Even when consummated, lust can imply a "proposed" joy underpinned by a "dream"; and in line 12, as two critics note, is "proposed not as a joy possible of consummation, but as one only to be known through the dream, by which lust leads itself on" (Graves and Riding, quoted in Shakespeare 1977: 446). Evoking these shifting and contrary emotional states, the poem's concluding couplet, once again, seems to defer any possibility of fulfillment as it yokes together "heav'n" and "hell" as the antithetical states of being that coexist in the struggling passions of "lust in action." Shakespeare's engagement with the exigencies of passion and sexual desire in sonnet 129 produces a taxonomy of emotional suffering and disorientation, rather than of fulfillment and serenity.

Such ebbs and flows of passion typify our experience of the sonnet sequence as a whole, taking us on an affective journey, following emotions that are dynamic and varied, but with few extended or static moments of fulfillment or joy. In most of the sonnets, of course, this emotional suffering permeates the poems written in praise of a specific addressee – the mysterious young man or a "dark lady" – albeit in somewhat satiric, even ambiguous terms. In sonnets 29–30, for instance (to be analyzed later in this essay), the speaker's feelings for the young man are overcast by despair and complaint: expressed in terms of his "outcast state," "woes," "grievances," and "bootless cries."

The speaker's expressions of emotional distress often prevent contemporary Anglo-American students from considering Shakespeare's sonnets as "love" poems. One of my students recently suggested, with some frustration, that Shakespeare's poems were more about suffering than love. In making this distinction, her response was structured by the normative cultural script of contemporary society, one that promotes instant gratification and therapeutic release as integral components of the experience of love. For this student, perhaps not untypically, expressions of loss and grief running through Shakespeare's sonnets went against the logic of gratification. Instead, she was asserting a familiar proprietary fulfillment of the consumer society, focused on the question: "What do I get from love?"

The student's unease was further complicated by her response to the sonnets addressed to the young man (1–126), since they did not speak to standard, heteronormative expectations of a love relationship. Such normative expectations often overlook the Renaissance fluidity of meaning ascribed to the terms "lover" and "friend," or to the possibilities of men's desire for and love of other men.[2] Such student engagements with the sonnets' treatment of the passions often lead me to pedagogically interrogate the terms of our reading of early modern affective expressions and experiences. Can we read affects and passions transhistorically and transculturally, by stressing similarities in emotional experiences? Or are we, as modern readers, likely to misread early modern social rules governing emotions?

Underpinning these questions are the familiar arguments about whether similarities in affective experiences reveal a biological and universal basis of human nature, or whether specific cultural discourses about passions and affections point to the multiplicity and variety of emotional expression. Such issues typically frame contemporary debates about the goals and limitations of ethnography (Reddy 2001: 34–62; Paster et al. 2004: 3–13). As we look afresh at Shakespeare's sonnets – with some emphasis on his pervasive representation of disquiet and anguish caused by passions – through the prism of an anthropology of emotions, we can see how early modern taxonomies of passion and affection differ from our current modes of classification, and yet continue to shape our preoccupation with emotions as a subject of study.

Of course, each sonnet by Shakespeare can be considered "its own distinct world, a compressed, often fantastically complex fourteen-line rehearsal of an emotional scenario" (Greenblatt 2004: 247); however, I wish to consider some of these scenarios in terms of the "normative emotion scripts that govern affective expression and exchange" (Paster et al. 2004: 10) and reveal the nature and scope of human emotions. Such an approach may lead us to reconsider the tensions between shifting passions and both poetic and social conventions in the sonnets, while addressing questions about the scope and power of the emotional regime of Renaissance England. What was the normative style of emotional management? Were some emotions privileged over others? Were sonneteers (and sonnet forms) at variance with moral philosophers in the formers' emphasis on the unpredictable affective journey rather than on moral goals?

Such questions call for an approach that considers the affective world of the sonnets in terms of the dominant "emotional regime" of the period. This is a term coined by anthropologist William Reddy for "a normative style of emotional management that is fundamental to every [society] and political regime, of every cultural hegemony" (2001:

121). In order to explain the dynamics of this structure, Reddy comes up with the concept of *emotives*. "If performatives are words that do things, emotives – the words we use to talk about our emotions – are terms with transformative impact on both the self and others . . . [And] if emotions are real and if they are expressed through emotives, then we can evaluate [societies and] political regimes by the emotives they permit" (Rosenwein 2002: 2). For instance, we can identify which kinds of emotional expressions are allowed or encouraged and which others are forbidden or frowned upon. Articulations of emotions – or "emotives" – according to Reddy, "are both self-exploring and self-altering," whereby a self embarks on a process of "emotional navigation" among a broad range of feelings and desired goals (2001: 122–3). In this formulation, emotional suffering results from the individual's experiencing tensions and conflicts among different goals, while facing the self-altering effects of emotional expression. In western societies, such a view of suffering is illustrated by unrequited love, as Reddy explains:

> Suffering that results from goal conflicts is seen also in love relationships . . . Seeking out a loved one may realize a high-priority desire to be with the person, but it may also expose one to rejection – and thus to the knowledge that one has not embraced the loved one's own goals. This happens most obviously when the loved one makes clear the desire to avoid the lover . . . When and in what ways ought one to seek out the loved one in order to bring about a change of heart? When and in what ways ought one to accept the loved one's expressed aversion for oneself? Emotional suffering occurs when high-priority goals are in conflict in this way. (p. 123)

Overall, Reddy's theory enables us to map a particular emotional regime as being either *rigid* in its normative goals or *loose* in allowing for greater self-exploration and navigation of feelings, especially in situations of frustrated emotions. In doing so, we can chart the taxonomies of various passions as evidenced in the literary and cultural texts of different societies governed by distinct emotional regimes. In this vein, it would be useful to consider the effects and prescriptions of the emotional regime of Jacobean England and the ways in which it determined the nature and scope of human passions.

II

Lawrence Stone's analysis of early modern English society as somewhat lacking in strong passionate and affective ties clearly falls short of capturing the range of affections and bonds available to people in the period. Nonetheless, he gives us a clear sense of the normative "emotional regime" as articulated in the political, social, and religious orthodoxies of the time. Stone defines societal expectations of marriage in sixteenth-century England in quite restrictive terms:

> Marriage was not an intimate association based on personal choice. Among the upper and middling ranks it was primarily a means of tying two kinship groups . . . Among

peasants, artisans and laborers, it was an economic necessity for partnership and division of labor . . . So far as society was concerned, it was a convenient way of channeling the powerful but potentially disruptive instinct of sexual desire. (1979: 5)

Stone recognizes that "romantic love and sexual intrigue were certainly the subject of much poetry of the sixteenth and seventeenth centuries and many of Shakespeare's plays." But he believes that romantic love was "a reality which existed in one very restricted social group . . . that is the household of the prince and great nobles." Early modern English society, in Stone's vision, is based on a restrictive emotional regime whereby "romantic love and lust were strongly condemned as ephemeral and irrational [especially] as grounds for marriage" (1979: 103, 86). Overall, Stone's argument implies that sexual desires and affective impulses in Renaissance England could be contained within specific social spheres and moral prescriptions; but recent criticism more persuasively offers less deterministic, and more varied and dynamic, evaluations of Renaissance passions and affective relationships. According to one critic, "most writers of moral philosophy [in the Jacobean period] approach man's nature and passions with either a physical or moralistic bias . . . [Either] moral issues, ethics, and man's spiritual nature are their main concerns . . . or [others], all physicians at some point in their careers, see human beings in terms of humors, spirits, complexions, temperaments, and natural heat" (Newbold, in Wright 1986: 25).

Thomas Wright's influential and representative study, *The Passions of the Mind in General* (1601), seems aware of this dual emphasis on passions in terms of morals and humors, while also reflecting on their potential for good as well as evil: "It hath been declared, I think sufficiently, how most men ordinarily follow the unbridled appetite of their sensual passions; yet no doubt but they may by virtue be guided, and many good men so moderate and mortify them that they rather serve them for instruments of virtue than foments of vice" (Wright 1986: 100). Like other Renaissance moral philosophers and thinkers, Wright counters the position of the Stoics, as he states: "Hereby we may conclude that Passions well used may consist with wisdom – against the Stoics – and if they be moderated, to be very serviceable to virtue; if they be abused and overruled by sin, to be the nursery of vices and pathway to all wickedness" (p. 102).

Overall, Wright's anti-Stoic interest in the uses of passion for moral ends typifies the prevailing Judeo-Christian Renaissance attitudes, described by Richard Strier as follows: "both the humanist and Reformation traditions provided powerful defenses of the validity and even the desirability of ordinary human emotions and passions . . . [and] the Renaissance and Reformation defenses of passion entered into English vernacular literature in the sixteenth and seventeenth centuries" (2004: 32). The centrality of affect in the Renaissance is important not only to the humanist defense of rhetoric, but also to religious expression, for instance, as modeled on the Psalms and on the passion of Christ (pp. 23–32).

In general, the "emotional regime" of Jacobean England depended upon its strong moral prescriptions, though not without some unease about the power of emotions to "disquiet the Mind and trouble the peacable state of this petty commonweal of our soul" (Wright 1986: 141). On the one hand, all moral philosophers and religious authorities warned against passions, which we should "undertake to reclaime and bring under the Empire of reason, and by the assistance of grace, to change them into virtues"; yet they also recognized that "Passions making up a part of our soul, they were not to be extirpated but by death" (Senault 1649: 20). Thus, defenses of passion typically reflected this emotional struggle. Again, Senault, in *The Use of Passions* (1649), charts out the dynamic of this struggle, when he addresses those who "have fought with Passions as with so many Monsters" (p. 20) and tries to defend God's creation of human nature:

> they know not that good use might be made of them [Passions], and tacitly blaming him [that] hath indowed us with them, they have labored to sweeten them, not seeking out to manage them; they imagined Passions were not otherwise requisite to vertue, save only to exercise her courage, they thought they were not otherwise useful for men, save only for trial; And that man could reape no other advantage by them, save only patiently to bear with them or to oppose them with resolution; but I pretend to defend their cause by defending God's cause, and to make it appeare in the pursuit of this work, that the same providence, which hath drawn our safety from our detriment or loss, will have us work our rest from out of the disorders of our Passions; and that by his grace we may tame these wild monsters, that we may reduce these rebels under their obedience, and that we make such souldiers march under the banners of vertue as have oftenest fought in the behalf of vice. (Senault 1649: 20)

In Henry Peacham's collection of emblems, *Minerva Britanna* (1612), the figure of Temperance articulates a similar call "to curb affection, that too farre aspires," holding in one hand a bridle, symbolizing restraint, and in the other a golden cup, suggesting excess (Peacham 1966: 93). While a victory over the passions is extolled, the figure of temperance vividly describes the nature of the endeavor:

> For when to lustes, I loosely let the raine,
> And yeeld to each suggesting appetite,
> Man to his ruine, headlong runnes amaine,
> To frendes great greife, and enimies delight:
> No conquest doubtles, may with that compare,
> Of our affectes, when we the victors are.
> (Peacham 1966: 93)

In this sense of a constant struggle or a battle with the "disorders" of their passions and affections, the normative emotional regime of the period repeatedly exhorted individual subjects to harness their passions to virtue. One critic astutely notes that classical and early modern thinkers "wanted not so much to banish the passions as to manage them carefully, redirecting them in virtuous directions" (Schoenfeldt 2004: 52). Yet ironically, the very profusion of writings on emotional experiences also opens a discursive and imaginative space for self-discovery and transformation – for "emotional navigation" among a broad array of affections and desired goals, as Reddy defines the process. Wright enables such a fluid process when he outlines the important reasons for the study of passions:

> But, finally, I will conclude that this subject I entreat of comprehendeth the chief object that all the ancient Philosophers aimed at, wherein they placed the most of their felicity: that was *Nosce teipsum*, "know thyself"; the which knowledge principally consisteth of a perfect experience every man hath of himself in particular, and an universal knowledge of men's inclinations in common. (1986: 92–3)

The quest for self-knowledge Wright mentions signals a process that despite the best ethical intentions can lead to a contingent and unexpected affective journey. If passions and affections are "disorders," "perturbations," and "appetites," they are inevitably ungovernable and inconsistent. In sum, as Schoenfeldt notes:

> Passions indeed occupy an unsettled status in early modern culture, at once dangerous and necessary to ethical and physical health. Not just the range of quotidian desires and disgusts that render for us the vagaries of human character and motivation, the early modern passions were powerful affective impulses that the individual was thought to suffer (thus, the etymology from the Latin *passus*, to suffer). (2004: 46)

The associations between passion and suffering are found not only in etymology, but also in the schemes of primary emotions listed by prominent moral philosophers and poets. According to Thomas Aquinas, "there are eleven different species of passions, six in the concupiscible appetite and five in the irascible" (Wright 1986: 38). These are love, desire, pleasure, hatred, and aversion in the first group, and hope, fear, despair, and courage in the second group. While Wright acknowledges the authority of Aquinas, he believes that all passions can be reduced to six: "And unto these six (love, desire, pleasure, hatred, fear, and sadness) all ordinate and inordinate passions may easily be reduced." He also challenges "that common division of Thomas Aquinas, admitted by Scholastic Doctors as very convenient, because we prove some notable differences in so many passions" (p. 108). Wright further undermines Aquinas in stating that the passion we experience most often and strongest is not desire, as the latter suggests, but grief or sadness.

He goes on to explain the order of passions as follows: "First of all, then, sadness most manifestly is known to us, because we suffer often and feel most sensible pain: then pleasure, then fear; the other[s] are not so open, but sometimes they may exceed and so show themselves, as ire, desperation, etc." (Wright 1986: 193). Even in lists of passions in which the order of emotions differs, "sadness" and "pleasure" coexist as two sides of a coin; if desire or "concupiscence" is a primary motivating emotion, then, as Wright asserts, "Love then most is felt when it is absent from the object [desired] beloved" (p. 192).

III

Passions caught up in a dynamic of desire, pain, and fleeting pleasure are what constitute the personal drama enacted in the world of the Renaissance sonneteers: for instance, Shakespeare, Sidney, Spenser. One can get a sense of the emotional direction of the sonneteers from Stephen Booth (1969), when he describes the Renaissance sonnet as a form of "aristocratic, secular love poetry." He goes on to explain: "Like the basic courtly love convention from which it grew, the sonnet convention is one of indecorum" (p. 177). Structurally, also, the sonnet form militates against the representation of any kind of totalizing and stable emotional experience. Again, Booth elaborates: "In all stages of its development, the courtly love tradition relies upon a reader's sense of the frame of reference in which the writer operates and the writer's apparent deviation from that pattern in a rhetorical pattern that both fits and violates the expectation" (p. 177).

While I focus on Shakespeare's sonnets, all sonneteers draw readers into a universe of passions and affections that is on the margins of the normative style of emotional management in Renaissance England. Typically in the sonnet tradition, passions do not figure as a sensual threat to reason and morals; rather, affective bonds are associated with the exigencies of fluctuating desires, so that even a sublimation of emotions, in some instances, remains unmoored from moral goals. Thus, while Petrarchism supplied an important socioliterary code through which the Renaissance typically explored its fictions of masculine selfhood, the self it created was a desiring, emotionally fraught subject always in pursuit, and one whose identity "depend[s] upon an anxious, sometimes volatile relation to 'objects' of knowledge, [desire], and interpretation that are forever outside [his] mastery" (Breitenberg 1992: 431).[3] Furthermore, if Petrarchism is most commonly associated with a masculine economy of desire based on the valorization of the female beloved, Shakespeare's sonnets addressed to the mysterious "young man" clearly complicate and move beyond this male–female dynamic; some critics note that they offer "an implicit challenge or redefinition [of Petrarchism] in eulogizing a young male friend, rather than a distant idealized woman, and in making almost no claims to spiritual enlightenment" (Duncan-Jones, in Shakespeare 1997: 49).

Despite referring to two – male and female – addressees, Shakespeare's sonnets do not radically deviate from the Petrarchan exploration of a desiring masculine subject experiencing a psychic and emotional vulnerability, whereby his persona is "emotionally scattered" (Breitenberg 1992: 435). The vocabulary of the passions deployed by Shakespeare's speaker, with its endlessly deferred fulfillment, reveals a radically different emotional regime from that endorsed by moral philosophers, physicians, and even religious thinkers in early modern England. While the orthodox institutions and moral certainties these latter proposed acknowledged the centrality of affectivity, they were preoccupied with *harnessing* passions to moral, ethical, therapeutic, and spiritual goals. Moral philosophers, particularly, often called for the control and transformation of passions from "rebels" to "souldiers [that] march under the banners of vertue as have oftenest fought in the behalf of vice" (Senault 1649: 20). The stirring and volatile emotions evoked by Shakespeare's speaker in the sonnets are more akin to tormenting rebels.

In fact, the speaker seems to follow the dictum of the moral philosophers, "Know thyself," in attempting to chart the "perturbations" and "disorders" that the latter associated with the passions, while being unable to control them. The poems' shifting tones also testify to how the "passions mightily change and alter . . . the disposition of the mind" (Wright 1986: 141).

Instead of harnessing his feelings toward ethical or spiritual goals, the speaker seems to endlessly desire and yet defer consummation scenarios. In doing so, he frequently reveals an impulse to *aestheticize* his passions, typically associated with the frustrations of desire, in the solace of memory of previously shared love – a poetic memorialization of something already lost. It seems that the poet is attempting simultaneously discursive control and emotional solace, both of which seem tenuous and ephemeral. These struggles are evident in the exigencies of "lust" in sonnet 129 and in the volatility of passions expressed in sonnets 29 and 30.

In mapping the emotional universe of Shakespeare's sonnets, critics have often made biographical conjectures about the identity of the addressee. Typically, the sonnets "excite the curiosity about the speaker's situation, and . . . powerfully express his emotions and private consciousness" (Magnusson 2004: 361).[4] Thus, the critic goes on to explain: "The first seventeen sonnets, often referred to as the procreation group, comprise an address of a humanist poet-educator to a youthful, highborn patron . . . [But] then in sonnet 20 the authoritative script of humanist advice-giving is interrupted, never to be wholly resumed, by a confession – of personal involvement, of an intimate love relationship" (pp. 363–4).

In addressing the beautiful, highborn young man, who is the addressee of the first 126 sonnets, and the female lover, the focus of a secondary relationship in the last 28 sonnets, the self that Shakespeare constructs in these poems complicates the courtly tradition and its well-worn conceit of mistress worship in order to evoke a morally and emotionally ambiguous and decentered experience. While one can only conjecture about the biographical correspondences between the speaker and Shakespeare, the affective power of the sonnets often leads readers and critics to listen to a personal voice in the sonnets: "[They] are a thrilling, deeply convincing staging of the poet's inner life . . . of Shakespeare's response to his tangled emotional relationships . . . and the sonnets are [also] a cunning sequence of beautiful locked boxes to which there are no keys" (Greenblatt 2004: 249). At whatever emotional level a reader is drawn to the sonnets, pertinent to my argument is the implication here that the emotional drama of the individual – poignant as it is – is nonetheless mediated by the conventions of courtly love literature with its complexities of wordplay and profusion of figurative language. As one critic notes, the "reader has constantly to cope with the multitudinous organization of a Shakespeare sonnet . . . He always has the comfort and security of a frame of reference, but the frames of reference are not constant and their number seems limitless" (Booth 1969: 187).

Let us now turn to a sequence of two sonnets – 29 and 30 – in particular to explore the speaker's affective engagement with wide-ranging, and generally painful, emotions of love as well with its poetic memorialization. Here, as often found in other sonnets, *poetic creation and emotional suffering seem to be mutually constitutive.* One critic has put these sonnets in a group of ten (29–39) entitled "my outcast state" (Giroux 1982: 37). While such a designation (taken from sonnet 29) does not suggest a clear autobiographical narrative, it nonetheless helps in focusing on the mood and tone of a cluster of poems in which the outcast, lonely speaker seeks solace in remembrance of the love he experienced in the past.

In sonnet 29, "When in disgrace with fortune and men's eyes," we must first note how the speaker of the sonnets is socially situated and that his relation to the addressee has both personal and worldly dimensions. The speaker feels alone and in disgrace, while desiring the "art" and "scope" of other men. In the opening nine lines, he desires worldly success and recognition of self-worth that seem to elude him:

> When in disgrace with fortune and men's eyes,
> I all alone beweep my outcast state,
> And trouble deaf heav'n with my bootless cries,
> And look upon myself and curse my fate,
> Wishing me like to one more rich in hope,
> Featured like him, like him with friends possessed,
> Desiring this man's art, and that man's scope,
> With what I most enjoy contented least;
> Yet in these thoughts myself almost despising,
>
> (ll. 1–9)

In this first segment of self-exploration, the speaker deploys the "emotives" of pain almost as a kind of self-fashioning, describing his identity in expressions of scarcity, jealousy, and self-hate: "I . . . beweep my outcast state," "curse my fate," "trouble heav'n with . . . my bootless cries," "myself almost despising." The source of his suffering seems diffuse and all-encompassing, evoking Thomas Wright's scheme of primary emotions, whereby "sadness" casts its shadow on desired or projected "pleasure"; but suffering here also implies a religious, Christian connotation of the "sin of despair," extending a metaphor between "material and spiritual well-being" (Shakespeare 1977: 180).

From line 10 onwards, the speaker attempts to transform his wide-ranging feelings of despair by harnessing them to the remembrance of the "sweet love" of his friend.

> Haply I think on thee, and then my state,
> Like to the lark at break of day arising
> From sullen earth, sings hymns at heaven's gate;
>   For thy sweet love remem'bred such wealth brings,
>   That then I scorn to change my state with kings.
>
> (ll. 10–14)

Here, "remem'bred," unlike the earlier "thoughts" (which could also imply griefs), has a stirring, transformative impact on the speaker. Yet, while marking a culmination of his changing spirits, implied by the speaker's "state" like the lark, both "arising" and singing "hymns," these lines also rhetorically displace grief into memory, eliding the gap between the speaker's desire for his friend and an acceptance of his absence. Furthermore, the loss implied by "rememb'red" is followed in the same line with the present tense, "brings," leaving us uneasy about the speaker's final state of mind. We are not sure whether this love "rememb'red" continues into the present, even though the speaker extols its power. Furthermore, the reference to "kings" in the final line displaces and even erases the emotional intensity of the opening lines of this passage. The concluding reference to kings could possibly be a topical allusion to "King James I who may have enjoyed the company of the poet's friend at a time when the poet did not" (Shakespeare 1997: 168). The final vision of sonnet 29 is further complicated if one extends the opening religious analogy whereby "the beloved's love [also] functions as the love of the deity does in Christian theology" (Shakespeare 1977: 180). It is not surprising for a Shakespearean sonnet to evoke multiple frames of reference, one blurring or overlapping the other. Yet the affective journey of the speaker remains one of self-expression and exploration – as much about his "bootless cries" to heaven and rising "hymns" as about his remembrance of absent love.

A movement through varied states of "woe" – past and present, expressed in legal and financial metaphors – followed by the consolation of remembering his "dear friend" marks the emotional self-exploration of Shakespeare's speaker in sonnet 30.

> When to the sessions of sweet silent thought
> I summon up remembrance of things past,
> I sigh the lack of many a thing I sought,
> And with old woes new wail my dear time's waste.
> Then can I drown an eye, unused to flow,
> For precious friends hid in death's dateless night,
> And weep afresh love's long since cancelled woe,
> And moan th' expense of many a vanished sight.
> Then can I grieve at grievances foregone,
> And heavily from woe to woe tell o'er
> The sad account of fore-bemoanèd moan,
> Which I new pay as if not paid before.
>
> (ll. 1–12)

In the opening twelve lines of the poem, the speaker issues a summons to things past, calling a court in which "thought" is the judge – "sessions of sweet . . . thought" – in order to bemoan his condition or estate in terms of "[his] dear time's waste," "th' expense of many a vanished sight," and the "sad account of fore-bemoanèd moan." In this accounting, the speaker offers a complex gradation of emotional suffering, which intersects with shifting senses of the notion of time. For instance, "my dear time's waste" can imply (1) "my costly, grievous, and useless expenditure of my precious time"; (2) "the grievous consumption of my span of life"; (3) "the precious remnants of my lifetime (= things past)"; (4) "time's grievous destruction of things precious to me" (Shakespeare 1977: 182). Time is typically a destroyer, laying waste both life and love.

Thus, from line 4 onwards, the speaker charts his grief and "grievances" through a disorientating emotional scenario in which past and present are blurred. Thus, he offers "new wail" for "old woes" and can "drown an eye" for "precious friends hid in death's dateless night." His sense of loss evokes a particular poignancy, as he seems to "weep afresh" at "cancelled" bonds that are no longer valid and "many a vanished sight." Despite the legal allusion here, the emotional "lack," which the sonnet sums up in line 3, remains palpable through these emotional expressions veering between past and present. Emotional loss also implies a paradoxical paying of "dues" in line 12 in the form of grieving for traumas of the past, which the speaker may have "foregone" to grieve.

At the conclusion of the sonnet, the speaker attempts to focus his feelings into a desired though conditional present: "*if* the while I think on thee," his "dear friend," then all "losses are restored, and sorrows end." But ultimately, as in so many other sonnets, the addressee, the "dear friend," is absent from the emotional scenario.

> But if the while I think on thee, dear friend,
> All losses are restored, and sorrows end.
> (ll. 13–14)

The only solace for the speaker lies in remembrance and aesthetic transmutation of his sense of loneliness. The opening "lack" is filled by the memory of his friend, through which he can at least temporarily imagine (via this poem) an end to his sorrows.

These two sonnets, while not representative of the sequence as a whole, nonetheless typify the speaker's frequent preoccupation with lack and desire, rather than with fulfillment and consummation. While they evoke Thomas Wright's scheme of primary emotions, whereby sadness casts his shadow on pleasure and "love is most felt when absent" from the lover or friend, they differ from the moral philosophers in that they do not approach passions as a sensual threat to reason and morals – and as requiring ethical control and sublimation. Like the moral philosophers, Shakespeare *understands* human struggles with passions, woes, and longings, especially as they reflect frustrations of desire. Yet, instead of harnessing these feelings to moral goals, he opens up an imaginative space in the sonnets to dramatize their challenges. Thus, in these poetic dramatizations, we can observe how Shakespeare's expressions of love under the pressures of loss and lack are a far cry from our contemporary, therapeutic culture that can sometimes estrange modern readers from the affective experience of the sonnets.

Author's Note

My special thanks to Randy McLeod for his useful (and witty!) comments on drafts of this essay.

My thanks also to the Early Modern Reading Group at Michigan State University, for our many discussions on the sonnets and my treatment of them in this essay.

NOTES

1   William Shakespeare, *Shakespeare's Sonnets*, ed. Stephen Booth (New Haven and London: Yale University Press, 1977), 111. All quotations from the sonnets are from this edition of the text.

2   For a detailed account of the shifting meanings of the terms, "lover, "love," and "friend," see Shakespeare 1977, "Notes," 431–2.

3   Breitenberg (1992: 435) offers a useful discussion of "Petrarchism as an enabling discourse of masculine heterosexual desire and as a socio-literary convention that provides a compensatory form of masculine empowerment in response to the perception of psychic and emotional vulnerability." However, he does not account for an erotic economy of masculine desire that is directed at a young man, as in Shakespeare's sonnets.

4   Magnusson (2004: 356–9) clearly shows the difficulties of identifying the addressee.

REFERENCES

Booth, Stephen (1969). *An Essay on Shakespeare's Sonnets*. New Haven and London: Yale University Press.

Breitenberg, Mark (1992). "The Anatomy of Masculine Desire in *Love's Labor's Lost*." *Shakespeare Quarterly* 43: 4 (Winter), 430–49.

Giroux, Robert (1982). *The Book Known as Q: A Consideration of Shakespeare's Sonnets*. New York: Atheneum.

Greenblatt, Stephen (2004). *Will in the World: How Shakespeare Became Shakespeare*. New York: Norton.

Magnusson, Lynne (2004). "Shakespeare's Sonnets: A Modern Perspective." In *Shakespeare's Sonnets*, ed. Barbara Mowat and Paul Werstine, 355–69. Washington DC: Folger Shakespeare Library.

Paster, Gail Kern; Rowe, Katherine; and Floyd-Wilson, Mary, eds. (2004). *Reading Early Modern Passions: Essays in the Cultural History of Emotion*. Philadelphia: University of Pennsylvania Press.

Peacham, Henry (1966). *Minerva Britanna or a Garden of Heroical Devices . . .* , Part I. Leeds: Scolar. (First publ. 1612.)

Reddy, William (2001). *The Navigation of Feeling: A Framework for the History of Emotions*. Cambridge, UK: Cambridge University Press.

Rosenwein, Barbara (2002). Review of *The Navigation of Feeling: A Framework for the History of Emotions*, by William Reddy. *American History Review* 107, Oct., 1–3.

Senault, J. F. (1649). *The Use of Passions*, trans. Henry Monmouth. London.

Schoenfeldt, Michael (2004). "'Commotion Strange': Passion in *Paradise Lost*." In Gail Kern Paster, Katherine Rowe, and Mary Floyd-Wilson (eds.), *Reading Early Modern Passions: Essays in the Cultural History of Emotion*, 43–67. Philadelphia: University of Pennsylvania Press.

Shakespeare, William (1977). *Shakespeare's Sonnets*, ed. Stephen Booth. New Haven: Yale University Press.

Shakespeare, William (1997). *Shakespeare's Sonnets*, ed. Katherine Duncan-Jones. London: Thomas Nelson. (The Arden Shakespeare.)

Stone, Lawrence (1979). *The Family, Sex, and Marriage 1500–1800*. New York: Harper & Row.

Strier, Richard (2004). "Against the Rule of Reason: Praise of Passion from Petrarch to Luther to Shakespeare to Herbert." In Gail Kern Paster, Katherine Rowe, and Mary Floyd-Wilson (eds.), *Reading Early Modern Passions: Essays in the Cultural History of Emotion*, 23–42.

Vickers, Nancy (1981). "Diana Described: Scattered Woman and Scattered Rhyme." *Critical Inquiry* 8, 265–79.

Wright, Thomas (1986). *The Passions of the Mind in General*. A Critical Edition, ed. William Webster Newbold, 23–42. London and New York: Garland. (First publ. 1601.)

PART VI
Ideas of Darkness in the Sonnets

18
Rethinking Shakespeare's Dark Lady

Ilona Bell

This thing of darkness I / Acknowledge mine.
The Tempest, V. i. 275–6

I

No writer was more capable of constructing an intricate plot with dramatic developments leading to a compelling resolution than Shakespeare. Why then do the dark lady sonnets seem so disjointed? And why does Shakespeare's sonnet sequence come to such a contradictory and befuddling end? The explanation this essay proposes by reading the sonnets as a private lyric dialogue, rooted in the practice of courtship and seduction and the laws of betrothal and marriage, substantially alters the traditional view of the dark lady and Shakespeare's sonnets as a whole. While scuttling deeply ingrained critical assumptions and introducing new material, this reinterpretation touches upon some of the most fundamental and frequently debated problems the sonnets pose: How do the sonnets represent and judge the three main characters: the speaker, the young man, and the dark lady? How meaningful and authoritative is the order of the poems in the 1609 first edition? Who was the audience, and how stable is the traditional two-part division between the young man sonnets (1–126) and the dark lady sonnets (127–54)? Finally, what is the connection between poet and sonnet speaker, life and art?

The sonnets as a whole are usually read as a morality play in which the young man plays "the better angel," the idealized spirit of male friendship (heightened by the sexual *frisson* of 20), while the dark lady plays "the worser spirit" (144. 3–4), the temptress who introduces lust, moral corruption, and deceit by seducing the man, Shakespeare, and countless others. The two groups are connected by sonnets 40–2 and 152–4, where, although the circumstances remain murky, the man goes to woo the lady on Shakespeare's behalf, turns the sonnets to his own use (40. 6), and ends up sleeping with the lady. Shakespeare's idealized view of the man becomes increasingly fraught and complicated as rumors and unfolding events cast shadows over his "bright" image.

By contrast, Shakespeare's view of the lady is generally thought to be readily know-able and indisputably negative. "The fair friend is found to be less than fair, though forgivable," John Kerrigan concludes, but the dark lady is "decidedly dark in the conduct of her love-life . . . morally she inhabits, as she enshrines, a hell" (Shakespeare 1986: 59, 61). She "is everything that should arouse revulsion," Stephen Greenblatt writes. "Dishonest, unchaste, and faithless," she "has infected [Shakespeare] with vene-real disease" (2004: 255). These critiques of the dark lady are so deeply entrenched that they permeate annotations and interpretations, even when the line being glossed, or the sonnet being explicated, makes no such claims, and even when the editor or critic pur-ports to read each sonnet as a discrete utterance.

Grounding one's reading of the sonnets on the *presumption* that the dark lady is a promiscuous married woman who sleeps with Shakespeare, seduces the man, and spreads venereal disease is rather like prosecuting a rape trial by attacking the victim's prior sexual experiences. Adultery and promiscuity were serious charges in Shakespearean England, where a woman's honor was virtually synonymous with chastity, with virginity before marriage and fidelity after marriage, where venereal disease was rampant and incurable, and where sex outside marriage was deeply illicit, not only immoral and illegal but also cause for legal action, as the numerous court cases of sexual slander demonstrate (Ingram 1987; Gowing 1996). This essay reads the dark lady sonnets afresh – without assuming either that the man is basically innocent and forgivable or that the dark lady is adulterous, promiscuous, deceitful, and thoroughly reprehensible.

A few of the dark lady sonnets have been widely read and brilliantly explicated, but the sequence has more often been disregarded, subordinated as a "subsequence," and disparaged as a "very disparate group," "disjunctive, wildly various" (Shakespeare 2002: 132; 1986: 57) – a view that is understandable since the sonnets are indeed murky and messy, fraught with unexplained complications, unforeseen conflicts, and unresolved contradictions. Some critics argue that discontinuity is inherent to the genre; yet if one assumes that sonnets are discrete utterances with no more than a few scattered mini-sequences, that is what one will find, in Shakespeare's sonnets as elsewhere. Other scholars have argued that the order of the poems is meaningless because the 1609 first edition was unauthorized. Some critics have even fabricated new and improved sequences; however, these reconstituted products, like orange juice from concentrate, are distinctly less satisfying than the original. Katherine Duncan-Jones has argued, very convincingly I think, that Shakespeare oversaw the 1609 printing; but even if the first edition was pirated, it was almost certainly based on a manuscript collection that stemmed from an authorial original. Two of the dark lady sonnets were pirated in *A Passionate Pilgrim* (1599), a small, miscellaneous collection of poems, but the rest could not have circulated beyond a few private friends because there is not one manuscript predating the 1609 edition. (By comparison, there are several thousand extant manuscripts predating the first edition of Donne's poems.) In the absence of evidence that the order is not authori-tative, the 1609 sequence deserves continuing exploration.

The connection between poet and sonnet speaker has also been much debated, theo-retical objections to biographical criticism vying with indications of autobiographical veracity: shameless punning on Shakespeare's name, "Will"; references to the sonnet speaker as poet; enigmatic allusions to information and circumstances that are assumed but never elucidated. This essay refers to the speaker as Shakespeare because I believe, as do many Shakespeareans, that the sonnets are imbricated in Shakespeare's life, "embodied in particular lived circumstances" that are known to the addressee but concealed from us (Barber 1987: 6–7; Greenblatt 2004: 226–55; Ramsey 1979: 15; Schalkwyk 2002: 5; Schiffer 1999: 14–32; Spiller 1992: 154).

Countless hours and acres of trees have been expended trying to identify the man and the dark lady. (For that matter, even more time and paper have been wasted trying to prove Shakespeare was not Shakespeare.) What I'd like to know is not, who were the young man and the dark lady, but what was their relationship to Shakespeare and to each other? Much of what happens in the dark lady sonnets and the intertwined young man sonnets is so intimate, so sexual, so fraught with desire and potential scandal that Shakespeare would rather not say – exactly. And to make matters even more baffling, there is a great deal he does not know and cannot understand about the man and the lady, and their relationship to each other, which raises another vexed interpretative problem: the question of Shakespeare's audience. Francis Meres' remark in his 1598 *Palladis Tamia*, "Shakespeare's sugard sonnets among his private friends," is frequently cited as evidence that Shakespeare's sonnets, like so many of the greatest English Renaissance sonnets and lyrics, were manuscript poems that circulated among a côterie audience. But who exactly were these "private friends"?

Recent critics (Marotti 1982; Sedgwick 1985; Wall 1993) posit a male côterie, but English Renaissance love poems were generally written to and for a beloved. In Shakespearean England love poetry was considered the language of, and was regularly used for, courtship and seduction (Bell 1998). Readers of the first edition would have assumed they were overhearing a private lyric dialogue between Shakespeare, the young man, and the dark lady. Indeed, much as Shakespeare's dramatic dialogues contain carefully embedded stage directions, the sonnets contain directions for reading them as one side of an ongoing private conversation between lovers. For example, sonnet 48 reminds the man that Shakespeare kept the sonnet texts "locked up" in his own safe keeping, thereby implying that the sonnets were read or recited to the man or the lady (cf. Wright 1999: 137) until the man left London to visit her, when the sonnets had to be sent via messenger:

> By those swift messengers returned from thee,
> Who ev'n but now come back again, assured
> Of thy fair health, recounting it to me.
>> This told, I joy, but then no longer glad,
>> I send them back again, and straight grow sad.
>>> (45: 10–14)

At this point, the sonnets comprise one side of a continuing epistolary dialogue – or trialogue because (as 40 implies) the man shows his sonnets to the lady in order to prove that Shakespeare loves him more than her. Although the other side of the conversation takes place outside the poems, tantalizing glimpses of it can still be detected in sonnets like these.

This essay reads the mysterious, unexplained gaps in the poems along with the allusions to an ongoing private lyric dialogue as provocation to imagine a set of characters and events: the poet/lover Shakespeare, whose sonnets are actions, or interventions, in relationships the poems initiate, manipulate, interrogate, and regret; the dark lady and the young man, whose actions on the margins of the poems, and whose responses in the white spaces between the poems, are implied, provoked, solicited, and obsessively re-examined by the sonnets themselves. Modern-day readers who distrust biographical interpretation can read the sonnets as a fictive representation of an unfolding private lyric dialogue that posits and incorporates the kind of responses the sonnets would have received from the dark lady and the young man had they been the original private lyric audience; I myself think Shakespeare would have produced a more successful plot and more fully embodied characters had he set out to construct a poetic fiction.

Shakespeare's sonnets, and especially the dark lady sonnets, do not *tell* a story; they are not primarily narrative or explanatory. Rather, they are performative utterances, written to be read or recited to the man or the lady, or epistolary persuasions, sent to one or both of them – or at least they were written to look as if that was the case for readers who were prepared to believe it was. Several of the young man sonnets adopt a magisterial, eternizing point of view (Ferry 1975), and two of the dark lady sonnets adopt a general, philosophical stance. Some sonnets meditate upon the speaker's rejection in miserable, solitary self-pity. But most are addressed directly to the man or the lady or both. Since English second-person pronouns do not distinguish between male and female, some of the young man sonnets may have been addressed to the lady, and vice versa (Dubrow 1999). Whether overt or covert, autobiographical or fictive, the purpose is rhetorical: by constructing persuasive dramatic situations and compelling analogies in rhyming quatrains, linked by logical connectives and capped or overturned by resounding epigrammatic couplets, the sonnets seek to shape the man's and the lady's responses so as to ameliorate Shakespeare's desires, frustrations, and anxieties.

The sonnets' rootedness in the world that surrounds their borders need not, and indeed should not, undermine the "specifically literary exigencies that begin before and continue after Shakespeare" (Fineman 1986: 300). Shakespeare uses the form masterfully, and individual sonnets exhibit a controlling vision and overarching perspective that the sequence lacks. Hence brilliantly crafted individual sonnets exist in tension with the unstable, distraught figure who is embroiled in events not fully known to him and relationships only partially comprehensible by him – the "Shakespeare" who is grappling with unbelievably thorny, tangled emotions and shifting, confused (and highly confusing) judgments. Simultaneously sonneteer and poet/lover, Shakespeare is not only author and actor; he is also a character in a drama he tries to, but cannot entirely, script or understand. Constantly fretting about what is occurring beyond his purview and anxiously imagining what will happen next, shifting moment by moment from dramatic intensity to tortured retrospection to prospective desire and dread, the point of view is as fluid as it is unpredictable.

II

The dark lady sonnets move from praise to blame with remarkable rapidity. The first poem extols the unconventional, natural beauty that makes this woman universally admired and sets her apart from the fashionable, painted beauties whom Shakespeare deplores for "Fairing the foul with art's false borrowed face" (127. 6). The second admires her sensuous playing of the virginals, suggesting that she is a well-educated, virginal gentlewoman. The third comprises a far-reaching denunciation of sexual experience, from desire to post-coital *tristesse*:

> Th' expense of spirit in a waste of shame
> Is lust in action, and till action lust
> Is perjured, murd'rous, bloody, full of blame
> (129. 1–3)

Although the third quatrain offers a momentary stay against the inevitable post-coital let-down, the balanced, chiasmic syntax and relentless temporal movement – "A bliss in proof, and proved, a very woe" (l. 11) – undercut the fleeting glimpses of sexual pleasure as soon as they are "proved" or experienced. Still, imagination and memory continue to rekindle desire: "Before, a joy proposed, behind, a dream" (l. 12). The sonnet ends, as it began, with the damning claim that "lust" is the fast track to hell. And yet, the irresistible logic of the syntax makes it impossible "To shun the heav'n that leads men to this hell" (l. 14).

Sonnet 129 may have been written after the sequence ended because its universal, impersonal point of view and continual fluctuation from "before" to "behind" suggest a proleptic prescience or retrospective understanding of what is to come in the ensuing sonnets. Its prominent position at the outset of the dark lady sonnets provides an overview of the intense feelings of desire and disgust that both characterize, and emerge from, the lovers' triangle.

This generalized critique of sexuality is applied directly to the lady two sonnets later, where fulsome praise yields a sudden about-face: "In nothing art thou black save in thy deeds, / And thence this slander as I think proceeds" (131. 13–14). In a culture where the courts were constantly adjudicating cases of sexual "slander," this biting attack carries too strong a moral and legal force to mean merely that "[t]he only bad (*black*) thing about you is how cruel (*tyrannous*) you are to me" (Vendler 1997: 560). What the lady has done to provoke this sexual insult the sonnet does not say, though presumably she and the man both know.

Instead of responding defensively or angrily, the lady expresses sympathy for Shakespeare's suffering, as the following sonnet relates. Acknowledging that what he writes in the sonnets is contingent upon what happens outside them, Shakespeare promises to retract his prior criticism if she shows him some "pity," meaning not only sympathy but also sexual favor:

> And suit thy pity like in every part.
> Then will I swear beauty herself is black,
> And all they foul that thy complexion lack.
>   (132. 12–14)

We soon learn exactly what she has done to provoke both the cutting critique of 131 and the more aggressive sexual pursuit of 132: she slept with the man. Worse yet, her affection was drawn from Shakespeare to the man when he showed her the adoring sonnets of idealized love he himself received from Shakespeare (40. 6–10). Shakespeare regrets losing her to the man, but is even more upset about losing the man to her, or at least that is what he writes the man:

> That thou hast her, it is not all my grief,
> And yet it may be said I loved her dearly;
> That she hath thee is of my wailing chief.
>   (42. 1–3)

Shakespeare suggests that the lady should take him in thrall instead. But she is not the least bit interested, so he is left to his own obsessive fantasies:

> Wilt thou, whose will is large and spacious,
> Not once vouchsafe to hide my will in thine?
> Shall will in others seem right gracious,
> And in my will no fair acceptance shine?
>   (135. 5–8)

The manic puns on "will" (meaning future intention, sexual desire, male and female genitalia) and Shakespeare's own name "Will" (the 1609 quarto capitalizes "Will" in lines 1–2 and 11–14) argue that she might as well sleep with Shakespeare, since she is already sleeping with the man (whose name may also be Will) and will no doubt sleep with countless "others."

These sonnets are generally read as evidence of the lady's promiscuity, but the only explicit reference to her multiple lovers is a question about her future behavior: "Shall will in others seem right gracious?" If she were indeed the promiscuous, sexually voracious woman that this conventional misogyny assumes, she might have agreed to "Think all but one, and me in that one will" (135. 14), or to "fill it full with wills, and my will one" (136. 6). But as this frenzy of hyperbolic requests reveals, she still refuses to sleep with Shakespeare. Certainly not Shakespeare's most magnanimous or appealing lyric persuasions, sonnets 135 and 136 seem more likely to titillate and amuse the man than to persuade the lady.

"About her sexual appetite and promiscuity," Schoenbaum writes (1980: 224), "there is no question; she is 'the bay where all men ride'." Critics never seem to notice that this phrase, which is constantly cited as evidence of the lady's promiscuity, is a question, made all the more hypothetical by Shakespeare's avowedly subjective point of view:

> If eyes corrupt by over-partial looks
> Be anchored in the bay where all men ride,
> Why of eyes' falsehood hast thou forgèd hooks,
> Whereto the judgement of my heart is tied?
> (137. 5–8)

"[M]uch virtue in If," as Touchstone remarks (*As You Like It*, V. iv. 103). Angry that she still won't sleep with him, and jealous of her hold on the man's attentions, Shakespeare imagines that she is available to anyone and everyone – everyone but himself, that is.

The dark lady sonnets draw us into a world where passion distorts judgment, where duplicity and role-playing are a mark of sophistication, and where it is difficult to distinguish truth from lies. Whereas sonnets 1–126 idealize and eternize the man, covering up or excusing his moral lapses, the dark lady sonnets set out to be honest about the woman's attractions and limitations. But Shakespeare's attempts to see and represent her accurately are foiled by his recognition that nothing she says to him and nothing he says about her can be trusted. The more he tries to report what is, rather than to portray what should be, the more desire befuddles judgment.

In the space between these sonnets and the next, the lady protests that his fantasies about her promiscuity are just that, fantasies: "my love swears that she is made of truth" (138. 1). Shakespeare pretends to believe her – "I do believe her though I know she lies" – because it flatters his ego "That she might think me some untutored youth" (138. 2–3). Although one may wonder why "critics have almost universally taken Shakespeare at his word on this point" (Schalkwyk 2002: 395; Stapleton 1983), even Shakespeare's most skeptical editors and critics, even the infinitely subtle Fineman, assume that "what she says is false" (1986: 170). Nonetheless, her declaration "that she is made of truth" lingers, offering an enticing hint of her outlying voice and contestatory point of view.

"No one questions the affair between the poet and the dark lady" (Schiffer 1999: 14), which is rather odd since almost everything else about Shakespeare's sonnets has been questioned. To be sure, he calls her "my mistress," which could mean a woman other than a wife with whom a man has a long-lasting sexual relationship. Yet in the sixteenth century "mistress" was more commonly used to mean: a woman who has control or authority; a woman loved or courted by a man, a sweetheart. If one begins with the assumption that the lady is sleeping with the speaker, then sonnet 138 means that he thinks she is lying when she says she is faithful to him. Yet the preceding and following sonnets make it clear that (1) she knows he knows she is sleeping with the man; (2) she continues to rebuff Shakespeare's sexual pursuit. In context, therefore, 138 means that he believes she is lying when she swears she cannot sleep with him because she is faithful to the man. Significantly, the pirated *Passionate Pilgrim* version, which was probably based on an early manuscript since it predates the first edition of the sonnets by a decade, makes it clear that Shakespeare's lies are an attempt to discredit the reasons she gives for sleeping with the man and not Shakespeare: "And wherefore sayes my love that she is young? / And wherefore say not I, that I am old" (138. 9–10). Moreover, *The Passionate Pilgrim* clearly concludes with a sexual fantasy: "Therefore I'll lie with Love, and Love with me": 138. 13).

Still, the 1609 text seems to disprove her claim to "truth" by revealing that she is indeed sleeping with Shakespeare:

> O love's best habit is in seeming trust,
> And age in love loves not to have years told.
> Therefore I lie with her, and she with me,
> And in our faults by lies we flattered be.
> (138. 11–14)

Yet, as the surrounding poems make clear, this witty sexual *double entendre* is the ultimate and most self-flattering lie of all, the lie the sonnet tells in order to make Shakespeare seem what he would like to be but is not: young and sexually triumphant.

Since 138 describes the lady in the third person, it was probably written not for her but for the man, and he, no doubt, would have been more amused than she by the poem's urbane sexual banter. At the same time, though, Shakespeare knew the man would probably show the sonnet to the lady, since that is how their relationship began. So what was the point? Is our beloved, many-minded Shakespeare trying to manipulate the lady by threatening to malign and misrepresent her if she refuses to have sex with him? Not a pretty thought, but one we must consider nonetheless, for two reasons. First, if the lyric dialogue is not a fiction, Shakespeare might, in fact, have circulated 138 to make those in the know think the lady was sleeping around; that would explain its appearance in the 1599 *Passionate Pilgrim*. (We will reconsider this point later.) Second, and more disturbing, only two sonnets later Shakespeare explicitly threatens to spread false reports about the lady unless she sleeps with him – "For if I should despair I should grow mad, / And in my madness might speak ill of thee" (140: 9–10) – which she still refuses to do: "do not press / My tongue-tied patience with too much disdain" (140: 1–2). If you cannot love me, Shakespeare tells her, at least act as if you do, or I will slander you.

If sonnets 135 and 136 are openly seductive and even a bit sleazy, and if 138 is clever and devious, then 140 is openly menacing, manipulative, and downright nasty – precisely the kind of irrational, immoral, predatory behavior predicted by 129: "till action lust / Is perjured, murd'rous, bloody, full of blame, / Savage, extreme, rude, cruel, not to trust" (ll. 2–4). Adopting a new, more distressed and (distressingly) aggressive tone, Shakespeare argues that his accusations will be believed, even if they are false: "Now this ill-wresting world is grown so bad, / Mad sland'rers by mad ears believèd be" (140. 11–12). Indeed, these "mad sland'rers" have been believed, for editors and critics continue to assume that the lady was a sexually voracious married woman, perhaps even a whore (Burrow [Shakespeare 2002: 648] "suggest[s] that the friend is paying for sex with the mistress") who slept with the sonnet speaker, the man, and countless others. But the reiterated allusion to the "mad" behavior prophesied by 129 – "no sooner had, / Past reason hated as a swallowed bait, / On purpose laid to make the taker mad; / Mad in pursuit, and in possession so" (ll. 6–9) – suggests that Shakespeare is threatening to add his voice to these "mad sland'rers" not because they speak truth, but because sexual frustration is driving him "mad." And what about the man? Sonnet 129 warns that "none" can "shun" the ill effects of "lust." Does that mean the man is "mad . . . in possession," "perjured" and "not to trust"?

In the following sonnets, Shakespeare's desire continues to grow, inflamed by the lady's rejection, while her resistance persists, fortified by her devotion to the man. Shakespeare admits that he is fantasizing about having sex with them both: "Nor taste, nor smell, desire to be invited / To any sensual feast with thee alone" (141. 7–8), which must have infuriated her because the next poem tries to make amends:

> Love is my sin, and thy dear virtue hate,
> Hate of my sin, grounded on sinful loving.
> O but with mine compare thou thine own state,
> And thou shalt find it merits not reproving,
> Or if it do, not from those lips of thine,
> That have profaned their scarlet ornaments,
> And sealed false bonds of love as oft as mine,
> Robbed others' beds' revénues of their rents.
> (142. 1–8)

Here, for the first time in the sequence, the language seems to suggest that the lady is a married woman who has betrayed her "bonds of love," her marriage vows, by distributing the "rents" or "revenues" – the marital "debt" or conjugal rights due her husband – to her various sexual partners. There is, however, another way to read the lines.

The comma at the end of line 7 is from the 1609 text, which (as Booth notes) frequently uses commas to mark a breathing pause. If you remove the grammatical break implied by modern usage, lines 7–8 mean that the lady's lips "sealed false bonds of love as oft as mine" – as often as Shakespeare's lips – "Robbed others' beds' revénues of their rents." In this case, the legal and financial terms "revenues" and "rents," with all the material and moral weight they bear, pertain not to the lady but to Shakespeare, who robbed his wife of the conjugal debt, the "revenues" to which his marriage vows entitled her, as well as the "rents," the financial gains that she and her children were legally entitled to share. Knowing that Shakespeare left Anne Hathaway behind in Stratford when he came to London to make his fame and fortune in the theater gives even greater weight to the root sense of "revenue" (from the French word, meaning that which returns or comes back). For the first time in the sequence, exoneration and blame are meted out equally.

With this concession, Shakespeare's hostility begins to abate, and the tone becomes considerably more ameliorative in the next sonnet, which represents the lady as a mother who puts her baby down to chase a fleeing fowl. Vendler, who is convinced of the lady's promiscuity, suggests she is chasing a "new lover" (1997: 602); Burrow cites "the other lovers whom she pursues" (Shakespeare 2002: 666). Yet Shakespeare's singular verb, "that which flies from thee," implies that she is chasing only "one of her feathered creatures" (143. 2). Indeed, the preceding poems make it clear that she is chasing the man, who is not an innocent barnyard creature but a "feathered" dandy (Kerrigan 1986: 374) whose fowl/foul flight threatens her dream of domesticity and motherhood – a scenario that is considerably more powerful and poignant if she is not already married to someone else.

She catches the man before he can run away, and they go off together, as we learn in the next poem, where Shakespeare's judgments seem more starkly black and white than ever: "The better angel is a man right fair, / The worser spirit a woman coloured ill" (144. 3–4). The pointed reference to "thy will" (143. 13), printed as "thy *Will*" in 1609, connects this sonnet to the two "will" sonnets that follow Shakespeare's discovery of their affair, and again hints that the man's name is also Will. Despite the blunt binarism of the opening lines, Shakespeare is beginning to suspect, as the sexual ambiguity of the conclusion hints, that they may have traded places: "I guess one angel in another's hell / Yet this shall I ne'er know, but live in doubt, / Till my bad angel fire my good one out" (144. 12–14).

The verb "fire," suggesting both coitus and inflammation, combined with the image of "one angel in another's hell" ["hell" being an idiomatic expression for vagina] has led scholars to infer that the lady gave the man venereal disease. Yet the sexually indefinite pronouns invite us to question that too. In their absence, Shakespeare can only "guess" and "suspect" but "not directly tell" "whether that my angel be turn'd fiend." By admitting that his doubts can be resolved only by ensuing events, Shakespeare again implies that the sonnets are contingent on circumstances they neither control nor fully comprehend. *The Passionate Pilgrim* version – "For being both to me: both, to each friend, / I guess one Angel in another's hell: / The truth I shall not know, but live in doubt" (144. 11–13) – multiplies the ambiguity and uncertainty, implying that the lady and the man are "both" "angel" and "fiend," "both to me" and to each other. Knowing that the man has run from domesticity in 143, there is reason to "suspect" that he may turn out to be the "bad angel" who "fire[s] my good one out." That raises the unsettling possibility that the lady may have been "coloured ill," put in a false light or represented unfairly, as the alternative meaning of "coloured" implies.

This suspicion is reiterated by the following sonnet, where "gentle day / Doth follow night, who like a fiend / From heav'n to hell is flown away," prompting us to ask again, more seriously, whether the man, who "flies from" the lady in 143, has turned "fiend" and flown away to hell, as 144 suspected he might. The truncated tetrameter lines, simple diction, and pun on Anne Hathaway's name ("hate away": 145. 13) have led critics (Gurr 1971; Booth, in Shakespeare 1977: 501) to think that 145 is an earlier sonnet, stuck in here; however, the pointed links to the preceding sonnets provide strong evidence to the contrary. Instead, as the simple clarity of the language and the missing fifth foot imply, 145 contains a discovery so revelatory that, like a visionary experience, it cannot be fully articulated or explained.

The structure of the sonnet, sandwiched between the two simple words, "I hate" (145. 2, 9, 13), and the two words that conclude the sentence and the sonnet, "not you," enacts the feeling of relief that comes flooding over Shakespeare as the clear light of day bursts through the dark clouds ("And taught it thus anew to greet" the day), clarifying the tortured, obsessive fantasies of 144. The effect is transformative: quite simply, her "mercy" "saved my life." Filled with hope for the first time since the man and the lady began sleeping together, another fear occurs to Shakespeare, the fear first raised by 143 that he now struggles to suppress (as the strained logic and syntax indicate) – the fear that his own marriage vows to Anne Hathaway could cast dark clouds over his reborn hope of winning the lady's love.

If so, are we now to believe, contrary to everything the sequence claimed earlier, that the man is actually the "worser spirit," and the dark lady, "the better angel"? But is it reasonable to place so much weight on one little simile ("who, like a fiend / From heaven to hell is flown away": 145. 11–12) and a single, possibly random echo of the preceding poem ("that my angel be turn'd fiend": 144. 9), especially when so many editors and critics have thought the dark lady sonnets are more disconnected, contradictory, and disordered than the young man sonnets? These qualms seem to be confirmed by the next sonnet, "Poor soul, the center of my sinful earth," generally considered the most disparate of the group. Still, connections among the dark lady sonnets are mounting.

When read in context, sonnet 146's sense of a "restored hierarchy" (Schoenfeldt 1999: 308) embodies the spiritual regeneration 145 describes. Now that the lady has raised hopes that he and she can start "anew" (145. 8), Shakespeare sets out to cleanse the negative thoughts that dominated the preceding sonnets. But, alas, as 129 prophesied, it is not so easy to escape the seemingly relentless cycle of "lust" and "disgust" that drove the man from the "heav'n" of sexual consummation to the "hell" of post-coital flight.

What follows is a dark night of the soul, where Shakespeare sounds more "desperate" and unhinged than ever before:

> Past cure I am, now reason is past care,
> And frantic mad with evermore unrest,
> My thoughts and my discourse as madmen's are,
> At random from the truth vainly expressed.
>
> (147: 9–12)

The emotional and interpretative crisis predicted by 129 reaches a climax in the couplet: "For I have sworn thee fair, and thought thee bright, / Who art as black as hell, as dark as night" (147. 13–14). The sonnets have repeatedly described the dark lady's "deeds" as "black," so whence comes the outraged shock and fury of this revelation – a revelation so unforeseen that Shakespeare claims it overturns everything he has previously "sworn" and "thought"?

To my knowledge no one has considered the possibility that 147 might be addressed to the man – not even Dubrow, who questions the division of the sonnets into two parts, or Fineman, who rests his argument on the foundational claim that, "unlike the young man," the dark lady "is not fair, and kind, and true" (1986: 174). Yet once alerted to the possibility, it seems obvious that what shines "bright" throughout the sonnets is not the lady, whose "eyes are nothing like the sun" (130. 1), who "make[s] me give the lie to my true sight, / And swear that brightness doth not grace the day" (150. 3–4), but the man, who is compared to a summer's day (18. 1) "That in black ink my love may still shine bright" (65. 14). And if it is not the lady but the man who is, and who has been all along, though unbeknownst to Shakespeare, "as black as hell, as dark as night" (147. 14), that would explain why Shakespeare is now in such a state of shock.

So "vexed with watching and with tears" (148. 10), Shakespeare no longer knows whether to trust his heart, which now seems to be madly in love with the lady, or his eyes, which find her fair even though he knows she has faults, or the world's judgment, which deems her more abhorrent than ever: "O, though I love what others do abhor" (150. 11). That he loves her is no longer in doubt; whether she deserves his love, or indeed whether he deserves her love, or whether she will return his love after all that has been said and done, remains in doubt.

The realization that everything he has "sworn" and "thought" to be true is now up for grabs throws Shakespeare into an emotional and hermeneutic crisis of unprecedented proportions. The following sonnets address themselves alternately to the man (148) and the lady (149), whose positions as good and bad angel seem to be in continual flux from this point on. The strain of trying to figure out who is being described and addressed forces us, like the sonnet speaker, to re-examine everything we know – everything we have taken for granted – about the lady and the man.

This deeply unsettling interpretative quandary reaches a climax in the last formal sonnet of the sequence, and, significantly, it is here that we encounter what seems to be conclusive proof of the dark lady's prior marriage to someone else: "In act thy bed-vow broke" (152. 3). The *OED* defines "bed-vow" as Shakespeareans have defined it, as a promise of fidelity to the marriage bed. Yet this is the first usage cited by the *OED*; the definition has no authority except the sonnet. To understand how to read "thy bed-vow broke," we need to place what has transpired between Shakespeare, the lady, and the man alongside English law and social practice.

According to the law, a promise to marry, followed by an oath made freely by both parties, constituted a legally binding betrothal, or marriage contract. Such an espousal *de futuro* could not be broken, except by mutual consent or for a "just" reason stipulated by law (if, for example, one of the parties was already pre-contracted to someone else, or if a familial tie precluded matrimony). After betrothal, most couples waited to solemnize their marriage in church until they had acquired sufficient goods and money to establish an independent household, or until they had convinced their kin to provide a dowry and marriage portion, or until the woman became pregnant. Yet many couples, especially in the lower and middling ranks but some in the upper ranks as well, began sleeping together once they were fast betrothed (Adair 1996), and for very good reason: an espousal, or promise to marry, even if made in the future tense and not confirmed by oath, comprised a legally binding common-law marriage when sealed by intercourse.

The coalescence of Elizabethan law and social practice make it more than likely if not all but certain that the lady and the man exchanged and then "broke" an espousal, a "bed-vow" that comprised a legally binding marriage when they solemnized their "vow" by going to "bed." The insistent, pervasive legal diction of sonnet 152 – "forsworn," "twice forsworn," "swearing," "bed-vow," "vowing," "two oaths' breach," "accuse," "perjured," "vows," "oaths," "sworn," "oaths," "oaths," "swear," "sworn," "perjured," "swear" – signifies that Shakespeare's interlocutor has not only broken faith – "all my honest faith in thee is lost" – but has also broken the law, which explains why "the sonnets portray a world dominated by legal, social, and verbal bonds" (Dubrow 1987, 246).

There is no need to posit a prior marriage to someone else to make the math work:

> In loving thee thou know'st I am forsworn,
> But thou art twice forsworn to me love swearing,
> In act thy bed-vow broke and new faith torn
> In vowing new hate after new love bearing.
> (152. 1–4)

The lady would be first "forsworn" by swearing her love to the man and then vowing "new hate" (as she does in sonnet 145); she would be "twice forsworn" by then swearing her love to Shakespeare. The problem is that the sonnets contain no indication that she ever swore her love to Shakespeare, as line 2 explicitly states. To be sure, that could have happened outside the sonnets, in the white spaces between 145 and 152 – except that the intervening sonnets contain numerous indications that Shakespeare is still trying to convince her to forgive his calumnies and return his love: "But, love, hate on, for now I know thy mind; / Those that can see thou lov'st, and I am blind" (149. 13–14). The dramatic situation fits the man *much* better: he was first "forsworn" when he swore his love to the dark lady after having sworn his love to Shakespeare (41. 12); he was "twice forsworn" when he abandoned the dark lady, denying that their "two oaths' breach" (152. 5) constituted a broken betrothal.

The end of sonnet 152 confirms this suspicion that it is the man, not the dark lady, who broke their bed-vow:

> And all my honest faith in thee is lost.
> For I have sworn deep oaths of thy deep kindness,
> Oaths of thy love, thy truth, thy constancy.
>
> (152. 8–10)

The plural "oaths" mentioned not once but twice, the doubly insistent "deep," "deep," intensified by the long vowel sounds, the continuing present perfect of "have sworn" – all this strengthens the force of "oaths" "sworn" repeatedly by Shakespeare over a long period of time. Yet the dark lady sonnets contain no such oaths. Shakespeare has twice entreated her to be "kind" ("Let no unkind, no fair beseechers kill" [135. 13]; "And play the mother's part, kiss me, be kind" [143. 12]), but he has repeatedly claimed she is "unkind": "So him I lose through my unkind abuse" (134. 12); "O call not me to justify the wrong / That thy unkindness lays upon my heart" (139. 1–2). It is not the lady but the man whom Shakespeare has called "kind": "For thou art covetous, and he is kind" (134. 6); "Kind is my love today, tomorrow kind, / Still constant in a wondrous excellence . . . Fair, kind, and true, is all my argument" (105. 5–9). To cinch the link to the man, "all my honest faith in thee is lost" could not be addressed to the dark lady because Shakespeare has never, ever, expressed any "honest faith" in her; on the contrary, he has repeatedly attacked her honesty and condemned her inconstancy: "When my love swears that she is made of truth, / . . . I know she lies" (138. 1–2).

"Oaths of thy love, thy truth, thy constancy" – that is precisely what Shakespeare has repeatedly "sworn" to the man, starting with the very earliest sonnets urging him to marry, where his eyes are "constant stars, in them I read such art / As truth and beauty shall together thrive" (14. 10–11). And that is what Shakespeare continues to swear in the sonnets where he is most enamored of the man: "Take all my comfort of thy worth and truth" (37. 4). When the man sleeps with the lady, Shakespeare complains, "thou art forced to break a twofold truth: / Hers, by thy beauty tempting her to thee, / Thine, by thy beauty being false to me" (41. 12–14); by sleeping with the man, the lady is false to herself, to her honor. By sleeping with her, the man is "false" to Shakespeare, but this doesn't stop Shakespeare from praising his "truth" and "constancy": "In all external grace you have some part, / But you like none, none you, for constant heart" (53. 13–14). Should any doubt remain, 152's penultimate line, "For I have sworn thee fair," echoes the first dark lady sonnet addressed to the man, repeating the very words that first signaled Shakespeare's loss of faith in the man – "For I have sworn thee fair, and thought thee bright" (147. 13).

Fair enough, but is this a circular argument? If some of the sonnets associated with the dark lady were actually addressed to the man, couldn't the poems describing the man as "fair," kind," "constant," and "true" have originally been addressed to the dark lady? A few, perhaps, but in most cases the pronouns and context make the reference to the man clear. The young man sonnets begin by urging him to marry; the dark lady sonnets begin by praising her unpainted beauty and skillful playing of the virginals, implying that she was a widely admired, well-educated, sensuous but virginal gentlewoman. Yet it never occurs to Shakespeare that the man and the lady were betrothed. Since the "Will sonnets" (135–6), "the bay where all men ride" (137), and the certitude that she was lying when she claimed she was "made of truth" (138) follow immediately after the revelation of their affair (132–4), the man must have represented her, not as his fiancée, but as a promiscuous seductress: "And when a woman woos, what woman's son / Will sourly leave her till he have prevailed?" (41. 7–8). Shakespeare was perfectly willing to forgive the man for succumbing to the lady's temptation. If, however, the man seduced, deceived, and slandered a virtuous virgin who had every reason to believe their "bed-vow" constituted an indissoluble marriage contract, that would be a very different matter. To be sure, Shakespeare himself threatened to spread rumors about her, but only after "Mad sland'rers by mad ears believèd be" (140. 12). Although Shakespeare may have begun to suspect it only when he wrote 140, the man was almost certainly the source of these "mad sland'rers," for he allowed the sonnets, which present the lady as promiscuous and deceitful, to circulate.

Shakespeare went to great lengths to keep the sonnet manuscripts carefully "locked up" (48. 9) in his own possession:

> How careful was I, when I took my way,
> Each trifle under truest bars to thrust,
> That to my use it might unusèd stay
> From hands of falsehood, in sure wards of trust!
>
> (48. 1–4)

But when the man went to visit the lady, Shakespeare was forced to relinquish the manuscripts to his safe keeping (45) – and was extremely upset to learn that the man allowed the sonnets to be stolen:

> But thou, to whom my jewels trifles are,
> Most worthy of comfort, now my greatest grief,
> Thou best of dearest, and mine only care,
> Art left the prey of every vulgar thief.
>
> (48. 5–8)

Shakespeare was too distressed about the consequences for himself and the man to worry about the lady; but now, in retrospect, it is clear that she is the one who suffered "the greatest grief."

Among the "just" reasons for dissolving an espousal *de futuro* are three that are directly pertinent to the rumors swirling around the lady: if one party is infected with some foul disease such as leprosy or the French pox; if a "deadly enmity" should spring up between the two parties; or if "there is a fame or common report, That there is some lawful impediment betwixt the Parties contracted, in which Case for fear of Scandal they are to be admonished, to abstain from marrying" (Swinburne 1686: 238–9). Even though espousals, once consummated, could not be dissolved in a court of law, by allowing the sonnets to circulate – and perhaps even arranging for 138 and 144 to be printed in *The Passionate Pilgrim* – the man created a climate "of fame or common report" that justified his rejection of the lady in the court of public opinion.

If the man not only seduced and abandoned a virtuous young virgin, but if he also lied to escape his moral and legal obligations to her, and if he then tried to justify his behavior by circulating poems and slanders insinuating that she was sleeping around and spreading venereal disease, that would make him not simply a jerk but a perjurer and a sinner – or, in the words of sonnets 144, 145, and 147, a "fiend" who deserves to burn in "hell" for destroying her honor and ruining her life. That would indeed change everything Shakespeare believed when he was writing the earlier sonnets to the man and the lady.

Shakespeare could hardly be more upset about his discovery of the man's duplicity – "all my honest faith in thee is lost" (152. 8). Yet he is even more upset, *much more* upset, by his own complicity and misjudgment: "I am perjured most, . . . / For I have sworn thee fair: more perjured eye, / To swear against the truth so foul a lie" (152. 6, 13–14). Shakespeare has been misled, first by his eye; second, by his sexual desires, his desire for her acquiescence, her "aye"; third by his ego, his "I"; and finally and most damningly, by his poet's delight in the play of language (eye/I/aye). With the unsettling and deeply disturbing discovery that his own sonneteering has affirmed and abetted the man's mad slanders, Shakespeare's sonnets come to an abrupt end.

The last formal sonnet in the young man sequence provides a premonition of the drama that is about to unfold in the dark lady sonnets that follow: "Hence, thou suborned informer! A true soul / When most impeached stands least in thy control" (125. 13–14). At this point, Shakespeare still believed, as the choice of the word "suborned" indicates, that the informer was using stealthy, underhand, or unlawful means to induce Shakespeare to give false testimony about the man. By 152, the end of the dark lady sequence, Shakespeare had discovered that the informer was more reliable, and his information more damning than Shakespeare was at first prepared to believe. (Are the numbers a hint that 152 reverses 125?)

The tone of shocked discovery and betrayal that concludes the dark lady sonnets provides powerful evidence that the sonnets continue to accrue complications as Shakespeare's relationships to the man and the lady unfold, reaching a paradigm-shattering revelation as the dark lady sonnets come to an end. The damning conclusion that it is the young man and not the dark lady who is "as black as hell, as dark as night" may seem to reverse, and thus to reaffirm, the binarism with which the sonnets began, but the effect is far more destabilizing than that. Rather than reaching a renewed sense of clarity and balance, Shakespeare is driven to the verge of madness by the discovery that his own desire to "swear" and "know," to make stark "black" and "bright" judgments, not only compounded but also to a large extent created the miserable misperceptions insinuated by the dark lady sonnets and repeated by scholars to this day.

III

Once we set aside the presumption of adultery, the dark lady sequence becomes a remarkably compelling representation of an intricate, unfolding, private lyric dialogue that ends, not with a stable resolution, but with a climactic, disruptive discovery. In theory, the dark lady sequence could be a fictional representation of a private lyric dialogue; however, it is difficult to argue that it is a successful fictional dialogue since the interactions between the characters and the interconnections teased out by this essay have eluded Shakespeare's commentators. More likely, the ambiguous language, enigmatic, unexplained conflicts, and veiled allusions to events occurring outside the sonnets were designed not to represent but to conceal Shakespeare's ongoing private lyric dialogue with the dark lady and the young man.

To clarify the abrupt ending somewhat, but not too much, Shakespeare added the two anacreontic sonnets and *A Lover's Complaint*. Sonnets 153 and 154 seek a cure for Shakespeare's lovesickness in a fountain where a virgin, dedicated to Diana, extinguished Cupid's flaming brand. These sonnets are usually seen as conventional fluff, designed to lighten the tone and bridge the gap between the dark lady sonnets and *A Lover's Complaint*. Yet the past tense, the overarching narrative perspective, the coded, allegorical language, and the story told not once but twice with the same tropes and only slightly different wording, reveal first, that a metamorphosis has occurred, bringing calm and clarity to the madness and torments of 147–52; second, that Shakespeare revisited the events enacted in the dark lady sonnets over and over again; third, that the only remedy for his former blindness lay in his mistress's eyes, where Cupid relit his brand and Shakespeare's love; fourth, that Shakespeare's continuing lovesickness can be cured only by his mistress – by the lady, not the man.

Cut to the opening of *A Lover's Complaint*, where the narrator observes a female complainant whose desperation verges on madness, echoing the distraction prophesied by sonnet 129 *and* dramatized by 147: "How have mine eyes out of their spheres been fitted / In the distraction of this madding fever!" (119. 7–8). As the male narrator watches the complainant weeping profusely, adding her tears to the stream's full course, the imagery recalls the fountain and tears of sonnets 153 and 154. The water imagery also summons up Shakespeare's response to learning that the young man and the lady were sleeping together (135. 9–12), hinting that *A Lover's Complaint* is a public apology for, and corrective to, earlier sonnets "coloured ill" with misrepresentations of the lady as "the bay where all men ride" (144. 4; 137. 6).

The male narrator observes the female complainant destroying her lover's tokens, letters, rings, and posies – material evidence that could have been used to corroborate a clandestine betrothal in a court of law (O'Hara 2000: 57–98). The story she tells makes it absolutely clear that the male lover, who bears an uncanny and irrefutable resemblance to the beautiful, androgynous young man of the sonnets (Bell 1999), pledged his "troth" with "holy vows" and a "strong-bonded oath" that comprised an espousal *de futuro* (*ALC*, ll. 177–80, 277–80). After convincing her to doff her "white stole of chastity" (l. 297), the male lover abandoned her to a life of dishonor, justifying his "bed-vow broke" (152. 3) with sanctimonious moral claptrap: "When he most burned in heart-wished luxury, / He preached pure maid and praised cold chastity" (ll. 314–15). The misery and near-madness that descend upon her fulfills the prophecy of sonnet 129: "Past reason hunted, and no sooner had, / Past reason hated as a swallow'd bait, / On purpose laid to make the taker mad / . . . / A bliss in proof, and proved, a very woe" (ll. 6–8, 11).

Because Shakespeareans have seen the dark lady as reprehensible and unforgivable, and the female complainant as "fickle" (*ALC*, l. 5) and unreliable, they have failed to realize that both women are maligned by an unscrupulous, dishonest, and fiendishly alluring young man – "with the garment of a grace / The naked and concealèd fiend he covered" (ll. 316–17) – which only goes to show that twentieth-century Shakespeareans were no less susceptible to deep-seated misogynistic assumptions than Shakespeare revealed himself to be when he fell for the young man: "A woman's gentle heart, but not acquainted / With shifting change, as is false women's fashion" (20. 3–4).

By giving the female complainant a voice, by allowing her to tell her story to the "reverend man" who listens sympathetically as she recounts the male lover's insidiously seductive proposal, *A Lover's Complaint* invites us to revisit the story discovered so belatedly and revealed so cryptically at the end of the dark lady sonnets. Dense with allusions to the sonnets (as Kerrigan's annotations and my essays delineate), *A Lover's Complaint*, like sonnet 129, provides an overview of, and guide to, the murky, mysterious drama the sonnets enact. Yet, Shakespeare being Shakespeare, it does so in an extremely intricate and challenging way. By making the male narrator an observer and eavesdropper whose perspective is subjective rather than omniscient, and by not bringing him back to sum up and assess what the male lover tells the female complainant and what she tells the reverend man, the complex layering of the narrative structure recreates the enigmatic interpretive challenge posed by the sonnets themselves.

The apparent disconnectedness of the sonnets, combined with the large number that could, in theory, have been addressed either to the young man or the dark lady, has led Heather Dubrow and others to question the traditional two-part division. In revisiting these questions, I have come to believe that the uncertainties about who is being addressed (and thus who is being praised or blamed) by any given sonnet, along with analogous uncertainties about who is to be believed or distrusted at any given moment in *A Lover's Complaint*, are not simply problems posed *for us* by the grammatical happenstance of the sonnets' second-person pronouns or the complaint's multiple speakers and shifting internal audiences. Rather, they are a dramatic enactment, and continuing re-enactment, of the shocking revelation and ensuing re-evaluation that Shakespeare himself experienced, much to his own consternation and bewilderment, as the dark lady sonnets drew to a close; the words the female complainant utters as the 1609 collection comes to an end – "Ay me! I fell; and yet do question make / What I would do again for such a sake" (*ALC*, ll. 321–2) – are, after all, Shakespeare's own.

In the end it turns out, just as sonnet 129 forewarned and as 137 and 138 might have alerted us if we had not been swayed by "lies" and "over-partial looks" (137. 5), that Shakespeare, as sonneteer and poet/lover, has been an unreliable narrator whose views we are "not to trust," not simply because like Prince Hal he deliberately cast a cloud over his true intentions, waiting for the right moment to reveal his carefully prepared plan of action, nor because, like Iago, he took a sheer villainous delight in manipulation, deception, and destruction, but because, like Othello and Antony, his own passions led him astray, driving him to the verge of madness, tempting him to endorse misogynist views that the situation seemed to support but that ensuing events revealed to be false. Upon discovering that he had unjustly promulgated the lady's dishonor and heartlessly magnified her misery, Shakespeare feels much as Antony does upon learning that Cleopatra was not a "Triple-turned whore," or as Othello does upon discovering that he has falsely abhorred and be-whored Desdemona.

The revelation that the young man made and "broke" a "bed-vow" induced Shakespeare to ask himself what we must now ask ourselves: Do the corruption and duplicity attributed to the dark lady and the female complainant belong instead to the young man and the male lover? And does the merciful forbearance shown the young man and the male lover deservedly belong to the dark lady and the female complainant? By not providing a definitive answer to these questions, Shakespeare implies that his own desire to "swear" and "know," to make binary "black" and "bright" judgments, not only compounded but also to a large extent created the miserable misperceptions promulgated by the sonnets and repeated by scholars to this day. Finally, by ending the sonnets with the interpretive crux of 147–152 and leaving the complaint's narrative frame unresolved, Shakespeare warns us not to seek or expect "simple truth" (138. 8).

By saving the more disturbing and accusatory sonnets to the young man for the end of the dark lady sequence, the first edition of *Shake-speares Sonnets* made it as difficult for us as it had been for Shakespeare himself to discover either the young man's perfidy or Shakespeare's confident but misguided complicity. Thus the analytic challenge bequeathed us by the 1609 sequence re-enacts the overarching hermeneutic crisis the dark lady sonnets confront – the hermeneutic problem that Shakespeare tried and failed to resolve in the later sonnets to the young man, that he revisited in 129, 153, and 154, retold in *A Lover's Complaint*, and re-enacted obsessively, over and over and over again, in *Much Ado About Nothing*, *All's Well That Ends Well*, *Measure For Measure*, *Hamlet*, *Othello*, *Antony and Cleopatra*, *Cymbeline*, and *A Winter's Tale*.

The widespread "revulsion" for the dark lady (Greenblatt 2004: 255) has prevented scholars from seeing crucial, clarifying links among the dark lady sonnets themselves. It has also occluded a large number of highly significant correlations between the sonnets and the plays. Moreover, it has raised unjustified doubts about Shakespeare's authorship of *A Lover's Complaint* by obscuring vital connections between the young man and the male lover, between the female complainant and the dark lady, and, even more revealingly, between the female complainant and Shakespeare. As sonnets 129 and 137 forewarned, Shakespeare has been an unreliable narrator, first as poet/lover who is too ready to say, "I know she lies" (138. 2), and later as observer/eavesdropper who is too quick to dub the female complainant "a fickle maid" (*ALC*, l. 5). Although he eventually acquires the knowledge and perspective that enables him to hear "this double voice" "reworded" (*ALC*, ll. 3, 1), like Claudio, Othello, Antony, and so many other misguided Shakespearean misogynists, his passions misled him, tempting him to see the situation from an "extreme" or "over-partial" point of view that ensuing events revealed to be "perjured, murd'rous, bloody, full of blame, / Savage, extreme, rude, cruel, not to trust."

References and Further Reading

Adair, Richard (1996). *Courtship, Illegitimacy, and Marriage in Early Modern England*. Manchester: Manchester University Press.

Barber, C. L. (1987). "An Essay on Shakespeare's Sonnets." In *Shakespeare's Sonnets*, ed. Harold Bloom, 5–27. New York: Chelsea House.

Bell, Ilona (1998). *Elizabethan Women and the Poetry of Courtship*. Cambridge, UK: Cambridge University Press.

Bell, Ilona (1999). "'That which thou has done': Shakespeare's Sonnets and *A Lover's Complaint*." In James Schiffer (ed.), *Shakespeare's Sonnets: Critical Essays*, 455–74. New York and London: Garland.

Bell, Ilona (2006). "Shakespeare's Exculpatory Complaint." In Shirley Sharon-Zisser (ed.), *Critical Essays on Shakespeare's "A Lover's Complaint": Suffering Ecstasy*. Aldershot: Ashgate.

Dubrow, Heather (1987). *Captive Victors: Shakespeare's Narrative Poems and Sonnets*, 169–257. Ithaca: Cornell University Press.

Dubrow, Heather (1999). "'Incertainties now crown themselves assur'd': The Politics of Plotting Shakespeare's Sonnets" (first publ. 1996). In James Schiffer (ed.), *Shakespeare's Sonnets: Critical Essays*, 113–34. New York and London: Garland.

Duncan-Jones, Katherine (1983). "Was the 1609 *Shake-speares Sonnets* Really Unauthorized?" *Review of English Studies* n.s. 34, 151–71.

Duncan-Jones, Katherine (1997). "Introduction." In *Shakespeare's Sonnets*, ed. Katherine Duncan-Jones. Nashville, Tenn.: Thomas Nelson. (The Arden Shakespeare.)

Edwards, Philip; Ewbank, Inga-Stina; and Hunter, G. K., eds. (1980). *Shakespeare's Styles: Essays in Honour of Kenneth Muir*. Cambridge, UK: Cambridge University Press.

Ferry, Anne (1975). "Shakespeare." In *All in War with Time: Love Poetry of Shakespeare, Donne, Jonson, Marvell*, 3–63. Cambridge, Mass.: Harvard University Press.

Fineman, Joel (1984). "Shakespeare's 'Perjur'd Eye'." *Representations* 7, 59–86.

Fineman, Joel (1986). *Shakespeare's Perjured Eye: The Invention of Poetic Subjectivity in the Sonnets*. Berkeley: University of California Press.

Fleissner, Robert F. (1973). "That 'cheek of night': Toward the Dark Lady." *College Language Association Journal* 16, 312–23.

Gowing, Laura (1996). *Domestic Dangers: Women, Words, and Sex in Early Modern London*. Oxford: Clarendon.

Greenblatt, Stephen (2004). *Will in the World: How Shakespeare Became Shakespeare*. New York: Norton.

Gurr, Andrew (1971). "Shakespeare's First Poem: Sonnet 145." *Essays in Criticism* 21, 221–6.

Hieatt, A. Kent; Hieatt, Charles W.; and Prescott, Anne Lake (1991). "When Did Shakespeare Write *Sonnets* 1609?" *Studies in Philology* 88, 69–109.

Hyland, Peter (2003). *An Introduction to Shakespeare's Poems*. Basingstoke: Palgrave Macmillan.

Ingram, Martin (1987). *Church Courts, Sex, and Marriage in England, 1570–1640*. Cambridge, UK: Cambridge University Press. (Past and Present Publications.)

Jackson, MacDonald P. (1999). "Shakespeare's Sonnets: Rhyme and Reason in the Dark Lady Sonnets." *Notes and Queries* 46, 219–22.

Marotti, Arthur (1982). "'Love is not love': Elizabethan Sonnet Sequences and the Social Order." *English Literary History* 49, 396–428.

Meres, Francis (1598). *Palladis Tamia*. London.

O'Hara, Diana (2000). *Courtship and Constraint: Rethinking the Making of Marriage in Tudor England*. Manchester: Manchester University Press.

Ramsey, Paul (1979). *The Fickle Glass: A Study of Shakespeare's Sonnets*. New York: AMS Press.

Schalkwyk, David (1994). "'She never told her love': Embodiment, Textuality, and Silence in Shakespeare's Sonnets and Plays." *Shakespeare Quarterly* 45, 381–407.

Schalkwyk, David (2002). *Speech and Performance in Shakespeare's Sonnets and Plays*. Cambridge, UK: Cambridge University Press.

Schiffer, James (1999). "Reading New Life into Shakespeare's Sonnets: A Survey of Criticism." Introduction to James Schiffer (ed.), *Shakespeare's Sonnets: Critical Essays*, 3–71. New York and London: Garland.

Schiffer, James, ed. (1999). *Shakespeare's Sonnets: Critical Essays*. New York and London: Garland.

Schoenbaum, Samuel (1980). "Shakespeare's Dark Lady: A Question of Identity." In Philip Edwards, Inga-Stina Ewbank, and G. K. Hunter (eds.), *Shakespeare's Styles: Essays in Honour of Kenneth Muir*, 221–39. Cambridge, UK: Cambridge University Press.

Schoenfeldt, Michael (1999). "The Matter of Inwardness: Shakespeare's Sonnets." In James Schiffer (ed.), *Shakespeare's Sonnets: Critical Essays*, 305–24. New York and London: Garland.

Sedgwick, Eve Kosofsky (1985). "Swan in Love: The Example of Shakespeare's Sonnets." In *Between Men: English Literature and Male Homosocial Desire*, 28–48. New York: Columbia University Press.

Shakespeare, William (1609). *Shake-speares sonnets Neuer before imprinted*. London.

Shakespeare, William (1599). *The passionate pilgrim*. London.

Shakespeare, William (1977). *Shakespeare's Sonnets*, ed. Stephen Booth. New Haven: Yale University Press.

Shakespeare, William (1986). *The Sonnets and A Lover's Complaint*, ed. John Kerrigan New York: Viking Penguin. (The New Penguin Shakespeare.)

Shakespeare, William (2002). *The Complete Sonnets and Poems*, ed. Colin Burrow. Oxford: Oxford University Press. (Oxford World's Classics.)

Spiller, Michael R. G. (1992). *The Development of the Sonnet: An Introduction*. London: Routledge.

Stapleton, M. L. (1983). " 'My false eyes': The Dark Lady and Self-Knowledge." *Studies in Philology* 90, 213–30.

Swinburne, Henry (1686). *A treatise of spousals*. London.

Vendler, Helen (1997). *The Art of Shakespeare's Sonnets*. Cambridge, Mass.: Harvard University Press.

Wall, Wendy (1993). *The Imprint of Gender: Authorship and Publication in the English Renaissance*. Ithaca, NY: Cornell University Press.

Wright, George T. (1999). "The Silent Speech of Shakespeare's Sonnets." In James Schiffer (ed.), *Shakespeare's Sonnets: Critical Essays*, 135–59. New York and London: Garland.

19

Flesh Colors and Shakespeare's Sonnets

Elizabeth D. Harvey

Our modern sense of the word "spectrum" as a "colored band into which a beam of light is decomposed by means of a prism" came into the English language in 1671 in Isaac Newton's writings on optics and the reflecting telescope.[1] Before Newton, however, the word meant an apparition or phantom, a sense that survives in our current meaning of "specter." Both spectrum and specter have the Latin *specere*, "to look," as their root, and both words raise questions about the nature of bodies and the role of the senses, particularly vision. The etymological coupling of these connotations of the spectral will inform this essay, for I will argue here that color is a discourse that haunts early modern poetics, not least in the commonplace phrase "the colors of rhetoric," which designated a linkage of language with visible color, an analogical modeling of rhetoric on painting. I will suggest, however, that the parallel between language and art was far from simple, and that rhetoric's colors depended upon a ghostly discourse of natural historical knowledge that invisibly shaped the chromatic lexicon of Shakespeare's sonnets and early modern poetry in general.

Readers of Shakespeare's sonnets have noted that the sequence moves along a gamut of color, from the "fairest creatures" of the first sonnet to the praise of "black" in sonnet 127. The narrative of the sequence is often described as an opposition between colors, a contrast between the fairness of the young man and the blackness of the dark lady. Recent critics have given us powerful readings that lend new cultural force to these categories of color, for they argue that darkness can be correlated with race and ethnicity: it is aligned in A. L. Rowse's early and highly problematic formulation with the dark skin of the Italianate Aemilia Lanyer, and in other more recent suggestions, advanced by such scholars of early modern colonialism as Kim Hall, with the negro or blackamoor.[2] The race argument has been intriguingly articulated by Margreta de Grazia, who suggests that the scandal of the sonnets is not the portrayal of homosexual love, but the representation of racial mixing, of miscegenation.[3] Sujata Iyengar's *Shades of Difference* makes the correlation between skin hue and race central to the arguments about England's early modern recognition of the cultural otherness within its own national boundaries.[4]

However, rather than seeing skin tone primarily in terms of race, a context in which words like "colored" or "black and white" carry a specifically racialized ideological and social charge that was not yet fully developed for early modern subjects, I will investigate here the place that the chromatic occupied in the early modern cultural imaginary. Color was more than the shade of skin visible to the eye; it was the expression of an entire bodily composition that included a relatively opaque interior. Attention to a more encompassing understanding of color is thus essential to a comprehension of the way the chromatic register works both in the sonnets and in the cultural imaginary of this period. Color had various sources that ranged from the philosophical and artistic to the medical and rhetorical, and the richness of this chromatic vocabulary laid the groundwork for a structure onto which discourses of race could ultimately graft themselves.

We might instructively approach this topic through Anne Carson's writing on Stesichorus in *The Autobiography of Red*. Stesichorus (650–555 BCE), the Greek lyric poet whose surviving poetic fragments recount Hercules' attempt to steal Geryon's red cattle, was according to Carson, the master of the adjective, those words that are appended, added, or foreign. This sense is derived from the Greek *epitheton*, "placed on top," and far from being simply dependent, ornamental lexical parts, adjectives are in Carson's view "the latches of being."[5] She suggests that whereas Homeric poetry attached adjectives to substantives as a kind of stable code, Stesichorus undid the latches, uncoupling objects and their epithets. The *OED*'s second definition for the adjective is "colors that are not permanent without a basis," a meaning that suggests both how frequently color occupies the adjectival position and also how complex the relationship between substance, what stands under, and the adjective, what is placed on top, actually is. Color and adjectives share a strange spatial quality: both are deemed to be simply additive, delicately attached to a substance, and yet, once joined, both can appear not only to modify but also to constitute an inherent property of the substance.

Aristotle's writings may help us to understand this apparently contradictory topography. He posits in *De sensu* that all bodies are transparent, and yet because all entities must have a defining boundary, that margin must be color.[6] Color, he suggests, is the limit or surface of a body. In *De anima* Aristotle tells us that color is what makes a body visible by "overlying" its transparency,[7] depending upon and making manifest the host body. Substance or flesh is diaphanous, transparent, and it is only pigmentation that gives it the visibility and solidity that we associate with flesh. Sir John Davies expatiates on this Aristotelian point in *Nosce teipsum*:

> For though our eyes can nought but Colors see;
> Yet colors give them not their power of sight;
> So though these fruites of Sense her objects bee,
> Yet she discerns them by her proper light.[8]

The chromatic, in other words, calls a body into sensuous life, rendering it accessible to the eye through the addition of light. In this interpretation, color is less an inherent property of the body than a necessary part of the sensory mechanism of vision, a quality that is brought into being through the interplay of object, light, and the faculty of sight.

These ideas are modified by Hippocratic and Galenic medical theory, according to which bodies were composed of a mixture of four humors (blood, phlegm, yellow bile, and black bile), each humor being designated by a color. The balance of the humoral mixture manifested itself in complexion, which plaited together not only elements of hot, cold, moist, and dry, but also the red, yellow, black, and white of the humoral spectrum.[9] Color in this medical sense is then a system of signs displayed on the exterior of the body that describes an interior imaginable through a semiotics of color. Hues on the surface of the body or in its excretions are messengers, carriers of information transported from an inscrutable centre to the body's margins. The vocabulary of color is thus most articulately developed in medicine and in erotic discourse, both of which from their respective diagnostic perspectives are preoccupied with reading the body's signs and structures, with surveying its surface for intelligence about a hidden interior.

Stephen Batman's 1582 Englishing of Bartholomaeus's thirteenth-century encyclopedia *De proprietatibus rerum*, a popular reference work of natural history, provides a representative account of color. The description draws heavily on Aristotle's *De sensu*, and it integrates humoral theory into its extended discussion of the way that vision and light make the eye receptive to color. All colors "abide in darknesse," we learn, and while light is necessary for the "spredd[ing]" of color in the aire, "light needeth not to the being of colour but onely to the shewing thereof."[10] Although they cannot be perceived in the dark, colors are nevertheless not "idle."[11] Hues are at war, constantly seeking mastery over each other, and all color is a function of the relative elemental proportions of moisture and heat. *De proprietatibus rerum* displays the convergence of the humors and the passions that becomes a characteristic of color theory (changes in the skin's hues "commeth sometime of humours inwarde and sometime of passions of the soule"[12]): not only does it delineate a system that explained human complexion and its accompanying manifestation of behavior, but the language Bartholomaeus uses to describe the optics of color is itself saturated with passionate agency: "Betweene whitnes and blacknes are many meane degrees following the mastrie of qualities that be active and passive, working and suffering, as they be more strong or feeble."[13] The ardent competition among colors is also a struggle among the elements: air continually propels substances toward the light and whiteness, and the density of earth incessantly pulls matter toward darkness. To understand these forces, argues Bartholomaeus, is to "grow from the spirit of death, singular, and plural, from the Adjective to the Substantive," to comprehend not just how colors "please the eye," but also how they "beautifie the soule."[14] Color is a lexicon of being, an expression of elemental combination that manifests itself in such natural bodies as fruit and flowers, and a chromatic language whose workings are specifically grammatical, revealing itself in the change from singular to plural and in the complex conjunction of adjective and substantive.

The language of color that characterizes early modern sonnets is thus already coded with a set of metaphysical and natural historical ideas about the world, language, the body, and the passions. While color is a predominant feature of the sonnet lady's canonical description – the familiar golden hair, the red and white of her complexion – this praise is also cognate with medical descriptions of lovesickness. In other words, the vocabulary of color is a feature of the objectifying and desiring gaze, but the chromatic also emerges from within the subject as part of the symptomology of erotic love. Jacques Ferrand's *Erotomania*, for instance, cites a "change of color" as one of the most recognizable signs of love melancholy.[15] His chapter on "The Cause of Paleness in Lovers" begins by noting that paleness is the "Color & Badge of Love," and then goes on in great detail to anatomize whiteness as an expression of green and yellow. His conclusion is that the humors, "unless they retire into the most inward parts of the Body, appears [*sic*] evidently in the skinne: but chiefly in the Face, because that the skinne of that part is more thin and fine, then of any other part; and therefore the more apt to receive the tincture of the Putrified Humors."[16]

That Shakespeare was fluent in this discourse of color is clearly evident in *The Rape of Lucrece*. When Tarquin first meets Lucrece, beauty and virtue strive for mastery in her face, a contest that manifests itself in color, a "silent war of lilies and of roses," a match between "beauty's red and virtue's white."[17] That the blood rushes to her cheeks and recedes in waves provides an image of the blush that resonates throughout the poem in its dialectic between the secrecy of the body's recesses and its surface, between color and how it is received and "read" by the eye. A few lines later, we learn that Tarquin "colored" his motives, disguising his intention by cloaking himself in hues. Lucrece cannot interpret his sign system, although she herself had already spoken eloquently in chromatic tones, an expression of what Luce Irigaray has called the *chroma soma*,[18] a fleshly body speaking through color. Tarquin and Lucrece exemplify the divergent, even contradictory history of color's meanings, for Lucrece embodies color's apparent capacity to express the body's inner secrecy, its hidden truths, whereas Tarquin figures color's capacity to disguise, to present a deceitful cover or corruption of correspondence between inner and outer.

Shakespeare begins to problematize the conventionalities of chromatic language in *The Rape of Lucrece* not only through his use of color to mean masking or concealing, but through his attention to the consequences of vision, the social implications of looking. To what extent does color express the invisibility or transparency of psychic operations, giving them bodily form and sensory existence? The blood that flows from Lucrece's breast when she kills herself stages a spectacular semiotics of color, dividing into two streams of pure red and seemingly tainted black blood, as if the hidden registers of color within her body could when externalized be interpreted as clear evidence of virtue.[19] The difficulty in *Lucrece* lies not only in the interpretation of this syntax of color, but in its transposition into the "colors of rhetoric," and this is, of course, the problem that Shakespeare grapples with in the sonnets: how to translate what Joel Fineman terms the "material logic of the person" into a language adequate to its expression.[20] Color is central to this process both because Shakespeare is working with an inherited vocabulary of praise that makes the chromatic a central feature and, more importantly, because color is one of the most potent early modern discourses about the material person, about the relations between psychic life, gender, and the increasingly inscrutable, unreadable surfaces of the body.

I want to test some of these claims by examining closely several sonnets. The first is sonnet 104:

> To me, fair friend, you never can be old,
> For as you were when first your eye I eyed,
> Such seems your beauty still. Three winters cold
> Have from the forests shook three summers' pride,
> Three beauteous springs to yellow autumn turned
> In process of the seasons have I seen,
> Three April pérfumes in three hot Junes burned,
> Since first I saw you fresh, which yet art green.
> Ah yet doth beauty, like a dial hand,
> Steal from his figure, and no pace perceived;
> So your sweet hue, which methinks still doth stand,
> Hath motion, and mine eye may be deceived:
>   For fear of which, hear this, thou age unbred,
>   Ere you were born was beauty's summer dead.[21]

The poem turns on an exchange of vision between the poet and the young man, crystallized in the "your eye I eyed," a phrase that joins the speaker and the fair friend in their reciprocal gaze. It makes the "eye" both an instrument of vision and a seen object, a mirroring that is both reproduced and distorted in the acoustic register through the insertion of the subject, the "I," between "eye" and "eyed." This specular echo anticipates the analogic reflection that informs the poem: the comparison between human age and seasonal change. Nature's cycles express themselves in caloric shifts that are in turn displayed as changes in color, from green spring to yellow autumn. Color functions as a temporal marker, and the potential for chromatic mutation is immanent, for just as one color becomes another through the addition of heat or cold, so does the human body contain the seeds of its own changing colors through time, as in the "sable curls all silvered o'er with white" of sonnet 12. Time writes on human bodies in cryptic signs, and color is one of its most dramatic markers. The reassurance that the speaker proffers in sonnet 104 is that the friend's beauty is "still," a word that is used twice in the poem: in both cases, the very oscillation between the sense of "still" as motionless and the adverbial meaning of "always" undermines the promise of stability that the word seems to hold. "Green" is the fulcrum of the analogy between natural and human worlds, a kind of chromatic seepage from one register to the other that carries with it the inevitable progress of seasonal change.[22] We are thus prepared for the representation of the gradual diminution of beauty, which, while it does not appear to alter, nevertheless, like the friend's "sweet hue" – a phrase that joins "Aprils perfume" with spring's green – only appears "still" to stand. The senses are deceived by their sensuous lingering on beauty, and the theft of youth's color is as inevitable as it is imperceptible.

The analogy between human bodies and plants is not just metaphorical, of course, but also relied in part on the Renaissance doctrine of signatures, the belief that natural objects expressed their purpose through a language of inscribed signs. Galen and Paracelsus allude to the way in which signatures reveal the essence of things and their curative potential through the attributes of shape and color, a theory that was codified in Jacob Boehme's *Signatura rerum* and enacted in herbal medicine by such practitioners as Nicholas Culpeper.[23] This chromatic homoeopathy is at work in the description in John Gerard's *Herball* of the virtues of plants like saffron, which was derived from the stigmas of the saffron crocus and could cure jaundice because the flower and the malady shared a yellow hue, and black hellebore, which was especially efficacious for purging the black bile that produced melancholy or for eradicating black spot on the skin.[24] Flowers, especially roses, often function in the sonnets in this analogic way, providing a natural language for human attributes; in sonnet 54 – "The canker blooms have full as deep a dye / As the perfumed tincture of the roses" – color serves as a delusive sign system that fails to distinguish the true rose from its false copy.[25] While the canker rose is the common name for the dog rose (*Rosa canina*) in such treatises as John Gerard's *Herball*,[26] the emphasis of the line falls on the canker, a word that evokes the fungal blight to which roses are particularly prone, a progressive infestation that ultimately turns the rose plant black. The flower's color deceives the eye, suggesting an interior depth and longevity that can be fully verified only by the olfactory sense, by the true rose's sweet odor. Lurking within the flower's color is a dye, color's afterlife, an infection of hue that usurps the native pigment in an ultimately fatal chromatic suffocation, registered in the homonymic dye/die.[27] A body's outside becomes by analogy an erotics of surface that gestures toward an inside; yet the correlation between inner and outer is radically unstable, contaminating erotic relations, not just in the canker that may lie at the flower's heart but in the lover's inability to distinguish between the rose and its bastard or counterfeit double.

Sonnet 99 is a blazon that draws on classical, biblical, and Petrarchan traditions of comparing the beloved's body to a catalogue of flowers. Shakespeare's speaker apostrophizes the violet, lily, marjoram, and rose, singling out their floral attributes – color and scent – and declaring each deficient by comparison to the beloved. He inverts the conventional analogy by insisting that the flowers have stolen their distinguishing characteristic from the beloved: "The purple pride / Which on thy soft cheek for complexion dwells, / In my love's veins thou hast too grossly dyed." What begins as analogic becomes in this comparison an infiltration and conceptual tangling, a transgression of the body's boundaries, as if the flower had invaded these venous passageways and mortally immersed itself there, its violet color the mark of that bloody saturation. The action of dyeing is a transfer not only of color but also of identity; like the "dyer's hand" of sonnet 111, its "nature is subdued / To what it works in." "Subdue," etymologically associated with seduction, carries the sense of deceit, theft, and overpowering, as if amorous and sexual relationships involved a tainting or blending of color that was also a transfer of fundamental nature. Early modern treatises on horticulture and natural history, such as Giambattista della Porta's *Natural Magick*, frequently refer to the practice of grafting as a way of altering or enhancing the color of flower and fruit. The term that della Porta uses to describe this floral grafting is "meddling," a word that is derived from the Latin *miscere*, to mix, but which also meant by extension either to have sexual intercourse or to interfere.[28] The metaphoric traffic between human and floral bodies inevitably evokes Ovid and the metamorphosis of Adonis and Clytie, intertexts that call up both sex and death as surely as the phrase "purple pride" suggests the sexual engorgement of blood.[29] Sonnet 99 is the only one of Shakespeare's sonnets to exceed fourteen lines, and the supernumerary line is usually considered to be line 5, "In my love's veins thou hast too grossly dyed."[30] The tincture of color appears not only to have exceeded the metaphoric border between flower and body, but also to have spilled over structurally, replicating itself in a suffusion of both color and rhyme. The parallelism of color and scent thus becomes an invasion of boundary, an imaging of the intimacy of sexual congress in language that is also a transgression of bodily and poetic limit.

Sonnets 97, 98, and 99 are often seen as linked by editors, who remark on the proliferation of seasonal and horticultural imagery and on the saturation of these metaphors with what Stephen Booth calls "the unexploited relevance to sexual love."[31] It is clear that Shakespeare is drawing on a rich medical, natural historical, and poetic tradition that conflates descriptions of human reproduction with the fecundity of the natural world. The "proud lap" of sonnet 98 that produces the "lily's white" and "the deep vermilion in the rose" refers most obviously to a hollow in the land that shelters and nurtures the flowers growing there, but "lap" just as frequently referred to the female pudendum. Helkiah Crooke in his English anatomy treatise of 1615, *Mikrocosmographia*, entitled Book 4, Chapter XVI on the female sexual organs "Of the Lap or Privitites," and the image on his title-page features a woman whose genitals are covered with a flower.[32] This representation was, of course, entirely conventional, depicting as it did what was already embedded in language: flowers, and the rose in particular, frequently figured (usually female) sexual organs, "flowers" was a euphemism for the "courses" or menstruation,[33] and defloration connoted the loss of virginity. The shared reproductive functions of plants and humans became a feature of medical description from its earliest formulations: the analogies between human and plant reproduction figure centrally in Hippocrates' treatises "On Seed" and "The Nature of the Child."[34] Because flowers have visible reproductive structures and because encoded desire is proclaimed in their color and perfume, they come to stand by analogy for a less manifest human sexual and reproductive longing, a conflation that sonnet 1 famously announces: "From fairest creatures we desire increase, / That thereby beauty's rose might never die." The displacement of sexuality into a botanical register, or of horticultural analogies into a human context, is in the young man sonnets an externalization of sexuality that is projected into a botanical landscape of color. The flowers that figure in Shakespeare's sonnets are distinguished not only by their fragrance and hue ("deep vermilion," "purple pride"), then, but also by the passions that they seem to exemplify. The roses of sonnet 99 "stand" "fearfully," "One blushing shame, another white despair." In sonnet 95, shame hides likes a canker in the rose, and in sonnet 67, the rose is again likened to the young man's blush, as if its appearance in his cheek testified not only to the surge of blood, but also to a vocabulary of affect and erotic possibility. Flowers do not function in the sonnets in any kind of simple analogic way. Rather, they infiltrate, expressing through color, scent, and emotional valence the intimacy of the body's inner psychic and imaginative life.

The erotic and chromatic aspects of horticulture are contrasted and extended through a second discourse of color: the language of painting and specifically of cosmetics. These references typically set the artifice of painting against nature, often depicting the young man's beauty as needing no cosmetic adornment, as in sonnet 83: "I never saw that you did painting need, / And therefore to you fair no painting set." Yet the opposition is never simple. The "deep vermilion in the rose" of sonnet 98 borrows the term from painting: the red crystalline mercuric sulphide that produced this brilliant red was a highly prized pigment used by painters and in sealing wax.[35] Sonnet 67 is especially pointed in its invocation of painting's counterfeit color:

> Ah wherefore with infection should he live
> And with his presence grace impiety
> That sin by him advantage should achieve,
> And lace itself with his society?
> Why should false painting imitate his cheek,
> And steal dead seeing of his living hue?
> Why should poor beauty indirectly seek
> Roses of shadow, since his rose is true?
> Why should he live, now nature bankrout is,
> Beggared of blood to blush through lively veins?

Shakespeare's use of "infection" in the sonnet's first line activates its root in the Latin *inficere*, to stain or taint. The poem is thus structured around the sense of infection as both dye and contagion, with this doubleness simultaneously figuring the duplicity of cosmetic counterfeiting and suggesting that painting contaminates or infects nature. As Giambattista della Porta's chapter on "Beautifying Women" in *Natural Magick* makes clear, almost all forms of cosmetic alteration involved changing color. Della Porta describes dyes for altering the color of the hair to gold, red, or black; he offers methods for painting the face white or rose, making the eyebrows black, coloring the body, taking away redness in the complexion, covering red pimples and black spots, even changing the color of children's eyes.[36] One recipe for whitening the complexion literalizes the floral metaphors of the sonnets, for it calls for washing the face repeatedly in a liquid of distilled lilies. Other methods are more drastic, such as the mercury and quicksilver sublimate he recommends, or – since Della Porta recognizes the intensely hazardous nature of this precipitate – the alternative he suggests: a less toxic concoction of white lead.[37] These sorts of cosmetic painting literally engendered infection, of course, because the metals and dyes seeped into the body, creating corrosive effects on the skin it was designed to improve, and causing irreparable harm to the internal organs and the nervous system. Sonnet 67's imaging of painting as a theft of the young man's storehouse of color, as a "beggar[ing] of blood to blush through lively veins," sets up an apparent contest between nature and artifice that aligns nature with life and painting with mortality, a monitory comment for those who sought to halt time through artifice. Yet as the sonnets repeatedly show, the depictions of color as natural or as deceptively contrived frequently overlap, ultimately blurring the distinction between reality or nature and its mimetic illusion.

Shakespeare's verse drew inevitably on the "flowers" and "colors" of rhetoric, a discourse codified in George Puttenham's *Arte of English Poesie*. Color as linguistic or rhetorical ornament is as necessary to the production of persuasive language as it was to Aristotle's sense of how the chromatic defines the bounds of a body. Nevertheless, Puttenham is forthright in his advice about the use of rhetorical figures, for, just as with cosmetic "art" or painting, the ornamental dimension of language must conform to the standards of decorum:

> This ornament we speake of is given to it by figures and figurative speaches, which be the flowers as it were and coulours that a Poet setteth upon his language by arte, as the embroderer doth his stone and perle, or passements of gold upon the stuffe of a Princely garment, or as th'excellent painter bestoweth the rich Orient coulours upon his table of pourtraite: so neverthelesse as if the same coulours in our arte of Poesie (as well as in those other mechanicall artes) be not well tempered, or not well layd, or be used in excesse, or never so little disordered or misplaced, they not onely give it no maner of grace at all, but rather do disfigure the stuffe and spill the whole workmanship taking away all bewtie and good liking from it, no lesse then if the crimson tainte, which should be laid upon a Ladies lips, or right in the center of her cheekes should by some oversight or mishap be applied to her forhead or chinne, it would make (ye would say) but a very ridiculous bewtie, wherfore the chief prayse and cunning of our Poet is in the discreet using of his figures, as the skilfull painters is in the good conveyance of his coulours and shadowing traits of his pensill, with a delectable varietie, by all measure and just proportion, and in places most aptly to be bestowed.[38]

Puttenham's description joins painting and the discourse of cosmetics with rhetoric (a conjunction that famously informs Plato's *Gorgias*), the ornamental coloring of language through the addition of figures and "flowers." Implicit in Puttenham's articulation is the idea that color is not, in fact, simply ornamental to portraiture, cosmetics, or poetry but constitutive of them. Indeed, the chromatic register may be said to be a language of its own. This primacy is evident in the vigorous Renaissance debates over painting, which set color and design in opposition to one another; colorists were often aligned with such fleshly and evanescent concerns as cosmetics, pleasure, and emotion, whereas the advocates of drawing were associated with abstract ideas, the intellect, and regulation.[39] Yet Renaissance defenders of painting such as Giorgio Vasari and Giovanni Paolo Lomazzo argued that painting had the capacity through color to represent not only the visible exterior form of the body but also its invisible interior, particularly the emotions.[40]

The notion of a chromatic language that could express what escaped the symbolic representation that is so important to Renaissance art theory is also central to more recent work on color, exemplified in Luce Irigaray's essay "Flesh Colors" and in Julia

Kristeva's analysis of painting, "Giotto's Joy."[41] Both theorists seek to explain how it is that through color the subject "escapes its alienation within a code (representational, ideological, symbolic, and so forth) that it, as conscious subject, accepts."[42] Kristeva claims that the "chromatic apparatus" is like rhythm in language: each functions outside of the symbolic dimensions of language, as an excess or a residue of meaning that cannot be processed within the existing linguistic or representational systems. Even though particular colors might be demanded by a particular historical necessity or form (such as, for instance, the sonnet lady's colors), color is still, according to Kristeva, "the space where the prohibition foresees and gives rise to its own immediate transgression."[43] In painting, she tells us, "color is pulled from the unconscious into the symbolic order." Even though the subject attempts to process color according to representational systems, through its own resistance color defies symbolic censorship and produces an irruption of the unconscious in representation. "[H]eavy with 'semantic latencies,'" color thus returns the subject to a more archaic moment in its development, to the beginning of its instantiation into the symbolic order.[44] The unconscious (or, for Irigaray, the imaginary) dimensions of color reveal how Shakespeare's use of color in the sonnets is powerfully linked to his imaging of interiority, affect, and the imagination.

The play of color as a correspondence between the body's appearance and its inner gendered or psychic nature is central to the treatment of color in sonnet 20, "A woman's face, with nature's own hand painted." The young man is described as "A man in hue all hues in his controlling," a line that has many interpretations, but whose interest for my purposes lies in the play between color as an involuntary revelation of interior thought and hue as an appearance that can be controlled or used to reveal an inner process that is feigned. The "living hue" of sonnet 67 that "blush[es] through lively veins" offers a more conventional representation of this humoral commerce, but in sonnet 20 the young man's ability to manage its ebbs and flows implies a camouflaging of somatic signs that would seem to master the vulnerability that erotic desire confers upon the subject. If "hue" refers to complexion, then to control the expression of color on the body's surface suggests a disruption of correspondence between face and mind, an intervention into and manipulation of the natural order. Stephen Booth reminds us that one meaning of "hue" was "phantasm or apparition," a spectral sense that figures the unseen and gestures toward the boundary of visibility, between beings and interiors that are legible to the eye only when color gathers at the edges of the spectral body.[45] In this sonnet, however, color registers not only affect and inner desire but also gender. Where women are associated with cosmetic "painting" and the vicissitudes of fashion, the young man is "with nature's own hand painted." Where women's "gentle heart[s]" express emotional turbulence on the skin, he seems able to "control" all hues, both his own and those in whom he kindles desire. Yet the bounds that differentiate the sexes are far from stable. This is one of only two Shakespearean sonnets that uses feminine rhymes throughout,[46] as if the poem's rhythms colluded in undermining the assertions of male self-sufficiency and affective imperviousness.

Readers have noticed the pun on female genitalia in "not acquainted," wordplay that prepares us for the second half of the sonnet with its playful mythology of sexual origin: "for a woman wert thou first created." The Galenic idea that male and female bodies are homologous subtends the sonnet, and behind the bawdy joke about adding "one thing" to the feminine "nothing" lies the territorialization of gender. Male and female bodies are, according to Galen, isomorphic except with respect to vision, for although they possess analogous sexual and reproductive organs, those parts are cloistered within the female body rather than being manifest to the eye. Galen's now well-known image of the female reproductive organs as similar to a mole's eyes, which was frequently repeated by early modern anatomists, drew on two discussions of the sense of sight in *Historia animalium*, where Aristotle singles out the mole as the only viviparous animal that does not have eyes.[47] Aristotle refines his assertion by suggesting that the mole has eyes of a sort; although they are not visible, they exist as undeveloped parts, hidden under a covering of skin. The interior of the female body is, consequently, associated with darkness, nothingness, and blindness, a linkage that begins to make a kind of gendered sense of the dark lady of the sonnets. The conventional association between darkness and female sexuality is registered in King Lear's invective against his daughters. In act four, scene six, where he encounters the blind Gloucester, Lear's lament for the loss of Gloucester's eyes converges with his curse on women's sexual and reproductive organs; situated below the waist, this place of lust and propagation is "hell" and "darkness," a description that resonates with Edgar's description of the "dark and vicious place" where Edmund was begotten and which "cost" Gloucester "his eyes."[48]

One striking aspect of the sonnet sequence as a whole is that after sonnet 126, the rare references to colors other than black occur in sonnets 130 and 146, chromatic allusions that are evoked only to be erased. Although sonnet 130, "My mistress' eyes are nothing like the sun" has rightly been read as Shakespeare's comic response to the exhaustion of the rhetorical conventions of praise in the sonnet tradition, Shakespeare's specific erasure of color (rather than, say, Donne's challenge to the metaphorics of comparison in Elegies like "The Comparison") is worth noticing. The color of the mistress's lip is negated through a failed analogy ("Coral is far more red than her lips' red," the anticipated white of her breasts are "dun," the conventional golden wires are in her "black," and the bloom of her cheeks is like no "rose damasked, red and white" the speaker has seen). The mistress's color, a surface expression of her beauty and her inner condition that makes her legible not only to the lover but to all who might choose to gaze upon her, is converted to black, a color noted for its inscrutability, its inaccessibility to vision. Black in the medical tradition is, of course, associated with a surfeit of black bile, the humor that produces melancholy. When the speaker praises black in sonnet 127, black becomes the color of mourning, a sign of woe and an expression of the body's physiology, which for early modern subjects was usually contiguous with its psychic or emotional condition. As we have seen with the discourse of color in general, blackness serves simultaneously as a perfectly corresponding outward expression of an inner condition and as a sign of the inscrutable nature of that innerness. In subsequent sonnets, darkness renders the mistress invisible to the gaze, investing her with a secrecy of motive that is cognate with her femininity. Whereas early modern culture conventionally fetishizes the outward surface of the female body, noting women's propensity to adorn and ornament those surfaces with cosmetic painting, these invectives displace a much larger cultural apprehension about femininity: that it is a cipher, an unknowable and unreadable interior.

The scandal of miscegenation to which de Grazia alludes is, then, multiple, for it includes not only potential racial intermixing, registered in the hue of the skin, but also the prevalent cultural fantasy that such intergrafting might occur. This fear is the sign of a more persuasive anxiety: that female desire and its attendant reproductive processes cannot be subject to ocular vigilance because they are eclipsed within the female body. The guarantee of paternity can only be female chastity, and the long debates in medical and midwifery treatises about the child's similarity to the mother and father, discussions that frequently include mention of a black child, testify to this concern.[49] If the first seventeen sonnets in Shakespeare's sequence urge the young man to procreate, this reproduction is imaged as the creation of sameness, a replication of the colors of youth, "the lovely April of her prime" (3), "that fresh blood" (11), "this fair child" (2). The Galenic homology would seem to proffer a mimetic comfort that is analogous to the somatic mirroring of the young man sonnets. Yet the very Galenic inversion that should guarantee knowledge produces the opposite, for in relegating the female sexual organs to a dark interior, it figured the unknowability and uncontrollability of female sexuality and its "colors," a darkness that haunts the early modern imaginary, a place where colors "abide," according to Batman's Bartholome, but are not "idle."

If darkness is a function of innerness, however, that interiority is predominately, though not exclusively, feminine. The secrecy of female generation is mirrored in the faculties of mind, the "children" "delivered from thy brain" (77) or the "brains beguiled / Which, lab'ring for invention, bear amiss / The second burthen of a former child" (59). The trope of poetic invention as childbirth relies in part on the early modern idea of a sympathetic linkage between womb and brain, although the transposition of this conjunction to a male body is a function of metaphor.[50] The dark innerness of the mind is the matrix of poetic creation, registered externally in the "black ink" of composition and more fully in such sonnets as 27:

> Weary with toil, I haste me to my bed,
> The dear repose for limbs with travel tired,
> But then begins a journey in my head
> To work my mind, when body's work's expired.
> For then my thoughts, from far where I abide,
> Intend a zealous pilgrimage to thee,
> And keep my drooping eyelids open wide,
> Looking on darkness which the blind do see.
> Save that my soul's imaginary sight
> Presents thy shadow to my sightless view,
> Which like a jewel hung in ghastly night,
> Makes black night beauteous, and her old face new.
>   Lo thus by day my limbs, by night my mind
>   For thee, and for myself, no quiet find.

The sonnet traces a movement of progressive interiority: the speaker retires to bed, and the rhyme accentuates the further retreat to the "head" and then to its inside, the mind. Looking into darkness, the speaker calls on the powers of the imagination, which summon the beloved in his shadowed form. This topography of the imaginary is a landscape of darkness and interiority that presages the dark lady sonnets, both in its exploration of night and in the mind's desiring capacity to see black night's "beauteous," rather than its "ghastly" aspect. Whereas Joel Fineman contrasts the young man sonnets with those that invoke the dark lady, juxtaposing vision and language, sameness and difference, the interiority of sonnet 27 aligns it much more closely with the dark lady sonnets, bound together as they are through their common representation of sightlessness and blackness. Darkness is gendered in so far as it is associated with the interiorized female reproductive organs and their unruly workings, which are frequently both demonized and celebrated as a matrix of uncontrollable creativity. Yet this gendering extends by analogy to the soul's "imaginary sight," which evokes not only the power that the imagination had to imprint the developing fetus, but also the generalized vision of desire and its creative manifestation in poetry.[51] If color both adorns and constitutes the ornamental exterior, it also figures the inscrutable interior, whether of the cryptic womb or the black mind with its imaginary power, the sightless view behind the eyelids, the vision of the imagination. In this interpretation, the colors of the spectrum are not contrasted with blackness. Rather, colors exist in darkness, a language of the passions, sexuality, and the unconscious, a world that subtends, participates in, and also continually escapes the regulations of symbolic language.

AUTHOR'S NOTE

I am grateful to the work of three excellent research assistants, Katherine Larson, Piers Brown, and Mingjun Lu, and to the perceptive comments of colleagues who heard or read an early version of this essay at the 2005 Renaissance Society of America and the 2006 Shakespeare Association of America conferences.

NOTES

1   *OED*, "spectrum," 3a; Paul Edwards (ed.), *The Encyclopedia of Philosophy* (New York: Macmillan; London: Collier Macmillan, 1967), vol. 5: 489–91.

2   Kim F. Hall, "'These bastard signs of fair': Literary Whiteness in Shakespeare's Sonnets," in Ania Loomba and Martin Orkin (eds.), *Post-Colonial Shakespeares* (London and New York: Routledge, 1998), 64–83 at 68. For a detailed history of the "darkness" readings of Shakespeare's Dark Lady, see Marvin Hunt, "Be Dark but Not Too Dark," in James Schiffer (ed.), *Shakespeare's Sonnets: Critical Essays* (New York and London: Garland, 1999), 368–89.

3   Margreta de Grazia, "The Scandal of Shakespeare's Sonnets," in Schiffer (ed.), *Shakespeare's Sonnets*, 89–112 at 106.

4   Sujata Iyengar, *Shades of Difference: Mythologies of Skin Color in Early Modern England* (Philadelphia: University of Pennsylvania Press, 2005).

5   Anne Carson, *Autobiography of Red* (Toronto: Vintage Canada, 1999), 4.

6   Aristotle, *De sensu*, in *Aristotle: On the Soul, Parva Naturalia, On Breath*, trans. W. S. Hett (Cambridge, Mass., and London: Harvard University Press, 1936; repr. 1995), 439a.

7   Aristotle, *De anima*, in *Aristotle: On the Soul, Parva Naturalia, On Breath*, 418b.

8   Sir John Davies, *Nosce teipsum*, in *The Poems of Sir John Davies*, ed. Robert Krueger (Oxford: Clarendon, 1975), 325–8.

9   See John Gage, *Color and Culture: Practice and Meaning from Antiquity to Abstraction* (Boston, Toronto, and London: Little, Brown, 1993), 29–30.

10 *Batman Uppon Bartholome, His Book, De Propri-etatibus Rerum* (London, 1582), 387. For this and other early modern prose texts, I have silently modernized "i," "j," "u," "v," and long "s," and I have expanded contractions.

11 *Batman Uppon Bartholome*, 387.

12 Ibid., 391.

13 Ibid., 387.

14 Ibid., 391.

15 Jacques Ferrand, *Erotomania* (London, 1640), 113.

16 Ibid., 123–4.

17 *The Rape of Lucrece*, in *William Shakespeare: Narrative Poems*, ed. Jonathan Crewe (New York and London: Penguin, 1999), ll. 65–71.

18 Luce Irigaray, "Flesh Colors," in *Sexes and Genealogies*, trans. Gillian C. Gill (New York: Columbia University Press, 1993), 160. (First publ. in French as *Sexes et parentés*, Paris: Minuit, 1987.)

19 William Shakespeare, *The Rape of Lucrece*, in *The Poems*, ed. F. T. Prince (London: Methuen, 1960; repr. Walton-on-Thames, Surrey: Thomas Nelson, 1998; [The Arden Shakespeare]), ll. 1737–50.

20 Joel Fineman, *Shakespeare's Perjured Eye: The Invention of Poetic Subjectivity in the Sonnets* (Berkeley: University of California Press, 1986).

21 All quotations from the sonnets are from Stephen Booth's edition: *Shakespeare's Sonnets* (New Haven and London: Yale University Press, 1977; repr. 2000).

22 For an evocative discussion of green, see Bruce Smith's essay, "Hearing Green," in Gail Kern Paster, Katherine Rowe, and Mary Floyd-Wilson (eds.), *Reading Early Modern Passions: Essays in the Cultural History of Emotion* (Philadelphia: University of Pennsylvania Press, 2004), 147–68.

23 Jacob Boehme's *Signatura rerum*, written in 1621 and translated into English at midcentury (*The signature of all things: shewing the sign, and signification of the severall forms and shapes in the creation*, London: printed by John Macock, 1651); Nicholas Culpeper, *The English Physitian Enlarged*, London: Peter Cole, 1653. See also William Coles, *The Art of Simpling. An introduction to the Knowledge and Gathering of Plants*, London, 1656.

24 See John Gerard, *Herball or Generall Historie of Plantes* (London: John Norton, 1597) on the saffron crocus (123–5) and black hellebor (824–7).

25 See Lisa Freinkel's essay, "The Name of the Rose: Christian Figurality and Shakespeare's Sonnets," in Schiffer (ed.), *Shakespeare's Sonnets*, 241–61.

26 Gerard, *Herball or Generall Historie of Plantes*.

27 Most editors gloss the canker rose as the dog rose (*Rosa canina*), though the term is sometimes also used to designate the wild poppy (*Papaver rhea*). In his *Herball*, John Gerard's description of the wild poppy is followed by an account of the "Bastarde Wilde Poppie" or "Winde Rose," whose juice is used to treat inflammation of the eye. It is especially efficacious for *Argema*, an ocular affliction that makes the white of the eye black and the black part of the eye white (300–1).

28 See Giambattista della Porta's *Natural Magick* (London, 1669; first publ. as *Magiae naturalis*, 1558, 1584), bk. 3, ch. XV, 94ff.

29 In Ovid's *Metamorphoses* (trans. Frank Justus Miller, Loeb Classical Library, Harvard University Press, 2 vols., 1916, repr. 1977), Clytie is the nymph who is changed into a violet (IV: 234–70). Adonis is transformed into an aenonome or wind flower (X: 681–739), though in early modern herbals he is also associated with the rose because of the flower's blood-red hue. Rembert Dodoens links him to the rose, for instance, in his *Nieuwe Herball*, trans. Henry Lyte (London, 1578), 655.

30 See Stephen Booth's headnote to sonnet 98 in *Shakespeare's Sonnets*, 317; Katherine Duncan-Jones's commentary in the Arden edition

(*Shakespeare's Sonnets*, London: Thomson Learning, 1997, 99, n. 50); and Helen Vendler, *The Art of Shakespeare's Sonnets* (Cambridge, Mass., and London: Harvard University Press, 1997), 422.

31 Booth, *Shakespeare's Sonnets*, 317.

32 Helkiah Crooke, *Mikrocosmographia. A Description of the Body of Man. Together with the Controversies thereto Belonging. Collected and Translated out of all the Best Authors of Anatomy, Especially out of Gasper Bauhinus and Andreas Laurentius* (London: William Jaggard, 1615), 237.

33 The connection between menstruation and flowers may have initially developed as a corruption of the French *fleur* and the Latin *fluor* (to flow). See the *OED* entry for *fluor*.

34 *Hippocratic Writings*, ed. G. E. R. Lloyd, trans. J. Chadwick et al., 1950; repr. with additional material (Harmondsworth: Penguin, 1978).

35 Victoria Finlay, *Colour* (London: Hodder & Stoughton, 2002), 182–3. *OED*, "vermilion, n." 1.a.

36 Giambattista della Porta, *Natural Magick* (London, 1669), 233–50.

37 Ibid., 239–43.

38 George Puttenham, *The Arte of English Poesie* (Menston, Yorks.: Scolar, 1968; facsimile of the 1589 edition), 115 (bk. 3, ch. 1).

39 Jacqueline Lichtenstein, *The Eloquence of Color: Rhetoric and Painting in the French Classical Age*, trans. Emily Mcvarish (Berkeley: University of California Press, 1993), 138–68. (First publ. Paris: Flammarion, 1989.)

40 Ibid., 156–9.

41 Irigaray, "Flesh Colors"; Julia Kristeva, "Giotto's Joy," in Leon S. Roudiez (ed.) *Desire in Language: A Semiotic Approach to Literature and Art*, trans. Thomas Gora, Alice Jardine, and Leon S. Roudiez (New York: Columbia University Press, 1980), 210–36.

42 Kristeva, "Giotto's Joy," 221.

43 Ibid.

44 Ibid., 221–2.

45 Booth, *Shakespeare's Sonnets*, 163.

46 Ibid.

47 Aristotle, *Historia animalium*, in *The Basic Works of Aristotle*, ed. Richard McKeon (New York: Random House, 1941), 1. 9; 4. 8.

48 William Shakespeare, *King Lear*, ed. Kenneth Muir (London: Methuen, 1972; The Arden Shakespeare), IV. vi, V. iii.

49 For a summary of accounts that were conventional in early modern medical texts, see the "Controversies" appended to bk. 5, "The History of the Infant," of Helkiah Crooke's *Mikrocosmographia*, esp. 299–300 and 311. For a discussion of the trope of black children and monstrous birth, see Valeria Finucci, "Maternal Imagination and Monstrous Birth: Tasso's *Gerusalemme liberata*," in Valeria Finucci and Kevin Brownlee (eds.), *Generation and Degeneration: Tropes of Reproduction in Literature and History from Antiquity to Early Modern Europe* (Durham, NC, and London: Duke University Press, 2001), 41–77.

50 For a fuller discussion of sympathy between organs, see Elizabeth D. Harvey, "Imaginary Anatomies," *Shakespeare Survey* 33, 2005, 80–6, and "Pleasure's Oblivion: Displacements of Generation in Spenser's *Faerie Queene*," in Christopher Ivic and Grant Williams (eds.), *Forgetting in Early Modern English Literature and Culture: Lethe's Legacies* (London and New York: Routledge, 2004), 53–64.

51 The tradition of linking the imagination and the development of the fetus extends from Hippocrates, Aristotle, Pliny, and Galen to such early modern writers as Marsilio Ficino, Ambroise Paré, and Nicholas Malebranche. See Finucci, "Maternal Imagination and Monstrous Birth," and Marie-Hélène Huet, *Monstrous Imgination* (Cambridge, Mass.: Harvard University Press, 1993).

PART VII
Memory and Repetition in the Sonnets

Voicing the Young Man: Memory, Forgetting, and Subjectivity in the Procreation Sonnets

Garrett A. Sullivan, Jr.

Shakespeare's sonnets have earned a privileged place in the history of subjectivity, but the subjectivity in question has invariably been that of the poet, not the young man.[1] As one critic puts it, "The desiring male subject has a clear, forceful voice. . . . But the desired male object in the sonnets has no voice."[2] As voiceless as the young man is, some sense of his subjectivity emerges through his noncompliance with the imperatives articulated by the poet.[3] Just as those imperatives are uttered in the service of memory, the reluctant young man can be seen as one who forgets himself. This essay will focus on memory and forgetting in the procreation sonnets, with attention paid to the significance of these categories for early modern conceptions of identity and subjectivity. It will also fantasize a voice for the young man, a fantasy enabled by his status as self-forgetter. Through the production of this fantasy, the procreation sonnets are revealed to be dialogic and agonistic; they record a conflict between the poet and the young man that hinges upon opposing notions of beauty, selfhood, and immortality. These sonnets conclude with the poet's seeming victory, as he advances a model of memory that neutralizes the problem of the young man's self-forgetting.

*

Can we feel sorry for a young man whose beauty renders him worthy of immortality? One might think not; but what of immortality's price tag, paid in the here and now of Shakespeare's sequence? Consider some of the poet's querulous, overlapping demands in the first seventeen sonnets: stop masturbating (4. 1–2; 9. 2) and instead reproduce, preferably again and again (6. 7–8); "Be not self-willed" (6. 13); don't just admire yourself in the glass, make *more* of yourself, both literally and figuratively (3), and, by doing so, perpetuate your beauty (1. 1–2); remember that you are moving ever closer to the grave, and so you need to produce offspring or die alone and "unlooked on" (7. 14); remember also that you have a duty to the world to reproduce (9. 3–12); and, finally, just be yourself (13. 1) – by doing what *I* tell you to do.[4] The young man of the procreation sonnets, then, is an object of admonition; the poet urgently seeks to make him change his ways, and, as we shall see, does so in the intertwined names of beauty and memory and in the face of oblivion.

If the poet works to engender obligation and fear in the young man, it is procreation and the immortality it promises that would supposedly grant consolation for "folly, age and cold decay" (11. 6). To achieve that consolation, however, the young man must take on a particular identity proffered by the poet, the nature of which is worth pausing over. In the face of death, the poet tells us, sexual reproduction promises to extend the young man's selfhood through time; he will live on through his children. And yet, both this form of immortality and the identity it presupposes might be seen as having precious little to offer. Imagine the young man mulling over the poet's cold comfort: "Should I reproduce, I'm told, my 'beauty' and my 'self' will live on (e.g. 4). But they won't, not really. My children will not be replicas of me, and whatever beauty they lay claim to will be their own, even granting my part in their genesis. (Moreover, I will find myself in the depressing position of watching their beauty grow while my own fades, watching through 'deep sunken eyes' (2. 7).) As for my 'selfhood,' it too will dissolve with my death. Having children may preserve the 'fair house' of my dynastic identity (13. 9; see also 10. 7), but what does it have to offer *me*?"

This fantasy of giving voice might meet with readerly skepticism on the grounds of anachronism. If the poet's demands are largely coercive, the young man's imagined resistance sounds decidedly modern, perhaps nowhere more significantly so than in the distinction made between himself (the italicized "me") and the "fair house" of his familial identity. Both the "fair house" of sonnet 13 and the potentially "ruinate[d]" "beauteous roof" of sonnet 10 are figures for the social identity of the young man. They function as does Bertram's "monumental ring" in *All's Well that Ends Well*, as emblems of an identity which weaves together "house, . . . honor, [and] life."[5] The ring is the instantiation of familial memory, "an honor 'longing to our house, / Bequeathed down from many ancestors" (IV. ii. 42–3). In sum, the ring symbolizes Bertram's dynastic identity, as the "fair house" does the young man's. Given this, what does it mean to distinguish between the "me" of the young man and his "fair house"? To do so would seem to install an anachronistic conception of the "individual" as one who can be comfortably differentiated from his social (and in this case dynastic) identity. The young man's "me" sounds quite modern, the "me" of "what have you done for *me* lately?" The fantasy of the young man's voice, then, is the fantasy of a subject who is our and not Shakespeare's contemporary.

Or is it? For all the obvious significance of Bertram's ring, the salient point in *All's Well* is that he *gives the ring away* to (he thinks) Diana, whom he later disingenuously alludes to as "a common gamester to the camp" (V. iii. 188). That is, Bertram *betrays* house, honor, and life in the pursuit of sexual desire. In handing over the ring, Bertram drives a wedge between "himself" (as represented by his desires) and his social identity. Moreover, such wedge-driving is a common object of Shakespearean representation – from Antony's inability to "hold [his] visible shape" (*Antony and Cleopatra*, IV. xiv. 14) to Tarquin's forsaking himself (his dynastic identity) for himself (his desires) (*The Rape of Lucrece*, l. 157).[6] Thus, anachronism lies not in distinguishing between "me" and the "fair house" of dynastic identity, but in imagining that that distinction can take only a 21st-century form. The "me" of both our fantasy of the young man's voice and of Bertram's renunciation of his monumental ring can be seen as a specifically early modern creature whose very existence articulates possibilities for selfhood not identical to dynastic identity. Such possibilities are drawn together under the name of self-forgetting.

Before we can accept the young man as self-forgetter, however, we first have to consider the role(s) of memory in the procreation sonnets. Both this cluster of seventeen sonnets and the entire sonnet sequence are marked not only by a preoccupation with the category of memory, but also by a fascination with the sheer capaciousness and complexity of that category.[7] For example, the sonnets itemize multiple objects that can preserve and/or provoke memory, including monuments (55), "tables" both physical and cognitive (77, 122), "children's eyes" that keep the young man's "shape in mind" for his widow (9. 8), the "picture" by which the young man is made "present still with [the poet]" (47. 9–10), and, most famously, the poet's "eternal lines" themselves (18. 12). (Of course, the sonnets prioritize some objects over others, as the poet's verse is said to outlast "unswept stone, besmeared with sluttish time" [55. 4].) The sonnets also offer a variety of metaphors for memory and its operations, including, in one sonnet alone, a court of law, a financial record, and a narrative "account" (30. 11). Some poems consider the complex relationship between the objects associated with memory and memory as a cognitive operation. In sonnet 77, the "waste blanks" of a notebook supplement the young man's memory – indeed, they serve as a kind of *off-board* memory in that they make it possible for written ideas to "take a new acquaintance of thy mind" (ll. 10–12)[8] – while in 122, the very notion that "tables" might function as an "adjunct" to the *on-board* memory of the poet "were to import forgetfulness in [him]" (ll. 12–14). The poet in the first sonnet advocates the utility of the notebook, while in the second the tables read as a kind of scandal.[9] Finally, one sonnet distinguishes between "historical" and "subjective" memory – between the "memory" out of which aging men "wear their brave state" (and thus pass into oblivion) and the poet's "conceit" which "sets" the young man "before [his] sight" (15. 8–10). All in all, then, these poems consider the multiple and sometimes conflicting forms, both physical and discursive, that memory can take.

In the procreation sonnets, the reader does not encounter the full variety of memory sketched above. This does not mean that memory appears as completely homogeneous, as the example from sonnet 15 suggests. However, a specific model of memory, advanced in the opening lines of the first poem, resonates throughout the procreation sonnets.

> From fairest creatures we desire increase,
> That thereby beauty's rose might never die,
> But as the riper should by time decease
> His tender heir might bear his memory.
>
> (1. 1–4)

The heir bears the memory of one of the "fairest creatures" simply by looking like him, and it is through the heir's very existence that "beauty's rose" lives on. Memory here has no significant cognitive component; for instance, we are not told (as we are in other sonnets, e.g. 9. 7–8) that the appearance of the heir will *remind* anyone of the fair creature who sired him.[10] Instead, the successful "bearing" of the "riper" creature's memory presumes only that the heir physically resemble that creature. It is through the perpetuation of such resemblance that beauty's rose "might never die." The "memory" borne by the heir, then, defines the heir himself, as the physical product of "increase," his very existence perpetuating "beauty's rose." And insofar as "his memory" is the embodiment of a fair creature, and the fair creature is the embodiment of beauty, the memory borne by the heir is equivalent to beauty in this sonnet. The business of memory is thus the perpetuation of beauty through sexual reproduction.

This inaugural model of memory as beauty reverberates throughout the procreation sonnets, even if it is not the only available model. For instance, sonnet 2 evokes this model in its reference to the "fair child" by whom the young man will "prov[e] his beauty by succession thine" (2. 10, 12). And yet, memory is not explicitly mentioned here. Instead, it makes its presence felt through the clear echo of the terms of memory presented in sonnet 1. Moreover, the final couplet of sonnet 2 expands these terms by suggesting that reproduction will preserve not just beauty, but the beautiful young man himself: "This were to be new made when thou art old, / And see thy blood warm when thou feel'st it cold" (13–14). The "tender heir" of sonnet 1 is refigured as one whose very being extends the life of the young man (and not just "beauty's rose") beyond its natural date. The young man will be "new made" through offspring.

There is a seemingly less palatable alternative offered in the poem, however. Contrasted with the inaugural model is a comparatively impoverished form of memory that is associated with physical decay:

> Then being asked, where all thy beauty lies,
> Where all the treasure of thy lusty days,
> To say, within thine own deep-sunken eyes,
> Were an all-eating shame and thriftless praise.
>
> (2. 5–8)

The memory of the young man's beauty exists here both as a "thriftless," non-generative "praise," the antithesis of the final couplet's new making, and in the "deep-sunken eyes" of his lost loveliness. That is, both praise and eyes are *reminders* of the young man's beauty – but reminders that stand in stark contrast to "new making," representing a model of memory that fails to overcome decay in the way that "increase" does. Indeed, eyes and praise serve as a form of memory on the brink of oblivion.

And yet, it is to this form of memory that, through his repeated exhortations to reform, the poet suggests the young man has a seemingly perverse commitment – memory in the face and in the service of oblivion.[11] Why this commitment? One answer lies in the limitations of "new making" as they are revealed in the final couplet of sonnet

2. To be new made is to "*see* thy blood warm when thou *feel'st* it cold" (14, emphasis added). The blood "seen" here is not contained in the (no longer) young man's body, but is simultaneously the *actual* blood of his child and the *dynastic* blood warmed on its passage from father to son. *Seeing* the warm-blooded child, then, does nothing to make the blood in his father's body *feel* any less cold, or to cause his eyes to be any less "deep-sunken." While the young man's social identity can be perpetuated through the production of offspring, doing so will not arrest the decay of his body, no matter what the poet says. The young man's perverse commitment, then, is in part a response to the limitations of the poet's model of memory-as-beauty, which finally will fail to keep its promise of warming the blood. It is also a refusal of the poet's equation of dynastic and actual blood – or of the notion that the young man's "fair house" is constitutive of who he is. More broadly, this commitment is the marker of the young man's identity distinct from the procreative role that the poet repeatedly urges on him. According to the poet, the failure of the young man to conform to this role constitutes a violence done to himself: "For having traffic with thyself alone, / Thou of thyself thy sweet self dost deceive" (4. 9–10). We might speculate that, in not capitulating to the poet's logic, the young man does not cede this point.

The association of the young man's failure to reproduce with a violence done to himself is reiterated throughout the procreation sonnets. In sonnet 8, not to marry and have children is an act of self-erasure – "'Thou single wilt prove none'" (l. 14) – while in sonnet 10, it is "'gainst thyself . . . to conspire" (l. 6). In sonnet 13, the exasperated poet exclaims "O that you were yourself!" (l. 1), assuming that the young man is not and will not be himself for as long as he does not sire an heir. In all of these examples, the young man's selfhood is threatened by his failure to procreate. More specifically, the poet will not grant him selfhood unless or until he has children. The example from sonnet 8 captures this logic clearly: if you remain single, you will prove to be nothing or no(o)ne; your selfhood hinges upon generation. Thus, the poet creates a model of selfhood for the young man that both is profoundly future-oriented and has implications for the young man in the here and now. Having children is not only the means by which the young man's "immortality" is secured, it is the grounds for his identity (or lack thereof) *in the present* of the sonnet sequence. To fail to generate is for the young man not to be himself. Self-trafficking is both self-deception and self-erasure. It is this stark view proffered by the poet that we can imagine the young man as rejecting. Instead, he might suggest that "traffic[king] with thyself alone" constitutes an *expression* of selfhood rather than its eradication or "deception."

How, then, do we describe the model of selfhood advanced by the young man through actions taken in noncompliance with the poet's imperatives? This is where our fantasy of the young-man-as-subject runs into a problem: the "voiceless" young man nowhere articulates such a model; we have only his noncompliance to go on. And yet, the *terms* of that noncompliance are telling, and they bring the procreation sonnets into dialogue with other Shakespearean models of selfhood. As suggested above, the poet's demands of the young man are, in the very first lines of the sonnet sequence, made in the name of beauty-as-memory. Moreover, procreation is figured as a memory technology that grounds the identity of the young man.[12] That the young man apparently does not accept the identity proffered him by the poet – that he does not produce offspring – means that he also does not accept memory's terms as the poet lays them out. Instead, the young man seems to settle for memory in the face of oblivion, the memory of deep-sunken eyes and thriftless praise. That is, the young man settles for what the poet would term oblivion. In conspiring against himself, or deceiving himself, or being untrue to himself, the young man also *forgets himself* – "forgets" the model of selfhood that the poet seeks to impose upon him.[13] In this regard, the young man bears a family resemblance to Bertram, Antony, Tarquin and a number of other Shakespearean characters that forget themselves.

But what does it mean for the young man to forget himself?[14] We can begin with the definition of self-forgetting on offer in the *OED*: "To lose remembrance of one's own station, position, or character; to lose sight of the requirements of dignity, propriety, or decorum; to behave unbecomingly."[15] Yet in the early modern period, more is at issue in self-forgetting than a mere violation of propriety. To "lose remembrance of one's own station" is, as in the case of Bertram and his ring, to be alienated from one's identity as it is articulated within a hierarchical society. A violation of propriety is also a betrayal of property (the two words are intertwined in the period) – a betrayal of the responsibilities and performances attendant upon ownership understood as a social office. In this sense, the young man recognizably forgets himself and, in not reproducing, takes action against the interests of his "fair house."

This formulation does not go quite far enough, however. While self-forgetting describes actions taken against the imperatives of "one's own station" – against, that is, one's social identity – it also offers a model of selfhood constituted in terms different from those of such imperatives. In dramatic examples of self-forgetting, this model of selfhood is the basis for subjectivity. Indeed, in early modern drama interiority often emerges around and through self-forgetting, in the gap between a character's social identity and his or her own desires or vital energies. It is in this gap that our fantasy of the young man's subjectivity is located. However, whereas a dramatic character can articulate his or her own desires, if not the ways in which those desires conflict with the imperatives of his or her identity, the young man's desires are not represented; they exist only through and as his noncapitulation to the poet. In this regard, the model of self-forgetting we encounter in the procreation sonnets is significantly different from the one on offer in Shakespearean drama (or even in poems like *Lucrece*, where Tarquin's subjectivity, presented here in the third person, emerges out of his self-forgetting: "Pawning his honor to obtain his lust, / . . . for himself himself he must forsake" [ll. 156–7]).

But *why* has the young man forgotten himself? His motives remain as opaque, while not as malign, as those of Iago.[16] Arguably we are bumping up against the limitations of treating the young man as a *character* (rather than as no more than the textual occasion for the production of the poet's subjectivity). Perhaps; but surely such treatment is offered at Shakespeare's invitation. The question why the young man does *not* remember himself by procreating is the inevitable product of a sequence of poems that repeatedly and in various ways make the case *for* his doing so. Such repetition implies that the case has not been successfully made and, if this is so, one inevitably wonders why. Just as the sequence as a whole has teased critics into various biographical speculations, so it raises (unanswerable but tantalizing) questions about the subjectivity of a young man who refuses procreative immortality.[17] What is important for this essay is the form the questions take, the ways in which they engage the categories of memory and forgetting. And it is through and in terms of these categories that our fantasy of the young man and his motives can further develop.

The young man's self-forgetting is partly attributable to his refusal of the logic underpinning the poet's demands, a logic in which "I" become identical to "[my] fair house." To see only refusal, however, is to figure the young man as entirely reactive. For the purposes of our fantasy, we will consider the refusal to procreate as active, as the expression of a desire – specifically, the desire for oblivion. But what does oblivion connote here, and what does the desire for it look like? One answer is to be found by returning to other Shakespearean self-forgetters, such as Bertram, Tarquin, and Antony. For each of these characters, self-forgetting is a violence done to identity (as well as to others) through the influence of overmastering sexual desire. Certainly there are significant differences among all these characters as self-forgetters, and there are also forms of self-forgetting that do not center on sexual desire. However, continuities between these characters and the young man are worth pondering. In pursuing Diana to the detriment of both his dynastic identity and his marriage, Bertram forgets himself. Bertram's would-be adultery is concomitant with the surrender of his "monumental ring"; sexual relations outside an economy of marital procreation are enacted at the expense of memory and in the service of oblivion.

The young man, then, seeks oblivion as a sexual agent operating outside a procreative economy. This is particularly obvious in the final sonnets of the larger sequence, in which both young man and poet are lovers of the dark lady, who, as Valerie Traub has argued, is a figure for "promiscuous unproductivity defying patriarchal reproduction."[18] However, such "promiscuous unproductivity" is also the condition of the young man's sexuality in the procreation poems, as in the case of sonnet 4's references to masturbation. In contrast to the procreative model of selfhood, which grounds identity in futurity, the poet associates masturbation with the present-centered activity of the spendthrift: "why dost thou spend / Upon thyself thy beauty's legacy?" (4. 1–2). Here a form of selfhood emerges through violence done to the future, "beauty's legacy." We are told that it is through such self-trafficking (4. 9) that the young man deceives himself – denies himself a selfhood grounded in futurity and in memory. In contrast to this view, we can see the young man performing a selfhood that is present-centered, figured in terms of nonreproductive sexuality and set in opposition to the reproductive model of memory – that is, a selfhood in the service of (what the poet would term) oblivion.

Masturbation is not the only nonreproductive sexual practice associated with the young man. Peter C. Herman has analyzed the language of usury in the procreation sonnets (e.g. 4, 6, 9), a language that has strong associations with both prostitution and sodomitical relations.[19] Indeed, usury is a common metaphor for nonreproductive sexuality, suggesting as it does "unnatural" "breeding."[20] In contrast to memory and procreation, then, the first seventeen sonnets associate oblivion with a range of non-reproductive sexual practices, from onanism to sex with prostitutes to sodomy.[21] The poet's privileging of memory is not narrowly heteronormative in its impulse. Indeed, if achieved, procreation would consolidate or affirm relations between the poet and the young man. Moreover, procreation in these sonnets is sometimes figured (and arguably most often thought of) quasi-parthenogenetically (e.g. 13. 14). The would-be mother of the young man's imagined heir appears only intermittently in these poems, usually as little more than another rhetorical arrow drawn from the poet's quiver (as in the example of the "private widow" [9. 7] conjured up by the poet to tug at the young man's heartstrings). While the difference between oblivion and memory, then, is also one between "illicit" and "licit" sexual practices, the latter distinction separates not the homoerotic from the heteroerotic, but the procreative from the nonprocreative.[22]

Oblivion, then, has as its domain a range of sexual activity defined through its incompatibility with memory's procreative imperatives. The young man as desiring agent responds to the appeal to posterity not by breeding but by seizing the day – by indulging in sexual practices divorced from the logic of memory. He has taken to heart the poet's claims about the ravaging effects of time – "For never-resting time leads summer on / To hideous winter, and confounds him there" (5. 5–6); "[T]hou among the wastes of time must go" (12. 10); "Make war upon this bloody tyrant, time" (16. 2) – but, like the "unthrift" he is repeatedly accused of being, he responds by consuming rather than perpetuating himself. That is, he aligns himself with oblivion and *carpe diem.*[23] What the young man has to offer is a model of beauty (and of sexuality) that is grounded in the here and now, in seizing the day. The poet rightly stresses the fragility of this notion of beauty – it is always already fading – but what he proposes in its place largely evacuates the present-ness of beauty in favor of its perpetuation.[24] That is, the ephemerality of physical beauty is figured by the poet not as beauty's very condition, but as a limitation to be overcome by means of sexual reproduction. On the other hand, the young man, in embracing oblivion and eschewing procreation, assumes and acts upon notions of sexuality and beauty that foreground their time-bound, present-centered nature.

In the poet's formulation, memory and beauty generate a particular notion of the future. The claim to memory is an assertion of authority and the projection of that authority onto the future – "you and your beauty must live on, and by the means that I prescribe." In rebuffing the procreative imperative in favor of oblivion, the young man does not accede to the poet's authority. Put differently, he reveals the obvious limits of that authority, as the poet cannot make the young man sire children. It is because of the poet's failure, perhaps, that he introduces an alternative to the procreative model of memory at the end of the sub-sequence. In sonnet 15, the poet pledges to "engraft [the young man] new" (ll. 13–14) in his verse. While brave states are commonly worn "out of memory," the poet "war[s] with time" in order to perpetuate the memory of the young man (ll. 8, 13). In other words, poetry emerges as an alternative memory technology to that of reproduction.

This notion recurs in the last of the procreation sonnets, in which the young man is imagined as twice perpetuated, in offspring and in the poet's "rhyme" (17. 14). The sub-sequence ends with procreation and poetry sharing pride of place. However, their equality is short-lived. Sonnet 18 proffers only the form of memory represented by the poet's "eternal lines" (l. 12). The poem closes with the assertion, repeatedly echoed in subsequent sonnets, that "this [poem] gives life to thee" (l. 14). In this sonnet, the procreative model is superseded by one in which the poet is the sole repository for the memory and identity – the "life" – of the young man. This new model thus solves for the poet the problem of (the young man's desire for) oblivion. The young man has not sired an heir in response to the poet's insistent demands, but now the poet's "eternal lines" ensure his friend's immortality. These lines succeed where the appeal to reproduce has failed – succeed not only in immortalizing the young man, but also in circumventing the problem of his resistance. Moreover, insofar as the procreation sonnets can be read as staging a conflict between the poet and the young man – or between memory and oblivion – the poet finally wins out, if only by shifting the terrain of memory from sexual reproduction to verse.

Of course, this is not where Shakespeare's sonnets leave relations between these two figures. The young man's affair with the dark lady, for instance, marks a new stage in his often agonistic relationship with the poet (e.g. sonnets 133, 134).[25] Moreover, these final sonnets place the poet in a position similar to the one we have seen the young man occupy; the dark lady is explicitly figured as the cause of the *poet*'s forgetting himself: "Do I not think on thee, when I forgot / Am of myself, all, tyrant, for thy sake?" (149. 3–4). One difference between the young man and the poet inheres in the anguished response of the latter to the prospect of oblivion, which he experiences as self-loss and self-abasement:

> What merit do I in myself respect
> That is so proud thy service to despise,
> When all my best doth worship thy defect,
> Commanded by the motion of thine eyes?
> (149. 9–12)

Relations among the characters shift over the course of the sequence, then, and whatever triumph of memory (and victory over the young man) the poet's "eternal lines" represent, it is a provisional one that punctuates the end of the procreation sonnets.

This essay has shown that the immortalizing project of the procreation sonnets is advanced at the expense of the young man's desires as well as his sense of self. In turn, that project is threatened by the young man's choice of oblivion over memory, nonproductive sexuality over progeny. The poet's "eternal lines," then, emerge as a model for memory that solves the problem of procreation by granting immortality to the young man (and, of course, to the poet) without having to secure his consent. And it is with the emergence of these lines that our fantasy of the young man must dissolve, for it is through his resistance to reproduction that this essay has been able to imagine him into being – as one who is eager to forget himself by embracing the oblivion of nonprocreative sexuality. Additionally, it is through this resistance that we have been able to trace the outlines of an early modern form of selfhood in which the (aristocratic) subject is not identical to his dynastic identity. Self-forgetting describes not the erasure but the recasting of the self, in terms antithetical to those laid down by the poet's conception of memory. Moreover, self-forgetting arguably has a strong affinity with a particular notion of fantasy – fantasy as an expression of possibility, the imaginative realization of that which is latent in a given literary or cultural document. This essay has indulged in the fantasy of voicing the young man in order to cast light upon his self-forgetting – in order, that is, to consider what it would mean to locate selfhood in terms of self-trafficking rather than self-perpetuation, ephemerality rather than eternity, oblivion rather than memory. It is a fantasy that emerges alongside but in critical relation to the poet's immortalizing project.[26] And yet, this fantasy arguably has an immortalizing project of its own, for it reads the procreation sonnets paradoxically, as a 400-year-old document of *resistance* to immortality. It is in this way that the sonnets "eternize" oblivion, by perpetuating the subjectivity that emerges out of forgetting oneself.

Notes

1 See esp. Joel Fineman, *Shakespeare's Perjured Eye: The Invention of Poetic Subjectivity in the Sonnets* (Berkeley: University of California Press, 1986).

  As James Schiffer points out in his superb introduction to a recent collection of essays on which this essay draws extensively, "scholarly opinions vary about whether these poems should be read as a poetic novel, as a series of dramatic monologues, as letters, as journal entries, as silent meditations, or as disparate, unrelated groups of related sonnets in a poetic miscellany" ("Reading New Life into Shakespeare's Sonnets: A Survey of Criticism," introduction to James Schiffer, ed., *Shakespeare's Sonnets: Critical Essays* [New York and London: Garland, 1999]: 3–71, esp. 12). This essay will treat the "poet" and "young man" as characters in a sonnet sequence understood as comprising a number of loosely sketched and overlapping narratives, one of which unfolds over the course of the procreation sonnets. Specifically, the essay assumes that the procreation sonnets together tell a story whose interest lies in the poet's lack of success

in convincing the young man to reproduce; and that the young man's refusal to capitulate to the poet's demands offers the reader the means by which to generate a sketch of the young man's "subjectivity" (through his status as one who forgets himself).

2 Bruce R. Smith, "I, You, He, She, and We: On the Sexual Politics of Shakespeare's Sonnets," in Schiffer, ed., *Shakespeare's Sonnets*, 411–29, esp. 420. Smith does argue that while the young has no voice, his is "an active subject" (p. 421), although Smith's evidence is drawn from late in the sonnet sequence.

3 Olga L. Valbuena has discussed "the rhetoric of coercion" deployed by the poet in these sonnets, suggesting that immortality will be the young man's only if he capitulates to the terms of the poet's project. See Valbuena, "'The dyer's hand': The Reproduction of Coercion and Blot in Shakespeare's Sonnets," in Schiffer, ed., *Shakespeare's Sonnets*, 325–45.

4 The sonnets are cited from William Shakespeare, *Shakespeare's Sonnets*, ed. Katherine Duncan-Jones (London: Thomson Learning, 1997).

5 William Shakespeare, *All's Well that Ends Well*, in *The Riverside Shakespeare*, ed. G. Blakemore Evans et al. (Boston: Houghton Mifflin, 1974), IV. iii. 17, IV. ii. 52. All references to Shakespeare's plays and to *Lucrece* are drawn from this text and will henceforth be made in the body of the essay. In turning to the plays, I assume representational continuities between Shakespeare's poetic and theatrical works. On such continuities, as well as the importance of theatrical discourse for the sonnets, see Patrick Cheney, *Shakespeare, National Poet-Playwright* (Cambridge: Cambridge University Press, 2004), esp. 207–38; and David Schalkwyk, *Speech and Performance in Shakespeare's Sonnets and Plays* (Cambridge: Cambridge University Press, 2002).

6 Garrett A. Sullivan, Jr., *Memory and Forgetting in English Renaissance Drama: Shakespeare, Marlowe, Webster* (Cambridge: Cambridge University Press, 2005), esp. 44–64.

7 On memory in the sonnets, see, among others, Colin Burrow, "Introduction," in William Shakespeare, *The Complete Sonnets and Poems*, ed. Colin Burrow (Oxford: Oxford University Press, 2002), 1–158, esp. 91–138; Burrow, "Life and Work in Shakespeare's Poems," the Chatterton Lecture on Poetry, *Proceedings of the British Academy* 97 (1998), 15–50; John Kerrigan, "Introduction," in William Shakespeare, *The Sonnets and A Lover's Complaint*, ed. John Kerrigan (London: Penguin, 1999 [first publ. 1986]), 7–63; and Joyce Sutphen, "'A dateless lively heat': Storing Loss in the Sonnets," in Schiffer, ed., *Shakespeare's Sonnets*, 199–217. An essay that is not about memory but that indirectly offers an illuminating account of its operations in the sonnets is Lars Engle, "Afloat in Thick Deeps: Shakespeare's Sonnets on Certainty," *PMLA* 104: 5 (1989), 832–43. It should be noted that memory is a much greater preoccupation of the young man sonnets than it is of those devoted to the dark lady.

8 The language of "on-board" and "off-board" memory complicates a simplistic distinction between a "real," internal memory and external memory "prompts"; it suggests that the inscriptions in the "waste blanks" of 77 *are* a form of memory. That the young man's lines will "take a new acquaintance of [his] mind" suggests that the "off-board" notebook will serve as the "in-board" memory does, to provide information necessary for the exercise of judgment. On material "tables" as a technology of memory, see Peter Stallybrass, Roger Chartier, J. Franklin Mowery, and Heather Wolfe, "Hamlet's Tables and the Technologies of Writing in Renaissance England," *Shakespeare Quarterly* 55: 4 (2004), 379–419.

9 For more on these two sonnets, see chapter 21 by Amanda Watson in this volume.

10 The poem also does not endorse the possibility that the heir bears the fair creature's memory by carrying in his head recollections of that creature. Memory in the poem is corporealized through "increase."

11 "Thriftless praise" is memory in the *service* of oblivion because, from the poet's perspective, it cannot compete with memory understood as the reproduction of beauty; it is memory in the *face* of oblivion because, from the young man's perspective, it is all that can survive his youth and beauty. It is striking that, for all of their interest in memory, the sonnets are largely indifferent both to the *memento mori* and *ars moriendi* traditions. Relatedly, the procreation sonnets do not concern themselves centrally with Christian immortality.

12 In sonnet 15, it is a technology implied to be less successful than that of poetry (ll. 13–14), while in sonnet 17, both child and poem have equal efficacy (ll. 13–14).

13 As suggested in Sullivan, *Memory and Forgetting*, "self-forgetting" describes not a cognitive activity – the young man does not literally forget who he is in a quasi-amnesiac fashion – but a pattern of behavior and a mode of being in the world. The young man's self-forgetting is thus the performance of a specific pattern of behavior (as well as the rejection of that pattern advocated by the poet).

14 The following two paragraphs draw upon Sullivan, *Memory and Forgetting*.

15 This is actually the most relevant of four definitions of the term, the other three of which are as follows: to omit care for oneself; to lose one's way; to lose consciousness.

16 On "strategic opacity" as a key to Shakespeare's representation of interiority, see Stephen

Greenblatt, *Will in the World: How Shakespeare Became Shakespeare* (New York: Norton, 2004).

17 On the sonnets as both inviting and frustrating biographical speculation, see Burrow, "Introduction" and "Life and Work."

18 Valerie Traub, "Sex without Issue: Sodomy, Reproduction, and Signification in Shakespeare's Sonnets," in Schiffer, ed., *Shakespeare's Sonnets*, 431–52, esp. 446. See also Michael Schoenfeldt, "Making Shakespeare's *Sonnets* Matter in the Classroom," in Patrick Cheney and Anne Lake Prescott, eds., *Approaches to Teaching Shorter Elizabethan Poetry* (New York: Modern Language Asssociation, 2000), 239–44, esp. 240; and Schoenfeldt, *Bodies and Selves in Early Modern England: Physiology and Inwardness in Spenser, Shakespeare, Herbert, and Milton* (Cambridge, UK: Cambridge University Press, 1999), 74–95, esp. 82–3.

19 Peter C. Herman, "What's the Use? Or, the Problematic of Economy in Shakespeare's Procreation Sonnets," in Schiffer, ed., *Shakespeare's Sonnets*, 263–83. See also Thomas M. Greene, "Pitiful Thrivers: Failed Husbandry in the Sonnets," in *The Vulnerable Text: Essays on Renaissance Literature* (New York: Columbia University Press, 1986), 175–93.

20 Of course, male sex with female prostitutes is not necessarily nonreproductive, but it is figured as such in the sonnets. As Herman puts it, "usury destabilizes the subject of the Petrarchan sonnet sequence itself by introducing overtones of unauthorized sexualities" ("What's the Use?," p. 270).

21 In the early modern period, sodomy can encompass nonreproductive sexual activity. As used here, the term refers more narrowly to "homosexual" activity. On the association of the nonprocreative sexuality of the dark lady with sodomy, see Jonathan Goldberg, "*Romeo and Juliet*'s Open Rs," in Goldberg, ed., *Queering the Renaissance* (Durham, NC: Duke University Press, 1994), 218–35, esp. 225;

Richard Halpern, *Shakespeare's Perfume: Sodomy and Sublimity in the Sonnets, Wilde, Freud, and Lacan* (Philadelphia: University of Pennsylvania Press, 2002), esp. 11–31.

22 It is obviously procreation within marriage that is valorized here, as an illegitimate child would not work to maintain the "fair house" of the young man's dynastic identity. It is for this reason that these seventeen poems are often referred to as the "marriage sonnets."

23 Gordon Braden asserts that the *carpe diem* topos is absent from Shakespeare's sonnets (as well as Petrarch's): "Shakespeare's Petrarchism," in Schiffer (ed.), *Shakespeare's Sonnets*, 163–83, esp. 169–70. In contrast, Heather Dubrow argues that the procreation sonnets evoke this topos: *Echoes of Desire: English Petrarchism and its Counterdiscourses* (Ithaca, NY: Cornell University Press, 1995). This essay suggests that the young man's actions can be seen as enacting the topos.

24 Here is a point of contact between this argument and those that have stressed the prevalence of economic language in these early sonnets. Procreation in the service of perpetuating beauty is "thriftiness," whereas illicit sex is a form of "squandering." To reproduce is to make an investment in the realization of future beauty. For more on the economic language of the sonnets, see Herman, "What's the Use?"; Lars Engle, "'I am that I am': Shakespeare's Sonnets and the Economy of Shame," in Schiffer (ed.), *Shakespeare's Sonnets*, 185–97.

25 The language of usury reappears in sonnet 134, with the dark lady now cast in the role of usurer (l. 10).

26 Insofar as this project strongly resembles Shakespeare's, bequeathed to him by his poetic forebears, the young man's self-forgetting could be read as Shakespeare's own meditation upon the identity he is called upon to adopt as writer of sonnets. That, however, is another fantasy.

"Full character'd": Competing Forms of Memory in Shakespeare's Sonnets

Amanda Watson

One motive for much if not all art (music is probably an exception) is . . . to keep memorable what deserves to be remembered. . . . The audience is enabled to call back the poem, or pieces of it, the poet to call back the thing itself, the subject, all that was to become the poem.

Donald Justice, "Meters and Memory"

Introduction: The Memory Arts in Shakespeare's England

How do we keep people in mind when they cease to be present in front of us, when we can no longer see or hear or touch them? How can we stop their features from fading? Photographs and drawings are static; individual memories blur; verbal descriptions fall short of the absent person's sharply particular presence. Shakespeare's sonnets return to and turn on the question of how to retain the memory of something as changeable, time-bound, and mortal as a beloved face. The sonnets that are generally considered to be addressed to the young man present this question in especially urgent terms.[1] The standard reading of the "young man" sonnets is that the sequence moves from commemorating the young man himself to exalting the poet's art. If we read the sonnets in the order of the 1609 quarto, the pronounced early emphasis on visual resemblance as the best way to memorialize the fair young man gives way to an equally pronounced later emphasis on poetry as the ideal means to that end. But this is not the whole story; the sonnets' speaker invokes a wide variety of discourses about memory, giving precedence now to one, now to another. At times the speaker's shifting commemorative strategies jar against each other, producing puzzling contrasts: is it the young man's appearance the speaker wants to preserve, or his "substance"? Who is really meant to be remembered: the young man or the speaker? Can poetry live up to the claims some of the sonnets make for its power to memorialize? In this chapter, I will, by way of background, discuss some of the rhetorical traditions that underlay the concept of memory in early modern England. I will then survey several of Shakespeare's main metaphors of commemoration; I read the sonnets as drawing on disparate and at times competing models for the way we retain and recollect ideas. Although the sonnets are often read as exalting poetry itself as the most lasting mnemonic, I conclude by suggesting the ways in which forgetting, as well as remembering, makes both Shakespeare's poetic and his commemorative project possible.

Remembering depends on the mind's ability to store information and to retrieve it again. In the second book of *The Faerie Queene*, Edmund Spenser allegorizes these two functions of memory as an elderly archivist and his page, Eumnestes and Anamestes, who preside over a room "all hangd about with rolles, / And old records from auncient times deriu'd" (II. x. 55. 5–6). Such metaphors are pervasive in the western tradition. As Douwe Draaisma summarizes, the various "storage space" metaphors that have been used to represent memory in the western tradition include spaces

> for information, such as archives and libraries; for goods, such as wine cellars and warehouses; for animals, such as dovecotes and aviaries; for valuables, such as treasure chests and vaults; for coins, such as leather purses or *sacculi* used by medieval moneychangers. . . . Buildings are also included in this imagery: places, abbeys, theatres. (Draaisma 2000: 3)

The concept of the memory as a repository holding some form of information was as current in the 1590s as it is today in the age of digital memory. To assist their own powers of recollection, Shakespeare's contemporaries would have had access to the classical "art of memory," a set of mnemonic storage-and-retrieval methods based on an architectural metaphor – much like the room of memory in *The Faerie Queene*.

Originally developed as a way for ancient Greek and Roman orators to remember their speeches, the art of memory enjoyed a long and varied history. As intellectual historians such as Frances Yates and Mary Carruthers have shown, the art of memory or *ars memorativa* tradition spread from classical Greece and Italy to the rest of Europe, gained traction in the Middle Ages, and took a wide variety of forms during the Renaissance. Among the oldest and the most popular of these mnemonic methods was the system of *loci* ("places") and figures. Yates summarizes this type of system, which is based upon three Latin works on rhetoric – the anonymous *Rhetorica ad herennium*, Cicero's *De oratore*, and Quintilian's *Institutio oratoria* – as follows:

> The first step was to imprint on the memory a series of loci or places. The commonest, though not the only, type of mnemonic place system was the architectural type. . . . The images by which the speech is to be remembered . . . are then placed in imagination on the places which have been memorised in the building. This done, as soon as the memory of the facts requires to be revived, all these places are visited in turn. (Yates 1966: 3)

Carruthers terms this system and its ilk "the architectural mnemonic" (Carruthers 1992: 71). The student of memory was expected to associate material to be remembered with symbolic images, and to place these images into an imaginary architectural setting (such as a palace, a church, a street, or a room with a series of niches in the walls) in order to remember in sequence.

Memory images, in this tradition, are sometimes images of objects and sometimes images of human figures. They can be direct representations of the memorized material or, more frequently, symbolic or metaphoric images. Quintilian, in the *Institutio oratoria*, offers the example of memory images "drawn from navigation, as, for instance, an anchor; or from warfare, as, for example, a weapon," to remind the user of the topics of navigation and warfare (quoted in Yates 1966: 22). The *Ad herennium* recommends that memory figures should be *imagines agentes*, or vividly "active" images: strikingly beautiful or ugly, dramatically clothed, bloodied, or comical, to make them harder to forget (Yates 1966: 10). This method was used to memorize words and phrases as well as concepts, but the classical authors conceded the greater difficulty of associating "an image for every single word" (Yates 1966: 9), and recommended word-for-word memorization only for limited use, as for "extracts from the poets" (Carruthers 1992: 73). The prominence of images in these early memory systems, however, does not mean that the *ars memorativa* was a nonverbal one. Memory, from the ancient Greeks onward, was imagined as a writing surface as well as a room full of images; it was frequently described as a book or a wax tablet ready to receive impressions that are also memory traces.[2]

We will see over the course of this essay how both verbal and pictorial models of memory inform Shakespeare's sonnets. They crop up in the work of other Elizabethan and Jacobean authors as well. Sir Philip Sidney, whose *Astrophel and Stella* helped to spark the sonnet craze that led to the publication of Shakespeare's own sonnets, considered the art of memory very much akin to the poet's art. "Now, that verse far exceedeth prose in the knitting up of the memory, the reason is manifest," he writes in the *Defence of Poesie*, "even they that have taught the art of memory have showed nothing so apt for it as a certain room divided into many places well and thoroughly known. Now, that hath the verse in effect perfectly, every word having his natural seat, which seat must needs make the word remembered" (Sidney 1983: 134–5).[3] Sidney correlates the "natural seat" of each word in a line of verse – presumably its metrical position – with the *loci* of the architectural mnemonic. But who are the figures occupying the "many places well and thoroughly known"? For Sidney, they are both the words themselves and the characters of epic poetry, such as Virgil's Aeneas: "the lofty image of such worthies most inflameth the mind with desire to be worthy" when the student of poetry remembers them (Sidney 1983: 131).

During the Renaissance, the arts of memory had connections with the theater as well: inventors of memory systems recommended architectural mnemonics resembling stage sets, which were sometimes called "memory theaters." The Italian author Giulio Camillio not only developed an amphitheater-shaped memory theater but built an elaborate wooden model of it filled with images.[4] The idea of the stage as a model for architectural mnemonics reached England during the sixteenth century (Yates 1966: 260). John Willis, author of a seventeeth-century memory treatise entitled *Mnemonica*, includes a diagram of a model background or "repository," which resembles an empty stage (Willis 1621: 6). Frances Yates has argued that Willis's contemporary Robert Fludd based his own theater memory system on Shakespeare's Globe (Yates 1966: 342–67); James Schiffer reads Hamlet's vow to remember "while memory holds a seat / In this distracted globe" as a punning allusion to the memory-theater system (Schiffer 1995: 76). Although these authors published their treatises after the composition and publication of Shakespeare's sonnets, English readers in the 1590s and 1600s would have had access to several translations of Italian memory treatises, as well as to works on rhetoric that described the classical memory arts. Yates concludes that the Elizabethan reader "would have known what the art of memory in its more normal forms was like," since "there had been a growing lay interest in the art" in England since the early 1500s (Yates 1966: 260).

"Much liker than your painted counterfeit": Memory Images

We have seen that Shakespeare's contemporaries and fellow writers, such as Sidney and Spenser, were aware of the tradition of associating remembered material with mental pictures. Memory images were considered most effective when they were visually unusual or striking, as the *Ad herennium* recommends. Later authors stressed the importance of using imagery that carried strong emotional associations (Carruthers 1992: 59–60). A similar rhetoric of passionate visual imagining and recollection informs many of Shakespeare's sonnets: the speaker, obsessed with the young man's image, looks for ways to keep that image vivid after the young man grows old. This is not surprising when we consider how early modern poets and medical theorists both connected erotic love with the act of seeing. Lina Bolzoni draws a persuasive parallel between the art of memory's *imagines agentes*, which stick in the memory by stirring the passions, and early modern theories of lovesickness:

> [S]ixteenth- and seventeenth-century medical treatises offer evidence that it was common practice to overheat the cranium of those obsessed by love. . . . It is commonly believed that the intensity of amorous desire causes the *phantasma* – that is, the image of the beloved – to concentrate within itself all the vital forces of the lover . . . If the zones of memory are like a mass of wax on which a seal leaves its imprint, lovesickness transforms them into a hard block in which the *phantasma* of the object is fixed. (Bolzoni 2001: 145)

Love makes the lover unable to think of anything else, literally stamping the beloved's picture into the brain, until the only way to remove it is to overheat the brain in the hopes of dissolving the memory. Love, in this theory, creates memory-images that work all too well. Bolzoni also connects the phantasmata of desire to the way some authors of mnemonic manuals recommended stocking one's mental theater with likenesses of beautiful women, whose attractiveness would make them more memorable (Bolzoni 2001: 146–51).

The obsessed and sometimes sleepless lover, haunted by the beloved's image, is an immediately recognizable figure for readers familiar with the Petrarchan tradition. Thanks to the Italian-influenced vogue for sonnets in the 1580s and 1590s, this tradition found its way into English sonnets as well.[5] We see it in Shakespeare's sonnet 113, in which the speaker's mind "shapes" everything it sees, be it "[t]he most sweet favor or deformèd'st creature," to the young man's form (ll. 12, 10). Several of the sonnets about sleeplessness, particularly 27, 43, and 61, emphasize the speaker's inability to stop visualizing the young man. In sonnet 27, the speaker's "soul's imaginary sight / Presents thy shadow to my sightless view" (ll. 9–10), keeping him awake at night. The same mental picture is an "image," a "shadow . . . like to thee," and a "spirit" in sonnet 61, before the speaker admits that the picture is entirely a product of his "own true love" (ll. 1, 4, 5, 11). Sonnet 43 finds him asleep, but dreaming incessantly of the young man's "shadow" (l. 5). (Sidney evokes the same topos in his own sonnet about sleeplessness, *Astrophel and Stella* 39, in which Astrophel bribes sleep to visit him by promising it a glimpse of "Stella's image" in his mind, "[l]ivelier than elsewhere" [l. 14].) In each of these sonnets, a simulacrum of the beloved possesses the lover's mind or heart. Shakespeare's speaker answers his own question – "Is it thy will thy image should keep open / My heavy eyelids to the weary night?" – with an emphatic "O no" (61. 1–2, 9); the image is not the young man, but a creation of the speaker's own untiring memory. And in one of the strangest moments in the sequence, the young man becomes, himself, a mnemonic, reminding the poet of past beloveds. Sonnet 31, "Thy bosom is endeared with all hearts," fantasizes a vision of the young man overlaid with the likenesses of "all those friends which I thought buried" (l. 4) and "Hung with the trophies of my lovers gone" (l. 10). Instead of simply surpassing all of these earlier friends, the young man *contains* them as well, as if he were a walking memory theater (or mausoleum): "Thou art the grave where buried love doth lie . . . Their images I loved I view in thee" (ll. 9, 13).

The first seventeen sonnets (the "procreation" sequence) refer to a somewhat different model of pictorial recall. Instead of internal and involuntarily recalled memory images, the procreation sonnets celebrate the deliberate creation of outward reminders of the young man's beauty.[6] To further the argument that the young man should marry and beget heirs, many of the sonnets in this group assert the commemorative value of children who resemble their parents. This claim emerges in the very first quatrain of sonnet 1:

> From fairest creatures we desire increase,
> That thereby beauty's rose might never die,
> But as the riper should by time increase,
> His tender heir might bear his memory:
>
> (1. 1–4)

This "memory" is explicitly an outward resemblance, and failure to reproduce is equated with oblivion. "But if thou live rememb'red not to be," warns the final couplet of sonnet

3, "Die single and thine image dies with thee" (ll. 13–14). At another point in this group of sonnets, the speaker again imagines the young man dying childless and mourned by the entire world, which will not be able to remember him properly without reminders of his "form":

> The world will be thy widow and still weep,
> That thou no form of thee hast left behind,
> When every private widow well may keep,
> By children's eyes, her husband's shape in mind.
>   (9. 5–8)

In some of these sonnets, the primary purpose of reproduction seems to be the making of a living memory-image to "[c]all . . . back" reminiscences of the young man's beauty (3. 10). As the speaker tells the young man, nature "carved thee for her seal, and meant thereby / Thou shouldst print more, not let that copy die" (11. 13–14). As in many of the later sonnets, the speaker wants everyone, not just himself, to remember the young man. Thus the memory image must be located out in the world rather than inside the speaker's mind and heart.

But the sonnets soon question the value of pictorial means for this end, signaling a shift in emphasis toward verbal forms of commemoration. Sonnet 16, near the end of the procreation sequence, asks the young man why he will not take advantage of "means more blessed than my barren rhyme" (l. 4) to immortalize himself. Here poetry appears for the first time in the sequence as a secondary, inferior option for preserving the young man's likeness; the youth must still "live . . . in eyes of men" by picturing himself "by [his] own sweet skill," i.e. by fathering children (ll. 12, 14). In later sonnets, however, the speaker begins to favor immortality through the written legacy of poetry over other methods. Sonnet 16's "barren rhyme" gives way to the "pow'rful rhyme" of sonnet 55, which the poet claims will outlive all "gilded monuments," "statues," and other commemorative objects (ll. 2, 1, 5). Readers who already know sonnet 18, "Shall I compare thee to a summer's day?", may not notice the move from the procreation sonnets to the more familiar claim that the young man's "eternal summer shall not fade" (l. 9). But, on close examination, the transition is a startling one. One minute, poetry is at best "a tomb, / Which hides your life and shows not half your parts" (17. 3–4). The next minute, the verse-tomb has become the "eternal lines" that promise to lift the young man out of death's "shade" (18. 12, 11). This moment is all the more surprising when one recalls that a reader who does not expect the claim for poetry's power is likely to anticipate – as Stephen Booth suggests in his commentary on sonnet 18 – "another exhortation to marry" in the final couplet. The procreation sonnets set up an implicit competition between visual commemoration and poetic commemoration, with the latter eventually prevailing.

Yet even in the later sonnets, the speaker invokes the power of images as spurs to recollection, as we have seen. The sonnets shift back and forth, at times boldly asserting that the young man's beautiful appearance can be captured and made to last, and at times conceding that "time will come and take my love away" (64. 12), leaving the poems themselves as his only memorial. This shift in emphasis away from visual memory may have to do with the Protestant outcry against images, which extended in some cases even to the imaginary imagery of the art of memory.[7] But the sonnets seem more concerned with the way in which any memorial must capture the beloved approximately rather than fully. The repeated paradox of the young man's fairness living on in "black ink" (65. 14) or "black lines" (63. 13) suggests that the replication is not exact. The young man's memory is a distillation rather than a perfect likeness. We can see the speaker working out the differences between essence and appearance, visual "counterfeit" and enduring substance, in a small group of sonnets that draw their metaphors from perfuming rather than from the visual arts.

Pressed Flowers and Olfactory Recall

Considering how strongly we associate the senses of smell and taste with memory, this kind of sensory recall seems oddly overlooked in the memory literature available to Shakespeare and his readers. The *ars memorativa* tradition emphasized sight over the other senses in its focus on the creation of imagery, and we have already noted the same emphasis on the visual in the sonnets. Sonnets 5 and 6, which share an image of preserving flowers' fragrance after the flowers die, stand out in the procreation sequence because they link commemoration not to sight but to smell. In sonnet 5, the young man is urged to distill his essence, a metaphor that de-emphasizes the lovely outward shape that the other sonnets praise:

> Then were not summer's distillation left
> A liquid pris'ner pent in walls of glass,
> Beauty's effect with beauty were bereft,
> Nor it nor no remembrance what it was.
> But flow'rs distilled, though they with winter meet,
> Leese but their show, their substance still lives sweet.
>
> (5. 9–14)

Theseus tries to persuade Hermia to marry in very similar terms in *A Midsummer Night's Dream*: "earthlier happy is the rose distill'd," he argues, "Than that which withering on the virgin thorn / Grows, lives, and dies in single blessedness" (I. i. 76–8) – though Theseus seems more concerned with the present than with the future. But both he and the sonnets' speaker imagine procreation as a means of preserving part of an otherwise mortal life. What is interesting in the procreation sonnets is the way in which the terms have shifted from outward appearance to inward substance.

Sonnet 6 picks up the argument where sonnet 5 leaves off, urging the young man to "let not winter's ragged hand deface / In thee thy summer ere thou be distilled" (ll. 1–2). Once beauty, whether that of young men or roses, dies (so the argument in this sonnet goes), some palpable "remembrance what it was" can remain if someone has taken the trouble to "distill" it into a more lasting form. Sonnet 6, like others in the procreation sequence, makes the claim that the young man will be "refigured" by his children (l. 10); but for once this refiguring is not a matter of re-creating his appearance. Sonnet 5's final couplet acknowledges that the young man's outward "show" will not, after all, survive. This is a far cry from the surrounding sonnets' imagery of the child as a "glass" (i.e. a mirror, 3. 1) or "sweet semblance" (13. 4) of its parents. It is a far cry, even, from the flower metaphor in sonnet 16, in which "maiden gardens" wait to bear the young man "living flowers, / Much liker than your painted counterfeit" (ll. 6–8). Here the young man is a flower propagating an identical flower, but the perfume sonnets offer an oddly mixed metaphor: distilling where we might expect grafting.

In *Shakespeare's Perfume*, Richard Halpern persuasively glosses the perfume bottle in sonnets 5 and 6 as a glass womb and the distillate of flowers as a metaphor for the young man's semen, providing the genetic material for children who will carry on his image (Halpern 2002: 14). But, Halpern notes, the glass bottle image is "perfectly suited to another, implied purpose: that of figuring *poetic* procreation," and thus "Sonnet 5 seems to offer a curiously material demonstration, even before the fact, of the Freudian thesis that sexual desire can be distilled into art" (p. 14). The miniature sequence comprising sonnets 5 and 6 stands out not only for its shift from one sense to another, but for its anticipation of the claims that the speaker will soon make for poetry – another art that relies on other kinds of mimesis than the visual.

The metaphor of distilled roses returns in sonnet 54. The perfume image keeps its association with immortality and continuing remembrance, but the vehicle and tenor of the metaphor have both shifted. In the earlier sonnets, the rose and its fragrance stand for the young man's short-lived beauty and its preservation in the form of future children, respectively. In 54, the rose's fragrance is a "sweet ornament" that enhances its visual beauty, as truth will enhance the young man's physical charms (l. 2). The fragrance prevents the rose from dying "unwooed, and unrespected," and gives it an afterlife as perfume: "Of their sweet deaths are sweetest odors made" (ll. 10–12). But instead of returning us, as we might expect, to the procreation argument, the couplet offers poetry as the distilling agent by which truth can be made to outlast beauty: "And so of you, beauteous and lovely youth, / When that shall vade, by verse distils your truth" (ll. 13–14). The perfume-making process, formerly a metaphor for offspring, has become a metaphor for the condensing and refining process of poetry.

I suspect that Emily Dickinson had these sonnets at the back of her mind when she composed her own meditation on distillation, perfume, immortality, and remembrance:

> Essential Oils – are wrung —
> The Attar from the Rose
> Be not expressed by Suns – alone —
> It is the gift of Screws —

> The General Rose – decay —
> But this – in Lady's Drawer
> Make Summer – When the Lady lie
> In Ceaseless Rosemary —
> > (Dickinson 1960: 335)

Where Shakespeare's perfume sonnets focus on distillation's final product in its glass vial, Dickinson dwells on the laborious and covertly violent process of pressing oil (the "gift of Screws") from flowers. But there is something thoroughly and eerily Shakespearean in the way this poem's second stanza focuses on the afterlife of the attar of roses, long after their initial "Summer" has ended, long after the "Lady" who pressed them lies "In Ceaseless Rosemary" (as if she, too, were being stored away in a drawer full of potpourri). In Dickinson's poem, the perfume – which can be read as a figure for both memory and artistic creation – survives at the expense of the rose itself. A similar logic underlies many of the commemorative gestures in the sonnets. The relentless march of time in sonnet 60 ("Like as the waves make towards the pebbled shore") will inevitably "[f]eed . . . on the rarities of nature's truth," leaving nothing but the poem itself to "stand" as a record of those rarities (ll. 1, 11, 13).

Writing and the Persistence of Memory

Where does this claim for poetry's survival originate? The permanence of poetry is one of the oldest western metaphors for eternal preservation; Horace's "exegi monumentum aere perennius" (*Odes*, III. 30) is a classic instance.[8] Verse itself is one of the oldest mnemonic devices, whether the material being remembered is the story of the fall of Troy or the number of days in April. And when Shakespeare's speaker begins to praise poetry, he hails it as both a worthy object to be remembered and an ideal means of preservation. In his "poor rhyme," he eventually finds a means to preserve the young man's memory and his own:

> Now with the drops of this most balmy time
> My love looks fresh, and death to me subscribes,
> Since spite of him *I'll* live in this poor rhyme,
> While he insults o'er dull and speechless tribes.
> And thou in this shalt find thy monument,
> When tyrants' crests and tombs of brass are spent.
> > (107. 9–14, emphasis added)

We might expect "you'll live" instead of "I'll live," but sonnet 107 guarantees commemoration for both the speaker and the addressee. The speaker's praise for the memorializing potential of poetry – as opposed to children, or imaginary inward portraiture – does several things at once. It introduces the topos of poetic immortality; it connects this topos with the various other means of commemoration explored in the sequence; and it emphasizes forms of memory that are both external and verbal.

The turn to verse at the end of the procreation sonnets introduces another set of models of memory, based on written and spoken words as well as (or instead of) moving images. From its classical beginnings onward, practitioners of the art of memory compared their methods to reading and writing, since both reading and picturing rely on the sense of sight (Carruthers 1992: 17). The mental portrait gallery of the architectural mnemonic was also a legible text composed of signs. Mary Carruthers argues that "[t]he connection between what is to be remembered and the device used to remember it is fundamentally through language, not through picture" (Carruthers 1992: 28). In the section on memory in his 1560 *Arte of Rhetorique*, Thomas Wilson (closely following the *Rhetorica ad herennium*) asserts that

> i. The places of Memorie are resembled vnto Waxe and Paper. ii. Images are compted like vnto Letters or a Seale. iii. The placing of these Images, is like vnto wordes written. iiii. The vtterance and vsing of them, is like vnto reading. (Wilson 1994: 237)

A trained memory, thus organized, could be and was seen as akin to a writing surface – the "Waxe and Paper" full of words or stamped imprints. Ernst Curtius has traced the metaphor of "the book of memory" from the ancient Greeks all the way to Shakespeare's plays and sonnets (Curtius 1953: 304, 339–40). In turn, poets such as Shakespeare saw writing as a vessel of memory. Sonnet 81 claims "immortal life" for poet and addressee long after both have died, "such virtue" (the poet confidently concludes) "hath my pen" (ll. 5, 13). This sonnet includes a scene of future reading that counterbalances the dispiriting vision of sonnet 17, in which the speaker imagines a skeptical posterity exclaiming " 'This poet lies' " (l. 7). No such fears occur in sonnet 81; instead, the poet predicts that "eyes not yet created shall o'er read" it, while "tongues to be" repeat the poems out loud (ll. 10–11). Here verse is a static "monument" to be viewed and read, but also a living remembrance "Where breath most breathes, ev'n in the mouths of men" (ll. 9, 14). It unites the ancient tradition of memorized oral poetry with the ink-and-paper medium in which Elizabethan readers encountered the sonnet.

Although medieval authors did not consider word-for-word recall so important as remembering the general gist of a text, the *ars memorativa* did offer guidelines for memorizing words and phrases, particularly from poems (Carruthers 1992: 86–7). In his *Mnemonica*, John Willis recommends that the reader memorize individual words, letters, and phrases by imagining them inscribed on a wall. "Scriptile Ideas," as Willis calls them, are "whereby the thing to be remembred, is supposed to be written in a plaine white table hanged vp in the midst of the opposite wall belonging to the roome wherein it is placed" (Willis 1621: 33). Willis considers poetry suitable for his "scriptile idea" method because of its distinctive shape on the page. He notes that "verses are to be distinguished by their seuerall lines," so they, and "generally all other kindes of sentences which haue . . . a peculiar kind of writing by it selfe," should be memorized by visualizing the shapes of the words (Willis 1621: 44). Willis's instructions resonate with the tradition that represented the mind itself as a "plaine white table." Mary Thomas Crane has observed how humanist pedagogical theory stressed the importance of collecting and memorizing sayings, or *sententiae*. A common metaphor for memorization was that of "[e]ngraving or carving sayings on the mind," which, as Crane notes, can be linked with the technique of memorizing words by visualizing them written on walls as well as with the actual practice of decorating walls with adages and sayings (Crane 1993: 74–5).

In Shakespeare's sonnets, the literary topos of poetry as perpetuation coexists – at times uneasily – with the pedagogical and physiological metaphor of inscription as memory. The poet's "verse" is a relatively abstract entity in the sonnets we have examined thus far. But elsewhere, commemoration in words takes a specific form: writing on paper. Sonnet 77, which commentators generally suggest originally accompanied the gift of a notebook, reminds its addressee that "vacant leaves [i.e. blank paper] thy mind's imprint will bear, / And of this book this learning mayst thou taste" (ll. 3–4). The pages extend the young man's memory by providing an external storage space for his thoughts, which he can later consult after he has forgotten them:

> Look what thy memory cannot contain,
> Commit to these waste blanks, and thou shalt find
> Those children nursed, delivered from thy brain,
> To take a new acquaintance of thy mind.
>
> (77. 9–12)

The early modern equivalents of the pocket notebook (or the portable digital assistant) were called "writing tables" or "table-books." Made of paper covered in wax for easier erasure, table-books could be used and reused for note-taking. As various critics have noticed, this type of notebook is what Hamlet thinks of when he vows to "wipe away all trivial fond records" from the "table of [his] memory," and when he later exclaims "My tables – meet it is I set it down / That one may smile, and smile, and be a villain" (*Hamlet*, I. v. 98–108). In a recent article, Peter Stallybrass and Roger Chartier describe sixteenth- and seventeenth-century table-books "composed of a printed twenty-four-year almanac and other printed material, bound together with blank pages of erasable paper or parchment" bearing the evidence of repeated erasings (Stallybrass et al. 2004: 386). Sonnet 77's "book" may be of this type. Writing tables, like the wax tablets that preceded them, served as a useful metaphor for memory because they could be erased as well as covered with inscriptions.

Sonnet 122 returns to the image of the writing tablet as a memory supplement, but with far less assurance. This time, the sonnet's addressee has given a book of tables to the speaker. The speaker has ventured "to give them from me" and asks for forgiveness because he trusts his own powers of recollection, "those tables that receive thee more," more than any external memorandum (ll. 11–12). In the first quatrain, the speaker seems ready to launch into the eternizing metaphors that have become so familiar over the course of the sequence:

> Thy gift, thy tables, are within my brain
> Full charactered with lasting memory,
> Which shall above that idle rank remain
> Beyond all date ev'n to eternity—
>
> (ll. 1–4)

These lines tie writing ("charactered" suggests letters as well as the young man's "character") to "lasting memory" in the way we have seen in sonnet 81. And yet, as soon as he makes this claim, the speaker finds himself forced to back away from it: "Or at the least, so long as brain and heart / Have faculty by nature to subsist" (ll. 5–6). Meanwhile, he insists that the tables are a poor substitute for the very powers of recollection whose mortality he has just admitted:

> That poor retention could not so much hold,
> Nor need I tallies thy dear love to score.
> Therefore to give them from me was I bold
> To trust those tables that receive thee more.
>   To keep an adjunct to remember thee
>   Were to impart forgetfulness in me.
>
> (ll. 9–14)

Crane argues that this sonnet engages with early modern practices of verbal memorization, since "Shakespeare here, unusually, depicts his record of the young man *not* as an image, but as a written 'record,' engraved on the memory as sayings were in humanist educational theory" (Crane 1993: 198). But sonnet 122 shares a key quality with some of the more image-centric sonnets in the sequence: it privileges the record "within [the] brain" over external means of commemoration. Like sonnets 46 and 47, which stage a debate between the speaker's "eye and heart" over which of them gets to keep the young man's picture (46. 1), 122 locates the young man's "record" inside the speaker himself. But the speaker undermines his own rhetoric of "lasting memory" by admitting that his mind and memory will last only as long as his body lives.

Stallybrass and Chartier see the erasable tablet metaphor as foregrounding "the difficulty of making any complete separation between remembering and forgetting," concluding that "[t]he claims to memory's endurance in Sonnet 122 differ significantly from the claims concerning the immortality of writing in earlier sonnets" (Stallybrass et al. 2004: 417). And yet the earlier sonnets' claims about writing, as we have seen, emerge from a complex array of memorial practices: portraiture, mental imagery, reproduction both sexual and textual, distillation, the monumental and the lyric. None of these practices is free from the speaker's doubts about the permanence of memory. When the writing metaphor emerges at the end of the procreation sequence, it emerges in an anxious quatrain about the survival of the sonnets themselves:

> So should my papers, yellowed with their age,
> Be scorned, like old men of less truth than tongue,

And your true rights be termed a poet's rage
And stretched meter of an antique song.

(17. 5–12)

Writing preserves but can also be lost; it can be both a metaphor for the mind's impression-making processes and a literal reference to the poet's manuscripts, which age and grow fragile like the poet's body. Sonnet 121, the last to concern itself at length with memory, ends on a pessimistic note that has already sounded near the beginning of the sequence.

Conclusion: Oblivion as a Way of Remembering

Sonnet 121 highlights a paradox of memory. To use physical objects as repositories of memory is to risk forgetting, as anyone who has forgotten appointments after writing them down in a datebook can attest. This is a claim at least as old as Plato's *Phaedrus*, in which Socrates tells a fable about the dangers of oblivion that result from entrusting one's ideas to writing.[9] And yet, without such potentially unreliable means of storage, individual memories die with the person who remembers them. Shakespeare's speaker's inner "tables" will preserve the young man only "so long as brain and heart / Have faculty by nature to subsist" (122. 5–6). Hence the increasing emphasis on the poems themselves as a means of preserving memory. And yet, as we have seen in sonnet 17, the sonnets also give voice to the fear that words alone are not vivid enough to keep the young man from being forgotten. The doubts that repeatedly plague the speaker, even as he argues for poetry's immortalizing power, indicate how profoundly the sonnets are haunted by forgetting. Again and again, time appears as the enemy of the poet's project and the beloved's youth and beauty, threatening to overthrow everything that looks permanent, leaving nothing to serve as a trigger for memory. The "Great princes' favorites" and "The painful warrior" of sonnet 25, not to mention "all the rest . . . for which he toiled," all end up "from the book of honour razèd quite" and "forgot" (25. 5, 9, 11–12).

So it is strange, and yet unsurprising, that even the process of forgetting can be pressed into memory's service in several of the sonnets. Sonnet 71 illustrates this strategy of commemorating through a demand to be forgotten. Here the speaker, ostensibly concerned that his death will make the young man suffer, asks not to be mourned. Even his poems should not be read as memorials, despite the preceding sonnets' claims to the contrary:

Nay, if you read this line, remember not
The hand that writ it, for I love you so,
That I in your sweet thoughts would be forgot,
If thinking on me then should make you woe.

(ll. 5–8)

We cannot quite take these lines literally. To tell someone to forget something is to make it harder for them to forget. As Umberto Eco remarks in his speculative essay on the "art of forgetting," any methodical attempt *not* to remember "allows one not to forget something but to remember that one wanted to forget it" (Eco 1988: 254). "Remember not" is like "Don't think of an elephant" – a command that undermines itself. Helen Vendler reads this sonnet as "a defensive construct hoping to awaken in the shallow young man the very depths of mourning that it affects to prohibit" (Vendler 1997: 329). We may also read it as an attempt to turn oblivion into yet another commemorative strategy.

Three more sonnets on the speaker's own aging and death follow this reverse-psychology appeal, culminating in a renewed assertion that the poems are what must survive:

> My life hath in this line some interest,
> Which for memorial still with thee shall stay.
> When thou reviewest this, thou dost review
> The very part was consecrate to thee.
> The earth can have but earth, which is his due;
> My spirit is thine, the better part of me.
>
> (74. 3–8)

This sonnet ends by arguing that the speaker's body is "[t]oo base . . . to be rememb'red," and what really matters is "this," the poem, which "with thee remains" (ll. 12, 14). As in the various sonnets about the young man's inevitable aging and death, the speaker admits that memory, including the kind of commemoration the sonnets promise, cannot preserve everything.

And perhaps this is where the sequence ends its exploration of what it means to commemorate: with the awareness that memories, like poems, are always representations and hence always partial. "Partialness is . . . characteristic of memory," Carruthers argues, "because a part of the original image is inevitably lost or 'forgotten' when the memory impresses the *imago* [image] of a *res* [thing]" (Carruthers 1992: 25). To remember one thing is to forget other things, as Hamlet promises to do by wiping his mental tables clean. To remember is also to symbolize, to turn people or things or events into signs of themselves, and to lose something of their immediacy. In some ways, the work of memory in these sonnets resembles the work of mourning that Peter Sacks identifies as the great project of the elegy – the acceptance of loss by substituting a symbolic reminder of the lost object which is also a "prize and sign of poethood" (Sacks 1985: 1, 5). But the sonnets do not memorialize an already lost beloved; instead, they look ahead to a time in the future when others, or at times the young man himself, will look back and try to remember. "Against that time" (in the words of the first line of sonnet 49), the speaker deploys as many strategies as he can to ensure that something remains. A memory image, a portrait, a written note, an inscription, a poem, a bottle of rosewater: all are made things, representations, likenesses that signify. Visual memory strategies appear to predominate in the earlier sonnets while verbal commemoration takes over in the later ones, but even if we read the ordering of the sequence as authorial, the "young man" sonnets do not conclude on the confident note of "Not marble nor the gilded monuments / Of princes shall outlive this pow'rful rhyme" (55. 1–2).

By way of comparison, we might consider some of the ways in which verbal and visual forms of recollection interact in Shakespeare's plays. I have already noted Hamlet's use of the table-book metaphor; elsewhere in the play, though, many of the triggers for recollection are visual. Hamlet chooses to remind Gertrude of her failings by showing her a pair of portraits of Claudius and King Hamlet, the "counterfeit presentment of two brothers" (III. iv. 54). James Schiffer cites this exchange, together with Hamlet's black clothing and the play-within-the-play, as instances of Hamlet's need for visible reminders of his mourning and his need for revenge (Schiffer 1995: 69–71). Indeed, the ghost's repeated visits to enjoin Hamlet to remember are themselves invocations of the concept of the phantasmatic memory image. In a less serious register, Viola woos Olivia with a familiar argument from the procreation sonnets – "Lady, you are the cruell'st she alive / If you will lead these graces to the grave / And leave the world no copy" (*Twelfth Night*, I. v. 241–3) – only to receive an ironic reassurance:

> O, sir, I will not be so hard-hearted; I will give out divers schedules of my beauty. It shall be inventoried, and every particle and utensil labell'd to my will: as, *item*, two lips, indifferent red; *item*, two grey eyes, with lids to them; *item*, one neck, one chin, and so forth. (I. v. 244–9)

Olivia mocks not only the rhetoric of the blazon and the love lyric, but also the very notion that a written record can accurately "copy" a face. What inventory of "lips, indifferent red" and "grey eyes, with lids to them" can make us imagine a face we have never seen? As in the sonnets, we encounter the gap between what can be seen and the words that memorialize it.

Not many of Shakespeare's plays throw verbal and visual recollection into as high relief as the sonnets do, but *The Winter's Tale* dramatizes some of the same tensions we have been examining. Leontes and other characters exhibit the same preoccupation with children's resemblance to their parents that informs the procreation sonnets. Many of the metaphors center on the acts of writing, copying, and printing. Leontes calls Mamillius's nose "a copy out of mine" (I. ii. 122). Paulina describes the infant Perdita as "Although the print be little, the whole matter / And copy of the father" (II. iii. 99–100), a metaphor that Leontes later repeats when he greets Florizel with "Your mother was most true to wedlock, Prince, / For she did print your royal father off, / Conceiving you" (V. i. 124–6). The imagery of these moments is drawn from the printing press; the child resembles its parents in a textual rather than an iconic manner. But in its last two acts, *The Winter's Tale* replaces the child Perdita, the "copy" of her father in small print, with the adolescent Perdita, who bears a striking physical resemblance to her mother, and the play begins to move toward its final scene of visual commemoration. After Leontes and Paulina imagine Hermione's ghost haunting him, Leontes agrees to marry another woman only if she is "as like Hermione as is her picture" and then only if Hermione is "again in breath" (V. i. 74, 83) – and he gets his wish when Hermione's statue comes to life. The statue scene gives us a classic "moving image" that prompts memory: the contrite Leontes comments that the statue "has / My evils conjur'd to remembrance" (V. iii. 39–40). Yet the statue is more than a figure for Leontes' and Paulina's gallery of memory; it turns out to be the very person it commemorates. This total correspondence between memory image and beloved (but lost or to-be-lost) character is what the speaker of the sonnets tries for, but can never quite achieve. Barring such a miracle, memory is always already a partial forgetting; but the forgetting is also a starting point for poetry.

NOTES

1   I follow the convention that divides the sonnets into two groups, 1–126 (those addressing the young man) and 127–54 (those addressing the dark lady). Although critics such as Heather Dubrow have made compelling arguments against treating 126 as the dividing line between the young man and dark lady sequences (Dubrow 1996), I focus on the sonnets before 126 for the pragmatic reason that memory is far less of an explicit concern in the sonnets that follow it. As Joyce Sutphen points out, "the word 'time,' which occurs over seventy times in the first 126 sonnets, never appears again after sonnet 126 – nor does 'memory.' Words connected with the memory motif – 'book,' 'page,' 'pen,' 'paper,' 'pencil,' 'line,' 'verse,' 'copy,' 'stamp,' and 'print' – are also absent after 126" (Sutphen 1999: 210).

2   On the metaphor of memory as a book or a wax tablet from Plato to Freud, see Draaisma (2000: 7–9, 24–46) and Carruthers (1992: 21–2). Peters (2004) provides an overview of the connections between the memory-as-theater and memory-as-book models.

3   In his discussion of the role of the art of memory in sonnet 15, Raymond Waddington also notes this passage from Sidney, as well as Spenser's memory room from *The Faerie Queene* (Waddington 1974: 108–12). For more on the connections between the art of memory and literature of the English Renaissance, see Plett (1989); for a discussion of the place of memory in relation to history in early modern England, see Woolf (1991).

4   See Yates (1966: 129–72) for a longer account of Camillo and his theater.

5   For a much longer study of English poets' responses to Petrarch, see Dubrow (1995). See also ch. 5 by Richard Strier in this volume.

6   For a longer and more detailed discussion of the procreation sonnets, see ch. 20 by Garrett Sullivan in this volume.

7   The history of iconoclasm in England during the Reformation is a larger subject than this essay can address, but Frances Yates provides an interesting perspective on the objections that image-based memory systems could raise among Protestant iconoclasts, one of whom complained in 1603 that "'A thing feigned in the mind by imagination is an idol'" (Yates 1966: 278). See also Booth's commentary on the word "images" in line 13 of sonnet 31 (Shakespeare 1977).

8   "I have finished a monument more lasting than bronze and loftier than the Pyramids' royal pile, one that no wasting rain, no furious north wind can destroy, or the countless chain of years and the ages' flight" (Loeb Classical Library edition, ed. C. F. Bennett, 1914). See E. R. Curtius's discussion of the "poetry as perpetuation" topos (Curtius 1953: 476–7).

9   In Socrates' fable, the Egyptian god Theuth invents the written alphabet and offers it to Thamuz, king of Thebes, as an "elixir of memory"; Thamuz replies that "this invention will produce forgetfulness in the minds of those who learn to use it, because they will not practice their memory" (*Phaedrus* 274E–

275A; Loeb Classical Library edition, trans. Harold North Fowler, 1914). Both Yates and Carruthers discuss this passage in their surveys of early theories of memory (Yates 1966: 36–9; Carruthers 1992: 30–1). Daniel Woolf argues that in the early modern period, writing was seen as both "a necessary evil" and "an acceptable, even a desirable, substitute for sheer reliance on memory" (Woolf 1991: 290). Peters (2004: 181–6) argues that the Platonic opposition between memory and writing underlies many of the critical studies of the *ars memorativa* since Yates, and argues instead that "a relationship of reciprocity" existed between memory and the early modern book (p. 185).

References and Further Reading

Bolzoni, Lina (2001). *The Gallery of Memory: Literary and Iconographic Models in the Age of the Printing Press*, trans. J. Parzen. Toronto: University of Toronto Press. (First publ. in Italian as *La stanza della memoria: modelli letterari e iconografi dell'età della stampa*, Torino: Einaudi, 1995.)

Carruthers, Mary (1992). *The Book of Memory: A Study of Memory in Medieval Culture*. Cambridge, UK: Cambridge University Press.

Crane, Mary Thomas (1993). *Framing Authority: Sayings, Self, and Society in Sixteenth-Century England*. Princeton: Princeton University Press.

Curtius, Ernst Robert (1953). *European Literature and the Latin Middle Ages*, trans. Willard R. Trask. Princeton: Princeton University Press. (First publ. in German as *Europäische Literatur und lateinisches Mittelalter*, Bern: A. Francke, 1948).

Dickinson, Emily (1960). *The Complete Poems of Emily Dickinson*, ed. T. H. Johnson. Boston: Little, Brown.

Draaisma, Douwe (2000). *Metaphors of Memory: A History of Ideas about the Mind*, trans. Paul Vincent. Cambridge, UK: Cambridge University Press. (First publ. in Dutch as *Metaforenmachine: een geschiedenis van het geheugen*, Groningen: Historische Uitgeverij, 1995.)

Dubrow, Heather (1995). *Echoes of Desire: English Petrarchism and Its Counterdiscourses*. Ithaca, NY: Cornell University Press.

Dubrow, Heather (1996). " 'Incertainties now crown themselves assur'd': The Politics of Plotting Shakespeare's Sonnets." *Shakespeare Quarterly* 47: 3, 291–305.

Eco, Umberto (1988). "An *ars oblivionalis*? Forget it!" *PMLA* 103: 3, 254–61.

Halpern, Richard (2002). *Shakespeare's Perfume: Sodomy and Sublimity in the Sonnets, Wilde, Freud, and Lacan*. Philadelphia: University of Pennsylvania Press.

Justice, Donald (1991). "Meters and Memory." In *A Donald Justice Reader*, 149–55. Hanover, NH: University Press of New England.

Peters, Julie Stone (2004). "Theater and Book in the History of Memory: Materializing Mnemosyne in the Age of Print." *Modern Philology* 102: 2, 179–206.

Plett, Heinrich (1989). "Ars memorativa: Mnemonic Architecture and English Renaissance Literature." *Texte: revue de critique et de théorie littéraire* 8–9, 147–58.

Sacks, Peter (1985). *The English Elegy: Studies in the Genre from Spenser to Yeats*. Baltimore: Johns Hopkins University Press.

Schiffer, James (1995). "Mnemonic Cues to Passion in *Hamlet*." *Renaissance Papers* 1995, 65–80.

Shakespeare, William (1977). *Shakespeare's Sonnets*, ed. Stephen Booth. New Haven: Yale University Press.

Sidney, Philip (1983). *Sir Philip Sidney: Selected Prose and Poetry*, ed. R. Kimbrough. Madison: University of Wisconsin Press.

Stallybrass, Peter; Chartier, Roger; Mowery, J. Franklin; and Wolfe, Heather (2004). "Hamlet's Tables and the Technologies of Writing in Renaissance England." *Shakespeare Quarterly* 55: 4, 379–419.

Sutphen, Joyce (1999). " 'A dateless lively heat': Storing Loss in the Sonnets." In J. Schiffer (ed.), *Shakespeare's Sonnets: Critical Essays*, 199–217. New York: Garland.

Vendler, Helen (1997). *The Art of Shakespeare's Sonnets*. Cambridge, Mass.: Harvard University Press.

Waddington, Raymond (1974). "Shakespeare's Sonnet 15 and the Art of Memory." In Thomas Sloan and Raymond Waddington (eds.), *The Rhetoric of Renaissance Poetry from Wyatt to Milton*, 96–122. Berkeley: University of California Press.

Willis, John (1621). *The Art of Memory So Far Forth as it Dependeth Vpon Places and Idea's*. London: Printed by W. Jones.

Wilson, Thomas (1994). *The Art of Rhetoric*, ed. P. E. Medine. University Park, Pa.: Pennsylvania State University Press. (First publ. 1560.)

Woolf, Daniel (1991). "Memory and Historical Culture in Early Modern England." *Journal of the Canadian Historical Association* 2, 283–308.

Yates, Frances (1966). *The Art of Memory*. Chicago: University of Chicago Press.

PART VIII
The Sonnets in/and the Plays

Halting Sonnets: Poetry and Theater in *Much Ado About Nothing*

Patrick Cheney

This chapter proposes to investigate the role of Shakespeare's sonnets within his larger theatrical career. *Much Ado About Nothing* is a useful site for such an investigation, because it concludes with two scenes of revelation: the first (more famous) about theater; the second (less discussed) about sonneteering. In the first revelation, Friar Francis and his acting troupe (Beatrice, Margaret, Ursula, Benedick, and Leonato) put on the play of Hero's resurrection before Don Pedro and Claudio: "The former Hero! Hero that is dead!"[1] In the second revelation, Claudio, newly reconciled with Hero, pulls a "halting sonnet" from Benedick's pocket, while Hero herself plucks "another" sonnet from the "pocket" of Beatrice (V. iv. 87–8). As Benedick remarks, "A miracle! here's our own hands against our hearts" (ll. 91–2). This double revelation in the final act intimates that Shakespeare's comedy might be processing more than the politics of gender difference (Findlay 2003; Suzuki 2000; Berger 1997; Paster 1995; Gay 1994; Howard 1987; Cook 1986; Neely 1985). *Much Ado* might also be processing a professional dynamic of authorship between two literary forms, often kept separate in mainstream Shakespeare scholarship: poetry and theater, sonneteering and playwriting. By looking further into this dynamic, we may discover a critical model that helps account for arguably the most anomalous contour of Shakespearean authorship: the fact that this consummate man of the theater wrote a sonnet sequence (Cheney 2004: ch. 7).[2]

While critics between Charles Gildon in 1710 (Cannan 2004) and David Schalkwyk in 2002 have studied in detail the connection between the sonnets and the plays, including *Much Ado*, most neglect the template of authorship underwriting the connection, especially the signature form this authorship takes: Shakespeare recurrently combines a discourse of and a fiction about sonneteering and theater. We can explain this signature most obviously by recalling that Shakespeare worked on poems and plays, sonnets and theater, throughout his writing career.[3] But we may profitably situate his writing practice within a broader cultural context: the combination of literary forms that is itself a sixteenth-century phenomenon in England and Europe.[4]

Shakespeare may be unusual in writing a sonnet sequence while deeply involved in the new commercial theater, but the anomaly draws attention to his practice as itself worth examining. Suggestively, the practice escapes our two main critical narratives about the presence of Shakespeare's poems in his otherwise theatrical career: that Shakespeare came to London to be a poet but then abandoned this early vocation for the theater (Schmidgall 1990: 1; Kermode 2000: 3, 17); or that he wrote poems only when the plague closed the theater, primarily in 1592–3 (McDonald 2001: 15). By including a fiction about sonneteering in *Much Ado*, Shakespeare affords an unusual opportunity to witness his distinct form of early modern authorship. Consequently, we may come to see Shakespeare's *Sonnets* not as peripheral to his theatrical canon but as intimately bound up with it.

Shakespeare's Theater of Sonnets: A New Critical Model

Surprisingly, critics have neglected Shakespeare's staging of sonneteering in *Much Ado*. Most simply ignore it (e.g. Rossiter 1965; Berger 1997; Cook 1986; Suzuki 2000); a few refer to it only in passing (Howard 1987: 182; Neely 1985: 56; Lewalski 1968: 245). In our most sustained and recent study of "Shakespeare's Sonnets and Plays," Schalkwyk offers the following brief discussion:

> Beatrice and Benedick's mutual engagement in the world of the sonnet – despite their shared ironical stance towards Petrarch – is decisive in breaking their solitary poses. Their alignment of hands and hearts reminds us that the sonnet is a form of action, something produced through and by the body towards the union of both bodies and souls. . . . Beatrice and Benedick require the publication of sonnets written separately to the beloved to attest to feelings that neither can finally deny. (2002: 69; see also 136)

Schalkwyk identifies two important features to Shakespeare's narrative. First, the playwright makes sonneteering a crucial "action" in the plot, the very device that "breaks" the "solitary poses" of the play's two most celebrated characters: once the sonnets are published, Benedick and Beatrice can no longer deny their love for each other. Second, and following from the first, Shakespeare presents the lovers' sonnets as material evidence for the mutuality of their emotions.

From Schalkwyk's brief analysis, we can discern an idea that taps into an important conversation in Shakespeare studies today: only through the material publication of sonnets does an individual's emotional character become visible (McCoy 1997; Paster 2004; Everett 1994: 71, 76). The sonnets, in other words, serve as written manifestations of an interior identity that is emotional in quality. Through his fiction, we might speculate, Shakespeare confronts and overcomes the primary limitation of theater, which must depend on the stage to perform an external action (or "show"): through sonneteering, the playwright permits the audience to become privy to what we cannot see, the hidden recesses of a character's emotional subjectivity.

In our most important recent study of Shakespeare's poems, Colin Burrow finds Shakespeare characteristically doing just the opposite, including in the 1609 *Sonnets* and in their companion poem, *A Lover's Complaint*. In this narrative poem, the country maid throws "deep-brain'd sonnets" (l. 209) in the river, leading Burrow to conclude that "in Shakespeare's poems objects do not reveal emotions; they encrypt them intriguingly, and start his readers on a quest for mind" (1998: 28). If this occlusion of emotional identity is characteristic of "Shakespeare" when he represents sonnets as objects, we might attend all the more to his use of sonnets in *Much Ado*, where sonnets do encrypt the passions. In fact, the dramatic scene concluding this comedy takes us into intriguing emotional territory, precisely where the divide between body and mind, hand and heart, "physiology and inwardness" (to use Schoenfeldt's words) ends.

The phrase "halting sonnet" serves as a clear signpost. Editors typically do not gloss the key word, "halting." The recent Folger edition offers "lame, limping" (Shakespeare 1995: 194), while David and Ben Crystal in *Shakespeare's Words: A Glossary and Language Companion* add "hesitating, . . . faltering" (2002: 211). Although providing a start, these glosses miss the pun on metric *foot*, a unit of rhythmic measure in poetry (noted only by the Oxford World's Classics edition [Shakespeare 1993: 200]): a halting sonnet is a poem with a limp or lame meter: a bad sonnet. In sonnet 89, Shakespeare presents his narrator, named Will in sonnet 136, resorting to the pun in addressing the young man: "Speak of my lameness, and I straight will halt" (l. 3). As Stephen Booth points out, this line does not identify Shakespeare himself as lame but portrays Will as lame in the exercise of his metric foot (Shakespeare 1977: 293; 1997c: 288; 1996: 196; 2002: 558). In *As You Like It*, Shakespeare pauses to insert a dialogue on a poem's halting metric feet. After Celia reads Orlando's poem, Rosalind agrees with her cousin that "the feet might bear the verses," adding, "but the feet were lame, and could not bear themselves without the verse, and therefore stood lamely in the verse" (III. ii. 167–71).

As the presence in a play of this metric discourse about poems intimates, Shakespeare could assign to the idea of halting verse not merely "poetic" but also theatrical significance. In *Hamlet*, for instance, the Prince responds to news about the arrival of the players at Elsinore with some animated wit: "He that plays the king shall be welcome – . . . and the [actor playing the] lady shall say her mind freely, or the blank verse shall halt for't" (II. ii. 319–25). The Riverside supplies this gloss: "the verse will not scan if she omits indecent words" (Shakespeare 1997b: 1204). Hamlet reminds us that not just sonnets but plays can speak in halting verse. The rhymed iambic pentameter of a sonnet and the blank verse or unrhymed iambic pentameter of a play can both exhibit the same stylistic failure.

It is the fiction of this failure that Shakespeare moves to center stage, in the sonnets as in *Much Ado*, and in such plays as *Love's Labor's Lost*, *As You Like It*, *Hamlet*, and even *Othello*, where Iago tries to produce a poem on Desdemona (II. i. 148–58), only to have Desdemona playfully retort, "O most lame and impotent conclusion" (l. 161). We might say, then, that the phrase "halting sonnet" constitutes a useful metonymy or syntactic model for Shakespeare's practice of yoking poetry to theater; a sonnet halting is a sonnet in action: poetry performed before the theater audience.

In *Much Ado*, the metonymic failure is not merely stylistic; as Schalkwyk indicates, the discourse of the halting sonnet certainly evokes questions of professional language or form but also questions of the body or physiology, and of the emotions or interiority. Benedick makes the connection explicit when he wittily identifies the revelation of the sonnets as a "miracle": "here's our own hearts against our hands." We shall return to the language of miracle later, but for now we may emphasize the form the miracle takes: the two sonnets inscript the truth of the lovers' (concealed) "hearts," and thus contradict (work "against") the evidence of their "hands," which previously have been at "merry war" (I. i. 62). Once the sonnet-evidence is produced, Benedick is compelled to tell Beatrice, "Come, I will have thee, but by this light, I take thee for pity" (V. iv. 92–3). In Shakespeare's theatrical staging, Benedick and Beatrice's mutual composition of "sonnets" becomes the spring to the comic dénouement leading to their marriage.

Staging Sonneteering in *Much Ado*

Let us look at Claudio's full speech on Benedick's "halting sonnet":

> And I'll be sworn upon't that he loves her,
> For here's a paper written in his hand,
> A halting sonnet of his own pure brain,
> Fashion'd to Beatrice.
>
> (V. iv. 85–8)

Claudio begins with an oath ("I'll be sworn") to support his claim that Benedick "loves" Beatrice. He produces as evidence a paper document written by and in his friend's hand. The phrase "of his pure brain" describing the sonnet recalls the "deep-brain'd sonnets" in *A Lover's Complaint*, suggesting how consistently Shakespeare imagines sonneteering as a practice inscripting the mind, whether deeply or purely. Claudio's final phrase, "Fashion'd to Beatrice," is resonant; rarely glossed, the word "Fashioned" means "addressed" (Shakespeare 1997a: 1442), while the Crystals (2002) add "form, shape, make [into]." Benedick both addresses his halting sonnet to Beatrice and shapes his pure brain to her, creating a form wherein they – or their "hearts" – meet. The sonnet is a purifying site for the mutual greeting between male and female: brains, hearts, hands.[5]

Here is Hero's full revelation of Beatrice's sonnet:

> And here's another
> Writ in my cousin's hand, stol'n from her pocket,
> Containing her affection unto Benedick.
>
> (V. iv. 88–90)

Like Benedick's sonnet, Beatrice's is "Writ" in her own "hand" and produced against her will ("stol'n"); it testifies against her public claims to warfare with her rival wit, "Containing her affection" for him. The sonnet is a container, or receptacle, for female affection, a passionately written inscription of emotional attachment.[6]

According to the *Oxford English Dictionary*, a pocket for Elizabethans was "A small bag or pouch worn on the person; spec. one inserted in or attached to a garment, for carrying a purse or other small articles" (def. 2.a). Thus, both Beatrice and Benedick have been carrying their sonnets around in small bags or purses attached to their clothing. Critics often remark on the importance of "fashion" and clothing to this play; the word "fashion" occurs significantly more in *Much Ado* than in any other Shakespearean work (twenty-one times with cognates; see Findlay 2003: 394). Carol Cook observes that the "characters talk a good deal about how they dress," and goes on to align "dressing well" with "talking well," suggesting that both "modes of decorous behavior serve similar functions": "to cover their emotional nakedness and to avoid exposure" (1986: 189). Although neglecting the "halting sonnet" conclusion to the play, Cook prepares us to formulate the significance of this dramatic climax: a "sonnet" concealed within a "pocket," a hidden document "Containing . . . affection," becomes the play's final image for the affective heart, at once pure and deep, within a social exchange between male and female. The comedy treats this exchange playfully, for a halting sonnet is also an "impotent" one, a sign especially of the male's lack of sexual vigor and thus an occasion for his cuckoldry (Paster 1995).

Petrarchan Theater

If Claudio can pull a "halting sonnet" out of Benedick's pocket, we might wonder how it got there. In act five, scene two, Shakespeare supplies an answer. He presents Benedick, "the Prince's jester" (II. i. 137), as a theatrical man who tries to write Petrarchan love poetry. The scene begins comically, when Benedick asks Margaret for "help" in writing a "speech of Beatrice" (ll. 2–3). As soon as Benedick realizes that he loves Beatrice, he turns to the Elizabethan convention of composing Petrarchan sonnets on her (Howard 1987: 182). Just as Desdemona will ask Iago to compose a poem to her, Margaret suggests to Benedick, "write me a sonnet in praise of my beauty" (V. ii. 5). Elizabethan women are complicit with men in the production of Petrarchan verse, which is programmed for (and by) men to "praise" female "beauty."[7] Benedick greets the prospect enthusiastically – too enthusiastically it turns out, since he claims with confidence, "In so high a style, Margaret, that no man living shall come over it" (ll. 6–7). Here Benedick betrays a paradox at the center of the Petrarchan enterprise: even though penning his intimate affection for the female, the sonneteer competes with other "m[e]n" in an economy of poetic fame (see Durling 1976: 27). Margaret quickly sees through the exaltation of Benedick's "high . . . style," punning on his word "over": "To have no man come over me?" (l. 9). Wickedly bawdy, her question speaks to the hierarchical thinking at the heart of the Petrarchan tradition, where men and women remain unequal – with the male "over" or above the female, at once on top of her (sexually) and superior to her (socially). This pun then reroutes the conversation from sonneteering to repartee, ended only when Benedick tells Margaret to bring Beatrice to him.

As soon as Margaret exits, Benedick, left alone on stage, breaks into song – an unusual form in Shakespeare that we might term a lyric soliloquy:

> The god of love,
> That sits above,
> And knows me, and knows me,
> How pitiful I deserve—
>   (V. ii. 26–9)

This may not appear much of a song, but that is what Shakespeare's fiction makes plain.[8] The great wit of the Men's Club of Messina (in Harry Berger's phrase) turns out to deserve only pity when it comes to producing sonnets on his lady, as Benedick himself confesses (l. 30). Indeed, the contents of the song trope the convention of pity central to the Petrarchan tradition (e.g. *Rime sparse* 1. 1. 8), betraying the lover's self-absorption. Nonetheless, we might acknowledge that Benedick's failure makes for fine drama.

His final speech before the arrival of Beatrice advances his failure in terms specific to the literary tradition, and brings that tradition up to date:

> . . . in loving, Leander the good swimmer, Troilus the first employer of pandars, and a whole bookful of these quondam carpet-mongers, whose names yet run smoothly in the even road of a blank verse, why, they were never so truly turn'd over and over as my poor self in love. Marry, I cannot show it in rhyme; I have tried. I can find out no rhyme to "lady" but "baby," an innocent rhyme; for "scorn," "horn," a hard rhyme; for "school," "fool," a babbling rhyme: very ominous endings. No, I was not born under a rhyming planet, nor can I woo in festival terms. (V. ii. 30–41)

Here, Shakespeare uses a soliloquy to stage failed sonneteering in considerable detail. The scene captures Benedick in the very throes of sonnet-invention. He compares himself to two famous lovers from classical culture: Leander, who loved the original woman named Hero but then died while swimming the Hellespont to visit her; and Troilus, who met Cressida through her uncle, the go-between Pandarus, only to be betrayed by her. Both Leander and Troilus are tragic lovers, and Benedick's failure to recognize this becomes part of his comedic failing. He imagines both Leander and Troilus as exemplary: Leander, for being a "good swimmer"; Troilus, for being the "first employer of pandars." Benedick is not simply a failed sonneteer; he is a failed reader of the Western tradition of love poetry. Not surprisingly, he criticizes the "whole bookful" of lovers as mere "carpet-mongers": they are arm-chair lovers. He is the true lover because he suffers – "truly turn'd over and over . . . in love." The word "turn'd" fuses the literary process of invention and the Ovidian idea of change or metamorphosis.[9]

Benedick does not mention the author of his own poetry book, but no doubt it is his own "self."

No sooner does he vaunt his success, however, than he confesses his failure: "I cannot show it in rhyme." The word "show" is Shakespeare's favorite word for theater (see e.g. *Hamlet* III. ii. 139–46), and here Benedick employs it to identify his attempt at rhyme as merely a show, an outward appearance, not a true work of poetry. He has "tried," but he can produce only a series of silly rhymes, each having a simplistic meaning, whether "innocent," "hard," or "babbling," and all are "ominous." His failure at rhyme leads to a measured conclusion: he has "not been born under a rhyming planet." He has not been born a poet, and he is not destined to become one. Accordingly, he will not use sonneteering to "woo in festival terms" – bring about the marital conclusion of Shakespeare's "festive comedy" (Barber 1959; cf. Neely 1985: 39, 55–7). Quite the opposite occurs: the conclusion is brought "against" him through the publication of a halting sonnet he claimed he could not compose.

The Prince's Jester

Shakespeare's presentation of Benedick as a failed sonneteer at the end of the play is important because, at the beginning, this witty lover is the consummate theatrical man. In act two, scene one, during the meta-theatrical Masque, Beatrice, herself wearing a mask, tells her rival wit, also masked, that Benedick is "the Prince's jester, a very dull fool; only his gift is in devising impossible slanders" (ll. 137–8), primarily against her. Later in this scene, Benedick expresses his dismay to Claudio: "that my Lady Beatrice should know me, and not know me! The Prince's fool!" (ll. 203–4). Yet a third time Benedick complains, this time to Don Pedro, "She told me, not thinking that I had been myself, that I was the Prince's jester" (ll. 242–3). Such hyperbolic dramaturgy marks Benedick as a professional fool, a man of the theater, a kinsman to Feste in *Twelfth Night*, the Fool in *King Lear*, and Autolycus in *The Winter's Tale*.

In act three, scene two, however, Claudio records a decisive – and little-discussed – character change in Benedick: "his jesting spirit . . . is now crept into a lute-string" (ll. 59–60). This seemingly innocuous remark also announces a career change: Benedick has turned from his role as the Prince's jester to a new part as a lutanist: effectively, he has turned from being a professional man of the theater to become a court poet. When Don Pedro replies, "Indeed that tells a heavy tale for him" (l. 61), Shakespeare draws attention to the narrative of Benedick's change of direction (cf. King 1964: 144 n. 5, 153–5). Let us look into the details of this heavy tale.

Just prior to this, the audience has witnessed the moment of change. To open act two, scene three, Benedick tells the Boy, "In my chamber-window lies a book, bring it hither to me in the orchard" (ll. 2–3). Seemingly a trivial detail, the directive alerts us to a neglected contour for this comedy: Benedick turns from stage to page, from theater to print shop, from performance to books (cf. Everett 1994: 82). Hence, during his subsequent monologue, he displaces his own change onto the change in Claudio, delivering a detailed analysis of his friend's "conversion" at falling in love with Hero, only to refer to his own falling in love with Beatrice:

> I have known when there was no music with him but the drum and the fife, and now had he rather hear the tabor and the pipe. . . . [N]ow is he turn'd orthography. . . . May I be so converted and see with these eyes? I cannot tell; I think not. I will not be sworn but love may transform me to an oyster. (II. iii. 12–24)

On the surface, Shakespeare rehearses no more than an Elizabethan convention: a soldier's turn from warfare to wooing, his exchange of one kind of "music" for another. Yet the terms evoke musical instruments in the Renaissance hierarchy of genres, specifically associated with the Virgilian progression from epic ("the drum and the fife") to amorous lyric and pastoral ("the tabor and the pipe").[10] Like Claudio, Benedick is moving down the Virgilian path, from higher to lower forms, undergoing Ovidian "transform[ation]." Hence, Benedick speaks the lines in the pastoral locale of the epic city, the "orchard," indicating that Shakespeare here nicely localizes his familiar comedic pattern of court and country (cf. Sullivan 2003; Lewalski 1968: 237; Krieger 1979: 54).

The young men's turn from warfare to wooing explains the precise design of the next event: Benedick "hide[s] . . . in the arbor" (l. 36) to overhear Don Pedro and Claudio persuading the professional musician Balthasar to sing a song he has sung to them earlier (l. 43). If the singer is not reluctant to sing, he is at least modest: "O good my lord," says Balthasar to Don Pedro, "tax not so bad a voice / To slander music any more than once" (ll. 44–5). Yet in Balthasar's vocational modesty, Don Pedro finds the mark of excellence: "It is the witness still of excellency / To put a strange face on his own perfection" (ll. 46–7). The phrasing relies on a theatrical metaphor for disguise familiar throughout the Shakespeare canon (Cheney 2004: 135–9): the singer puts a mask on his face as "witness" to his "perfection." Everywhere we look, Shakespeare does not separate poetry and theater; here, he uses theater as a metaphor for poetry.

Such playful banter on the theatrical vocation of the singer leads to the pun at the center of a play called *Much Ado About Nothing*, marking this scene at the structural midpoint the pivotal one of the comedy:

> *D. Pedro.* Do it in notes.
> *Balth.*   Note this before my notes:
> There's not a note of mine that's worth noting.
> *D. Pedro.* Why, these are very crotchets that he speaks—
> Note notes, forsooth, and nothing.
>
>   (II. iii. 54–7)

As critics often observe, the comedy that makes much ado about "nothing" puns on the concept of "noting," which lies at the heart of the dramatic action: the use of language to make observations on others (Shakespeare 1999: xxxii; Rossiter 1965: 54;

Berry 1972). Long ago, Harold C. Goddard wrote, "in all of Shakespeare's immense vocabulary, there are few more interesting words. . . . Nothing is . . . practically a synonym for creativity" (1951: 273; cf. Bloom 1998: 200). As Goddard helps us see, the halting sonnets produced at the end of the play from the recesses of the two lovers' pockets evoke the "creativity" of making musical notes, literally placing lyric song in the title of this play. *Much Ado about Nothing* / *Much Ado about Noting*: this is a dramatic comedy about the theatrical art of lyric song.[11]

Consequently, it is right at this moment – hovering around the play's central pun – that Benedick speaks a theatrical aside about the Orphic power of lyric:

> Now, divine air! now is his soul ravish'd! Is it not strange that sheep's guts should hale souls out of men's bodies? (II. iii. 58–60)

Benedick does not just wittily detach himself from the art of the singer; he uses inspired discourse (as if against his will) to participate in that art. He refers to the Orphic power of music to ravish the soul, to draw the soul out of the body to experience the joyful condition of transcendence, and to the practice of stringing musical instruments – here the lute – with "sheep's guts."[12]

At the heart of Benedick's wit, then, is a paradox: such a seemingly low body part of a dead animal can produce the most "divine air" from a human. This is what Benedick finds "strange": the mystery of the material giving birth to the spiritual, of an animal's organ being able to elevate the soul to its highest mystery of exaltation. We can be even more precise: through the material process of Orphic music, the interior organ of a dead sheep can metamorphose the interior organ of a human being into a state of religious ecstasy.

On the surface, Benedick may be mocking the idea of Orphic poetry to ravish the soul; but for his part Shakespeare prepares to deliver one of the most remarkable lyric songs in his theatrical canon:

> Sigh no more, ladies, sigh no more.
> Men were deceivers ever,
> One foot in sea, and one on shore,
> To one thing constant never.
> Then sigh not so, but let them go,
> And be you blithe and bonny,
> Converting all your sounds of woe
> Into hey nonny nonny.
> Sing no more ditties, sing no moe,
> Of dumps so dull and heavy,
> The fraud of men was ever so,
> Since summer first was leavy,
> Then sigh not so, etc.
>
> (II. iii. 62–74)

A surprising dearth of commentary exists on this song (cf. Paster 1995: 217; Shakespeare 1999: xxxvi; 1993: 203–6; 1981/2002: 236–7). As readers will recognize, "songs and sonnets" were closely linked both as a phrase during the English Renaissance and as lyric forms. Shakespeare himself uses the phrase in *The Merry Wives of Windsor*, when Slender says, "I had rather than forty shillings I had my Book of Songs and Sonnets here" (I. i. 198–9), an allusion to Tottel's famous miscellany of this title (Shakespeare 1997b: 326). The close connection between songs and sonnets in Shakespeare, as in his culture, helps explain the allied discourse of songs and sonnets in *Much Ado*; the two forms are kinds of lyric, and both operate as separate or lyric spaces, important to distinguish from theatrical "show" (cf. Shakespeare 1993: 203).

For up until this point in the play, theater has been fully within the hands of Don Pedro and his brother, Don John, as has been widely discussed (Howard 1987; Paster 1995: 225–6; Greenblatt 1997: 1382–4). The play begins with Don Pedro, and focuses immediately upon his authority and agency: "I learn in this letter," says Leonato, "that Don [Pedro] of Arragon comes this night to Messina" (I. i. 1–2). By turning down the Virgilian path from war to wooing, Don Pedro prepares for a different kind of "action" (l. 6) – and one that formally organizes the plot until act three, scene two; at the Masque scene of "reveling" (I. i. 320), Don Pedro uses theatrical costume to woo Hero on behalf of Claudio: "I will assume thy part in some disguise / And tell fair Hero I am Claudio. . . . / In practice let us put it presently" (ll. 321–8).

For the first half of the play, this theatrical "practice" turns out to be much ado about noting, undergoing a strange afterlife, as characters report that they have overheard the plan. In act one, scene two, for instance, Antonio's servant overhears Don Pedro's plan and tells his master of it; Antonio then tells Leonato, "The Prince and Count Claudio, walking in a thick-pleach'd ally in mine orchard, were thus much overheard by a man of mine. The Prince discover'd to Claudio that he lov'd my niece your daughter, and meant to acknowledge it this night in a dance" (ll. 8–13). It is not clear whether the servant or Antonio misconstrues the plan, but immediately we become privy to the vulnerability of Don Pedro's comedic theater of courtly wooing. In the tightly woven community of Messina, theater is subject to "noting": to overhearing and thus to misconstruing.

Subsequently, in act one, scene three, Borachio reports to Don John that he, too, has overheard the plan, but his terms suggest that he also misconstrues the details, even though he catches the drift: "I whipt me behind the arras and there heard it agreed upon that the Prince should woo Hero for himself, and having obtain'd her, give her to Count Claudio" (ll. 60–4). Then, in act two, scene one, Leonato tells Hero that Don Pedro will court her for marriage: "Daughter, remember what I told you. If the Prince do solicit you in that kind, you know your answer" (ll. 66–8). It is in this scene that we witness the plan in operation. During the wooing, the masked Don Pedro wants to know when Hero will "walk" with him "in company" (ll. 90–1), and she replies, "When I like your favor, for God defend the lute should be like the case" (ll. 94–5). The comparison is important, because Hero likens the masked suitor with his desiring heart to a lute in its musical case. That is to say, Shakespeare likens theater to poetry.

Later in this scene, we see the anti-theater of Don John set in, when the villain tells Claudio of Don Pedro, "He is enamor'd on Hero. . . . I heard him swear his affection" (ll. 164–8). The formal moment of crossover in the authority of masculine theater then occurs momentously in act three, scene two, when Don Pedro and Claudio extend their theater of comedic wooing to their plot against Benedick and Beatrice (ll. 76–9), only to be interrupted by the dramatic entry of Don John, who announces of Hero: "The lady is disloyal" (l. 104). Don John goes on to deploy his villainous theater designed to break up marriage, when he brings his brother and Claudio to Hero's window, to witness the performed playlet of Margaret in disguise as Hero making love to Borachio (III. iii).

Initially, then, the plot's focus on this double theatrical action shows a patriarchal conflict between the two brothers (cf. Neely 1985: 40–1). While Don Pedro uses theater to bring about marriage, Don John uses theater to break marriage up. Finally, however, the plot shows a succession from the one to the other. The succession depends on a shared patriarchal attitude toward the female: both brothers use theater to target the female, betraying the goal of festive comedy, companionate marriage (McDonald 2001: 261–2; Paster 1995: 218).

Once we recognize this theatrical design, we are prepared to see what is radical in Balthasar's lyric song. The dramatic context of his song presents another paradox: the leading patriarch of the play, the theatrical Don Pedro, asks Balthasar to sing "Sigh no more, ladies" ("again"); yet, as this opening line reveals, the song itself addresses ladies (who are absent). The paradox is no doubt amusing; it reveals that even the arch-patriarch is instinctively sympathetic to a song opposing his project. But the paradox also has an edge; its address to "ladies" takes the song out of the fiction to ladies in the theater audience. In other words, Balthasar's song constitutes a visible moment of *authorship*.

Accordingly, the contents of the song first introduce a counter-voice into the play – the voice of lyric poetry: a male song encourages ladies to turn away from the authority of men to find authority in themselves. The song criticizes masculinity for its *deceptive agency* ("Men were deceivers ever") and its *unfaithful desire* ("One foot in the sea, and one on shore, / To one thing constant never"), in the end inviting women to "let them go." The song advises women to locate their love and faith elsewhere than in men, and to be happy on their own: "be you blithe and bonny." While several recent critics have expressed unwillingness to find here a feminist manifesto, we might alternatively discover a *lyric manifesto*, critiquing masculine *theater* for its deceptive agency and its unfaithful desire, and re-locating authority in a *feminine-based song*, in *music*, in *lyric poetry*: "Converting all your sounds of woe / Into hey nonny nonny." Women should turn from love of and faith in the deceptive theater of men to love of and faith in their own lyric voice. The word "nonny" is not merely enigmatic, it is gnomic; but the *Oxford English Dictionary* suggests one primary meaning: "Used in songs as (part of) a refrain. . . . Often with allusion to Shakespeare" (def. 1.a). The word "nonny," then, is a vocational term for the art of song itself – and specifically for Shakespearean song. We might, then, see a verbal connection between the key word for lyric in Balthasar's song, "nonny," and the lyric pun on "noting" in the key word in the play's title, "nothing."[13] Balthasar's song is a mournful song of loss, of separation, of women choosing to separate themselves from men; but it also constructs a new female identity and voice, in which women learn to live independently of men and find happiness without them, on their own, through their own art form: in the lyric of song. In other words, Shakespeare selects lyric, not theater, as a private space for an intimate (evidently premarital) phase in the formation of female identity, through which a woman discovers her autonomy independently of men.

"The Story is Printed in Her blood": Reading the Petrarchan Book

The opposition between lyric poetry and staged theater in acts one to three sets up the similar opposition in the potentially tragic catastrophe of act four. As we should expect, Claudio's calumny of Hero at the church in scene 1 depends on a particular charge. Not simply has she falsified feminine desire, she has falsified masculine theater:

> Behold how like a maid she blushes here!
> O, what authority and show of truth
> Can cunning sin cover itself withal!
>   (IV. i. 34–6)

Readers are often irritated at Hero; she has so little to say, including for herself. Yet, as Claudio's first line indicates, what absorbs Shakespeare, here and throughout his canon, should not surprise us: *the masculine perception of the female as the cause of tragic suffering and death* (cf. Neely 1985: 53). Nowhere is this idea on more concentrated display than in *Much Ado*, and nowhere in this play is it more concentrated than in this scene.

In his calumnizing speech, Claudio directs the viewers on stage (and thus in the audience) to focus on Hero's face, and to interpret the blush suffusing her cheeks. Himself a man of theater, he reads into his beloved's blush a "show of truth," an "exterior show" (l. 40) of modesty "cover[ing]" her "guiltiness" (l. 42). Importantly, Claudio assigns theatrical agency and will to Hero's blush, convinced that she controls her "blood" for the purpose of deception.

When Claudio's assault on her integrity causes Hero to faint, Don Pedro, Don John, and Claudio march swiftly off. To his credit, Benedick stays, marking a moment of separation, the breaking up of the Messina Men's Club: "How doth the lady?" (l. 113). Similarly, Beatrice depends, not on the theatrical proof offered by men, but on the authority of her own "soul": "My cousin is belied" (l. 146). Then a community of men and women hover over the fallen body of a lady; two men step forward to deliver *readings* of her facial blush. First, the humiliated father is decisive in his interpretation: "The story . . . is printed in her blood . . . O she is fall'n / Into a pit of ink, that the wide sea / Hath drops too few to wash her clean again" (ll. 122–41). After Macbeth, we know we are standing on the threshold of Shakespeare's most intense tragic territory (cf. *Macbeth* II. ii. 57–60).

Unlike Macbeth, Leonato selects a metaphor from Elizabethan print culture. Not simply a convention, the metaphor draws attention to a particular masculine economy, rooted in the material conditions of books. In particular, Leonato gives voice to the "stigma of print," through which "Gentlemen . . . shunned print" because it was beneath their dignity (Saunders 1951: 140); Leonato also betrays the fear that lies beneath the stigma: fear of the effeminized falsification of manly identity (see Wall 1993: 227–78). Leonato imagines his daughter's face as a book that men may read to discover the truth about female "virginity" (l. 47). He looks at his daughter's face to see a blush stamped on her unconscious form, and is convinced the outward blush reveals an inner truth. The "blood" in her cheeks "print[s]" the "story" of her whoredom. The key to the feminine narrative is the blood suffusing her face; a blush manifests the truth of emotional character, revealing the inwardness we cannot otherwise see.

Yet Friar Francis intervenes to deliver a different interpretation of the feminized text:

> By noting of the lady[,] I have mark'd
> A thousand blushing apparitions
> To start into her face, a thousand innocent shames
> In angel whiteness beat away those blushes,
> And in her eye there hath appear'd a fire
> To burn the errors that these princes hold
> Against her maiden truth. Call me a fool,
> Trust not my reading, nor my observations,
> Which with experimental seal doth warrant
> The tenure of my book; trust not my age,
> My reverence, calling, nor divinity,
> If this sweet lady lie not guiltless here
> Under some biting error.
>
> (IV. i. 158–70)

Noting of the lady: by punning on the key word in the title of the play, "nothing," Friar Francis centralizes this moment of interpretation, transposing the action of "noting" from the theater of the two Dons to a purified reading of the female. As a member of the clergy, the Friar witnesses nothing less than a religious epiphany occurring in the face of an unconscious girl: a dramatic metaphysical action beyond human agency.

First, the Friar sees a "thousand blushing apparitions . . . start into her face," the word "apparitions" identifying the rush of red blood as a militant, ghostly presence. Next, a second set of spirits, equal in number, arrive on the scene, but with a different character, color, and action: "a thousand innocent shames / In angel whiteness beat away those blushes." In this war in heaven, the thousand white angels beat away the thousand red apparitions, as the force of innocence defeats the invading army. Miraculously, the Friar can peer into Hero's "eye" to see something apocalyptic: a burning "fire" that purifies the "errors" of the "Princes." This fire is righteous indignation itself, an interior (Christian) armor protecting the female against patriarchal corruption (cf. Lewalski 1968: 249).

The Friar calls his interpretation of Hero's innocence a "reading" of a lady's "book." Unlike the angry Leonato, this visionary clergyman does not suffer from the stigma of print, and thus he voices a masculine integrity having clear access to the metaphysical truth about female interiority. If the lady is a book, we might wonder who the author of her book is. Shakespeare's representation of agency here is striking. On the one hand, only Hero can be her own author (as Coriolanus says memorably of himself [V. iii. 36]); on the other, she has fainted. Yet even in her unconscious state Hero continues to author her integrity, and this is the book that the Friar discovers and reads. Shakespeare does not here objectify truth as living outside Hero's psyche; but neither does he reduce that psyche to mere psychology. Rather, he invests the psyche with a glowing metaphysics, and that is the story printed in Hero's blood (cf. Findlay 2003: 406). Shakespeare's dramaturgy lends credence to the recent groundbreaking thesis of Lukas Erne, who uses textual scholarship to argue that Shakespeare writes plays both for the stage and for the page, concerned not merely with the next performance but also with his literary reputation. In *Much Ado*, we might discover Erne's "literary dramatist" at work: a playwright with a deep commitment to print culture.

Shakespeare's concern with printed books as a form of identity allows us to determine that in this scene he also deploys a unique version of the standard Petrarchan blazon (cf. e.g. Vickers 1985). Instead of dismembering the female body by inventorying its parts for masculine titillation, Shakespeare concentrates on the face, but discovers the outward form to be the "print" of an emotional "story." This scene constitutes a bold counter-Petrarchan moment, and its imagery of an eroticized book with metaphysical power coheres both with Balthasar's song about female identity and with Benedick's haplessly acquired interest in the feminine art of lyric.

Epitaphs, Lyric Songs, and Theater

Through excavating Shakespeare's narrative about poetry and theater in acts one to four, we prepare ourselves to return to act five. In scene three, the newly reformed Claudio, repentant about the (supposed) death of Hero, and willing to listen to Leonato's advice about marrying the (fictional) daughter of Antonio, "Almost a copy of my child that's dead" (V. i. 289), visits Hero's tomb in command not of theater but of poetry. The term "copy," also from print culture (see sonnet 11. 14), communicates Claudio's changed attitude, including toward printed poetry. Accordingly, Shakespeare presents the new Claudio as a poet, the author of a funeral "epitaph," which he reads out loud before hanging it on Hero's tomb:

"Done to death by slanderous tongues
Was the Hero that here lies.
Death, in guerdon of her wrongs,
Gives her fame which never dies.
So the life that died with shame
Lives in death with glorious fame."
                              (V. iii. 3–8)

In his epitaph, Claudio accepts blame for his beloved's death but finds consolation in Hero's virtue; through her "Death," she achieves "glorious fame." As such, the epitaph lines up with Shakespeare's sonnets, and even achieves genuine intensity in the last three lines, each of which includes the Christian trope of life-in-death (cf. *Faerie Queene* 1. 1. 2), moving the epitaph out from classical fame to the immortality of Christian glory (see Cheney 1993: ix–xiii, 7–8; cf. Findlay 2003: 404). While critics often indict Claudio for his shallowness, the artistic quality of his lyric lends access to a more profound interiority than we might initially have imagined (Lewalski 1986: 248–50; Shakespeare 1981/2002: 54–9).

The earliest editions of *Much Ado* do not identify the singer of the following "Song," but Claudio's directive in line 11, "Now, music, sound, and sing your solemn hymn," prompted Edward Capell (and subsequent editors, such as A. R. Humphreys [Shakespeare 1981/2002: 210]) to assign the lyric to Balthasar; it is another stunning poem within a play:

Pardon, goddess of the night,
Those that slew thy virgin knight,
For the which, with songs of woe,
Round about her tomb they go.
          Midnight, assist our moan,
          Help us to sigh and groan,
                    Heavily, heavily.
Graves, yawn and yield your dead,
Till death be uttered,
                    Heavily, heavily.
                              (V. iii. 12–21)

Addressed initially to Diana, classical goddess of the moon and of virginity, the song is paradoxically Christianized as a "solemn hymn." Rather than erasing death, this religious lyric confronts darkness head-on: "Midnight, assist our moan." Yet Shakespeare takes the tragic tenor of the lyric to its limit, when the song concludes by addressing "Graves," evoking the superb disturbance of pagan resurrection (as in *Hamlet* I. i. 114–25): the dead "yawn" and the tombs "utter" the word "death, / Heavily, heavily." Here Shakespeare uses lyric as a haunting space to mark the male's change in attitude, including about the two literary forms making up the author's own professional career: poetry and theater.

"Strike Up, Pipers"

The playlet next staged by Friar Francis and his acting troupe (combining men with women) introduces a model of theater radically opposed to the one with which the play began. In the earlier theater of Don Pedro, the Don was the principal playwright and lead actor, performing with his friend Claudio, while Hero was both their target and an actor unaware she was rehearsing their script. Here at the close, however, Hero is the lead actor, while Don Pedro and Claudio become merely members of the audience:

> *Hero.* [*Unmasking.*] And when I liv'd, I was your other wife,
> And when you lov'd you were my other husband.
> *Claudio.* Another Hero!
> . . .
> *Don Pedro.* The former Hero! Hero that is dead!
> (V. iii. 60–5)

The language evokes the miracle of resurrection, Hero come back from the grave. Shakespeare rewrites scripture, in which a male messiah undergoes a spiritual resurrection (Lewalski 1968: 251; cf. Findlay 2003: 405). Throughout his canon, the author discovers fresh ways to relocate redemption in the female, from Romeo's dream of Juliet reviving her dead lover through her kiss (V. i. 1–11), to the resurrection of Hermione in *The Winter's Tale* (V. iii. 98–121). In Shakespeare's Elizabethan comedy, "Hero that is dead" enacts a new emotional theater designed to affect the hearts of the patriarchal audience.

This theatrical revelation then gives way to the final discovery, in which Claudio and Hero pull halting sonnets out of the pockets of Benedick and Beatrice. In perhaps the most important statement on this discovery, Stephen Greenblatt finds an incident of Renaissance self-fashioning:

> Near the play's close, we see Benedick struggle to compose the required sonnet to Beatrice – an entirely conventional exercise performed to fulfill the theatrical role in which he has been cast [by Don Pedro]. . . . And in the final moments, when the deception is revealed, it is this exercise rather than any feelings of the heart that confirms the match. . . . When a similar sonnet by Beatrice is produced, Benedick cries "A miracle! Here's our own hands against our hearts". . . . Many readers of the play, and most performers, have tried to reverse this formulation. . . . But what if we do not dismiss their own words?. . . . Beatrice and Benedick would not in that case "love" each other. . . . They are tricked into marriage against their hearts. (1997: 1385–6)

The present argument has tried to find a way out of this interpretive impasse, neither asserting the romanticism of "love" in the amusing sonneteering nor reducing "marriage" to a "social conspiracy" cemented by two sonnets that lack "authentic inward feelings" (Greenblatt 1997: 1386, 1385). Instead, the goal has been to discern a rather compelling fiction of English Renaissance authorship, cut right along the divide of outward practice and inner feeling, with the sonnets being the material object that gives access to the concealed emotion. In a surprising move, Shakespeare creates a dramatic plot that moves from theater to poetry, transacting a succession from plays to sonnets, and thereby validating the art of the sonnet as an important cultural institution for individual identity and social relationships.

Newly exposed as the author of a bad sonnet, it is Benedick, not Don Pedro, who steps forward to bring the play to its conclusion, after learning that Don John has been captured:

> Think not on him till to-morrow. I'll devise thee brave punishments for him. Strike up, pipers.
> *Dance.*
>
> (V. iv. 127–9)

The intrusion of Don John in the play's final lines is not surprising but structural, because this deceptive "villain" (I. iii. 32) has declared at the outset, "I have decreed not to sing in my cage" (l. 34). *Don John is the theatrical man devoid of lyric.* He is the dark antithesis to the lyric comedian who becomes his witty judge – a judge willing to engage in an art for the Other even when he is so inept at it. At the close, Benedick jocularly revises judicial affairs in the counter-terms of artistic invention ("devise," "brave"), to become the comedy's master of ceremonies. The jesting sonneteer uses his new cultural authority to address the pastoral pipers of the city, to strike up their instruments for the performance of dance. Benedick becomes a man of the theater who composes halting sonnets. In *Much Ado about Not{h}ing*, Shakespeare playfully uses the Elizabethan comedic stage to fictionalize the complexities of his own compound form of authorship as a new English poet-playwright.

NOTES

1 *Much Ado About Nothing* (written 1598; published 1600), V. iv. 65. All quotations from Shakespeare come from the Riverside edition (Shakespeare 1997b).
2 Most mainstream criticism focuses on Shakespeare's plays, with most recent work on the poems a detached enterprise.
3 On the *Sonnets* as "Shakespeare's life's work," see Burrow (1998: 17). See also Shakespeare (1997c: 1–28). This paragraph and the next draw on Cheney (2004: ch. 7).
4 Petrarch composed his famous sequence, the *Rime sparse*, but also a lost comedy, *Philologia*

(Cheney 2004: 26 n. 14). During Shakespeare's time, Torquato Tasso was writing his tragedy *Torismondo* and his *Rime* in Italy, and Lope de Vega was writing his comedy *Fuente Ovejuna* and his *Rimas* in Spain. Around 1613–14, Leonard Diggs connected Shakespeare with Lope as sonneteering playwrights (Morgan 1963).
5 In his introduction to the Norton edition of the play, Greenblatt sees the word "fashioned" as "the play's term for the social system in which all the characters . . . are involved." Shakespeare deftly uses the term

... both to designate the images that elicit emotions and to describe the process that shapes these images" (1997: 1385). We shall return to Greenblatt at the end of this chapter.

6 Might we also see here an instance of Greenblatt's model of subversion and containment (1980: 1–9), allowed by the *OED*? The verb *contain* can mean "To keep or retain in a certain state or order, under control, in subjection" (def. 10). Thus, Beatrice's sonnet becomes a masculine form that *contains* her desire within a patriarchal economy.

7 See *Henry V*, where the French Dolphin transports this sonnet program to his horse (III. vii. 39–40).

8 According to Humphreys, Benedick sings the opening lines "of a song by the actor and balladist William Elderton, printed in 1562 and often quoted or imitated" (Shakespeare 1981/2002: 236).

9 Cf. Wall 1993: 36–7 on *Love's Labor's Lost* I. ii. 184: "I shall turn sonnet"; *Two Gentlemen* III. ii. 92: "I have a sonnet that will serve the turn."

10 For the pastoral association of these musical instruments, see *Winter's Tale* IV. iv. 182–3; Spenser, *Maye* 20–2, *Epithalamion* 129–31.

11 Greenblatt links "nothing" and "noting" only with theatricality (1997: 1383). For a full "theatrical" model, with Benedick and Beatrice as merely "comic" and "surrogate playwrights," see Traugott 1982: 170, 175.

12 For the Orphic significance of the image, see *Two Gentlemen of Verona* III. ii. 76–9; cf. Spenser, *October*, 25–30.

13 Is it then coincidental that "nonny" and "nothing" share a second meaning: the female womb? The *OED* also defines "nonny" as "The vulva," while Holland cites the Elizabethan meaning of "nothing" as "the female genitals" (Shakespeare 1999: xxxii).

References

Barber, C. L. (1959). *Shakespeare's Festive Comedy: A Study of Dramatic Form and Its Relation to Social Custom*. Princeton: Princeton University Press.

Berger, Harry, Jr. (1997). "Against the Sink-a-Pace: Sexual and Family Politics in *Much Ado about Nothing*." In Peter Erickson, ed., *Making Trifles of Terrors: Redistributing Complicities in Shakespeare*, 10–24. Stanford: Stanford University Press.

Berry, Ralph (1972). "Problems of Knowing." In *Shakespeare's Comedies: Explorations in Form*, 154–74. Princeton: Princeton University Press.

Bloom, Harold (1998). *Shakespeare: The Invention of the Human*. New York: Riverhead-Penguin Putnam.

Burrow, Colin (1998). "Life and Work in Shakespeare's Poems." The Chatterton Lecture on Poetry. *Proceedings of the British Academy* 97, 15–50.

Cannan, Paul D. (2004). "Early Shakespeare Criticism, Charles Gildon, and the Making of Shakespeare the Playwright-Poet." *Modern Philology* 102: 35–55.

Cheney, Patrick (1993). *Spenser's Famous Flight: A Renaissance Idea of a Literary Career*. Toronto: University of Toronto Press.

Cheney, Patrick (2004). *Shakespeare, National Poet-Playwright*. Cambridge, UK: Cambridge University Press.

Cook, Carol (1986). "'The sign and semblance of her honor': Reading Gender Difference in *Much Ado about Nothing*." *PMLA* 101, 186–202.

Crystal, David, and Crystal, Ben (2002). *Shakespeare's Words: A Glossary and Language Companion*. Harmondsworth: Penguin.

Dutton, Richard, and Howard, Jean E., eds. (2003). *A Companion to Shakespeare's Works: The Comedies*. Oxford: Blackwell.

Erne, Lukas (2003). *Shakespeare as Literary Dramatist*. Cambridge, UK: Cambridge University Press.

Everett, Barbara (1994). "*Much Ado about Nothing*: The Unsociable Comedy." In Michael Cordner, Peter Holland, and John Kerrigan, eds., *English Comedy*, 68–84. Cambridge, UK: Cambridge University Press.

Findlay, Alison (2003). "*Much Ado about Nothing*." In Richard Dutton and Jean Howard, eds., *A Companion to Shakespeare's Works: The Comedies*, 393–410. Oxford: Blackwell.

Gay, Penny (1994). "*Much Ado about Nothing*: A King of Merry War." In *As She Likes It:*

Shakespeare's Unruly Women, 143–77. London: Routledge.

Goddard, Harold C. (1951, 1960): *The Meaning of Shakespeare*, 2 vols. Chicago: University of Chicago Press/Phoenix.

Greenblatt, Stephen (1980). *Renaissance Self-Fashioning: From More to Shakespeare*. Chicago: University of Chicago Press.

Greenblatt, Stephen, ed. (1997). Introduction to *Much Ado about Nothing*. In the *Norton Shakespeare*, 1381–7. New York: Norton.

Howard, Jean E. (1987). "Renaissance Antitheatricality and the Politics of Gender and Rank in *Much Ado about Nothing*." In Jean E. Howard and Marion F. O'Conner, eds., *Shakespeare Reproduced: The Text in History and Ideology*, 163–87. New York: Methuen.

Kermode, Frank (2000). *Shakespeare's Language*. London: Allen Lane/Penguin.

King, Walter N. (1964). "Much Ado About Something." *Shakespeare Quarterly* 15, 143–55.

Krieger, Elliot (1979). "Social Relations and the Social Order in *Much Ado about Nothing*." *Shakespeare Survey* 32, 49–61.

Lewalski, Barbara K. (1968). "Love, Appearance, and Reality: Much Ado about Something." *Studies in English Literature 1500–1900* 8, 235–51.

McCoy, Richard C. (1997). "Love's Martyrs: Shakespeare's 'Phoenix and Turtle' and the Sacrificial Sonnets." In Claire McEachern and Debora Shuger, eds., *Religion and Culture in Renaissance England*, 188–208. Cambridge, UK: Cambridge University Press.

McDonald, Russ (2001). *The Bedford Companion to Shakespeare: An Introduction with Documents*, 2nd edn. Boston: Bedford/St. Martin's.

Morgan, Paul (1963). "'Our Will Shakespeare' and Lope de Vega: An Unrecorded Contemporary Document." *Shakespeare Survey* 16, 118–20.

Neely, Carol Thomas (1985). "Broken Nuptials in Shakespeare's Comedies: *Much Ado about Nothing*." In *Broken Nuptials in Shakespeare's Plays*, 24–57. New Haven: Yale University Press.

Paster, Gail Kern (1995). "*Much Ado about Nothing*: A Modern Perspective." In William Shakespeare, *Much Ado about Nothing*, ed. Barbara A. Mowat and Paul Werstine, 213–29. New York: Washington Square Press. (Folger Shakespeare.)

Paster, Gail Kern (2004). *Humoring the Body: Emotions and the Shakespearean Stage*. Chicago: University of Chicago Press.

Petrarch, Francis (1976). *Petrarch's Lyric Poems: The "Rime sparse" and Other Lyrics*, ed. and trans. Robert M. Durling. Cambridge, Mass.: Harvard University Press.

Rossiter, A. P. (1965). "*Much Ado About Nothing*." In Kenneth Muir, ed., *Shakespeare: The Comedies*, 47–57. Englewood Cliffs, NJ: Prentice-Hall.

Saunders, J. W. (1951). "The Stigma of Print: A Note on the Social Bases of Tudor Poetry." *Essays in Criticism* 1: 139–64.

Schalkwyk, David (2002). *Speech and Performance in Shakespeare's Sonnets and Plays*. Cambridge, UK: Cambridge University Press.

Schmidgall, Gary (1990). *Shakespeare and the Poet's Life*. Lexington: University Press of Kentucky.

Schoenfeldt, Michael C. (1999). *Bodies and Selves in Early Modern England: Physiology and Inwardness in Spenser, Shakespeare, Herbert and Milton*. Cambridge, UK: Cambridge University Press.

Shakespeare, William (1977). *Shakespeare's Sonnets*, ed. Stephen Booth. New Haven: Yale University Press.

Shakespeare, William (1981, 2002). *Much Ado about Nothing*, ed. A. R. Humphreys. London: Thomson Learning. (The Arden Shakespeare, 2nd ser.)

Shakespeare, William (1993). *Much Ado about Nothing*, ed. Sheldon P. Zitner. Oxford: Oxford University Press. (Oxford World's Classics.)

Shakespeare, William (1995). *Much Ado about Nothing*, ed. Barbara A. Mowat and Paul Werstine. New York: Washington Square Press. (Folger Shakespeare.)

Shakespeare, William (1996). *The Sonnets*, ed. G. Blakemore Evans, intr. Anthony Hecht. Cambridge, UK: Cambridge University Press. (The New Cambridge Edition.)

Shakespeare, William (1997a). *The Norton Shakespeare: Based on the Oxford Edition*, ed. Stephen Greenblatt et al. New York: Norton.

Shakespeare, William (1997b). *The Riverside Shakespeare*, ed. G. Blakemore Evans et al., 2nd edn. Boston: Houghton Mifflin.

Shakespeare, William (1997c). *Shakespeare's Sonnets*, ed. Katherine Duncan-Jones. London: Thomas Nelson. (The Arden Shakespeare, 3rd series.)

Shakespeare, William (1999). *Much Ado about Nothing*, ed. Peter Holland. Harmondsworth: Penguin. (Pelican Shakespeare.)

Shakespeare, William (2002). *William Shakespeare: The Complete Sonnets and Poems*, ed. Colin Burrow. Oxford: Oxford University Press. (Oxford World's Classics.)

Spenser, Edmund (1909–10). *The Poetical Works of Edmund Spenser*, ed. J. C. Smith and Ernest de Sélincourt. 3 vols. Oxford: Clarendon.

Sullivan, Garrett A. (2003). "Shakespeare's Comic Geographies." In Richard Dutton and Jean Howard, eds., *A Companion to Shakespeare's Works: The Comedies*, 182–99. Oxford: Blackwell.

Suzuki, Mihoko (2000). "Gender, Class, and the Ideology of Comic Form: *Much Ado about Nothing* and *Twelfth Night*." In Dympna Callaghan, ed.,

A Feminist Companion to Shakespeare, 121–43. Oxford: Blackwell.

Traugott, John (1982). "Creating a Rational Rinaldo: A Study in the Mixture of the Genres of Comedy and Romance in *Much Ado about Nothing*." *Genre* 15, 157–81.

Vickers, Nancy J. (1985). " 'The blazon of sweet beauty's best': Shakespeare's *Lucrece*." In Patricia Parker and Geoffrey Hartman, eds., *Shakespeare and the Question of Theory*, 95–115. New York: Methuen.

Wall, Wendy (1993). *The Imprint of Gender: Authorship and Publication in the English Renaissance*. Ithaca, NY: Cornell University Press.

23

Personal Identity and Vicarious Experience in Shakespeare's Sonnets

William Flesch

Given their claim to eternize their subjects, Shakespeare's sonnets have done a remarkably poor job of making us admire anything besides the superficial attractiveness of the young man (the sonnets to whom I'll be concentrating on in what follows) and the dark lady. I think this is a notable fact. No doubt it indicates the bitter irony Shakespeare expresses in the sonnets, but it also casts some interesting light on how he thought about representing human beings, especially if we juxtapose his thinking in the sonnets with his practices and themes in the plays.

I

I want to begin by pursuing an insight of William Empson's, in his great reading of sonnet 94, generally regarded as one of the most important essays ever written on the sonnets.[1] Empson suggests that the relation between Shakespeare, or at least the speaker of the sonnets, and the young man parallels that between Falstaff and Hal. In each case a needy and essentially transparent older man tries unsuccessfully to move the cold and to-temptation-slow object of his desire.

One aspect of this similarity is that both appeal more to the young man's vanity than to a sense of virtue within him. The sonnets, as Harold Bloom has noted,[2] show strangely little obvious expression of resentment or vituperation toward the young man – as can be seen by comparison with the later sonnets to the dark lady, or indeed any contemporaneous sequence of sonnets lamenting the indifference of the cruel fair. Indeed, sonnet 94 is striking for the unusual hostility it expresses (in the suggestion that the young man risks being compared to a festering lily). It is the relatively palpable aggression in sonnet 94 that appealed to Empson: the hostility is still deniable, but not hard to spot, which makes it possible to argue more generally for hostility disguised by irony in the sonnets to the young man.

I agree that the sonnets allow one to infer that the young man is cold and indifferent to their speaker. But I don't think they are only documents of ironic bitterness; just as often, they are anguished and always psychologically subtle attempts to woo him, and to find some way to make do with whatever the speaker can get from him.

I am interested in the insightfulness of their appeal to the young man's psychology, which seems to me to be of a piece with the psychological acuity that Shakespeare displays in his thinking about drama. The fact that dramatic representation can have so powerful an effect on its spectators is itself a prominent psychological feature in Shakespeare's depiction of character: only consider Hamlet's "guilty creatures sitting at a play" speech, or his reaction to the player's "dream of passion." Conversely, the idea that their stories may be displayed to later spectators can have a powerful effect. People care about their future reputations as imaginary spectators of their own stories. By way of negative reaction, consider Cleopatra's "And I shall see / Some squeaking Cleopatra boy my greatness," or, more positively, recall Cassius's anticipation of how "states unborn in accents yet unknown," will replay the conspirators' actions on stage. (The self-referential jokes in these passages connect the way drama features as a psychological fact in which he's interested to Shakespeare's actual drama and dramatic practice.) This last appeal to the memory of a future yet uncreated is to be found in the sonnets as well: "Your monument shall be my gentle verse, / Which eyes yet not created shall o'er-read" (sonnet 81).

The sonnets depict their speaker as hoping to affect the young man through his vanity, and as failing to do so. The attempt and the failure represent two basic types in Shakespeare's "characteristics," his delineation of different modes of character. They correspond to two versions of narcissism as analyzed by Freud: roughly speaking, the primary narcissism, whereby someone is indifferent to what anyone thinks about him or her, since the primary narcissist essentially doesn't acknowledge the existence of others at all; and the secondary narcissism, which looks to the esteem of others to heal a narcissistic wound. The secondary narcissist displays vanity, which means a need or desire to impress others with his own superiority and privilege. The primary narcissist is cold, rather than vain. Both essentially belong to the type or position of the beloved and not of the lover, but the secondary narcissist is at least interested in what others think, and therefore potentially wooable.

In contrast to the beloved, the lover corresponds to Freud's third erotic category (the "anaclitic type"). Such lovers seek another's good, care about the happiness of others as well as of themselves. Perfect requital for such a person would consist in the idea that it makes the beloved happy that the lover loves him or her. A modern Aristophanes might therefore distinguish different types of couples: those in which the devotion of the lover gratifies the narcissist; those in which two anaclitic lovers take joy in the pleasure that each gives the other; and those in which two narcissists feed each other's vanity.

Shakespeare will tend to represent only anaclitic love as stable in his plays, and we could instance, more or less uncontroversially, Romeo and Juliet or Hermia and Lysander. Mutuality between wounded narcissists, each feeding the other's vanity, might be found to achieve some arguable success with Vincentio and Isabella, if nowhere else in Shakespeare; a failed version of such a relation can be seen in Troilus and Cressida, perhaps.

For the anaclitic type catering to the narcissist, there might be more debate, but Macbeth could provide one example, Ophelia another, and Portia, before Bassanio's come-uppance, a third. These examples are complicated by the very instability of the relation, so that one or both partners change. Perhaps the clearest instance, though, might be Hero's anaclitic love for the deeply narcissistic Claudio, at least until he learns his lesson (if we are satisfied that he does), or Helena's for Demetrius, both before and after he is subjected to the aphrodisiac that makes him fall in love with her.

This is nevertheless the relation that obtains between the speaker of the sonnets and the young man, as it does between Falstaff and Hal. Let's stipulate this about Shakespeare: that his own erotic life (as we can guess from the sonnets) was passionate, anguished, and real, rather than the exfoliation of vanity, and that his psychological acuity and insight were at least as great as Freud credited them with being. We can paraphrase this stipulation (which would apply to many great writers: Proust for another obvious example) by saying that he could see with pure lucidity the impossibility of finding erotic satisfaction in loving the cruel fair or narcissistic object to whom (on the evidence of the sonnets) he seems to have been particularly attracted.

Both the speaker of the sonnets and Falstaff appeal to what they hope will be the vanity of their young men. But Falstaff at least is ultimately deceived in his hopes because Hal turns out to be personally indifferent to the judgments of the world. (Concerning Hal, the terminology of narcissism, itself perhaps an item from the vocabulary of resentment and disparagement, doesn't seem particularly helpful any more.) Hal belongs to a class of Shakespearean characters that would include the Bullingbrook of *Richard II*, Octavius Caesar, Hamlet, and even Claudio and Iago, at least in some of their aspects – men who do not care what the world thinks of them. They do or may care about power, but they don't care about being understood. They don't care, that is to say, about publishing the truth about their own characters, and so fundamentally we could say they care about power and not about truth. Their reputation is a means to an end, not an end in itself.

Here we may superimpose a second distinction, or trace Shakespeare's distinction, between this kind of character, personally indifferent to being understood, and the kind that does care that the truth be known, whether out of vanity or out of passion. Othello, at least in his last speech, represents wounded vanity more perhaps than he represents love. With everything that he is guilty of, with all the humiliations heaped upon his head, he still wishes to preserve some shred of integrity – as though, realistically, that integrity would matter to anyone besides him. In this he is not unlike Malvolio, absurd whether gulled or not, since it is just his vain liability to be gulled through his own rapaciousness that makes him atrocious. Or, to take one more example, Mowbray in *Richard II* is intent on confuting all false accusations, thereby confirming the even more deplorable ones he doesn't confute.

Othello may, however, be taken as an example also of someone who wishes to express the ultimate truth of his love. The desire to express the truth of one's inner passions generally takes the form of a sense of their ontological seriousness. Here again it doesn't pay to distinguish sharply between the vain narcissist and the altruist – or perhaps we could say that selfish and unselfish motivations become inextricable. Hamlet loved Ophelia, and wants everyone to understand his unexampled passion. Cordelia's "no cause at all" is more purely unselfish than Hamlet's declaration of love, but Hamlet's is genuine for all that. Antony and Cleopatra are certainly intent both on themselves and on each other when they express themselves, and act, on behalf of their own peerlessness. Any genuine appeal for pardon, from Lear's to Cleopatra's, combines a sense of the significance of one's feelings in virtue of the fact that they are one's own with the hope that those feelings, truly known, will make a genuine difference to the other person.

Let's return to the example of vanity, so central to the sonnets (as in the eternizing fame they offer, which we shall consider shortly) and consider what is implied by Shakespeare's appeal to the vanity of the beloved. Such an appeal – as we know from sonnets 18 and 130 – has to address something that's true. The witty inventiveness of sonnet 130 is in its persuasive verisimilitude. The lady is beautiful, and does not need to be belied by false compare. People want to be admired not for qualities they know they don't have, but for qualities they do: the trick is to pick qualities the object of flattery thinks admirable, or at least to make those qualities seem admirable. (To forestall an objection, I'll say that an older person wants to be admired for youthfulness, not for youth, even if the admirer calls it youth. Only a young person wants to be admired for youth itself.) Thus does Falstaff appeal primarily to what he takes Hal's vanity to be: his status as heir apparent. He appeals as well to what he thinks is Hal's fear for his own status, through the rebuke of his father or the attack of the rebels. So too the speaker of the sonnets wishes to appeal to the young man through a catalogue of his virtues.

Consider sonnet 94 again. If we can summarize it (rather crudely) as attempting to prevent the young man from using his power to hurt, it does so in several ways. It praises him for restraint as well as for beauty, and therefore attempts to make restraint part of the young man's calculus of vanity. It praises him, to say the same thing differently, for having the power to hurt: a power which derives from his beauty and from his restraint. It also warns against the use of the power to hurt, since such use will injure his reputation for restraint and sour the effect of his beauty. To the extent that the young man cares for his reputation, he will attempt to act so as to make it endure.

Of course, we can tell a lot about both the young man and the speaker of the sonnets from the fact that it is in this way that the speaker attempts to affect the young man: we learn that the speaker is anxious about what the young man will do, and that this anxiety verges on bitterness; and that his hostility results from seeing pretty clearly that the young man is not in love with the speaker and is only to be approached through the vanity the speaker can recognize in him. Generally the speaker of the sonnets attempts to excuse the young man's vanity even to himself, as well as to blame himself and his own betrayals for anything that goes wrong. But these attitudes are two sides of the same coin: the young man is more or less indifferent to the speaker, and the speaker recognizes this and therefore refrains from any expression of a sense of being entitled to make demands of him.

One of the deep peculiarities of Shakespeare's speaker is the way he doesn't rely on the notion to which most sonneteers implicitly do appeal: the idea that communicating his own love earnestly and accurately enough will win him the reciprocity he desires. There is none of Sidney's or Spenser's wishful expectation (familiar to a fault in Yeats) that the passion of the poetry should persuade the beloved, that if only they can express themselves urgently enough they will make themselves understood and loved. Of course Shakespeare wants to convince the young man that his own poetic powers are a reason for the young man to gratify him. But he represents himself as experienced enough not to imagine them a direct reason. He doesn't think, "If you knew how much and how purely I loved you, you would love me back." He represents such characters in his plays – for example, Benedick, Othello, and Orsino; but he doesn't represent himself this way in the sonnets.

Nevertheless, we can see a trace of this outgrown attitude in the hope that the young man cares about the fact that the speaker sees and praises his virtues with accurate extravagance. The young man would be appreciated for what is true about him; and his praiser would be appreciated for seeing the young man's qualities. There's still a trace of the "If you knew how much I loved you" gesture in the sonnets, then; but the praise redounds to the addressee, not the unique poetic soul of the speaker. The only quality in himself the speaker can appeal to is the fact that he somehow understands the young man's virtues better than anyone else does, or expresses them better than anyone else does.

II

I said before that among the psychological features of human beings in which Shakespeare is interested are those that seem connected to what theater can offer. Vanity is or can be such a feature. One version of vanity is the love of fame, and one version of fame is the immortality that future theatrical representation can assure. Cassius and Cleopatra and the young man of the sonnets (or so the speaker hopes) anticipate their future reputations, as represented by tragedians personating them. Enobarbus follows the ruined fate of Antony beyond what he regards as the dictates of reason, in order to earn a place in the story. Henry V's men will be remembered on St. Crispin's Day, no matter what happens to them; Hamlet and Othello are both concerned with their reputations after their deaths.

Such a concern also helps illustrate the overlap between the earnest lover's desire to be understood truly by his beloved and any person's desire to be the hero of some memorable and memorializing story. The former is an intensification of the latter; the latter a generalization of the former. When Othello laments "the pity of it," he is imagining his self-pity as something that should be universally shared by all who understand the truth, a truth which shows the nobility of his character. This fits perfectly with his desire to be remembered as one who loved not wisely but too well. To know all is to forgive all, indeed to pity all, and perhaps in the end to love entirely. As we have seen, this attitude finds its complement in the idea that you can appeal to people through

their vanity, by praising them. The idea is that people care what others think about
them, sometimes even when they want others to think they don't care. If Hal is genuinely indifferent to what others think of him (by which I mean personally indifferent,
since he wishes only to do what is expedient to his consolidation of his power, not to
reveal the depth and purity of his soul), he ought to be regarded as more like Claudius
than like Hamlet, who is very anxious that those around him should know that he is
indifferent to what they think of him: "I have that within that passes show, / These
but the trappings and the suits of woe."

It might seem natural that we care what others think about us, and that we should
want others to appreciate us for our genuine qualities, although a philosophical tradition
originating with Hume (and to be found today in some of the subtler treatments of
evolutionary psychology) will treat this fact as noteworthy. It may seem natural, but I
think that Shakespeare wondered about this concern when it got stretched to breaking
point, as it sometimes must, in theatrical representation. For it is not clear whom we
care about when we care about a character we see on stage or screen. Is it Hamlet or
Burbage? Is it Jerry Travers or Fred Astaire? This is not much of an issue when it comes
to a purely fictional character, when there is no real Hamlet to compare to the fictional
one, as there was a real and living Cole Porter (for example) to compare to Cary Grant's
portrayal of Cole Porter in the biopic. But from the real person's point of view, theatrical
representation by someone else might have a peculiar and dissatisfying element in it.
Cleopatra anticipates that the actor who plays her will be a ludicrous and humiliating
impostor. Cassius looks forward to his personification by others who will preserve the
story of his courage and principle. But in the case of Cassius we can wonder what personal investment he can have in his memorialization on stage by an actor not himself.
And we can also ask the obvious counter-question: to what extent does a Shakespearean
actor wish to be admired as an actor, and to what extent does he wish instead to elicit
responses to the character he plays? (Hamlet's instructions to the players attempt to
make them disappear into their characters.)

I'll be more explicitly interested in the first question – how someone like Cassius or
Cole Porter might feel about being admired in the person of someone else – than in
the second, but they are related questions, and plays like *Much Ado About Nothing* or
Cyrano de Bergerac thematize the issue in both directions. I don't deny the likelihood
that seeing oneself portrayed as a hero would be gratifying, as Claudio was ambivalently
gratified by seeing Don Pedro portray him. Thomas Nashe, who had a hand in *1 Henry
VI*, makes the issue explicit, when he writes of Talbot:

> How it would have ioyed braue Talbot (the terror of the French) to thinke that after he
> had lyne two hundred yeares in his Tombe, hee should triumph againe on the Stage, and
> haue his bones newe embalmed with the teares of ten thousand spectators at least, (at
> seuerall times) who in the Tragedian that represents his person, imagine they behold him
> fresh bleeding. (*Pierce Pennilesse*)

The idea of being gratified by being a secret audience to one's own story may be
found as far back as the *Odyssey*, when the disguised Odysseus hears the singer Demodekos

tell the story of his adventures at the court of the Phaeikians – and as recently as the last time someone Googled himself. Enobarbus stays loyal to Antony (for a while) because he wants a place in the story; Henry V wants to know what people are saying about him; Hamlet worries about his reputation after his death. What is striking about the Talbot episode is the pleasure Nashe imagines Talbot taking in the vicarious experience of his own life.

Let's look at the passage a little bit more carefully: Nashe is marveling at the great and underappreciated fact that real people have powerful emotional responses to events and characters they know to be fictional. Why should this be? Why should we care about the fates of persons whose nonexistence must make them supremely unimportant to our own lives? It is clear that such interest must bespeak a highly developed potential or capacity in human beings for vicarious experience. A playwright like Nashe or, pre-eminently, Shakespeare, is likely to wonder what the nature and limits of vicarious experience are. In fact, Shakespeare's career can be seen as a series of more and more radical experiments testing the limits of vicarious emotion.

One of the fascinating things about Nashe's little thought experiment here is the psychologically plausible idea that the imagined Talbot would have a vicarious experience of the audience's response to his own plight. Such an experience might also have been Nashe's, since he had a hand in *1 Henry VI*, taking pleasure in the audience's sorrow over the representation of Talbot dying on stage. And we can imagine Burbage, playing Talbot, delighting in the sorrow that he is causing his audience. Vicarious experience is so far from being dependent on direct experience that is becomes possible to imagine (as in the anaclitic couples we've considered already) a series of mutually inter-refering experiences, all of them vicarious.

At any rate, Talbot takes joy in seeing an audience weeping over his sorrow, and the joy derives from the fact that they are weeping over him. Or over a representation of him. But let's push the question a little farther. What about seeing oneself portrayed as a hero when one isn't one? The question we are broaching here is that of the relation between subjective or internal identity and one's identity in the eyes of others. Vanity and passion alike imagine the possibility of its mattering that it is myself, my true self, that is being represented, and that the world will care about it when that self is represented in the world. It matters to Talbot that it's Talbot the audience is weeping for, and that he's done the things they admire. But what if he hadn't? Or, to take a different way representation might misfire, what if they'd got his name wrong? Would it smell as sweet? What if they'd meant a different Talbot?

By laying out this array of questions I am trying to show a connection between issues that come out in the vicarious experience essential to dramatic representation – experience vicarious from the point of view of audience, but also actor, and, most surprisingly perhaps, represented person – and those that come out in the sonnets' portrayal of the vicarious experience essential to erotic life and the expression of erotic need – experience vicarious from the point of view of the speaker and also of his projection of the point of view of the addressee.

I suggested above that the speaker of the sonnets has thought through the question of how he appears to the young man. He has given up the tempting idea that a true expression of his passion would move the young man to reciprocate. But for this he substitutes a more subtle but roughly parallel attitude: that a true expression of his appreciation for what he perceives in the young man will move him. This is, of course, part of the adolescent idea that "If you knew how much I loved you, you would love me back," carrying the implicit suggestion that it is I alone who understand how wonderful you are. The speaker has toned such a claim down considerably, but the posture is still roughly the same. The form it takes now is that the speaker alone can blazon the young man's virtues to the world accurately or powerfully enough.

This idea recurs in the sonnets, but can be explored most interestingly in sonnets 78–86. We could see these as constituting a sequence, but don't need to. They do, however, circle around a single issue: the sonneteer's erotic rivalry with other poets in love with and praising the young man. Thus in sonnet 86 he despairs because of the success his rival's "great verse" has, a success the young man ratifies; that rival is presumably the "poet" of sonnet 79 and "better spirit" of sonnet 80; in 85 several others are more eloquent than he in the young man's praise, no doubt those who wield the "alien pen[s]" of 78; in 82 he pursues the topos of modesty by acknowledging[s] that the young man needs fresher praise than he is able to afford.

The modesty he expresses is part of a rhetorical move, not unlike what Antony practices in his funeral oration on Caesar. The trick in most of this group is to sustain the kind of humility that would show his tractability to the young man's dominance while appealing to the young man's vanity. Accordingly, he asserts that in the modesty to which they are compelled by the young man's virtues, his sonnets will nevertheless best serve the publication of those virtues. These sonnets all share the claim and conceit that the best way to praise the young man is through plain-spoken accuracy, phrased "In true plain words by thy true-telling friend" (82: 12). Such Kent-like plainness wants the glib and oily art which is its own contradiction, since the others devote their attention to rhetorical flourishes and not to the person who should be praised, even as he is beyond praise. It's the young man's being beyond praise that makes the speaker dumb and mute (84) with his own insufficiency. (Sonnet 23 explicitly connects a related idea with the theater, through the speaker's comparison of himself to "an unperfect actor on the stage / Who with his fear is put besides [forgets] his part" and is therefore unable to declare his love in person.) Sonnet 84 (which may be regarded as a kind of counterpart to sonnet 130) summarizes these issues, conceding greater artfulness to the rival, but turning that artfulness against itself:

> Who is it that says most, which can say more
> Than this rich praise, that you alone are you,
> In whose confine immured is the store
> Which should example where your equal grew?
> Lean penury within that pen doth dwell,
> That to his subject lends not some small glory,
> But he that writes of you, if he can tell
> That you are you, so dignifies his story.
> Let him but copy what in you is writ,

> Not making worse what nature made so clear,
> And such a counterpart shall fame his wit,
> Making his style admired everywhere.
>> You to your beauteous blessings add a curse,
>> Being fond on praise, which makes your praises worse.

The idea here is one to be found as well in some of the plays, as in *Antony and Cleopatra*, where Enobarbus quotes Lepidus saying of Caesar, "Would you praise Caesar, say 'Caesar': go no further" (III. ii. 13). The idea is that the most accurate praise of the young man will also be the highest praise, since he is nature's work 'gainst fancy. Perspicacity trumps eloquence, and even the speaker's very dumbness should testify to that perspicacity. He sees a truth that renders the praise of others necessarily inaccurate. Any alteration meant to contribute to the praise of the young man diminishes it. The poet's gain is the young man's loss, whereas for Shakespeare his own loss is the young man's gain. (This silence is just what Theseus appreciates in the silence of the learned clerks who meant to praise him in *A Midsummer Night's Dream*.) As with sonnet 94, the speaker attempts to influence what the young man does by appealing to his vanity: in this case his vain belief that he is without vanity, since the last couplet withholds the praise he wants so long as he shows himself fond of praise. But then it is of course appealing to his fondness for praise, and praises him by suggesting that he needs no praise.

All of this gives a sense of the extent to which the speaker appeals to the young man's reputation in the eyes of others – to the young man's vicarious experience of his own admirers (Shakespeare among them), which includes his sense of their vicarious experience of him. Let's list the modes in which reputation can matter can matter to someone. There is, first of all, the admiration that others have for one. One might wish to be admired, to be the cynosure of every glance or the law of fashion and the mold of form. This is the love of praise that sonnet 84 chastises and manipulates. Then there is the more subtle sense that some representation of oneself might allow one to take pleasure in one's own virtues. We might, like Talbot, have something like the same perspective on ourselves as others do. But to this would be added the additional pleasure that it was on ourselves that we and the others had this perspective. A third way of taking a kind of vicarious pleasure in something in which we are still known to have an important and determining interest is to be what is called being proud of someone. One aspect of vicarious experience is that of feeling such emotions as pride or embarrassment because of our connection with another person: feeling pride or embarrassment in a parent, for example.

This experience can stretch still farther, so that we may be proud of the person we are in love with. Part of this is that if the love is requited then we can boast, "I love thee in such sort / As thou, being mine, mine is thy good report" (sonnet 36). But the absolute construction in "being mine," which doesn't make it certain that the young man is entirely his, since it leaves the meaning of "As" ambiguous between assertion and hope, also reminds us that we may be proud simply to be in love with a person, whether they reciprocate or not. The pride taken in unrequited love may seem almost incoherent, since anyone who admired us for the object of our love would have to be more or less in love with them as well; and if they didn't feel as we do, there would be nothing in our love that would entitle us, in their estimation, to the pride we feel. Titania is aware of this, even in the throes of her love for Bottom, since she knows that no one else will find him anything but an ass. But the general and incoherent attitude takes the form of thinking that everyone will agree with our overestimation (as Freud calls it), while also being impressed with the uniqueness of our own feeling.

The sonnets connect these issues, these ways of thinking about representation, self-representation, and love. To take one example, the opening sonnets are a sequence urging the young man to marry and beget a child. They take as their major premise the implacability of time, and try what conclusions follow. There are two possible responses to the inevitability of time's erosion of the young man's beauty: he can beget a child; he can hope to live on in Shakespeare's verse. Both these possibilities are broached and promoted in sonnet 17, in which the young man can anticipate living twice, in a child and in Shakespeare's rhyme. Both offer ways of surviving time's depredations; but such survival is necessarily vicarious. We've already begun exploring the ways that survival in literary representation means a kind of far-fetching vicarious experience of oneself: like Nashe's Talbot, we take pleasure in thinking of others admiring – not ourselves but – a representation or "counterpart" (sonnet 84, again) of ourselves. The same would be true of the pride one takes in a child, especially if we think of that pride as redounding to our credit.

It's a commonplace that part of the studied irony of the sonnets consists in the way they warn the young man that he too will one day be like the speaker. This too has a vicarious component in it, to the extent that the speaker can offer himself as a representation of the young man too. Sonnet 73 would be a case in point here: the young man must not only leave the speaker ere long; he will become old and twilit ere long as well, just as the speaker is now. Similarly, the opening sonnets, especially if they constitute a well-formed sequence, warn the young man by example as well as by precept. That child would preserve the young man's beauty when he himself has lost it, and the speaker shows him what it would be like to lose it. Such a warning is implicit in sonnet 22, which shows the lover attempting to apply to himself something like the compensation he has pressed upon the young man in the sonnets encouraging him to have a child:

> My glass shall not persuade me I am old
> So long as youth and thou are of one date;
> But when in thee time's furrows I behold,
> Then look I death my days should expiate.
> For all that beauty that doth cover thee
> Is but the seemly raiment of my heart,
> Which in thy breast doth live, as thine in me:
> How can I then be elder than thou art?
> O! therefore, love, be of thyself so wary

> As I, not for myself, but for thee will;
> Bearing thy heart, which I will keep so chary
> As tender nurse her babe from faring ill.
>> Presume not on thy heart when mine is slain;
>> Thou gav'st me thine not to give back again.

The argument of this sonnet, let me note, is somewhat difficult to make sound reasonable. The point may be to abuse a conceit, Browning-like, in the hope that the young man won't notice that he is not so bound as the metaphor would suggest, since after all the speaker's possession of his heart doesn't mean that he can keep it when the young man ceases to love him. But we can make a less euphuistic sense of the lines if we paraphrase the last couplet like this: "You really did love me, and won't love another as you loved me; and besides you are aging and won't be able to tempt people with your beauty much longer."

It's certainly the case that the sonnet is rhetorically devious, intentionally equating two different meanings in the ambiguity of the metaphor of one's heart living in another's breast. The speaker's heart lives in the young man's breast because he loves the young man and takes his desires and interests as his own; the young man's heart lives in the speaker's breast in another sense, since this just means the speaker loves him. But once the sonnet establishes the symmetry of a relationship that in fact depends on two different interpretations of a metaphor, he can push that symmetry, allowing the young man's beauty to be his own praise and pleasure – but thereby also warning of the converse: that his decrepitude is what the young man should anticipate if he transfers his affections elsewhere. (Antony will find such symmetry is not reliable, when he fulminates against Cleopatra "whose heart I thought I had for she had mine.")

What interests me here, however, is how and why the speaker may be proud of the young man's beauty. This is not a case of making the young man into a trophy, which is one way that people boast of the beauty of those who love them. Here the speaker describes a vicarious experience of the young man's youth, as though the youth were his own – which is just what he has promised the young man a child will procure him. And indeed the speaker even describes himself in a parental or at least care-taking relation to the young man, whose heart he treats as his babe. There is no question that among the things the sonnet describes is the genuine revivification, joy, and pride that he feels in the young man's beauty. But the pride seems to be at the base of joy and revivification: if he didn't feel proud, he wouldn't feel delighted either. The most elemental question the sonnet raises, then, is how one person may be a proxy for another: how a child or a lover can be the focus of one's own experience and sense of oneself: in brief, how vicarious experience can itself be a fundamental, irreducible element of human experience.

This may amount to saying that theater is a fundamental element of human experience. It's certainly the case that Shakespeare over and over considers the relation of love to theater. One exemplary moment may be found in *A Midsummer Night's Dream*, when Oberon and Titania trade accusations of jealousy. It's a strange jealousy, however, for each of them is jealous of the way the other panders to the happiness of their respective human protégés, Hippolyta and Theseus. Oberon and Titania want Hippolyta and Theseus to find erotic happiness, and they take vicarious pleasure in the prospect, the pleasure they express when they bless the house at the end of the play. This is what we want too, and in *A Midsummer Night's Dream* as in the sonnets (and as in most of the comedies as well as some of the tragedies) Shakespeare is exploring how large a component vicarious experience constitutes in all erotic experience. To what extent is caring about what happens to the characters in a story like being in love with them? To what extent is being in love like caring what happens to a character in a story?

One difference might be that the audience's response is more purely selfless than the lover's interest. But I think Shakespeare was interested in the similarities, not the differences. Or perhaps we could say (what is ultimately the same thing) that the implicit self-representation of the plays and the narrative poems differs from that in the sonnets in that the other works allow Shakespeare a domain of serene command of his powers and insights that the sonnets are so conspicuously tortured by lacking. At any rate, the deeply philosophical issues that the sonnets raise are highly germane to the philosophical issues that arise not only in Shakespeare's plays but in all narrative which makes audiences feel anxiety about how things will turn out.

Another sonnet can help make this connection clearer. We've noticed that the early sonnets encourage the young man to beget his own image as a way of preserving it – a kind of precursor to Robert Trivers's selfish gene theory, popularized by Richard Dawkins. The speaker also thinks of the young man as a proxy for him, someone in whom he can take vicarious pleasure, although without the possibility of seeing the young man as his literal image. This doesn't prevent a parallel structure of representation, however, as sonnet 37 makes clear, where the speaker imagines the young man as his own child:

> As a decrepit father takes delight
> To see his active child do deeds of youth,
> So I, made lame by Fortune's dearest spite,
> Take all my comfort of thy worth and truth.
> For whether beauty, birth, or wealth, or wit,
> Or any of these all, or all, or more,
> Entitled in their parts do crowned sit,
> I make my love engrafted to this store.
> So then I am not lame, poor, nor despised
> Whilst that this shadow doth such substance give
> That I in thy abundance am sufficed
> And by a part of all they glory live.
> > Look what is best, that best I wish in thee.
> > This wish I have, then times happy me.

His love is engrafted to the store of the young man's qualities. This means both that those qualities produce his love and that his love allows him to see himself as represented by the young man. Again, this means that there is something irreducible in vicarious experience: he takes pleasure in the young man's powers and qualities, and that pleasure is fundamentally unselfish. It isn't even pleasure that the young man loves him. It is pleasure in loving the young man.

Of course he appeals to the young man's vanity in saying this: he has designs on him. But those designs themselves assume that the young man would take pleasure in considering the experience of the person who appreciates his virtues, loves him for them, takes pleasure in them.

III

I believe that Shakespeare is thinking through some thorny philosophical issues about self-representation and self-reference in noticing the highly practical and therefore highly salient fact of vicarious experience, salient in erotic life as in theater. Some recent philosophical accounts of how to talk about oneself and about others may be helpful here, since I think they schematize just the most difficult aspects of what Shakespeare was thinking through.

Thomas Nagel, following a line of argument originated by Wittgenstein, asks what, in an exhaustive series of objective propositions about the world, could indicate who I am, in the world?[3] You and I might read the same list; but we are different people, and the list can't tell us who is who. David Lewis summarizes this line of argument by denying that self-knowledge is propositional.[4] I know who I am, but this isn't propositional knowledge, because no proposition tells me which propositions are true of me unless I already know who I am. There is no meaningful proposition which says that I am I. My being myself is not a tautology but a first-person experience that no third-person description could convey (just because all a third-person description could convey is the apparent tautology).

Let's reconsider Nashe's account of Talbot. Imagine with Nashe that the new-risen Talbot is watching the audience absorbed in the play; but now imagine that death causes amnesia, and he doesn't know that he is the Talbot the play is representing. In such a case, what would happen to the joy Nashe imagines he will take in seeing himself portrayed so heroically and mourned so passionately? He might still like the play, or like its spectators, but his response would be the same as any other person's in the same position. What would make him take joy is only the recognition that the Talbot on the stage was a representation of him himself, so that he would feel personal satisfaction through the emotional response devoted to the tragedian impersonating him.

Would he be right to feel such satisfaction? What does it matter that he himself was Talbot? If he approves of what the *History* indicates Talbot has done, that should be enough. It doesn't add anything to Talbot's achievement for the person applauding that achievement to be Talbot himself. Nor is he himself the beneficiary of the applause of the audience, which is directed to his representation or his "counterpart" or (as computer gamers now call it) his avatar. No further fact becomes true of Talbot, real or representational, by virtue of the fact that it is he who is being represented.

I agree that this goes against our intuitions and our own desires. I want to win a race myself; it's peculiarly unsatisfying to think that it doesn't matter who wins the race, so long as someone does; and it's peculiarly unsatisfying to be told that if Algernon wins the race I could console myself by just imagining that I myself am Algernon and that therefore it's as though I have won the race, since whether I am he or not can make no difference to anyone else, since in fact there is no objective fact of the matter about whether I'm he or whether I'm myself – the subjective fact being available in principle only to the two of us and no one else. To an audience that knows nothing else about us except that we are racing each other, it makes no difference that it's I who win the race. (I myself can mean no more to those who watch the race than I do to "Julie," the friendly automated voice of the Amtrak reservation system, nor can they distinguish my subjectivity from Algernon's any more than Julie can.) If Algernon and I are both amnesiacs and we watch a replay of the race, there is no way for either of us to decide our personal investment in who won. The spectators of the race are in a similar position: they may be rooting for Flesch to win, but this is not the same thing as saying that they are rooting for me. They may be rooting for Flesch, but it never enters into their rooting – how could it? – that I am he. They are rooting for a third-person entity, not a first-person entity; for an object, not a subject; for my objective counterpart, but not for me.

In sonnets like number 94 Shakespeare both acknowledges and turns away from the young man's investment in its being he who has power. The acknowledgment of his power, I have said, is an appeal to the young man's vanity; or we might say the vanity is just the idea that it matters that he's the one who has the power to hurt, as though that said any more than saying some have power to hurt (which is in fact all that the sonnet does explicitly say). The sweetness of the summer's flower is not finally a fact that makes any difference to the flower, which only lives and dies; it makes a difference only to the summer that enjoys it. And yet the intuitive desire which vanity intensifies is the desire to be oneself that flower, as though its praisers could be saying something more than "what a singularly sweet flower that singularly sweet flower is," as though they could say you are that sweet flower, where you could mean something different applied to me from what was meant when applied to someone else. But it doesn't mean anything different to the person who addresses the addressee as you; the pronoun doesn't pick out the fact that it is I being addressed rather than another. For if I were someone else instead, a possibility that would entail no objective change – that is if I happened to be someone else instead – then it wouldn't be I who was being addressed. But everything else would remain exactly the same.

This is a pretty abstract summary, but I think it's a central issue in many of the sonnets of praise, focused particularly in the eternizing trope. Consider the young man's point of view. What does it mean to be remembered when you're dead? What picks him out as the person remembered? There isn't even an I there anymore to be able so say, "When they remember the young man it's I they're remembering." Who is the young man besides the purely objective person of whom things are predicated in Shakespeare's sonnets, and who could be anyone?

IV

We hazard and argue other predicates about him, guess at his identity, whether South-ampton or Willie Hughes. But even if any of these are proved, they are mere predicates. Can we still ask who is he besides the sum of his predicates, now that he is dead? But what else besides the sum of his predicates can immortality in verse mean? The sonnets, by tautology, can say nothing about him that is not in the end propositional. Can such propositions make a difference, gratify his narcissism or his vanity, when there is no subjective self they can pick out? The questions are all the more acute because there is no subjective self left.

This isn't a fact peculiar to the sonnets, of course. Homer's work, the old joke goes, was composed not by Homer but by a poet of the same name. The distinction is an empty one, like saying that Shakespeare's sonnets to the young man weren't addressed to the young man we conventionally call him, but to another young man of whom we know just as much or just as little, and just the same things. What if the name of Caesar and all the things that he had done actually applied to another person, and not Caesar? Would we still be praising Caesar by saying Caesar and going no further?

But it does feel as though knowing the name of the young man might make a dif-ference, just as knowing what he looks like individuates him a little bit more. The sonnets themselves say that they seek to portray him; in addition to his being young, for example, we know that he is fair. It is natural to human psychology that it does matter to us what others think of us, even if we don't gain by it: it matters how they remember us, for example.

In general, it is one's name that comes closest to making one feel that propositions can refer to oneself, can capture or express attitudes towards our first-person selves, can pick out the subject that I am, someone not only objectively but also subjectively indis-tinguishable from me, as though someone else could, as I could, tell me from a replica exact down to the atomic level of each cell (a replica who would believe himself real and me to be the replica).

It is therefore notable that the sonnets that praise the young man do not name him, notable that he is never named (unlike, say, the broad hints of Penelope Rich's name in *Astrophel and Stella*). The beloveds in the sonnets aren't even given nonce-names (Stella, Delia, or the like), which they might take as at least specifying them as uniquely as their real names would. Now, we needn't make too much of this: it is probable that everyone who counted knew who the young man was, whether he was Mr. W.H. or not. But we shouldn't make too little of it either, since Shakespeare does promise him immortality in the minds of those not yet born, those therefore who can know him only through the records made of his beauty. Such records would come closest to picking him out if they named him, since what they would say is that a person with a particular name had these other qualities – beauty, virtue, and the rest – which is close to, but not identical to, picking out that particular person.

This argument may help solve the moral or psychological problem (if it is one) of why the vain want to be praised for qualities they actually have. Like their names, such qualities go some way towards uniquely specifying them. If they're praised for qualities they know they don't have, the praise will be that much farther from picking them out, from making them the objects of praise. If I get praised for winning a race that I have lost, I will come to conclude that the praisers are mistaking me for the winner. "False compare" belies the person it is supposed to praise, and may fail even to look like praise of that person. False predicates may make me realize that "you have but mistook me all this while: . . . how can you say to me I am a king?" (*Richard II*, III. ii). *Twelfth Night* presents a hilarious version of this truth when Viola recites her praise of Olivia, but then pauses to make sure that it is Olivia, whom she's never before seen, that she's addressing. Predicates can go farther than mere physical objectivity, and can include, for example, family members. Olivia falls in love with Sebastian, and this partly redounds to Viola's credit. Sebastian is a representation of Viola in the same way that her own beauty is a representation of her, and just as the young man's child would be a representation of him. We can, with Shakespeare, take this one step farther still and say that the beauty or poetic skill of the person who loves me is a representation to the world of my own qualities, another predication made of me, just as my qualities are predications made of me.

Here we can say that we have come full circle, since in loving someone I also hope that the reality and expression of my love is a predication of my true self, and that this predication will matter to the person I love. It is in this way, as we have seen, that the love the speaker feels and the vanity of the beloved are essentially two facets of the same interest in what others will think of the predicates that represent or fail to represent oneself. And it is therefore in this way that we can also argue for an element of disinterestedness in love. We can say that vicarious experience, the experience of satisfaction that Titania and Oberon take in seeing Theseus and Hippolyta happily married, is disinterested. This is so even if we take it as important that the characters are likely to be doubled, with a single actor playing Oberon and Theseus, and another playing Titania and Hippolyta. Praise of Hippolyta is even so not praise of Titania; and this teaches the more radical lesson that praise of Titania is not praise of Titania either, since there's a sense that if I am Titania, or if my name is Titania, praise of Titania is still not praise of me. Titania is still only my counterpart, not my subjective self. No proposition can actually refer to me (subjectively). Any Shakespearean character could rightly say, with Iago, "I am not what I am." We can conclude, therefore, that vicarious experience is primordial, since our experience of ourselves in the world of relation to others is irreducibly vicarious.[5]

V

As ought to be obvious, I think that these were issues that Shakespeare thought about at some length, in both drama and poetry. I think he explored them, but I also think he used them for his own varying purposes, from the expert solicitation of audience interest in fictional characters to the moral and philosophical analysis of the relations between those characters. Stanley Cavell, in considering the attitudes that Shakespeare's characters take toward others, sees a crucial moral issue in moments of acknowledgment of what we might call the unpredicable subjectivity of the other.[6] Some characters acknowledge, some avoid acknowledgment, some never think even to acknowledge. Claudio, in allowing Pedro to represent him, is more or less indifferent to the relation of subjectivity to objectivity, more or less indifferent to the question whether any representation can pick him out from everyone else in the world. He is also, worrisomely, indifferent enough (as is Olivia) to the question whether he will marry Hero or her cousin at the end. By contrast, Beatrice and Benedick know each other at the end, as do Antony and Cleopatra.

In the sonnets Shakespeare puts these issues to use as a way of attempting to put pressure on the young man, which is one of his constant goals. The most he can offer the young man is something close to a set of predicates that will really pick him out, refer (impossibly) to the young man's subjectivity, to the young man's primary narcissism, even after he is dead. The most punishment he can inflict on the young man is to withhold these predicates. One of the modes of such withholding is to explore the idea of their impossibility.

It is often the case in the sonnets that rebuke of the young man takes the form of irony. I want to end by citing a couple of sonnets I take to be ironic, in effect even if not in intention. Sonnet 53 is a kind of summary of the issues that I have raised here: all the attributes of the young man may be found elsewhere, in descriptions of Helen or of Adonis (or, contrariwise, the young man can be taken as a useful representation of Helen or Adonis); only his "substance," whereof he is made, is inaccessible. The last line of 53 may look like conventional praise as well, even as it denies that it falls into the pattern of conventional praise offered by the quatrains. But it is also highly ambiguous, its irony suggesting that the young man's heart in fact deserves no praise (it might be the most inconstant heart of all). What I want to stress, though, is that the ambiguity and the irony derive from the fact that the heart is inscrutable and inaccessible: that we know nothing of the young man's heart, and that the speaker is representing the young man's heart as inaccessible to him as well.

Even the conventional praise is no praise at all, of course. Yet all language is conventional, and the only knowledge we can have of the young man after his death is that which conventional praise offers.

Like the sonnets that say you only have to describe the young man to make your poetry great, but then don't describe him, therefore don't eternize him, sonnet 59 also withholds any specifying information. If description isn't enough, if naming isn't enough, how much does this sonnet offer?

> If there be nothing new, but that which is
> Hath been before, how are our brains beguil'd,
> Which labouring for invention bear amiss
> The second burthen of a former child!
> O! that record could with a backward look,
> Even of five hundred courses of the sun,
> Show me your image in some antique book,
> Since mind at first in character was done!

That I might see what the old world could say
To this composed wonder of your frame;
Whether we are mended, or whe'r better they,
Or whether revolution be the same.
    O! sure I am the wits of former days,
    To subjects worse have given admiring praise.

Although this sonnet ends by asserting the young man's unique and unexampled virtue, it concedes that a description of the young man might well be found five hundred years before his birth. So the description has nothing to do with the young man himself. What is attributed to him *de dicto* (as the philosophers say) has no necessary connection with the subjectivity he could ascribe to himself *de se*. The burden of description has already been borne, by some counterpart real or imagined, and the fact that the description isn't applied to subjectively the same person doesn't prevent its being verbally the same: a collection of superlatives.

But what do we know about the young man when we know that he is the object of a passel of superlatives? Nothing at all except that those superlatives applied (so Shakespeare claims) to some person. But we know nothing more than (at most) that he was some person.

The inaccessibility of subjectivity to characterization by propositions makes subjectivity the diametrical opposite of drama, where everything we need to know about a character we do know. There is nothing lacking in the propositions that characterize a fictional character, since the character is simply the artifact created by these propositions. But the young man, the speaker of the sonnets, the writer of the plays, and their audience all share a particular relation to being described. We are interested in others and interested in the interest of others. We place ourselves in the world through the vicarious interest we take in their vicarious interest in us.

The limitations to overcoming the radical separations between people are the limitations imposed by subjectivity and by the fact that propositions cannot reach subjectivity itself, when what we share with others is the representable or propositional world. This is to share an enormous amount, and Shakespeare is the playwright of the most enormous social vision. But in the sonnets he brings himself to the limits of being able to speak of himself or of another in their subjectivity. The painfulness of the great sonnets finds an explanation, one consonant with his lifelong literary vocation as a playwright, in the somewhat less well-known sonnets I have for the most part been analyzing here: sonnets in which Shakespeare considers more analytically what can and what cannot be genuinely communicated between real people, no matter how intimate they are.

NOTES

1 This essay first appeared in *Some Versions of Pastoral* (New York: New Directions, 1974; first publ. 1935.)

2 In conversation. See Harold Bloom, *The Anatomy of Influence* (New York: Farrar, Straus, Giroux, forthcoming 2008).

3   See Thomas Nagel, "The Objective Self," in C. Genet and S. Shoemaker (eds.), *Mind and Knowledge* (New York: Oxford University Press, 1983).

4   See in particular David Lewis, "Attitudes de dicto and de se," *Philosophical Review* 88 (1979), pp. 513–43.

5   The depiction of Sinon in *The Rape of Lucrece* makes this point as well. Lucrece is amazed by the innocence on the depicted face of this hypocrite. But Sinon looks innocent only because the painter has depicted an innocent man; that innocent man stands for the "real Sinon," but there is nothing astonishing about being able to depict someone innocent.

6   See in particular Stanley Cavell, "Disowning Knowledge," in *Seven Plays of Shakespeare*, 2nd edn. (New York: Cambridge University Press, 2003), and *Must We Mean What We Say?*, 2nd edn. (New York: Cambridge University Press, 2004).

PART IX
The Sonnets and
A Lover's Complaint

"Making the quadrangle round": Alchemy's Protean Forms in Shakespeare's Sonnets and *A Lover's Complaint*

Margaret Healy

When thou hast made the quadrangle round, then is all the secrett found.
(George Ripley, *The Compound of Alchymie*, 1591)

Reflecting on a lifetime's study of the sketchbooks of Renaissance architects and artists, the historian Rudolf Wittkower "forcibly" concluded that "the geometry of the circle had an almost magical power over these men" (1977: 19). Indeed, Alberti's survey of the best designs for churches (*De re aedificatoria*, 1450) began with an eulogy of the circle: "Nature herself . . . enjoys the round form above all others as is proved by her own creations" (Wittkower 1977: 3). At least from the time of the Orphic poets of antiquity, the circle and its center had been apprehended as symbols of God, and later neoplatonic philosophy had done much to invigorate this notion. Furthermore, the ancient philosopher Vitruvius had famously inscribed a well-proportioned man with extended limbs inside a square and circle and this symbol, with its mystic geometry embodying the harmonies of the universe, had a hold on the Renaissance artist's imagination which, Wittkower declared, "can hardly be overestimated" (p. 14). The well-tempered individual – man's body in equilibrium and in harmony with nature – was considered a microcosm of the world and of God; so much so that, according to Alberti, the Vitruvian figure conveyed an ideal of beauty that the harmonious soul apprehended instinctively (p. 27). Beautiful architecture, paintings, and poetry, too, had, of necessity, to be informed by this ideal. Quite simply, this was an age in which "all art was thought of spatially" and "formal elements" and "spatial patterns" could not be separated from substantive concerns (Fowler 1970: ix).

It is strange, given the current critical emphasis on the importance of original contexts, that the early modern obsession with form and spatial pattern has been largely ignored over recent decades. Studies of Shakespeare's sonnets have been dominated by such topics as sexual desire, gender, and racial politics, with the pursuit of linear narratives and recognizable subjectivities – all very modern preoccupations. My intention is not to denigrate such projects; rather, I wish to emphasize the interpretative dissonance that can result from ignoring questions that were central to the mindset of our forebears, thereby effectively effacing the considerable difference of the past. As I hope to show, commencing an exploration of the sonnets by returning to the focal concerns of Renaissance poets and commentators can yield significant additional insights into Shakespeare's richly mysterious, multi-faceted sequence. Importantly, this approach will demonstrate that the *representation* of the pursuit of spiritual improvement *is* a key feature of the sequence – something strenuously rejected by most modern editors – and that the enigmatic *A Lover's Complaint* (which contains an allegory of the Resurrection) was undoubtedly an integral part, indeed fitting culmination of, Shakespeare's sonnet project.

Samuel Daniel's *A Defence of Ryme* (?1603) provides us with the most extensive account of what a sonneteer writing at the cusp of the seventeenth century sought to achieve through his art. Daniel addressed his treatise to William Herbert and, by way of an eulogy to Herbert's mother the Countess of Pembroke, declared that her Wilton home was his "best Schoole" for learning "the formall ordering of those compositions" (Daniel 1904: 358). Philip Sidney's sister was indeed renowned as a "Great Favourer of Phoebus' offspring" (Hall 1995: 107). Of the sonnet Daniel observes:

> In an eminent spirit, whome Nature hath fitted for that mysterie, Ryme is no impediment to his conceit, but rather gives him wings to mount, and carries him, not out of his course, but as it were beyond his power to a farre happier flight. Al excellencies being sold us at the hard price of labour, it followes, where we bestow most thereof we buy the best successe: and Ryme, being farre more laborious than loose measures . . . , must needs, meeting with wit and industry, breed greater and worthier effects in our language . . . Nor is this certaine limit observed in Sonnets, any tyrannical bounding of the conceit, but rather reducing it in *girum* and a just forme, neither too long for the shortest project, nor too short for the longest, being but onely imployed for a present passion. For the body of our imagination being as an unformed *Chaos* without fashion, without day, if by the divine power of the spirit it be wrought into an Orbe of order and forme, is it not more pleasing to Nature, that desires a certaintie and comports not with that which is infinite, to have these clozes, rather than not to know where to end, or how farre to goe, especially seeing our passions are often without measure? (1904: 365–6)

Sonnets are particularly associated here with "passions," which can get out of hand. The sonnet's limited length and the demands of its rhyme scheme constrain them healthfully, as in an "Orbe of order," or "*girum*" [circle] – a "just forme." Sonnets are thus the product of disciplined restraint bred by "wit and industry." This is certainly not, then, the spontaneous outflow of personal feelings so prized three centuries later by the Romantics. Control and moderation are paramount in this account, as is the very Renaissance veneration of divine circular form.

Daniel's "eminent spirit" with "wings to mount" is highly reminiscent of Sir Philip Sidney's poet as delineated in his seminal *Apologie for Poetrie* (c.1583). Inspired by the "heavenly Maker," poets can, in Sidney's estimation, "deliver . . . golden" worlds surpassing Nature's (Sidney 1904: 156):

When with the force of a divine breath he bringeth things forth far surpassing her doings, with no small arguments to the incredulous of that first accursed fall of Adam: sith our erected wit maketh us know what perfection is, and yet our infected will keepeth us from reaching unto it. But these arguments wil by fewe be understood, and by fewer granted. (p. 157)

Somehow – and "fewe" (only initiates, we might think) will understand or "grant" [believe] it – the inspired poet can overcome his "infected will" and thereby recapture "golden" worlds lost at the Fall.

Sidney's taunts are tantalizing: who did understand and how was this effacing of the "infected" will achieved? John Donne's poetic evocation of the sonnet form in "The Canonization" is enlightening. Like many of Shakespeare's sonnets, this poem appears on the surface blasphemous in its representation of the self-absorbed lovers: "For Godsake hold your tongue, and let me love" (Donne 1912: 14–15). They will even be "approve(d)," "*Canoniz'd* for Love" by sonnet "hymnes":

> And if no peece of Chronicle wee prove,
> We'll build in sonnets pretty roomes;
> As well a well wrought urne becomes
> The greatest ashes, as halfe-acre tombes
> (ll. 31–4)

This beautiful analogy of the "pretty" stanza [room] of the sonnet with a memorializing "well wrought urne" is evocative of divine circular form, and the "ashes" resonate with the "Phoenix ridle" of the preceding stanza:

> We'are Tapers too, and at our owne cost die,
> And wee in us finde the'Eagle and the Dove.
> The Phoenix ridle hath more wit
> By us, we two being one, are it.
> So to one neutrall thing both sexes fit,
> Wee dye and rise the same, and prove
> Mysterious by this love.
> (ll. 21–7)

The copulation of the lovers, which is associated with burning ("tapers"), will result in their death and resurrection from the ashes ("The Phoenix ridle") as "one neutrall thing" incorporating "both sexes" – the hermaphrodite, which was widely understood in the Renaissance as the prelapsarian perfect human form (Gilbert 2002: 15). Here, I suggest, is the clue to the mystery: the conjunction of lovers, the Phoenix, and the hermaphrodite are the central symbols of the spiritual alchemy that Donne alludes to in his sermons and poetry. He even imagined God as a consummate alchemist: "*For brass, I will bring gold*, says God in *Esay*; *and for iron, silver*. God can work in all metals and transmute all metals: he can make a Moral man, a Christian; and a Superstitious Christian, a sincere Christian" (Donne 1953–62: vol. 4, 110). This, too, is the "heavenly alchemy" operating to "gild" nature, which Shakespeare associates with his own art in sonnet 33. Both these writers adapt the witty and sophisticated enigmas of alchemical thought to poetic expression. Alchemy is a discarded art today, however, and in order to understand Shakespeare's extensive use of its lexicon in his sonnets we must strive to resurrect it from the ashes of near-oblivion.

First, however, we would do well to attend to Martin Ruland's warning in his *A Lexicon of Alchemy*, published in 1612:

> In the writings of Hermetic Science, the Philosophers never express the true significance of their thoughts in the vulgar tongue and they must not be interpreted according to the literal sense of the expression. *The sense which is presented on the surface is not the true sense.* They discourse in enigmas, metaphors, allegories, fables, similitudes, and each Philosopher adapts them after his own manner. (381 [emphasis added])

One of alchemy's most famous adepts, Geber, confirms in his *Summa* (thirteenth century) that while the "wise man" will understand, "the foolish and the ignorant" will not (Burckhardt 1967: 29). This deliberate obfuscation was intended to lead astray "covetous" fools – those who, like Ben Jonson's "false alchemists," imagined that the art was all about extracting real gold from base metals and getting rich quickly. The hazard is obvious: if we read alchemical images literally we run the risk of situating ourselves among the foolish. While many Renaissance alchemists *were* metalworkers and chemists, their true goals were of a rather different kind, as the words of the seventeenth-century practitioner Thomas Vaughan suggest: "Give me an art then, that is a perfect intire *Map* of the *Creation* that can lead me directly to the *Knowledge* of the true *God* . . . and by which I can attain to all the *Secrets* and *Mysteries* in *Nature*" (1984: 166).

In recent decades historians of science have demonstrated that – rather ironically – it was this mystical "chymical" dream which fueled the explosion of science in the mid-seventeenth century – the so-called "Scientific Enlightenment." If the "secrets" of nature could be unraveled, the ravages of the Fall might be repaired and earthly Paradise restored. Initially, however, inner alchemy had to be applied to purify the soul of its drosses, cleansing its infected will and transmuting it into spiritual "gold" – the rebirth of the soul of the artist himself. This sounds like a remarkably esoteric preoccupation, but George Puttenham's *The Arte of English Poesie* suggests that the transformations wrought by alchemy or metalwork were quite readily applied to the operation of the poet's psyche. Of the latter Puttenham declared, "his inward conceits be the mettall of his minde," and "as his minde is tempered and qualified, so are his speeches and language" (Puttenham 1904: 154). As we shall see, inner alchemy could be a remarkably painful and torturous process fraught with danger and incorporating retrograde as well as forward movement. It is this hazardous "craft" – designated the "opus circulatorium" (the circular work) – which is encoded in Shakespeare's highly emblematic, riddling and paradoxical sonnets and *A Lover's Complaint*; and it is this which accounts for the "cool framework of order and steadying artifice" that Colin Burrow has located in the sequence (Shakespeare 2002: 116).

Originally an Egyptian art associated with its legendary founder, Hermes Trismegistus, alchemy was absorbed into and developed by Chinese, Indian, Greco-Egyptian, and Hebraic cultures (Linden 2003: 1–9; Abraham 1998: xv). Platonism and Christianity formed a ready alliance with alchemy, and the Christian hermeticists placed pagan and Christian prophets "in the same genealogical lines, interconnecting them" (Abraham 1990: 173). The success of this integration can be readily apprehended merely by stepping over the threshold of the cathedral in Siena: the striking black-and-white mosaic pavement images (*c.*1480) include a huge representation of Hermes Trismegistus with sibyls bearing prophecies about the coming of Christianity and an inscription proclaiming: "Hermes Mercurius Contemporaneous Moyse" [Moses]. After the conquest of Alexandria, Islamic culture, too, had readily absorbed Trismegistus' teachings, embellishing the art and producing some of its most famous adepts, whose works were translated into the European vernaculars throughout the sixteenth and seventeenth centuries (Burckhardt 1967: 18–19). A focal revelation of Trismegistus had been that "all things proceed from One alone by meditation on One alone" (*The Emerald Tablet*). This philosophy was incorporated into Plato's *Symposium* (which also construed androgyny as the original state), but it was in the Islamic works that the doctrine of "oneness of existence" reached its fullest flowering (Burckhardt 1967: 19). The famous alchemist Khunrath said of this mystery: "Out of the gross and impure One there cometh an exceeding pure and subtle One" (Abraham 1990: 44). The ultimate alchemical goal was to recapture the original "nobility" of human nature and achieve illumination of the soul through "oneing" with the eternal spiritual realm (Burckhardt 1967: 40, 26–7). In Christian hermeticism this "oneing" was with Christ – the philosopher's stone. Undoubtedly this is the inspiration behind the "wondrous excellence" and "One thing expressing" of Shakespeare's famously enigmatic sonnet 105, which invokes the Trinity and begins (as though to head off misinterpretation of the sonnets through literal reading):

> Let not my love be called idolatry,
> Nor my beloved as an idol show,
> Since all alike my songs and praises be,
> To one, of one, still such, and ever so.

The angry annotation on a 1609 quarto of the sonnets – "What a heap of wretched Infidel Stuff" – has been attributed to the sequence's "flamboyantly blasphemous extremes" (Duncan-Jones, in Shakespeare 1997: 49), but the choice of the word "Infidel" suggests, rather, a rejection of the Islamic taint of Shakespeare's alchemy.

Paging through the vivid imaginative landscape of the beautifully engraved alchemical textbooks of the late sixteenth and seventeenth centuries, it is not difficult to understand the appeal of this richly symbolic art to Renaissance wits in pursuit of new invention. Some of these volumes even present the stages of the "opus circulatorium" in the form of theatrical scenes complete with audiences; others are more like allegorical romances. Their surreal imagery certainly opens a window of understanding onto some of Shakespeare's most obscure lines and makes sense of the Pythagorean geometry, with its divine implications, which many scholars have found in Shakespeare's sequence, but are at a loss to explain in the context of an entirely secular sequence. Take François Beroalde de Verveille's *Le Tableau des riche inventions* (Paris, 1600), for example (figure 24.1): here we find at the top of the title-page a lion with its paws cut off (symbol of sulfur which has fixed volatile mercury), an eagle (symbol of mercury), a fire sprouting a tree of life topped by a phoenix (philosopher's stone), an hourglass (indicating the need for both time and patience), and myrtle branches growing in all directions signifying that the origin, cause, and end of all things is Love (De Rola 1979: 25, 28). Its author tantalizingly warns that its rich inventions are "covered with the veil of amorous deceits" (title-page; De Rola 1979: 25–6). Lovers kissing, copulating, dying in a fire, and rising anew as one hermaphrodite are the key recurring "amorous deceits" of all of these alchemical volumes.

Read against the backdrop of these engravings, even the bizarre images of Shakespeare's particularly enigmatic sonnet 19 resonate with meaning:

> Devouring time, blunt thou the lion's paws,
> And make the earth devour her own sweet brood;
> Pluck the keen teeth from the fierce tiger's jaws,
> And burn the long-lived Phoenix in her blood.
>
> (ll. 1–4)

Time (who, as Saturn, devoured his own children) is being invoked to assist sulfur (the lion) in the process of fixing mercury. The tiger probably alludes to the acid added to the alchemist's alembic, which gradually "loses its teeth" or abates as it aids the dissolution or devouring of the distinct, male and female, raw "materia" into a chemical soup from which the refined new androgynous birth will emerge (Simonds 1999: 103).

The poet is having immense fun here playing with these highly evocative arcane images; to try to pin down the exact meaning of each of them is actually a rather foolish pursuit (alchemical symbols are remarkably labile and ambiguous); it is their cumulative significance that is important. In this context they refer, of course, to psychic, imaginative transformations rather than to material chemical processes. Together they confirm that an "opus circulatorium" is in progress and that the poet, through his mercurial verse (the adept's head is his "still"), will "distil" and thus preserve "beauty's pattern" for eternity. Importantly, the next sonnet (20) produces the wondrous "master-mistress" – suggestively, an alchemical hermaphrodite. Martin Ruland's *Lexicon* affirms that the "hermetick art" was imagined to produce truly marvelous effects:

> The Adepts assure us that it is possible not only to prolong life, but also to renew youth. To renew youth is to enter once again into that beautiful season when the forces of our being were at the spring and freshness of early power. Paracelsus, by means of his celebrated Mercury of Life, claimed to metamorphose an old into a young man. (441)

Significantly, the perfecting, eternalizing work of alchemy was expressed geometrically through divine mathematics and always commenced with the completion of a circle – a "marriage."

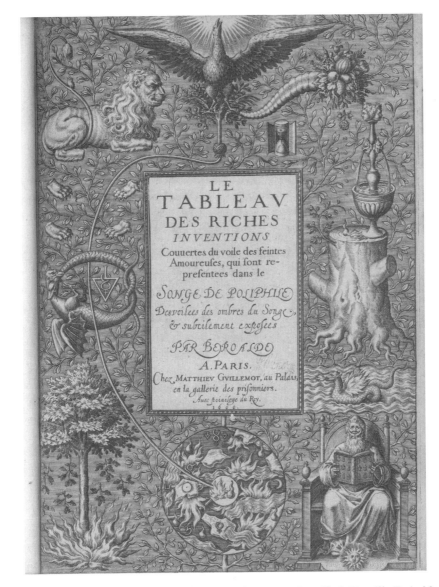

Figure 24.1 Title-page, *Le Tableau Des Riches Inventions*, by François Beroalde de Verveille (Paris: Mattieu Guillemot, 1600). Reprinted with permission of the J. R. Ritman Library, Amsterdam.

Emblem XXI of Michael Maier's *Atalanta fugiens* (1618) depicts an alchemist, compasses in hand, inscribing on a wall a Vitruvian-type image, incorporating a man and woman holding hands, which represents the following wisdom: "Make from the male and female a circle, then a square, afterwards a triangle, from which make a circle, and thou shalt have the Philosopher's Stone" (De Rola 1979: 81) (figure 24.2). The whole

Figure 24.2   Illustration accompanying Emblema XXI, Michael Maier, *Atalanta fugiens* (Oppenheim: Theodor de Bry, 1618). © *British Library, London.*

operation of the *opus* was aimed at recapturing man's "Adamic" undivided state of wholeness and this necessitated an initial "conjunctio" of opposites – of male and female, Sol and Luna, Sulfur and Mercury, fixed and volatile – through their distillation by fire in the alchemist's alembic or "head" (Burckhardt 1967: 149). The "chemical wedding" or "marriage" was, in fact, *the* key symbol of alchemy, and by commencing his sonnet sequence in such an unconventional way with a repetitive call to the male beloved to beget an heir through union with his female opposite, Shakespeare was undoubtedly signaling the alchemical trajectory of his sequence; a trajectory gradually reinforced through an accretion of suggestive images. The "rose" (emblem of the philosopher's stone), "flame," and "fuel" of sonnet 1, though conventional emblems of love, point the wise reader in the right direction; with the introduction in sonnets 4 and 5 of the two most important protagonists (aside from the mercurial poet) in the "theater" of the alembic – Nature and Time – any lingering doubts vanish.

The philosopher-alchemist had to imitate nature, laboring with her assistance to distil and "store" beauty's "essence," because the soul must be "pregnant with ideal Beauty" before the secrets of this divine art could be accessed (de Rola 1979: 24). This

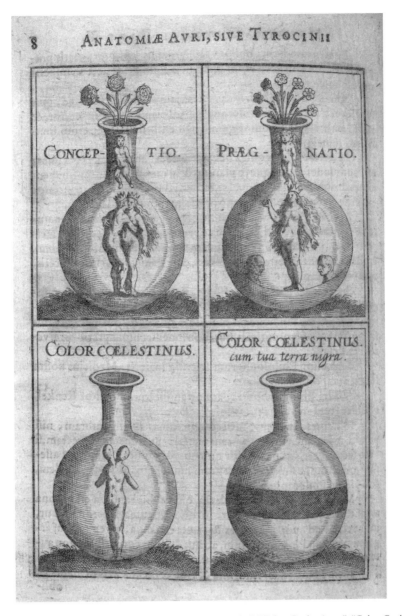

Figure 24.3 Johann Daniel Mylius, "Conceptio," "Praegnatio," "Color Coelestinus," "Color Coelestinus cum tua terra nigra." © *British Library, London.*

was a process that necessitated patience, time, and toil but which, paradoxically, was simultaneously opposed by Time (Saturn) and his scythe. Saturn was also the base metal (the darkened soul) from which gold was extracted. In order for Beauty's essence to be distilled the beloved must, as sonnet 5 rather disturbingly asserts, become "A liquid prisoner pent in walls of glass" (the alembic) – a highly evocative image and an

extremely common one in the alchemical textbooks (figure 24.3). The alchemist-poet
– needing time but at war with time – labors to "give life" to his beloved in "eternal
lines" (sonnet 18): "flowers distilled" (sonnet 5). With the fixing of volatile mercury in
sonnet 19, considerable progress is signaled, and the triumphant note of sonnet 20 registers success – "Beauty" is now an alchemical fusion of male and female qualities. The
operations of the poet's "head" have produced a hermaphrodite (also called Mercurius
by adepts) – the master-mistress of the poet's passion.

Crucially, however, the "opus" has really only just begun. Time that gives, takes
away: the "conjunctio" mediated by the alchemist is actually a curious deathly embrace
– the beloved must die and be resurrected again and again from the ashes of the adept's
"head" for the philosopher's stone to be brought to fruition. Spiritually, this meant that
the "substance" of the soul had to be repeatedly dissolved and crystallized anew through
intense meditation and prayer: luminosity demanded the painful integration of all the
dark impulses of the soul (Burckhardt 1967: 27). In the alchemists' language, the
"womb" of generation inevitably becomes a "grave," "tomb," or "prison" of decay, and
the workman must proceed to grapple with the mental torments of "hell" – the dark
phase or "nigredo" of the cycle. As the adept Artephius explains, this was an essential
phase in the cycle of purification: "that which does not make black cannot make white,
because blackness is the beginning of whiteness and a sign of putrefaction and alteration" (Abraham 1998: 27).

Shakespeare's sonnets are dense with the melancholic symbolism of the "nigredo."
A gloomy litany of "darkness," "ghastly night" (27), "oppression," "clouds," "grief"
(28), "bootless cries" (29), and "sorrows" (30), culminates in the overt alchemical symbolism of 31:

> Thou art the grave where buried love doth live,
> Hung with the trophies of my lovers gone.

The "grave" was the alchemist's vessel during the "nigredo," and it was of course here
that the bodies of the lovers were "imprisoned," burned, and purified. Inevitably, this
involves loss, as only one androgynous body can be resurrected from the fire. Sometimes
in alchemical texts (as in Mylius's *Philosophia reformata*, 1622) the dead bodies are ma-
cabrely pictured in a coffin or tomb. Shakespeare's frequent allusions to "clouds and
eclipses," as in sonnet 35, and his designation of his inventive "brain" as both "tomb"
and "womb" of generation for his "in-hearse[d]" "ripe thoughts" (86), are similarly
alchemically inspired. The poet-alchemist's confrontation with the dark side of his
psyche is, however, thankfully rewarded by periodic glimmers of light, and the "blessed
shape" of Adonis/Helen in sonnet 53 is surely a "triumph" of luminosity: perfect
androgynous neoplatonic Beauty is now "stilled" and "stored" – a "trophy" to the
alchemist's art. But, as we learn in sonnet 54, distillation must begin again immediately,
and tinctured "truth" is now the goal.

"Like as the waves make towards the pebbled shore / . . . Each changing place with
that which goes before" (60. 1–3), the progress of the alchemical opus always incorporates erosive movement and counter-movement – both loss and hard-won gain – and

the latter is paradoxically facilitated by and yet obstructed by time. This spiraling movement back and forth is symbolized by the entwined serpents of Mercury's caduceus. Shakespeare's metaphors are particularly appropriate because mercurial water was known as the "sea" which dissolved the base metals and nourished the infant stone which "crawls to maturity," continually set back by "Crooked eclipses": phases of putrefaction and death which, negative as they may seem, lead to new understanding and thus to "growth." This "fight" for "glory" –"Nativity" (birth of the stone) – necessitated extreme concentration and sustained toil, and sonnet 60 brilliantly captures the intensity, working energy, and excitement of an obsessed, brow-mopping scientist who feels he is at last gaining ground and bringing something truly momentous to fruition – Mary Shelley's Dr Frankenstein springs to mind. The analogy is indeed more appropriate than it may at first seem, for, as in Frankenstein's case, the moral status of the projected "birth" is not guaranteed. Thus sonnet 93 anxiously reflects: "How like Eve's apple doth thy beauty grow, / If thy sweet virtue answer not thy show," and 94 notes: "Lilies that fester smell far worse than weeds." The lily was an emblem of the philosopher's stone.

As the opus "crawls" haltingly but progressively forth, the poet-alchemist's "distraction," "fears," and "hopes" reach "fever" pitch (sonnet 119):

> What potions have I drunk of siren tears
> Distilled from limbecks foul as hell within,
> Applying fears to hopes, and hopes to fears,
> Still losing when I saw myself to win?

"Tears" are the drops of moisture that condense at the top of the still and rain down upon the blackened body lying at the bottom of the alembic, cleansing it of its impurities. The foul medicine produced by the "evil still" seems to have worked, however, for the sonnet moves into the third quatrain on a positive note, affirming in true Christian fashion the value or "gains" of suffering:

> O benefit of ill: now I find true
> That better is by evil still made better,
> And ruined love when it is built anew
> Grows fairer than at first, more strong, far greater.

Spiritual improvement consequent upon torturous inner alchemy is registered in these lines and confirmed by sonnet 124. The poet's "dear love"

> . . . was builded far from accident;
> It suffers not in smiling pomp, nor falls
> Under the blow of thralled discontent,
> Wherto th'inviting time our fashion calls:
> It fears not policy, that heretic,
> Which works on leases of short-numbered hours,
> But all alone stands hugely politic.

Constancy and simplicity are now the essence of the speaker's love, and by sonnet 125 it is clear that the body of his beloved has merged, mysteriously, with that of Christ:

> No, let me be obsequious in thy heart,
> And take thou my oblation, poor but free,
> Which is not mixed with seconds, knows no art,
> But mutual render, only me for thee.

"Oblation" is the sacramental bread-and-wine offering to God, and "mutual render" refers to Christ's crucifixion and the redemption of humankind. The echo from Leviticus 1: 13 ("it is a burnt offering, an oblation made by fire for a sweete savour unto the Lord") in the earlier line (7), "For compound sweet forgoing simple savour," is significant in this context: alchemical purifications were, of course, brought about through "fire." Has distilled "truth" been captured? Certainly, the poet's earlier preoccupation with secular desire for his beloved "lovely Boy" merges and is even at times replaced with meditations on divine love in this group of sonnets. To the "sensual" he has indeed brought in "sense," as he promises in sonnet 35. It would seem that two of the "trinity" of Platonic virtues might have been harnessed – beauty and truth. The third, goodness or kindness, will be the preoccupation of the culminating 28 sonnets. According to Ficino's commentary on Plato's *Symposium*, these three attributes reside as a trinity within the divine mind.

Like most recent commentators, Katherine Duncan-Jones finds no hint of "Petrarch's treatment of secular love as a route to religious transcendence" (Shakespeare 1997: 49) in Shakespeare's sequence; but, if we allow that sixteenth-century neoplatonism as transformed by Ficino incorporated the sensual and erotic, we must surely revise this finding. Here, for example, is a description of "virtuous love" generated by "reason" from an influential sixteenth-century work by Tullia d'Aragona:

> It has for its chief end the transformation of self into the beloved object, with the desire that should be transformed into the self, so that out of two, one alone is made. Of this transformation, Francis Petrarch and the most reverend Cardinal Bembo have written, often and with great subtlety . . . It is certainly true that the lover, who beyond this spiritual union desires also the union of the bodies, to make him one, as far as he can, with the beloved. (*Dialogue dell'Infinita d'Amore*, Venice, 1547, quoted in Spiller 1992: 73)

Our poet-speaker's "friend-worship" and desire for oneness with his beloved seems far less "flamboyantly blasphemous" (Duncan-Jones, in Shakespeare 1997: 49) in this hermetic context.

The complex numerology that various scholars have located in Shakespeare's sonnet sequence certainly supports a spiritual, hermetic reading; indeed, the poet's "divine mathematics," which he advertises in sonnet 38 ("he that calls on thee, let him bring forth / Eternal numbers to outlive long date") makes no sense without it. Equally, as the physician-alchemist Robert Fludd describes, there can be no inner alchemy in the absence of the Pythagorean study and application of harmonic ratios: "the true and profound music of the wise" (Debus 1979: 6). As Fludd's *Tractus apologeticus* (1617) explains, without a knowledge of the "mysteries of occult music" it is "impossible for anyone to know himself. And without this he will be unable to reach a perfect knowledge of God, for he who understands himself truly and intrinsically perceives in himself the idea of the divine Trinity" (Debus 1979: 9).

That Shakespeare was aware of this hermetic wisdom is evident from an outstandingly beautiful passage in *The Merchant of Venice*:

> There's not the smallest orb which thou behold'st
> But in his motion like an angel sings,
> Still quiring to the young ey'd cherubins;
> Such harmonie is in immortall soules,
> But whilst this muddy vesture of decay
> Doth grossly close it in, we cannot heare it:
>
> (V. i. 60–5)

and

> The man that has no music in himself,
> Nor is not mov'd with concord of sweet sounds,
> Is fit for treasons, stratagems, and spoiles;
> The motions of his spirit are dull as night.
>
> (ll. 83–6)

"Mark the music," this lyrical passage concludes: the man with no music simply cannot be trusted. In this context it is deeply significant that, as Fred Blick has demonstrated, all Shakespeare's sonnets except 126 "exhibit the rhyming concord of unison" in their rhyme scheme and sonnet 8 "exploits to an extraordinary degree, rhyming concord of unison" (1999: 152–3). This is appropriate because the number 8 denotes the octave or diapason in music, described by Francis Bacon as "the sweetest Concord: in so much as it is in effect an Unison" (*Sylva*, 1626; Blick 1999: 154). Blick has admirably shown how, through doubled use of words and chiasmus, word chimes, flurries of puns, as well as visual and musical rhymes, sonnet 8 achieves this effect (1999: 153); but his analysis falters when he attempts to marry the poem's substantive concerns to the intricacies of its formal patterning. This is how the poem "sweetly chides" the young, tune-deaf beauty to marry:

> If the true concord of well-tuned sounds
> By unions married, do offend thine ear,
> They do but sweetly chide thee, who confounds
> In singleness the parts that thou shouldst bear:
> Mark how one string, sweet husband to another,
> Strikes each in each by mutual ordering,

> Resembling sire, and child, and happy mother,
> Who all in one, one pleasing note do sing:
>> Whose speechless song being many, seeming one,
>> Sings this to thee: "Thou single wilt prove none."

Read literally, this simply does not make musical sense. As Blick points out, such a family, "due to age and sex," is unlikely to "sing on one note at one pitch in unison" (1999: 157). Read alchemically, however, the riddle is solved: the union of two would result not in three separate bodies, but in one hermaphrodite ("all in one" "seeming one") and thus "one pleasing note."

There is now a general consensus among editors that the sonnets were most likely prepared and sequentially ordered by the poet prior to publication, a hypothesis underpinned by the "numerological finesses" of the collection, indicating "sophisticated principles of organisation at work" (Shakespeare 1997: 100–1). Duncan-Jones's edition foregrounds many instances of deliberate counterpointing between subject and numbering, like sonnet 66, for example, which rants against worldly corruption in many guises ("Tired with all these"), its number simultaneously invoking the biblical beast of Revelation. While repeatedly affirming the "insistently secular" nature of the Bard's sonnets, Duncan-Jones nevertheless highlights the "pioneering analysis" (p. 97) of their pyramidal structure by Alistair Fowler – an analysis that has profound religious implications. In his groundbreaking book *Triumphal Forms* (1970), Fowler demonstrated the almost unprecedented numerological complexities of Shakespeare's sequence, pointing out that the substance of several of the sonnets resonates with that of the Penitential Psalms bearing the same numbers in the Book of Common Prayer (1970: 190; see also Roche 1989: 420). His erudite study locates a range of further mathematical-substantive intricacies, but it is his finding of a significant pyramidal structure within the sequence that most excites me; for the triangle or pyramid is an essential form in the alchemical opus.

Commencing with the axiom that any self-referring sonnets should be taken seriously as commenting on their own form, and that structural analysis must examine the pattern created by any irregular sonnets (in this case 99, 126, and 145), Fowler proceeds to unravel an elaborate structural symmetry. If the self-referring sonnet 136 ("Then in the number let me pass untold") is counted out, a total of 153 sonnets emerges – "one of the best known of all symbolic numbers" (Fowler 1970: 184). The religious significance of 153 resided in this being the total catch of fish in John 21: 11, fulfilling prophecies in Ezekiel and Matthew 13: 47, 48, 49 : "the kingdome of heaven is like unto a draw net cast into the sea, that gathereth of all kinds of things. Which, when it is full, men draw to land, and fit and gather the good into vessels, and cast the bad away. So shall it be at the end of the world." In fact 153 had kept the Church Fathers especially busy, attracting many interpretations, but the dominant recurring theme was that of the elect – of "believers risen in Christ and endowed with the spirit" (Fowler 1970: 185, 189). Furthermore, among Shakespeare's contemporaries, Fowler suggests, the especial importance of 153 resided in its triangularity. Set out in Pythagorean manner, 153 forms an equilateral triangle with a base of 17; and when the irregular stanzas, 99, 126, and 145, are located in the sequence pattern "each is denoted by a triangular number within the greater triangle 153" (p. 186). Sonnet 145 thus commences a culminating ten-sonnet triangle and 126 begins a twenty-eight-sonnet triangle – and both these numbers were profoundly significant: ten was the principle of divine creativity, and twenty-eight that of moral perfection, eternity, and "the perfect bliss in heaven towards which saints yearn" (pp. 186, 187). Additionally, a Trinitarian interpretation of 153 took the triangular faces to represent the threefold creative principle: we might recall here the speaker's repetitive insistence on "Fair, kind and true" being all his "argument" (105). Symbolic pyramids abound in Shakespeare's sequence; no wonder sonnet 123 declares, addressing Time, "Thy pyramids, built up with newer might, / To me are nothing novel, nothing strange."

It would seem that 126 might form the "great base" of a pyramid leading to "eternity" (alluded to in sonnet 125); if this is so, then the triangle demanded by the adept in *Atalanta fugiens* has been inscribed in the sequence through divine mathematics. In fact, pyramids with Trinitarian, eternalizing significances abound in alchemical texts. Fludd described how light "streaminge from the presence of God shining out of darkenes may be reduced into a formall pyramis" linking the spiritual with the material world and vice versa (Debus 1979: 152). Significantly, too, Puttenham's *Arte of English Poesie*, commenting on the form of "the Spire or Taper called Pyramis," likens it to a flame which is always pointed "and naturally by his forme covets to clymbe" (Puttenham 1904: 99). "A flame . . . coveting to climb": sonnet 126 would appear to warrant our closer scrutiny from the fiery, alchemical perspective. The following lines surely register the poet-alchemist's pleasure and success; he is almost crooning over his creation:

> O thou my lovely Boy, who in thy power
> Dost hold time's fickle glass, his sickle hour,
> Who hast by waning grown, and therin sho'st
> Thy lovers withering, as thy sweet self grow'st.[1]

Through repeated operations of the opus – incorporating union, death of the lovers, and regeneration – "my" (signifying proud ownership) "sweet" distillation has "grown." The power to stay the destructive effects of time is now within the "lovely Boy's" "power." However, a warning comes next; "fear" Nature:

> If nature, sovereign mistress over wrack,
> As thou goest onwards still will pluck thee back,
> She keeps thee to this purpose: that her skill
> May time disgrace, and wretched minute kill.
> Yet fear her, O thou minion of her pleasure:
> She may detain, but not still keep her treasure.

This "sovereign mistress" might "pluck thee back" as a "minion of her pleasure" (to "kill" minutes), but she can't keep you – you must eventually be "rendered" – fired, melted down again. The second line here captures the ebb and flow of the alchemical opus – the "still" *will* hold him back. It would seem that Mistress Nature's purposeful "skill" is necessary at this stage in the opus in order to "disgrace" time (to achieve eternity?). The sonnet is abruptly terminated, two coffin-like parentheses mark the spot, and "black beauty" makes her dramatic debut.

Who or what is "black beauty"? Mysterious mutability is the hallmark of alchemical writing, and just as the speaker's "friend" dissolves in and out of material existence, sometimes seeming a "he," sometimes a "he–she," sometimes an aspect of the poet's psyche, and occasionally even a "she," so the dark lady defies our inevitable attempts to stabilize her. Indeed, the troubled *ménage à trois* we witness from time to time throughout the sequence could well be a dramatized projection of the speaker's inner conflict ("Two loves I have, of comfort and despair": 144. 1). Suggestively, in sonnet 127 the dark lady is even "beauty's successive heir" – the "lovely boy's "bastard" offspring, his "successor" in the opus. A "cunning," whimsical tyrant in love, sometimes entirely Circean and sometimes incorporating maternal qualities (as when she is called upon to comfort blubbering Will in sonnet 148), she is certainly a complex and ambivalent literary creation. In fact, one of her most dominant guises is that of Mistress or Dame Nature herself. In the alchemical context this is entirely appropriate, for her "skill" as "Kind" [Nature] is necessary to engender "kindness" (the third aspect of the triangle or trinity – "Fair, kind and true") and to complete "Will's" – the artist's – spiritual transformation. Adepts frequently asserted that "covetousness" ("attachment to one's limited ego in thrall to passion": Burckhardt 1967: 32) was the obstacle to the soul's transcendence. This is what Will is striving to overcome in the last sonnets: exercising reason he must eradicate "Will in overplus," tame his sensual self, and lighten his darkened spiritual nature and vision. He must in fact negate himself – "Myself I'll forfeit" (134), "for nothing hold me" (136). Alchemists insisted that a too dominant "I" could be overcome only by kindness – "compassion alone delivers us from the artfulness of the ego" and Nature's "skill" in engendering this was crucial (Burckhardt 1967: 32).

As Titus Burckhardt describes, this final stage of the alchemical opus, which culminates in the liberation of the spirit, can only be achieved, "by means of a natural vibration of the soul," when Nature comes to the aid of the art, according to the alchemical adage: "The progress of the art pleases nature greatly" (1967: 123). Always female, Nature is both the "power of desire and longing in man" and a potent force that "develops all the capacities hidden in the soul, against or in keeping with the desires of the ego, depending on whether the latter assimilates the power of nature, or becomes its victim." As Sophia or "wisdom" she is a positive, nurturing power, but as blind passion or Circe she binds the soul and blocks spiritual progression (p. 118). Her ambivalent, shifting nature – actually a reflection of her lover's conflicting desires – and her taming, spiritually improving potential help us to understand seemingly ironic Shakespearean lines such as the opening to sonnet 142 and the close of 141: "Love is my sin, and thy dear virtue hate, / Hate of my sin, grounded on sinful loving"; "Only my plague thus far I count my gain, / That she that makes me sin, awards me pain."

Both the Bible and classical legend contain many "types" of dark Nature: notably, Cleopatra, Medea, Sheba, and Solomon's Bride ("I am blacke . . . but comely," *Salomons Song*, 1: 4, Geneva Bible, 1599 edn.). Like Solomon's Bride, Shakespeare's enigmatic lady is dark or fair only according to her lover's perception; hence "Thy black is fairest in my judgment's place," and others may view her differently: " 'tis my heart that loves what they despise" (sonnets 131, 141). His quest to see correctly seems fraught and urgent – he is undergoing a spiritual struggle with grave implications. The analogy with the *Song of Solomon* is important, because this was read in the early modern period as an alchemical text which, according to the Geneva Bible gloss (1599), "by most sweete and comfortable allegories . . . describeth the perfite love of Jesus Christ . . . and the faithfull soule or his Church." Duncan-Jones finds a perplexing echo of the *Song of Solomon* in the final line of sonnet 154, "water cools not love" ("for love is strong as death . . . the coales therof are fiery coales, and a vehement flame. Much water cannot quench love" [8: 6, 7]). Significantly, the Geneva Bible gloss decodes this as, "The spouse desireth Christ to be joined in perpetuall love with him" – undoubtedly an allusion to "oneing" with Christ.

Shakespeare was by no means the first writer to allude to the *Song* in his sonnets. The Italian hermeticist Giordano Bruno modeled his *Deggli eroici furori* (dedicated to Sir Philip Sidney) on it and, deploying many motifs that are also found in Shakespeare's last twenty-nine sonnets (the eye–heart debate, for example), he makes it clear in his second dialogue that women are not the cause of man's enslavement to their beauty, but a Circe whom men seek out and who blinds them (Roche 1989: 152). Such blinded men can be restored only by a nymph of Diana (Roche 1979: 152). It is, of course, just such a nymph who disarms "the general of hot desire" in Shakespeare's concluding sonnet. In alchemy Diana was the symbol of the pure white stone cleansed of its impurities on the completion of the "opus circulatorium" (Abraham 1998: 54) – the circular work.

The artist would appear to have "made the quadrangle round," but – rather frustratingly – whether or not he has found "all the secrett" promised by the adepts' adage ("When thou hast made the quadrangle round, then is all the secrett found") remains a mystery at the close of the sequence. If, however, *A Lover's Complaint* is read as a companion poem or coda to the sonnets, as editors from John Kerrigan (1986) onwards have argued it should, some surprising revelations emerge – not least, the extreme degree to which alchemical poetry could engage in the humanistic rhetorical strategy, "serio ludere" or playing seriously. Unaware of the alchemical symbolism in the sonnets or its coda, Colin Burrow is a representative commentator when he declares, "its [the *Complaint's*] language is so full of innovation that it is difficult even to penetrate its literal sense, let alone to grasp what the objects . . . mean" (Shakespeare 2002: 141), and laments the lack of a closing frame and the return of the "I" voice at the end. Ironically, these observations foreground two key features of thinking and writing that serve to amplify the marked difference of the past and its subjectivities from the present and ours: from the point of view of the alchemical artist *c.*1600, the literal meaning did not even have to make sense because it was not the true meaning (merely one designed to lead "covetous" fools astray, and with which you could have a great deal of fun in the process); and, furthermore, the "real" spiritual goal of alchemy involved divesting oneself of the artful ego – the "I" voice so prized by our own culture. Indeed, if our poet-alchemist has succeeded at all in his quest for spiritual refinement we might expect him to be listening instead of declaiming for a change.

This is precisely, of course, how we do find him: in *A Lover's Complaint*, we encounter the speaker's liberated "spirits" eavesdropping and being granted a strange vision of a

Figure 24.4 "Rosea Rubea," last emblem, *Praetiosum Donum Dei*, sixteenth century, University of Glasgow Library, Ferguson MS 148, illus. 34, "the red elixir, red rose and red king." Reprinted with permission of Glasgow University Library, Department of Special Collections.

rather comic, ingenious kind, though not without deeply serious implications. The *Complaint*'s plot is uncanny in the extreme. The "concave," echoing "womb" setting is surely the alchemist's circular vessel in which the Stone is conceived and generated (figure 24.4). As the poem unfolds, it becomes increasingly clear that there are pervasive and insistent shadowy connections between the sonnets and the *Complaint*, which serve to increase the mysterious prismatic complexity of both. The tearful maid – "The carcass of a beauty spent and done" (l. 11) (spent "materia" left in the bottom of the alembic) – who has been subjected to Time's scythe (l. 12) and is, notably, "seared," having undergone "many a blasting hour" (l. 72), is one of the beautiful youth's "trophies of affections hot" (l. 218), and that youth seems to correspond to the sonnets' "lovely Boy." What we hear next is an account of the heated drama in the alembic – as portrayed by the sonnets – but from the maid's perspective as one of the lovely boy's / the youth's "withered" lovers (sonnet 126). She is, in fact, the last maiden he copulated with in the artist's "head" or alembic in order to "grow." That he *has* grown through his former liaisons is attested by his "plants" sprouting in "orchards" – alchemical symbols of philosophical enrichment. Since the youth (like the lovely boy) is the "combined sum" (l. 231) of former "marriages" (chemical weddings) – "the broken bosoms that to me belong" (l. 254) – whose "burning lungs" have raised "Hallowed . . . sighs" (l. 228), "all these hearts" eventually depend on his final "conjunctio" with his "origin and ender" – the mercurial female "materia" (the virgin maid of the *Complaint*) that will give birth to "ultima materia," the pure original stuff of creation receptive to all forms (Abraham 1998: 35, 153). This is the mysterious Stone, philosophical Mercury, or the fifth essence that can cure all diseases (even Will's venereal malady) and guarantee eternity – Christ the Redeemer.

However, as our alchemist-poet has hinted several times along the way, a divine conclusion to his intrepid art is by no means guaranteed ("And whether that my angel be turned fiend / Suspect I may, yet not directly tell": sonnet 144) – occult practices have black as well as white outcomes and, as this age was only too aware, fiends can masquerade as angels. That his labors have produced a mercurial "type" is clear, and the *Complaint* provides us with a brilliantly witty description of the lovely boy's growth and progress from the "trophy" maid's perspective. A beautiful youth with conjoined male and female attributes, his visage "termless" with "phoenix down," and a microcosm of "paradise," such that "maidens' eyes stuck over all his face" ("the eyes of all that were in the Synagogue were fastened on him": Luke 4: 20), Love, the maid confides, made him her "dwelling." This Christ-like figure, "Accomplished in himself, not in his case" (l. 116), the embodiment of "grace," "reigns" in "the general bosom" (cf. sonnet 20) commanding "duty" from all. On the consummation of his relationship with the virgin maid, a brinish mercurial current streams from his face and gives rise to symbolism of the final "rubedo" stage of an alchemical opus: "Who glazed with crystal gate the glowing roses / That flame through water which their hue encloses!" (ll. 286–7). According to the alchemical textbooks, the tincture of red (recalling the Passion) blushing through crystal heralds the birth of philosophical Mercurius (Abraham 1998: 125) – the Stone. Significantly, the maid's words resonate with those of Revelation 15: 2:

"And I saw as it were a glassie sea, mingled with fire, and them that had gotten victorie of the beast . . . stand at the glassie sea."

Paradoxically, however, this type of Christ is also, in the maid's estimation, a poisoner given to "foul beguiling" (l. 170). What are we to make of this "cherubin"-like "tempter" whom the "fickle" maid yet so desires? Is this a vision of "saint" or "devil," of "comfort" or "despair"? Actually, it is neither: rather, Shakespeare has given us a wonderfully vivid, dramatic evocation of the alchemical hermaphrodite or dual-natured Mercurius: "a protean, elusive, duplicitous, inconstant, teasing spirit." He is "the water which killeth and reviveth," both destructive and creative (Abraham 1998: 126). As Abraham's alchemical dictionary describes, the fact that Mercurius can freely participate in both light and dark worlds without taint makes him "the perfect mediating bridge, able to unite the division which was thought to have occurred at man's fall from the garden of Eden" (1998: 126). By the end of the successful opus, however, the alchemist should have tamed "inconstant" Mercurius into a helpful ally. The maid's final description of her seducer as a "fiend" whose "grace" is a mere "garment" could lead us to suspect that our alchemist has not succeeded, but things are rather more complex. The disheveled maid is not only the unclean matter left at the bottom of the vessel after a firing but, as female "materia," she also has a mercurial, inconstant nature, which makes her a very "fickle," unreliable story-teller indeed. Whether or not our alchemist's "spirits" are granted a culminating vision of "the perfect bliss in heaven towards which saints yearn" (see above, p. 16) or of a reprobate's hell, eludes us. Brilliantly and wittily capturing the bewilderingly paradoxical, mysterious, yet seductive character of the alchemical quest, the poem ends with the maid's repeated equivocal exclamations of ecstatic wonder and/or Complaint – significantly a sequence of "O"s, or circles upon the page.

I conclude with the illuminating reflections of Martin Luther:

> The science of alchemy I like very well . . . I like it not only for the profits it brings in melting metals . . . I like it also for the sake of the allegory and secret signification, which is exceedingly fine, touching the resurrection of the dead at the last day. For, as in a furnace the fire extracts and separates . . . and carries upward the spirit, the life, the sap . . . while the unclean matter, the dregs, remain at the bottom, like a dead and worthless carcass; even so God, at the day of judgment, will separate all things through fire . . . The Christians and righteous shall ascend upwards into heaven, and there live everlastingly, but the wicked and the ungodly, as the dross and filth, shall remain in hell, and there be damned. (Luther 1992: DCCCV)

NOTE

1 Duncan-Jones's edition inserts an apostrophe, altering the meaning to signify one lover: "lover's." I follow Colin Burrow's edition here: "lovers" is far more appropriate in this overtly alchemical context.

References and Further Reading

Abraham, Lyndy (1990). *Marvell and Alchemy*. Aldershot: Scolar.

Abraham, Lyndy (1998). *A Dictionary of Alchemical Imagery*. Cambridge, UK: Cambridge University Press.

Blick, Fred (1999). "Shakespeare's Musical Sonnets: Numbers 8, 128, and Pythagoras." *Upstart Crow* 19, 152–68.

Burckhardt, Titus (1967). *Alchemy*. Dorset: Element.

Daniel, Samuel (1904). *A Defence of Ryme*. In Gregory Smith (ed.), *Elizabethan Critical Essays*, vol. 2, 365–84. Oxford: Oxford University Press. (First publ. 1603.)

Debus, Allen G. (1979). *Robert Fludd and His Philosophicall Key*. New York: Science History Publications.

de Rola, Stanislas Klossowski (1988). *The Golden Game*. London: Thames & Hudson.

Donne, John (1912). *Poetical Works*, vol. 1, ed. H. J. C. Grierson. Oxford: Oxford University Press.

Donne, John (1953–62). *The Sermons of John Donne*, 10 vols., ed. George R. Potter and Evelyn M. Simpson. Berkeley and Los Angeles: University of California Press.

Fowler, Alastair (1970). *Triumphal Forms: Structural Patterns in Elizabethan Poetry*. Cambridge, UK: Cambridge University Press.

Geneva Bible (1990). Facsimile of the 1599 edition. Ozark, Mo.: L. L. Brown Publishing.

Gilbert, Ruth (2002). *Early Modern Hermaphrodites: Sex and other Stories*. Basingstoke: Palgrave.

Hall, Kim (1995) *Things of Darkness*. Ithaca, NY: Cornell University Press.

Jones, Thomas O. (1995). *Renaissance Magic and Hermeticism in the Shakespeare Sonnets*. Lewiston: Edwin Mellen.

Linden, Stanton J. (1996). *Dark Hieroglyphicks: Alchemy in English Literature from Chaucer to the Restoration*. Lexington: University Press of Kentucky.

Linden, Stanton J. (2003). *The Alchemy Reader: From Hermes Trismegistus to Isaac Newton*. Cambridge, UK: Cambridge University Press.

Luther, Martin (1992). *The Table Talk of Martin Luther*, trans. William Hazlitt. London: Bell.

Puttenham, George (1904). *The arte of English Poesie*. In Gregory Smith (ed.), *Elizabethan Critical Essays*, vol. 2, 1–193. Oxford: Oxford University Press. (First publ. 1589.)

Roche, Thomas P., Jr. (1989). *Petrarch and the English Sonnet Sequences*. New York: AMS Press.

Ruland, Martin (1612). *A Lexicon of Alchemy*. London: British Library C54 C11.

Shakespeare, William (1997). *Shakespeare's Sonnets*, ed. Katherine Duncan-Jones. London: Thomas Nelson. (The Arden Shakespeare.)

Shakespeare, William (2002). *The Complete Sonnets and Poems*, ed. Colin Burrow. Oxford: Oxford University Press. (Oxford World's Classics.)

Sidney, Sir Philip (1904). *The arte of English Poesie*. In Gregory Smith (ed.), *Elizabethan Critical Essays*, vol. 1, 148–207. Oxford: Oxford University Press. (First publ. 1595.)

Simonds, Peggy Munoz (1999). "Sex in a Bottle: The Alchemical Distillation of Shakespeare's Hermaphrodite in Sonnet 20." *Renaissance Papers* 97–105.

Spiller, Michael R. G. (1992). *The Development of the Sonnet: An Introduction*. London: Routledge.

Vaughan, Thomas (1984). *The Works of Thomas Vaughan*, ed. Alan Rudrum. Oxford: Clarendon.

Wittkower, Rudolf (1977). *Architectural Principles in the Age of Humanism*. London: Academy Editions. (First publ. 1949.)

25

The Enigma of
A Lover's Complaint

Catherine Bates

A Lover's Complaint – the poem published as an end-piece to the 1609 quarto of the sonnets – has to be the most abjected part of the Shakespeare canon: slighted, sidelined, passed over, ignored, and not only by a tradition that, rightly or wrongly, has bestowed a higher critical value on the plays than on the poems, but even by an earlier readership that, if the popularity of *Venus and Adonis* and *The Rape of Lucrece* are anything to go by, prized Shakespeare as a poet more highly than anything else. In marked contrast to the narrative poems (which went through numerous editions throughout Shakespeare's lifetime and the seventeenth century, inspired hosts of enthusiastic imitations, and, in the case of *Venus and Adonis* at least, received more allusions than anything else that Shakespeare wrote), *A Lover's Complaint* left not a ripple and sank without trace. And, if current popular and scholarly interest in the sonnets might be thought to make up for the relative neglect of the lyrics in the seventeenth century (there were fewer allusions to the sonnets than to any other of Shakespeare's works, the only exception being *A Lover's Complaint*), then such compensation, if that is what it is, has not extended as far as the latter, publications on the sonnets currently outnumbering those on the *Complaint* by a ratio of hundreds to one. When the poem *is* addressed, furthermore, it leaves its readers exercised, chary, and somewhat bemused: put on the spot by a poem that challenges norms and fails to conform to expectations of either Shakespeare or the genre.

What causes dismay is not only the poem's syntax and diction – which strike everyone as difficult and strange ("perplexing," "complex," "contorted," "obscure," "dense," "compressed," "unfamiliar," "curious," and "odd" being just a few of the words used to describe them) – but also its imagery, its presentation of character, its narrative structure, and its tone. There is a general charge of obscurity: this "abstruse and virtually unexplicated" poem that is "hard to understand and difficult to love" (Bell 1999: 455), that "does not read easily" (Roe, in Shakespeare 1992: 73), that even "verges on impenetrability" (Craik 2002: 437), is said to have "abandoned the forceful clarity of" the other narrative poems (Muir 1973: 218). One critic alone describes the poem and various aspects of it as "most peculiar" (Roche 1989: 440, 456), "extraordinary" (p. 441), "mysterious" (p. 441), "astonishing" (p. 442), "complicated" (p. 444), "bewildering" (p. 445), "perplexing" (p. 457), and "strange" (pp. 441, 444, 448, 454, 458). Indeed, the one word that is used to describe the poem more than any other is "enigmatic" (Roche 1989: 444, 446, 447, 453; Rees 1991: 167; Burrow, in Shakespeare 2002: 141, 142).

This sense of the poem as maverick and strange, moreover, periodically breaks out into doubt over whether Shakespeare wrote it at all: debate over the authorship of *A Lover's Complaint* has a long history. Although the poem was championed by Edmond Malone, its Shakespearean credentials were disputed by Hazlitt, doubted from the middle of the nineteenth century, and vigorously rejected early in the twentieth, when the poem was attributed to the rival poet of the sonnets (Mackail 1912). Although energetic efforts were made from the 1960s to restore the poem to the canon (Jackson 1965; Muir 1973), the question has recently been thrown open again, stylometric tests developed in part to gauge the authenticity of "A Funeral Elegy by W. S." having cast renewed doubt on that of *A Lover's Complaint* (Elliott and Valenza 1997). The most recent candidate to be proposed as its author is John Davies of Hereford (Vickers 2003).

For my purposes, however, the question of who wrote *A Lover's Complaint* seems less important, or less interesting at any rate, than the fact that the question should get asked at all (let alone so often). In what follows, therefore, I am not so concerned with the claims of this or that candidate or with the merits of any particular case as with what this strained and sometimes dismissive reaction has to say about *A Lover's Complaint* itself. For there is clearly something about this poem that nags, troubles, and complains – that piques and irritates but that clearly refuses to go away, for every time the authorship question is decided in favor of Shakespeare uncertainty breaks out again, drawing readers back to reconsider the old problem and to worry at it obsessively like an unhealed scar. For although on the face of it there are no external reasons for doubting that "*A Lovers Complaint BY WILLIAM SHAKE-SPEARE*" – as the drop-title announces the poem in the quarto – is indeed his (Duncan-Jones 1983), the internal properties of the poem that register as quirky and odd nevertheless urge with particular insistence that this question of authorship and authenticity be addressed. And, for some readers, these properties are anomalous enough for what is unusual or untypical to shade into what is "unShakespearean" (Mackail 1912: 63; Vickers 2003: 13), as if, while the "problem" – whatever that is – cannot be solved or made to go away, it can at least be firmly separated from Shakespeare's name.

A notional benchmark of propriety is being brought into play here: some norm or expectation against which what is experienced as different or excessive is implicitly being measured. And with this comes a sense of something endangered, of a need to protect and preserve, as if the imperiled object were the iconic image of the writing subject as Master Poet, and as if notions of authorial self-consistency and orthodoxy (in which the critic may have a certain investment) were somehow at stake. From this perspective, the poem's long relegation to the margins begins to look a little more motivated than accidental, more defensive than benign – not so much a polite indifference

as an embarrassed aversion of the gaze, as if critics have turned away from this trouble-
some piece, either excising it from the canon or (which amounts to much the same
thing) ignoring its existence altogether. There is no doubt that the general air of dubi-
ousness that hangs over the poem has contributed in good measure to its long-term
neglect. Judged difficult, doubted, or denied: in none of these scenarios, it seems to me,
does the poem meet with an entirely neutral response. At best a source of unease, at
worst something to be cut away or effectively disavowed, in all events *A Lover's Complaint* has been treated as a problem, as something that draws quantities of cathexis to
it like a hystericized limb, a chronic complaint of the Shakespeare corpus that, whatever
action is taken, it seems, remains stubbornly resistant to cure.

In this respect, the reception history of *A Lover's Complaint* has much in common
with that of the sonnets: for the compulsive reordering, re-presenting, and "straighten-
ing" of those poems has recently been read as a "hysterical symptom" (Stallybrass 1999:
77, 86) – a complex response to their culturally disturbing representation of love
between men and a felt need to deny, apologize for, or one way and another accommo-
date it. Except that, if the editorial history of the sonnets can be seen to symptomize
the "moral panic" (p. 77) induced in earlier generations of readers by the prospect of
the heterosexual, "manly" Shakespeare under threat, then whatever it is in *A Lover's
Complaint* that unsettles and perturbs evidently possesses a still greater power to alarm
– the reception it has met with being more akin, perhaps, to the "similar panic when
the cry goes up that Throne and Altar are in danger" identified by Freud in his essay
on fetishism (Freud 1927: vol. 21, 153) – since Shakespeare's involvement in this poem
is perennially thrown into doubt (no matter how elusive the proof) while, however
energetically imputations of homosexuality to Shakespeare may have been rejected in
some quarters and at certain times, it was never seriously suggested that the sonnets
were not his.

This disturbing effect that *A Lover's Complaint* has on its readers may have something
to do with the way in which the poem deviates from the tradition of female complaint
to which it otherwise belongs, and a clue for the way this happens is to be found within
the poem itself. The opening lines – which announce a "plaintful story" (l. 2) and a
"sad-tuned tale" (l. 4) – clearly identify the poem's allegiance to the complaint tradition
and invite us to assume that the letters and other objects which the weeping girl is
casting into the stream on whose banks she sits are, as would be entirely conventional,
those of the faithless lover who has deserted her. This assumption, moreover, is personified in the figure of the old man (himself the classic figure of the *senex* who has withdrawn from the court to a life of contemplation and retreat) who soon enters the scene
and, like the reader or critic, "desires to know" (l. 62) and "desires" to hear (l. 66) the
cause of her grief. Given his former experience "Of court, of city" (l. 59), it is quite
logical that he should be presented as assuming that the scenario before him conforms
to the generic expectations of courtly complaint. Yet, however acutely this old philosopher may have "observèd" (l. 60) the ins and outs of courtly life and love, he turns out
– if that is his assumption – to be wrong. And it is a sign, perhaps, of his being out
of place – of his not being in the poem or tradition he thought he was in – that he

does not reappear again, and that the ending that he (and we) might well, following the complaint tradition, have expected (in which the girl dies of a broken heart, say, and the old man, having prepared for her a modest grave, weeps "wise tears in a passage of concluding pathos" (as one editor speculates: Shakespeare 1992: 72) is, in the event, shown up as being trite and banal by comparison with the strange and unsettling ending that we actually get. That *A Lover's Complaint* is departing from convention here and overturning all expectation is suggested by something that, along with John Kerrigan, although for different reasons, I think is "of the greatest significance" (Shakespeare 1986: 17): namely, the fact that the girl is not, as it happens, discarding the favors of her former lover but, rather, those of other *women*. How this (which neither the old man nor the reader expected) came to be is the burden of the story that, by way of explanation, she proceeds to tell in the long speech that follows.

This unusual scenario demands inspection, and, on looking more closely at the objects that the girl is weeping over, what is immediately striking is (even allowing for hyperbole) their quantity – "A thousand favours" (l. 36), "many" (ll. 43, 45), "yet more" (l. 47) – and their diversity: "papers" and "rings" (l. 6), a "napkin" (l. 15), favours of "amber crystal and of beaded jet" (l. 37), "folded schedules" (l. 43), rings of "gold and bone" (l. 45), "letters" (l. 47) – as well as (as she proceeds with her story, further items get added to the list) "tributes" of rubies and pearls (l. 197), "talents of their hair" (l. 204), "deep-brained sonnets" (l. 209), "trophies" (l. 218), "similes" (l. 227), and a "device" (l. 232). All these, it transpires, are love tokens that were originally given to the youth by other women and then passed on by him to the girl.

The first thing to notice about this multitude of objects, apart from the fact that they originate with women, is – and it is a point on which the poem is emphatic – that they are all objects that signify: that is to say, they are all, to that extent, *texts*. The "napkin," for example, is embroidered with "conceited characters" (l. 16) and "silken figures" (l. 17) that the girl reads ("often reading what contents it bears," l. 19); the "folded schedules" are similarly "perused" (l. 44); the rings of gold and bone are "posied" (l. 45), that is, inscribed with rhymes or mottoes; and the letters "penned in blood" (l. 47) with "lines" (l. 55) and "contents" (l. 56) that she reads and tears. As for the various jewels – amber, crystal, jet (l. 37), rubies and pearls (l. 198), a diamond (l. 211), an emerald (l. 213), a sapphire and opal (l. 215), locks of hair entwined with gold (l. 205), and so forth – these belong to a long history of lapidary symbolism and are to be treated as signifiers loaded with meaning. Emeralds and opals, for example, were traditionally believed to cure weak sight, so presumably the women originally sent them to the youth meaning either that he should see them and their love more clearly and/or that their sight had been dazzled by him. The pearls and rubies, moreover, set off a chain of signification. As synecdoches of the women who sent them, they are signifiers of signifiers – the "bloodless white" (l. 201) of the pearls "figuring" (l. 199) the women's pallor which in turn signifies the "Effects of terror" (l. 202), "grief" (l. 200), "pensived and subdued desires" (l. 219), while the "encrimsoned mood" (l. 201) of the rubies stands for the women's blushes, themselves "aptly understood" (l. 200) as signs of either "dear modesty" (l. 202) or "affections hot" (l. 218). Should there be any doubt about the signification of these metaphorical objects (the youth offers all these to the girl as "similes," l. 227), they come attached (see "annexions," l. 208) with more straightforwardly literary texts: that is, with "deep-brained sonnets" that "did amplify" (l. 209) and "blazon" (l. 217) – the specifically rhetorical and literary senses being implied here – their intended meaning. In this respect, the jewels have an affinity with the "device" (l. 232) that was given to the youth by an infatuated nun and which, although not specified as such, was presumably some combination of image and text as would have been familiar from the tradition of emblem-books and courtly *imprese*.

The objects which the girl throws into the stream, then – having read and perused their contents, sighed and wept over them, and then torn, broken, cracked, or rent them – are, emphatically, all texts; and the poem suggests that in each case they derived originally from women. The question has been raised whether the youth himself might not have written directly to the girl and have authored at least some of these missives; her exclamation, "O false blood, thou register of lies!" (l. 52), for example, has been cited as evidence that the "letters sadly penned in blood" must have been composed by the seducer whose faithlessness she here laments. Yet, although we know from her own testimony that the youth is capable of seducing as much by written words as by speech – she found his "characters and words" (l. 174) equally deceiving – these apply, in the context, specifically to persuasions he had directed at others. And, even here, there remains the possibility that these "characters" with which he wooed former mistresses might, in turn, originally have been sent to him by earlier paramours still – his habit of passing on second-hand favors being, as we shall see, an unfailingly successful seductive ploy – a possibility that opens up an interesting scenario of infinite regress as the origin of those letters is pushed back ever further into the poem's murky narrative past (that this question of whether or not the youth wrote the letters rehearses the similar question of whether or not Shakespeare wrote *A Lover's Complaint* should not, in the circumstances, go unnoticed).

The poem, in fact, seems to taunt us with the undecidability of the issue, making great play of the enigmatic and indecipherable nature of these texts, the contents of which remain teasingly hidden from us and "sealed to curious secrecy" (l. 49). As far as the girl in the poem is concerned, in any case, there is no incontrovertible evidence that the youth has ever written to her directly at all; the emphasis, rather, is on the fact that the objects he gives her have all been inscribed – posied, penned, amplified, blazoned, and so forth – by women. In line with this goes the distinct impression that this windy boy prefers to speak than to write, the stress throughout being specifically on his verbal skills. He is described, for example, as "maiden-tongued" (l. 100), as the possessor of a "subduing tongue" (l. 120); as skilled in "arguments" (l. 121), in "question deep" (l. 121), in "replication [that is, repartee] prompt," in "dialect [that is, the art of dialectic or argumentation]" (l. 125), and in "passions" (ll. 126, 295), that is, passionate speeches. Those who fall for him imagine "what he would say" (l. 132), not what he would write, and it is his winning speech that the girl recites to the old man. The youth's abilities to move and persuade ("To make the weeper laugh, the laugher weep," l. 124), to captivate an audience that is dazzled by what it sees and hears, to use deception (see especially ll. 302–15) and disguise (he did "livery falseness," l. 105, and wear the "garment of a grace," l. 316), all add up to the impression that he is above all else a consummate actor (he even knows, where necessary, how to act as a convincing audience, "to weep at woes, / Or to turn white and sound [i.e. swoon] at tragic shows," ll. 307–8).

What we have here, then, is a situation in which, contrary to expectation, a female complainant responds to texts most if not all of which are by women; a scene in which women write and women read, where these texts ("many" and "deep") both derive from and end up in women's hands; a scenario in which, to be specific, these texts that are being written, sent, passed on, and read are ones that address and importune, blazon, and praise a beautiful man. Put this way, the poem rather strikingly reverses the far more familiar scheme of things in which male poets write elaborately conceited Petrarchan poems to and about beautiful women and circulate them among themselves. What gradually unfolds in *A Lover's Complaint*, that is to say, is a scene of female "homosociality" in which the structure that clearly manifests itself in the practices of male côterie writing (where poems about or addressed to women are designed to establish a relation – even if mainly a competitive one – with other men) is reproduced (Sedgwick 1985) – only here, of course, the other way round.

The two situations are not, it is true, exactly parallel, since here the exchange of texts is mediated by the youth: it is he who passes them on to the girl (as proof of his desirability) and not the women themselves (as proof of their ability), they being presented – albeit through the distorting lenses of the youth's words which are, in turn, reported by the girl – as expressing their desire for him in "good faith" rather than as aiming directly at showing off or dazzling a fellow rival. But the basic model remains the same. Although it is the youth who markets himself – he who raises his own price by passing on the accumulated capital of others' love as "tender" (l. 219) and "combinèd sums" (l. 231), he who circulates himself – he nevertheless remains a commodity, an item of value that is exchanged, as the poems about him are, between women. The poem thus reproduces the structure basic to homosocial relations: that is, a triangle in which an ostensibly heterosexual relation, however ardently expressed, is accompanied by if not subordinated to a homosocial one. And it is that homosocial relation between women on which *A Lover's Complaint* rather unexpectedly insists.

The girl's primary relation, then, is one of identification: before she desires the youth she *identifies* with those who desire him, and any relation she comes to have with him is mediated from the outset by the fact that he is already in relation with others. She desires him not for himself but because he is desired of others – it is their desire and nothing else that motivates her own – and this, indeed, is the point of the long speech she makes by way of explanation to the old man who seeks to know the "grounds and motives" (l. 63) of her woe: the content of most of lines 71–147 – the first part of her speech – is an account of how she came to fall for the youth in the first place. For what she details – in describing the reactions of a besotted community, "the general bosom" (l. 127), that is "enchanted" (l. 128) and "bewitched" (l. 131), driven to an erotic frenzy, prompted to speculation and debate, moved to laughter and tears by this male equivalent of

Zuleika Dobson – is not so much the youth himself, his particular attractions and charms, as the devastating effect these have on others. If her description is anything to go by, then this is ultimately of greater concern to her than the youth himself – who always remains a somewhat distanced figure, pedestalized and seen from afar – the important thing, it seems, being not so much the boy as the vantage point from which he is seen: that is, her identification with those others who are so enthralled. Her descriptions of the youth thus periodically slide over to descriptions of those who are looking at him: "Each eye that saw him did enchant the mind" (l. 89), "Many there were that did his picture get / To serve their eyes" (ll. 134–5). Right from the start, then, the girl sees the youth through others' eyes, viewing him from the position of the admiring audience with which she has already identified, relating herself not to him, in the first instance, but to those in fascinated thrall. And although these include men as well as women – since this youth (like that of the sonnets – a connection that has not gone unnoticed) appeals to "sexes both" (l. 128) – the group with whom she identifies most particularly are his female fans, those who "Sweetly supposed them mistress of his heart" (l. 142). That she has already identified with this group before he even approaches her or begins to woo her is suggested by an image that has struck several editors and commentators as in need of explanation: the youth's beauty was such, she says, that he had "maidens' eyes stuck over all his face" (l. 81). If in looking at him what she is primarily doing is looking at others looking, then it makes sense that what she sees there is not so much his good looks as the looks of the other women gazing thereon. Her relation with him, that is, comes to be overshadowed by what prompts and structures it: namely, her relation (conscious or otherwise) with the other maidens.

This, moreover, explains the point and content of the next part of the girl's story (ll. 148–77) in which she describes how, *unlike* those others, "some my equals" (l. 148) with whom she otherwise identifies, she did not yield straight away but held out for a while and defended her "honour" (l. 151) from his advances. For the purpose of this narrative delay – which creates a space within which the youth has to court her, persuade her, and win her round, the ultimate weapon in his armory being the love tokens he has received from others – is less to impress us with her virtue than to demonstrate the compelling force of her identification. Critics have struggled to explain why, right from the start, the girl is described as a "fickle maid" (l. 5), but if she has identified herself with the youth's other admirers from the beginning, then the description is wholly appropriate. Ironically, her "resistance" merely provides an opportunity for proving her complete susceptibility to his ploy. For if she identifies with the youth's other devotees then his tactic of giving her the love tokens he had previously received from them only confirms and validates that prior relation. That is why his ruse works – why, indeed, it cannot fail – for it was this identificatory relation with the other women that initially established him as an object of longing and the existence of such tokens of devotion that aroused her desire in the first place. The girl, in fact, more or less admits this when she tells the old man that she knew the youth's devious tactics all too well but went on desiring him all the same: she "knew the patterns of his foul beguiling" (l. 170), "patterns" here referring both to examples of those he had already deceived and to his particular mode of beguilement. It is as if she knew that he had persuaded others as he would persuade her, by exploiting their mutual identification, but that she was as helpless as they.

To this extent, the girl is pre-persuaded, already in love, although in a more complex way, perhaps, than Kenneth Muir suggests when he says that she had "fallen in love with him before he began to woo" (Muir 1973: 216). For she responds to the youth in the way that she does because she is already in identificatory relation with the doting women. The seducer's trick succeeds so well because, by putting the women who collectively adore him in touch with one another, he is effectively closing the loop – or, more accurately, the triangle – that structures homosocial desire. While some find it odd, therefore, that the youth should approach the girl by referring to his previous conquests, in the light of the bond that exists between the women it makes perfect sense to do so and, indeed – insofar as it taps into this powerful (if not necessarily conscious) relation – it explains why the girl should find it so irresistible. That is why she insists to the old man that she had no choice in the matter and that her fall was inevitable ("whoever shunned by precedent / The destined ill she must herself assay?," ll. 155–6); why she argues that anyone like her, or like the others, would have been so persuaded ("who, young and simple, would not be so lovered?," l. 320); and why (in a move that is, in the circumstances, entirely logical, even if some have taken exception to it on moral grounds) she says that she would do it all again: "Ay me, I fell; and yet do question make / What I should do again for such a sake" (ll. 321–2). For one critic, that anyone "with even a modicum of logic and a minimal knowledge of human behaviour" should succumb to the youth's persuasions – let alone go into the situation with their eyes open and knowingly be prepared to repeat the whole experience – seems "unbelievable" (Roche 1989: 452). But to the extent that it demonstrates the identificatory relation between the women and the homosocial bond that subtends their heterosexual desire, it seems psychologically all too plausible – a shrewd, even compelling depiction of the wayward workings of human desire.

Moreover, the youth's tactic has worked not only with this particular girl but also, conceivably, with the entire group. The possibility suggested earlier on that he may have used the same trick on the very women with whom the girl identifies – that he may have given them each others' love tokens or those of supposedly earlier lovers still – seems, now, ever more likely. If so, he would have succeeded with them as smoothly as with the girl because they, too, are in the same position – all madly identifying with one another – that being precisely the situation he is exploiting. Indeed, there is no one who does not desire him in this way, no love for him that is not mediated by an existing relation with fellow rivals, for the prospect of there ever having been one originating, "authenticating" passion for him and him alone recedes ever further into the fictional past to become nothing other than the illusion by means of which he panders himself. As with collective hysteria over a celebrity or a media icon, the youth is never desired directly or for "himself" but only as the deflected object of others' desires – he is the mediatory relay (albeit a crucial one) that allows desire to circulate among his adoring fans.

That this, indeed, is the model of desire that the poem presents – a triangulated structure in which the heterosexual relation is to some extent also a homosocial one – is reinforced by the repeated emphasis on the sheer quantity of women who are enamored of him – "Many there were" (l. 134), "So many" (l. 141), "Among the many" (l. 190), "many a several fair" (l. 206), "all these hearts" (l. 274). Such a multitude of devotees can only suggest a model in which desire is produced and proliferated by identification with others. And, although the youth singles out an infatuated nun – the "sister sanctified, of holiest note" (l. 233) – as a particularly notable example of his success, the poem is not structured in such a way as to suggest that the girl is moved to love him by identifying with a single conquest alone. Rather, the poem works to create a sense of collective frenzy – a crowd of numerous, mostly undifferentiated others, all spurred on to desire the youth by one another. Indeed, not only is an entire community shown to be united in the same mutual identification: the very environment gets caught up in the hysteria and comes to be identified as a desiring woman itself. Thus, the girl finds herself in a landscape that is not only populated by figures like herself – she being one "afflicted fancy" (l. 61) among many "wounded fancies" (l. 197), "proofs new bleeding" (l. 153), "broken bosoms" (l. 254), and so forth – but that is also, by means of transferred epithets (the river's "weeping margin," l. 39) and the pathetic fallacy (the "concave womb," line 1, of the resounding hill and its "sist'ring vale," l. 2; the "world" of the poem being stormed by the girl's sighs and tears, "sorrow's wind and rain," l. 7) in danger of being personified as a clamorous woman itself, the entire locality metamorphosing into a choric complainant that threatens finally to disappear once and for all into a vanishing, echoing voice.

This has some interesting consequences for our interpretation and understanding of the poem. To begin with, it reorientates any pre-existing notions we may have had about its genre or, indeed, about the genre of the complaint form more generally. For if the girl identifies with the other desiring women (and they with one another), then to *be* a desiring woman is her (and their) heart's desire. She (and they) *want* to want the youth – on that rests their whole identity. Instead, therefore, of seeing the girl as a tragic victim who has been abandoned and is "complaining" about it, the poem invites us to see her as someone who has exactly what she desires – which is to be someone who desires – that being her position, after all, from beginning to end. She does not, that is, seek to change her situation, any more than a crowd of screaming fans is calling for urgent assistance. Like them, the girl wants and chooses to be in that state and, indeed, works it up to a fine pitch. "Big discontent" (l. 56) is paradoxically what contents her, the state of privation, lack, "castration," her masochistic mode of choice. She means it when she tells the old man that it gives no "satisfaction to our blood / That we must curb it upon others' proofs" (ll. 162–3) because, insofar as she identifies with the "proofs new bleeding" (l. 153) of the youth's previous conquests, she positively desires to "bleed" like them – that to her is "sweet" and "good" (l. 164). Callous as it might seem, the youth's statement of his former mistresses – that "They sought their shame that so their shame did find" (l. 187) – is, in the light of this more complex vision of desire, largely true.

A hint that this is the correct reading, moreover, is to be found once again in the fate of the old man. Old-fashioned and possessed, perhaps, of a simpler understanding of human motivation and desire, he bustles in and, full of good intentions, assumes that the girl wants to alleviate her pain, offering to "assuage" her "suffering" (l. 69) and so to effect some curative change to her condition. That the girl does not actually want this and that his understanding of the situation is therefore largely off-target is suggested by the fact that he completely disappears, never to close the frame. The old man's disappearance leaves space for a darker and more compelling depiction of human desire – one, indeed, more in keeping with the sonnets (the later ones, at any rate) – in which heterosexual desire is complicated and triangulated by homosocial identification, and in which it is (for that reason) irrational, insane, obsessive, driven, self-destructive, addictive, masochistic in a compulsively repetitive way, wholly immune from considerations of worth or desert or from the pursuit of happiness or satisfaction, but no less irresistible for that. The speaker of the sonnets, like the girl of *A Lover's Complaint*, "well knows" the heaven that leads to this hell (sonnet 129) but remains as incapable of shunning it as she. In a recent article on Ovid and Shakespeare, Gordon Braden has suggested that the most fitting epigraph to the sonnets might come not from the "ameliorative end" of the *Metamorphoses*, but rather from the lips of one of Ovid's most famous complaining heroines, Medea: "I see the better and approve it," she cries, describing her fateful passion for Jason, "but I follow the worse" (Braden 2000: 109). The same desire for desire – the same compulsion to choose the worse over the better, pain over pleasure, guaranteed separation and loss over marriage and a "happy ending" – could make this the right epigraph for *A Lover's Complaint* as well, were that poem not, in articulating the same message more or less to the letter, itself the true epigraph for the sonnets that the critic perhaps is looking for.

There is no doubt that the girl and women of *A Lover's Complaint* are presented as being driven to repeat their painful experiences. Indeed, if the poem is about anything it is about repetition: its landscape is littered with women who have succumbed (and, as an echoing voice, that landscape reduplicates their story a thousand times), and, in a way has seemed so baffling to many, the particular speaker maintains that she would do it all again, go through the same painful experience any number of times. As Heather Dubrow notes (citing sonnet 129 again), repetition of this kind both "writes and is written by erotic desire" (Dubrow 1995: 36–7) because it demonstrates how "that impulse is never finally satisfied and hence never finally controlled – 'Had, having, and in quest to have, extreme'." In the case of *A Lover's Complaint*, desire is necessarily repetitive, structurally incapable of resolution or closure, because the poem specifically activates the homosocial triangle by means of which desire circulates between its three elements – the women, the youth, and the girl – round and round without end. As Colin Burrow comments, there is "no escaping from a loop in which someone is desired for having treated others so badly that they longed for him, and no escape from the consciousness that when you have been abandoned by him too that might make him even more desirable" (Shakespeare 2002: 146). Hence the circularity of *A Lover's Complaint* – the sense that it never seems to get anywhere, to change or achieve anything – which has led to complaints about the poem's "pointlessness" (Kerrigan 1991: 50) as critics are obliged to admit that, unlike more openly homiletic and thereby conventional examples of the complaint tradition, *A Lover's Complaint* is bound by no such didacticism and "promulgates no forthright moral" (p. 50); the desire for an ethical reading that would wind up the story, redeem the wrong done, and satisfy readerly expectations finding itself here well and truly stumped, silenced, and seen off as effectively as the old man.

Attempts on the part of the reader to introduce the moral standpoint which the poem so conspicuously leaves out – such as the "unremitting Christian outlook of the Renaissance" that one critic brings in to try to adjudicate the situation (Roche 1989: 443) – seem as out of place as the old man, and fail not only to make sense of the poem but somehow to do justice to it as well. While Lucrece, Burrow notes, manages to "break out of the potentially endless process of complaining" by taking her own life (Shakespeare 2002: 145), there is no such promised end for the girl of *A Lover's Complaint*, who goes on and on and keeps the cycle repeating itself indefinitely. Where Lucrece protests loudly, both before and after the rape, her suicide being the ultimate refusal of the way she has been treated, the girl and women of *A Lover's Complaint* positively court and invite such mistreatment. If Lucrece, at great length and in no uncertain terms, says "no" to what happens to her, then the girl and women of *A Lover's Complaint* say "yes," "more," and "again" – not to being raped, of course, but certainly to being seduced. In her reading of *The Rape of Lucrece*, Lynn Enterline suggests that Shakespeare is critiquing the male homosociality of the more traditional Petrarchan scenario – where men commodify woman and trade her between themselves – by asking what that woman as subject might have to say about such violent objectification (Enterline 2000). But if Shakespeare's "ethical inquiry" into Petrarchanism seeks in part to recuperate woman by giving her a voice and a subjectivity otherwise denied her, *A Lover's Complaint* (unsettling the desire for ethical readings once again) puts a new and disturbing angle on the whole scene. For although the poem turns conventional homosociality on its head by making it a man who circulates as the object of female desire, it neither "recuperates" that man by making him protest at such objectification (quite the reverse), nor "empowers" the women by making them active agents, the willful mistresses of their own erotic desire: on the contrary, they are shown to choose dereliction and abandonment every time. Or rather, if this reversal does position the women as subjects, then the poem reveals that subjectivity to be the very opposite of masterly – willfully self-destructive and masochistic.

It is not surprising, then, that critics seeking an "ethical" reading of *A Lover's Complaint* should find themselves at a loss, for what emerges is that the poem presents a view of human motivation and desire that is profoundly at odds with all that might seem logical or reasonable, let alone ethical, and that it promulgates the strange but undeniable reality that Freud found himself having to confront (and that, in the form of the death drive, is still balked at by some, now as it was then) – namely, that human beings are not necessarily driven by gain, greed, or self-interest but, as often as not, by impulses that are obviously harmful, self-destructive, and masochistic, a clinical and all too observable fact that forced Freud to the conclusion that, peculiar as it may seem, "there really does exist in the mind a compulsion to repeat which over-rides the pleasure principle" (Freud 1920: 18. 22). Since the masochistic impulse remained, even to Freud, "mysterious," "incomprehensible," and "obscure" (Freud 1924: 19. 159, 161), it no longer seems so strange that *A Lover's Complaint* should so often have been described in similar terms; in which case, "enigmatic," the epithet applied to it more frequently than any other, might now be seen as an apt descriptor – as indicating the poem's depiction of a truly masochistic subjectivity and desire – rather than as the faintly disgruntled response of readers who feel they cannot get to the bottom of it and sense that the poem is somehow withholding something from them.

It seems to me that *A Lover's Complaint* is best understood if it is seen as a text that looks ahead to recent developments in psychoanalytic theory – developments which suggest that an originary masochism is constitutive of all human subjectivity. Indeed, the poem begins to make sense when it is seen to anticipate recent suggestions that the figure of the seduced girl might, perhaps, be the prototype of all human sexuality, "male" no less than "female." For according to these speculations, "feminine" masochism is not some weird perversion, a distinct pathology which afflicts a few, nor even a sub-category within a slightly wider field (one that includes, classically, "erotogenic" and "moral" masochism as well), but, rather, the fundamental point of origin in the psychic history of all human beings. In this account, the figure of the seduced girl comes to exemplify the foundation of all subsequent psychic development, in men as well as women, because, in the words of Jacques André, it "presents a privileged affinity with the originary position of seduction of the child vis-à-vis the adult" (André 2002: 111). Like the seduced girl, the child too is situated as the passive recipient of a sexuality that comes to it from the outside in the form of enigmatic, untranslatable messages from the other, a sexuality that is intrusive and exogenous, penetrative and traumatic, that breaks in upon and "shatters" the child into subjectivity and sexuality alike (Laplanche 1999).

The scene of female homosociality that *A Lover's Complaint* unfolds, then, has much to say about the position of the women in the poem, for they now seem less the victims of a heartless brute than a group who are bound together in a willed and self-chosen masochistic identity. It also has something to say, furthermore, about the women's attitude to poetry, metaphor, and art. For if the youth is a mere pretext – the mediatory relay for the interpersonal relations that exist between them – then it no longer seems so surprising that the women should all fall for someone who is so openly wicked. As a means to an end, the youth was never desired for himself or on his own merits (nor was anyone under any illusion that he was), because he was never really the object of interest or attention at all. Some critics register a sense of outrage at the youth's blatant manipulativeness and assume that the writer of the poem is as appalled and horrified as they. As the girl (along with her fellow sufferers) is a "victim" (Shakespeare 1986: 18) of the youth's false praise and empty rhetoric, so the author of the poem is taken to be delivering a devastating critique of such falseness – a lesson powerful enough, in one case, to orientate the critic's interpretation not just of *A Lover's Complaint* but of the sonnets as well, the entire sequence now seen, in the light (or shadow) cast back over it by the concluding complaint, to be a bitter warning against the "mendacity of metaphor" (Shakespeare 1986: 23) and the "perils of invidious hyperbole" (p. 23). This reading – which sees Shakespeare as a scrupled poet who, "alert to the ethical implications of his art" (p. 29), warns against the power of metaphor to falsify – seeks to redeem the situation by restoring what is real and true, the essential "nature of things" (p. 23) that lies behind the deceptive surface of smoky words. The narrative of *A Lover's Complaint*, however, suggests that the girl and women of the poem are *not* so deceived. As the girl confesses to the old man, "further I could say this man's untrue, / And knew the patterns of his foul beguiling . . . Saw how deceits were gilded in his smiling, / Knew vows were ever brokers to defiling" (ll. 169–70, 172–3), and no doubt the other women would have added their own voices to hers, in the same collective conviction. The implication, in other words, is that the women knew the youth's dastardly tactics all too well but went on desiring him all the same. They were never deceived by his false vows; they never believed the content of his words – least of all his transparent claim never to have loved "Till now" (l. 182). Never under any illusion about the falseness of his words, they allowed themselves, rather, to be moved – stirred to a passion, no less – precisely *because* those words were specious and empty and never pretended to be anything otherwise. What galvanizes the women is specifically the surface and not the content of the youth's words.

The situation might be compared to an episode similar enough to have struck one critic at least (Rees 1991) as being a likely analogue or source for *A Lover's Complaint*, namely the story of Dido and Pamphilus in Book II of Sidney's *New Arcadia*. There, too, a group of women are driven to erotic frenzy by a callous youth who manipulates them in exactly the same way as the youth of the complaint: in "the stirring of our own passions," explains Dido, the inamorata who speaks for herself and the other unfortunates, " . . . there lay his master's part of cunning, making us now jealous; now envious; now, proud of what we had, desirous of more; now giving one the triumph to see him, that was prince of many, subject to her; now with an estranged look making her fear the loss of that mind which, indeed, could never be had . . ." (Skretkowicz 1987: 238). As with their fellows in *A Lover's Complaint*, moreover, these women were never deceived by Pamphilus – they were fully apprised of his faults from the beginning, never thought he was anything other than a worthless, exploitative deceiver – and yet, enigmatic though it might seem, that did not warn them off him in the least; quite the opposite. "And, which is strangest," Dido continues, "I must confess even in the greatest tempest of my judgement was I never driven to think him excellent, and yet so could set my mind both to get and keep him as though therein had lain my felicity – like them I have seen play at the ball grow extremely earnest who should have the ball, and yet everyone knew it was but a ball." Quite apart from exemplifying with peculiar neatness the homosocial situation in which, as a mediatory relay for relations between women, the man finds himself passed around like an object from one to the other, the image of the ball-game also suggests much about the women's attitude to fiction and art. For the women here, like those of *A Lover's Complaint*, never doubt that the ball is "but a ball," but that does not motivate them any the less to enter with full gusto and enthusiasm into the spirit of the game. They "believe" in the youth's words, that is, in the same way that an audience or readership of poetic fictions "believes" in poetic fictions that never made any claim to be true – that ball that "was but a ball" having echoes, after all, with that stage-play door marked "Thebes" that (Sidney suggests in the *Defence of Poetry*) a theater audience is no less willing to accept for the duration, no matter how clear they are that it is not Thebes. In which case, the women of *A Lover's Complaint* might seem less the tragic victims of a vile seducer than the all too willing players and spectators of a tragic play. Rather than seeing the poem as an attack on metaphor that belies the inner truth or essential reality of things "in themselves," then, it is possible to see it as an experiment (for good or ill or what you will) in the power of fictions, if not to teach or to delight then most certainly to move.

References and Further Reading

André, Jacques (2002). "Feminine Sexuality: A Return to Sources." *new formations* 48, 77–112.

Bell, Ilona (1999). " 'That which thou hast done': Shakespeare's Sonnets and *A Lover's Complaint*." In James Schiffer (ed.), *Shakespeare's Sonnets: Critical Essays*, 455–74. New York: Garland.

Braden, Gordon (2000). "Ovid, Petrarch, and Shakespeare's *Sonnets*." In A. B. Taylor (ed.), *Shakespeare's Ovid: The Metamorphoses in the Plays and the Poems*, 96–112. Cambridge, UK: Cambridge University Press.

Craik, Katharine A. (2002). "Shakespeare's *A Lover's Complaint* and Early Modern Criminal Confession." *Shakespeare Quarterly* 53, 437–57.

Dubrow, Heather (1995). *Echoes of Desire: English Petrarchism and Its Counterdiscourses*. Ithaca, NY: Cornell University Press.

Duncan-Jones, Katherine (1983). "Was the 1609 *Shake-Speares Sonnets* Really Unauthorized?" *Review of English Studies* n.s. 34, 151–71.

Elliott, Ward E. Y., and Valenza, Robert J. (1997). "Glass Slippers and Seven-League Boots: C-prompted Doubts about Ascribing *A Funeral Elegy* and *A Lover's Complaint* to Shakespeare." *Shakespeare Quarterly* 48, 177–207.

Enterline, Lynn (2000). *The Rhetoric of the Body from Ovid to Shakespeare*. Cambridge, UK: Cambridge University Press.

Freud, Sigmund (1920). *Beyond the Pleasure Principle*. In *The Standard Edition of the Complete Psychological Works of Sigmund Freud*, ed. James Strachey, 24 vols., vol. 18, 1–64. London: Hogarth.

Freud, Sigmund (1924). "The Economic Problem of Masochism." In *Works*, ed. Strachey, vol. 19, 155–70.

Freud, Sigmund (1927). "Fetishism." In *Works*, ed. Strachey, vol. 21, 147–57.

Jackson, Macdonald P. (1965). "Shakespeare's *A Lover's Complaint*: Its Date and Authenticity." *University of Auckland Bulletin* 72.

Kerrigan, John (1991). *Motives of Woe: Shakespeare and "Female Complaint."* Oxford: Clarendon.

Laplanche, Jean (1999). "Masochism and the general theory of seduction." In John Fletcher (ed.), *Essays on Otherness*, 197–213. London: Routledge.

Mackail, J. W. (1912). "*A Lover's Complaint*." *Essays and Studies* 3, 51–70.

Muir, Kenneth (1973). " '*A Lover's Complaint*': A Reconsideration." In *Shakespeare the Professional*, 204–19. London: Heinemann.

Rees, Joan (1991). "Sidney and *A Lover's Complaint*." *Review of English Studies* 42, 157–67.

Roche, Thomas P., Jr. (1989). *Petrarch and the English Sonnet Sequences*. New York: AMS Press.

Sedgwick, Eve Kosofsky (1985). *Between Men: English Literature and Male Homosocial Desire*. New York: Columbia University Press.

Shakespeare, William (1986). *The Sonnets and A Lover's Complaint*, ed. John Kerrigan. Harmondsworth: Penguin. (The New Penguin Shakespeare.)

Shakespeare, William (1992). *The Poems: Venus and Adonis, The Rape of Lucrece, The Phoenix and the*

Turtle, The Passionate Pilgrim, A Lover's Complaint, ed. John Roe. Cambridge, UK: Cambridge University Press.

Shakespeare, William (2002). *The Complete Sonnets and Poems*, ed. Colin Burrow. Oxford: Oxford University Press. (Oxford World's Classics.)

Skretkowicz, Victor, ed. (1987). *The New Arcadia*. Oxford: Clarendon.

Stallybrass, Peter (1999). "Editing as Cultural Formation: The Sexing of Shakespeare's Sonnets." In James Schiffer (ed.), *Shakespeare's Sonnets: Critical Essays*, 75–88. New York: Garland. (First publ. in *Modern Language Quarterly* 54, 1993, 91–103.)

Vickers, Brian (2003). "A Rum 'Do': The Likely Authorship of 'A Lover's Complaint.'" *Times Literary Supplement*, 5 Dec., 13–15.

Appendix:
The 1609 Text of Shakespeare's
Sonnets and *A Lover's Complaint*

SHAKE-SPEARES

SONNETS.

Neuer before Imprinted.

AT LONDON
By G. Eld for T. T. and are
to be folde by *William Afpley.*
1609.

TO. THE.ONLIE.BEGETTER.OF.
THESE.INSVING.SONNETS.
Mr. W. H. ALL.HAPPINESSE.
AND.THAT.ETERNITIE.
PROMISED.

BY.

OVR.EVER-LIVING.POET.

WISHETH.

THE.WELL-WISHING.
ADVENTVRER.IN.
SETTING.
FORTH.

T. T.

S H A K E - S P E A R E S,
SONNETS.

FRom fairest creatures we desire increase,
  That thereby beauties *Rose* might neuer die,
But as the riper should by time decease,
His tender heire might beare his memory:
But thou contracted to thine owne bright eyes,
Feed'st thy lights flame with selfe substantiall fewell,
Making a famine where aboundance lies,
Thy selfe thy foe, to thy sweet selfe too cruell:
Thou that art now the worlds fresh ornament,
And only herauld to the gaudy spring,
Within thine owne bud buriest thy content,
And tender chorle makst wast in niggarding:
   Pitty the world, or else this glutton be,
   To eate the worlds due, by the graue and thee.

2

VVHen fortie Winters shall beseige thy brow,
  And digge deep trenches in thy beauties field,
Thy youthes proud liuery so gaz'd on now,
Wil be a totter'd weed of smal worth held:
Then being askt, where all thy beautie lies,
Where all the treasure of thy lusty daies;
To say within thine owne deepe sunken eyes,
Were an all-eating shame, and thriftlesse praise.
How much more praise deseru'd thy beauties vse,
If thou couldst answere this faire child of mine
Shall sum my count, and make my old excuse
Proouing his beautie by succession thine.
   This were to be new made when thou art ould,
   And see thy blood warme when thou feel'st it could,

3

LOoke in thy glasse and tell the face thou vewest,
  Now is the time that face should forme an other,
Whose fresh repaire if now thou not renewest,
Thou doo'st beguile the world, vnblesse some mother.
For where is she so faire whose vn-eard wombe
Disdaines the tillage of thy husbandry?
Or who is he so fond will be the tombe,
Of his selfe loue to stop posterity?
Thou art thy mothers glasse and she in thee
Calls backe the louely Aprill of her prime,
So thou through windowes of thine age shalt see,
Dispight of wrinkles this thy goulden time.
   But if thou liue remembred not to be,
   Die single and thine Image dies with thee.

4

VNthrifty louelinesse why dost thou spend,
 Vpon thy selfe thy beauties legacy?
Natures bequest giues nothing but doth lend,
And being franck she lends to those are free:
Then beautious nigard why doost thou abuse,
The bountious largesse giuen thee to giue?
Profitles vserer why doost thou vse
So great a summe of summes yet can'st not liue?
For hauing traffike with thy selfe alone,
Thou of thy selfe thy sweet selfe dost deceaue,
Then how when nature calls thee to be gone,
What acceptable *Audit* can'st thou leaue?
    Thy vnus'd beauty must be tomb'd with thee,
    Which vsed liues th'executor to be.

5

THose howers that with gentle worke did frame,
 The louely gaze where euery eye doth dwell
Will play the tirants to the very same,
And that vnfaire which fairely doth excell:
For neuer resting time leads Summer on,
To hidious winter and confounds him there,
Sap checkt with frost and lustie leau's quite gon.
Beauty ore-snow'd and barenes euery where,
Then were not summers distillation left
A liquid prisoner pent in walls of glasse,
Beauties effect with beauty were bereft,
Nor it nor noe remembrance what it was.
    But flowers distil'd though they with winter meete,
    Leese but their show, their substance still liues sweet.

6

THen let not winters wragged hand deface,
 In thee thy summer ere thou be distil'd:
Make sweet some viall; treasure thou some place,
With beautits treasure ere it be selfe kil'd:
That vse is not forbidden vsery,
Which happies those that pay the willing lone;
That's for thy selfe to breed an other thee,
Or ten times happier be it ten for one,
Ten times thy selfe were happier then thou art,
If ten of thine ten times refigur'd thee,
Then what could death doe if thou should'st depart,
Leauing thee liuing in posterity?
    Be not selfe-wild for thou art much too faire,
    To be deaths conquest and make wormes thine heire.

7

L Oe in the Orient when the gracious light,
   Lifts vp his burning head, each vnder eye
Doth homage to his new appearing sight,
Seruing with lookes his sacred maiesty,
And hauing climb'd the steepe vp heauenly hill,
Resembling strong youth in his middle age,
Yet mortall lookes adore his beauty still,
Attending on his goulden pilgrimage:
But when from high-most pich with wery car,
Like feeble age he reeleth from the day,
The eyes (fore dutious) now conuerted are
From his low tract and looke an other way:
    So thou, thy selfe out-going in thy noon:
    Vnlok'd on diest vnlesse thou get a sonne.

8

M Vsick to heare, why hear'st thou musick sadly,
   Sweets with sweets warre not, ioy delights in ioy:
Why lou'st thou that which thou receaust not gladly,
Or else receau'st with pleasure thine annoy?
If the true concord of well tuned sounds,
By vnions married do offend thine eare,
They do but sweetly chide thee, who confounds
In singlenesse the parts that thou should'st beare:
Marke how one string sweet husband to an other,
Strikes each in each by mutuall ordering;
Resembling sier, and child, and happy mother,
Who all in one, one pleasing note do sing:
    Whose speechlesse song being many, seeming one,
    Sings this to thee thou single wilt proue none.

9

I S it for feare to wet a widdowes eye,
  That thou consum'st thy selfe in single life?
Ah; if thou issulesse shalt hap to die,
The world will waile thee like a makelesse wife,
The world wilbe thy widdow and still weepe,
That thou no forme of thee hast left behind,
When euery priuat widdow well may keepe,
By childrens eyes, her husbands shape in minde:
Looke what an vnthrift in the world doth spend
Shifts but his place, for still the world inioyes it
But beauties waste hath in the world an end,
And kept vnvsde the vser so destroyes it:
    No loue toward others in that bosome sits
    That on himselfe such murdrous shame commits.

10

FOr shame deny that thou bear'st loue to any
Who for thy selfe art so vnprouident
Graunt if thou wilt, thou art belou'd of many,
But that thou none lou'st is most euident:
For thou art so possest with murdrous hate,
That gainst thy selfe thou stickst not to conspire,
Seeking that beautious roofe to ruinate
Which to repaire should be thy chiefe desire:
O change thy thought, that I may change my minde,
Shall hate be fairer log'd then gentle loue?
Be as thy presence is gracious and kind,
Or to thy selfe at least kind harted proue,
    Make thee an other selfe for loue of me,
    That beauty still may liue in thine or thee.

11

AS fast as thou shalt wane so fast thou grow'st,
In one of thine, from that which thou departest,
And that fresh bloud which yongly thou bestow'st,
Thou maist call thine, when thou from youth conuertest,
Herein liues wisdome, beauty, and increase,
Without this follie, age, and could decay,
If all were minded so, the times should cease,
And threescoore yeare would make the world away:
Let those whom nature hath not made for store,
Harsh, featurelesse, and rude, barrenly perrish,
Looke whom she best indow'd, she gaue the more;
Which bountious guift thou shouldst in bounty cherrish,
    She caru'd thee for her seale, and ment therby,
    Thou shouldst print more, not let that coppy die.

12

VVHen I doe count the clock that tels the time,
And see the braue day sunck in hidious night,
When I behold the violet past prime,
And sable curls or siluer'd ore with white:
When lofty trees I see barren of leaues,
Which erst from heat did canopie the herd
And Sommers greene all girded vp in sheaues
Borne on the beare with white and bristly beard:
Then of thy beauty do I question make
That thou among the wastes of time must goe,
Since sweets and beauties do them-selues forsake,
And die as fast as they see others grow,
    And nothing gainst Times sieth can make defence
    Saue breed to braue him, when he takes thee hence.

13

OThat you were your selfe, but loue you are
  No longer yours, then you your selfe here liue,
Against this cumming end you should prepare,
And your sweet semblance to some other giue.
So should that beauty which you hold in lease
Find no determination, then you were
You selfe again after your selfes decease,
When your sweet issue your sweet forme should beare.
Who lets so faire a house fall to decay,
Which husbandry in honour might vphold,
Against the stormy gusts of winters day
And barren rage of deaths eternall cold?
    O none but vnthrifts, deare my loue you know,
    You had a Father, let your Son say so.

14

NOt from the stars do I my iudgement plucke,
  And yet me thinkes I haue Astronomy,
But not to tell of good, or euil lucke,
Of plagues, of dearths, or seasons quallity,
Nor can I fortune to breefe mynuits tell;
Pointing to each his thunder, raine and winde,
Or say with Princes if it shal go wel
By oft predict that I in heauen finde.
But from thine eies my knowledge I deriue,
And constant stars in them I read such art
As truth and beautie shal together thriue
If from thy selfe, to store thou wouldst conuert:
    Or else of thee this I prognosticate,
    Thy end is Truthes and Beauties doome and date.

15

WHen I consider euery thing that growes
  Holds in perfection but a little moment.
That this huge stage presenteth nought but showes
Whereon the Stars in secret influence comment.
When I perceiue that men as plants increase,
Cheared and checkt euen by the selfe-same skie:
Vaunt in their youthfull sap, at height decrease,
And were their braue state out of memory.
Then the conceit of this inconstant stay,
Sets you most rich in youth before my sight,
Where wastfull time debateth with decay
To change your day of youth to sullied night,
    And all in war with Time for loue of you
    As he takes from you, I ingraft you new.

16

BVt wherefore do not you a mightier waie
Make warre vppon this bloudie tirant time?
And fortifie your selfe in your decay
With meanes more blessed then my barren rime?
Now stand you on the top of happie houres,
And many maiden gardens yet vnset,
With vertuous wish would beare your liuing flowers,
Much liker then your painted counterfeit:
So should the lines of life that life repaire
Which this (Times pensel or my pupill pen)
Neither in inward worth nor outward faire
Can make you liue your selfe in eies of men,
    To giue away your selfe, keeps your selfe still,
    And you must liue drawne by your owne sweet skill,

17

VVHo will beleeue my verse in time to come
If it were fild with your most high deserts?
Though yet heauen knowes it is but as a tombe
Which hides your life, and shewes not halfe your parts:
If I could write the beauty of your eyes,
And in fresh numbers number all your graces,
The age to come would say this Poet lies,
Such heauenly touches nere toucht earthly faces.
So should my papers (yellowed with their age)
Be scorn'd, like old men of lesse truth then tongue,
And your true rights be termd a Poets rage,
And stretched miter of an Antique song.
    But were some childe of yours aliue that time,
    You should liue twise in it, and in my rime.

18

SHall I compare thee to a Summers day?
Thou art more louely and more temperate:
Rough windes do shake the darling buds of Maie,
And Sommers lease hath all too short a date:
Sometime too hot the eye of heauen shines,
And often is his gold complexion dimm'd,
And euery faire from faire some-time declines,
By chance, or natures changing course vntrim'd:
But thy eternall Sommer shall not fade,
Nor loose possession of that faire thou ow'st,
Nor shall death brag thou wandr'st in his shade,
When in eternall lines to time thou grow'st,
    So long as men can breath or eyes can see,
    So long liues this, and this giues life to thee,

19

DEuouring time blunt thou the Lyons pawes,
And make the earth deuoure her owne sweet brood,
Plucke the keene teeth from the fierce Tygers yawes,
And burne the long liu'd Phænix in her blood,
Make glad and sorry seasons as thou fleet'st,
And do what ere thou wilt swift-footed time
To the wide world and all her fading sweets:
But I forbid thee one most hainous crime,
O carue not with thy howers my loues faire brow,
Nor draw noe lines there with thine antique pen,
Him in thy course vntainted doe allow,
For beauties patterne to succeding men.
    Yet doe thy worst ould Time dispight thy wrong,
    My loue shall in my verse euer liue young.

20

AWomans face with natures owne hand painted,
Haste thou the Master Mistris of my passion,
A womans gentle hart but not acquainted
With shifting change as is false womens fashion,
An eye more bright then theirs, lesse false in rowling:
Gilding the obiect where-vpon it gazeth,
A man in hew all *Hews* in his controwling,
Which steales mens eyes and womens soules amaseth.
And for a woman wert thou first created,
Till Nature as she wrought thee fell a dotinge,
And by addition me of thee defeated,
By adding one thing to my purpose nothing.
    But since she prickt thee out for womens pleasure,
    Mine be thy loue and thy loues vse their treasure.

21

SO is it not with me as with that Muse,
Stird by a painted beauty to his verse,
Who heauen it selfe for ornament doth vse,
And euery faire with his faire doth reherse,
Making a coopelment of proud compare
With Sunne and Moone, with earth and seas rich gems:
With Aprills first borne flowers and all things rare,
That heauens ayre in this huge rondure hems,
O let me true in loue but truly write,
And then beleeue me, my loue is as faire,
As any mothers childe, though not so bright
As those gould candells fixt in heauens ayer:
    Let them say more that like of heare-say well,
    I will not prayse that purpose not to sell.

22

MY glasse shall not perswade me I am ould,
So long as youth and thou are of one date,
But when in thee times forrwes I behould,
Then look I death my daies should expiate.
For all that beauty that doth couer thee,
Is but the seemely rayment of my heart,
Which in thy brest doth liue, as thine in me,
How can I then be elder then thou art?
O therefore loue be of thy selfe so wary,
As I not for my selfe, but for thee will,
Bearing thy heart which I will keepe so chary
As tender nurse her babe from faring ill,
    Presume not on thy heart when mine is slaine,
    Thou gau'st me thine not to giue backe againe.

23

AS an vnperfect actor on the stage,
Who with his feare is put besides his part,
Or some fierce thing repleat with too much rage,
Whose strengths abondance weakens his owne heart;
So I for feare of trust, forget to say,
The perfect ceremony of loues right,
And in mine owne loues strength seeme to decay,
Ore-charg'd with burthen of mine owne loues might:
O let my books be then the eloquence,
And domb presagers of my speaking brest,
Who pleade for loue, and look for recompence,
More then that tonge that more hath more exprest.
    O learne to read what silent loue hath writ,
    To heare wit eies belongs to loues fine wiht.

24

MIne eye hath play'd the painter and hath steeld,
Thy beauties forme in table of my heart,
My body is the frame wherein ti's held,
And perspectiue it is best Painters art.
For through the Painter must you see his skill,
To finde where your true Image pictur'd lies,
Which in my bosomes shop is hanging stil,
That hath his windowes glazed with thine eyes:
Now see what good-turnes eyes for eies haue done,
Mine eyes haue drawne thy shape, and thine for me
Are windowes to my brest, where-through the Sun
Delights to peepe, to gaze therein on thee
    Yet eyes this cunning want to grace their art
    They draw but what they see, know not the hart.

25

L Et those who are in fauor with their stars,
Of publike honour and proud titles bost,
Whilst I whome fortune of such tryumph bars
Vnlookt for ioy in that I honour most;
Great Princes fauorites their faire leaues spread,
But as the Marygold at the suns eye,
And in them-selues their pride lies buried,
For at a frowne they in their glory die.
The painefull warrier famosed for worth,
After a thousand victories once foild,
Is from the booke of honour rased quite,
And all the rest forgot for which he toild:
    Then happy I that loue and am beloued
    Where I may not remoue, nor be remoued.

26

L Ord of my loue, to whome in vassalage
Thy merrit hath my dutie strongly knit;
To thee I send this written ambassage
To witnesse duty, not to shew my wit.
Duty so great, which wit so poore as mine
May make seeme bare, in wanting words to shew it;
But that I hope some good conceipt of thine
In thy soules thought (all naked) will bestow it:
Til whatsoeuer star that guides my mouing,
Points on me gratiously with faire aspect,
And puts apparrell on my tottered louing,
To show me worthy of their sweet respect,
    Then may I dare to boast how I doe loue thee,
    Til then, not show my head where thou maist proue me

27

W Eary with toyle, I hast me to my bed,
The deare repose for lims with trauaill tired,
But then begins a iourny in my head
To worke my mind, when boddies work's expired.
For then my thoughts (from far where I abide)
Intend a zelous pilgrimage to thee,
And keepe my drooping eye-lids open wide,
Looking on darknes which the blind doe see.
Saue that my soules imaginary sight
Presents their shaddoe to my sightles view,
Which like a iewel (hunge in gastly night)
Makes blacke night beautious, and her old face new.
    Loe thus by day my lims, by night my mind,
    For thee, and for my selfe, noe quiet finde.

28

HOw can I then returne in happy plight
That am debard the benifit of rest?
When daies oppression is not eazd by night,
But day by night and night by day oprest.
And each (though enimes to ethers raigne)
Doe in consent shake hands to torture me,
The one by toyle, the other to complaine
How far I toyle, still farther off from thee.
I tell the Day to please him thou art bright,
And do'st him grace when clouds doe blot the heauen:
So flatter I the swart complexiond night,
When sparkling stars twire not thou guil'st th' eauen.
    But day doth daily draw my sorrowes longer,
    And night doth nightly make greefes length seeme stronger.

29

VVHen in disgrace with Fortune and mens eyes,
I all alone beweepe my out-cast state,
And trouble deafe heauen with my bootlesse cries,
And looke vpon my selfe and curse my fate.
Wishing me like to one more rich in hope,
Featur'd like him, like him with friends possest,
Desiring this mans art, and that mans skope,
With what I most inioy contented least,
Yet in these thoughts my selfe almost despising,
Haplye I thinke on thee, and then my state,
(Like to the Larke at breake of daye arising)
From sullen earth sings himns at Heauens gate,
    For thy sweet loue remembred such welth brings,
    That then I skorne to change my state with Kings.

30

VVHen to the Sessions of sweet silent thought,
I sommon vp remembrance of things past,
I sigh the lacke of many a thing I sought,
And with old woes new waile my deare times waste:
Then can I drowne an eye (vn-vs'd to flow)
For precious friends hid in deaths dateles night,
And weepe a fresh loues long since canceld woe,
And mone th'expence of many a vannisht sight.
Then can I greeue at greeuances fore-gon,
And heauily from woe to woe tell ore
The sad account of fore-bemoned mone,
Which I new pay as if not payd before.
    But if the while I thinke on thee (deare friend)
    All losses are restord, and sorrowes end.

31

Thy bosome is indeared with all hearts,
  Which I by lacking haue supposed dead,
And there raignes Loue and all Loues louing parts,
And all those friends which I thought buried.
How many a holy and obsequious teare
Hath deare religious loue stolne from mine eye,
As interest of the dead, which now appeare,
But things remou'd that hidden in there lie.
Thou art the graue where buried loue doth liue,
Hung with the tropheis of my louers gon,
Who all their parts of me to thee did giue,
That due of many, now is thine alone.
    Their images I lou'd, I view in thee,
    And thou (all they) hast all the all of me.

32

IF thou suruiue my well contented daie,
  When that churle death my bones with dust shall couer
And shalt by fortune once more re-suruay:
These poore rude lines of thy deceased Louer:
Compare them with the bett'ring of the time,
And though they be out-stript by euery pen,
Reserue them for my loue, not for their rime,
Exceeded by the hight of happier men.
Oh then voutsafe me but this louing thought,
Had my friends Muse growne with this growing age,
A dearer birth then this his loue had brought
To march in ranckes of better equipage:
    But since he died and Poets better proue,
    Theirs for their stile ile read, his for his loue.

33

FVll many a glorious morning haue I seene,
  Flatter the mountaine tops with soueraine eie,
Kissing with golden face the meddowes greene;
Guilding pale streames with heauenly alcumy:
Anon permit the basest cloudes to ride,
With ougly rack on his celestiall face,
And from the for-lorne world his visage hide
Stealing vnseene to west with this disgrace:
Euen so my Sunne one early morne did shine,
With all triumphant splendor on my brow,
But out alack, he was but one houre mine,
The region cloude hath mask'd him from me now.
    Yet him for this, my loue no whit disdaineth,
    Suns of the world may staine, whe[n] heauens sun staineth.

34

VVHy didst thou promise such a beautious day,
   And make me trauaile forth without my cloake,
To let bace cloudes ore-take me in my way,
Hiding thy brau'ry in their rotten smoke.
Tis not enough that through the cloude thou breake,
To dry the raine on my storme-beaten face,
For no man well of such a salue can speake,
That heales the wound, and cures not the disgrace:
Nor can thy shame giue phisicke to my griefe,
Though thou repent, yet I haue still the losse,
Th'offenders sorrow lends but weake reliefe
To him that beares the strong offenses losse.
   Ah but those teares are pearle which thy loue sheeds,
   And they are ritch, and ransome all ill deeds.

35

NO more bee greeu'd at that which thou hast done,
   Roses haue thornes, and siluer fountaines mud,
Cloudes and eclipses staine both Moone and Sunne,
And loathsome canker liues in sweetest bud.
All men make faults, and euen I in this,
Authorizing thy trespas with compare,
My selfe corrupting saluing thy amisse,
Excusing their sins more then their sins are:
For to thy sensuall fault I bring in sence,
Thy aduerse party is thy Aduocate,
And gainst my selfe a lawfull plea commence,
Such ciuill war is in my loue and hate,
   That I an accessary needs must be,
   To that sweet theefe which sourely robs from me,

36

LEt me confesse that we two must be twaine,
   Although our vndeuided loues are one:
So shall those blots that do with me remaine,
Without thy helpe, by me be borne alone.
In our two loues there is but one respect,
Though in our liues a seperable spight,
Which though it alter not loues sole effect,
Yet doth it steale sweet houres from loues delight,
I may not euer-more acknowledge thee,
Least my bewailed guilt should do thee shame,
Nor thou with publike kindnesse honour me,
Vnlesse thou take that honour from thy name:
   But doe not so, I loue thee in such sort,
   As thou being mine, mine is thy good report.

37

AS a decrepit father takes delight,
  To see his actiue childe do deeds of youth,
So I, made lame by Fortunes dearest spight
Take all my comfort of thy worth and truth.
For whether beauty, birth, or wealth, or wit,
Or any of these all, or all, or more
Intitled in their parts, do crowned sit,
I make my loue ingrafted to this store:
So then I am not lame, poore, nor dispis'd,
Whilst that this shadow doth such substance giue,
That I in thy abundance am suffic'd,
And by a part of all thy glory liue:
  Looke what is best, that best I wish in thee,
  This wish I haue, then ten times happy me.

38

HOw can my Muse want subiect to inuent
  While thou dost breath that poor'st into my verse,
Thine owne sweet argument, to excellent,
For euery vulgar paper to rehearse:
Oh giue thy selfe the thankes if ought in me,
Worthy perusal stand against thy sight,
For who's so dumbe that cannot write to thee,
When thou thy selfe dost giue inuention light?
Be thou the tenth Muse, ten times more in worth
Then those old nine which rimers inuocate,
And he that calls on thee, let him bring forth
Eternal numbers to out-liue long date.
  If my slight Muse doe please these curious daies,
  The paine be mine, but thine shal be the praise.

39

OH how thy worth with manners may I singe,
  When thou art all the better part of me?
What can mine owne praise to mine owne selfe bring;
And what is't but mine owne when I praise thee,
Euen for this, let vs deuided liue,
And our deare loue loose name of single one,
That by this seperation I may giue:
That due to thee which thou deseru'st alone:
Oh absence what a torment wouldst thou proue,
Were it not thy soure leisure gaue sweet leaue,
To entertaine the time with thoughts of loue,
VVhich time and thoughts so sweetly dost deceiue.
  And that thou teachest how to make one twaine,
  By praising him here who doth hence remaine.

40

TAke all my loues, my loue, yea take them all,
　What hast thou then more then thou hadst before?
No loue, my loue, that thou maist true loue call,
All mine was thine, before thou hadst this more:
Then if for my loue, thou my loue receiuest,
I cannot blame thee, for my loue thou vsest,
But yet be blam'd, if thou this selfe deceauest
By wilfull taste of what thy selfe refusest.
I doe forgiue thy robb'rie gentle theefe
Although thou steale thee all my pouerty:
And yet loue knowes it is a greater griefe
To beare loues wrong, then hates knowne iniury.
　　Lasciuious grace, in whom all il wel showes,
　　Kill me with spights yet we must not be foes.

41

THose pretty wrongs that liberty commits,
　When I am some-time absent from thy heart,
Thy beautie, and thy yeares full well befits,
For still temptation followes where thou art.
Gentle thou art, and therefore to be wonne,
Beautious thou art, therefore to be assailed.
And when a woman woes, what womans sonne,
Will sourely leaue her till he haue preuailed.
Aye me, but yet thou mightst my seate forbeare,
And chide thy beauty, and thy straying youth,
Who lead thee in their ryot euen there
Where thou art forst to breake a two-fold truth:
　　Hers by thy beauty tempting her to thee,
　　Thine by thy beautie beeing false to me.

42

THat thou hast her it is not all my griefe,
　And yet it may be said I lou'd her deerely,
That she hath thee is of my wayling cheefe,
A losse in loue that touches me more neerely.
Louing offendors thus I will excuse yee,
Thou doost loue her, because thou knowst I loue her,
And for my sake euen so doth she abuse me,
Suffring my friend for my sake to approoue her,
If I loose thee, my losse is my loues gaine,
And loosing her, my friend hath found that losse,
Both finde each other, and I loose both twaine,
And both for my sake lay on me this crosse,
　　But here's the ioy, my friend and I are one,
　　Sweete flattery, then she loues but me alone.

43

WHen most I winke then doe mine eyes best see,
 For all the day they view things vnrespected,
But when I sleepe, in dreames they looke on thee,
And darkely bright, are bright in darke directed.
Then thou whose shaddow shaddowes doth make bright,
How would thy shadowes forme, forme happy show,
To the cleere day with thy much cleerer light,
When to vn-seeing eyes thy shade shines so?
How would (I say) mine eyes be blessed made,
By looking on thee in the liuing day?
When in dead night their faire imperfect shade,
Through heauy sleepe on sightlesse eyes doth stay?
  All dayes are nights to see till I see thee,
  And nights bright daies when dreams do shew thee me.

44

IF the dull substance of my flesh were thought,
 Iniurious distance should not stop my way,
For then dispight of space I would be brought,
From limits farre remote, where thou doost stay,
No matter then although my foote did stand
Vpon the farthest earth remoou'd from thee,
For nimble thought can iumpe both sea and land,
As soone as thinke the place where he would be.
But ah, thought kills me that I am not thought
To leape large lengths of miles when thou art gone,
But that so much of earth and water wrought,
I must attend, times leasure with my mone.
  Receiuing naughts by elements so sloe,
  But heauie teares, badges of eithers woe.

45

THe other two, slight ayre, and purging fire,
 Are both with thee, where euer I abide,
The first my thought, the other my desire,
These present absent with swift motion slide.
For when these quicker Elements are gone
In tender Embassie of loue to thee,
My life being made of foure, with two alone,
Sinkes downe to death, opprest with melancholie.
Vntill liues composition be recured,
By those swift messengers return'd from thee,
Who euen but now come back againe assured,
Of their faire health, recounting it to me.
  This told, I ioy, but then no longer glad,
  I send them back againe and straight grow sad.

46

Mine eye and heart are at a mortall warre,
How to deuide the conquest of thy sight,
Mine eye, my heart their pictures sight would barre,
My heart, mine eye the freedome of that right,
My heart doth plead that thou in him doost lye,
(A closet neuer pearst with christall eyes)
But the defendant doth that plea deny,
And sayes in him their faire appearance lyes.
To side this title is impannelled
A quest of thoughts, all tennants to the heart,
And by their verdict is determined
The cleere eyes moyitie, and the deare hearts part.
  As thus, mine eyes due is their outward part,
  And my hearts right, their inward loue of heart.

47

Betwixt mine eye and heart a league is tooke,
And each doth good turnes now vnto the other,
When that mine eye is famisht for a looke,
Or heart in loue with sighes himselfe doth smother;
With my loues picture then my eye doth feast,
And to the painted banquet bids my heart:
An other time mine eye is my hearts guest,
And in his thoughts of loue doth share a part.
So either by thy picture or my loue,
Thy seife away, are present still with me,
For thou nor farther then my thoughts canst moue,
And I am still with them, and they with thee.
  Or if they sleepe, thy picture in my sight
  Awakes my heart, to hearts and eyes delight.

48

How carefull was I when I tooke my way,
Each trifle vnder truest barres to thrust,
That to my vse it might vn-vsed stay
From hands of falsehood, in sure wards of trust?
But thou, to whom my iewels trifles are,
Most worthy comfort, now my greatest griefe,
Thou best of deerest, and mine onely care,
Art left the prey of euery vulgar theefe.
Thee haue I not lockt vp in any chest,
Saue where thou art not, though I feele thou art,
Within the gentle closure of my brest,
From whence at pleasure thou maist come and part,
  And euen thence thou wilt be stolne I feare,
  For truth prooues theeuish for a prize so deare.

49

AGainst that time (if euer that time come)
When I shall see thee frowne on my defects,
When as thy loue hath cast his vtmost summe,
Cauld to that audite by aduis'd respects,
Against that time when thou shalt strangely passe,
And scarcely greete me with that sunne thine eye,
When loue conuerted from the thing it was
Shall reasons finde of setled grauitie.
Against that time do I insconce me here
Within the knowledge of mine own desart,
And this my hand, against my selfe vpreare,
To guard the lawfull reasons on thy part,
    To leaue poore me, thou hast the strength of lawes,
    Since why to loue, I can alledge no cause.

50

HOw heauie doe I iourney on the way,
When what I seeke (my wearie trauels end)
Doth teach that ease and that repose to say
Thus farre the miles are measurde from thy friend.
The beast that beares me, tired with my woe,
Plods duly on, to beare that waight in me,
As if by some instinct the wretch did know
His rider lou'd not speed being made from thee:
The bloody spurre cannot prouoke him on,
That some-times anger thrusts into his hide,
Which heauily he answers with a grone,
More sharpe to me then spurring to his side,
    For that same grone doth put this in my mind,
    My greefe lies onward and my ioy behind.

51

THus can my loue excuse the slow offence,
Of my dull bearer, when from thee I speed,
From where thou art, why shoulld I hast me thence,
Till I returne of posting is noe need.
O what excuse will my poore beast then find,
When swift extremity can seeme but slow,
Then should I spurre though mounted on the wind,
In winged speed no motion shall I know,
Then can no horse with my desire keepe pace,
Therefore desire (of perfects loue being made)
Shall naigh noe dull flesh in his fiery race,
But loue, for loue, thus shall excuse my iade,
    Since from thee going, he went wilfull slow,
    Towards thee ile run, and giue him leaue to goe.

52

SO am I as the rich whose blessed key,
Can bring him to his sweet vp-locked treasure,
The which he will not eu'ry hower suruay,
For blunting the fine point of seldome pleasure.
Therefore are feasts so sollemne and so rare,
Since sildom comming in the long yeare set,
Like stones of worth they thinly placed are,
Or captaine Iewells in the carconet.
So is the time that keepes you as my chest,
Or as the ward-robe which the robe doth hide,
To make some speciall instant speciall blest,
By new vnfoulding his imprison'd pride.
　　Blessed are you whose worthinesse giues skope,
　　Being had to tryumph, being lackt to hope.

53

VVHat is your substance, whereof are you made,
That millions of strange shaddowes on you tend?
Since euery one, hath euery one, one shade,
And you but one, can euery shaddow lend:
Describe *Adonis* and the counterfet,
Is poorely immitated after you,
On *Hellens* cheeke all art of beautie set,
And you in *Grecian* tires are painted new:
Speake of the spring, and foyzon of the yeare,
The one doth shaddow of your beautie show,
The other as your bountie doth appeare,
And you in euery blessed shape we know.
　　In all externall grace you haue some part,
　　But you like none, none you for constant heart.

54

OH how much more doth beautie beautious seeme,
By that sweet ornament which truth doth giue,
The Rose lookes faire, but fairer we it deeme
For that sweet odor, which doth in it liue:
The Canker bloomes haue full as deepe a die,
As the perfumed tincture of the Roses,
Hang on such thornes, and play as wantonly,
When sommers breath their masked buds discloses:
But for their virtue only is their show,
They liue vnwoo'd, and vnrespected fade,
Die to themselues. Sweet Roses doe not so,
Of their sweet deathes, are sweetest odors made:
　　And so of you, beautious and louely youth,
　　When that shall vade, by verse distils your truth.

55

NOt marble, nor the guilded monument,
Of Princes shall out-liue this powrefull rime,
But you shall shine more bright in these contents
Then vnswept stone, besmeer'd with sluttish time.
When wastefull warre shall *Statues* ouer-turne,
And broiles roote out the worke of masonry,
Nor *Mars* his sword, nor warres quick fire shall burne:
The liuing record of your memory.
Gainst death, and all obliuious emnity
Shall you pace forth, your praise shall stil finde roome,
Euen in the eyes of all posterity
That weare this world out to the ending doome.
    So til the iudgement that your selfe arise,
    You liue in this, and dwell in louers eies.

56

Sweet loue renew thy force, be it not said
Thy edge should blunter be then apetite,
Which but too daie by feeding is alaied,
To morrow sharpned in his former might.
So loue be thou, although too daie thou fill
Thy hungrie eies, euen till they winck with fulnesse,
Too morrow see againe, and doe not kill
The spirit of Loue, with a perpetual dulnesse:
Let this sad *Intrim* like the Ocean be
Which parts the shore, where two contracted new,
Come daily to the banckes, that when they see:
Returne of loue, more blest may be the view.
    As cal it Winter, which being ful of care,
    Makes Somers welcome, thrice more wish'd, more rare:

57

BEing your slaue what should I doe but tend,
Vpon the houres, and times of your desire?
I haue no precious time at al to spend;
Nor seruices to doe til you require.
Nor dare I chide the world without end houre,
Whilst I (my soueraine) watch the clock for you,
Nor thinke the bitternesse of absence sowre,
VVhen you haue bid your seruant once adieue.
Nor dare I question with my iealious thought,
VVhere you may be, or your affaires suppose,
But like a sad slaue stay and thinke of nought
Saue where you are, how happy you make those.
    So true a foole is loue, that in your Will,
    (Though you doe any thing) he thinkes no ill.

58

THat God forbid, that made me first your slaue,
    I should in thought controule your times of pleasure,
Or at your hand th' account of houres to craue,
Being your vassail bound to staie your leisure.
Oh let me suffer (being at your beck)
Th' imprison'd absence of your libertie,
And patience tame, to sufferance bide each check,
Without accusing you of iniury.
Be where you list, your charter is so strong,
That you your selfe may priuiledge your time
To what you will, to you it doth belong,
Your selfe to pardon of selfe-doing crime.
    I am to waite, though waiting so be hell,
    Not blame your pleasure be it ill or well.

59

IF their bee nothing new, but that which is,
    Hath beene before, how are our braines beguild,
Which laboring for inuention beare amisse
The second burthen of a former child?
Oh that record could with a back-ward looke,
Euen of fiue hundreth courses of the Sunne,
Show me your image in some antique booke,
Since minde at first in carrecter was done.
That I might see what the old world could say,
To this composed wonder of your frame,
Whether we are mended, or where better they,
Or whether reuolution be the same.
    Oh sure I am the wits of former daies,
    To subiects worse haue giuen admiring praise.

60

LIke as the waues make towards the pibled shore,
    So do our minuites hasten to their end,
Each changing place with that which goes before,
In sequent toile all forwards do contend.
Natiuity once in the maine of light.
Crawles to maturity, wherewith being crown'd,
Crooked eclipses gainst his glory fight,
And time that gaue, doth now his gift confound.
Time doth transfixe the florish set on youth,
And delues the paralels in beauties brow,
Feedes on the rarities of natures truth,
And nothing stands but for his sieth to mow.
    And yet to times in hope, my verse shall stand
    Praising thy worth, dispight his cruell hand.

61

IS it thy wil, thy Image should keepe open
My heauy eielids to the weary night?
Dost thou desire my slumbers should be broken,
While shadowes like to thee do mocke my sight?
Is it thy spirit that thou send'st from thee
So farre from home into my deeds to prye,
To find out shames and idle houres in me,
The skope and tenure of thy Ielousie?
O no, thy loue though much, is not so great,
It is my loue that keepes mine eie awake,
Mine owne true loue that doth my rest defeat,
To plaie the watch-man euer for thy sake.
      For thee watch I, whilst thou dost wake elsewhere,
      From me farre of, with others all to neere.

62

SInne of selfe-loue possesseth al mine eie,
And all my soule, and al my euery part;
And for this sinne there is no remedie,
It is so grounded inward in my heart.
Me thinkes no face so gratious is as mine,
No shape so true, no truth of such account,
And for my selfe mine owne worth do define,
As I all other in all worths surmount.
But when my glasse shewes me my selfe indeed
Beated and chopt with tand antiquitie,
Mint owne selfe loue quite contrary I read
Selfe, so selfe louing were iniquity,
      T'is thee (my selfe) that for my selfe I praise,
      Painting my age with beauty of thy daies,

63

AGainst my loue shall be as I am now
With times iniurious hand chrusht and ore-worne,
When houres haue dreind his blood and fild his brow
With lines and wrincles, when his youthfull morne
Hath trauaild on to Ages steepie night,
And all those beauties whereof now he's King
Are vanishing, or vanisht out of sight,
Stealing away the treasure of his Spring.
For such a time do I now fortifie
Against confounding Ages cruell knife,
That he shall neuer cut from memory
My sweet loues beauty, though my louers life.
      His beautie shall in these blacke lines be seene,
      And they shall liue, and he in them still greene.

64

VVHen I haue seene by times fell hand defaced
 The rich proud cost of outworne buried age,
When sometime loftie towers I see down rased,
And brasse eternall slaue to mortall rage.
When I haue seene the hungry Ocean gaine
Aduantage on the Kingdome of the shoare,
And the firme soile win of the watry maine,
Increasing store with losse, and losse with store.
When I haue seene such interchange of state,
Or state it selfe confounded, to decay,
Ruine hath taught me thus to ruminate
That Time will come and take my loue away.
  This thought is as a death which cannot choose
  But weepe to haue, that which it feares to loose.

65

SInce brasse, nor stone, nor earth, nor boundlesse sea,
 But sad mortallity ore-swaies their power,
How with this rage shall beautie hold a plea,
Whose action is no stronger then a flower?
O how shall summers hunny breath hold out,
Against the wrackfull siedge of battring dayes,
When rocks impregnable are not so stoute,
Nor gates of steele so strong but time decayes?
O fearefull meditation, where alack,
Shall times best Iewell from times chest lie hid?
Or what strong hand can hold his swift foote back,
Or who his spoile or beautie can forbid?
  O none, vnlesse this miracle haue might,
  That in black inck my loue may still shine bright.

66

TYr'd with all these for restfull death I cry,
 As to behold desert a begger borne,
And needie Nothing trimd in iollitie,
And purest faith vnhappily forsworne,
And gilded honor shamefully misplast,
And maiden vertue rudely strumpeted,
And right perfection wrongfully disgrac'd,
And strength by limping sway disabled,
And arte made tung-tide by authoritie,
And Folly (Doctor-like) controuling skill,
And simple-Truth miscalde Simplicitie,
And captiue-good attending Captaine ill.
  Tyr'd with all these, from these would I be gone,
  Saue that to dye, I leaue my loue alone.

67

AH wherefore with infection should he liue,
And with his presence grace impietie,
That sinne by him aduantage should atchiue,
And lace it selfe with his societie?
Why should false painting immitate his cheeke,
And steale dead seeing of his liuing hew?
Why should poore beautie indirectly seeke,
Roses of shaddow, since his Rose is true?
Why should he liue, now nature banckrout is,
Beggerd of blood to blush through liuely vaines,
For she hath no exchecker now but his,
And proud of many, liues vpon his gaines?
   O him she stores, to show what welth she had,
   In daies long since, before these last so bad.

68

THus is his cheeke the map of daies out-worne,
When beauty liu'd and dy'ed as flowers do now,
Before these bastard signes of faire were borne,
Or durst inhabit on a liuing brow:
Before the goulden tresses of the dead,
The right of sepulchers, were shorne away,
To liue a scond life on second head,
Ere beauties dead fleece made another gay:
In him those holy antique howers are seene,
Without all ornament, it selfe and true,
Making no summer of an others greene,
Robbing no ould to dresse his beauty new,
   And him as for a map doth Nature store,
   To shew faulse Art what beauty was of yore.

69

THose parts of thee that the worlds eye doth view,
Want nothing that the thought of hearts can mend:
All toungs (the voice of soules) giue thee that end,
Vttring bare truth, euen so as foes Commend.
Their outward thus with outward praise is crownd,
But those same toungs that giue thee so thine owne,
In other accents doe this praise confound
By seeing farther then the eye hath showne.
They looke into the beauty of thy mind,
And that in guesse they measure by thy deeds,
Then churls their thoughts (although their eies were kind)
To thy faire flower ad the rancke smell of weeds,
   But why thy odor matcheth not thy show,
   The solye is this, that thou doest common grow.

70

THat thou are blam'd shall not be thy defect,
For slanders marke was euer yet the faire,
The ornament of beauty is suspect,
A Crow that flies in heauens sweetest ayre.
So thou be good, slander doth but approue,
Their worth the greater beeing woo'd of time,
For Canker vice the sweetest buds doth loue,
And thou present'st a pure vnstayined prime.
Thou hast past by the ambush of young daies,
Either not assayld, or victor beeing charg'd,
Yet this thy praise cannot be soe thy praise,
To tye vp enuy, euermore inlarged,
    If some suspect of ill maskt not thy show,
    Then thou alone kingdomes of hearts shouldst owe.

71

NOe Longer mourne for me when I am dead,
Then you shall heare the surly sullen bell
Giue warning to the world that I am fled
From this vile world with vildest wormes to dwell:
Nay if you read this line, remember not,
The hand that writ it, for I loue you so,
That I in your sweet thoughts would be forgot,
If thinking on me then should make you woe.
O if (I say) you looke vpon this verse,
When I (perhaps) compounded am with clay,
Do not so much as my poore name reherse;
But let your loue euen with my life decay.
    Least the wise world should looke into your mone,
    And mocke you with me after I am gon.

72

OLeast the world should taske you to recite,
What merit liu'd in me that you should loue
After my death (deare loue) for get me quite,
For you in me can nothing worthy proue.
Vnlesse you would deuise some vertuous lye,
To doe more for me then mine owne desert,
And hang more praise vpon deceased I,
Then nigard truth would willingly impart:
O least your true loue may seeme falce in this,
That you for loue speake well of me vntrue,
My name be buried where my body is,
And liue no more to shame nor me, nor you.
    For I am shamd by that which I bring forth,
    And so should you, to loue things nothing worth.

73

THat time of yeeare thou maist in me behold,
When yellow leaues, or none, or few doe hange
Vpon those boughes which shake against the could,
Bare rn'wd quiers, where late the sweet birds sang.
In me thou seest the twi-light of such day,
As after Sun-set fadeth in the West,
Which by and by blacke night doth take away,
Deaths second selfe that seals vp all in rest.
In me thou seest the glowing of such fire,
That on the ashes of his youth doth lye,
As the death bed, whereon it must expire,
Consum'd with that which it was nurrisht by.
    This thou perceu'st, which makes thy loue more strong,
    To loue that well, which thou must leaue are long.

74

BVt be contented when that fell arest,
With out all bayle shall carry me away,
My life hath in this line some interest,
Which for memoriall still with thee shall stay.
When thou reuewest this, thou doest reuew,
The very part was consecrate to thee,
The earth can haue but earth, which is his due,
My spirit is thine the better part of me,
So then thou hast but lost the dregs of life,
The pray of wormes, my body being dead,
The coward conquest of a wretches knife,
To base of thee to be remembred,
    The worth of that, is that which it containes,
    And that is this, and this with thee remaines.

75

SO are you to my thoughts as food to life,
Or as sweet season'd shewers are to the ground;
And for the peace of you I hold such strife,
As twixt a miser and his wealth is found.
Now proud as an inioyer, and anon
Doubting the filching age will steale his treasure,
Now counting best to be with you alone,
Then betterd that the world may see my pleasure,
Some-time all ful with feasting on your sight,
And by and by cleane starued for a looke,
Possessing or pursuing no delight
Saue what is had, or must from you be tooke.
    Thus do I pine and surfet day by day,
    Or gluttoning on all, or all away,

76

VVHy is my verse so barren of new pride?
So far from variation or quicke change?
Why with the time do I not glance aside
To new found methods, and to compounds strange?
Why write I still all one, euer the same,
And keepe inuention in a noted weed,
That euery word doth almost fel my name,
Shewing their birth, and where they did proceed?
O know sweet loue I alwaies write of you,
And you and loue are still my argument:
So all my best is dressing old words new,
Spending againe what is already spent:
    For as the Sun is daily new and old,
    So is my loue still telling what is told,

77

THy glasse will shew thee how thy beauties were,
Thy dyall how thy pretious mynuits waste,
The vacant leaues thy mindes imprint will beare,
And of this booke, this learning maist thou taste.
The wrinckles which thy glasse will truly show,
Of mouthed graues will giue thee memorie,
Thou by thy dyals shady stealth maist know,
Times theeuish progresse to eternitie.
Looke what thy memorie cannot containe,
Commit to these waste blacks, and thou shalt finde
Those children nurst, deliuerd from thy braine,
To take a new acquaintance of thy minde.
    These offices, so oft as thou wilt looke,
    Shall profit thee, and much inrich thy booke.

78

SO oft haue I inuok'd thee for my Muse,
And found such faire assistance in my verse,
As euery *Alien* pen hath got my vse,
And vnder thee their poesie disperse.
Thine eyes, that taught the dumbe on high to sing,
And heauie ignorance aloft to flie,
Haue added fethers to the learneds wing,
And giuen grace a double Maiestie.
Yet be most proud of that which I compile,
Whose influence is thine, and borne of thee,
In others workes thou doost but mend the stile,
And Arts with thy sweete graces graced be.
    But thou art all my art, and doost aduance
    As high as learning, my rude ignorance.

79

WHilst I alone did call vpon thy ayde,
  My verse alone had all thy gentle grace,
But now my gracious numbers are decayde,
And my sick Muse doth giue an other place.
I grant (sweet loue) thy louely argument
Deserues the trauaile of a worthier pen,
Yet what of thee thy Poet doth inuent,
He robs thee of, and payes it thee againe,
He lends thee vertue, and he stole that word,
From thy behauiour, beautie doth he giue
And found it in thy cheeke: he can affoord
No praise to thee, but what in thee doth liue.
    Then thanke him not for that which he doth say,
    Since what he owes thee, thou thy selfe doost pay,

80

O How I faint when I of you do write,
  Knowing a better spirit doth vse your name,
And in the praise thereof spends all his might,
To make me toung-tide speaking of your fame.
But since your worth (wide as the Ocean is)
The humble as the proudest saile doth beare,
My sawsie barke (inferior farre to his)
On your broad maine doth wilfully appeare.
Your shallowest helpe will hold me vp a floate,
Whilst he vpon your soundlesse deepe doth ride,
Or (being wrackt) I am a worthlesse bote,
He of tall building, and of goodly pride.
    Then If he thriue and I be cast away,
    The worst was this, my loue was my decay.

81

OR I shall liue your Epitaph to make,
  Or you suruiue when I in earth am rotten,
From hence your memory death cannot take,
Although in me each part will be forgotten.
Your name from hence immortall life shall haue,
Though I (once gone) to all the world must dye,
The earth can yeeld me but a common graue,
When you intombed in mens eyes shall lye,
Your monument shall be my gentle verse,
Which eyes not yet created shall ore-read,
And toungs to be, your beeing shall rehearse,
When all the breathers of this world are dead,
    You still shall liue (such vertue hath my Pen)
    Where breath most breaths, euen in the mouths of men.

82

I Grant thou wert not married to my Muse,
And therefore maiest without attaint ore-looke
The dedicated words which writers vse
Of their faire subiect, blessing euery booke.
Thou art as faire in knowledge as in hew,
Finding thy worth a limmit past my praise,
And therefore art inforc'd to seeke anew,
Some fresher stampe of the time bettering dayes.
And do so loue, yet when they haue deuisde,
What strained touches Rhethorick can lend,
Thou truly faire, wert truly simpathizde,
In true plaine words, by thy true telling friend.
        And their grosse painting might be better vs'd,
        Where cheekes need blood, in thee it is abus'd.

83

I Neuer saw that you did painting need,
And therefore to your faire no painting set,
I found (or thought I found) you did exceed,
The barren tender of a Poets debt:
And therefore haue I slept in your report,
That you your selfe being extant well might show,
How farre a moderne quill doth come to short,
Speaking of worth, what worth in you doth grow,
This silence for my sinne you did impute,
Which shall be most my glory being dombe,
For I impaire not beautie being mute,
When others would giue life, and bring a tombe.
        There liues more life in one of your faire eyes,
        Then both your Poets can in praise deuise.

84

WHo is it that sayes most, which can say more,
Then this rich praise, that you alone, are you,
In whose confine immured is the store,
Which should example where your equall grew,
Leane penurie within that Pen doth dwell,
That to his subiect lends not some small glory,
But he that writes of you, if he can tell,
That you are you, so dignifies his story.
Let him but coppy what in you is writ,
Not making worse what nature made so cleere,
And such a counter-part shall fame his wit,
Making his stile admired euery where.
        You to your beautious blessings adde a curse,
        Being fond on praise, which makes your praises worse.

85

MY toung-tide Muse in manners holds her still,
  While comments of your praise richly compil'd,
Reserue their Character with goulden quill,
And precious phrase by all the Muses fil'd.
I thinke good thoughts, whilst other write good wordes,
And like vnlettered clarke still crie Amen,
To euery Himne that able spirit affords,
In polisht forme of well refined pen.
Hearing you praisd, I say 'tis so, 'tis true,
And to the most of praise adde some-thing more,
But that is in my thought, whose loue to you
(Though words come hind-most) holds his ranke before,
    Then others, for the breath of words respect,
    Me for my dombe thoughts, speaking in effect.

86

VVAs it the proud full saile of his great verse,
   Bound for the prize of (all to precious) you,
That did my ripe thoughts in my braine inhearce,
Making their tomb the wombe wherein they grew?
Was it his spirit, by spirits taught to write,
Aboue a mortall pitch, that struck me dead?
No, neither he, nor his compiers by night
Giuing him ayde, my verse astonished.
He nor that affable familiar ghost
Which nightly gulls him with intelligence,
As victors of my silence cannot boast,
I was not sick of any feare from thence.
    But when your countinance fild vp his line,
    Then lackt I matter, that infeebled mine.

87

FArewell thou art too deare for my possessing,
  And like enough thou knows thy estimate,
The Charter of thy worth giues thee releasing:
My bonds in thee are all determinate.
For how do I hold thee but by thy granting,
And for that ritches where is my deseruing?
Thy cause of this faire guift in me is wanting,
And so my pattent back againe is sweruing.
Thy selfe thou gau'st, thy owne worth then not knowing,
Or mee to whom thou gau'st it, else mistaking,
So thy great guift vpon misprision growing,
Comes home againe, on better iudgement making.
    Thus haue I had thee as a dreame doth flatter,
    In sleepe a King, but waking no such matter.

88

VVHen thou shalt be dispode to set me light,
And place my merrit in the eie of skorne,
Vpon thy side, against my selfe ile fight,
And proue thee virtuous, though thou art forsworne:
With mine owne weakenesse being best acquainted,
Vpon thy part I can set downe a story
Of faults conceald, wherein I am attainted:
That thou in loosing me shall win much glory:
And I by this wil be a gainer too,
For bending all my louing thoughts on thee,
The iniuries that to my selfe I doe,
Doing thee vantage, duble vantage me.
    Such is my loue, to thee I so belong,
    That for thy right, my selfe will beare all wrong.

89

SAy that thou didst forsake mee for some falt,
And I will comment vpon that offence,
Speake of my lamenesse, and I straight will halt:
Against thy reasons making no defence.
Thou canst not (loue) disgrace me halfe so ill,
To set a forme vpon desired change,
As ile my selfe disgrace, knowing thy wil,
I will acquaintance strangle and looke strange:
Be absent from thy walkes and in my tongue,
Thy sweet beloued name no more shall dwell,
Least I (too much prophane) should do it wronge:
And haplie of our old acquaintance tell.
    For thee, against my selfe ile vow debate,
    For I must nere loue him whom thou dost hate.

90

THen hate me when thou wilt, if euer, now,
Now while the world is bent my deeds to crosse,
Ioyne with the spight of fortune, make me bow,
And doe not drop in for an after losse;
Ah doe not, when my heart hath scapte this sorrow,
Come in the rereward of a conquerd woe,
Giue not a windy night a rainie morrow.
To linger out a purposd ouer-throw.
If thou wilt leaue me, do not leaue me last,
When other pettie griefes haue done their spight,
But in the onset come, so stall I taste
At first the very worst of fortunes might.
    And other straines of woe, which now seeme woe,
    Compar'd with losse of thee, will not seeme so.

91

SOme glory in their birth, some in their skill,
Some in their wealth, some in their bodies force,
Some in their garments though new-fangled ill:
Some in their Hawkes and Hounds, some in their Horse.
And euery humor hath his adiunct pleasure,
Wherein it findes a ioy aboue the rest,
But these perticulers are not my measure,
All these I better in one generall best.
Thy loue is bitter then high birth to me,
Richer then wealth, prouder then garments cost,
Of more delight then Hawkes or Horses bee:
And hauing thee, of all mens pride I boast.
　　Wretched in this alone, that thou maist take,
　　All this away, and me most wretched make.

92

BVt doe thy worst to steale thy selfe away,
For tearme of life thou art assured mine,
And life no longer then thy loue will stay,
For it depends vpon that loue of thine.
Then need I not to feare the worst of wrongs,
When in the least of them my life hath end,
I see, a better state to me belongs
Then that, which no thy humor doth depend.
Thou canst not vex me with inconstant minde,
Since that my life on thy reuolt doth lie,
Oh what a happy title do I finde,
Happy to haue thy loue, happy to die!
　　But whats so blessed faire that feares no blot,
　　Thou maist be falce, and yet I know it not.

93

SO shall I liue, supposing thou art true,
Like a deceiued husband, so loues face,
May still seeme loue to me, though alter'd new:
Thy lookes with me, thy heart in other place.
For their can liue no hatred in thine eye,
Therefore in that I cannot know thy change,
In manies lookes, the falce hearts history
Is writ in moods and frounes and wrinckles strange.
But heauen in thy creation did decree,
That in thy face sweet loue should euer dwell,
What ere thy thoughts, or thy hearts workings be,
Thy lookes should nothing thence, but sweetnesse tell.
　　How like *Eaues* apple doth thy beauty grow,
　　If thy sweet vertue answere not thy show.

94

THey that haue powre to hurt, and will doe none,
  That doe not do the thing, they most do showe,
Who mouing others, are themselues as stone,
Vnmooued, could, and to temptation slow:
They rightly do inherrit heauens graces,
And husband natures ritches from expence,
They are the Lords and owners of their faces,
Others, but stewards of their excellence:
The sommers flowre is to the sommer sweet,
Though to it selfe, it onely liue and die,
But if that flowre with base infection meete,
The basest weed out-braues his dignity:
    For sweetest things turne sowrest by their deedes,
    Lillies that fester, smell far worse then weeds.

95

HOw sweet and louely dost thou make the shame,
  Which like a canker in the fragrant Rose,
Doth spot the beautie of thy budding name?
Oh in what sweets doest thou thy sinnes inclose!
That tongue that tells the story of thy daies,
(Making lasciuious comments on thy sport)
Cannot dispraise, but in a kinde of praise,
Naming thy name, blesses an ill report.
Oh what a mansion haue those vices got,
Which for their habitation chose out thee,
Where beauties vaile doth couer euery blot,
And all things turnes to faire, that eies can see!
    Take heed (deare heart) of this large priuiledge,
    The hardest knife ill vs'd doth loose his edge.

96

SOme say thy fault is youth, some wantonesse,
  Some say thy grace is youth and gentle sport,
Both grace and faults are lou'd of more and lesse:
Thou makst faults graces, that to thee resort:
As on the finger of a throned Queene,
The basest Iewell wil be well esteem'd:
So are those errors that in thee are seene,
To truths translated, and for true things deem'd.
How many Lambs might the sterne Wolfe betray,
If like a Lambe he could his lookes translate.
How many gazers mighst thou lead away,
If thou wouldst vse the strength of all thy state?
    But doe not so, I loue thee in such sort,
    As thou being mine, mine is thy good report.

97

HOw like a Winter hath my absence beene
From thee, the pleasure of the fleeting yeare?
What freezings haue I felt, what darke daies seene?
What old Decembers barenesse euery where?
And yet this time remou'd was sommers time,
The teeming Autumne big with ritch increase,
Bearing the wanton burthen of the prime,
Like widdowed wombes after their Lords decease:
Yet this aboundant issue seem'd to me,
But hope of Orphans, and vn-fathered fruite,
For Sommer and his pleasures waite on thee,
And thou away, the very birds are mute.
    Or if they sing, tis with so dull a cheere,
      That leaues looke pale, dreading the Winters neere.

98

FRom you haue I beene absent in the spring,
When proud pide Aprill (drest in all his trim)
Hath put a spirit of youth in euery thing:
That heauie *Saturne* laught and leapt with him.
Yet nor the laies of birds, nor the sweet smell
Of different flowers in odor and in hew,
Could make me any summers story tell:
Or from their proud lap pluck them where they grew:
Nor did I wonder at the Lillies white,
Nor praise the deepe vermillion in the Rose,
They weare but sweet, but figures of delight:
Drawne after you, you patterne of all those.
    Yet seem'd it Winter still, and you away,
      As with your shaddow I with these did play.

99

THe forward violet thus did I chide,
Sweet theefe whence didst thou steale thy sweet that smels
If not from my loues breath, the purple pride,
Which on thy soft cheeke for complexion dwells?
In my loues veines thou hast too grosely died,
The Lillie I condemned for thy hand,
And buds of marierom had stolne thy haire,
The Roses fearefully on thornes did stand,
Our blushing shame, an other white dispaire:
A third nor red, nor white, had stolne of both,
And to his robbry had annext thy breath,
But for his theft in pride of all his growth
A vengfull canker eate him vp to death.
    More flowers I noted, yet I none could see,
      But sweet, or culler it had stolne from thee.

100

VVHere art thou Muse that thou forgetst so long,
  To speake of that which giues thee all thy might?
Spendst thou thy furie on some worthlesse songe,
Darkning thy powre to lend base subiects light.
Returne forgetfull Muse, and straight redeeme,
In gentle numbers time so idely spent,
Sing to the eare that doth thy laies esteeme,
And giues thy pen both skill and argument.
Rise resty Muse, my loues sweet face suruay,
If time haue any wrinkle grauen there,
If any, be a *Satire* to decay,
And make times spoiles dispised euery where.
  Giue my loue fame faster then time wasts life,
  So thou preuenst his sieth, and crooked knife.

101

OH truant Muse what shalbe thy amends,
  For thy neglect of truth in beauty di'd?
Both truth and beauty on my loue depends:
So dost thou too, and therein dignifi'd:
Make answere Muse, wilt thou not haply saie,
Truth needs no collour with his collour fixt,
Beautie no pensell, beauties truth to lay:
But best is best, if neuer intermixt.
Because he needs no praise, wilt thou be dumb?
Excuse not silence so, for't lies in thee,
To make him much out-liue a gilded tombe:
And to be praisd of ages yet to be.
  Then do thy office Muse, I teach thee how,
  To make him seeme long hence, as he showes now.

102

MY loue is strengthned though more weake in see-ming
  I loue not lesse, thogh lesse the show appeare,
That loue is marchandiz'd, whose ritch esteeming,
The owners tongue doth publish euery where.
Our loue was new, and then but in the spring,
When I was wont to greet it with my laies,
As *Philomell* in summers front doth singe,
And stops his pipe in growth of riper daies:
Not that the summer is lesse pleasant now
Then when her mournefull himns did hush the night,
But that wild musick burthens euery bow,
And sweets growne common loose their deare delight.
  Therefore like her, I some-time hold my tongue:
  Because I would not dull you with my songe.

103

A Lack what pouerty my Muse brings forth,
That hauing such a skope to show her pride,
The argument all bare is of more worth
Then when it hath my added praise beside.
Oh blame me not if I no more can write!
Looke in your glasse and there appeares a face,
That ouer-goes my blunt inuention quite,
Dulling my lines, and doing me disgrace.
Were it not sinfull then striuing to mend,
To marre the subiect that before was well,
For to no other passe my verses tend,
Then of your graces and your gifts to tell.
　　And more, much more then in my verse can sit,
　　Your owne glasse showes you, when you looke in it.

104

TO me faire friend you neuer can be old,
For as you were when first your eye I eyde,
Such seemes your beautie still: Three Winters colde,
Haue from the forrests shooke three summers pride,
Three beautious springs to yellow *Autumne* turn'd,
In processe of the seasons haue I seene,
Three Aprill perfumes in three hot Iunes burn'd,
Since first I saw you fresh which yet are greene.
Ah yet doth beauty like a Dyall hand,
Steale from his figure, and no pace perceiu'd,
So your sweete hew, which me thinkes still doth stand
Hath motion, and mine eye may be deceaued.
　　For feare of which, heare this thou age vnbred,
　　Ere you were borne was beauties summer dead.

105

L Et not my loue be cal'd Idolatrie,
Nor my beloued as an Idoll show,
Since all alike my songs and praises be
To one, of one, still such, and euer so.
Kinde is my loue to day, to morrow kinde,
Still constant in a wondrous excellence,
Therefore my verse to constancie confin'de,
One thing expressing, leaues out difference.
Faire, kinde, and true, is all my argument,
Faire, kinde and true, varrying to other words,
And in this change is my inuention spent,
Three theams in one, which wondrous scope affords.
　　Faire, kinde, and true, haue often liu'd alone.
　　Which three till now, neuer kept seate in one.

106

WHen in the Chronicle of wasted time,
    I see discriptions of the fairest wights,
And beautie making beautifull old rime,
In praise of Ladies dead, and louely Knights,
Then in the blazon of sweet beauties best,
Of hand, of foote, of lip, of eye, of brow,
I see their antique Pen would haue exprest,
Euen such a beauty as you maister now.
So all their praises are but prophesies
Of this our time, all you prefiguring,
And for they look'd but with deuining eyes,
They had not still enough your worth to sing:
    For we which now behold these present dayes,
    Haue eyes to wonder, but lack toungs to praise.

107

NOt mine owne feares, nor the prophetick soule,
    Of the wide world, dreaming on things to come,
Can yet the lease of my true loue controule,
Supposde as forfeit to a confin'd doome.
The mortall Moone hath her eclipse indur'de,
And the sad Augurs mock their owne presage,
Incertenties now crowne them-selues assur'de,
And peace proclaimes Oliues of endlesse age,
Now with the drops of this most balmie time,
My loue lookes fresh, and death to me subscribes,
Since spight of him Ile liue in this poore rime,
While he insults ore dull and speachlesse tribes.
    And thou in this shalt finde thy monument,
    When tyrants crests and tombs of brasse are spent.

108

VVHat's in the braine that Inck may character,
    Which hath not figur'd to thee my true spirit,
What's new to speake, what now to register,
That may expresse my loue, or thy deare merit?
Nothing sweet boy, but yet like prayers diuine,
I must each day say ore the very same,
Counting no old thing old, thou mine, I thine,
Euen as when first I hallowed thy faire name.
So that eternall loue in loues fresh case,
Waighes not the dust and iniury of age,
Nor giues to necessary wrinckles place,
But makes antiquitie for aye his page,
    Finding the first conceit of loue there bred,
    Where time and outward forme would shew it dead,

109

O Neuer say that I was false of heart,
  Though absence seem'd my flame to quallifie,
As easie might I from my selfe depart,
As from my soule which in thy brest doth lye:
That is my home of loue, if I haue rang'd,
Like him that trauels I returne againe,
Iust to the time, not with the time exchang'd,
So that my selfe bring water for my staine,
Neuer beleeue though in my nature raign'd,
All frailties that besiege all kindes of blood,
That it could so preposterouslie be stain'd,
To leaue for nothing all thy summe of good:
    For nothing this wide Vniuerse I call,
    Saue thou my Rose, in it thou art my all.

110

A Las 'tis true, I haue gone here and there,
  And made my selfe a motley to the view,
Gor'd mine own thoughts, sold cheap what is most deare,
Made old offences of affections new.
Most true it is, that I haue lookt on truth
Asconce and strangely: But by all aboue,
These blenches gaue my heart an other youth,
And worse essaies prou'd thee my best of loue,
Now all is done, haue what shall haue no end,
Mine appetite I neuer more will grin'de
On newer proofe, to trie an older friend,
A God in loue, to whom I am confin'd.
    Then giue me welcome, next my heauen the best,
    Euen to thy pure and most most louing brest.

111

O For my sake doe you with fortune chide,
  The guiltie goddesse of my harmfull deeds,
That did not better for my life prouide,
Then publick meanes which publick manners breeds.
Thence comes it that my name receiues a brand,
And almost thence my nature is subdu'd
To what it workes in, like the Dyers hand,
Pitty me then, and wish I were renu'de,
Whilst like a willing pacient I will drinke,
Potions of Eysell gainst my strong infection,
No bitternesse that I will bitter thinke,
Nor double pennance to correct correction.
    Pittie me then deare friend, and I assure yee,
    Euen that your pittie is enough to cure mee.

112

YOur loue and pittie both th'impression fill,
  Which vulgar scandall stampt vpon my brow,
For what care I who calles me well or ill,
So you ore-greene my bad, my good alow?
You are my All the world, and I must striue,
To know my shames and praises from your tounge,
None else to me, nor I to none aliue,
That my steel'd sence or changes right or wrong,
In so profound *Abisme* I throw all care
Of others voyces, that my Adders sence,
To cryttick and to flatterer stopped are:
Marke how with my neglect I doe dispence.
    You are so strongly in my purpose bred,
    That all the world besides me thinkes y'are dead.

113

SInce I left you, mine eye is in my minde,
  And that which gouernes me to goe about,
Doth part his function, and is partly blind,
Seemes seeing, but effectually is out:
For it no forme deliuers to the heart
Of bird, of flowre, or shape which it doth lack,
Of his quick obiects hath the minde no part,
Nor his owne vision houlds what it doth catch:
For if it see the rud'st or gentlest sight,
The most sweet-fauor or deformedst creature,
The mountaine, or the sea, the day, or night:
The Croe, or Doue, it shapes them to your feature.
    Incapable of more repleat, with you,
    My most true minde thus maketh mine vntrue.

114

OR whether doth my minde being crown'd with you
  Drinke vp the monarks plague this flattery?
Or whether shall I say mine eie saith true,
And that your loue taught it this *Alcumie?*
To make of monsters, and things indigest,
Such cherubines as your sweet selfe resemble,
Creating euery bad a perfect best
As fast as obiects to his beames assemble:
Oh tis the first, tis flatry in my seeing,
And my great minde most kingly drinkes it vp,
Mine eie well knowes what with his gust is greeing,
And to his pallat doth prepare the cup.
    If it be poison'd, tis the lesser sinne,
    That mine eye loues it and doth first beginne.

115

THose lines that I before haue writ doe lie,
　Euen those that said I could not loue you deerer,
Yet then my iudgement knew no reason why,
My most full flame should afterwards burne cleerer.
But reckening time, whose milliond accidents
Creepe in twixt vowes, and change decrees of Kings,
Tan sacred beautie, blunt the sharp'st intents,
Diuert strong mindes to th' course of altring things:
Alas why fearing of times tiranie,
Might I not then say now I loue you best,
When I was certaine ore in-certainty,
Crowning the present, doubting of the rest:
　　Loue is a Babe, then might I not say so
　　To giue full growth to that which still doth grow.

116

LEt me not to the marriage of true mindes
　Admit impediments, loue is not loue
Which alters when it alteration findes,
Or bends with the remouer to remoue.
O no, it is an euer fixed marke
That lookes on tempests and is neuer shaken;
It is the star to euery wandring barke,
Whose worths vnknowne, although his higth be taken.
Lou's not Times foole, though rosie lips and cheeks
Within his bending sickles compasse come,
Loue alters not with his breefe houres and weekes,
But beares it out euen to the edge of doome:
　　If this be error and vpon me proued,
　　I neuer writ, nor no man euer loued.

117

ACcuse me thus, that I haue scanted all,
　Wherein I should your great deserts repay,
Forgot vpon your dearest loue to call,
Whereto al bonds do tie me day by day,
That I haue frequent binne with vnknown mindes,
And giuen to time your owne deare purchas'd right,
That I haue hoysted saile to al the windes
Which should transport me farthest from your sight.
Booke both my wilfulnesse and errors downe,
And on iust proofe surmise, accumilate,
Bring me within the leuel of your frowne,
But shoote not at me in your wakened hate:
　　Since my appeale saies I did striue to prooue
　　The constancy and virtue of your loue

118

Ike as to make our appetites more keene
With eager compounds we our pallat vrge,
As to preuent our malladies vnseene,
We sicken to shun sicknesse when we purge.
Euen so being full of your nere cloying sweetnesse,
To bitter sawces did I frame my feeding;
And sicke of wel-fare found a kind of meetnesse,
To be diseas'd ere that there was true needing.
Thus pollicie in loue t'anticipate
The ills that were, not grew to faults assured,
And brought to medicine a healthfull state
Which rancke of goodnesse would by ill be cured.
But thence I learne and find the lesson true,
Drugs poyson him that so fell sicke of you.

119

What potions haue I drunke of *Syren* teares
Distil'd from Lymbecks foule as hell within,
Applying feares to hopes, and hopes to feares,
Still loosing when I saw my selfe to win?
What wretched errors hath my heart committed,
Whilst it hath thought it selfe so blessed neuer?
How haue mine eies out of their Spheares bene fitted
In the distraction of this madding feuer?
O benefit of ill, now I finde true
That better is, by euil still made better.
And ruin'd loue when it is built anew
Growes fairer then at first, more strong, far greater.
So I returne rebukt to my content,
And gaine by ills thrise more then I haue spent.

120

That you were once vnkind be-friends mee now,
And for that sorrow, which I then didde feele,
Needes must I vnder my transgression bow,
Vnlesse my Nerues were brasse or hammered steele.
For if you were by my vnkindnesse shaken
As I by yours, y'haue past a hell of Time,
And I a tyrant haue no leasure taken
To waigh how once I suffered in your crime.
O that our night of wo might haue remembred
My deepest sence, how hard true sorrow hits,
And soone to you, as you to me then tendred
The humble salue, which wounded bosomes fits!
But that your trespasse now becomes a fee,
Mine ransoms yours, and yours must ransome mee.

121

TIS better to be vile then vile esteemed,
When not to be, receiues reproach of being,
And the iust pleasure lost, which is so deemed,
Not by our feeling, but by others seeing.
For why should others false adulterat eyes
Giue saluation to my sportiue blood?
Or on my frailties why are frailer spies;
Which in their wils count bad what I think good?
Noe, I am that I am, and they that leuell
At my abuses, reckon vp their owne,
I may be straight though they them-selues be beuel
By their rancke thoughtes, my deedes must not be shown
Vnlesse this generall euill they maintaine,
All men are bad and in their badnesse raigne.

122

T Thy guift, thy tables, are within my braine
Full characterd with lasting memory,
Which shall aboue that idle rancke remaine
Beyond all date euen to eternity.
Or at the least, so long as braine and heart
Haue facultie by nature to subsist,
Til each to raz'd obliuion yeeld his part
Of thee, thy record neuer can be mist:
That poore retention could not so much hold,
Nor need I tallies thy deare loue to skore,
Therefore to giue them from me was I bold,
To trust those tables that receaue thee more,
To keepe an adiunckt to remember thee,
Were to import forgetfulnesse in mee.

123

NO! Time, thou shalt not bost that I doe change,
Thy pyramyds buylt vp with newer might
To me are nothing nouell, nothing strange,
They are but dressings of a former sight:
Our dates are breefe, and therefor we admire,
What thou dost foyst vpon vs that is ould,
And rather make them borne to our desire,
Then thinke that we before haue heard them tould:
Thy registers and thee I both defie,
Not wondring at the present, nor the past,
For thy records, and what we see doth lye,
Made more or les by thy continuall hast:
This I doe vow and this shall euer be,
I will be true dispight thy syeth and thee.

124

Y F my deare loue were but the childe of state,
It might for fortunes basterd be vnfathered,
As subiect to times loue, or to times hate,
Weeds among weeds, or flowers with flowers gatherd.
No it was buylded far from accident,
It suffers not in smilinge pomp, nor falls
Vnder the blow of thralled discontent,
Whereto th'inuiting time our fashion calls:
It feares not policy that *Heriticke*,
Which workes on leases of short numbred howers,
But all alone stands hugely pollitick,
That it nor growes with heat, nor drownes with showres.
  To this I witnes call the foles of time,
  Which die for goodnes, who haue liu'd for crime.

125

VV Er't ought to me I bore the canopy,
With my extern the outward honoring,
Or layd great bases for eternity,
Which proues more short then wast or ruining?
Haue I not seene dwellers on forme and fauor
Lose all, and more by paying too much rent
For compound sweet; Forgoing simple sauor,
Pittifull thriuors in their gazing spent.
Noe, let me be obsequious in thy heart,
And take thou my oblacion, poore but free,
Which is not mixt with seconds, knows no art,
But mutuall render, onely me for thee.
  Hence, thou subbornd *Informer*, a trew soule
  When most impeacht, stands least in thy controule.

126

O Thou my louely Boy who in thy power,
Doest hould times fickle glasse, his fickle, hower:
Who hast by wayning growne, and therein shou'st,
Thy louers withering, as thy sweet selfe grow'st.
If Nature (soueraine misteres ouer wrack)
As thou goest onwards still will plucke thee backe,
She keepes thee to this purpose, that her skill.
May time disgrace, and wretched mynuit kill.
Yet feare her O thou minnion of her pleasure,
She may detaine, but not still keepe her tresure!
Her *Audite* (though delayd) answer'd must be,
And her *Quietus* is to render thee.
  (   )
  (   )

127

IN the ould age blacke was not counted faire,
Or if it weare it bore not beauties name:
But now is blacke beauties successiue heire,
And Beautie slanderd with a bastard shame,
For since each hand hath put on Natures power,
Fairing the foule with Arts faulse borrow'd face,
Sweet beauty hath no name no holy boure,
But is prophan'd, if not liues in disgrace.
Therefore my Mistresse eyes are Rauen blacke,
Her eyes so suted, and they mourners seeme,
At such who not borne faire no beauty lack,
Slandring Creation with a false esteeme,
　　Yet so they mourne becomming of their woe,
　　That euery toung saies beauty should looke so.

128

HOw oft when thou my musike musike playst,
Vpon that blessed wood whose motion sounds
With thy sweet fingers when thou gently swayst,
The wiry concord that mine eare confounds,
Do I enuie those Iackes that nimble leape,
To kisse the tender inward of thy hand,
Whilst my poore lips which should that haruest reape,
At the woods bouldnes by thee blushing stand.
To be so tikled they would change their state,
And situation with those dancing chips,
Ore whome their fingers walke with gentle gate,
Making dead wood more blest then liuing lips,
　　Since sausie Iackes so happy are in this,
　　Giue them their fingers, me thy lips to kisse.

129

TH'expence of Spirit in a waste of shame
Is lust in action, and till action, lust
Is periurd, murdrous, blouddy full of blame,
Sauage, extreame, rude, cruell, not to trust,
Inioyd no sooner but dispised straight,
Past reason hunted, and no sooner had
Past reason hated as a swollowed bayt,
On purpose layd to make the taker mad.
Made In pursut and in possession so,
Had, hauing, and in quest, to haue extreame,
A blisse in proofe and proud and very wo,
Before a ioy proposd behind a dreame,
　　All this the world well knowes yet none knowes well,
　　To shun the heauen that leads men to this hell.

130

MY Mistres eyes are nothing like the Sunne,
Currall is farre more red, then her lips red,
If snow be white, why then her brests are dun:
If haires be wiers, black wiers grow on her head:
I haue seene Roses damaskt, red and white,
But no such Roses see I in her cheekes,
And in some perfumes is there more delight,
Then in the breath that from my Mistres reekes.
I loue to heare her speake, yet well I know,
That Musicke hath a farre more pleasing sound:
I graunt I neuer saw a goddesse goe,
My Mistres when shee walkes treads on the ground.
  And yet by heauen I thinke my loue as rare,
  As any she beli'd with false compare.

131

THou art as tiranous, so as thou art,
As those whose beauties proudly make them cruell;
For well thou know'st to my deare doting hart
Thou art the fairest and most precious Iewell.
Yet in good faith some say that thee behold,
Thy face hath not the power to make loue grone;
To say they erre, I dare not be so bold,
Although I sweare it to my selfe alone.
And to be sure that is not false I sweare
A thousand grones but thinking on thy face,
One on anothers necke do witnesse beare
Thy blacke is fairest in my iudgements place.
  In nothing art thou blacke saue in thy deeds,
  And thence this slaunder as I thinke proceeds.

132

THine eies I loue, and they as pittying me,
Knowing thy heart torment me with disdaine,
Haue put on black, and louing mourners bee,
Looking with pretty ruth vpon my paine.
And truly not the morning Sun of Heauen
Better becomes the gray cheeks of th'East,
Nor that full Starre that vshers in the Eauen
Doth halfe that glory to the sober West
As those two morning eyes become thy face:
O let it then as well beseeme thy heart
To mourne for me since mourning doth thee grace,
And sute thy pitty like in euery part.
  Then will I sweare beauty her selfe is blacke,
  And all they foule that thy complexion lacke.

133

BEshrew that heart that makes my heart to groane
For that deepe wound it giues my friend and me;
I'st not ynough to torture me alone,
But slaue to slauery my sweet'st friend must be.
Me from my selfe thy cruell eye hath taken,
And my next selfe thou harder hast ingrossed,
Of him, my selfe, and thee I am forsaken,
A torment thrice three-fold thus to be crossed:
Prison my heart in thy steele bosomes warde,
But then my friends heart let my poore heart bale,
Who ere keepes me, let my heart be his garde,
Thou canst not then vse rigor in my Iaile.
    And yet thou wilt, for I being pent in thee,
    Perforce am thine and all that is in me.

134

SO now I haue confest that he is thine,
And I my selfe am morgag'd to thy will,
My selfe Ile forfeit, so that other mine,
Thou wilt restore to be my comfort still:
But thou wilt not, nor he will not be free,
For thou art couetous, and he is kinde,
He learnd but suretie-like to write for me,
Vnder that bond that him as fast doth binde.
The statute of thy beauty thou wilt take,
Thou vsurer that put'st forth all to vse,
And sue a friend, came debter for my sake,
So him I loose through my vnkinde abuse.
    Him haue I lost, thou hast both him and me,
    He paies the whole, and yet am I not free.

135

WHo euer hath her wish, thou hast thy *Will*,
And *Will* too boote, and *Will* in ouer-plus,
More then enough am I that vexe thee still,
To thy sweet will making addition thus.
Wilt thou whose will is large and spatious,
Not once vouchsafe to hide my will in thine,
Shall will in others seeme right gracious,
And in my will no faire acceptance shine:
The sea all water, yet receiues raine still,
And in aboundance addeth to his store,
So thou beeing rich in *Will* adde to thy *Will*,
One will of mine to make thy large *Will* more.
    Let no vnkinde, no faire beseechers kill,
    Thinke all but one, and me in that one *Will*.

136

IF thy soule check thee that I come so neere,
Sweare to thy blind soule that I was thy *Will*,
And will thy soule knowes is admitted there,
Thus farre for loue, my loue-sute sweet fullfill.
Will, will fulfill the treasure of thy loue,
I fill it full with wils, and my will one,
In things of great receit with ease we prooue.
Among a number one is reckon'd none.
Then in the number let me passe vntold,
Though in thy stores account I one must be,
For nothing hold me, so it please thee hold,
That nothing me, a some-thing sweet to thee.
    Make but my name thy loue, and loue that still,
    And then thou louest me for my name is *Will*.

137

THou blinde foole loue, what doost thou to mine eyes,
That they behold and see not what they see:
They know what beautie is, see where it lyes,
Yet what the best is, take the worst to be.
If eyes corrupt by ouer-partiall lookes,
Be anchord in the baye where all men ride,
Why of eyes falsehood hast thou forged hookes,
Whereto the iudgement of my heart is tide?
Why should my heart thinke that a seuerall plot,
Which my heart knowes the wide worlds common place?
Or mine eyes seeing this, say this is not
To put faire truth vpon so foule a face,
    In things right true my heart and eyes haue erred,
    And to this false plague are they now transferred.

138

WHen my loue sweares that she is made of truth,
I do beleeue her though I know she lyes,
That she might thinke me some vntuterd youth,
Vnlearned in the worlds false subtilties.
Thus vainely thinking that she thinkes me young,
Although she knowes my dayes are past the best,
Simply I credit her false speaking tongue,
On both sides thus is simple truth supprest:
But wherefore sayes she not she is vniust?
And wherefore say not I that I am old?
O loues best habit is in seeming trust,
And age in loue, loues not t'haue yeares told.
    Therefore I lye with her, and she with me,
    And in our faults by lyes we flattered be.

139

O Call not me to iustifie the wrong,
  That thy vnkindnesse layes vpon my heart,
Wound me not with thine eye but with thy toung,
Vse power with power, and slay me not by Art,
Tell me thou lou'st else-where; but in my sight,
Deare heart forbeare to glance thine eye aside,
What needst thou wound with cunning when thy might
Is more then my ore-prest defence can bide?
Let me excuse thee, ah my loue well knowes,
Her prettie lookes haue beene mine enemies,
And therefore from my face she turnes my foes,
That they else-where might dart their iniuries:
    Yet do not so, but since I am neere slaine,
    Kill me out-right with lookes, and rid my paine.

140

B E wise as thou art cruell, do not presse
  My toung-tide patience with too much disdaine:
Least sorrow lend me words and words expresse,
The manner of my pittie wanting paine.
If I might teach thee witte better it weare,
Though not to loue, yet loue to tell me so,
As testie sick-men when their deaths be neere,
No newes but health from their Phisitions know.
For if I should dispaire I should grow madde,
And in my madnesse might speake ill of thee,
Now this ill wresting world is growne so bad,
Madde slanderers by madde eares beleeued be.
    That I may not be so, nor thou be lyde,
    Beare thine eyes straight, though thy proud heart goe wide.

141

I N faith I doe not loue thee with mine eyes,
  For they in thee a thousand errors note,
But 'tis my heart that loues what they dispise,
Who in dispight of view is pleasd to dote.
Nor are mine eares with thy toungs tune delighted,
Nor tender feeling to base touches prone,
Nor taste, nor smell, desire to be inuited
To any sensuall feast with thee alone:
But my fiue wits, nor my fiue sences can
Diswade one foolish heart from seruing thee,
Who leaues vnswai'd the likenesse of a man,
Thy proud hearts slaue and vassall wretch to be:
    Onely my plague thus farre I count my gaine,
    That she that makes me sinne, awards me paine.

142

LOue is my sinne, and thy deare vertue hate,
Hate of my sinne, grounded on sinfull louing,
O but with mine, compare thou thine owne state,
And thou shalt finde it merrits not reproouing,
Or if it do, not from those lips of thine,
That haue prophan'd their scarlet ornaments,
And seald false bonds of loue as oft as mine,
Robd others beds reuenues of their rents.
Be it lawfull I loue thee as thou lou'st those,
Whome thine eyes wooe as mine importune thee,
Roote pittie in thy heart that when it growes,
Thy pitty may deserue to pittied bee.
   If thou doost seeke to haue what thou doost hide,
   By selfe example mai'st thou be denide.

143

LOe as a carefull huswife runnes to catch,
One of her fethered creatures broake away,
Sets downe her babe and makes all swift dispatch
In pursuit of the thing she would haue stay:
Whilst her neglected child holds her in chace,
Cries to catch her whose busie care is bent,
To follow that which flies before her face:
Not prizing her poore infants discontent;
So runst thou after that which flies from thee,
Whilst I thy babe chace thee a farre behind,
But if thou catch thy hope turne back to me:
And play the mothers part kisse me, be kind.
   So will I pray that thou maist haue thy *Will*,
   If thou turne back and my loude crying still.

144

TWo loues I haue of comfort and dispaire,
Which like two spirits do sugiest me still,
The better angell is a man right faire:
The worser spirit a woman collour'd il.
To win me soone to hell my femall euill,
Tempteth my better angel from my sight,
And would corrupt my saint to be a diuel:
Wooing his purity with her fowle pride.
And whether that my angel be turn'd finde,
Suspect I may, yet not directly tell,
But being both from me both to each friend,
I gesse one angel in an others hel.
   Yet this shal I nere know but liue in doubt,
   Till my bad angel fire my good one out.

145

THose lips that Loues owne hand did make,
     Breath'd forth the sound that said I hate,
To me that languisht for her sake:
But when she saw my wofull state,
Straight in her heart did mercie come,
Chiding that tongue that euer sweet,
Was vsde in giuing gentle dome:
And tought it thus a new to greete:
I hate she alterd with an end,
That follow'd it as gentle day,
Doth follow night who like a fiend
From heauen to hell is flowne away.
     I hate, from hate away she threw,
     And sau'd my life saying not you.

146

POore soule the center of my sinfull earth,
     My sinfull earth these rebbell powres that thee array,
Why dost thou pine within and suffer dearth
Painting thy outward walls so costlie gay?
Why so large cost hauing so short a lease,
Dost thou vpon thy fading mansion spend?
Shall wormes inheritors of this excesse
Eate vp thy charge? is this thy bodies end?
Then soule liue thou vpon thy seruants losse,
And let that pine to aggrauat thy store;
Buy tearmes diuine in selling houres of drosse:
Within be fed, without be rich no more,
     So shalt thou feed on death, that feeds on men,
     And death once dead, ther's no more dying then.

147

MY loue is as a feauer longing still,
     For that which longer nurseth the disease,
Feeding on that which doth preserue the ill,
Th'vncertaine sicklie appetite to please:
My reason the Phisition to my loue,
Angry that his prescriptions are not kept
Hath left me, and I desperate now approoue,
Desire is death, which Phisick did except.
Past cure I am, now Reason is past care,
And frantick madde with euer-more vnrest,
My thoughts and my discourse as mad mens are,
At randon from the truth vainely exprest.
     For I haue sworne thee faire, and thought thee bright,
     Who art as black as hell, as darke as night.

148

OMe! what eyes hath loue put in my head,
  Which haue no correspondence with true sight,
Or if they haue, where is my iudgment fled,
That censures falsely what they see aright?
If that be faire whereon my false eyes dote,
What meanes the world to say it is not so?
If it be not, then loue doth well denote,
Loues eye is not so true as all mens: no,
How can it? O how can loues eye be true,
That is so vext with watching and with teares?
No maruaile then though I mistake my view,
The sunne it selfe sees not, till heauen cleeres.
  O cunning loue, with teares thou keepst me blinde,
  Least eyes well seeing thy foule faults should finde.

149

CAnst thou O cruell, say I loue thee not,
  When I against my selfe with thee pertake:
Doe I not thinke on thee when I forgot
Am of my selfe, all tirant for thy sake?
Who hateth thee that I doe call my friend,
On whom froun'st thou that I doe faune vpon,
Nay if thou lowrst on me doe I not spend
Reuenge vpon my selfe with present mone?
What merrit do I in my selfe respect,
That is so proude thy seruice to dispise,
When all my best doth worship thy defect,
Commanded by the motion of thine eyes.
  But loue hate on for now I know thy minde,
  Those that can see thou lou'st, and I am blind.

150

OH from what powre hast thou this powrefull might,
  VVith insufficiency my heart to sway,
To make me giue the lie to my true sight,
And swere that brightnesse doth not grace the day?
Whence hast thou this becomming of things il,
That in the very refuse of thy deeds,
There is such strength and warrantise of skill,
That in my minde thy worst all best exceeds?
Who taught thee how to make me loue thee more,
The more I heare and see iust cause of hate,
Oh though I loue what others doe abhor,
VVith others thou shouldst not abhor my state.
  If thy vnworthinesse raisd loue in me,
  More worthy I to be belou'd of thee.

151

LOue is too young to know what conscience is,
Yet who knowes not conscience is borne of loue,
Then gentle cheater vrge not my amisse,
Least guilty of my faults thy sweet selfe proue.
For thou betraying me, I doe betray
My nobler part to my grose bodies treason,
My soule doth tell my body that he may,
Triumph in loue, flesh staies no farther reason.
But rysing at thy name doth point out thee,
As his triumphant prize, proud of this pride,
He is contented thy poore drudge to be
To stand in thy affaires, fall by thy side.
    No want of conscience hold it that I call,
    Her loue, for whose deare loue I rise and fall.

152

IN louing thee thou know'st I am forsworne,
But thou art twice forsworne to me loue swearing,
In act thy bed-vow broake and new faith torne,
In vowing new hate after new loue bearing:
But why of two othes breach doe I accuse thee,
When I breake twenty: I am periur'd most,
For all my vowes are othes but to misuse thee:
And all my honest faith in thee is lost
For I haue sworne deepe othes of thy deepe kindnesse:
Othes of thy loue, thy truth, thy constancie,
And to inlighten thee gaue eyes to blindnesse,
Or made them swere against the thing they see.
    For I haue sworne thee faire: more periurde eye,
    To swere against the truth fo foule a lie.

153

CVpid laid by his brand and fell a sleepe,
A maide of *Dyans* this aduantage found,
And his loue-kindling fire did quickly steepe
In a could vallie-fountaine of that ground:
Which borrowd from this holie fire of loue,
A datelesse liuely heat still to indure,
And grew a seething bath which yet men proue,
Against strange malladies a soueraigne cure:
But at my mistres eie loues brand new fired,
The boy for triall needes would touch my brest,
I sick withall the helpe of bath desired,
And thether hied a sad distemperd guest.
    But found no cure, the bath for my helpe lies,
    Where *Cupid* got new fire; my mistres eye.

154

THe little Loue-God lying once a sleepe,
　　Laid by his side his heart inflaming brand,
Whilst many Nymphes that vou'd chast life to keep,
Came tripping by, but in her maiden hand,
The fayrest votary tooke vp that fire,
Which many Legions of true hearts had warm'd,
And so the Generall of hot desire,
Was sleeping by a Virgin hand disarm'd.
This brand she quenched in a coole Well by,
Which from loues fire tooke heat perpetuall,
Growing a bath and healthfull remedy,
For men diseasd, but I my Mistrisse thrall,
　　Came there for cure and this by that I proue,
　　Loues fire heates water, water cooles not loue.

⌈FINIS.⌉

A L o u e r s C o m p l a i n t.
BY

W i l l i a m S h a k e - s p e a r e.

FRom off a hill whose concaue wombe reworded,
A plaintfull story from a sistring vale
My spirrits t'attend this doble voyce accorded,
And downe I laid to list the sad tun'd tale,
Ere long espied a fickle maid full pale
Tearing of papers breaking rings a twaine,
Storming her world with sorrowes, wind and raine.

Vpon her head a plattid hiue of straw,
Which fortified her visage from the Sunne,
Whereon the thought might thinke sometime it saw
The carkas of a beauty spent and donne,
Time had not sithed all that youth begun,
Nor youth all quit, but spight of heauens fell rage,
Some beauty peept, through lettice of sear'd age.

Oft did she heaue her Napkin to her eyne,
Which on it had conceited charecters:
Laundring the silken figures in the brine,
That seasoned woe had pelleted in teares,
And often reading what contents it beares:
As often shriking vndistinguisht wo,
In clamours of all size both high and low.

Some-times her leueld eyes their carriage ride,
As they did battry to the spheres intend:
Sometime diuerted their poore balls are tide,
To th'orbed earth; sometimes they do extend,
Their view right on, anon their gases lend,
To euery place at once and no where fixt,
The mind and sight distractedly commixt.

Her haire nor loose nor ti'd in formall plat,
Proclaimd in her a carelesse hand of pride;
For some vntuck'd descended her sheu'd hat,
Hanging her pale and pined cheeke beside,
Some in her threeden fillet still did bide,
And trew to bondage would not breake from thence,
Though slackly braided in loose negligence.

A thousand fauours from a maund she drew,
Of amber christall and of bedded Iet,
Which one by one she in a riuer threw,
Vpon whose weeping margent she was set,
Like vsery applying wet to wet,
Or Monarches hands that lets not bounty fall,
Where want cries some; but where excesse begs all.

Of folded schedulls had she many a one,
Which she perus'd, sighd, tore and gaue the flud,
Crackt many a ring of Posied gold and bone,
Bidding them find their Sepulchers in mud,
Found yet mo letters sadly pend in blood,
With sleided silke, feate and affectedly
Enswath'd and seald to curious secrecy.

These often bath'd she in her fluxiue eies,
And often kist, and often gaue to teare,
Cried O false blood thou register of lies,
What vnapproued witnes doost thou beare!
Inke would haue seem'd more blacke and damned heare!
This said in top of rage the lines she rents,
Big discontent, so breaking their contents.

A reuerend man that graz'd his catell ny,
Sometime a blusterer that the ruffle knew
Of Court of Cittie, and had let go by
The swiftest houres obserued as they flew,
Towards this afflicted fancy fastly drew:
And priuiledg'd by age desires to know
In breefe the grounds and motiues of her wo.

So slides he downe vppon his greyned bat;
And comely distant sits he by her side,
When hee againe desires her, being satte,
Her greeuance with his hearing to deuide:
If that from him there may be ought applied
Which may her suffering extasie asswage
Tis promist in the charitie of age.

Father she saies, though in mee you behold
The iniury of many a blasting houre;
Let it not tell your Iudgement I am old,
Not age, but sorrow, ouer me hath power;
I might as yet haue bene a spreading flower
Fresh to my selfe, if I had selfe applyed
Loue to my selfe, and to no Loue beside.

But wo is mee, too early I attended
A youthfull suit, it was to gaine my grace;
O one by natures outwards so commended,
That maidens eyes stucke ouer all his face,
Loue lackt a dwelling and made him her place.
And when in his faire parts shee didde abide,
Shee was new lodg'd and newly Deified.

His browny locks did hang in crooked curles,
And euery light occasion of the wind
Vpon his lippes their silken parcels hurles,
Whats sweet to do, to do wil aptly find,
Each eye that saw him did inchaunt the minde:
For on his visage was in little drawne,
What largenesse thinkes in parradise was sawne.

Smal shew of man was yet vpon his chinne,
His phenix downe began but to appeare
Like vnshorne veluet, on that termlesse skin
Whose bare out-brag'd the web it seem'd to were.
Yet shewed his visage by that cost more deare,
And nice affections wauering stood in doubt
If best were as it was, or best without.

His qualities were beautious as his forme,
For maiden tongu'd he was and thereof free;
Yet if men mou'd him, was he such a storme
As oft twixt May and Aprill is to see,
When windes breath sweet, vnruly though they bee.
His rudenesse so with his authoriz'd youth,
Did liuery falsenesse in a pride of truth.

Wel could hee ride, and often men would say
That horse his mettell from his rider takes
Proud of subiection, noble by the swaie,
What rounds, what bounds, what course, what stop he makes
And controuersie hence a question takes,
Whether the horse by him became his deed,
Or he his mannad'g, by' th wel doing Steed.

But quickly on this side the verdict went,
His reall habitude gaue life and grace
To appertainings and to ornament,
Accomplisht in him-selfe not in his case:
All ayds them-selues made fairer by their place,
Can for addicions, yet their purpos'd trimme
Peec'd not his grace but were al grac'd by him.

So on the tip of his subduing tongue
All kinde of arguments and question deepe,
Al replication prompt, and reason strong
For his aduantage still did wake and sleep,
To make the weeper laugh, the laugher weepe:
He had the dialect and different skil,
Catching al passions in his craft of will.

That hee didde in the general bosome raigne
Of young, of old, and sexes both inchanted,
To dwel with him in thoughts, or to remaine
In personal duty, following where he haunted,
Consent's bewitcht, ere he desire haue granted,
And dialogu'd for him what he would say,
Askt their own wils and made their wils obey.

Many there were that did his picture gette
To serue their eies, and in it put their mind,
Like fooles that in th' imagination set
The goodly obiects which abroad they find
Of lands and mansions, theirs in thought assign'd,
And labouring in moe pleasures to bestow them,
Then the true gouty Land-lord which doth owe them.

So many haue that neuer toucht his hand
Sweetly suppos'd them mistresse of his heart:
My wofull selfe that did in freedome stand,
And was my owne fee simple (not in part)
What with his art in youth and youth in art
Threw my affections in his charmed power,
Reseru'd the stalke and gaue him al my flower.

Yet did I not as some my equals did
Demaund of him, nor being desired yeelded,
Finding my selfe in honour so forbidde,
With safest distance I mine honour sheelded,
Experience for me many bulwarkes builded
Of proofs new bleeding which remaind the foile
Of this false Iewell, and his amorous spoile.

But ah who euer shun'd by precedent,
The destin'd ill she must her selfe assay,
Or forc'd examples gainst her owne content
To put the by-past perrils in her way?
Counsaile may stop a while what will not stay:
For when we rage, aduise is often seene
By blunting vs to make our wits more keene.

Nor giues it satisfaction to our blood,
That wee must curbe it vppon others proofe,
To be forbod the sweets that seemes so good,
For feare of harmes that preach in our behoofe;
O appetite from iudgement stand aloofe!
The one a pallate hath that needs will taste,
Though reason weepe and cry it is thy last.

For further I could say this mans vntrue,
And knew the patternes of his foule beguiling,
Heard where his plants in others Orchards grew,
Saw how deceits were guilded in his smiling,
Knew vowes were euer brokers to defiling,
Thought Characters and words meerly but art,
And bastards of his foule adulterat heart.

And long vpon these termes I held my Citty,
Till thus hee gan besiege me: Gentle maid
Haue of my suffering youth some feeling pitty
And be not of my holy vowes affraid,
Thats to ye sworne to none was euer said,
For feasts of loue I haue bene call'd vnto
Till now did nere inuite nor neuer vovv.

All my offences that abroad you see
Are errors of the blood none of the mind:
Loue made them not, with acture they may be,
Where neither Party is nor trew nor kind,
They sought their shame that so their shame did find,
And so much lesse of shame in me remaines,
By how much of me their reproch containes.

Among the many that mine eyes haue seene,
Not one whose flame my hart so much as warmed,
Or my affection put to th, smallest teene,
Or any of my leisures euer Charmed,
Harme haue I done to them but nere was harmed,
Kept hearts in liueries, but mine owne was free,
And raignd commaunding in his monarchy.

Looke heare what tributes wounded fancies sent me,
Of palyd pearles and rubies red as blood:
Figuring that they their passions likewise lent me
Of greefe and blushes, aptly vnderstood
In bloodlesse white, and the encrimson'd mood,
Effects of terror and deare modesty,
Encampt in hearts but fighting outwardly.

And Lo behold these tallents of their heir,
With twisted mettle amorously empleacht
I haue receau'd from many a seuerall faire,
Their kind acceptance, wepingly beseecht,
With th' annexions of faire gems inricht,
And deepe brain'd sonnets that did amplifie
Each stones deare Nature, worth and quallity.

The Diamond? why twas beautifull and hard,
Whereto his inuis'd properties did tend,
The deepe greene Emrald in whose fresh regard,
Weake sights their sickly radience do amend.
The heauen hewd Saphir and the Opall blend
With obiects manyfold; each seuerall stone,
With wit well blazond smil'd or made some mone.

Lo all these trophies of affections hot,
Of pensiu'd and subdew'd desires the tender,
Nature hath chargd me that I hoord them not,
But yeeld them vp where I my selfe must render:
That is to you my origin and ender:
For these of force must your oblations be,
Since I their Aulter, you en patrone me.

Oh then aduance (of yours) that phraseles hand,
Whose white weighes downe the airy scale of praise,
Take all these similies to your owne command,
Hollowed with sighes that burning lunges did raise:
What me your minister for you obaies
Workes vnder you, and to your audit comes
Their distract parcells, in combined summes.

Lo this deuice was sent me from a Nun,
Or Sister sanctified of holiest note,
Which late her noble suit in court did shun,
Whose rarest hauings made the blossoms dote,
For she was sought by spirits of ritchest cote,
But kept cold distance, and did thence remoue,
To spend her liuing in eternall loue.

But oh my sweet what labour ist to leaue,
The thing we haue not, mastring what not striues,
Playing the Place which did no forme receiue,
Playing patient sports in vnconstraind giues,
She that her fame so to her selfe contriues,
The scarres of battaile scapeth by the flight,
And makes her absence valiant, not her might.

Oh pardon me in that my boast is true,
The accident which brought me to her eie,
Vpon the moment did her force subdewe,
And now she would the caged cloister flie:
Religious loue put out religions eye:
Not to be tempted would she be enur'd,
And now to tempt all liberty procur'd.

How mightie then you are, Oh heare me tell,
The broken bosoms that to me belong,
Haue emptied all their fountaines in my well:
And mine I powre your Ocean all amonge:
I strong ore them and you ore me being strong,
Must for your victorie vs all congest,
As compound loue to phisick your cold brest.

My parts had powre to charme a sacred Sunne,
Who disciplin'd I dieted in grace,
Beleeu'd her eies, when they t' assaile begun,
All vowes and consecrations giuing place:
O most potentiall loue, vowe, bond, nor space
In thee hath neither sting, knot, nor confine
For thou art all and all things els are thine.

When thou impressest what are precepts worth
Of stale example? when thou wilt inflame,
How coldly those impediments stand forth
Of wealth of filliall feare, lawe, kindred fame,
Loues armes are peace, gainst rule, gainst sence, gainst shame
And sweetens in the suffring pangues it beares,
The *Alloes* of all forces, shockes and feares.

Now all these hearts that doe on mine depend,
Feeling it breake, with bleeding groanes they pine,
And supplicant their sighes to you extend
To leaue the battrie that you make gainst mine,
Lending soft audience, to my sweet designe,
And credent soule, to that strong bonded oth,
That shall preferre and vndertake my troth.

This said, his watrie eies he did dismount,
Whose sightes till then were leaueld on my face,
Each cheeke a riuer running from a fount,
With brynish currant downe-ward flowed a pace:
Oh how the channell to the streame gaue grace!
Who glaz'd with Christall gate the glowing Roses,
That flame through water which their hew incloses,

Oh father, what a hell of witch-craft lies,
In the small orb of one particular teare?
But with the invndation of the eies:
What rocky heart to water will not weare?
What brest so cold that is not warmed heare,
Or cleft effect, cold modesty hot wrath:
Both fire from hence, and chill extincture hath.

For loe his passion but an art of craft,
Euen there resolu'd my reason into teares,
There my white stole of chastity I daft,
Shooke off my sober gardes, and ciuill feares,
Appeare to him as he to me appeares:
All melting, though our drops this diffrence bore,
His poison'd me, and mine did him restore.

In him a plenitude of subtle matter,
Applied to Cautills, all straing formes receiues,
Of burning blushes, or of weeping water,
Or sounding palenesse: and he takes and leaues,
In eithers aptnesse as it best deceiues:
To blush at speeches ranck, to weepe at woes
Or to turne white and sound at tragick showes.

That not a heart which in his leuell came,
Could scape the haile of his all hurting ayme,
Shewing faire Nature is both kinde and tame:
And vaild in them did winne whom he would maime,
Against the thing he sought, he would exclaime,
When he most burnt in hart-wisht luxurie,
He preacht pure maide, and praisd cold chastitie.

Thus meerely with the garment of a grace,
The naked and concealed feind he couerd,
That th'vnexperient gaue the tempter place,
Which like a Cherubin aboue them houerd,
Who young and simple would not be so louerd.
Aye me I fell, and yet do question make,
What I should doe againe for such a sake.

O that infected moysture of his eye,
O that false fire which in his cheeke so glowd:
O that forc'd thunder from his heart did flye,
O that sad breath his spungie lungs bestowed,
O all that borrowed motion seeming owed,
Would yet againe betray the fore-betrayed,
And new peruert a reconciled Maide.

FINIS

Index

Page numbers in *italic* refer to illustrations.

Ad herennium see *Rhetorica ad herennium*
Adamson, Sylvia   244
adjectives: relationship to substance   315
Adonis   320
adultery   29, 294
Aeneid (Virgil)   17–18
Akrigg, G. P. V.   123, 125
Alberti, Leon Battista   405
alchemy   405–25
   images and emblems   410, 412
   metaphors   111, 112, 413–14, 415–16, 419,
     423–4
Alexander, William   209
All's Well that Ends Well (Shakespeare)   332–3,
   337
allegory   30
Allen, Michael J. B.   51, 52
alliteration   26, 33, 109
Alpers, Paul   174
Amoretti (Sidney)   212–13
anagrams   40
Anatomi auri (Mylius)   *413*
André, Jacques   437
androgyny   29
   see also hermaphrodites
antanaclasis   243
antithesis   37, 42
Antony and Cleopatra (Shakespeare)
   Cleopatra's fear of dramatic
     representation   384, 388
   concern for reputation in   387
   nature of praise   391
   Octavian Caesar's character   385

   personal and social identity   332, 337
   symmetry of love   393
   types of love   386
Apologie for Poetrie (Sidney)   406–7
Aquinas, Thomas   283
Arcadia (Sidney)   21, 112, 192, 209, 211–12
archaism   59–60
Arden, Mary   131
argument, development of   33–6
Aristotle   315, 324
art
   and order   15–26
   see also poetry; writing, act of
Arte of English Poesie (Puttenham)   60, 64, 322,
   408, 419
Arte of Rhetorique (Wilson)   352
Artephius   414
As You Like It (Shakespeare)   114, 365
Ashbery, John   40
astronomical metaphors   23–5
Astrophel and Stella (Sidney)
   carpe diem theme   114–15
   gestation metaphors   61
   identity of characters   397
   lovesickness   347
   and MS circulation   139, 211
   organization of text   52
   published editions   209, 210
   resolution   228
Atalanta fugiens (Maier)   411–12, *412*
Auden, W. H.   177–8
audience: sonnets   50, 115
Augustine of Hippo, St   75, 85, 86

Aurora (Alexander)   209
autobiography *see* biography

Bacon, Sir Francis   62, 193, 195, 417
Barnes, Barnabe
    A Divine Centurie   204, 208, 214
    linking devices   217
    MS circulation   215
    Parthenophil and Parthenophe   211, 212, 217
Barnfield, Richard
    Cynthia   92, 204, 208, 220
    MS circulation   214
    organization of texts   58, 91, 92, 96
    and same-sex love   5
    sonnets to Ganymede   97, 204, 208
Baron, Hans   87
Bartholomaeus   316, 325
Bassano, Emilia *see* Lanier, Emilia
Basse, William   200
Bate, Jonathan   115, 116, 129–30
Bates, Catherine   8
Batman, Stephen   316, 325
Beal, Peter   187–8, 201, 214
Beckett, Samuel   28
bed-vow: meaning   304–6
"Before that antient time that man & wife"
    196–7
Bell, Ilona   8, 92, 100, 426
Bellasis, Margaret   194
Bellay, J. du   204
Benbow, Lady   194
Benn, Antony   194
Benson, John   7, 53–4, 58, 140, 148–9, 188,
    189
Berger, Harry   368
betrothals: Elizabethan   304–5, 307
Bible
    Coverdale's   118
    Ecclesiastes   60–1
    Isaiah   118
    John   418
    Leviticus   416
    Luke   423
    Revelation   418, 423–4
    Song of Solomon   421
biography
    Empson on authorial   163–82
    sonnets as autobiography   45–56, 121–36,
        228–41
        emotional identity with sonnets' speaker
        169–81, 267–71, 285

relationship with "dark lady" and "fair
    youth"   294–313, 339, 383–6, 420
BL MSS
    Add. 10309   190, 194
    Add. 15226   193
    Add. 21433   190, 194
    Add. 25303   190, 194
    Add. 30982   190, 192–3
    Sloane 1792   190, 191–2
black: significance   324
Blick, Fred   417
Bloom, Harold   383
Bodleian MS Rawlinson Poetical 152   199
body, human
    female   320, 323–6
    as fleshly substance   227, 248–57
    horticultural imagery   318–21
    Petrarch and Shakespeare's attitudes compared
        73–89
    relationship with color   316–26
    substance vs shadow   252–7
Boehme, Jacob   319
Bolzoni, Lina   346
books
    as form of identity   376
    as metaphors   374–6
    see also printing
Booth, Stephen
    approach to sonnets as autobiography   169, 228
    commentary style   33, 175–6, 181
    on meaning of "hue"   323
    overview of commentary and edition by   142
    overview of contribution   7
    on punctuation of 1609 quarto   301
    on Renaissance sonnets   284
    on Shakespeare's frames of reference   285
    on sonnet 1   113–14
    on sonnet 3   274
    on sonnet 18   348
    on sonnet 35   178–9
    on sonnet 44   259
    on sonnet 53   227
    on sonnet 59   62
    on sonnet 89   365
    on sonnets 97–9   320
    on sonnet 105   231
    on sonnet 113   88
    on sonnet 130   80, 81
    on sonnet 138   89
    on sonnets' ambiguity   244–5
    Vendler on his structure theories   30, 31

botanical metaphors   23–5, 318–21, 349–51
Bowers, Fredson   155
Bradbrook, M. C.   126–7
Braden, Gordon   85–6, 88, 342, 435
Bradley, A. C.   46–7
Breitenberg, Mark   284
Breton, Nicholas   197
Bruno, Giordano   421
Büdel, Oscar   77, 84, 85
Burbage, Richard   126
Burbage, Winifred   126
Burckhardt, Titus   420
Burgess, Anthony   122–3
Burghley, William Cecil, Lord   129
Burke, Kenneth   249
Burrow, Colin
    and 1609 quarto   205, 206, 210
    on "dark lady"   294, 301, 302
    on *A Lover's Complaint*   100, 421, 427, 435
    on MS version of sonnet 106   198
    overview of contribution   8
    overview of edition by   143–4, 161
    on Shakespeare and classical allusions   242–3
    on sonnet 43   253
    on sonnets 153–4   59
    on sonnets' nature and structure   51–2
    on sonnets' power to reveal emotion   365
Butler, Samuel   54

Caelia (Murray)   209
Caelica (Greville)   211
caesura   60
Callaghan, Dympna   8
Camillio, Giulio   345
"The Canonization" (Donne)   407
Capell, Edward   150
Carew, Thomas   186, 187, 192, 194, 197
carpe diem theme   113–15, 338
Carruthers, Mary   344–5, 352, 356, 359
Carson, Anne   315
Cartwright, William   191
Castiglione, Baldassare: *The Courtier*   227, 240
catachesis   268, 269
Cavell, Stanley   398–9
Cecil, William *see* Burghley, William Cecil, Lord
Certain Small Works (Daniel)   209
Certain Sonnets (Sidney)   210–11, 219
change
    and color   318–19
    cyclical nature of life   57–70
    sonnet 15   24–5

sonnets as attempt to halt   65–6, 231–2, 238–9
    as theme   4–5
    time and change in the sonnets   106–8
    see also memory and memorialization; time
Chapman, George   133, 215
characterization   28–30, 383–401
    see also speaker
Chartier, Roger   353, 354
Chaucer, Geoffrey   60
chemical weddings   410–14
Cheney, Patrick   8, 134–5, 206
chiasmus   37, 267–8
Chloris (Smith)   212, 213
Christ Church, Oxford: anthologies and poets   190–3, 194
Christianity
    and alchemy   409
    and Petrarch   80
    religious significance of sonnet numbering   418–19
    Shakespeare and blasphemy   80
    Shakespeare and Catholicism   169–70
    Shakespeare's rejection of   33
    Shakespeare's use of Christian themes
        A Lover's Complaint   423
        Much Ado   377
        sonnet 29   287
        sonnet 105   231
        sonnet 125   416
        sonnet 146   85
    and sonnet conventions   20–1
    sonnets as theological sequence   268
churl: Shakespeare's meaning   114
Cicero   259, 344
classical references
    and Shakespeare   242–60
    Shakespeare's allusions   33, 242–3
    Shakespeare and Ovid   77, 106–7, 108, 116
Cleopatra (Daniel)   93
Coelia (Percy)   212
Colie, Rosalie   34
Colin Clouts (Spenser)   209
"The Collar" (Herbert)   28
Collier, John Payne   202
color
    ancient and early modern attitudes   315–17
    darkness and the sonnets   324–6
    darkness and writing   325–6
    and nature   318–19
    relationship with the body   316–26

as revealer of inner nature   323
and the sonnets   314–28
and time/change   318–19
commemoration *see* memory and
  memorialization
"The Comparison" (Donne)   324
complaint genre   59–60, 91–101, 428–9
  see also A Lover's Complaint
The Complaint of Rosamond (Daniel)   59, 93, 97,
  98–9, 209
Complaints (Spenser)   204, 215
complexion
  cosmetics for   321–2, 323
  as mirror of bodily humors   316, 317
  as mirror of feelings   323, 374–6
The Compound of Alchymie (Ripley)   405
Constable, Henry   214, 217
contracts
  early modern   110
  as metaphors   305
Cook, Carol   367
Cooke, Sir Anthony   214
Corbett, Richard   190, 191, 197
Coriolanus (Shakespeare)   376
Cormack, Bradin   8
"Corona" (Donne)   214
coronas   220
Coryate, Thomas   146
cosmetics   321–2, 323
couplets, Shakespearean   34–6, 100
The Courtier (Castiglione)   227, 240
courtly love conventions   20–2, 284
Cousins, A. D.   258
Coverdale, Miles   118
Craig, Alexander   91
Craik, Katharine A.   96, 426
Crane, Mary Thomas   353, 354
Crashaw, Richard   187
Crewe, Jonathan   139
Crooke, Helkiah   320, 328
Crum, Margaret   191, 201, 215
Crystal, David and Ben   365, 366
Cuffe, Henry   197
Culpeper, Nicholas   319
Curtius, Ernst   352
Cynthia (Barnfield)   92, 204, 208, 220
Cynthia (Nugent)   215

Daniel, Samuel
  Certain Small Works   209
  Cleopatra   93

The Complaint of Rosamond   59, 93, 97, 98–9,
  209
A Defence of Ryme   406
his sister and Southampton   129
MS circulation   197, 214
preferred medium of circulation   185
repetition   218
as "rival poet"   133
see also Delia
Dante Alighieri   87
"dark lady"
  alchemical view   420, 421
  character   293–4, 297–311, 337
  darkness and female sexuality   324
  darkness and the sonnets   324–6
  identity   51, 100, 123–34, 225, 314
  as love object   225–41
  and *A Lover's Complaint*   100, 309–10
  and nature   267, 420
  relationship with "fair youth" and poet
    294–311, 339, 420
  Shakespeare's disgust with   230
  and sonnet 40   235
"dark lady" sequence
  and color   324–6
  dating   215
  narrative in   293, 297–309
  and privacy   186
dating (calendrical), and Shakespeare   110
Davies, John, of Hereford   209, 215, 216, 427
Davies, Sir John   214, 215, 315
Davison, Francis   209
De proprietatibus rerum (Bartholomaeus)   316
De re aedificatoria (Alberti)   405
death
  and distillation   112
  and Petrarch   78–80, 106
  and sex   112
  sonnet 12   43–4, 109
  sonnet 15   24–5
  sonnet 32   196
  sonnet 60   41–3
  as theme   4–5, 65
  writing as immortality   231–2, 238–9, 338–9,
    345, 348–9, 350, 351–6
  see also change; memory and memorialization
deception
  in *A Lover's Complaint*   438
  in *New Arcadia*   438–9
  in the sonnets   437–8
deconstructivism   167

dedicatee
    Pembroke   9, 122, 130, 131–3
    Shakespeare himself   130
    Southampton   9, 122
    Who He?   143
    William Hart   152
    Willie Hughes   54, 121, 152
Defence of Poesie (Sidney)   345, 439
A Defence of Ryme (Daniel)   406
Deggli eroica furori (Bruno)   421
Delia (Daniel)
    côterie images   213–14
    the Delian tradition   4, 91–101
    editions   220
    linking devices   217
    material conventions   207, 208
    revisions   216
    structure   58
desire *see* sexual desire
"Dialogue" (Herbert)   29
Diana   421
Diana (Constable)   217
Dickinson, Emily   350–1
Dictionary of National Biography (*DNB*)   121–2
Diella (Lynche)   91, 92, 93, 94, 97
Digby, Venetia   191
Diggs, Leonard   379
distance theme   246–51, 254–7
distillation
    alchemical process   412, 413–14
    images   111, 112, 414, 415–16, 419, 423–4
    and memory   349–51
A Divine Centurie (Barnes)   204, 208, 214
DNB see Dictionary of National Biography
Dodoens, Rembert   320
Donne, John
    and alchemy   407–8
    attitude to the body   73–4
    "The Canonization"   407
    and comparison   324
    "Corona"   214
    coronas   220
    MS circulation   139, 185, 186, 193, 194, 195,
        196, 214
    Petrarch's influence   78
    poetry's dramatic qualities   6
    poetry's shifting moods   52
Dowland, John   197
Draaisma, Douwe   344
Drayton, Michael   185, 207, 209, 214, 216, 218
Drummond, William   209, 214

Dryden, John: *Aeneid* version   17–18
Dubrow, Heather
    on *carpe diem* theme   342
    on lyric and narrative   49
    on nature of desire   435
    overview of contribution   7–8
    on Petrarch   80, 87
    on sonnets' addressees   233, 304
    on sonnets' disconcerting effect   51
    on sonnets' sequence   45, 46, 218, 228, 310
Duncan-Jones, Katherine
    on 1609 quarto   33, 47, 53, 88, 205, 294
    and authorial biography   166
    on modernizing spelling   160
    on MS versions of sonnets   189–90, 193, 199
    on same-sex love   284
    on Shakespeare and Petrarch   416
    on sonnet 40   235, 236
    on sonnet 113   88
    on sonnet 126   262
    on sonnet 154   421
    on sonnets' biographical context   131–3
    on sonnets' sequence and numbering   91, 418
Durling, Robert M.   86–7
Dutton, Richard   8
dyeing: Shakespeare's meaning   319

E.C.: *Emaricdulfe*   214, 215, 218
Ecclesiastes   60–1
Eco, Umberto   356
economic metaphors *see* legal and financial
    metaphors
education: Elizabethan   259
Eld, George   145
Elderton, William   380
Eliot, T. S.   28
Elizabeth I, queen of England
    as "dark lady"   225
    references in sonnets   125, 128, 130
    Shakespeare's feelings for   132
Emaricdulfe (E.C.)   214, 215, 218
emblems   30, 410, 412
emotions
    early modern emotional regime   279–83,
        284
    in Shakespeare   284–8
    sonnet conventions   284
    sonnets' power to evoke   363–82
    and speaker's authenticity   29
    see also love
emotives   280

Empson, William 163–82
  and Auden 178
  life 170
  Seven Types of Ambiguity 163, 164–6, 168–72,
    175
  Some Versions of Pastoral 168, 173–5, 178
  on sonnet 94 173–6, 383
  The Structure of Complex Words 164, 169
Engle, Lars 8, 83, 341
Enterline, Lynn 436
enumeration 39–40
epideixis 239, 270
Erasmus, Desiderius 262
Erne, Lukas 135, 376
Erotomania (Ferrand) 317
ethics *see* morality
etymology, Elizabethan knowledge of 244

face *see* complexion
Faerie Queene (Spenser) 108–9, 166, 344
"fair youth"
  character 293, 302–11
  faults 233
  historical identity 54, 121–34, 225
  as love object 225–41
  personal identity and selfhood 331–42
  relationship with "dark lady" and poet
    294–313, 339, 383–6, 420
  Shakespeare's disgust with 230
  as subject as well as object 265–6
  see also same-sex love
"fair youth" sequence
  characterization 383–401
  dating 215
  erotic rivalry 390–1
  memory in 343–57
  and privacy 186
  procreation sequence 215, 231–2, 331–42,
    347–8, 349–51
Falstaff: Shakespeare as 383–6
fame
  importance to Shakespearean characters 387
  Petrarch on 79
family relationships 100–1, 133–4
famine 113
fancifulness 39, 143
fashioned: meaning 366, 379–80
feminist criticism 28
Ferrand, Jacques 229, 317
Ficino, Marsilio 227, 230, 240, 416
Field, Richard 159

figures of speech 258
  catachesis 268, 269
  chiasmus 37, 267–8
  syllepsis 243
financial metaphors *see* legal and financial
  metaphors
Fineman, Joel
  on contrast between "dark lady" and "fair
    youth" sequences 326
  on "dark lady" 299, 304
  and epideixis 239
  on influence of sonnet convention 296
  and Shakespeare's sexuality 226
  on Shakespeare's uniqueness 82
  on sonnet 44 249
  on sonnet 45 250
  on sonnet 105 64, 231, 232
  on sonnets as autobiography 228, 267–71
Finucci, Valeria 325
Fitton, Mary 135, 225
flattery
  Shakespeare's meaning 84
  see also praise
Flesch, William 8
Fletcher, Giles
  Licia 92, 95, 96, 97
  MS circulation 215
  organization of texts 58, 91
Florio, John 129
flowers
  as alchemical emblems 412, 415, *422*
  floral imagery 319–21, 349–51
Fludd, Robert 346, 416–17, 419
Folger MSS
  V.a.139 196–7
  V.a.148 187–9
  V.a.162 194–6
  V.a.170 190, 191
  V.a.345 190, 193
Forbis, J. F. 51
Ford, John (film director) 121
Ford, John (writer) 144
forgetting
  self-forgetting 336–9, 340
  Shakespeare's exhortations to 355–6
Forman, Simon 124
forms, Platonic 252–7
Foster, Donald 48
Foucault, Michel 167
Fowler, Alastair 418
Frankenstein, Dr 415

Fraser, Russell   127
Freccero, John   73–4
Freeman, Arthur   143
Freinkel, Lisa   268–9
Freud, Sigmund   384, 392, 428, 436–7
Fry, Paul   163
Fuller, Thomas   187
"A Funeral Elegy by W. S." (Shakespeare?; Davies?)
   427
"Funeral Elegy for William Peter" (Ford)   144

Galen   247, 250, 316, 319, 323–4
Ganymede sonnets (Barnfield)   97, 204, 208
Gardiner, Judith Kegan   228
Geber   408
gender relations
   and alchemy   410–14
   feminine masochism   437
   Galen's view of male and female bodies
      323–4
   in *A Lover's Complaint*   429–39
   in *Much Ado*   371–6
   and nature vs artifice   323
   in Petrarchan tradition   367–8
   relational view   237
   sexual politics in *Venus* and *Lucrece*   139
   Vendler on Shakespeare's attitude   29–30
   see also heterosexuality; same-sex love; women
Genette, Gerard   211
genres, literary: social significance   167
Gerard, John   319
Gibbon, J.   187
Gildon, Charles   149, 383
Giroux, Robert   286
Goddard, Harold C.   371
"Gods love"   196
Gorgias (Plato)   322
grafting   320
Graves, Robert   153, 156, 168, 278
Grazia, Margreta de   7, 53, 154, 266, 269, 314
green: significance   318
Greenblatt, Stephen
   on "dark lady"   294
   on distinctness of each sonnet   279
   on *Much Ado*   378–9, 380
   on Shakespeare's verbal invention   245
   on social tension in "fair youth" sequence   130
   on sonnets as autobiography   166, 285
   on subversion and containment   380
   on Wyatt   168, 172
Greene, Robert   129, 130
Greene, Thomas M.   78, 87, 118, 259

Greg, W. W.   155
Greville, Fulke   211, 214
Griffin, B.   215
A Groatsworth of Wit (Greene)   129
guilt   99
"Gulling Sonnets" (Davies)   214
Gurr, Andrew   33, 127

Habington, William   195–6
Haffenden, John   163
Hall, Joseph   196
Hall, Kim   314
Halpern, Richard   65, 350
halt and halting: meaning   365
Hamlet (Shakespeare)
   concern for reputation in   387, 388, 389
   contemporary popularity   137
   on halting verse   365
   Hamlet's character   385, 386
   links between sex and death   112
   play within the play   384
   possible memory-theater allusions   346
   table-book metaphor   353
   triggers for memory   357
   types of love   385, 386
Hardy, Barbara   48, 50
Harington, Sir John   159, 194
harmonic ratios   417
Hart, William   152
Harvey, Elizabeth   8
Hathaway, Anne   127, 133, 301–2, 303
Healy, Margaret   8
hell: idiomatic meaning   302
Henry IV, Parts 1 and 2 (Shakespeare):
   Shakespeare and "fair youth" as Falstaff and
      Hal   383–6
Henry V (Shakespeare)   380, 387, 389
Henry VI, Part 1 (Shakespeare)   388–9
Herbert, George   20–1, 28–9, 74, 195
Herbert, Mary *see* Pembroke, Countess of
Herbert, William *see* Pembroke, third Earl of
Herman, Peter   116, 337, 342
hermaphrodites   407, 414, 418, 424
   see also androgyny
Hermes Trismegistus   409
Hero and Leander (Marlowe)   139
Heroical Epistles (Drayton)   209
Herrick, Robert   185
heterosexuality
   and Shakespeare   132, 225–41
   sonnets' attitude to   5, 30
Heywood, Thomas   149

Hieatt, A. Kent 33, 48
Hieatt, Charles W. 48
Hippocrates 316, 320
Hobbs, Mary 201
Hoby, Thomas 240
Holland, Peter 122, 380
Hollander, John 228, 244
Homer 80, 388–9
homoeroticism *see* same-sex love
Honan, Park 130–1
Honigmann, Ernst A. J. 130, 133, 135
Horace 106, 351
horticultural metaphors *see* botanical metaphors
hourglasses 261–7, 271–5
hue: meaning 323
Hughes, Willie 54, 121, 152
Humes, James C. 130
humors, bodily 247, 250, 316
Humphreys, A. R. 377, 380
A Hundred Points of Good Husbandry (Tusser)
    110–11
Hunsdon, Lord 124

iconoclasm 349
Idea (Drayton) 209, 216
identity
    alchemy and the ego 420, 422
    early modern notions of social and personal
        331–42
    sexual desire's effect on 337, 339
    Shakespeare's exploration 383–401
    sonnets' power to reveal 363–82
    theater's power to reveal 364
imagery *see* metaphor
infection: Shakespeare's meaning 321
Ingram, W. G. 142
Inns of Court: poetry associated with 194, 245
interiority: Shakespeare's representation 336
inventories 39
Irigaray, Luce 317, 322–3
irony 34, 399–400
Isaiah 118
Islam, and alchemy 409
Iyengar, Sujata 314

Jackson, Stephen 195
Jaggard, William 89, 146–7, 185, 199
James I, king of Scotland 59
James I and VI, king of England and Scotland
    poems about 191
    references in sonnets 62, 125, 128, 130, 133,
        287

Jameson, Fredric 63
John's Gospel 418
Johnson, Samuel 60
Jonson, Ben
    1616 first folio 137–8, 159
    MS circulation 187, 191, 197
    preferred media of circulation 185
    as "rival poet" 133
    and Shakespeare 115, 240
    Thorpe's editions 139, 146
Joseph, Miriam 258
Julius Caesar (Shakespeare) 118, 384, 388, 390
Justice, Donald 343

Kalas, Rayna 8
Kalstone, David 78
Kastan, David Scott 205
Keats, John 43–4, 109
Kerrigan, John
    on alternative authorial versions of sonnets
        202
    on contrast in the sonnets 52
    on "dark lady" 294
    on deception in the sonnets 438
    on *Delia* 91
    and *A Lover's Complaint* 3–4, 57–8, 100, 436
    overview of edition by 142
    on sonnets 40–2 235
    on sonnet 126 263
    on sonnets 153 and 154 59
    on sonnets' disconcerting effect 51
    on sonnets' sequence 47–8, 90, 91, 99
    on time in the sonnets 108
Khunrath 409
King, Henry 187, 191
King, John 191
King Lear (Shakespeare) 324, 386
King's Men 138
The Kingis Quair (James I of Scotland) 59
knots: in Petrarch 75–80
Koskimies, Rafael 226–7
Kott, Jan 36
Kreiger, Murray 274
Kristeva, Julia 322–3
Kuin, Roger 92

lame: meaning 365
Lampus, Lord 194
land leases 110
language
    chromatic 322–3
    early variation of English 259

language   (*cont'd*)
    Latin's effect on sonnets   242–60
    sonnets as social speech   9
    see also figures of speech; rhetoric; wordplay
Lanier, Alfonso   124
Lanier, Emilia (Aemilia Lanyer; *née* Bassano)
    124–5, 128, 134, 225, 314
lap: Shakespeare's meaning   320
Latin, and Shakespeare   242–60
"A Law Cause"   192
Lawes, Henry   193
Leare, Daniel   192
Lee, Sir Sidney   121
legal and financial metaphors   287, 288, 337–8,
    342
Leishman, J. B.   117, 240
Lennard, John   262
Lever, J. W.   85
Levi, Peter   127–8
Levin, Richard   89
Leviticus   416
Lewis, C. S.   28
Lewis, David   395
A Lexicon of Alchemy (Ruland)   408, 410
Licia (Fletcher)   92, 95, 96, 97
Licia (Griffin)   215
lilies   415
Ling, Sir Edmond   192
Lintott, Bernard   149–50
Lodge, Thomas
    MS circulation   214
    Phillis   4, 58, 92, 208, 212
    The Tragical Complaint of Estred   59
Lok, H.   215
Lomazzo, Giovanni Paolo   322
love
    effect on sight   230, 346–7
    impossibility of characterizing the beloved
        383–401
    psychoanalytic types   384
    and Shakespeare   4–6, 228–41
    taking pride in the beloved   391–5
    types in Shakespeare's plays   384–5
    see also emotions; same-sex love
Love's Labour's Lost (Shakespeare)   185
A Lover's Complaint (Shakespeare)   426–40
    acceptance in canon   139
    alchemical influence   421–4
    archaism   59–60
    authorship   427
    contemporary popularity   426

    divergence from complaint genre   428–9
    identity of characters   100
    Levi on   128
    lyric and narrative   49
    mentions of sonnets   365, 366
    and morality   436–7
    nature of desire in   429–39
    obscurity   426–7
    place in the sonnet sequence   3–4, 57–9,
        90–103, 309–11, 408
    surrogacy   96, 100
lovesickness: effects   230, 346–7
Lucrece see *The Rape of Lucrece*
Luke's Gospel   423
Luther, Martin   424
Lydgate, John   60
Lynche, Richard
    Diella   91, 92, 93, 94, 97
    MS circulation   215
lyrics: historical contextual influences   167

Macbeth (Shakespeare)   385
McKerrow, R. B.   155
McLeod, Randall   154, 155–6
Magnusson, Lynne   285
Maier, Michael: books by   411–12, *412*
Malone, Edmond   46, 54, 137, 140–1, 150–3,
    158, 160, 269
Man, Paul de   167
The Man Who Shot Liberty Valence (film)   121
Manningham, John   132
manuscripts
    Shakespeare's   147–8, 185–203, 294
    sonnet sequences   212–16, 219
Marianus Scholasticus   59
Marlowe, Christopher
    Hero and Leander   139
    publishing history   146
    as "rival poet"   133
    and same-sex love   5
Marotti, Arthur   8, 46, 206, 210, 211
marriage
    alchemical   410–14
    early modern concept   280–1, 304–5, 307
Martial   78
masochism
    feminine   437
    and *A Lover's Complaint*   434–7
masturbation   337
mathematics, divine   416, 418–19
Measure for Measure (Shakespeare)   101, 384

Medcalf, Stephen   227
meddling: etymology and meaning   320
Medea (Ovid)   435
medical theory   247, 250, 316, 319, 323–4
melancholy   250
Melchiori, Giorgio   89, 269
memory and memorialization
  as beauty   334
  and distillation   349–51
  early modern concept   343–6
  in "fair youth" sonnets   343–57
  metaphors for   333
  mnemonic methods   344–6, 352–3
  and physical decay   334
  poetry as   338–9, 345, 348–9, 350, 351–6
  procreation as   331–42, 347–8
  and sight   344–6, 352, 354
  and smell   349–51
memory theaters   345–6
menstruation, and flowers   320
The Merchant of Venice (Shakespeare)   134, 385, 417
Mercurius   424
Meres, Francis   3, 50, 139, 185
The Merry Wives of Windsor (Shakespeare)   372
Metamorphoses (Ovid)   106–7, 108, 116, 258, 320
metaphor
  alchemical
    alchemical emblems   410, 412
    used by Shakespeare   111, 112, 413–14, 415–16, 419, 423–4
  botanical   23–5, 318–21, 349–51
  contract metaphors   305
  fluidity of reference   41–2, 44
  importance of context   32
  legal and financial   287, 288, 337–8, 342
  for memory   333
  for non-reproductive sex   337–8
  printing metaphors   374–6
  Shakespeare's warnings against falsity of   438
  sonnet 12   44
  sonnet 15   23–5
  sonnet 30   287, 288
  sonnet 34   38
  theatrical   23–5, 370, 390
  water metaphors   309
  writing metaphors   61–2, 325, 357
meter   261, 365
A Midsummer Night's Dream (Shakespeare)
  learned clerks' silence   391
  procreation as immortality   349

types of love   384, 385, 392
vicarious experience in   393–4
Mikrocosmographia (Crooke)   320, 328
Mill, J. S.   28
Milton, John   6, 18, 61
Minerva Britanna (Peacham)   282
mirrors   271–4
miscegenation   314–15, 325
Miscellany (Tottel)   185–6
mistress: early modern meaning   299
Mnemonica (Willis)   345–6, 352–3
morality
  of constancy   256
  early modern emotional regime   279–83, 284
  Elizabethan sexual   294
  and *A Lover's Complaint*   436–7
  sexual   29–30
  and Shakespeare   83, 284–8
  sonnet conventions   284
  and sonnet-writing   230
More, Thomas   264–5
Morley, George   190, 197
Much Ado About Nothing (Shakespeare)
  Claudio's character   399
  on importance of Shakespeare's sonnets to his œuvre   363–82
  misprision   51
  occurrence of "fashion"   367
  "Pardon, goddess of the night"   377
  "Sigh no more ladies, sigh no more"   371–4
  time and patience   110
  types of love   385
Muir, Kenneth   426, 433
Murray, Sir David, of Gorthy   91, 209
Musa, Mark   117
Musaeus   229
Muses Sacrifice (Davies)   209
music
  musical instruments   370
  musical performance of the sonnets   193–4
  of the spheres   417
Mylius, Johann Daniel: books by   *413*

Nagel, Thomas   395
narcissism   384
narrative
  love-triangle version   293–313
  narrative order   38–9
  sonnets as *see* structure: order and sequences
  sonnets' anti-narrativity   45–56
  and surrogacy   96–7

Nashe, Thomas   210, 388–9
Natural Magick (della Porta)   319–20, 321
nature
    alchemical view   419–20
    and color   318–19
    and "dark lady"   267, 420
    vs painting   321–2, 323
Negro, Lucy   225
neoplatonism
    forms   252–7
    and Petrarch   73–80
    and Shakespeare   226–7, 238–9, 252–3, 416
New Arcadia (Sidney)   438–9
niggard: Shakespeare's meaning   113–14
nigredo   414
nonny: meaning   373–4
Norris, Christopher   163
North, Marcy   8, 189
Nosce teipsum (Davies)   315
notebooks *see* table-books
Nothing Like the Sun (Burgess)   122–3
Nugent, Richard   215
numerology   416
NYPL MS Drexel 4257   193

oaths   305–6
O'Connor, Garry   130
Odyssey (Homer)   388–9
"On a made not marriageable" (anon.)   192–3
"On his Mistress Beauty" (Shakespeare and
    Pembroke?)   197–8
O'Neill, Onora   157–8
order
    in art   15–16, 25–6
    narrative order   38–9
    in the sonnets *see* structure
organization
    poetic forms   16–18, 25–6
    in the sonnets *see* structure
orgasm   4
Orgel, Stephen   8, 231
Othello (Shakespeare)   259, 365, 385, 387
Overbury, Sir Thomas   195, 201
Ovid
    Medea   435
    Metamorphoses   106–7, 108, 116, 258, 320
    as poet-playwright   134
    and Shakespeare   77, 106–7, 108, 116, 245,
        258, 259
Oxford Dictionary of National Biography see
    Dictionary of National Biography

painting
    color and the unconscious   323
    Renaissance debates over   322
    vs nature   321–2, 323
Palladis Tamia (Meres)   3, 185
Pamphilia to Amphilanthus (Wroth)   215
Paracelsus   319, 410
Paradise Lost (Milton)   61
Parrot, Henry   195
Parry, Robert   91
Parthenophil and Parthenophe (Barnes)   211, 212,
    217
Partridge, John   111
The Passionate Pilgrim (anthology)
    1599 edition   3, 89, 146–7, 185
    1612 edition   9, 146–7, 149, 185
    and Benson   9
    and Folger MS V.a.339   196
    sources   199
    version of sonnet 138   300
passions *see* emotions
Paster, Gail Kern   279
paternity: early modern attitude   325
patronage
    and "fair youth" sonnets   186–7
    influence on Shakespeare's work   115–16
    Southampton as Shakespeare's patron   115,
        124, 125, 138
    workings of   138
Peacham, Henry   282
Peele, George   138
Pembroke, Mary Herbert (née Sidney), Countess
    of   133, 211–12, 406
Pembroke, William Herbert, third Earl of
    and Samuel Daniel   406
    date of first meeting Shakespeare   130
    as dedicatee of sonnets   9, 122, 130, 131–3
    as "fair youth"   47, 122, 126, 131–3
    poems by   197–8
Pequigney, Joseph   54–5, 226, 234, 265–6
perception, and speaker's authenticity   30
Percy, William   212, 215
Perry, R.   215
persona *see* speaker
persuasiveness, Shakespeare's art of   387, 389–95
Peters, Julie Stone   359
Petrarch, Francis
    Canzoniere   74–84, 105
    and Daniel   99
    influence   347
    and Ovid   259

Secretum 73–4, 77, 79
  and Shakespeare 73–89, 416
  and Spenser 94
  and time 104–6
Phaedrus (Plato) 258, 355
Phillis (Lodge) 4, 58, 92, 208, 212
philosopher's stone 414–15
philosophical ideas, and speaker's authenticity 29–30
The Phoenix and the Turtle (Shakespeare) 139, 227
Pico della Mirandola, Giovanni 227
Pinder, Sir Paul 195
pity: Shakespeare's meaning 298
plants
  herbal medicine 319
  as metaphors 23–5, 318–21, 349–51
Plato 258, 322, 355, 409, 416
Platonism *see* neoplatonism
playfulness 38, 143
pocket: early modern definition 367
Poetical Rhapsody (Davison) 209
poetry
  as memory 338–9, 345, 348–9, 350, 351–6
  as perpetuation 351–5, 356
  as Shakespeare's love object 225–41
  ways of memorizing 352
  see also writing, act of
Pope, Alexander 157
Porta, Giambattista della 319–20, 321
Praetiosum Donum Dei 422
praise
  Petrarchan 29, 37, 324
  Shakespeare's methods of 383–7, 389–91, 396, 397–400
  sonnet 130 30
Prescott, Anne Lake 48
printing
  effect on texts' accuracy 155–6, 159
  material aspects of sonnet sequences 206–14
  as memory 231–2
  metaphors 374–6
  printing conventions and authorial intention 92–3
procreation
  avoidance of as suicide 112
  as immortality 107
  metaphorical use 61–2, 325–6
  metaphors for 320
  Spenser on 108–9

procreation sonnets
  dating 215
  printing as memory 231–2
  procreation as memory 231–2, 331–42, 347–8
  smell as memory 349–51
pronouns 269
Proust, Marcel 385
proverbs, use of 35–6
Psalms (Sidney) 215
psychoanalysis
  masochism and sexuality 437
  psychoanalytic types of love 384
  see also Freud, Sigmund
punctuation: modernizing 159–60
puns *see* wordplay
purification: alchemical 414
Puritanism, and Shakespeare 170
Puttenham, George 60, 64, 322, 408, 419
pyramids 62, 418–19

Quintilian 344, 345

race issues 314–15, 325
Ralegh, Sir Walter 125, 185, 194
The Rape of Lucrece (Shakespeare)
  color in 317–18
  composition date 125, 127, 135
  contemporary popularity 137, 426
  dedicatee 2
  gender relations and morality 436
  overview and sexual politics 138–9
  personal and social identity 332, 336, 337
  publishing history 53, 138
  Sinon's depiction 401
Ravenshaw, J. 187
reading literature: Empson's approach 163–82
reciprocity 256–7
Reddy, William 279–80, 283
redemption 378
Redpath, Theodore 142
Rees, Joan 427, 438
religion *see* Christianity; Islam
remembrance *see* memory and memorialization
repetition
  and desire 435–6
  phonetic 65
  as theme 57–70
reproduction, human *see* procreation

reputation
  importance to Shakespeare's characters 387,
    388, 389–91
  see also fame
resurrection 378, 414
Revelation 418, 423–4
rhetoric
  and color 322
  and memory 344–5
  Shakespeare's persuasiveness 387, 389–95
Rhetorica ad herennium 344, 345, 352
rhyme
  functions 17–18
  Shakespeare's use of feminine 323
  sonnet 8 417
Rich, Penelope 397
Richard II (Shakespeare) 137, 385
Richard III (Shakespeare) 137
Ricks, Christopher 83–4
Riding, Laura 153, 156, 168, 278
Ringler, William 210
Ripley, George 405
"rival poet": identity 133
Roberts, Sasha 53, 92, 189–90, 199–200, 201,
  206
Robinson, Thomas 138–9
Roche, Thomas P., Jr.
  and the Delian tradition 58, 91
  on *A Lover's Complaint* 427, 433, 436
  on Petrarch's *Secretum* 86
Roe, John 92, 99, 102, 147, 227, 426
Rogers, T. 215
Rollins, Hyde E. 149, 150
Romeo and Juliet (Shakespeare)
  contemporary popularity 137
  contracts 110
  meaning of "churl" 114
  redemption 378
  types of love 384
Rosenbach MSS
  1083/16 197–8
  1083/17 147–8, 190
roses 319–21, 349–51, 412, *422*
Rowe, Nicholas 140
Rowse, A. L. 123–5, 314
Royalist anthologies 193
Rudyerd, Sir Benjamin 198
Ruland, Martin 408, 410

Sacks, Peter 356
Sagaser, Elizabeth Harris 102

Samburne, Sheriff of Oxford 192
same-sex love
  in alchemical context 416
  early modern attitude 279
  "fair youth" as subject as well as
    object 265–6
  gender pronouns changed in
    transcription 53–4, 140, 141–2, 149, 190
  Malone's attitude 151–2
  and other writers 5
  reproductive vs non-reproductive sex 337–8
  and Shakespeare 122–34, 141–2, 225–41
  sonnets' attitude to 5, 29, 101
  see also "fair youth"
Sands, Sir William 193
Schalkwyk, David 54–5, 299, 383, 384, 366
Schiffer, James 7, 299, 340, 346, 357
Schoenbaum, Samuel 125–6, 299
Schoenfeldt, Michael 247, 260, 282, 283
Scholes, Robert 50, 52
Secretum (Petrarch) 73–4, 77, 79
Sedgwick, Eve Kosofsky 226, 233
seduction
  fundamentality to human psychic history
    437
  in *A Lover's Complaint* 429–39
  in the sonnets 387, 389–95
Senault, J. F. 282, 284
Sewell, George 149
sexual activity: reproductive vs non-reproductive
  337–8
sexual desire
  color as indicator of 323
  effect on identity 337, 339
  in *A Lover's Complaint* 429–39
  repetitive nature 435–6
  in the sonnets 4–6, 435
sexual intercourse 4–6, 237
sexuality
  darkness and female sexuality 324–6
  floral imagery 320
  psychoanalytic view 437
  sonnets' attitude to 29–30
shadow vs substance 252–7
Shakespeare, Hamnet (son) 133–4
Shakespeare, William: CHARACTER AND LIFE
  Basse's epitaph 200
  circle of friends 295
  grain hoarding 113
  and Latin 242–60
  "lost" years 130

nature of erotic life   385
reasons for writing   115–16
sexuality   122–34, 141–2, 225–41
sonnets as autobiography   45–56, 121–36,
    228–41
    emotional identity with sonnets' speaker
        169–81, 267–71, 285
    relationship with "dark lady" and "fair
        youth"   294–313, 339, 383–6, 420
Shakespeare, William: COLLECTED WORKS
First Folio   137–8
Shakespeare, William: PLAYS
importance to Shakespeare the writer   363–82
publishing history   6
Shakespeare's psychological acuity   384
types of love portrayed   384–5
see also individual plays by title
Shakespeare, William: SONNETS, EDITIONS
1609 quarto   2–3, 50, 139–40, 145–8, 186
    authorization   126, 127, 128, 131, 134,
        139–40, 146, 187, 205, 210, 219, 294
    material aspects and context   204–21
1640 (Benson)   7, 53–4, 58, 140, 148–9, 188,
    189
1711 (Lintott)   149–50
1780 (Malone)   46, 54, 137, 140–1, 150–3,
    158, 160, 269
later editions   142–4, 154–61
Shakespeare, William: SONNETS, GENERAL
audience   50, 115
as autobiography   45–56, 121–36, 228–41
    relationship between characters   293–313,
        339, 383–6, 420
    Shakespeare's emotional identity with
        sonnets' speaker   169–81, 267–71, 285
centrality to Shakespeare's writing career
    363–82
circulation means   58, 139, 143
compared to other sonnet sequences   20–5,
    90–103, 204–21
composition dates   2, 33, 125, 129, 135, 215
composition process   216–19
contemporary popularity   53, 137, 140
contrast in   52
dedicatee
    Pembroke   9, 122, 130, 131–3
    Shakespeare himself   130
    Southampton   9, 122
    Who He?   143
    William Hart   152
    Willie Hughes   54, 121, 152

dedication   2–3
dramatic qualities   6, 30, 48–50
exclusion from First Folio   138
form and rhythm   6
identity of characters   50–1, 54, 100, 121–34,
    225
internal reading directions   295
length   68, 261
material aspects and context   204–21
MS versions   147–8, 185–203
musical performance   193–4
objects and subjects   265–75
order and sequences
    126's place   261–76
    alchemical view   418–19, 421–4
    Booth on multiple levels   15–26, 31
    coherence of tone, pace, and tempo
        115
    compared to Delian tradition   90–103,
        204–21
    and composition date   33
    "dark lady" sequence   186, 215, 293,
        297–309, 324–6
    "fair youth" sequence   186, 215, 343–57,
        383–401
    A Lover's Complaint's place   3–4, 57–9,
        90–103, 309–11, 408
    overview   3–4
    pairing   217–18
    patterns emerging from   57–60
    procreation sequence   215, 231–2, 331–42,
        347–8, 349–51
    pyramidical   418–19
    reasons for open-endedness   228–40
    Shakespeare's awareness of   215, 218–19
    significance of numbering   109, 418–19
    skeptical view   45–56
    thematic clusters   217–18
    Vendler on multiple levels   31–4
transcribers' changes   53–4, 140, 141–2, 149,
    190
Shakespeare, William: SONNETS, INDIVIDUAL
sonnet 1
    alchemy's influence   412
    influence of Shakespeare's classicism
        243–4
    as introduction to sequence   65, 212
    Lintott's version   150
    memory in   333–4, 347
    tenderness in   251–2
    time in   113–14

Shakespeare, William: SONNETS, INDIVIDUAL
  (*cont'd*)
  sonnet 2
    memory in   334–5
    MS versions   187, 190–4
    reasons for popularity   201
    surrogacy   100
    versions compared   147–8
  sonnet 3   273–4, 347–8
  sonnet 4   109, 337
  sonnet 5
    alchemy's influence   413–14
    smell and memory in   349–51
    time in   106–7, 108, 110
  sonnet 6
    smell and memory in   349–51
    time in   107, 111–12, 113
  sonnet 7   40, 107
  sonnet 8
    alchemy's influence   417–18
    MS versions   187, 193
    threat to selfhood   335
  sonnet 9   348
  sonnet 10   335
  sonnet 11   348
  sonnet 12   43–4, 119
  sonnet 13   188, 335
  sonnet 14   39
  sonnet 15
    alliteration   26
    form and organization   18–20, 22–5
    memory in   333, 338
    metaphor   23–5
    and Prudence tradition   258
    sonnet convention in   22
  sonnet 16
    Empson on   168
    floral metaphors   350
    memory in   348, 350
    self-doubt   230
  sonnet 17
    memory in   339, 348, 354–5, 392
    on poetry and distance   255
    use of "tomb"   172
  sonnet 18   4, 339, 348
  sonnet 19   410
  sonnet 20
    alchemy's influence   414
    androgyny   29
    color in   323
    MS versions   188
    place in the sequence   49

    relationship to 126   266–7
    same-sex love   5
    sonnet convention in   22
    textual cruces   157
  sonnet 21   37
  sonnet 22   392–3
  sonnet 23   390
  sonnet 25   33, 125, 151
  sonnet 26
    as dedicatory epistle   2, 218
    and patronage   186–7
    textual cruces   157
  sonnet 27
    alchemy's influence   414
    darkness   325–6
    lovesickness   347
    shadow and substance   253
  sonnet 28   188, 414
  sonnet 29
    alchemy's influence   414
    expression of emotion   278, 285–7
    MS versions   188–9
    textual cruces   160
  sonnet 30   278, 285–7, 333
  sonnet 31   100, 347, 414
  sonnet 32
    awareness of sonnets as sequence in   218
    Malone on   151–2
    MS versions   187, 195–6
  sonnet 33   38, 187
  sonnet 34   38
  sonnet 35   100, 178–81, 414
  sonnet 36   227, 240
  sonnet 37   253, 394–5
  sonnet 38   218, 245–6, 416
  sonnet 40   35–6, 235–7, 298
  sonnet 42   298
  sonnet 43   39, 253, 347
  sonnet 44   247–9
  sonnet 45   249–51, 295
  sonnet 46   39
  sonnet 47   39
  sonnet 52   149
  sonnet 53
    alchemy's influence   414
    irony   399
    materiality in   252, 253, 254
    possible neoplatonism   227
  sonnet 54
    alchemy's influence   414
    fluidity of reference   40–1
    MS versions   188

perceptive qualities   30
poetry as memory in   350
sonnet 55   348
sonnet 57   38
sonnet 59   61–4, 399–400
sonnet 60
    alchemy's influence   414–15
    fluidity of reference   41–3
    models of existence   29
    poetry as memory in   351
    reciprocity   256
    time in   109
sonnet 61   34, 253, 347
sonnet 62   39, 188
sonnet 63   112
sonnet 66
    allegory   30
    antithesis   37
    counterpointing between number and subject
        418
    enumeration   39–40
    grammatical and syntactical significance   33
sonnet 67
    Benson's version   149
    color in   323
    floral imagery   320–1
    nature vs artifice   321
    shadow and reality   253
sonnet 68   149, 187
sonnet 69   149
sonnet 71
    Benson's version   149
    commemoration and forgetting   355–6
    MS versions   187, 195
sonnet 73
    conceptual models   43
    Empson on historical and biographical context
        169
    structure   37
    textual cruces   156–7
    vicarious experience   392
sonnet 74   356
sonnet 76   30, 37, 217
sonnet 77   333, 353
sonnet 78
    fancifulness   39
    influence of Shakespeare's classicism   243
    phonetic repetition   65
    satire   37
sonnet 79   37
sonnet 81   352
sonnet 83   170–2, 257

sonnet 84   37, 390–1
sonnet 85   37
sonnet 86   414
sonnet 87   84
sonnet 89   233, 365
sonnet 92   230
sonnet 93   415
sonnet 94
    alchemy's influence   415
    Empson on   173–5, 175–6, 383
    persuasiveness   386
    proverbial expression   35
sonnet 95   37, 233, 320
sonnet 96   233
sonnet 97   39, 189, 320
sonnet 98   320
sonnet 99
    fancifulness   39
    horticultural imagery   319–20
    length   68, 261
    narrative in   45
sonnet 100   218
sonnet 101   218
sonnet 102   188
sonnet 104
    color in   318
    imprecision of dating in   110
    perceptive qualities   30
    Petrarchan notes   81
    phonetic repetition   65, 318
sonnet 105
    alchemy's influence   409
    attitude to love object   231–4
    philosophical concepts   29
    on repetition   64
    subversion   37
sonnet 106
    MS versions   187, 197–8
    Petrarchan notes   80
    philosophical concepts   29
    textual cruces   155–6
sonnet 107
    external references   125, 128, 130
    memorialization   233, 351–2
    MS versions   187
sonnet 108   81, 149, 234
sonnet 110   129, 130, 230
sonnet 111   129, 130
sonnet 112   129, 130
sonnet 113
    on love's disturbing effects   230,
        347

Shakespeare, William: SONNETS, INDIVIDUAL
  sonnet 113 (*cont'd*)
    Petrarchan notes   81
    textual cruces   88
  sonnet 114   81–2, 84, 230
  sonnet 116
    dramatic qualities   30
    love and sex in   29–30
    on love's permanence   52–3
    MS versions   187, 188, 193
    Petrarchan notes   82
    place in sequence   88
    subversion   37
    tenderness in   4
    on writing   237–8, 239
  sonnet 117   30
  sonnet 119   230, 415
  sonnet 120   46–7
  sonnet 121   40, 83, 355
  sonnet 122
    Benson's version   149
    memory in   333, 353–4
    subversion   37
  sonnet 123   133
  sonnet 124   188, 415
  sonnet 125   133, 308, 416
  sonnet 126
    alchemy's influence   419–20
    length   68, 261
    place in sequence   261–76, 419
    subject and object   270
  sonnet 127   66–7, 267, 324
  sonnet 128   187, 199
  sonnet 129
    composition date   297
    enumeration   39
    grammatical and syntactical
      significance   33
    Graves and Riding on   168, 278
    Malone's version   140–1, 153
    nature of love and sexuality   4, 30, 277–8,
      297
    Petrarchan notes   84
    place in sequence   49, 300
    subversion   37
  sonnet 130
    color in   324
    parody   36
    Petrarchan notes   80–1
    on praise of female beauty   30,
      324

    sonnet convention in   22
    wittiness   386
  sonnet 131   297
  sonnet 132   188, 298
  sonnet 133   267
  sonnet 134   267, 420
  sonnet 135   227, 298
  sonnet 136   298, 418, 420
  sonnet 137   130, 299
  sonnet 138
    first publication   3, 89, 146, 185
    implication in   38
    MS versions   187, 196–7
    Petrarchan notes   83–4
    place in sequence   299–300
    reasons for variants   199
    versions compared   146–7
  sonnet 140   300–1
  sonnet 141   82–3, 301, 420
  sonnet 142   188, 301, 420
  sonnet 143   37, 45, 302
  sonnet 144
    first publication   3, 185
    male/female binary   240
    Passionate Pilgrim version   302
    place in sequence   49, 302
    reasons for variants   199
    same-sex love   5
    sonnet convention in   22
    subversion   37
  sonnet 145
    and Anne Hathaway   127, 303
    composition date   33, 133
    meter   261
    place in sequence   302–3
    rhyme pattern   275
  sonnet 146
    Petrarchan notes   85
    place in sequence   303
    textual cruces   1–2, 158–9
  sonnet 147
    addressee   304
    nature of love   4, 85
    place in sequence   49, 303–4
  sonnet 148
    addressee   304
    Petrarchan notes   83
    place in sequence   304
    proverbial expression   35–6
  sonnet 149   304, 339
  sonnet 150   83

sonnet 151
  double meanings 142
  dramatic qualities 30
  Petrarchan notes 85
  sonnet convention in 22
sonnet 152
  addressee 304–6
  on adultery 30
  place in sequence 304–6, 308
  repetition in 67
  sexual congress 237
sonnet 153
  archaism 59, 60
  nature of love 4
  place in sequence 57–9, 309
sonnet 154
  allusion to *Song of Solomon* 421
  archaism 59, 60
  nature of love 4
  place in sequence 57–9, 309
  venereal disease 228
Shapiro, Marianne 87
Shelley, Mary 415
show: Shakespeare's use 369
Sidney, Mary *see* Pembroke, Countess of
Sidney, Robert 215, 220
Sidney, Sir Philip
  Amoretti 212–13
  Apologie for Poetrie 406–7
  Arcadia 21, 112, 192, 209, 211–12
  and Bruno 421
  Certain Sonnets 210–11, 219
  contemporary popularity of sonnets
    140
  Defence of Poesie 345, 439
  influence of editions on 1609 quarto 210–12,
    219
  linking devices 217
  on memory 345
  MS circulation 192, 197, 211, 215
  New Arcadia 438–9
  and persuasion 387
  Psalms 215
  and Smith 213
  sonnets 21, 206–7
  see also Astrophel and Stella
Siena cathedral 409
sight
  love's effect on 230, 346–7
  and memory 344–6, 352, 354
  and Shakespeare 317, 318

Signatura rerum (Boehme) 319
signatures, doctrine of 319
Singh, Jyotsna 8
sleeplessness 347
"A Slumber Did My Spirit Seal" (Wordsworth)
  167
smell, and memory 349–51
Smith, Bruce 50, 266, 269, 327, 340
Smith, William 212, 213, 215, 217
Snow, Edward 89
sodomy 338
solitude, human attitude to 117
Song of Solomon 421
sonnets, Shakespeare's *see under* Shakespeare
sonnets and sonnet sequences, non-Shakespearean
  aims 406–7
  collected editions 209
  and color 317
  composition process 214, 216–19
  conventions
    arrangement and layout 207, 209–11
    emotional 20–2, 284
    introductory matter 207–8, 209,
      211–14
    length 207
    material 206–14
    title-pages 207, 209
  fashionable period 186, 206
  form 18, 406
  linking devices 217
  MS circulation 212–16, 219
  Petrarchan tradition satirized in *Much
    Ado* 367–9
  published 1591–99 204
  published 1603–12 209
  second editions 209
sound patterns: sonnet 15 19, 23
Southampton, Henry Wriothesley, Earl of
  Akrigg's study 123
  as dedicatee of sonnets 9, 122
  as "fair youth" 2, 121–31
  release from prison 125, 128, 130
  as Shakespeare's patron 115, 124, 125, 138
  Wood on character 133
speaker
  authenticity and characterization 28–30
  development of arguments 33–6
  and irony 34
  as Shakespeare *see* biography
spectrum: etymology 314
spelling: modernizing 160–1

Spenser, Edmund
  1595 volume   91, 94, 95
  archaism   60
  Colin Clouts   209
  Complaints   204, 215
  Faerie Queene   108–9, 166, 344
  MS circulation   214, 215
  and persuasion   387
  preferred medium of circulation   185
  Two Cantos of Mutabilitie   238–9
Spurgeon, Caroline   42
Stallybrass, Peter   265, 353, 354, 428
Steevens, George   141, 150, 151
Stesichorus   315
Stock, Brian   117
Stone, Benjamin   192, 194
Stone, Lawrence   280–1
Strier, Richard   7, 164, 281
Strode, William   187, 190–1, 192, 193, 194
structure: in the sonnets *see under Shakespeare:*
  sonnets, general
subdue: Shakespeare's meaning   319
substitution *see* surrogacy
subversion   37, 380
Suckling, Sir John   196
Sullivan, Garrett   8
Surrey, Henry Howard, Earl of   17
surrogacy   90, 96–9, 100–1
Sutphen, Joyce   358
Swinburne, Henry   307
syllepsis   243
Sylvester, Joshua   197
Symposium (Plato)   409, 416

table-books   353, 354
Le Tableau des riches inventions (Verville)   410,
  411
Tacitus   202
Tanselle, Thomas   155
Tasso, Torquato   379
Taylor, Gary   51, 148, 199, 201
Taylor, John   111
Tears of Fancy   215
The Tempest (Shakespeare)   293
The Temple (Herbert)   74
tender and tenderness: Shakespeare's meaning
  251–2, 254–7
theatrical metaphors   23–5, 370, 390
Thomson, Peter   128
Thorpe, Thomas   2–3, 50, 139–40, 145–6, 185,
  204–21

thrift   111–12, 113
time
  archaism in sonnets   59–60
  artifice as means to halt   322
  and change   106–8
  and color   318–19
  cyclical pattern of life   57–70
  distilled and mechanized   108–10
  Elizabethan obsession with   108
  Empson on human time-scales   164–5
  financial   112–13
  frequency of occurrence in sonnets   358
  and husbandry   110–12
  Petrarchan   104–6
  saving   113–16
  sonnet 30   287
  sonnet 126 and the hourglass   261–7, 271–5
  and the sonnets   104–18
  and speaker's authenticity   29
  see also change; memory and memorialization
Tottel, Richard   185–6
Tractatus apologeticus (Fludd)   417
The Tragical Complaint of Estred (Lodge)   59
transformation *see* change
Traub, Valerie   226, 337
Trevor, Douglas   8
Troilus and Cressida (Shakespeare)   146, 227,
  384
trust   230
Tullia d'Aragona   416
turn: meaning   368
Tusser, Thomas   110–11
Twelfth Night (Shakespeare)   357, 385
Two Cantos of Mutabilitie (Spenser)   238–9

University of Nottingham, Portland MS Pw V 37
  190
usury metaphors   337–8, 342
Utopia (More)   264–5

Valbuena, Olga L.   340
vanity: poet's appeal to "fair youth's"   383–7,
  391, 396
Vasari, Giorgio   322
Vaughan, Thomas   408
Vega, Lope de   379
Vendler, Helen
  commentary style   9, 175, 176–8, 181
  on "dark lady"   297, 302
  overview of contribution   7
  overview of edition by   143

on sonnet 35   179–81
on sonnet 71   356
on sonnet 105   233, 240
on sonnet 116   237–8
on sonnet 151   142
on sonnet 152   67
on sonnets' disconcerting effect   52
venereal disease   4, 110, 228, 302
Venus and Adonis (Shakespeare)
  Adonis's refusal of Venus   113
  composition date   125, 135
  contemporary popularity   137, 426
  overview and sexual politics   138–9
  publishing history   53, 138
Verveille, François Beroalde de: books by   410,
  411
Virgil   17–18, 80
vision *see* sight
Vitruvius   405
voice *see* speaker

W.H.: identity
  Pembroke   9, 122, 130, 131–3
  Shakespeare himself   130
  Southampton   9, 122
  Who He?   143
  William Hart   152
  Willie Hughes   54, 121, 152
Waddington, Raymond   258, 358
waiting
  and Petrarch   105
  and Shakespeare   116
Waley, Arthur   164
Wall, Wendy   97, 102, 206, 213–14, 220
water metaphors   309
Watson, Amanda   8
Wells, Stanley   158, 159, 266
Westminster Abbey MS 41   190
Wharton, Thomas   152
"When that thine eye hath chose the dame"
  (Shakespeare?)   192
Wilde, Oscar   54, 225
Wilkins, Ernest Hatch   87
"will" pun   298, 302, 420
Willis, John   345–6, 352–3
Wilson, John Dover   263, 270
Wilson, Thomas   352
Wimsatt, William   177
The Winter's Tale (Shakespeare)   357–8, 378
Wittes Pilgrimage (Davies of Hereford)   209, 215,
  216

Wittgenstein, Ludwig   395
Wittkower, Rudolf   405
women
  body   320, 323–6
  Elizabethan sexual morality   294
  homosocial relations between in *A Lover's
    Complaint*   429–39
  lack of voice in the sonnets   28
  and masochism   437
  in Petrarchan tradition   367–8
  and redemption   378
  role in the sonnets   5
  sexual organs
    and flowers   320
    words for   320, 323, 380
  sexuality linked to darkness   324–6
  Shakespeare's view   371–6, 378
  sexual politics in *Venus* and *Lucrece*   139
  see also "dark lady"; gender relations
Wood, Michael   133–4
Woolf, Daniel   359
wordplay
  influence of Shakespeare's classicism   242–60
  Much Ado   367, 370–1, 375
  reasons for   237
  sonnet 43   39
  sonnet 105   233
  sonnet 121   40
  sonnet 135   227, 298
  sonnet 145   127, 303
  "will/Will"   298, 302, 420
Wordsworth, William   18, 25–6, 167
Wotton, Henry   194
Wright, Thomas   277, 281–2, 283, 285
writing, act of
  and darkness   325–6
  as immortality   231–2, 238–9, 338–9, 345,
    348–9, 350, 351–6
  metaphors   61–2, 325, 357
  see also poetry
writing tables *see* table-books
Wroth, Mary   215, 220
Wyatt, Sir Thomas   89, 168, 172
Wyndham, George   152

Yale Osborn Collection MS b 205   190
Yates, Francis   344–5, 346, 358, 359
Yeats, W. B.   387
"young friend" *see* "fair youth"

Zepheria   215